ERNESTO

ERNESTO

THE UNTOLD STORY OF HEMINGWAY IN REVOLUTIONARY CUBA

• • • • •

Andrew Feldman

MELVILLE HOUSE
BROOKLYN • LONDON

ERNESTO

First Melville House Printing: May 2019

Melville House Publishing
46 John Street
Brooklyn, NY 11201
and
Suite 2000
16/18 Woodford Rd.
London E7 oHA

mhpbooks.com
@melvillehouse

Design by Betty Lew

ISBN: 978-1-61219-638-1
ISBN: 978-1-61219-639-8 (eBook)

Printed in the United States of America

1 2 3 4 5 6 7 8 9 10

Library of Congress Cataloging-in-Publication Data

Names: Feldman, Andrew, 1973- author.
Title: Ernesto : the untold story of Hemingway in revolutionary Cuba / Andrew Feldman.
Description: Brooklyn : Melville House, [2019] | Includes bibliographical references.
Identifiers: LCCN 2018050528 (print) | LCCN 2018055010 (ebook) | ISBN 9781612196398 (reflowable) | ISBN 9781612196381 | ISBN 9781612196381 (hardcover) | ISBN 9781612196398 (eBook)
Subjects: LCSH: Hemingway, Ernest, 1899-1961--Homes and haunts--Cuba. | Hemingway, Ernest, 1899-1961--Knowledge--Cuba. | Authors, American--20th century--Biography. | Americans--Cuba--Biography.
Classification: LCC PS3515.E37 (ebook) | LCC PS3515.E37 Z5897 2019 (print) | DDC 813/.52--dc23
LC record available at https://lccn.loc.gov/2018050528

To my father, who challenged me,
To my mother, who accepted me,
To my wife, still standing her ground,
and to my daughter, *que adora las sorpresas.*

CONTENTS

• • • • •

INTRODUCTION

• • • • •

Along the windswept banks of a fishing village a few miles from Havana, there is a bust dedicated to the memory of a writer, set there by its inhabitants, the fishermen of Cojímar. When they first heard the news that Hemingway was dead, it felt as if they had received a blow from the long beam of their sail as wind changed and the boat came suddenly about. Still, some of them doubted the validity of the news; after all, the papers had declared his death on more than one occasion and were obliged to retract their stories when Mr. Way (as many of the fishermen, finding his full name difficult to pronounce, called him) returned from the dead, indestructible and immortal, like some hero of ancient lore.[1] Others, sneering at the headlines, rejected the suggestion, repeating itself like a vulgar joke in the newspapers and on the radio, that his death had been a suicide. In this way, they were able for a time to maintain the fiction that their friend, Ernest Hemingway, was alive and that he had never faltered in the face of death.

For thirty years, the villagers had shared the sea and fished with Hemingway, so they believed that they knew him well. They came to love him naturally and simply, like a brother, as was their custom, and he came to love them back. Whenever he, in his motored craft, encountered them after a long day of fishing, rowing back beneath the sun, *el americano* would throw out a line and tow their boats back to port. Often, he would invite them for a drink in La Terraza, the village restaurant-bar beside the docks where they could talk, exchange tips about sea conditions, and enjoy some rum and one another's company. Asking many questions, Ernest Hemingway, the writer, listened intently to their responses, to their sentiments, and to their manner of speaking—slowly gathering details for his work and strengthening ties of friendship with these men.

In Cojímar where his first mate Gregorio Fuentes also lived, Hemingway kept his boat, the *Pilar*. It was safe there. Everyone in the village knew who owned it, and they looked after it as if it were their own. As the years passed, he had become part of their community; when Gregorio Fuentes's daughters married, Hemingway, along with the other fishermen, attended their weddings.[2]

Hemingway's experiences in Cojímar provided the material that allowed him to write the novel that rescued his career and restored his readers' faith in his astonishing talent. His previous novel, *Across the River and into the Trees*, had been considered a failure. This awkward work of "fiction" indulgently explored two of his infatuations: his World War I wounds and nineteen-year-old Venetian beauty Adriana Ivancich, with whom he had become enamored while deep in the throes of a middle-age crisis. The book was ill received by both the public and his critics, who ridiculed its self-indulgent style, gossiped about the disgraceful goings-on of its aging author, and declared his career over. Like a counterpunch, Hemingway then released a much shorter work, over a decade in the making, condensing his experiences accumulated during a lifetime of fishing the Gulf Stream—with the fishermen he had come to admire. He called this novella, about an aging fisherman and his Cuban village of Cojímar, *The Old Man and the Sea*.

The work achieved immediate success and widespread praise from many of the very critics who had so roughly criticized his previous work. It won him a Pulitzer Prize and, one year later, resulted in the achievement of literature's highest honor, the Nobel Prize—solidifying his place as a literary legend. Recognizing his debt to the village and to Cuba, Hemingway immediately announced to the press that he had won the prize "as a citizen of Cojímar . . . as a *Cubano sato*."[3] It was a gesture that ran countercurrent to prevailing politics of his day, one that underlined his respect for the Cuban people and affirmed his identity as a world citizen and a member of the Caribbean community in which he lived. Keeping a promise that he had made to himself and to an old friend, he donated his prize medal to the church of La Virgen de la Caridad del Cobre, the people's patron saint who, Cubans believe, possesses the supernatural power to grant or to withhold great favors.[4] His gift not only underlined his gratitude but also suggested that, after twenty-two years of residence in Cuba, Hemingway believed in La Virgen too.

In the pages of *Life* magazine, *The Old Man and the Sea* first appeared with pictures of Hemingway walking along the shores of Cojímar village on its cover. Warner Brothers offered Hemingway $150,000 for the movie rights and another $75,000 to serve as the film's technical advisor, an unprecedented sum for a writer to receive in 1953.[5] Drawing from the film's $5 million budget, the author also insisted upon employing all of Cojímar's fishermen to assist in the production, in order to lend the film some authenticity, to recognize them, and to bring their struggling families some much-needed income.

• • • • •

Hemingway Dead of Shotgun Wound; Wife Says He Was Cleaning Weapon," said the newspaper, which Cojímar's fishermen read before wrapping it around the baitfish that they would bring on the boat that day.[6] Reflecting upon it, they saw Mary's denial was merely her grief, and after long hours spent at sea, the realization that they were also grieving floated slowly to the surface. When they returned to port and observed his ship, the *Pilar*, anchored there, floating without a captain, their throats thickened from the emptiness, for they understood they missed a friend and a man that they had admired. They could not bring themselves to judge this man that they respected and loved. Gathering at La Terraza, they stood silently along the bar where their friend no longer appeared. But they wanted to do something more to honor him.

They decided to commission a sculpture and place it at the entrance of the harbor of their town. They were very poor, and they did not have enough money to purchase the material, so they melted down the propellers from their boats for a sculptor to fashion into a bust. Today the bust remains, its eyes fixed forever, gazing into the waters of the Gulf, a source of life and mystery that the writer loved and so often wrote about.

As a Hemingway scholar completing my dissertation at the Université de Paris IV, La Sorbonne, and following my research in Spain, I stumbled upon a story of Hemingway's friendship with America's persistent enemy. Then I read an article in a French newspaper announcing that the Finca Vigía Museum in Havana would be opening its doors and archives to foreign researchers like me. Following Hemingway's example, I wanted to "go to the source" to investigate.

What I found there was an untold and remarkable story of Hemingway in Cuba, which has been eclipsed by fifty-seven years of Cold War blockade. The blockade, which continues to this day, has defined Cuban-American relations for the last half century and has had many regrettable consequences: it severed many of our cultural, intellectual, familial, and economic ties, and the prolonged separation has complicated our capacity to understand each other and the history that we "Americans" inevitably share. As Hemingway's own story shows, the difficult lessons are not received easily, but those lessons are invaluable when attained in struggle against our own wayward natures—over time.

As the first North American permitted to study in residence at the Finca Vigía Museum and Research Center, I spent two years conducting interviews and examining documents that had previously been unavailable to other researchers. My investigations bore many fruitful discoveries, and when I myself "became Cuban," through marriage, I believe that my perspective increased and continues increasing, a little each day, and in ways that I hope will add depth to this narrative.

Formerly, numerous respected researchers, unable to consult Cuban sources, had concluded that Hemingway lived in Cuba in isolation, as an expatriate American writer who did not associate with the Cuban people; yet my research in that country in consultation with Cuban sources revealed a completely different Hemingway, one who enjoyed a long and enriching friendship with Cuban fishermen like

Gregorio Fuentes and Carlos Gutierrez, and with Cuban writers like Enrique Serpa and Fernando G. Campoamor, as well as an enduring affair and tender friendship with Leopoldina Rodríguez.

In Cuba, it is often said that Hemingway loved Cuba and that Cuba loved him back, and everywhere one goes in Havana this emotion appears in plaques that pay homage to the author, in statues, in Cojímar, in Habana Vieja's Floridita Bar, at the Bodeguita del Medio, at the "Marina Hemingway," in the affection with which Cubans speak of him, and in the way they maintain his boat, the *Pilar*, and his Finca Vigía home—as a monument and as a museum—as a shrine to the friendship that might have been.[7]

ERNESTO

CHAPTER 1

Key West by Way of Havana, Newlyweds Passing Through (1928)

• • • • •

The long steamship lumbered and crashed over the shifting swells of a dark and turbulent sea. Two quadruple-expansion engines burned in the hull, turning twin screws, and heaving 9,266 tons and 485 feet of steel forward. Mile after mile, she plunged ahead.[1] If it were not for the smokestack on her back, billowing clouds of smoke into the air, one might have mistaken her for a whale leaping amidst the waves, or a ghost wandering among the black dunes of the sea. Thunder cracked, and after a heartbeat, lightning spread through the sky and lashed the waves. Lying in the narrow beds of their cramped quarters, Mr. and Mrs. Hemingway and the other 802 passengers aboard the Royal Mail Steamer *Orita* closed their eyes, murmured their prayers, and attempted to fall asleep as the ship tumbled over the rollercoaster crosscurrents of the great Atlantic Ocean.[2]

In the morning, the wind and the rain were gone. A single drop fell from a faucet and splashed into a wash basin—like a period punctuating the silence after the storm. Illuminating the floating dust, the first rays of daylight traversed a quietly creaking cabin. The bulkheads and bed sheets were gleaming as white as the new places and life awaiting Ernest and Pauline Hemingway. As the ship slowed, Ernest's eyelids flickered, then opened as he glanced about the cabin and got his bearings.

Grinning as he came to his feet, he slipped into trousers, while in the bunk beside him, his wife, Pauline, slept. It was a new day dawning, and he would soon be arriving in a place he had never been.[3] An early riser ordinarily, Pauline was exhausted by her sixth month of pregnancy and by weeks of rough seas.[4] Back in America, she hoped to deliver a baby soon, her first and her husband's second, in the safe haven of her family home in Piggott, Arkansas. It was a town that, for all intents and purposes, her family, the Pfeiffers, owned. After a stopover in Havana, they would continue to Key West, then overland to Arkansas.

Shutting the cabin door softly behind him, Ernest stepped out into the humming corridor. Following the curve along the steel bulkhead, he found the hatch to the exterior deck. Leaning over the railing and breathing the air, wild and alive with the sea, he first gazed upon the shores that a Genoese explorer called "the most beautiful land that human eyes had ever seen" on the day he encountered a "New World."[5] Later, when Ernest neared the end of his days on Cuba, he would write that "all things to be truly wicked must start from an innocence."[6] And so it must have started as the first explorer peered down his telescope to survey brown bodies cutting across the hazy waters of a promised land. With "good bodies and handsome features," the natives emerged "naked, tawny and full of wonder" from huts of littoral villages to swim out and greet the big boats arriving from the sea.[7]

Cocking their heads at the strange-talking men, the Taíno, Guanahatabey, and Ciboney offered parrots, spears, balls of cotton, and food and extended their hands in friendship.[8] Their beauty, affection, and freedom from material possessions at first enchanted Columbus and his crew. But when the explorers saw their gold ornaments and inferior weapons, they seized them as their prisoners and ordered to be taken to the gold.[9] The captain christened the island "Juana," the name of the royal princess, and claimed it for the Spanish throne.[10] Before he and his men had finished their conquest of the island, they would have exterminated approximately 8 million souls.[11]

As night fell and the ship approached the port, Hemingway could feel the engines shift, grumbling in a lower gear, and smell the scent of land. Their steamship rounded a peninsula and he could see the old Spanish fortress, the Castle of the Three Kings, on the hill.[12] In the semidarkness, buoys clanged and moaned out in the bay. In the moonlight as he drifted by, Hemingway could see the stone garrets and high walls, which King Charles V of Spain had ordered built after the misadventure of Colón to protect his wealth as his colony grew.[13]

At the mouth of the harbor, sailboats, tugboats, and rowboats deftly intermingled, returning to port from the open sea. Black and copper-skinned men rowed weather-beaten skiffs, gathered lines, and recast them into the current with a persistent rhythm. Four centuries after Columbus, the natives had changed. Unseen in the eventide, their wrinkled faces now contained the features from not only Taíno ancestors but also of Iberian, African, and Eurasian peoples immigrating freely and under duress to another land.[14] When the steamer plowed by beneath the moon, their eyes flashed as they took stock of the ship and the bulky author leaning over the railing of its upper deck framed by electric lights. More prudent than their great-great-grandparents, these natives maintained a distance, resigning themselves to the ritual of their daily bread.

Flirting with the salty-sour air of the sea, breezes scented with mangoes and mariposas came overland from the island's interior, greeting another arrival with their sickly-sweet promise.

In the distance overhead, seagulls cried as the ship turned and a citadel came into view. Holding their position beneath the stars, the massive fortresses known to *Habaneros* as *El Morro* and *La Cabaña* sprawled across a two-hundred-foot hill and conquered the horizon.[15] Throughout the Colonial Era, these fortifications had permitted the Spanish to control the harbor (although they would lose it to the British for a year from 1792 to 1793). The American Army seized control of the fortress and the island in 1898, when Spain lost the Spanish-American War. Later, Cuban dictators as diverse and as similar as Machado, Batista, Castro, and Guevara would make consistent use of the fort's labyrinth of stone chambers to imprison their abundant enemies. on the spine of the peninsula above the fortress called La Cabaña, the Christ of Havana watched over the old city, raising a stone hand to bless arrivals while his wrinkled brow expressed some measure of hesitation.Having just converted to Catholicism to marry Pauline, Ernest noted the Divine Trinity in the statue's extended index finger, middle finger, and folded thumb. Before the time of Christ, the gesture had evoked a trinity in a supernatural family—a mother, a son, and a spirit of light—in Aphrodite, Zeus, and Chronos—Venus, Jupiter, and Saturn—terrestrial beings and celestial sources, mystical origins in the stars, a falling, an isolation, and an aspiration to return. As he ascended in the literary world, Ernest included an epitaph serving also as title for his first novel, *The Sun Also Rises*: "One generation passeth away, and another generation cometh: but the earth abideth forever. The sun also ariseth, and the sun goeth down, and hasteth to his place where he arose" (Ecclesiastes 1:4–7).

A tugboat appeared to pull the large ship through the ramparts on either side of the canal.[16] In the old days they ran a chain between the fortresses on either side of the water to block the entrance of raiding ships. That day, atop the aging parapets, stood modern sentinels in white sailors' uniforms armed with wooden-stock rifles, slung loosely about their shoulders with green webbed straps. People strolling along the seawall gathered in the park along the water's edge to watch the grand entrance of the great ship. As RMS *Orita* neared the massive cement slab, sailors tossed her lines over the edges of the tall hull. The docksmen below recovered the lines and attached them to bollards. A whistle shattered weeks of vast ocean silence. Then the boat buzzed with activity as passengers prepared for debarkation.

Ducking through the hatch, Ernest stepped aside as passengers departed with large suitcases. Opening the door of his cabin, he found Pauline sitting inside, pinning her hair in front of the vanity, with her fine reflection looking back as he came in. Rising to greet her prize, a writer as clever as he was determined, she pulled herself tightly into the alcoves of his thick body.

Had he had a marvelous time outside? How was she feeling? Had she been able to sleep? And the movements of "Petit Pilar" . . . ? "Pilar," the code name that they had used while she was his mistress had now become the nickname for the daughter that they hoped she would deliver.[17] Glancing at Pauline's swelling belly, he wondered if it was a girl as she predicted. Excitedly describing his views of the port, he put on the brown suit that she had laid out for him, then sat on the bed behind her and watched as she finished painting her lashes and lips. Her hair was "clipped close like a boy's" and "coarsely silky," accentuating the nape of her neck, just like later descriptions of several of his fictional heroines.[18]

As Mr. and Mrs. Hemingway exited the passageway into a humid spring evening, they longed for a bath and a night's sleep on solid land to sustain them during the last leg of a long journey across the Straits of Florida toward home.[19] Along with seven packets of mail, Ernest and Pauline were thus delivered to Havana.[20]

Nearly twenty-nine years old and soon to be the father of two, Ernest stood six feet tall with a mustache accentuating his adulthood and his authority. Pauline was four years older, but five inches shorter, and smaller, making her look much younger than he. She wore a dark floral scarf and a draping silk dress hung like a cloak over her emergent abdomen. A felt cloche hat extended over sharp, acquiescent eyes; a friend once described her as "very winning, very bright. Her face was not beautiful, but so intelligent and alert that she became attractive."[21]

In front of the terminal was a bustling street where clucking horse carriages competed with tooting Model T roadsters, and motorbikes squawked alongside porters dragging wheelbarrows stacked with suitcases and heavy trunks. On the other side of the melee was a high hedge and, beyond that, Saint Francis Square, or Plaza de San Francisco, commonly known by Habaneros as the Plaza de las Palomas with the Fuente de los Leones as its centerpiece, which a flock of pigeons had claimed as *baignoire* for their exclusive use.[22] From the mouths of its four kneeling lions, four streams of water were trickling serenely toward the four corners of the square. As the Hemingways passed through, eighteen iron bells in the towers of the church rang out, shaking the plaza and sending the pigeons into flight. Every hour it occurred: the birds took center stage with demonstrations of aerobatics for passers by before settling back into their bath and returning tranquility to the square with their *coocoorrucoos*.

Exiting the plaza to cross Oficios, Amagura, Obrapía, and Mercaderes Streets, Ernest and Pauline followed other arrivals, blending in with locals and expatriates that composed Habana Vieja—Old Havana—at the time. On Calle Obispo (Bishop Street), they came face-to-face with the newly constructed five-story Hotel Ambos Mundos, "the best of both worlds," where their room awaited.[23] As they approached, a fine looking white-uniformed mulatto doorman greeted them grandly in the foyer and escorted them through the lobby to reception. Marble-tiled floors, high ceilings, chaise longes, fresh flowers, interior fountains, and a polished bar—all contributed to the hotel's Art Deco elegance.

They received a room key and took the elevator to the highest floor. In the corner room, 511, there was a large mahogany bed, a nightstand with a chrome water pitcher, a dresser, a bookshelf, and a writing desk. The porter opened the double windows to let the air flow into the room and showed them how to close the shutters during storms and how to draw the curtains to shield themselves from the sun. Having tipped the porter, Ernest stepped out on the fifth-floor balcony to discover a privileged view of the harbor below. After they had bathed, they lay beside each other on the creaking mattress, settling into the clean dryness of their sheets and the wonderful dark stillness of the room. Having spent more than a month at sea, they listened to the muffled screeches of wind outside, across waves, and beyond, and soon both vanished into dreamless sleep.

In the morning Ernest sat at the desk to write letters while his wife continued to sleep. After his third letter, he stood, approached the window, and watched the silence. "To the north, over the old cathedral, the entrance to the harbor, and the sea, and to the east to Casablanca peninsula, the roofs of all houses in between and the width of the harbor."[24] Abandoning correspondence, he moved his chair next to the balcony. In the distance, he could make out dozens of small fishing boats like those they had passed coming in. Peering out toward the boats as they rowed over the waves he remembered that he had already seen them—untroubled amidst sharks, leaning back against their skiffs, rising and falling over waters turning every shade of blue.

He had seen them in paintings with his first wife years ago during the first week they had spent together. And they had loved each other very much. It was just after the War when his mother had kicked him out of the house and he had moved in with his friends—fellow ambulance driver Bill Horne, and Bill and Katy Smith from Walloon Lake—with whom he had shared a Chicago flophouse.[25]

Now memories of Winslow Homer's watercolors from a visit to the Chicago Art Institute returned.[26]

• • • • •

After an ordeal of caring for her dying mother, Hadley Richardson had come to Chicago in October 1920 to recover with Katy Smith, her friend and roommate from Bryn Mawr, but Katy saw less and less of her friend after Hadley and Ernest met and sparked a romance that continued through tender letters long after Hadley's return to Saint Louis. A redhead with hints of gold, Hadley had lovely hands and a beautiful heart.[27] She emanated clarity and empathy, wholesome sexiness and generosity. When she came into the room, an intense feeling overcame him: he had met the girl he was going to marry.[28]

A "beautiful physical specimen," Ernest was eight years younger than she; he was "slender and moved well. His face had the symmetry of fine bony structure and he had a small elastic mouth that stretched from ear to ear when he laughed. He laughed aloud a lot from quick humor and from sheer joy of being alive."[29] He had been aptly named, for what charmed her more than anything was his "flattering habit" of listening to her, "focusing his entire attention on a person, gazing out from watchful brown eyes," suggesting that he was sincere and "not interested in anyone but her."[30]

The spark between them resulted in visits back and forth between Saint Louis and Chicago, but it was through letters that they created the sort of intimacy that might have made them blush had they been face-to-face: "I must not . . . hold back from you. It would poison me," she wrote.[31] In ever more affectionate letters, they gave each other nicknames, like "Nesto" and "Hasovitch," invented a language, and solidified an alliance.[32] While separated, the letters expressed erotic imaginings, passionate longings, and sexual awakenings: "Your hands can make me do all sorts of nice things for you by the littlest touch—make me want to, I mean, but then, so can your eyes. I'd do anything your eyes said."[33] It was difficult, she said, to put the letters containing so much of herself into the mailbox and let them go.[34]

When he struggled in Chicago to earn forty dollars per week at the magazine *Cooperative Commonwealth*, she reassured him, "We are PARTNERS . . . if I hadn't been aware of my ability to back my single self financially . . . I wouldn't have let you, ever take me on," and when Sherwood Anderson prodded him with the knowledge that the place for any aspiring writer was Paris, Hadley let it be known that her inheritance assured them financial independence.[35] Marrying on Horton's Bay, Michigan, in September 1921, they honeymooned at the family cabin before moving into a dingy flat at 1239 North Dearborn Street.

Supporting him heart and soul, she believed in Ernest and his writing: "I never expected to find anyone into whose life I could fling my spirit—and now I can—every side of me backs you up . . . I love your ambitions. Don't think I am ambitious except to be a balanced, happy, intelligent lady, making the man happy and using everything lovely he has to give me, very hard."[36] In November, just after he had lost the job at *Cooperative Commonwealth* and secured another with the *Toronto Star*'s Parisian office, they booked passage aboard SS *Leopoldina*, bound for Paris.

During the early days, they had lived in the Latin Quarter at 74 rue du Cardinal Lemoine in an apartment with no running water and a bucket for a lavatory on the landing of the stairs. When they returned to Paris after the birth of their first son in Toronto, they lived at 113 rue Notre-Dame des Champs just above a sawmill in a working-class neighborhood near Montparnasse.[37] They called their boy "Bumby" because of the "round, solid feel of him" in their arms, but his Christian name was John Hadley Nicanor Hemingway, after his mother and a bullfighter they admired.[38]

Hadley had been Hemingway's closest friend and the loveliest and most sincere person that he had ever known.[39] From the middle of the Atlantic Ocean during his transatlantic crossing, he had calculated the time in Paris and wondered if Bumby and Hadley might have been still sleeping in their beds, or if they might have been awakening at that moment, or brushing their teeth, or if they were in the kitchen having *café avec tartines de beurre et marmelade*.[40] From the bridge of the steamship, he had even sent her a telegram: "FAREWELL."[41]

Now through the translucent curtains of his hotel in Cuba, he watched Pauline, his second wife. When he first met her at the Fitzgeralds', he had not thought much of her, preferring her sister, Virginia, as the more attractive of the two.[42] He remembered that he and Hadley had just met Zelda and Scott, read Scott's new novel *The Great Gatsby*, and agreed it was very good.[43] Scott took it upon himself to mentor Ernest and introduce him and Hadley to their wealthy friends, such as Gerald and Sara Murphy with whom they had become enamored and summered in Antibes.[44] Weary of poverty and eager for a publisher to give real publicity to his work, Ernest accepted Scott's help.

Petite and flat chested, Pauline attended a private Catholic school in Saint Louis before coming to Paris to work for *Vogue*. Dressing the part in long strings of pearls and short-fringed dresses, she looked as if she had stepped out of the pages of the magazine. Seeing Ernest occasionally at the Dingo Bar while he was having a drink with Scott or with John Dos Passos, the Pfeiffer sisters threw around the latest slang (everything was "positively ambrosial," the superlative of the moment), smoked cigarettes from ivory stems, and flirted openly with the boys.[45] Scott said the rumor was Pauline had come to Paris to shop for a husband; the sisters' clothes and manners announced just how much money their family possessed.[46]

The trouble started one afternoon just after Ernest and Hadley had returned from skiing in Schruns, and Hadley received an invitation for tea at Kitty Cannell's apartment near the Eiffel Tower. There was an American girl from Saint Louis who, Kitty said, had recently arrived in Paris whom Hadley had to meet, because she was from Saint Louis, too. When Hadley, aged thirty-four, arrived looking matronly and plain, she found the Pfeiffer sisters slender with delicate bones like small birds, exquisitely dressed, and with silky bobbed black hair like Japanese dolls.[47]

Pauline wore a trendy chipmunk coat, one of its kind.[48] After boxing, Ernest and Harold Loeb turned up, faces flushed with virility and vitality, and Ernest ended up chatting with Virginia, mostly about their hometown and the family fortune, and showing much more than polite interest.[49] Ernest later joked to Kitty that he would have gladly taken Virginia in her sister's coat.[50]

Hearing Hadley and Ernest had a son, the Pfeiffers dropped in on the Hemingways' meager apartment one day for a visit with an expensive toy from a store on rue Saint-Honoré. Doting on Hadley also, they brought fashion magazines, invited her to shows, and took her to tea at the Hôtel de Crillon on the Place de la Concorde. Even though Pauline initially protested such a pig of a man, shabby and unshaven, could allow his wife to live in such abject conditions, soon the witty, well-to-do sisters were dropping by the room Ernest rented as an office on the fifth floor of the rue Mouffetard, bringing their good cheer, lively talk, and admiring eyes to the end of long days spent in front of an uncooperative typewriter.[51] Afterward, appearing only was Pauline, well dressed, clever, flattering, offering to take him, a married man, to dinner.[52]

Owning the corn, the wheat, most of the land, the bank, and the cotton gin in Piggott, Pauline's father was very wealthy, and her uncle Gus, who was even wealthier (with investments in drug stores, pharmaceuticals, liniment, and perfume) and who had no children of his own, made doubly certain that Pauline never wanted for anything.[53] She was a rich girl who was accustomed to getting exactly what she desired, and when she realized that she wanted Ernest, she set out to take him, regardless of whether he was already married to Hadley and to Bumby.[54] In the end, he accepted the deal.

• • • • •

From the balcony of the Ambos Mundos Hotel, he watched Pauline sleeping, exhausted, on the big bed and looked out at the boats fishing in front of the castle, and he decided to take a walk and let "Fife" rest. At the bar, he ordered a coffee, and a barman in a white jacket brought it out. Reinvigorated, he walked outside, then following the street passing in front of their hotel, he drifted toward the city center with the vague intention of hiring a car so they could see some of the town when his wife woke up.[55]

Without restrictions and following the current, he wandered up the main commercial thoroughfare of Calle Obispo where fabric traders, printers, booksellers, tailors, spice vendors, restaurateurs, and tavern keepers attracted an unending river of pedestrian traffic. There, he saw merchants, veiled matrons, well-tailored businessmen, Creoles in white garments, mothers and daughters eyeing merchandise and being watched by others in their long, flowing dresses amidst shoeshine boys, priests, tourists, beggars, speculators, and fortune seekers. After a long gray Parisian winter and a rough crossing, the streets of Havana offered firm soil, sunshine, and a reassuring breeze.

A vanguard in the Americas, the Creole capital of Havana had already achieved notoriety by 1928. Fueled by depressed economies at home and the proliferation of advertisements promising easier fortunes, Europeans, Asians, and North Americans flocked at the turn of the century in greater and greater numbers to the island in pursuit of amusement, adventure, and opportunity. Havana, which writers described as a feminine and alluring city that gave herself freely and held nothing back from those who would venture to her shores, had become a refuge for these émigrés, though hundreds of thousands incoming would also be cut down by illness and disease or robbed by the unlawful schemes of financial predators proliferating in Havana at that time.

As he came upon Parque Central (Central Park), he observed businessmen sitting on rows of benches beneath the trees and boys kneeling on the pavement in front of them to shine their shoes. Two eras of *taxistas* lined up: horse buggies and automobiles.[56] On a pedestal in the center of the park stood a high statue of a short man, José Martí.[57] Tucking his left arm meekly behind his back, the white-marble likeness with a thick mustache, taut bow tie, and flowing overcoat pointed his right finger ahead.

As he crossed the park, Ernest looked up into Martí's white granite eyes—fixed firmly ahead—incarnating all he had accomplished and all he had not. An activist for liberty as a boy, Martí was accused of treason at the age of sixteen, imprisoned by the Spanish government, and exiled from Cuba. Living in Spain, in Mexico and Guatemala, in the United States and Venezuela, Martí studied, became a lawyer, organized a movement, and returned with an army to reclaim his homeland. As the forefather of a Cuban democracy, Martí united disparate peoples—Creoles and former slaves—as they took a stand after years of servitude for freedom.[58] As a poet, he wrote movingly with a mighty pen. As a general, he participated stubbornly with a feeble sword during the first battle of the Cuban War of Independence at Dos Ríos. Despite his diminutive stature, Martí became his country's most beloved hero by living and dying for his cause four years before Ernest Hemingway was born.

Ernest looked down El Malecón, a wall weaving lazily along the waves crashing across the rocks at its base, then gazed into "the mirror of the sea," waters that Conrad, an author he admired,[59] had said had no memory.[60] The balustrade, running the length of the sidewalk between the city and the sea, from Vedado to El Morro fort, were reminiscent of many he had seen on the Riviera and on Spanish coasts. To have no memory sounded wonderful as in his mind the entanglements of his past turned over.[61]

• • • • •

As winter approached in December 1925, Ernest, Hadley, and Bumby took refuge from the gray dankness of Paris, skiing in the white powdered mountains of Schruns, Austria. On Christmas eve, Pauline arrived too, by now the maidenly friend of the family, and checked into a neighboring room of the Hotel Taube.[62] It was the oldest trick probably that there was, wrote Ernest later, for a rich young unmarried woman to become the temporary best friend of the wife, then stealthily, innocently, and unrelentingly set out to marry her husband.[63] Every morning in the Austrian chalet, the writer wrote as was his routine, and in the afternoons while he and Hadley were skiing, the rich, unmarried woman who had joined them sat reading by the fire.

At first she seemed little more than a casual friend. After all, she was good company for Hadley while Ernest was writing, and it was not unusual for them to be in the company of female friends.[64] In the evenings, the three of them played bridge or conversed cozily indoors, but soon Pauline was spending more time with Ernest, reading from works in progress, complimenting him, and giving him editorial feedback.[65] "The husband has two attractive girls around when he has finished work. One is new and strange and if he has bad luck he gets to love them both. Then the one who is relentless wins," he later wrote. Yet when Pauline returned to Paris in January, he pursued, leaving wife and son behind in Schruns.[66]

He had told Hadley the trip was necessary to advance his career. Emboldened by critics' praise for his first story collection, *In Our Time*, but disappointed with his publisher's promotional efforts, Ernest had been concocting a scheme to wriggle out of his first contract and fast-track his career with the firm that represented F. Scott Fitzgerald.[67] Fitzgerald had raved about Ernest's writing to his editor at Scribner's, Max Perkins, who then offered Ernest a deal. His current agreement with Boni and Liveright allowed him to publish elsewhere only if they rejected his work. Consequently, he created *The Torrents of Spring*, a parody of his former mentor, Sherwood Anderson, knowing that Boni and Liveright would refuse a work so damaging to their top author. Hadley remembered Anderson's kindness to them, and she urged her husband not to betray a friend. But Pauline supported Ernest in the power move.[68]

Receiving telegrams in Schruns from both publishers, Ernest insisted he had to go to New York to sign a new contract for *The Torrents of Spring* and *The Sun Also Rises*.[69] His wife had always believed in putting his writing career first, and she agreed to stay behind in Austria with their son. However, passing through Paris on the way there and back he stayed with Pauline in her apartment on rue Picot even though he told his wife that he was staying at the Hôtel Venézia in Montparnasse.[70] In one stroke, Ernest had betrayed both the family and the friends who had enabled him to attain his dream.[71] When he came back to Schruns, he found his wife and son waiting for him there. As he held her close, he felt the pangs of regret and told himself that he would set himself straight.[72] He would work well, love her and no one else. They would be happy, and he would forget Pauline. After coming out of the mountains in the spring, however, he and Pauline started up again.

Likely not wanting to see, Hadley did not notice Ernest's affair until the end of April when Virginia and Pauline invited her on a tour of the castles of the Loire in Virginia's car.[73] After a short time on the road, Pauline, perhaps pregnant with Ernest's child at the time, snapped at Hadley over a trifle, then withdrew into a sullen silence.[74]

Sensing that something was wrong, Hadley softly asked Virginia, "Don't you think Pauline and Ernest get along awfully well with each other?"

"Well," Virginia announced, "I think they're *very* fond of each other."[75]

From "the way she said it," Hadley "seized the situation. Suddenly it was immediately clear."[76]

When she asked her husband if he was having an affair, he so insisted that she drop the subject that she felt ashamed for having brought it up.[77] Afraid to lose him by pushing him about it, Hadley yielded, but when Kitty Cannell ran into her in the streets of Paris and asked after Ernest, Hadley blurted out: "Well, you know what's happening, she's taking my husband."[78] Meanwhile, Hadley and Ernest had been planning a trip to Madrid to attend the bullfights of San Isidro, then to travel to the south of France to meet the Fitzgeralds, the MacLeishes, and the Murphys as invited guests in a rented villa in Cap d'Antibes, the Mediterranean village where the Murphys anchored a sleek one-hundred-foot yacht, *Weatherbird*. When Bumby fell ill, Hadley went to the warmer weather of the Côte d'Azur while Ernest decided to go to Madrid alone.[79]

It is likely that Ernest rendezvoused in Madrid with his mistress, "Pilar"—Pauline—to terminate a pregnancy.[80] While it would have been a sin for her as a Catholic to abort, at that time it would have also been mortifying for a fashionable young lady in a prominent family from a tiny rural community to explain a pregnancy conceived out of wedlock.[81] The story Ernest set to paper one year later takes the form of a tense conversation at a junction-station bar somewhere between Barcelona and Madrid: an unnamed man pressures a woman, Jig, to get a "simple operation," just to "let the air in."[82] The title of the story, "Hills Like White Elephants," refers to the hills of Spain's Ebro valley that the couple watched during their suppressed argument and to the "white elephant" they had to dispose of.[83] Just after Madrid and before rejoining his family on the Riviera, Ernest would write to his Protestant parents to confess that he had attended Catholic mass in Madrid (with Pauline, most likely after her upsetting operation), to inform them of his "shift" to another publisher, and to mention the name of a new woman with whom he planned to winter in Piggott.[84]

Fearing that Bumby's whooping cough would infect her children, Sara Murphy ordered Hadley and her boy quarantined in a villa separate from the beautiful people. In a letter Hadley informed Ernest that the Murphys had been keeping "a grand distance from us poisonous ones."[85] In her mounting anxiety and isolation, Hadley employed radical measures to get her husband to appear, even demeaning herself by inviting his lover, who she said was immune to whooping cough, to assist her with their son.[86] While his mistress's presence was unpleasant to Hadley, Pauline and Ernest running off together was much worse. "Fife," Pauline, could stop off here if she wanted to, wrote Hadley, then rued that it would be a "swell joke on *tout le monde*" if she, Ernest, and Pauline spent the summer *ensemble*.[87]

Soon Ernest and Pauline showed their faces in Antibes. When Bumby stopped whooping and the jet set's lease on their villa ran out, Ernest rented basic rooms for himself, his wife, and his mistress at the Hôtel de la Pinède in Juan-les-Pins. Then there were three breakfast trays, three wet bathing suits on the line, three bicycles, and a mistress who tried to teach a wife how to dive, but the wife would not be a success. Ernest wanted them to play bridge together, but Hadley found it hard to concentrate, so they spent mornings on the beach, sunning or swimming, and lunched in their little garden. After siestas, they took long bicycle rides along the Golfe-Juan; descriptions of the not-so-utopic sun-soaked threesome would later reappear in his wicked posthumous novel *The Garden of Eden*.[88]

When the reviews of his early works, like the *In Our Time* collection, appeared, their comparisons irritated Ernest to such an extent that he felt compelled to distance himself by firing off shots in the form of lengthy parodies written about former mentors Sherwood Anderson and Gertrude Stein. In 1926 Scribner's released the Anderson parody, *The Torrents of Spring*, and by February 1927, the *New Yorker* published the Steinesque story, "My Own Life." These works advanced his career, but ultimately derailed friendships by ridiculing two writers who had arguably helped him the most, and resulted in return fire, like *The Autobiography of Alice B. Toklas.*[89] In his novel *The Sun Also Rises*, which was in progress at that time, Hemingway's character Pedro Romero, the matador, declares, "The bulls are my best friends." Pedro's lover, the debauched heroine Lady Brett, asks him, "You kill your friends?" The matador answers, "Always. So they don't kill me."[90] The moral is clear: one has to seize the upper hand before others have a chance.

Still an ally in June 1926, F. Scott Fitzgerald sent Ernest a four-page letter full of encouragement and detailed feedback for his first novel's first draft: "The novel [was] damned good . . . a proof of brilliance"; but he suggested that Ernest cut all wordy descriptions, backstories, ineffectual bits (which he specified), snobbery, sneers, glibness, nose-thumbings, and style for style's sake. He advised him to reduce the word count from seventy-five thousand to fifty thousand.[91] Although the criticism might have at first been difficult to stomach, Ernest wrote Scott later that year to thank him and joke that he should dedicate the book to him. The dedication page would read "*The Sun Also Rises* (Like Your Cock if You Have One), A Greater Gatsby (Written with the friendship of F. Scott Fitzgerald) (Prophet of the Jazz Age)."[92] Following Scott's advice, Ernest wrote Perkins in June that he would be making some cuts that "Scott agreed with."[93] Whatever Fitzgerald's faults, he attempted to be Ernest's friend, offering his time, editing, and counsel, and later graciously downplayed his influence on Ernest's novelistic debut.[94]

The tension with Hadley grew throughout the summer and peaked in July in Pamplona where they were accompanied by the Murphys and Pauline, and in Valencia where they were alone while Ernest was revising *The Sun Also Rises*. Returning to Antibes, the Hemingways informed the Murphys, their sponsors, that they could accompany them no farther. Their marriage was over. After a final, strained train ride in a closed compartment with a woman and her caged canary, Hadley and Ernest returned to Paris to set up separate residences.[95] Making it easier, well-heeled Gerald Murphy told Ernest that he and Pauline might make a better match, and he deposited four hundred dollars into Ernest's account and offered his pied-à-terre at 69 rue de Froidevaux, overlooking Montparnasse cemetery, as an alternate residence for Ernest while Hadley and Bumby sought refuge in Hôtel Beauvoir.[96] In August in Gerald Murphy's apartment, Ernest continued reworking *The Sun Also Rises*, a manuscript scandalizing former friends, personages immortalized in the name of a noble cause. Meeting him in Deux Margots that summer, Samuel Putnam, who knew Ernest in Chicago, reported that his ego had swollen since the early days: he was behaving much less like the humble reporter he had known and more like a "literary celebrity," "tarzan of the printed page."[97]

Unable to comprehend her husband's callousness and still hoping his feelings for Pauline were a passing infatuation, Hadley made one last attempt to save her marriage by promising a divorce on one condition: he must agree to separate from his lover for one hundred days. If they still desired each other afterward, Hadley would not stand in the way. Hearing this, Pauline set course directly, via steamship departing from Boulogne on September 24, for a self-imposed exile in Piggott. Was it remorse? Penance? A last rite out of respect for Hadley's dying marriage? Or her merger with Ernest as sure as a profit margin, patiently accrued like the rent collected from one of her father's tenant farms?

By October, Hadley was sounding somewhat suicidal and rather brokenhearted in her letters and asking Ernest not to see her.

> Dearest Tatie, I think it will be the very best thing for you and me to keep apart and I am sure you feel so too . . . [In] case anything should happen to me Marie and the concierge could get hold of you for Umpster. Not trying to suggest disasters but you are responsible for Umpster after me. Anyway my awfully tender, sorry love, dear Chickie and I don't think Pauline is a rotter and I'm sure some day—if let alone—my old trusting affection will come back . . . I promise to try for it. But to forget you both in the meanwhile. You see, I can't afford to think about you two for a while, or

> I'm going to break down completely. Your loving, oh so sorry we *talked* again. Cat.[98]

By November 16, she saw the futility in her demands and took back control of her life. Yes, she cared deeply for Ernest, but she could no longer bear the back and forth, the ups and downs. Frostily, she inventoried her belongings and requested that Ernest move everything on the list from their old apartment at rue Notre-Dame des Champs to her new one at rue de Fleurus. In a letter to Ernest that month, John Dos Passos comforted and teased his friend that "Pauline was an awfully nice girl. Why don't you [become] a Mormon?"[99]

While Ernest was moving Hadley's possessions one by one by handcart through the bumpy streets of Paris, it dawned on him what he was losing, and he began to weep. When he saw his father in such a state, Bumby asked what the matter was. Papa pointed to a cut on his hand, so Bumby brought a bandage, spoke to him in the only language that he knew, *"Je t'aime, Papa . . . la vie est beau avec Papa,"* and caused his father to feel much worse.[100] Just after, Hadley cancelled all conditions and asked Ernest to initiate divorce proceedings immediately.[101] Declaring *fin* to the hundred-day siege, Ernest dispatched Virginia to send a telegram to her sister.[102] His divorce, which he filed in December, was granted in April 1927 by the court. As the divorce was pronounced final, Hadley and Bumby fled from Paris on a steamer to America.

In gold-embossed invitations from Cartier, Pauline invited a few guests to a reception at the MacLeishes' apartment at 44 rue de Bac. Friends Ada and Archibald MacLeish agreed to host the luncheon, but declined to attend the ceremony, for they found Ernest's conversion to Catholicism, which annulled his first marriage and made his son a bastard in the eyes of the church, to be distasteful.[103] After their civil ceremony at the Hôtel de Ville and a small service in the side chapel of l'Église de Saint-Honoré d'Eylau, a large Catholic church in Paris's well-heeled sixteenth arrondissement, Ernest and Pauline became husband and wife on May 10.[104] The bride appeared in an off-white chemise designed for her by Lanvin, a strand of Cartier pearls, and her close-cropped *coiffure en rigueur,* while the groom wore a frowzy tweed suit dressed up with a new necktie.[105] Unable to travel to Paris,

Mary Pfeiffer, Pauline's mother, struggled to accept the "crooked circumstances" through which her daughter had come to be married, but she sent her best wishes, prayers, and a check, hoping that the Lord's guidance would straighten their pathway to peace and happiness.[106] At the end of May, Hadley took Bumby to visit the Hemingway grandparents, whom he had never met, in Oak Park.

Eager to make a new life work amidst Parisian ghosts, Pauline had also bid Ernest to pray and rented a sumptuous apartment "to suit their tastes" at 6 rue Férou, with a large master bedroom, maid's room, writer's study, and expensive antiques.[107] Like a genie from a lamp, Uncle Gus appeared at the end of March to check in on the happy couple and to furnish another check to pay for all desired. Ernest could never have written *The Sun Also Rises*, as well as *In Our Time* and *The Torrents of Spring*, without Hadley, he said, so he dedicated the book to her and Bumby and gave them all the royalties.[108] His every need would also be thereafter assured by the Pfeiffer clan, so it was the right thing to do.

After a dazzling honeymoon on France's Mediterranean coast, in the Basque Country, and in Galicia, the Hemingways returned to their new apartment in Paris in mid-September. Hadley also returned to Paris, in October, renting an apartment for Bumby and herself at 98 boulevard Auguste Blanqui.[109] While Pauline did her best to make their life there work, Paris had been poisoned for her and could never be quite the same. Haunted, Ernest had never intended to lose a family, Paris, or to betray someone so close to him, Hadley, his most trusted friend. By mid-March 1928, Pauline and Ernest, retaining the rented apartment at rue Férou, had decided to depart for America. Adrift in pursuit of Ernest's writing and in flight from another life, they nomadically visited family and friends, and rented rooms, *sans domicile fixe* during the next three years.[110]

• • • • •

On the other side of the Atlantic Ocean, Ernest walked along the Malecón of the harbor of Havana and gazed at the water that now separated him from it all: the painful divorce, the turbulent affair, his first family, the enchanted postwar period that he had known with Hadley, the trenches of World War I, the drunken dissolution of the artist class. He had taken his licks, come through it, and extracted all he could, from Stein, Pound, Joyce, Fitzgerald, and the rest of them, and at last the critics were hailing him as the new talent. He was a literary conqueror arriving home.

Returning along the walkway that separated the Old Town from the port, he looked over turquoise waters and really could not believe his luck; he wondered if he could put the bad part behind him. The scene of the Caribbean crossroads embodied origins and terminus. Like Ernest, Cuba's capital was *"ambos mundos,"* the best of both worlds, old and new. At that time tinny announcements over black-and-white newsreels lured would-be visitors with descriptions of the contrast in her cityscapes: the thrilling rebirth of a new capital amidst antique cultures, sophistication, and charm. But it had been Dos Passos's gushing descriptions of a "tropical, maritime, and unspoiled" paradise that had really primed his appetite.[111]

The two writers met as ambulance drivers in Italy during the war and became friends in Paris.[112] Dos Passos decided to hitchhike to Key West and returned to Paris to sing the glories of his "dreamlike crossing of the keys" and the tarpon fishing there he had seen. "A vacation paradise like no other in Florida. You ought to try it."[113] "The air smelt of the Gulf Stream" and there was "an island . . . Cayo Hueso, as half the people called it . . . linked by car-ferries with Havana," where "cigar factories had attracted a part Cuban, part Spanish population."[114] When Dos Passos told him about it, he had to see it for himself.

Turning his back on the sea, he looked toward the city of Havana. Her buildings, avenues, the faces of her people, the way they breathed and talked—details of an island at the edge of progress, caught between contending worlds. Her walls along the sea, Art Deco skyscrapers rising into the clouds, iron-railed balconies wrapping around the aging buildings of Old Havana, bells resounding on the hour, stone arches framing window displays, and the movements of people on promenade and between the shops—yes, here, he thought, he might really make a fresh start.

A phase of awakening in Paris was ending. His career was finally taking off, but not without considerable costs. Although now free from poverty, the financial security offered by his second marriage would not guarantee his independence.[115] The island of Cuba found itself in a similar knot as she emerged from colonial past to neocolonial present. As a long war for autonomy ended, she had become dependent upon the United States. Following a divorce from Spain, a prickly affair with a powerful northern neighbor would complicate Cuba's struggle for identity and independence.

Studying a storm as it travelled along the horizon, Ernest walked along the sea. His eyes wandered along the fortifications of an ancient city, and he daydreamed about raids of buccaneers whom he had often read about as a boy—pirates like François "Peg Leg" le Clerc (1554), the "Exterminating Angel" Jacques de Sores (1555), or Sir Francis Drake, who sent terror into Spaniards' hearts when he appeared in the spring of 1586 with twenty-three ships at the mouth of Havana's harbor, only to shark-circle and turn away. Or the Dutchman Piet Heyn (1628), who had captured the Spanish treasure fleet in the Bay of Matanzas. Or the Englishman Henry Morgan (1662), who had taken the castle guarding Santiago Bay and plundered the city—stealing everything of value, including the church's bells. Majestic renegades in square-rigged galleons with towering masts and puffing sails laid siege, lobbing cannonballs at the defenses of a forsaken Spanish fort. Ernest imagined the raiders as they leaped, blades in their teeth, seizing fortunes from marooned servants of the crown, from power assiduously amassed.[116]

Later that evening along the Malecón, passersby, perhaps the Hemingways among them, stood agape as a cannonball hopped over the high wall of the fort and plunked to the bottom of the sea while mulatto soldiers in white powdered wigs, tricornes, and red petticoats, retired colors, extinguished torches, and executed an about-face with the setting sun. The Havana tradition owed its origin to the Seven Years' War, when the British navy, encountering the weaknesses in Spain's defenses, seized the city of Havana for ten months. When the English returned Havana in exchange for Florida in 1762, Spanish sentinels reinforced fortifications and implemented the *cañonazo*, a "canon blast" advising citizens to return within the city gates by curfew, a tradition upheld at nine o'clock every day to this day.[117]

Ernest followed the wall to the seaport where the ledge along the water opened into the cobbled courtyard called the Plaza de Armas, a square containing Castillo de la Fuerza Real (the four-cornered Castle of the Royal Forces), formerly known as the Plaza de la Iglesia for the simple church there, Havana's first. In that square, the Spanish army had lived for over a century and trained their army to protect the settlers. In 1829, they added El Templete to the square, a neoclassical temple to commemorate the city's founding in 1519. At the base of the temple grew Havana's most visited resident, a ceiba tree, a living shrine to thousands of believers from the Yoruba faith taken from their home to work the soil in the white man's promised land. Following the locals' example, Ernest touched the tree for good luck.

Hibiscus, begonia, and jasmine sprouted from the garden island in the middle of the Plaza de Armas and emitted an intense bouquet. Around the flowers rose trunks of poplar, palm, and bamboo, reaching their branches over the square and lending it shade and sanctuary. In the twirling shadows of falling leaves stood a stone likeness of "the despot," King Fernando VII, smiling confidently with his cape about his shoulders. Later, Cubans would remove his statue and replace it with that of Carlos Manuel de Céspedes, the Cuban landowner who, on October 10, 1868, became a *héroe nacional* for his decision to free his slaves, setting the sparks in motion for Cuba's long-desired war for freedom.[118]

Wiping the sweat accumulating on his brow, Ernest sat on a bench in front of the statue of the Spanish king, and he observed the passersby with African features and many shades of mulatto skin. When the Spanish had been unable to enslave the natives, they abducted Africans from Angola, Zaire, Congo, Nigeria, Cameroon, Benin, Sierra Leone, and Ghana or purchased them from warring tribes, to use them in a lucrative tobacco and sugar trade.[119] Shackled tightly together below the deck of ships, hundreds of seasick slaves endured agony, extreme heat, drownings, and death by disease during the two-to-three-month crossing of the Middle Passage. Historians estimate 11 million Africans survived the arduous crossing and enslavement in the Americas, while approximately 17.8 million (or three out of every five) died en route.[120] Those Africans who survived mixed with each other, with native peoples, with other immigrants, and with their Spanish masters to become *Criollos*, or Creoles: mixed-race peoples born in America, recipients of discrimination from colonists reinforcing control of territory and resources.

For centuries, Creoles and slaves arose in isolated rebellions, only to be put down again. After decades of illicit meetings, mountain militias on the move, funds elicited from dissidents abroad, and armies trained on the other side of the sea, slave-owners and slaves united in the fight against their Spanish oppressors. As the story goes, plantation owner Carlos Manuel de Céspedes rang the bell of his house in Bayamo, not to summon slaves to supper or to work the fields, but to announce that they were free. Céspedes then asked these freed men if they would join him in battle against the Spanish, and all present answered "*¡Que sí!*"[121] When the rebel "mambí" forces surprised the Spanish colonial army and took Bayamo, Cuba's national anthem, "La Bayamesa," was born: "Run to battle, men of Bayamo. The motherland looks proudly to you. Do not fear a glorious death. Because to die for the motherland is to live. To live in chains is to live mired in shame and disgrace. From the bugle hear the sound. Run, brave ones, to battle!"[122]

"There are things that never get to be what they're supposed to be," writes Manuel Pereiras García. Cuban writer Eliseo Alberto adds, "In Cuba the past never passes."[123] After three hundred fifty years of slavery and colonial rule, Cuba fought three separate wars for independence between 1868 and 1898, the last one ending the year before Ernest was born. Céspedes's "*grito de Yara*" ("battle cry of Yara") was a defining moment in the island's history, for it was the spark inspiring mixed-race peoples of Cuban birth to rise up decisively against colonial rule, led by figures like Agramonte, Figueredo, Gutiérrez, Máximo Gómez, and Antonio Maceo.[124] Of the forty-two thousand mambí resistance fighters, 80 to 90 percent descended from African slaves, and two generals, Antonio Maceo and Quintín Bandera, were Creole. Historians have often described the Cuban War of Independence as the largest slave rebellion in the New World.[125] However, Cuba's story of revolt started, not with Céspedes, José Martí, or even Fidel Castro, but with a defiant Taíno native chief named Hatuey, who was burned at the stake in 1512 for guerrilla attacks on Iberian explorers. From early in her history, uprisings became, lamentably, inseparable from the island's identity.

Ernest removed his jacket and tie and hung them beside him on the bench; he leaned back to behold the giant flamboyant tree rising behind him and spreading resplendent branches overhead. When the wind rushed through the plaza, the bright orange petals of her flowers detached, twirling as they fell to the cobbled ground. In the sedative splendor of the historic square, Ernest's restless mind reeled as it took measure of the possibilities of an island whose stylish hotels would cost him only two American dollars per day.[126]

A boy carrying a box of brushes raised his eyebrows and made a clicking sound with his mouth as he looked at Ernest's shoes. Smiling kindly at him, Ernest extended a foot and watched as the boy ran his rag across. The boy was about a year older than Bumby. It was then that Ernest, with a faint smile glimmering beneath his clean mustache, noticed that he was being observed by natives assessing him at the edges of the square. Some still equated Americans with opportunity while others were always wary of the appetites that awakened predictably soon after foreign landings on their blinding white coasts. At the corner of the plaza, there were tables set out. When a waiter walked by carrying two Hatuey beers, Ernest looked at the cold bottles sweating in the sun, thinking he might like to try one that afternoon. What would Hatuey himself have had to say, if he had known about the beer that would later bear his name?

Among new arrivals, Cuba had often been called "*la manzana*"—the apple from which they longed to take a bite.[127] Even President Thomas Jefferson openly coveted the isle, admitting to his successor, James Madison, "I candidly confess that I have ever looked upon Cuba as the most interesting addition that can be made to our system of States," after he failed to purchase it from Spain in 1808. If we could acquire Cuba and Canada, Jefferson reasoned, "we should have such an empire for liberty as she has never surveyed since the creation."[128] In 1820, Thomas Jefferson pressed US War Secretary John Calhoun to just "take Cuba . . . at the first possible opportunity."[129]

After the Seminole Wars in Florida, suppressing unruly Indians and slaves there, General Andrew Jackson and President John Quincy Adams compelled Spain to cede these territories to the United States in 1819; four years later, Adams outlined a theory known as "*la fruta madura*" ("the ripe fruit"), which reasoned that the "ripe fruit" of Cuba, once separated from Spain by a passing storm, would not fall to the ground but gravitate toward the North American "bosom."[130] In 1823, President James Monroe further propagated the pursuit of manifest destiny in Latin America when he enacted the foreign policy known as the Monroe Doctrine, warning the nations of Europe to leave "America to the Americans": any meddling by European countries in the Western Hemisphere would compel the United States to defend its interests.[131]

As slavery ended in the United States, owners of large plantations—like John Quitman who became Governor of Mississippi—plotted to move operations south, supported by other politicians, such as John Henderson (a senator from Mississippi), and by journalists, like Laurence J. Sigur (an editor advocating in *New Orleans Delta*).[132] Ambitions blazing, these Southern leaders creatively funded several private forays into Latin America, like those by Narciso López, William Crittenden, and William Walker, as well as public incursions like the Banana Wars denounced by Major General Smedley Butler. The longing for Latin American territories had not dissipated by the end of the nineteenth century, when Assistant Secretary of the Navy Theodore Roosevelt was rapidly increasing the United States' fleet, acquiring territories, and advocating an open declaration of war against Spain, a leading global-economic competitor at that time.[133] Having lived in the United States, José Martí prophesized of American expansionism, "I have lived in the monster; I know its guts. My sling is that of David"[134]—words uttered on the eve of his death, echoing on the lips of every cubano today, because their prediction came true.

• • • • •

Gracias," said Ernest Hemingway as he paid for the shine; he gathered his jacket and crossed the plaza beneath the arid vines of a two-hundred-year-old banyan tree. Through its canopy, he could see the balcony window of his hotel room and that the shutters were open.

After breakfast on the terrace the next morning, Pauline and Ernest came down into the lobby, met their driver, and circled the town by autocar. As they passed along the newly inaugurated Fifth Avenue, connecting the city center to the new developments along the sea, the driver pointed to Biltmore Yacht and Country Club, and showcased a two-thousand-acre estate where prospector John McEntee Bowman was building enticing vacation homes in the Playa, Miramar, Country Club Park, and Marianao districts in Spanish and neocolonial style. It was becoming increasingly fashionable for the wealthy families, like that of American chemicals tycoon Irénée du Pont,[135] to own one, which a girl from the Pfeiffer family would have already known. Returning through Vedado, they passed Taganana Hill, where the soon-to-be celebrated Hotel Nacional was under construction.

On a hill beside the sea, workers were digging a private swimming pool. In front of the hill were two columns, a monument inaugurated three years earlier, in 1925, to honor the soldiers who died in the event that sparked the Spanish-American War.[136] With busts of William McKinley, the US president who declared war; General Leonard Wood, the second American governor of Cuba; and Theodore Roosevelt, the *Maine* memorial remembers the 226 men who died there on February 15, 1898, when their ship exploded.[137] After the explosion, the wreckage of the sunken ship, with its mast protruding just above water, blocked Havana harbor and became a point of interest among sightseers until an act of Congress and the US Army Corps of Engineers removed it, repatriated the sailors' remains, and dragged the wreck four miles out to sea in 1912.

The last shots of the Spanish-American War had been fired one year before Ernest was born. During Lieutenant Colonel Teddy Roosevelt's "splendid little" ten-week war, the Rough Riders took San Juan Hill, becoming the living embodiment of American expansionism. At the Treaty of Paris on December 10, 1898, Spain surrendered Cuba, Puerto Rico, Guam, Wake Island, and the Philippines to the United States (which also annexed Hawaii and Samoa during the conflict), but Cuba's representatives were conspicuously absent. At the end of a thirty-year struggle for autonomy, Cuba found itself a protectorate in "America's care," for its future good.[138]

One of Cuba's most respected military leaders, General Máximo Gómez, nicknamed "the Fox" by his Spanish adversaries, declined an invitation to attend the ceremony where the American flag was to be raised over Castillo del Morro in Havana, writing in his diary on January 8, 1899: "Ours is the Cuban flag, the one for which so many tears and blood have been shed. We must remain united to bring to an end this unjustified military occupation."[139] The intervention and expansionism at the outset of the twentieth century ultimately led to a "century of mistrust" in Cuba and in Latin America.[140]

The Platt Amendment to Cuba's constitution, added on Christmas of 1901, granted the US military the right to intervene in Cuban affairs if necessary "for the preservation of Cuban independence" and to maintain bases on the island. American General John R. Brooke governed for a year, then turned his post over to General Leonard Wood, who continued American supervision of the transition to full democracy for three more years before an "election" occurred. In a neocolonial, neoconquistador manner, the new governor conceptualized his job in both racial and religious terms:

> It is our God-given mission, and the whole Christian World is watching to see if the great American republic is equal to the strain. We are dealing with a race that has steadily been going down for one hundred years and into which we have to infuse new life, new principles, and new methods of doing things.[141]

Among the candidates for president during Cuba's first election was Bartolomé Masó, a staunch opponent of US occupation and the Platt Amendment, until he withdrew under US pressure.[142] His opponent, Estrada Palma, won the election by default. To quiet rising civil unrest, US troops returned in 1906, when Ernest was seven years old, and did not depart until he was turning ten. Until 1909, American governors William Howard Taft and Charles Edward Magoon ruled the protectorate, then relinquished power in 1913 to a marionette.

"On to Cuba!" proclaimed the *New York Journal* when war against Spain had ended and US occupation ensued. "The war-ridden isle is expected to be a veritable Klondike of wealth," "a new country," a "virgin land," and "the land of promise."[143] Soon there were dozens of homesteading companies, such as the Cuban Land and Steamship Company in 1899, reselling subdivided, marked-up land plots that they had snatched up cheaply right after the war: "Such a field of wealth has never before been opened. It may mean a fortune to you. It certainly means happiness, comfort, and competence to those who accept our offer . . . Why toil, starve, and freeze, when by at once taking advantage of this offer you can reap a golden harvest, and live a life of comparative ease."[144] After the Panic of 1893 and a depression until 1898, thousands of unfulfilled and unemployed Americans began arriving on the island that promoters described as the next frontier, the new California, a fruit farmer's dream, the promised land, their destiny itself manifesting.[145]

After decades of war, Cuba found itself in ruins and without the financial capital to recover. Bolstered by favorable legislation, speculators descended upon the island like vultures on a carcass and North American investments increased tenfold. By purchasing the land at rock-bottom prices, stakeholders created modern American mills, called latifundia,[146] which would come to dominate the agricultural economy and push out small farmers dependent on antiquated equipment.[147] In cahoots with American investors like United Fruit, Cuban-American Sugar, American Sugar Refining, and Milton Hershey (the "Chocolate King" who still has a town named after him in Cuba), a new breed of dictators ascended to power: José Miguel Gómez (1908–1912), Mario García Menocal (1912–1920), Alfredo Zayas (1920–1924), who erected an opulent presidential palace in 1921, and culminating with Gerardo Machado (1924–1933) and Fulgencio Batista's 1940 coup.

During this time, illicit deals flourished and unprecedented riches flowed in, filling state's coffers with loans from robber barons like J. P. Morgan and John D. Rockefeller, advancing $9 million and $100 million for "public works"[148] and creating one of the most spectacular capitols that Latin America had ever seen, as Cuba miraculously emerged from the ashes after decades of war, resurrecting itself.[149] While their governors were making deals, the other 99 percent of Cuba's citizens remained in distant *barrios marginales* in thin-roofed *solars*,[150] with dirt floors and crumbling walls, until they objected to not sharing in the profits extracted from the nation's resources and land, to their abject conditions, and to the manufacturing infrastructures built to support foreign companies from public funds.[151]

After World War I devastated the farms of European beet sugar, the value of Cuban cane sugar spiked, and landowners repositioned themselves to provide American buyers with much more of the lucrative crop.[152] Those who cashed in on the gold mine of sugar tasted a period of opulence that rivaled American standards—in the words of American visitors to Cuba at that time: "Cubans spend money with both hands . . . and they could teach us Americans about the art of extravagance in the construction of beautiful houses and the purchase of jewelry, clothing from Paris, and large automobiles."[153]

To attend to the boom in Cuban sugar, seasonal workers poured in from all over the Caribbean to collect the Cuban harvest, or *zafra*. Perversely, many Cuban farmers no longer owning land found themselves working the *colonias* of foreign owners and competing for jobs with migrants from Haiti, Jamaica, and Barbados.[154] During the period from 1900 to 1930, sugar mills proliferated in the east of the island and railroads expanded to transport the cane, and Cuba became the world's premier sugar producer with American investors owning 40 to 50 percent.[155]

A common Cuban expression laments, "*Sin azúcar no hay país*" ("Without sugar, there is no country"), but Cuban sugar often made promises it could not keep. Cuban agriculture's focus on a single crop and a single customer made for a roller-coaster economy when the price of sugar rose and fell in the mid-1920s from 4.2 cents per pound in 1924 to 2.6 in 1926.[156] When the people protested that they were not benefiting from the resources extracted from their country's soil, governors begged and borrowed money from American banks to launch projects of public works, laying roads and inaugurating buildings—while taking advantage of the large disbursements by dipping hands in the cookie jar in varied and creative ways.

After the War of Independence ended, Americans and Spaniards still owned much of the land and resources in Cuba, but Cuban leaders demonstrated resourcefulness: it has often been said by Cuban historians that the second zafra in Cuba during the early twentieth century was politics. Gerardo Machado, the son of a tobacco and cattle farmer, had distinguished himself in combat during the War of Independence. Riding waves of protest in 1925 to include the founding of the Cuban Communist Party during that year, Machado ran for president as a member of the Liberal Party, promising "Water, Roads, and Schools" and depicting himself "on foot, with the people," in contrast to the conservative candidate, General Mario García Menocal, who was often seen on horseback. The campaign won him the presidency.[157] Having sworn he would fix everything from the crumbling infrastructure to the injustices of the Platt Amendment, Machado insisted on presidential term limits, pledged to eliminate corruption, and barnstormed for fair trade and autonomy from the United States. With a gleam in his eye, he proclaimed that he would soon make Cuba the "Switzerland of the Americas," but instead he soon became one of the worst dictators in Cuban history.[158]

Restoring order to angry people would present a significant challenge. While Cuba's president Machado's commitment to law and order was laudable, uncompromising tactics revealed the dictatorial inclinations in the school of recent rulers like Miguel Primo de Rivera, António de Oliveira Salazar, or Benito Mussolini, during an era where fascism was on the rise. Ushering in the new era, Mussolini cynically announced in 1928, the same year Hemingway arrived in Cuba: "Democracy is beautiful in theory; in practice, it's a fallacy. You in America will see that someday."[159] The first two years of Machado's presidency fulfilled many hopes by passing laws to protect Cuban architecture; regulating the sugar industry; and commissioning projects to build roads (like the new National Highway), railroads, bridges, and discernable buildings like the Capitol dome and the Hotel Nacional. Initially at least, Machado walked a line by encouraging foreign investment while advocating Cuban autonomy and development.

As public works deals proliferated and public funds evaporated, the public's suspicions piqued concerning money siphoned behind the scenes. When a pro-Machado "Constitutional Assembly" broke his key campaign promise by passing a new law extending presidential term length from four to six years, officials at the American embassy suspected that he had used public funds to bribe members of the opposing parties. Diverse factions unified against him, including the Directorio Estudiantil Universitario in 1927 that organized protests on the steps of the University of Havana.[160] Students demanded democratic processes be reinstated and the president, whom they considered a "tropical Mussolini," removed.[161] The university administration, taking orders from Machado's cabinet, convened a tribunal and permanently expelled several students for speaking out.[162] The students responded by organizing workers and intellectuals all over the island to put pressure on what they now considered to be an illegitimate government. With a pregnant bride in tow and eager to return home, Ernest may not have read about the students' expulsion in the local newspaper, but the attentive writer and his wife would have noted the ambition, corruption, insurgence, and suppression in Havana, in conversation at the street corners, in the strides of passersby, and in their eyes.

After two days in Cuba, Pauline and Ernest boarded another steamer, Peninsular and Occidental's SS *Cuba*, carrying them over the last ninety-mile stretch to Key West, Florida. Cleaving north, the ship left a streak of wake like a white scar across the purple belly of the sea. Holding her husband's hand and leaning into his shoulder, Pauline placed the other hand on her abdomen to feel the movements of a child she would have now with the man she had desired and won.[163] They turned a moment later toward the horizon and crossed it in pursuit of ever-elusive happiness.

CHAPTER 2

Oak Park and the War, *Fathers and Sons* (1899–1932)

• • • • •

Arriving in Key West, the couple was advised that the Model T roadster that Pauline's Uncle Gus had bought them had not yet arrived. No matter. What could bother "a writer writing" when he was on the water and on a roll—with a new story already taking hold?[1] While they waited for the automobile, the Ford Motor Company accommodated them at an agency apartment at 314 Simonton Street.[2] There, Ernest sunk himself into scenes familiar to him from the Great War and combined them with others imagined from a humbling retreat after the Battle of Caporetto.[3] Struggling with a previous manuscript, he had failed to produce a book, but he had the feeling now that he was onto something big.[4]

After being wounded on the Italian front, Frederic Henry from *A Farewell to Arms* finds himself in a hospital in Milan and falls in love with an American nurse, Catherine Barkley. Deserting his unit and "the War," Henry seeks a separate peace, and he finds a brief idyll in Switzerland with Catherine before death returns and steals his wife and child during birth. Ernest, determined to make his story and characters more vivid than those in *The Sun Also Rises*, would employ a favorite technique of returning to experiences that he had lived firsthand—the war wound and recovery at the hospital in Milan, the rejection by the twenty-seven-year-old American nurse Agnes von Kurowsky, and moments with Hadley in Chamby during their matrimonial bliss—then combining them with recent events that were still unfolding, such as the retreat from Paris with Pauline and the upcoming and complicated birth of his second son.[5]

As the dawn faded in humid Key West, he scribbled and sweated to convey the scenes of love and war that had affected him in the snowy Italian mountains and everything he had lost since then.[6] In the afternoons exhausted, he recuperated by fishing beneath an offshore breeze in the turquoise waters of the Gulf.

Approaching delivery, Pauline longed to finish the journey home to Piggott, Arkansas, but she also loved seeing her husband this way: truly happy only when he was writing well. When she looked in on him each morning, she dared not disturb his rhythm, for she could see it in his eyes and in his forward-lean in his chair while rereading the day's results. Soon the Ford arrived, but Ernest could not risk leaving this place where his story was at last unfolding. So they lingered in Key West, the scanty island town where he and his story were coming alive.[7]

While fishing in Key West in 1928, Ernest had met several people who became influential and longtime friends, like rumrunner and speakeasy-owner Joe Russell, and bait-and-tackle-shop owner Charles Thompson. When Ernest received a visit from friends from Paris, writer John Dos Passos and painter Waldo Peirce, the Bahamian captain Bra Saunders took "the Mob" charter fishing on his boat. When a tropical storm appeared without warning, they had to seek shelter at Fort Jefferson.[8] Stranded for seventeen days, they survived on canned goods and whatever fish they could catch.

There, Ernest encountered two Cuban fishing captains, also marooned on the island, named Carlos Gutierrez and Gregorio Fuentes.[9] When Ernest's party ran out of supplies, Gregorio gave them food and rum. Gregorio also took him in his broken-down boat, the *Joaquín Cisto*, across unsafe waters through a storm to a neighboring cay where Gregorio knew the lighthouse operators so that Ernest could use the telephone.[10] Carlos, captain of the schooner *Paco*, also insisted on giving Ernest's party some food, and on their last night in Dry Tortugas, Ernest invited Carlos and his crew over to share some rum.[11] A night of jug passing and tall tales ensued. Carlos, a commercial fisherman who had been going to sea with his father since 1884 when he was six years old, told his own tales of 120-foot whale sharks, of a fight between a shark and a dolphin, of 20-foot rattlesnakes that swam off the coast of the Gulf of Mexico, and of the crocodiles floating lazily there many miles out at sea.[12]

Respected among Havana fishermen, Carlos held the record for the highest number of marlin caught in a single season, bettering hundreds of others, even other commercial fishermen working out of Casablanca docks.[13] That evening, Carlos told Ernest about the marlin that swam off the coast of Cuba every summer season, rising from the depths of the sea, leaping into the air, and crashing into the waves.[14] If Ernest ever wanted to return to Cuba, Carlos agreed to teach him all he knew about these noble creatures, out "on the blue water."[15]

On April 10, Ernest's parents unexpectedly arrived in Key West by ferry, returning from a vacation in Havana and accompanied by Uncle Willoughby on hiatus from missionary duties in the Far East. Neither son nor parents had communicated their plans to the other: their meeting was unexpected.[16] Dr. Clarence "Ed" Hemingway and his wife Grace had not seen their son in four years, and they had never met Pauline. The five of them hurriedly toured the island together that day.

The afternoon's photographs offer glimpses of Pauline heavy with child and Ernest leaning across his new bright yellow automobile. The writer is wearing a casual sweater vest, and his father a three-piece suit. In the photograph, his "hawk-nosed" father gapes at his son with admiration and concern, while Ernest smiles, red faced, and crosses his arms conspicuously in front of his crotch.[17] His father's diminishing weight, vacant stare, and graying complexion depict a man in sharp decline, but too close-lipped or proud to say it to his son. Before the parents continued that evening to Saint Petersburg as planned, they said choked-up farewells on the docks.

The visit, however brief, had done them all some good. Despite differences, they were family. In the letters that followed this visit, Dr. Hemingway said that they had gone much too long without seeing each other and that he was eager to see Ernest and his family again in Oak Park in a few months. He did not mention his worsening health, financial difficulties, and unpaid taxes on bad investments in Florida.[18]

These were problems that his son, a successful writer married to a wealthy family, might have done something about. From a cabin in the Smoky Mountains, Ed wrote his son, "Ernest, How I wish you and Leicester [Ernest's brother] were here with me in this wonderful trout country."

• • • • •

Ernest grew up in a suburb of Chicago in the heartland of the United States, a country town that took pleasure both in its increasing affluence and its separation from the "big city."

All over America during the early twentieth century, farms, homesteads, and open country were rapidly industrializing and assuming the frenzied, mechanized paces of the new epoch they were calling the Modern Age. The family's passion was a cabin in the Michigan woods, which offered wide spaces and "wild, open country" for their lionhearted children to explore and overcome.[19]

As the boy grew, more and more of his town's members had electricity, automobiles, and telephones, surrendering provincial insulation and attaining the amenities and vices of a modern world.[20] While the eldest members of Ernest's community had pursued Sioux Indians across the plains and shot real bison along the outer reaches of the American frontier, neither Ernest nor his father would do so. Within commuting distance of the urban jungle of Chicago, the conservative, affluent, and genteel community of Oak Park, Illinois, looked forward pragmatically, offered one of the best school systems in the nation, awarded cultural achievements, and provided numerous examples for its children to emulate. Thus Ernest re-created the frontier in his imagination and his weapon of choice became a Corona typewriter.

Oak Park employed competent teachers, like Fannie Biggs, and supported parents as they required that children apply themselves. In her journalism class, structured "as though the classroom were a newspaper office," and in extracurriculars like *The Trapeze*, the school paper, Biggs applauded Ernest's stories, no matter how amateurish they might have been.[21] Ernest's mother, Grace, the parent primarily responsible for her children's upbringing, was as quick to praise her children's achievements as she was to criticize the weakening of their resolve.[22]

Just before Ernest entered Oak Park High School, the American military returned to Cuba to suppress an uprising of ten thousand Afro-Cubans, members of the Independent Party of Color who had revolted, and to slay more than two thousand of the same. Back home, Ernest benefited not only from a first-rate education but also from his family's connections. Henry Haskell, Uncle Tyler Hemingway's classmate at Oberlin College, was chief editorial writer at the *Kansas City Star.* When Ernest graduated, Ed Hemingway asked his brother, Tyler, to contact Haskell to give Ernest a chance. The *Star* agreed to employ him on a thirty-day trial period as a cub reporter from eight to five, six days per week, at fifteen dollars per week.

His iconic editor, "Pete" Wellington, ordered him to memorize the 110 items of his style sheet, transforming the high schooler's clumsy sentences into vigorous prose. Among the items were maxims such as "Use short sentences. Use short first paragraphs. Use vigorous English. Be positive, not negative."[23] Hemingway later remembered Wellington as a "stern disciplinarian, very just and very harsh," and that those were "the best rules I ever learned for the business of writing. I've never forgotten them."[24]

Every year, Ernest's grandfathers, who had fought for the Union during the Civil War, donned their uniforms, marched with the Military Order of the Loyal Legion or the Grand Army of the Republic, and were honored by their community.[25] Their sacrifice and their moral duty composed a mythology, an ethos for Oak Park, shared by President Woodrow Wilson and by Secretary of the Navy Theodore Roosevelt, preaching and practicing a "strenuous life," "manly virtue," and "service to the common good."[26] During the Spanish-American War, Teddy Roosevelt and his band of Rough Riders had taken San Juan Hill, the year before the writer was born, and brought his country's ethics to the islands of the Caribbean and the Pacific.

• • • • •

Ernest's generation had heard the stories. When they came of age, it was their turn.

Extra, extra, read all about it: "Archduke Assassinated," "Lusitania Sunk," "Germany Declares War," "All Europe is in Arms," "Germany Invades France," "French Resist at Marne," "Austria Has Chosen War," "Italy Declares War," "US Declares War," "Wilson Signs War Decree," "War Declared by All." Daily newspapers and weekly newsreels bombarded an entire generation of young people with fabulous stories and movie-screen-sized scenes from "the Great War." It was all larger-than-life, the most magnificent occurrence in their tender lives; none need be told to respond to the call of duty in the next great American "adventure," but their elders did encourage and recruit them to participate as soldiers, sailors, airmen, corpsmen, nurses, and ambulance drivers.

Every young fella whom Ernest knew would be volunteering just as soon as he could. Those who "shirked their duty" or did not wish to follow would be branded "yellow," weaklings, cowards to the core. Henry Serrano Villard, who had responded to Red Cross recruitment with Ernest, recalls they were both "fired by patriotic fervor, bent on helping to make the world safe for democracy," and that they saw the war as an event that nobody dare miss: "Not for anything would I have missed the opportunity for a ringside view of the greatest spectacle to unfold in our time. To many of us the war in Europe resembled a gigantic stage on which the most exciting drama ever produced was being played out." As the poet Archibald MacLeish described the war, "It was something you 'went to' from a place called Paris."[27] Along with 4.8 million other men, Ernest put his career on hold and shipped out.[28]

At the front, these young men would discover firsthand just how strenuous the "strenuous life" could be: artillery bombardments, mustard gas, modern fighter planes, machine guns, the first tanks, and trench warfare. If they survived to see the armistice on November 11, 1918, they then discovered on January 6, 1919, that Roosevelt, an indestructible model of manly virtue, had died. Six months later, they watched as a flawed peace process at Versailles sowed the seeds of a second world war, and it became more difficult to understand why hundreds of thousands of young men and women, family and friends, had been lost.[29] As a "Lost Generation" of shell-shocked fighters returned home, financial booms and busts complicated their employment, "flappers" confounded their sensibilities, Prohibition obstructed their anesthetization, and other upheavals emerged throughout the "Roaring Twenties."[30]

Hobbling in uniform in his hometown once again, a young Hemingway had survived, was greeted as a hero, and asked to speak at several functions. At his high school, he took the stage and imparted the wisdom he had acquired in the war.[31] To the *Oak Parker* newspaper, he declared, "I went because I wanted to go . . . I was big and strong, my country needed me, and I went and did whatever I was told—and anything I did outside of that was simply my duty."[32] Just after that, however, his nurse, Agnes von Kurowsky, who had left nineteen-year-old "Ernie" smitten at the *l'opspedale della croce rossa* in Milan, dropped another bombshell in a letter notifying him that she had decided to marry another man, a real one rather than a kid like him.[33]

Taking this bruise to his manhood rather badly, the boy wonder recoiled to the woods to camp, hunt, fish, and write—alone or in the company of William Horne (a fellow ambulance driver) or Bill and Katy Smith (childhood friends) during the medicinal summer of 1919. Likely suffering from post-traumatic stress disorder and certainly from a broken heart, Ernest now focused on writing various short stories.[34] He enjoyed a brief but ultimately unsatisfying relationship with seventeen-year-old Marjorie Bump, a pudgy, red-headed, freckle-faced waitress and daughter of a hardware store dealer in the logging town of Petoskey. Then to write, he holed up in a lake cottage in Michigan throughout the summer, then stayed after its end. There, to ease his loneliness, he had a mechanical affair with Liz Dilworth, a waitress and neighbor.[35]

By fall, Ernest escaped to a boardinghouse on Horton Bay to continue his writing in dogged yet fruitless attempts rejected by editors at the *Saturday Evening Post* and *Popular Magazine*.[36] One day, he put on his uniform and delivered another "war lecture" at the local library, which produced lucrative results: in attendance were his mother's wealthy friend Harriet Connable and her invalid son, Ralph Connable, Jr. They were so dazzled by the war hero and aspiring writer that they offered him a position in Toronto as Ralph Jr.'s caretaker at fifty dollars per month with all expenses paid.

In mid-January, Ernest accepted and moved into their mansion. Ralph Sr., an influential businessman expanding the Woolworth department store chain into Canada, presented Ernest to his friends at the *Toronto Star Daily*, namely, to Gregory Clark, features editor.[37] While Clark was not initially impressed with the lumbering boy-braggart, he warmed to him during a fishing and skiing trip and introduced him to the chief editor, J. H. Cranston, when they returned. Cranston could pay him only ten dollars per story, he said, but in February, Ernest became a regular contributor to the *Star*.[38] By mid-May, he had published eleven stories in the newspaper.[39]

Attempting to while away another summer on Walloon Lake in 1920, Ernest and buddies snuck his sisters out for a midnight picnic when his parents' tolerance for his lack of direction was already wearing thin. When his sisters' absence was discovered, it caused a scandal. Weary of his idleness, mother and father criticized their son's joblessness, his spending habits, his vanity, his lust, his godlessness, and his corrosive influence on his sisters.[40] In her "bankruptcy letter," Grace tallied his numerous transgressions by which he had depleted the emotional account between mother and son: "There is nothing before you but bankruptcy: *You have overdrawn.*"[41] In alliance with Ernest's father, Grace insisted that her son get his act together. In his own letter, the father reiterated her marching orders: to vacate the family cabin and to make something of his life at once.[42] Ernest and Bill Horne moved into a friend's apartment at 100 East Chicago Avenue while they looked for work, but in 1920 and 1921, an economic recession took hold, accompanied by labor strikes with thousands of unemployed veterans marching for their "bonus."

Responding to an advertisement, Ernest found a job at forty dollars per week writing for *Cooperative Commonwealth*, a magazine for Midwestern farmers. After Christmas, Ernest's living arrangement expired, so he moved into a seven-room apartment on 63 East Division Street with Bill and Katy Smith's big brother, Y. K. By mid-January, Y. K. had introduced Ernest to his friend Sherwood Anderson, who was a well-known writer at the time.

When the president of *Cooperative Commonwealth* defrauded

the company of millions and left Ernest without employment, the twenty–year-old journalist wrote John Bone, managing editor of the *Toronto Star Daily* for a job, perhaps in Toronto or in Italy, and Bone offered him a spot at the Paris office of the *Star* at seventy-five dollars per week, plus expenses. Sherwood Anderson provided letters of introduction addressed to all his "Parisian" friends: Lewis Galantière, Gertrude Stein, and Ezra Pound. Armed with these letters, Ernest and his first wife, Hadley, alias "Wemedge" and "Wicky Poo," booked passage aboard SS *Leopoldina* and arrived just before the Christmas of 1921. As the Hemingways arrived in Paris, the US Marines' occupation of Cuba, known as the "Sugar Intervention," marked its fourth consecutive year, leaving a permanent guard in the east at Guantánamo Bay in 1922 to ensure that production continued unimpeded by revolt or popular protest.

During his first spring in Paris in 1922, Ernest Hemingway met the mentors and friends that would connect him and teach him what he needed to know: Stein, Pound, James Joyce, John Dos Passos, F. Scott Fitzgerald, and Ford Madox Ford, with whom he edited the *Transatlantic Review.*[43] Residing first in the Latin Quarter at 74 rue Cardinale Lemoine, he and Hadley borrowed books from Sylvia Beach's Shakespeare and Company library and bought others at the bookstalls along the quais of the river Seine: Tolstoy, Turgenev, Gogol, Chekhov, Dostoyevsky, Stendhal, Flaubert, Maupassant, Baudelaire, Proust, Marryat, Thomas Mann, Henry James, D. H. Lawrence, James Joyce, T. S. Elliot, Fielding, Anderson, Kipling, Crane, Conrad, Melville, Twain, Hawthorne, Thoreau, Donne, and Shakespeare.[44] Ernest travelled extensively as a foreign correspondent for the *Toronto Star,* covering the important European events such as the Lausanne peace conference, the burning of Smyrna, and the Greco-Turkish Wars, while also squeezing in skiing, fishing, bullfights, and swimming on holiday in Switzerland, Spain, and along the *côte Atlantique.*[45]

After a brief return to Toronto for their first child's birth in October 1923, Ernest and Hadley arrived back in Paris in January, relocating to the working-class neighborhood near Montparnasse in the apartment above a sawmill at 113 rue Notre-Dame des Champs. During their absence, Robert McAlmon's small press, Contact Editions, had published just three hundred copies of *Three Stories and Ten Poems* by Ernest Hemingway (containing "Up in Michigan," "Out of Season," and "My Old Man") locally in Paris, putting it in the hands of fellow artists who were in the know. The *Transatlantic Review* published "Indian Camp" along with pieces of the unfinished manuscript of Joyce's *Finnegans Wake*.[46]

From afar, Ernest read of the millions of US veterans struggling to make ends meet petition for "a compensation adjustment" for wages lost while serving overseas. The opposition was quick to label them as "bonus seekers," and among members of Ernest's generation, a sense of betrayal simmered. Insisting on fiscal integrity, President Warren Harding had first vetoed their "bonus bill" in September 1922. When Harding died suddenly of a heart attack halfway through his third year in office, President Calvin Coolidge vetoed the bonus bill again and chided veterans as he held the line again in May 1924: "Patriotism . . . bought and paid for is not patriotism."[47] A few days later, two-thirds of Congress overrode the president's veto by agreeing to pay the veterans $1.00 for each day of service at home and $1.25 for each day of service abroad, but with a catch: they would not receive the money until the bonds matured twenty-one years later, in 1945. A provision of the bill required the government to pay vets immediately in the event of their untimely death, which earned it the nickname of the "tombstone bonus." For a time, the vets seemed to be placated.

Practicing the "discipline of hunger" in Paris, Ernest observed the paintings in the galleries of the Jardin du Luxembourg and Musée d'Orsay, and found a clean, well-lit space to write in the cafés of the Left Bank, where he filled his lined notebooks with the hard-boiled vignettes and stories of *In Our Time*, published first with Three Mountains Press in 1924, and later expanded and republished with Boni and Liveright in 1925. Its fragmented, brutal, and unrelenting style expressed itself in eighteen vignettes and stories, like "On the Quai at Smyrna," "L'Envoi," "Indian Camp," "The Doctor and the Doctor's Wife," "The End of Something," "The Three-Day Blow," "A Very Short Story," "Soldier's Home," "The Revolutionist," "The Battler," "Out of Season," and "Big Two-Hearted River."

"Big Two-Hearted River"—the story of a young man's fishing

trip—was at once simple and profound. After much training and discipline, and many false starts, Ernest was grasping his craft, finding his rhythm, and making art look effortless—it was a magical period of artistic awakening when he discovered his astonishing talent. Reminiscing about his creative process for the story, Ernest wrote, "I sat in a corner with the afternoon light coming in over my shoulder and wrote in the notebook . . . When I stopped writing I did not want to leave the river where I could see the trout in the pool, its surface pushing and swelling smooth against the resistance of the log-driven piles of the bridge. The story was about coming back from the war but there was no mention of the war in it."[48] Drawing from what he had learned from the artists whom he respected, from scenes of war and nature, and from his powers of observation, Ernest created a new style and techniques. Through the "art of omission," Ernest evoked and tapped into emotions running beneath the surface, connecting with readers in powerful ways.[49] His stories had a unique quality about them in those early years and attracted a great deal of critical attention.

When Scribner's published his first novel, *The Sun Also Rises*, in October 1926, Sylvia Beach—who had known Ernest from the early days, when he had come to Paris looking for a lucky break—threw him a party to celebrate and perhaps to cheer him up. It had upset Ernest to hear Gertrude Stein and others of his elders throwing around the phrase "Lost Generation" without any appreciation of what it was about. Ms. Stein lamented the youth of their time who appeared to be ruined by the war, a *"génération perdue,"* good for nothing, drinking themselves to death, and Ernest took umbrage with her assessment of his generation and her misreading of his book: "The hell with her lost-generation talk and all the dirty, easy labels."[50] His novel not only tried to reveal his generation truthfully, but it also underscored that he "thought that all generations were lost by something and always had been and always would be."[51] He added, "I thought of Miss. Stein and Sherwood Anderson and egoism and mental laziness versus discipline and I thought who is calling who a lost generation?"[52]

Nevertheless, many understood Hemingway's unique voice, his literary technique, and his attempt to strike at the core of a society.

On October 31, 1926, the *New York Times Book Review* declared his victory:

> No amount of analysis can convey the quality of *The Sun Also Rises*. It is a truly gripping story, told in a lean, hard, athletic narrative prose that puts more literary English to shame . . . Mr. Hemingway knows how not only to make words be specific but how to arrange a collection of words which shall betray a great deal more than is to be found in the individual parts. It is magnificent writing, filled with that organic action which gives a compelling picture of character. This novel is unquestionably one of the events of an unusually rich year in literature.[53]

Building on the acclaim for *In Our Time, The Sun Also Rises* would establish Ernest's reputation as a modernist writer who rocked the foundations of a society's arrogance, who questioned the betrayal of youth and the mechanization of violence and deceit; but some critics, like the local paper and his own mother, would wonder if he was prostituting his talent by glorifying a degraded stratum of humanity.

Responding to his mother's criticism after a two-month silence, Ernest apologized for the delay, explaining that he preferred not to write in anger, particularly to his mother, but precised that he did not feel at all ashamed of the book except where he failed to represent the broken people he was trying to portray.[54] Responding to his son and to rumors in the papers regarding his son's divorce, his father answered this time, expressing both parents' sincere concern, asking his son to take care of his family and to pray. Gored and bucking against the reins, Ernest in his later letters likewise betrayed a fear: he was letting his parents and himself down.[55] Like his novel's protagonist, he was wounded, unable to advance as cleanly as he had hoped, impotent, cut down, bleeding, bound to capitulate . . . flawed. In the next novel, he vowed that he would not make the same mistakes and would express himself with such clarity and simplicity that even readers from Oak Park could not fail to understand.

• • • • •

Back in the States, they commenced a whirlwind tour: Pauline's prolonged and precarious childbirth in a Kansas City hospital, where they welcomed their son Patrick; numerous hunting trips near Sheridan, Wyoming; extended visits with family in Piggott and Oak Park; and rendezvous with friends like the MacLeishes in Massachusetts, the Fitzgeralds in Philadelphia and Delaware, and Max Perkins, Waldo Peirce, and Mike Strater in New York. The Hemingways returned to Key West in November 1928. They rented an apartment at 1100 South Street, which Charlie Thompson's wife, Lorine, had procured on their behalf; Pauline attempted to settle in while Ernest had to depart three days later aboard a red-eye express train bound screaming for New York.

Concerned about Bumby's ongoing cough and flu in November 1928, Hadley decided to spare her son another gray winter in Paris by sending him to spend some time with his father. Hadley and Bumby had to cross the Atlantic aboard the *Île de France* to make the handoff in Manhattan, a midway point. She asked Ernest to take the train up from Key West and meet her there, and he agreed. Kissing Pauline goodbye at Key West Station, Ernest caught the train northbound.[56] He carried in his leather haversack the manuscript of *A Farewell to Arms* to revise on the way.

Thirty-seven hours and forty-five minutes later, he emerged dog tired on a winter morning, amidst the steaming grates, asphalt streets, and hustle and bustle at the entrance to New York City's Penn Station. He met his ex-wife in the lobby of her hotel, Hotel Earle, near Washington Square, to retrieve their son.[57] She was now with another man, Paul Mowrer, whom she had met in the spring, just after their divorce.[58] Ernest and Hadley's meeting, the first since their separation, was a strained and awkward reunion. But afterward a reunited father and son adventured happily in the green spaces of the parks, between towering buildings, stopping in to see whatever caught their interest in the shops, and then they gaily called upon Daddy's editor, Max, at his building on Fifth Avenue. Then, crossing over Sixth and Seventh Avenues, father and son boarded the return train south.

Back in Oak Park, Bumby's grandfather, Ernest's father, having spent the morning fretting over finances in his office, returned home at noon, incinerated some papers in the basement, went upstairs, drew the shades, and sat down in semidarkness at the edge of his bed. Amidst frequent headaches, diabetes, and hypertension, he could not sleep and had been pursued by dark feelings at every turn. As a doctor, he might have diagnosed his own condition or seen that these obstacles were surmountable and that these feelings would soon pass.[59] Instead, he placed the muzzle of his .32 caliber Smith & Wesson pistol behind his ear, seeing no possibility of a way through. The difficulties had become overwhelming and unbearable. As emotion and frustration overcame his mind, he pulled the trigger, and its explosion echoed throughout the rooms of Ernest's childhood home.

Ernest's thirteen-year-old brother, Leicester, at home sick from school, heard the noise, rushed to his parents' bedroom, and forced his way in.

"It sounded like a shot!"

He knocked at the door. "Daddy!" He tried the door. It opened, and in the darkened room all shades were drawn except one; there on the bed lay his father, making hoarse breathing noises. His eyes were closed, and in that first instant as Leicester saw him there in the half dark, nothing looked wrong. He put his hand under his father's head. His hand slipped under easily and when he brought it out again, it was wet-warm with blood.[60]

Their mother, Grace, sent a panicked telegram to Scribner's: "TRY TO LOCATE ERNEST HEMINGWAY IN NEW YORK ADVISE HIM OF DEATH OF HIS FATHER TODAY ASK HIM TO COMMUNICATE WITH HOME IMMEDIATELY."[61] He had already left, so his sister Carol sent another message to his train en route. The train porter hurried to hand him the news: "father died this morning arrange to stop here if possible."[62]

The shock of the news washed over him as he struggled to keep his composure in front of young Bumby and to focus on the business at hand: getting off the train at the next stop in Philadelphia, wiring for enough money to make it to Chicago, and finding a suitable escort for the boy to continue to Key West. Entrusting his son to a porter named McIntyre, Ernest waved goodbye through the window of the departing train, and, once inside the Philadelphia station, telegrammed Max Perkins: "PLEASE WIRE $100 IMMEDIATELY WESTERN UNION NORTH PHILADELPHIA STATION. MY FATHER IS DEAD. MUST GET FIRST TRAIN TO CHICAGO."[63] Unsure the message would reach his editor, he called Mike Strater in New York, left a message, and hung up. Then he dialed his friend F. Scott Fitzgerald at his home in Delaware. Scott answered immediately and sent him the money, which Ernest received via Western Union minutes before his train departed.

In Oak Park, Ernest assumed the role of the "man of the family," coaching his little brother: "At the funeral, I want no crying. You understand, kid? There will be some others who will weep, and let them. But not in our family. We're here to honor him for the kind of life he lived, and the people he taught and helped. And, if you will, really pray as hard as you can, to help get his soul out of purgatory."[64] Then at the funeral, he informed his sister Marcelline that their father's soul was condemned to burn in everlasting hellfire.[65] Returning to Key West, he wrote Perkins en route: "What makes me feel the worst is my father is the one I cared about."[66]

• • • • •

Ernest took charge of his father's messy financial affairs and paid six hundred dollars in taxes on his properties. He combined a monthly contribution from his income with a sizeable donation from Pauline's family to assure his mother, sister, and brother an income of one hundred dollars per month. He ordered his mother to move into a smaller place at River Forest and to enlist Uncle George to help her to sell their large family home at a profit. Haunted by the thought that he had contributed to his father's death by refusing to help him in his time of need, Ernest wrote that it was the least Uncle George could do; Grace, suddenly dependent upon her son and still grieving, acquiesced to her son's command.[67] Of the mother who had once thrown him out of the house after he had returned from war, who had once criticized his first novel's success, and who had judged him for divorcing his first wife, he was now in full control, asserting his manhood.

From Oak Park, he wrote Scott Fitzgerald a few days after his father's funeral to thank him for wiring the money: "My father shot himself as I suppose you may have read in the papers . . . Will send you the $100 as soon as I reach Key West. I was fond as hell of my father and feel too punk—also sick, etc.—to write a letter but wanted to thank you."[68] Having returned to Key West in the middle of December, Ernest, perhaps attempting to confront the pain or acquire an object that memorialized his old man, asked his mother to send him the gun once the police returned it to her. From Oak Park, she answered, "Les wants you to leave it to him, when you are thru with it—but you have first choice . . . Old Long John was the pistol I learned to shoot with when you were a baby in my arms. You always loved to cuddle into my neck when the gun fired."[69]

When the box arrived, he left it for months unopened. "For Heaven's sake, Ernest, haven't you opened your mother's box yet?" asked childhood friend Katy Smith while visiting Key West in April.[70] Opening the package, they found some of Grace's paintings that she hoped Ernest would sell for her, cookies for Sunny (Ernest's younger sister visiting in Key West), a cake for Pauline that by then had turned rancid, a book for Bumby, and the Smith & Wesson that had killed Grace's husband of thirty-two years.

Later Ernest told Leicester that their father had written him that he needed money and that Ernest had responded with a check that was delivered to the house, but he'd found the envelope amidst his father's affairs unopened.[71] This story was most likely a lie, the ever-resourceful echoes of a guilt-ridden conscience, an imagination that however clever could not find a way through.[72] The writer's perhaps most honest sentiments on the subject appeared on a scrap of paper among his papers three years later: "To commit suicide except as a means of ending unbearable pain may be compared to cheating at solitaire, but a man making such a comparison is a confident fool."[73] Every person must face eternity, or lack of it, alone.

• • • • •

For Thanksgiving, Ernest's sister Madelaine, or "Sunny," had come down to Key West for a visit and stayed to help with the children,

Patrick and Bumby, and by January 1929 she was helping her brother to type the first draft of his nearly completed manuscript. He was still struggling with the ending and allegedly rewrote it forty-nine times to "get the words right." When Ernest finished *A Farewell to Arms* in February, he invited his editor to Key West to receive the manuscript and to fish. On the train ride back to New York, Max Perkins finished reading it and elatedly declared it a triumph—he offered Ernest sixteen thousand dollars, an unprecedented sum, to serialize it in *Scribner's Magazine* in May.[74] During yet another fishing visit, from mid-February to mid-March, Ernest's guests Mike Strater, Waldo Peirce, and Dos Passos also read it and pronounced their friend's second novel a success.

As newsmen and fans pursued him and threatened the privacy essential to his work, Ernest took flight to isolated and foreign places out of their reach: writing and hunting in the monastic wildernesses of North America, chasing corridas in Spain, and repairing to the cafés and avenues of Paris. Ernest, with Pauline, Patrick, Bumby, and his trusted and helpful sister Sunny, passed through Havana via steamship, again staying briefly at the Ambos Mundos, before departing for Europe aboard the *Yorck* on April 5, 1929, with another new car, a Ford Model T purchased by Pauline's Uncle Gus.[75] In Paris, they returned Bumby to his mother and checked back into the apartment at 6 rue Férou. At the end of September, *A Farewell to Arms* appeared in book form with a dedication to its generous benefactor, Uncle Gus.[76] In spite of the stock market crash on October 24, 1929, and the Great Depression that followed, sales of Ernest's novel reached thirty-six thousand copies that same month.[77]

The shockwaves of "Black Thursday" were felt the world over, particularly back in Cuba, a nation still dependent upon trade with the United States. Foreign trade dropped to 10 percent of its former level; the price of sugar tumbled from 2.18 cents per pound in 1928 to its lowest point of 0.57 cents in 1932. As these effects rippled, businesses went bankrupt, unemployment spiked, and salary reductions went into effect across the island, creating conditions of scarcity for the majority of Cubans that rivaled the days of slavery.[78] Suspending the purchase of Cuban bonds, creditors lending Cuba funds to keep operations afloat froze future lines of credit. As three-quarters of a million veterans from the War of Independence came of age, the island's economy was collapsing, and they would find themselves without a way to enter the workforce—many of these young people joined militant groups.[79] Many others were drawn to the lights of the Havana night where the yanqui dollars never seemed to disappear completely as long as there were music, *mujeres*, and rum. Since Prohibition in 1920, it had been illegal for a yanqui to have a drink, but with a little money, a yanqui could have all that his heart desired in the city belonging not to politicians or to religious moralists but to bootleggers, pimps, and the underworld that was Havana, Cuba, in her emergent glory.

The critical reception for *A Farewell to Arms* was mostly favorable: Hutchinson in the *New York Times Book Review* said it was "a moving and beautiful book"; Hazlitt of the *New York Sun* called Hemingway's description of the retreat from Caporetto "unforgettable," and the novel "in depth, in range, drama . . . the finest thing Hemingway has yet done." Malcolm Cowley thought it showed greater maturity and thoughtfulness than previous works, and even his mother's local beacon of artistic appreciation, Fanny Butcher, approved of it, naming it "the most interesting novel of the year." Grace clipped the article from the *Chicago Tribune*, sent it to her son, and told him she thought it deserved the high praise that it was receiving and that she was proud of him, too.[80]

While Ernest's élan vital was rising, Scott's seemed to be waning, with Zelda suffering from a nervous breakdown, his own tensions and drinking on the rise, and his writing stalled. From New York, Max Perkins wrote Ernest to express his concern with Scott, who was "in a bad way, on account of Zelda," who had been "desperately sick": "In a very recent and brief letter, he says 'Zelda is sick as hell' and he speaks of himself as 'somewhat harassed and anxious about life.' I wouldn't quote these phrases to anyone else but you, but you ought to know about it. He does not like to admit—at least to me—that he is worried, and when he does, there is no doubt of it. I sometimes even think of going over there."[81]

From a hunting ranch in Wyoming, Ernest responded to his editor concerning Fitzgerald, his frustrating friend, "Please if I speak rudely in letters never take it personally—I'm working damned hard and a letter about some bloody problem or other is only a damned Interuption [*sic*] and Curse . . . We'll have a good time in March at Tortugas!"[82] In another letter, three weeks later, Ernest explained to Max that he had to "stick to one thing" when he was writing a book and keep that in his head and nothing else. He stressed: "The Example of Scott ought to be evidence enough that a man has to stay in a book in his head until it's finished—I don't want excuses for not finishing my present book—I want to write it."[83] Rather than become distracted by Scott's alcoholism, anxiety, and marital problems, Ernest would be determined to get his own writing done. Just before returning to Paris in 1929, Ernest wrote his editor to tell him not to give Scott his new address on the Left Bank.[84]

• • • • •

From April 21, 1929, until January 10, 1930, Ernest and Pauline resided in Paris in the sixth arrondissement apartment beside the Jardin du Luxembourg. They travelled in Spain throughout the year, made a side trip to Berlin in November for a six-day bicycle race, and paid their respects to Gerald and Sara Murphy in Switzerland in December. In January they boarded the ocean liner *La Bourdonnais* and returned to the States via New York and Havana, arriving in Key West in February. Amidst a torrent of houseguests staying in their large rented house at 1425 Pearl Street and innumerable fishing trips into the Gulf Stream, Ernest started a new project in March 1930, his most ambitious undertaking yet; having scored a commercial and critical victory with *A Farewell to Arms* the previous year, he would now plunge into a nonfiction treatise on *tauromachia* (bullfighting), exploring the matador's "dance with death" and titling it *Death in the Afternoon*.[85] Just miles away from Ernest in Key West, two hundred thousand workers from the National Workers Confederation of Cuba, led by Rubén Martínez Villena, organized an illegal strike, the first one against Machado's presidency, and many of them were killed.[86] Before a union rally began in Artemisa in May, Cuban police appeared and fired shots to disperse the panic-stricken crowd, and summarily imprisoned all of the attendees that they could round up.[87]

In August, *Scribner's Magazine* published "Wine of Wyoming," and in September, Paramount Pictures purchased screen rights for *A Farewell to Arms* from Scribner's for eighty thousand dollars, with twenty-four thousand of it going to the author.[88] Increasingly accident prone, Ernest had a serious car accident in November, which kept him in the hospital until January 1931.[89]

Back in Cuba tensions were on the rise after the police, following a tip, appeared at the University of Havana with batons raised, attacked students planning a protest, and fatally wounded one of them named Rafael Trejo on September 30, 1930. Suspecting universities and high schools as hotbeds of sedition, and responding to protests across the country that November, President Machado pushed a measure through congress suspending constitutional guarantees, arresting all members of the Directorio Estudiantíl Universitario (DEU), and shutting down educational institutions on December 15.[90]

On December 30, Cuba inaugurated the Hotel Nacional de Cuba. The $4 million project, awarded in 1928 to New York construction company McKim, Mead, and White, created Havana's iconic five-hundred-room hotel in two years, blending elements of classical Spanish, Moorish, and Art Deco architecture. It was what historian Rosalie Schwartz called "a fitting monument to the president's surging self-importance, fed by bankers and businessmen who honored him with banquets and saluted him as he sat in the presidential box at Oriental Park."[91] While in exile in Mexico, Julio Antonio Mella, the founder of the Cuban Communist Party, was hunted down by the henchmen of President Machado and assassinated.

In January 1931, President Machado stopped the presses of fifteen newspapers and magazines—those of his critics.[92] Ultimately, these moves backfired, however, as unemployed journalists and energized students became full-time protesters and organizers of subversive activity. Drawing anti-imperialist ire and observing that nearly every civic leader on the island "was opposed to the government except those being paid by it," Ambassador Harry F. Guggenheim in the American embassy advised President Machado to reconcile with the opposition, while Secretary of State Henry L. Stimson expressed concern about the large number of dissidents accumulating in Cuban prisons.[93] The bodies of Machado's enemies were washing up in Havana, fishermen were finding their limbs in the bellies of sharks, and in Cuba, his reputation as a man who fed his enemies to the sharks grew.[94]

To keep itself afloat, the Cuban government by the end of January issued an emergency tax on monies sent out of Cuba, alcohol, tobacco, petroleum, radios, and numerous other items.[95] Activating an army and a navy of twelve thousand men during the same month, Machado dug in for a fight: "Me resign? Never resign," he declared to his countrymen and the watching world.[96]

Other factions attempted to negotiate, such as Machado's political rivals, insurgent conservatives like Mario García Menocal, dissident liberals such as Miguel Mariano Gómez, and moderate reformists like Carlos Mendieta, leader of the National Union party. But by 1931 other more radical factions were forming, such as the Students' Left Wing, and the Abecedarios, or ABC, made up of the more "moderate" members of the DEU after its dissolution: young men and women, middle-class students, and professionals whose class-conscious manifesto expressed anti-imperialism and a need for the Cubanization of the island's economy.[97] Using an alphabetized cellular structure, the ABC responded to governmental acts of violence with bombings, armed struggle, and assassinations of elected officials to spread fear among them and influence reforms.[98] One of their first attempted acts of violence was to dynamite the Havana aqueduct and cut off the city's water supply.

While the rest of the country indulged in violent acts in the name of progress, in Hershey, Cuba, the natives, hungry in their poverty, continued to work as "complacent as oxen in the cane fields," according to the *Chicago Tribune*.[99] The secret of Hershey Chocolate's "prosper[ity] in spite of depressed general conditions," concluded E. E. Allen, Jr., in *Barron's* weekly financial newspaper five months later, was Milton Hershey's capacity to secure steady "inventories of low-cost raw materials sufficient for quite some time."[100]

In the middle of February, eighty-five professors were dismissed from the University of Havana on grounds of conspiracy, including physics professor and future president Dr. Ramón Grau San Martín. On February 24, 1931, the Machado administration announced the completion of a major project of public works initiated in 1927: the

National Highway, running 705.6 miles from Pinar del Río to Santiago, costing the country $74,870,000 dollars ($107,000 per mile) and constructed in record time, three years and nine months, at an average of 15.72 miles per month. The new highway subsequently guaranteed a cheaper rate of freight for the transport of sugar, tobacco, and fruit.[101] Those investors with the closest ties to Machado received the construction contracts and the privilege to determine the route of the highway at every turn.[102]

• • • • •

While her husband was fishing in Dry Tortugas with the gang in March,[103] Pauline Hemingway discovered that she was pregnant again.[104] On April 29, Pauline's wealthy Uncle Gus bought a belated wedding gift for his niece and her husband, paying eight thousand dollars cash for the property 907 Whitehead Street: it was the largest house in Key West and sure to keep the couple closer to home.[105]

Ernest wrote his editor in April, asking Perkins to let him keep the money he owed and attempting to explain his difficult nature. He asked Max forgiveness in advance if he ever sounded rude in a letter. He was naturally "a rude bastard," he said, and the only way to avoid that was to be always formally polite, but that had stopped between them long ago when Max asked him to un-mister him. "So please remember that when I am loud mouthed, bitter, rude, son-of-a-bitching and mistrustful I am really very reasonable and have great confidence and absolute trust in you. The thing is I get so damned tired of being careful in letters—Christ, here I am starting to loud mouth again."[106]

To follow corrida season in Spain with American bullfighter Sidney Franklin as "research" for Ernest's book, the Hemingways sailed to Europe in May from Havana aboard the *Volendam*.[107] Pauline packed up belongings from their rue Férou apartment in Paris and shipped all their antique furniture before they returned to the United States aboard the *Île de France*. On board, their friends Mr. and Mrs. Don Stewart introduced Ernest and Pauline to Mrs. Jane Mason, the bewitching twenty-one-year-old wife of Grant Mason. Mrs. Stewart and Mrs. Hemingway, both pregnant, spent most of the trip resting in their rooms, leaving Don and Ernest free to "squire" Mrs. Mason, during what Ernest would later describe as a "drunken and merry" crossing.[108] Discovering that the Masons lived across the water in Havana, the Hemingways promised to visit just as soon as they could.

• • • • •

In August, elder Cuban leadership organized by Menocal and Mandieta attempted an armed uprising from the interior of Cuba and were effortlessly and unceremoniously captured by Machado's men in Pinar del Río; Mendieta was sent to prison on the Isle of Pines, while Menocal sought extradition in the Brazilian embassy.[109] Their clumsiness and lack of popular support legitimized and energized the younger and more radicalized groups like the ABC, but obstinately Machado announced by the end of that year that he would leave office on May 20, 1935: "Not a minute more or a minute less."[110] By August, the *Nation*, reporting "Cuba Revolts Again," appeared bored of Cuba's revolutions.[111]

After twelve hours of labor and another complicated caesarian operation at a hospital in Kansas City, on November 12, 1931, Gregory Hancock, Ernest's third son, was born. His father would brag about the boy's size, "9 lbs 7 ounces or 19 pounds 17 ounces. Heck of a big baby anyway with gigantic sexual equipment and deep bass voice."[112] The doctor's warning that another pregnancy could be fatal to Pauline complicated their marital life. Pauline's Catholic beliefs caused her to reject traditional forms of contraception, so the danger of pregnancy hindered their sex life, causing subsequent conflicts and estrangement.[113] And baby Gregory, their second unplanned child of the wrong sex who nearly killed his mother during childbirth and for whom she had to care and provide, would frequently hinder Pauline's ability to keep up with her husband's adventures and cause her to feel a significant measure of resentment.[114]

Just after Gregory was born, Ernest wrote his mother-in-law to explain why family had to take a back seat to his writing. "If this book [*Death in the Afternoon*] is punk it won't do any good to take . . . readers . . . aside and say, 'But you ought to see what a big boy Gregory is and just look at the big scar on my arm and you ought to see our wonderful water-work system and I go to church every Sunday and am a good father to my family or as good as I can be.'"[115] He was in a "tough business," and there were "no alibis." Thus he declared his hatred against excuse makers, Paris café posers, and fakers of the mojo.[116] Unrepentant, Ernest put ambition first.[117]

Ernest wired Max Perkins on January 21, 1932, that he had finished the first draft of his treatise on bullfighting. Then until March he fished and explored the Keys with Pauline, Carol, Bra Saunders, Joe Russell, Mike Strater, Archibald MacLeish, Uncle Gus, Charlie and Lorine Thompson, John and Katy Dos Passos, and other friends and invited guests. Even so, he found the time to write "After the Storm," a diver's frantic attempt to recover buried treasure from the sunken liner *Valbanera* that had just capsized during a hurricane. Having lifted the story from a real Caribbean pirate whom he admired, Bra Saunders, he polished it in March for publication in *Cosmopolitan* magazine two months later. It became one of his most haunting stories contrasting human frailty with the power of the sea.

At the same time, the Cuban president assured his people that the protection of the republic justified suspension of civil liberties, imprisonments, and acts of violence in secret prisons, attempting to eliminate all enemies of the state.[118] On New Year's Day, the first bomb interrupted a meeting of the Tobacco Selectors' Union in Santa Clara; on the twelfth of January, twelve separate bombs exploded all over Havana; on the twenty-fifth, police discovered a car packed with dynamite, nails, and glass; before the end of the month, the ABC had mined a house on Flores Street and killed two police officers in their booby trap; on February 19 terrorists threw a bomb onto a bus to injure three passengers; and on February 28 synchronized attacks during the primary election resulted in the shooting and bombing a man and a woman and two bombs exploding in Santiago with no casualties.[119] Back in the United States, there was also unrest as twenty-five thousand men of the Bonus Army, Ernest's World War I comrades in arms, marched on the capital and established a "Hooverville," a camp where they would wait for President Herbert Hoover and Congress to hand over the $2.39 billion that they believed the US Treasury had pocketed from their retirement pay.[120]

CHAPTER 3

Adventures as Close as Cuba (1932–1934)

• • • • •

It was quiet in the center of Key West. On the street there were few vehicles, aside from the occasional bicycle. Sitting on their covered porches, some residents smoked pipes, the floors creaking as they rocked back on their chairs' hindquarters, listening to rumba on the radio, its faint clamor escaping as a screen door creaked open, then snapped shut. At the shaded corner of a grocery store, two men loafed beneath the branches of a tree, and a group of children played in front of what townspeople called the "old Negro church."[1]

Rows of small wooden houses, built closely together, continued for several blocks; the sun had baked the thin walls brittle, and the sea wind had taken their paint away, leaving them as colorless and forgotten as abandoned bones.[2] As you left the center of town, the tight rows of houses ended abruptly. Behind a tall iron fence, the landscape opened into a grassy lawn surrounded by palm trees. Among the trees sat a fortresslike house in Spanish Colonial style, as old and grand as any in New Orleans: arched, shuttered windows, covered wraparound balcony, black ironwork zigzagging between the rails. Built during the Civil War, it had withstood the weather, remaining there while hurricanes lifted rows of other houses clean away.

In a round fisherman's hat with a turned-up brim and a striped, long-sleeved Basque jersey, Ernest looked like a figure from an Impressionist painting as he emerged merrily from his door with his cousin from Kansas City, Bud White, in tow. Swooping overhead, the beacon of the lighthouse came 'round in front of his house, over the town, and out to sea, and Ernest looked up through trails of clouds at stars—sparkling as clean as raindrops in the sky after the rain. They set off walking beneath the royal palms on either side of Whitehead Street toward the marina, where Ernest would soon depart for Cuba. As the night freshened, they could smell the bougainvillea mingling with the ocean breeze. In the high grass between the shotgun houses, toads croaked and crickets fiddled in a symphony aching with desire.

Having kissed her husband at the threshold, Pauline shuffled up the stairs with newborn Gregory in her arms, and standing behind a balcony rail, stared at the *homme de lettres et d'aventure,*[3] bounding through the village where they had recently made their home. The renovation of 907 Whitehead Street dragged on, requiring her to respond to carpenters, painters, plumbers, and electricians, trying to make the historic building a hospitable home.[4] They had hung Ernest's hunting trophies on the walls, elk heads from numerous trips west, and arranged the antiques they'd recently imported from France. After Gregory had been born, and with the renovation, Ernest's writing, the fishing, and other trips, they had been seeing rather less of each other, so she planned to take a steamer over to join him in a couple of days.[5]

Watching him until he was gone, she called out "Ada!" and grew impatient as she awaited the new nanny. Handing off the baby, just five months old, she looked in on his brother Patrick who was nearly three years old. Coming to as his mother entered the room with fine hair clinging to his warm forehead, the boy asked her for the news, "Has Papa gone to Cuba yet?"

"Yes. Now go to sleep, darling," she said, sweeping the fine hair from his brow and sneering at her likeness in his somber eyes. The boy turned on his side, and his mother continued to caress his hair. A few minutes later he fell asleep, and she got up and left him just as she heard the baby cry out in the next room.

Dusk burned off along the edges of Key West harbor as Ernest and Bud ducked into Thompson's Hardware to retrieve tackle and Charlie Thompson, by then one of Ernest's closest friends. The three men slogged across the hollow planks of the dock toward the *Anita*, Joe Russell's boat, anchored at the end of the pier. They could hear Joe

Russell, whom Ernest had nicknamed "Josie Grunts," aboard, grunting as he tended to do, loading the gear, and running the engines.[6] In the sky the moon was shining bright and casting her clear reflection on the surface of the murky water, between the boats.[7] Earlier in the day, they had loaded iceboxes with their provisions, leaving one compartment empty for the bait they could buy fresh the next morning on the other side.

The other side. Having heard the stories, embroidered by the fishermen he knew, Ernest now needed to see one of those majestic creatures for himself. The fish running off the coast of Cuba were said to grow to enormous size. Over there, he could rent a room for next to nothing and fish as much as he liked. In the morning there would be a quiet space for his writing. There would be no children, only his work, the sea, and Havana.

It was true that chasing those fish would require considerable expense, but seeing those monsters of mythical proportions would be worth it. Besides, "Josie" said they could do it on ten dollars per person, counting fuel and expenses . . . and if they loaded up the boat with liquid "Hoover gold" on the return trip . . . ?[8] The ban on alcohol was only enforced on the northern side of the Straits, so carrying sacs of rum from Havana to Key West could not only pay for the trip but might also turn an attractive profit *if* all went right.

Josie had been the first to bring a load of liquor across the straights from Cuba to Key West.[9] Claiming more than 150 trips to his credit, Josie was an experienced smuggler who operated a Key West drinking and gambling joint known as the Blind Pig (a generic Florida term for a bar operating outside the law), and he propositioned Ernest to come in as a "silent partner."[10] Each trip across could thus serve the dual purpose of hunting marlin and turning profit from contraband liquor, but the better part of valor being discretion, Josie preferred to make their crossings by night.[11]

The moon shining across the surface of an inky sea, Charlie and Ernest untied the boat, pushed the bow clear, and leapt in, giggling, as she drifted off the end of the dock. The Kermath engine sputtered and grumbled in the dark water. As the engine took hold, pushing the weight of the ship, they steered her slowly out of the harbor and into the currents of the sea. When they passed the rusty orange buoy that marked the harbor's end, they could see gulls sleeping in the cages at the top of it, though the gulls took little notice of them.

At last the boat was plunging southward through the dark water, and Josie was sitting on a stool in front of the helm. His captain's hat, with shining bill and embroidered gold leaf, was cocked back. In the shadowy recesses of the cockpit, they drank coffee from the thermos Charlie had filled at the store before they left. The deafening noise of the engine was everywhere, and the boat skipped steadily ahead. Josie produced a flask, brandy he had been saving for the trip. Steering the boat while extending it to his friend, Josie looked at Ernest from the crazy corners of his eyes as he took a sip. Having tasted it, Ernest licked it from the ends of his mustache, then felt an unanticipated burn deep in his throat, a cough escaped, and another, and another, so he stepped aft into the open air so that he could catch his breath. Josie laughed and slapped his friend across the back. Holding on firmly to the rail of the ship, Ernest looked out across black waves, whose shards were bright as the clouds, and drew a deep breath of night into his broad chest and felt happy to be alive.

Cutting through the current, the low-slung thirty-four-foot "bootlegger boat" moved slowly out in the open.[12] Riding high in the water, with a one-hundred-horsepower engine, she could do no more than eight knots an hour. The low roof offered little headroom but cut down her wind resistance and offered some protection from the sun. But she trolled well, would save gas, and her wide stern gave them the space to set up two fighting chairs and to work the lines, to bring in the bigger fish.[13] All in all, she was a good boat for fishing, and they were glad to have her.[14] So it was on April 23, 1932, that Ernest Hemingway departed on his first fishing expedition to Cuba.[15]

• • • • •

The lighthouse informed their approach as they passed between El Morro and La Punta off their starboard side. In the semidarkness, they could hear oars lapping as fishermen rowed intently out to sea. The rising sun painted the colors of morning across the sky. Checking in at the Coast Guard station at the entrance to the bay, they motored the *Anita* gently through and moored her to the old pier, San Francisco, and they went ashore in quest of a hot breakfast.[16] At the Pearl Café, a waiter in a black bow tie and vest set the table with toasted Cuban bread, fresh butter, guava jelly, boiled eggs, and steaming hot *café con leche.* With spoonfuls of island sugar, they sweetened the strong Cuban coffee that had been mixed with creamy dollops of steaming milk. They moistened the billowy bread by dipping it into the hot coffee and savored its sweet and simple richness.

As the pale dawn seeped in at the corners of the horizon, they could see at the entrance of the harbor a small cluster of fishing smacks, bobbing afloat, with their lines reaching deep into the water. Working the coral bottom for muttonfish, mackerel, snapper, kingfish, and baitfish to sell along the docks, men sat or stood with hands in their pockets waiting in their boats.

When they had finished eating and were feeling better, Josie asked the waiter if he knew a good "jig," a man for rigging baits, an honest day's work.[17] Folding his apron and sucking at the spaces between his teeth, the waiter walked out along the pier and spoke with several men sitting there waiting along the railing of the docks. A Negro man in his late fifties jumped to his feet with his hat in his hand and nodded at them across the way. Josie and Ernest looked at each other, rose from their table, and approached, extending a hand in greeting.

In a single word of heavily accented but functional Spanish, Josie got down to business: "*¿Carnada?*" Nodding, the old man pointed to the end of the dock and walked ahead of them to ask around for the bait they required. Another man opened a chest filled with ice and the bait-sized mackerel and kingfish he had to sell, while all stared at one another with direct and attentive eyes.

After they bought the bait, the jig wrapped it for them in a newspaper. They walked down the dock and aboard the *Anita*. Looking like he had always been there, the old jig sat down on the deck of their ship, and his fingers went to work immediately, agilely rigging the baits. Then they cast off, Josie steering them across the harbor and around the peninsula.[18] After the night's crossing, they might have been exhausted if it had not been for the coffee racing through their blood and the excitement of their first day's fishing ahead. There would be plenty of time for sleep once they had pulled their first monster from the sea.

Along the peninsula, a single gray heron walking gracefully atop its slender legs turned its *S*-shaped neck to glare back at them with beady yellow eyes before slinging its wings downward and taking flight gloriously over them as they approached. Beyond the harbor, scattered in the dark blue and silver-speckled water as far as they could see, were hazy silhouettes becoming the sharp outlines of weathered fishing smacks as the day awakened. Drifting with the current, these fishermen were hunting marlin travelling deep, with four to six lines at forty to sixty fathoms.[19]

To trap schools of fish between them, marlins often hunt in pairs. With impressive speed, the jig assembled a mobile made of baitfish, like the set of stringed figures hanging above a baby's bed, a sort of mackerel chandelier, which underwater would resemble the small schools that marlins feed upon. By using "teasers," or baitfish tied to slightly longer lines, the jig even simulated the stragglers that become separated from the school as the marlin closes in.

Hearts jumped when they felt a series of strikes on the line set sixty fathoms below, but then the strikes were gone, and they had not hooked anything. When the bites stopped altogether, and the sun was high above, they decided to return to port and rest for the following day. When they brought in the line, the jig showed them the hook. They could see that a large fish deep below had been eating at the bait.[20]

Bunking aboard the *Anita*, the four friends took their turns standing watch, and as luck would have it, it did not rain, or possibly they had been too tired to notice or hear any of the many noises in the port.[21] Arising early the next morning, they had a simple breakfast and lost no time in motoring out. Seeing so many rowboats in the waters off the Morro, Josie suggested that they use the motor to their advantage by trolling marlin that might be travelling at fifteen to twenty fathoms. Ernest and Charlie nodded. Attached at the *Anita*'s rear corners were two long poles with lines dragging in the wake, churning amidst the waves and looking from a distance like two giant whips. They ran from east to west, trolling for marlin swimming against the current.

They fished throughout the morning without a bite, and it was turning into afternoon when a dorsal fin broke the surface of the water; drumming Ernest's shoulder, Josie pointed at it as he licked his lips. Beneath the surface of the waves the fish's pectoral fins were spread such that it seemed to be flying through the blue water like some magnificent aquatic bird, but in its great hunger, it had abandoned its fear and was coming for the bait.

When the marlin came up to strike, it smashed at the bait, its bill slapping the water like a Chinese firecracker—then its tail rose above the surface as it pounced.[22] The jig had already taken the rod, and he handed it to Ernest while Charlie and Bud hurried to help him put on a harness and set himself in a chair. Josie urged him to be patient—to let the marlin take the bait.

Wait, darn it, be patient, now, be patient, Ernest, oh jeez . . . well, what are we waiting for? Yank back now! Ernest pulled back hard on the rod, striking once, several times, and hoping with all his might that he had driven the hook into the fish's jaw rather than yanked it right out of his mouth. Then a pause . . . five eternal seconds of agony when all imagined the worst, the unthinkable—that after spending two days hunting, they had blown it again. *Lost him? Oh crickets, had they lost him? Oh, Heaven, please make it that it was not so.*[23]

The line screeched hot off the reel, for the fish, summoning all his strength, took it and began to run. The great weight of the marlin shot straight out into the stretch of water in front of them, then dove down, down, down toward the bottom like a derailed train, nearly yanking the rod from Ernest's hands. Charlie and the jig came over to help. Forgetting to steer, Josie was shouting, "Give the fish some line!"

When they had given all five hundred yards of line that they had to give, Josie turned the *Anita* to follow in the direction of the fish and instructed Ernest to bring the line in as carefully as he could. Trying to keep it from slipping in his hands, Ernest slowly turned the crank of the reel. On the right side of his forehead, in a receding hairline, the large hook-shaped scar that he had acquired one drunken night in Paris by pulling a skylight on top of himself was now turning bright red, like a hot brand on a bull. Of course, he knew that he had to give the fish some line, then make him fight for it, but how much could he take back and not break it?

The rod was pinned to the boat with half of it underwater, so he lifted it cautiously, until he managed to place the butt into the socket of the harness. Then, pulling slowly, he tested with gentle pressure against the fish's great strength. Noticing that he was drenched in sweat, feeling the great ache in his arms, and noting the spots of lights in his peripherals, he realized that the contest had just begun.

Gathering his senses, he balanced the rod in the harness bit and turned the reel over slowly in his hands. There was an unexpected click, and the rod bent back, alarming as it doubled from the resistance of the line. Then the line was no longer moving at all. Afraid that he would break it, Ernest held firmly and did not move. In the boat, there were Ernest, the Cuban jig, Josie, Charlie, with the gaff in his hands, and cousin Bud, all connected in one impulse, awaiting . . . the marlin at the other end. There was an unbroken synchrony, a trance of exhilaration. There was this fight, this action, and nothing else. It was an old feeling that he had first known as a boy with his father on the lake, but those trout were a child's game compared to this.

It went on like that for hours. Each time the fish's heavy pull subsided, they convinced themselves they were near the end. Then the fight began again. Ernest reeled the line in slowly, working for every painful inch, lifting the rod upright, terrified that he would break it against the force of the fish. Then he felt something new, and he allowed himself to believe that the fish was coming up. Yes, it was there, rising in the water. The fish was coming up. When he told Charlie to get ready with the gaff, the fish, having other ideas, changed directions and shot beneath their boat in a silver streak just like a torpedo, pulling the line behind him persuasively in the opposite direction that they had been travelling.

The chair hit the deck of the boat and nearly tumbled into the water as Ernest stood up and, stumbling to the other side of the boat, tried to hold on to the rod that the fish was pulling from his hands. Ernest roared at Josie to "Bring the boat around!" rather uselessly, because he was already bringing the boat around. Clutching the seat back, Josie twisted his body to glare at Ernest (and to swear at him) while he piloted the boat in a new direction. Then on a gamble, Josie reached up and pulled the accelerator to kill the motor. They floated.

All was silent except the waves, the friction of the line, and the bearings spinning in Ernest's reel. To their surprise, the fish was now swimming straight out behind the boat and dragging them as a tugboat drags a freight ship. They had attempted to chase him in the direction he had been choosing, but the fish had called their bluff, and they were now playing a game of tug-of-war with a fish at fifty fathoms at the other end of the rope. By turning the ship to follow the direction the fish was choosing, they brought the boat around so that they could get closer and closer during the better part of an hour. At intervals they could see a blurred outline shimmer as it passed beneath the waves. With growing confidence, Ernest pulled more forcefully to bring him in, but he backed off as he felt the fish's great strength pull against the slackening line. "Then, astern of the boat and off to starboard, the calm of the ocean broke open and the great fish rose out of it, rising, shining dark blue and silver, seeming to come endlessly out of the water, unbelievable as his length and bulk rose out of the sea and into the air and seemed to hang there until he fell with a splash that drove the water up high and white."[24] Hanging on, Ernest watched in awe as the fish leaped from the water and bucked with all his savage, power, like a four-hundred-pound horse, hovering weightless for a suspended second as he jumped—sunlight gleaming across azure, silver, and indigo flanks.

The marlin leaped out of the water in ten long, clean jumps while, stunned, they watched the creature and gulped. He was magnificent. His sword was blue, and when he jumped, "it was like the whole sea was bursting open . . . The ocean was flat and empty where he had jumped but the circle made where the water had been broken was still widening."[25] His pointed scythe-like tail and great dorsal fin opened like a sail, and he jerked his head from side to side as he tried to shake the hook loose. Then the great weight of him crashed down . . . leaping and crashing, again and again, and throwing water like a racing motorboat as he staggered and surged ahead, fighting the unknown with every atom of courage, strength, and intelligence against an adversary at the other end that he had never seen, against the hook in his tongue, against the line between his teeth, against the deadly force behind him. They only noticed how long the fight had been when daytime turned to dusk.

In the sunset, the fish's outlines appeared in the murky water, a shimmering casket whose misfortune they had drudged up from the deep. Finally they succeeded in bringing the boat close enough to put a gaff in, and as they collaborated to finish the crime, a cloud of shadowy blood fanned out and enveloped the great fish still in the water below. Grunting, Josie leaned in, grabbed the cable, and felt the full weight of the fish in his hands. When at first it did not budge, they heaved together until they managed to get him on board—he was longer than the width of their boat, they noticed ecstatically and nauseously. They stood over the quivering fish, studying the creature extracted from the ocean as it moved on to another place. The large eye stared back at them, full of rage, confusion, frustration, then fear, before becoming very still suddenly, frozen, and leaving nothing of its great spirit but silence.[26]

The tarnished silver body lying across the deck had meat for a hundred men. Conquering any lingering qualms for the killing of such a marvelous animal, they motored to port with their trophy of flesh and bone strapped across the bow. With jubilation, some envy, and much hunger, the Cuban fishermen in the port watched *los americanos* returning and congratulated them. Driving a steel hook into the marlin's mouth, they lifted it upright with a cable and pulley on a thick timber crane at the end the dock. When they had washed the blood, they took their photographs, then watched as the knives went to work along the flesh to slice the steaks they would eat that evening. There was too much meat for the four of them to consume or store, but they would make good use of it at the market in Havana where it was selling for ten cents a pound.[27] Soon they were giving some of it away to the people along docks who had helped them when they returned, simple people with hungry children at home. The jig hacked off the sword and plopped it into Ernest's hands. After a second of hesitation, he broke into a watertight grin, and the old jig grinned back, returning to the carcass to cut the gringos' steaks.

Before their feast there would be abundant rum at Sloppy Joe's at the corner of Zuleta and Animas streets—a modest grocery store, converted to a tavern by José Abeal, an immigrant from Spain. This establishment was fast becoming one of the most well-known drinking destinations in the world. Its name, Sloppy Joe's, came from the seafood its owner kept for patrons at the bar. When the ice invariably melted onto the floor below, it caused some of his American patrons to kid one afternoon, "Why, Joe, this place is certainly sloppy; just look at the filthy water running from underneath the counter onto the floor."[28] The name stuck. The joint also served a *ropa vieja* sandwich of pulled beef with creole tomato sauce called the "Sloppy Special," whose bastardized American version appears in middle-school lunchrooms today. When Prohibition ended the following year, it was Ernest who had the bright idea to plagiarize the name from the Cuban bar, changing their Key West joint's name from the Blind Pig to Sloppy Joe's after the Old Havana establishment. The rebranding gave it an air of respectability and disassociated it from illicit activities.

After aperitifs at Joe's, they would head just a block and a half away to La Zaragozana, where the capable chefs would grill their marlin steaks to delectable perfection.[29] If the night before they had slept aboard the *Anita*, trading night watches like swashbuckling pirates or eunuch monks, that night they delegated the watch to an indigenous boy and celebrated in grand style, in all likelihood in the brothel backrooms along Merced and Economica streets, stumbling-distance from the old wharf. The "discreet" code word at the time for these establishments was "*los clubes de sesenta y nueve*"—"sixty-nine clubs."[30]

In the tapestried and mirrored rooms of the red light district, "the prurient spot resorted to by courtesans," explained T. Philip Terry, a popular travel writer at that time, a great variety of women were available, ranging in "complexion from peach white to coal black . . . 15-year-old flappers and ebony antiques . . . who unblushingly loll about heavy-eyed and languorous . . . in abbreviated and diaphanous costumes; nictitating with incendiary eyes at passing masculinity; studiously displaying physical charms or luring the stranger by flaming words or maliciously imperious gestures."[31] Another travel writer, Sydney Clark, described Havana at that time as the place "where conscience takes a holiday."[32] "Ernest said he liked Cuba because they had both fishing and fucking there. I believe they had him try out all the houses of prostitution," reported boat builder and angler John Rybovich, a longtime friend.[33] In Havana at that time there were 7,400 prostitutes on patrol.[34]

Military judges had found Rubén de León, Ramiro Valdés Daussá, and Rafael Escalona guilty the previous week of a violation of an 1894 explosives ordinance law. On April 26, they sentenced the three youths to eight years in the sinister Príncipe Castle, an isolated prison on the Isle of Pines. When Marianao police and army officials had entered their shared house in the Almendares suburb, they found a cache of arms and ammunitions, and in a nearby garage, a car loaded with dynamite, rigged to detonate via remote control. The students' intention had been to set off the explosives near President Machado. Per military police, this had been their sixth attempt to assassinate the president. Senator William E. Borah bemoaned the youths' plight before the United States Senate on April 11, 1932. Throwing them in dungeons, Cuban authorities had not permitted the students to see family or lawyers, which Cuban officials recognized to be true, but explained their sequestration was a necessary precaution to prevent further assassination plots.

Just a week before, on April 19, the police had found another car bomb at the home of Antonio Chivas, an engineering professor at the University of Havana: "An infernal machine which was in reality an automobile made into a monster bomb," said the police report. Some "youths planned to abandon the car close to police headquarters so that when the handbrake was released to remove the car from the streets, the circuit would be closed, exploding the huge [350-pound] TNT charge, thus wrecking the headquarters building and killing the majority of police reserves quartered there."[35]

• • • • •

After Ernest's first week in Havana, a steamer emerged from the haze with vapor following her like a bridal train as she puffed and sputtered across the bay.[36] Looking up from the paper, Ernest watched her now with anticipation as she came in, and he rose to greet her as the docks men attached a gangplank to her side, like an assembly of fathers giving their daughter away. Pauline's hair had been newly styled for her arrival, and descending the catwalk in her finest apparel, she looked like a present that had been wrapped for Ernest's birthday.[37] Despite best intentions not to, she shivered when she finally stepped down and held him in her arms, happiness swelling in their throats during the first moments that they saw each other again.[38]

While the *Anita* trolled for fish along the coast with Pauline newly on board, police raids and bomb blast reprisals continued to spread fear throughout the city of Havana. Now a year and a half after the president shut down the press, the remaining newspapers no longer reported the news. Among abrupt notices of curfews, detentions, and disappearances, were fashion shows, casserole recipes, gossip columns, quaint stories of human interest, and interviews such as the one Ernest gave when approached by reporters along the docks. *Mr. Hemingway, why have you come to Cuba this summer?* "The Cuban coast offers one of the best fishing grounds in the world to the fisherman who is looking for big game. In three days of fishing we have caught four marlins and three sailfish, one of which was landed by Mrs. Hemingway."[39] If the interview makes the writer appear oblivious to the insurrection, it's because broaching such subjects in the newspapers was simply not allowed. Conceivably still determined to write the story about revolutionaries that he had failed to finish, *A New Slain Knight*, Ernest wrote Perkins in May that his current research in Cuba was about much more than fish.[40]

After a few days out on the water with the boys, Pauline telephoned Jane Mason from her Ambos Mundos room.[41] Jane would join them on the boat the following day. Then the Hemingways were invited for drinks at Mr. and Mrs. Mason's home and, afterward, a proper initiation to Havana's glamour spots.[42]

Pauline might have been just as taken with the Masons' exquisiteness and money as her husband seemed to be. Jane was a perfect strawberry-blond beauty with an athletic body, crystalline eyes, and a racy disposition that contrasted strongly with her innocent visage and her husband's dusty old money.[43] Not only did Jane aim to have fun at all costs, but like the Fitzgeralds and the Murphys in Paris and on the Riviera, the Masons were beautiful people—multilingual and cultivated—as admired for their physical splendor as for their extravagant parties. Like the Murphys, they playfully and pretentiously collected books, paintings, and the artists that created them like feathers of exotic birds.

Jane was married to Grant Mason, Jr., an executive expanding Pan Am Airlines' operations in the Caribbean and the heir to a sizeable family fortune. A good-looking graduate of Yale University, Grant was the charmed descendant of James Henry Smith, a successful Wall Street speculator. For her radiance, attractiveness, and style, Jane's 1926 debut instantly made her an object of admiration. With "large eyes and fine features," the lovely Jane Mason had "Madonna-like" qualities, accented by a middle part in her smoothed back pale-gold hair.[44] During Jane's visit to the nation's capital, first lady Grace Coolidge called her "the prettiest girl ever to enter the White House."[45] Fond of sculpting, dancing, and singing, Jane Mason was a creative soul and patron of the arts and had opened her own art gallery in Havana. Her marriage to Grant had been the talk of the town, an event reported by more than thirty newspapers and magazines.[46] Whatever the consequences, the Masons' glamour and amusement would have been difficult for the Hemingways to resist.

After the day's fishing, the Hemingways joined the Masons at their villa, recently erected in Jaimanitas, a suburb à la mode along the water at the outskirts of Havana. As a wobbly red sun dissolved insouciantly into the horizon, they sipped daiquiris prepared by Cuban servants and rested tired, sun-bronzed bodies in pool chairs on the terrace of the Masons' extravagant home. Standing inside the sculpted stone banisters, the two couples chatted courteously, drank steadily, and took careful measure of each other.

When conversation waned, Grant pointed at a neighboring mansion across the way and said that it belonged to Ambassador Guggenheim. Then he showed them his forty-five-foot yacht, the *Pelican II*, anchored to a private pier at the end of a footpath from his stunning garden to the shining sea. Admiring the grounds, ship, sunset, and swaying water, the couples awaited the entrance of evening while breezes refreshed and restored their senses. When all was dark except for the tiki torches and the bright sparkling of the stars, the Masons joked that they should take a spin see the show at the Gran Casino Nacional, and throw some of their good money away.

• • • • •

After nearly a week in his wife's company, Ernest accompanied her to the ferry station and watched her ship shrink in the distance and disappear. Fearful of the approaching May Day holiday, Pauline returned to Key West to recuperate and to check on the house and the children. Writing to Ernest every day as his weeklong fishing and writing expedition extended into months, she was ever supportive of his work and his adventures, devoted to his needs, interested in his hobbies, taking care of bills, errands, and trip planning, attempting to do whatever she could to give the space and freedom he required to thrive.[47] Occasionally, her Catholic conscience did remind him: she had taken him from Hadley, so he was forever hers.[48]

That Cuban summer, Ernest fished fifty-four out of fifty-eight days, trolling the northern coast of an island paradise and often in Jane Mason's company without the supervision of her husband or his wife.[49] Pauline and Ernest's fifth wedding anniversary came and went with him in Havana and her in Key West and nothing to commemorate the occasion except a congratulatory telegram from Jane to Pauline, and Ernest's note in the ship's log that he "saw largest tarpon I ever saw."[50]

At first, Jane Mason's growing closeness with Ernest appeared to be out in the open, for she communicated with both Hemingway "friends" frequently in gay and attentive letters—in much the same way Pauline had written letters addressed to both Ernest and Hadley back in during her "Pilar" days.[51]

While a brave blond bombshell spending hours at sea with one's husband might sound like a wife's worst nightmare, Pauline did not seem, at least initially, to view Jane Mason as a threat, treating her as a friend and leaving her unattended in Ernest's company. The wealth and beauty seemed to inoculate both Hemingways at first. Besides, she must have been fine company in Havana. Pauline might have misguidedly placed her faith in her husband's low tolerance for high-strung women and so believed that their relationship would be short lived.[52]

In all probability bipolar himself, Ernest came to intimately identify with and understand Jane's capriciousness; she was his Zelda, a biographer would remark.[53] His short story "A Way You'll Never Be," crafted during the "Jane period," suggested identification with turbulent personalities; it was, he said, written "to cheer up a girl who was going crazy from day to day."[54] As Jane's friend would later report, "Jane Mason not only drank a bit, but was one of the wildest, hairiest, most drinking, wrenching, sexy superwomen in the world."[55]

Though in theory Ernest liked the company of men, his increasing fame, smugness, swagger, and drunkenness were making it much more difficult for other men to remain in the same room as him. After ruptures with Sherwood Anderson (the manliest writer of all), Harold Loeb (the Princeton athlete), and Gertrude Stein (his matriarchal nemesis), Ernest began to quarrel with and lose of other "friends." During a fishing trip when they were marooned on Dry Tortugas, Archie MacLeish recalled that he and Ernest consequently "saw a little too much of each other," and many years later Archie remembered Ernest's temper and attacks caused by Archie's slow reaction to a fire aboard: "I told him somebody ought to prick his balloon and that led to ribald observations about my not having a big enough prick . . . That began eating at him and he went on and on and on from there."[56] Back in New York, Archie had written trying to patch things up, but their friendship would subsequently decline: "The thing that troubled me always was that you seemed to be on the defensive against me and not to trust me. I know that you do not believe in trusting people but I thought I had given you about every proof a man could of the fact of my very deep and now long-lasting affection and admiration for you and it puzzled me that you should be so ready to take offense at what I did."[57]

At a time when he was wearing other friendships thin, Jane, in awe of his accomplishments, was remarkably tolerant, not to mention someone who certainly would not think to test his ego or his desires during alcohol-enriched escapades at sea. Handling the rod beautifully, never getting seasick, and even delivering provisions and helping with the cooking aboard, she was the perfect drinking and fishing partner; it was the ideal setup, one that Ernest relished.[58] And so that summer, in the logbook of the *Anita*, someone inscribed "Ernest loves Jane," like the initials of two wayward lovers scratched at the base of a rotting oak.[59] Taking the occasional day off to write at the Ambos Mundos Hotel, Ernest spent most of the end of April and the beginning of May fishing, at sea with Jane, Charlie Thompson, Charlie's brother Norberg, Josie, Bra Saunders, and their old bait-rigging jig.[60] On May 11, Jane departed via airplane for New York, and Pauline returned on the nineteenth to her place at her husband's side on the *Anita* just before a fresh volley of violence kicked off.[61]

• • • • •

The day after Pauline's return to Cuba, the political situation there got much uglier. As democracy on the island neared its historic birthday of May 20, 1902, the police were uncovering new "plots to overthrow the government" every day, it seemed, and arresting hundreds of journalists, engineers, politicians, professors, and students from respected families. On the day Pauline cruised in on USS *Florida*, President Machado had ordered the cancellation of Independence Day, prohibited all celebrations, increased security, suspended constitutional rights, and fled the city. "Machado Bans Freedom Fetes in Cuba Today—Troops Guard Island in Threat of Revolt."[62] Having raided athletic clubs, schools, and sewing circles, his administration warned through the propaganda mill that it had beefed up security around the presidential palace, appropriated arms, seized membership ledgers, and confiscated seditious literature urging citizens to revolt.

Advising military officials to lock up "everyone of a suspicious character and to adopt full precautions," a government communiqué adverted that it could not reveal the identities of those who had been arrested, but it promised that citizens would be surprised when the identities of the incarcerated were revealed, for many of them "would never have been suspected because of their high positions."[63] All government officials and their residences would be closely guarded. No assemblies of more than three people would be permitted. People would not be allowed to idle and would be ordered to keep moving. The military governor, a colonel, would clear the streets at midnight. The police and soldiers would stand guard throughout the night.[64] Despite these precautions, or perhaps in direct disobedience, the ABC initiated its campaign precisely as it had planned, launching a series of bombs at military brass like Major Rasco, Captain Samaniego, and Lieutenant Diego Diaz. Some arrived in boxes via post, still others by letter, while many were simply hurled at the officers' homes.[65]

• • • • •

The fish were not biting, and duty was calling. With pressure from Perkins to complete *Death in the Afternoon*, Ernest holed himself up at Ambos Mundos with the solitary task of reviewing the galleys of his manuscript.[66] Sounding lonesome in his letter, Ernest wrote Dos Passos to invite him to join him in Havana and to thank him for his feedback on his nonfiction work in progress.[67]

Further along in the letter, his advice to Dos Passos, or perhaps to himself, was clear: Do not get caught up in politics, do not allow the nose-picking twerps and critics to spoil their day. Hadn't they had their fill of dogma at the front? Now was the time to relish the moment, to create their art, to embrace the mystery in their immediate world. Life was too short and nasty to become involved in politics, and human weakness too formidable a foe to conquer.[68] Likewise, the following month Ernest got into a rankle when a random fan, Paul Romaine, wrote him a letter to tell him he admired his writing, then informed him that he did not appreciate his refusal to take up the political causes of their day. The writer responded that he would not follow fashion by "swinging to the left"; putting one's politics into one's writing was "horseshit."[69] By 1932, Ernest had already lived "the old lie" that dying for one's country was "sweet and right."[70]

In *Death in the Afternoon*, Ernest expounded on bullfighting, death, beloved Spain, the art of writing, fear, honor, and "grace under pressure."[71] Grace under pressure was something different from "guts," he had written Scott Fitzgerald in a letter eight years before: "Guts never made any money for anybody except violin string manufacturers."[72] The experimental mode in *Death* permitted him to interview himself so that he could elucidate previous works, theorize about literature, wax poetic, muse philosophical, and joke impudently about life, death, the craft of storytelling, and anything else under the sun.

When it seemed Cuban politics could not get any worse, it did, the following month of June 1932.[73] Militants detonated bombs in Havana's private schools and tried again to kill the president, inciting hundreds of additional arrests and raids.[74] When the rebels assassinated Captain Calvo, chief of the secret police, the following month, the US embassy increased its security to prevent any indiscretions.[75] Tensions were running high and fierce against soldiers in America as well. It was business as usual, Ernest wrote in *Esquire*, disgusted when President Hoover ordered police to drive the veterans of the Bonus Army from their encampment on the National Mall.[76] The police killed William Hushka and Eric Carlson, two vets who had served in the trenches in World War I, and President Hoover ordered General MacArthur's Twelfth Army Regiment to roll tanks, fix bayonets, and release riot gas to clear the rest.[77] There were ferocious clashes and resentment from veterans who had loyally served, making Hoover so unpopular that he lost the next election against Franklin D. Roosevelt in November of that year.[78]

Four days before Ernest left Havana, Machado declared a state of emergency in Cuba and imposed conditions of military law on the island to protect his power and the peace.[79]

• • • • •

Having already advanced too much money to Scott and Zelda Fitzgerald, Max Perkins stopped to check in on them at their new place in Baltimore. In a letter to Ernest, his star author, Max reported that the place had nice trees between which he would have liked walking had Scott not been so intent on sitting down to drink gin rickeys.[80] These days, Zelda was looking "less pretty," but had "more reality in her talk," an improvement by Max's calculations and a sign of better days to come. From Wyoming, Ernest wrote back fed up with both Zelda and Scott and in full harmony with Max: "Poor old Scott—He should have swapped Zelda when she was at her craziest but still saleable back 5 or 6 years ago before she was diagnosed as nutty—He is the great tragedy of talent in our bloody generation."[81] In 1935, Zelda was admitted to a psychiatric facility in Highland Hospital for chronic schizophrenia, and it became harder for the darlings of the Jazz Age to see each other without upsetting each other.

In November, Ernest began a new story that he called "Fathers and Sons," a title he borrowed from Ivan Turgenev. The young son in the story said he would not like his father to be buried overseas where he could not visit the grave, and his father agreed: they had to find a convenient place to be buried in America. "Couldn't we all be buried out at the ranch?" the son asks, a suggestion that now evokes Ernest's own eventual grave in Ketchum, Idaho, near which his son Bumby, or Jack, decided to live.[82]

After arousing the ire of so many real people with *The Sun Also Rises*, the narrator of "Fathers and Sons" expresses a new resolution not to betray the living. His art was important, but there were people he cared about that he had to protect.

From Thanksgiving to the Christmas holiday, Ernest stayed with his son and the Pfeiffers in Piggott and wrote another story about death and life called "A Clean, Well-Lighted Place." Two waiters in a café serve brandy to a lonely old man who they know had tried to kill himself. They want to go home, but the old man does not want to leave the "clean and well-lighted" café where he finds some comfort. The younger waiter, who has a wife waiting at home, objects to the old man's hanging around. The older waiter doesn't mind as much. He understands how the old man feels. Perhaps, one day, darkness will come to him, and someone will help him to find the light. "With all those who do not want to go to bed. With all those who need a light for the night."[83] Four years after his father's death, Ernest was purging intense emotions and defending empathy and solidarity in a simple story that many readers understood and appreciated.[84]

• • • • •

When Paramount unveiled the film version of *A Farewell to Arms* at the end of 1932, the Hollywood adaptation of his work so irritated Ernest that he declined the studio's invitation to the premiere hosted for him in Piggott. After a fire in the barn where he had been working at the Pfeiffer house, Ernest took leave of Piggott, inviting Max Perkins down to meet him and blast ducks—the sort of shooting that only their grandfathers and great-grandfathers had known, while the ducks descended on the rice fields along the White River in December in southeastern Arkansas. Ernest had already rented a houseboat for them and wrote persuasively and insistently in his letter to his editor that it would be good for him and good for business. Max later wrote of those days as "some of the coldest hours of [his] life." "There was just a powdering of snow on the steep banks . . . where we waited for ducks to drop to the water. It was just like the rivers in *Harper's Weekly* Civil War pictures."[85]

Stopping over in New York en route to Key West, Ernest advanced his career by meeting with his literary rivals Fitzgerald and Thomas Wolfe (for the first time), and with critic Edmund Wilson, who observed during an intimate dinner one evening, during which Scott became quite drunk, that "Hemingway was now a great man and Scott so much overcome with his greatness that he embarrassed me by his self-abasement."[86]

He also met Arnold Gingrich during this trip at Louis Henry Cohn's rare-book shop, who flirted and stroked Ernest's ego by mentioning his growing collection of "Hemingway first editions." Receptive to flattery, Ernest wrote Gingrich in a letter: "Am glad you liked the last chapter in the last book [*Death in the Afternoon*]—it is what the book is about but nobody seems to notice that . . . Papa feels pretty good."[87]

Back in Key West on Whitehead Street in his writing barbican, Ernest surveyed the three peacocks preening across his grassed enclosure as he continued his letter exchange with Gingrich, who was openly courting him and informed him that he would soon be launching a magazine. It would be "to the American male what *Vogue* is to the female," he said, "but it won't be the least damn bit like *Vanity Fair*. It aims to have ample hair on its chest, to say nothing of adequate cojones." Ernest would be guaranteed top billing and could write about whatever he pleased: "You write and I print."[88] The rising writer dictated his terms to the man that he would later call a weasel: "This is a very I, me, mine letter, but you said you were interested." The $250 per article fee was nonnegotiable, and Ernest would write four dispatches: the first letter would be from Cuba, the second from Spain, and the third and fourth from Africa.[89]

• • • • •

By the end of the January 1933, as Ernest was in Key West and fishing from Bra Saunders's boat with other invited guests, the newspapers made the situation in Cuba sound hopeless: "REVOLT BY TERROR GOING ON IN CUBA; FEAR OF RIOT GROWS. 150 DEATHS LAID TO POLICE . . . Killings Augmented by Retaliatory Bombings by ABC . . . MANY URGE INTERVENTION. Americans in Cuba Are Ready to Close Business."[90] *New York Times* reporter Russell Porter had gathered his facts in Havana and returned to the United States to publish where he would not be censored: The political situation was "very ugly," and no one could predict when it would end. President Machado had ruled with an iron hand and put down rebellion after rebellion using repressive measures to kill off the competition, which only increased opposition and terrorist acts. Cuban prisons were overcrowded with students, young doctors, lawyers, labor leaders, and others. Based on Porter's sources, 150 to 200 people had been killed in secret that year, such as the journalist Armando André, who dared to publish an article against Machado before he was murdered in secret by the police.[91]

Writing by morning and fishing most afternoons, Ernest completed two more stories by the end of February, and three and a half chapters of a new novel, *To Have and Have Not*. Self-promoting and schmoozing via letter with his new business partner Mr. Gingrich, he pushed Gingrich to visit him in Havana so that they could talk business, fish, and chin-wag.[92] Ernest departed on April 12 in a rented boat for his second annual two-month fishing trip to Cuba, during which he would happily receive a visit from Gus Pfeiffer and Pauline's brother, Karl. That month, "Homage to Switzerland" appeared in *Scribner's Magazine*, about Mr. Johnson, Mr. Wheeler, and Mr. Harris, stuck in the train station due to heavy snows while attempting to return to Paris. The story showcases an ear for dialogue and dialect, as well as much persistent regret about the author's divorce and his father's suicide. Ernest also published "God Rest You Merry, Gentlemen," rounding out a lucrative season of magazine pieces. In conversation with an ambulance driver resembling the author, two doctors, one Christian and one Jewish, tell the story of a young man distraught with lust who came to see them requesting a castration. When the doctors refused, the man's troubled conscience ultimately compelled him to perform the operation himself, resulting in his death.

By that time, international newspapers were now also calling for an end to Machado's "reign of terror." As a military junta composed of Machado opponents assembled in Miami, the world watched, optimistic that a new US president would mean military intervention to stop the flow of blood. Others, remembering previous invasions, remained skeptical. Flanks exposed and pretenses irrecoverable, Machado retaliated against anybody who appeared to deceive. Under pressure, Roosevelt shuffled the deck, changed the guard, and appointed Sumner Welles to assistant secretary of state. A Harvard graduate from New York City whose family had long been connected with the Roosevelts, Sumner spoke Spanish, had some experience in Latin America, but no obvious ties to big sugar, and was "generally familiar with the Cuban situation."[93] The watching world hoped Welles could deliver some relief to a tense situation. All wondered if the new statesman in Washington could calm an ever-increasing dictatorship and the violent protests.[94] From Key West where she had returned to attend to the house and children, Pauline wrote, missing her husband still in Havana: "No papa to admire with red-orange brown skin and handsome moustache over tightly closed mouth."[95]

• • • • •

One of the first Cubans to sniff Papa out at the taverns and along the docks of Havana was a sociable and enterprising newspaperman. Having himself received an education in the United States, José Antonio

Fernández de Castro loved American artists and writers with whom he could hold a stimulating conversation in English. As a young man, José Antonio revolted with twelve other concerned intellectuals (called "the Thirteen") against President Alfredo Zayas, one of the island's shadiest leaders who had "won" the lottery twice and erected statues of himself while still alive. Subsequently, young José Antonio had been imprisoned and exiled.[96] Returning to Cuba after the situation had cooled, José Antonio became editor-in-chief of *Orbe*, the magazine produced by *Diario de la Marina*, Havana's most respected newspaper. When José Antonio heard the author of *In Our Time*, *The Sun Also Rises*, and *A Farewell to Arms* was in town, the resourceful newsman tracked him down and seduced him by telling him he wanted to interview him about his fishing exploits.[97]

Urbane, street savvy, and daring, José Antonio was invited frequently aboard the *Anita* after his "fishing interview" in May 1933 and led Ernest along the soft, lovely underbelly of Havana throughout the summers of thirty-three and thirty-four.[98] Also in that world was Walker Evans, who had travelled to Cuba to take photographs for *The Crime of Cuba*, a book by journalist Carleton Beals. Soon Evans and Hemingway became drinking buddies. Hemingway encouraged him to continue his work, lent him some money, and, aboard the *Anita*, helped him to smuggle his provocative photographs out of the country during the oppressive regime.[99] "Dinner with Walker Evans," marked Ernest in the *Anita* logs; he later reminisced that he and Walker "were both working against Machado at the time."[100]

• • • • •

When she swerved her Packard to evade a bus in the other lane, Mrs. Mason splashed Ernest's name across the national newspapers. Her car dropped off the soft shoulder, rolling down a forty-foot embankment into a ravine, with Tony, her adopted three-year-old boy, and two of Ernest's sons, Patrick and Jack, entrusted to her company.[101] Miraculously, the car landed on its feet: four wheels on the ground. "Don't worry, Mrs. Mason. I'll get you right out," Bumby, who was nine years old, reassured Jane.[102] Pushing their way out of a window as bystanders watched from the road, they were shaken up, having escaped disaster with only a few bruises.

Outwardly calm, Jane kept an obligation to attend a dinner at the embassy that very evening. But as she was retelling the story of the accident, the ambassador made the mistake of laughing and she slapped him across the face, making a horrible scene.[103] Afterward, Jane had to inform Mr. Hemingway about the "massacre" she had brought upon their sons.[104]

"Well they have got to have a motor accident sometime in their life and I am very glad they started with you, Mrs. M.," he joked nervously, perhaps to release her from the guilt.[105] Appearing with a hangover at the docks to fish with him the following day, she wrestled in two marlins. But something had broken between them, she could sense it: she had now become the insane woman who had endangered his sons.[106] Sending the children and their nanny back to Key West, Ernest went out with Josie and Jane; she caught three tunas but showed signs of more unstable behavior, jumping from an open window the following day, May 29.[107] By the thirtieth, Pauline had arrived in Havana. After fishing all day with Ernest aboard the *Anita*, she insisted that they visit Jane to check on her condition at her Jaimanitas home.

Did Jane jump because her husband told her to stay, and she refused to be told what to do? Was she overcome by a sudden desire to patch things up with Ernest before his wife arrived the following day? Had Ernest's conscience or his preoccupation for the safety of his sons compelled him to break off this vacant, uncontrollable, and potentially destructive relationship by suggesting that he would be travelling with his wife to Africa without Jane? Only Jane knows for sure what was passing through her mind the moment she jumped. The impact broke her back, and she spent the next five months in a hospital in a body cast. The surgery left a seven-inch scar down of the back of the former beauty queen and another on her pretty leg, where the doctors took a bone graft to repair her fractured vertebrae. From the hospital in New York, Jane wrote the Hemingways to advise them that they were fitting her for a new "iron virgin" body cast, which she would have to wear for a year.[108]

Like Ernest, Jane would later be diagnosed as a manic-depressive personality.[109] "If only she had been at rest with herself, with her own talents," lamented her son in an interview years later as a sort of explanation for a phrase they had had inscribed in an open stone book atop her grave: "Talents too many, not enough of any."[110]

• • • • •

In June, a rumor rustled through Havana that Machado would be stepping down, so the president took to the podium to announce defiantly that he would remain.[111] Though his countrymen possessed many interesting opposing opinions, he said, they could rest assured that everything he did, he did for the good of the republic, and cheekily, he suggested a measure for them to reform: "Why not reinstate the office of vice president?" A gratuitous insult for an angry mob.[112]

Like a stray sniper's bullet, a review of *Death in the Afternoon* appeared in June. It was written by a colleague and former friend from the early years when they were journalists covering events in Europe just after the war. Shooting from the *New Republic*, Max Eastman's review, "Bull in the Afternoon," attacked Hemingway for "False Hair on the Chest School of Writing" and challenged him to "Come out from behind that false hair on your chest, Ernest. We all know you."[113] Frothing, Ernest returned fire with a formal letter of complaint to the editors and threats to sue the magazine if they did not issue an apology. Complaining to Perkins about Eastman, a fellow author at Scribner and Sons, Hemingway called him a "groper in sex (with the hands, I mean), [and] a traitor in politics" and announced that he was no longer a friend, but an enemy whom he would soon be beating with his fists.[114]

With the heat rising to a boiling point at the end of July, the city's bus drivers had had enough and declared a strike. By August 1, the streetcar drivers joined in, and by the seventh, it was a general strike, with masses of people gathering in the streets of the capital as the president declared a state of emergency and martial law. Crowds advancing up the Paseo del Prado clashed with cavalry and infantry units sent to squelch the rebellion. Killing dozens of people, the army attempted to slow the advance of an angry mob by firing shots into the crowd, but they were unable to do so, or halt the street celebrations that erupted when the rumor circulated that Machado had agreed to resign (caused by Welles's suggestion that he take a "leave of absence"). The protestors overtook the presidential palace and summarily executed several members of the homicidal secret police that they had long endured.

Refusing to surrender without a fight, the dictator sent his death squads to gun down hundreds of young activists in the street.[115] On a short stop in Cuba from August 4 to 7, Ernest, Patrick, Bumby (Gregory, not yet two, was left in the care of nanny Ada in Key West), Pauline, and Virginia Pfeiffer witnessed violent clashes between the rebels and Machado's army firsthand just before departing for Paris. Having witnessed *partidos de la porra* billy-club and machine-gun Cuban youth in the back (*la ley de la fuga* demanded that all who fled were guilty by implication and must be shot) and leave their bleeding corpses in the street, Ernest wrote Perkins on the tenth: "I hope to Christ they get rid of that lousy tyrant. Saw everything that happened—No not everything—but what one person could see—keeping in the streets when supposed to be fatal and with my customary fragility or whatever G. Stein called it had no marks—Pauline and Jinny both fired on in the streets—food cut off for 3 days."[116]

On a Pan Am seaplane arranged by the American ambassador, President Machado and his entourage fled safely with twenty-two pieces of luggage to the Bahamas before dawn on the twelfth of August and soon after obtained asylum in the United States where he happily lived out his days on Miami Beach.[117]

On the first of September, another hurricane pounded the Cuban coast, causing extensive damage and inciting looting in a country with a rapidly deteriorating rule of law.[118] A social cyclone would follow, a coup d'état dizzying in its velocity and effects. Gifting asylum to Machado, President Roosevelt deployed US destroyers *Taylor*, *Claxton*, and *Hamilton* to the Cuban coast. Roosevelt told members of the press that he was compelled to respond to rising instability, but he emphasized he did so only to protect Americans and that he had "full knowledge and approval" from the provisional president, Dr. Carlos Manuel de Céspedes.[119] A former ambassador to the United States and a personal friend of Sumner Welles, Céspedes was the son of the legendary plantation owner who freed his slaves, the founding father of Cuban independence, but this bloodline, during tense times, inspired a brittle confidence.

After Machado's flight to Nassau, Bahamas, the discovery of the bodies of sergeant Miguel Ángel Hernández, student Félix Alpízar, and labor leader Margarito Iglesias, tortured then murdered in the military fortress of Atarés, fueled the anger of dozens of enlisted men hitherto humiliated by their superiors.[120] On September 4, under the emboldened direction of a lowly sergeant named Fulgencio Batista, a cadre of sergeants from Camp Colombia commenced arresting officers in what would later be known as the "Sergeants' Revolt."[121] The tables turned on Machado's death squads, who now found themselves at the mercy of an angry mob or behind the walls of the secret dungeons like Principe Hill, where many of them had once been wardens. US warships moved into position on September 5 but did not attack; their mission was to keep the peace, not incite more disorder, violence, and instability.[122] In the vacuum of power left by Machado, a five-man pentarchy formed, composed of José M. Irisarri, Porfirio Franca, Guillermo Portela, Ramón Grau San Martín, and Sergio Carbó.[123]

Of mixed race and from a family of cane cutters from Banes in Oriente Province, Batista originated from humble roots, a product of the masses and possessing the intelligence and industry to work his way up through unassuming professions (barber, tailor, carpenter, cane worker, railroader on the sugar central lines, and later a solider and stenographer). From his unglamorous billet of stenographer, he observed Machado's trials make mockery of justice in Cuba's courts and saw the suppressed anger of the attendees. Representing the enlisted men, Batista benefited from an army at his back and formed alliances with the pentarchy that represented the interests of students, teachers, journalists, doctors, and workers of the ABC and DEU.[124] The younger student militant groups distanced themselves from charismatic old guard members like Menocal. The pentarchy, specifically Sergio Carbó, a respected journalist and a key link between the students and the sergeants, told Batista on September 8 that they had voted to promote him to the rank of colonel and make him military chief of staff.[125]

When President Céspedes returned on September 9 from a visit to the hurricane-strewn provinces of Santa Clara and Matanzas, the pentarchy was awaiting him in the presidential palace, supported by Batista's sergeants. They forced Céspedes to resign and named Dr. Ramón Grau San Martín as their new president and Antonio Guiteras, a proponent of revolutionary socialism, as their vice president, to the American ambassador's surprise. With warships floating in Havana harbor, President Roosevelt, Ambassador Welles, and his successor Jefferson Caffery reiterated the United States' "commitment to nonintervention and Cuban autonomy," yet privately discussed their options. In their communications, their distaste for the left-leaning elements coming to power was clear: Grau San Martín's group was "utterly impractical," "communistic," "radicals," "irresponsible," and "mislead[ing] the people" with "utopian dreams."[126]

• • • • •

Depositing their children in a maid's care in an apartment in Paris, the Hemingways set sail for African adventures while his first "Cuban Letter" surfaced in *Esquire*. Reeling readers in as the star of the new magazine, Ernest crowed to the largely male audience of *Esquire* that "they are a fish all right!" and he ought to know, for that summer he had bagged fifty-two marlins and two sailfish.[127] The article appearing in the autumn of 1933 was called "Marlin off the Morro: A Cuban Letter." It would be the first in a series of four others, called "Out in the Stream," "On the Blue Water," "There She Breaches! Or Moby Dick off the Morro," and "The Great Blue River"—articles vividly describing the marvels of marlin fishing off the Cuban coast. Though he had occasionally resisted the legend, the *Esquire* articles seemingly embraced it, calcifying a sensationalized version of himself—a sporting, adventuring, larger-than-life, and international man of letters. In total, he would write twenty-five articles and six stories for *Esquire*, whose editor had agreed that he would remain the highest paid contributor. The first edition of the magazine sold 105,000 copies, and two years later, it sold half a million copies per month: a record number due to the fame phenomenon that was becoming "Ernest Hemingway."[128]

In *Esquire*, this character, called Hemingway, told readers how to sleep with the hotel curtains open in Havana so the sun hit them in the morning (not too harshly but just early enough so that they could get up in time for fishing), what kind of breakfast to eat so that they would not get nauseated on the boat, what brands of beer were best to drink, what varieties of mangoes and avocados best accompanied a sandwich, and he even suggested a recipe for a delightful "French" dressing.[129]

As his ship churned through the Red Sea toward Africa, Ernest wrote his five-year-old son Patrick, whom he had nicknamed "Mexican Mouse," a letter describing all the animals, birds, and trees that he had seen along the way, telling him they would soon be arriving to the Indian Ocean, and ending: "I miss you, old Mex, and will be glad to see you again. Will have plenty of good stories when we come back . . . Give my best to everybody in Piggott. Go easy on the beer and lay off the hard liquor until I get back. Don't forget to blow your nose and turn around three times before you go to bed. Your affectionate papa."[130]

• • • • •

Back in Cuba, President Grau San Martín and Vice President Guiteras succeeded in passing a series of reforms that Cuban people believed to be long overdue—raising the minimum wage, guaranteeing free university tuition to the poor, and nullifying the Platt Amendment and Permanent Treaty May 22, 1903. They replaced them with the Treaty of Relations, which guaranteed the United States' right to rent Guantánamo base, established the Labor Department, conceded women's suffrage, established an eight-hour workday, helped leasing farmers to buy land, granted autonomy to the University of Havana, and nationalized the Cuban Electric Company. Though the Grau San Martín–Guiteras government courted the American ambassador, the progressive agenda—what would later be known as "the Government of 100 days"—worried Welles, and Caffey, his successor, who both gravitated toward Batista as a source of authority, stability, and prosperity, for he controlled the army, could crush the Communists, and protect American businesses on the island.[131]

Retreating from Batista's sergeants, four hundred of Machado's army officers holed up in the Hotel Nacional, which was also the temporary residence to the American ambassador and other diplomats. The sergeants and their student allies encircled the hotel in September and would not allow them to leave.[132] On October 2, they ended the siege with light shelling and a frontal assault; during the "Battle of Hotel Nacional," Batista's artillery guns from positions on land and sea sent projectiles crashing through the outer walls of the hotel and into its deluxe suites. When the fog of battle lifted, Batista's sergeants had taken the day with each side suffering twenty casualties. More than 280 more officers were in prison, and the opposition's hopes were squashed.[133]

As astute at business as he was at politics, Batista benefited from the financial support of the Mob.[134] That the Sicilian Mafia had been importing rum from Cuba since the era of Prohibition was no great secret. The Atlantic coasts of the island—privileged leeward and windward, yet offering plentiful coves and inlets for smugglers—were known as "rum row." The "smugglers' paradise" that was Cuba blossomed into a hotbed of black-market business through the perfect marriage of mafia bosses and politicians, like Jimmy Walker, the Irish-American New York mayor who visited Havana in 1927 and was given first-class treatment by a gang of real estate developers, bank presidents, the president of the Cuban Tourism Commission, the mayor of Havana, and the chief of police as he visited Oriental Park Racetrack and the Jockey Club.[135] When the boisterous Chicago mobster Al Capone came to Havana, he took full advantage of the city and made no attempt to hide his presence: booking the entire sixth floor of the Sevilla-Biltmore Hotel, staying in room 615, and visiting the racetrack and opera house. In 1928, the same year that Ernest and Pauline first arrived from Paris, Capone had opened a pool hall near Oriental Park Racetrack in Marianao but closed it soon afterward; leering, he told a reporter from the *Havana Post* that Havana had not been the right fit for "this particular type of business." He had pulled one over by using the joint as a distraction and control point for the import of contraband.[136]

In Havana on business during the twenties, mobsters Joseph "Doc" Stacher and Meyer Lansky guided Fulgencio Batista into their room at the Hotel Nacional and opened a suitcase of money. After gaping at it for a long moment, Batista understood and shook their hands. Before leaving the room, the mobsters had guaranteed Batista $3 to $5 million in cash annually and a percentage of their profits in exchange for a monopoly on his island's casinos, but the timing could not have been worse.[137]

The stock market crash and the Great Depression gutted tourism in Cuba and revenues plummeted from $26 million in 1928–29 to less than $5 million in 1933–34. The economic downslide, combined with political upheaval, cooled prospects and put mafia plans for expansion on hold until complications could be resolved. Brutality and chaos were bad for business, repugnant to the international press, and ever more unbearable for inhabitants.

President Roosevelt, hoping to stimulate positive change, sent Jefferson Caffery, Welles's replacement, to Cuba on December 18 as the new ambassador.[138] Though expectations were high that a new man in Havana would mean a change in policy, Caffery's arrival dampened the mood. "My country's policy toward Cuba will remain the same."[139] Or as he put it shortly after: "Diplomacy, as I interpret it, nowadays consists largely in cooperation with American business," assuring his place as the American ambassador for the next three years.[140] With support from Caffery and the army, Batista pressured Grau San Martín and Guiteras to tender their resignations and depart for Mexico, leaving Carlos Hevia as provisional president for six hours and setting off a workers' strike. By January 20, 1934, the National Union had negotiated a place at the table, with Carlos Mendieta as their puppet president. But as commander in chief with American support, Batista secured the reins, ruling the island as a strongman for stabilization of legal and illegal business during the next fifteen years as presidents came and went.

• • • • •

Laid up with dysentery at the well-appointed New Stanley Hotel in Nairobi during the first two weeks of the safari, Ernest returned to the hunt with something to prove and spent the rest of their African trip competing with gentle Charlie Thompson and feeling like an inferior hunter.[141] According to his own nonfictional account, he entangled himself in rivalry, comparing every shot, pelt, and act of bravery with those of his friend in a vain compulsion to demonstrate his superiority that he could not for the life of himself shake. Charlie's shots seemed to hit their marks while his were always slightly off-center. Next to Charlie's kudus, rhinos, and lions, his own kudus, rhinos, and lions appeared small and insignificant. Recognizing the pointlessness of his inferiority complex, Ernest made a joke later of his inimical tendencies in *Green Hills of Africa*, a book in which he poked fun at himself in the pursuit of waterbucks, elands, buffaloes, oryx, zebra, greater kudus, rhinos, leopards, and lions, and chased meaning in the spectacular open country of East Africa—an experience that surpassed his expectations, improved his marriage, and stimulated his imagination tenfold. Pauline's enlistment of her uncle's funds for this expedition, her willingness to accompany her husband when other friends had bailed out, and the time that they spent together during the safari seemed to benefit and sustain a marriage . . . during the following year.[142]

Travelling back through Paris, the Hemingways retrieved their children and visited old friends, like Sylvia Beach and James Joyce, who got so sozzled during dinner that Hemingway had to sling the Irish writer over his back like a "sack of potatoes" and lug him up several flights of stairs.[143] Boarding the liner *Paris* at Cherbourg, they traversed the ocean to return home via New York. While at sea, Ernest ensorcelled Marlene Dietrich by standing in as her date one evening at dinner with six other couples. Afterward, he began a correspondence and a more-or-less platonic relationship with the famous German-American actress, to whom he often referred fondly thereafter as "the Kraut." Passing through New York, the Hemingways called on the Murphys, Waldo Peirce, Max Perkins, and Scott Fitzgerald, who was struggling in his personal life and to finish his novel, *Tender Is the Night*.

In addition to the heads of three lions, a rhino, a wildebeest, impalas, kudus, and many other beasts—twenty-nine kills in total—the

African expedition would inspire much material during that year: journalism, nonfiction, and fiction. The "Tanganyika Letters" were the first three trophies of the page, producing spending cash from the good graces of Arnold Gingrich's bankbook. Like the Cuban Letters, they spread his fame as a hunter and as an explorer far and wide. Read mostly by American males, the letters in *Esquire* instructed, "there are two ways to murder a lion": as a "shootist" or as a "sportsman," so typifying their recurring theme—the authenticity of the experience he had to offer.[144] The pact with readers was to take them on the ride of their life. Unlike competitors or would-be imitators, he would not waste time with tourism or cowardly simulations but confront the marvelous mysteries of the great unknown while allowing them to follow.

Reinvesting the capital that he garnered from the articles, he financed future adventures that he could again write home about. As *Death in the Afternoon* discovered bullfighting from his perspective, *Green Hills of Africa*, published in October 1935, solidified his larger-than-life persona. The experiential travelogue was reinvented as a genre.

• • • • •

The previous year, Mr. Wheeler, of Wheeler Shipyard in Brooklyn, had smartly taken it upon himself to send Ernest one of their catalogues. Though he had been studying it for months—carrying it with him since the previous summer, even taking it to Africa with him—he continued to inspect the specifications and cabin arrangements inside the tent under a kerosene lamp of a custom-made fishing boat whose components would later become as familiar to him as a father's voice or as any number of childhood dreams. The advertisement read, "If you are looking for a fine roomy cruiser with lots of comforts, and ability for long offshore cruising and fishing trips, we suggest that you look this boat over very carefully . . . Afloat at the plant. For rail or steamer deliveries add $175 for cradle and cover."[145]

In March, while still in Paris just before boarding his return ship for New York, Ernest had written his *Esquire* editor to ask him for an advance against articles he had not yet written about his African exploits.[146] The boat cost $7,000, but he had only $3,500, Ernest explained to his editor, who immediately sent him $3,000 to make his down payment on the boat. Before he had even unpacked his travel trunk, he was passing through New York in April on the way to Key West and took a taxi out to the Brooklyn shipyard to order his thirty-eight-foot twin cabin cruiser, designed for offshore cruising and fishing.

She should be painted black, he specified, except for a green roof and her polished mahogany cockpit. The name *Pilar* would be scripted across the stern along with the name of her home port, *Key West*. At its origin, *Pilar* was the name of the Virgin of Saragossa, patron saint of Spain, a country he had held close to heart since the days he first travelled there as a young man with Hadley. Then, *Pilar* had become his macho-tender, Hispano-military code name for Pauline during their affair and when they met in Madrid while Hadley awaited quarantined with Bumby in Juan-les-Pins. Later, *Pilar* referred to the daughter Pauline and Ernest had hoped for but who never arrived. Finally, it was the name he gave the heroine of his later novel about the Spanish Civil War, *For Whom the Bell Tolls*.[147]

• • • • •

With his boat ordered, Hemingway again set his sights on Cuba, where corruption, frustration, and revolution were rising to a boiling point, though not nine months had passed since Machado's retreat. Students, intellectuals, journalists, laborers, the DEU, and ABC irregulars had supported revolutionary candidates Grau San Martín and Guiteras only to see them shuffled off the stage by Colonel Batista and Ambassador Caffery and replaced with labor leader Carlos Mendieta. These factions from the left, who had seen their causes tabled for corruption and business as usual, grew angrier and bolder every day. In April, one of Cuba's most popular magazines, *Bohemia*, printed the alarming words of writer/militant Pablo de la Torriente Brau (whom Ernest would later meet in civil-war Spain), drawing their inspiration from George-Jacques Danton: "Compromise, compromise is always the advice of those false revolutionaries who never understand the real lesson of Danton: that in Cuba, as in any other place, what a revolutionary needs is audacity, audacity and more audacity."[148]

The forces of law and order anxiously anticipated the massive demonstrations being planned by labor movements for May Day.[149] While police reinforced defenses and distributed riot gear, labor leaders organized two hundred thousand workers to shut down buses, trains, factories, cane fields, refineries, and resorts on the first of the month. Caffery advised the Secretary of State that there had been rumors that Communists would attempt to loot American business that day: "It is therefore expected that the government will take special measures to protect such property."[150]

As a student of revolution and as a man who was itching with expectation as he awaited his boat's arrival, Ernest convinced leftie John Dos Passos to accompany him to Havana to witness the May Day activities and to pre-book a dock for the *Pilar*'s first fishing season.[151] The two writers found the city on the brink of war, an entanglement of protesters and police.[152] They called on Carlos Gutierrez and Manuel Asper, owner of the Ambos Mundos Hotel, who said the situation was extremely serious.[153] Twenty-five thousand had gathered in Parque Central to protest a government that did not represent their interests. When police confiscated the protestors' banners and ordered them to disperse, they retreated to reassemble at Cristal Stadium, and sharpshooters then opened fire to disperse the crowd. Though there were no fatalities, eleven were wounded in the shootings.

Just after Ernest's return to calmer Key West, a young stranger appeared on the author's doorstep. Arnold Samuelson, a twenty-two-year-old valedictorian of his tiny class from White Earth, Minnesota, was struggling to write when he read "One Trip Across": a Cuban story that formed the basis of the novel *To Have and Have Not* and which appeared in *Cosmopolitan* along with a picture of Ernest Hemingway returning from an African safari. This was the way he wanted to write, and this was just the sort of man who could teach him, one whose education came from life itself. Arnold, son of a sharecropping wheat farmer, had completed every course for a degree in journalism at the University of Minnesota but had been so bored and frustrated by formal education that he refused to pay the final fee of five dollars to issue his diploma. Perhaps troubled by the brutal murder of his elder sister or unable during the Depression to secure a job in journalism, Arnold decided to "bum" across the country, hopping railroad trains to make a pilgrimage and learn the craft from a living master.

Summoning up the courage to knock at his idol's door, Samuelson was suddenly face-to-face with him—a massive man irritated with him for interrupting his writing and not respecting his privacy, but who soon softened under Arnold's admiring eyes and invited him to return the following afternoon.[154] Samuelson could hardly believe it when Hemingway offered him a job aboard the *Pilar*, a writing "apprenticeship," and one dollar per day salary.

Just before Ernest left for Miami with Pauline and Bra to meet the Wheeler representative who had come down from Brooklyn to deliver his boat, another worshipper, this time a blood relative, appeared at his door: Ernest's kid brother, Leicester, whom he'd nicknamed "Baron," with his buddy Al Dudek. They had blown the trust fund Ernest had set up for him with the movie rights of *A Farewell to Arms* to build a boat they called the *Hankshaw* and sail it down from Alabama for high-sea adventure. Cashing in favors with his friends, Ernest found them a place to park it in the naval yard. It had taken them twenty-three days to make a trip down to Key West, though it should have required only ten.[155] When Bra Saunders saw the rickety, top-heavy boat, he told Leicester he would give him five dollars for it just to make sure he did not die by trying to take it out to sea again.[156] Leicester's arrival surprised Ernest, as did his declaration that he dreamed of sea adventures and becoming a writer too.

From Miami harbor, the Wheeler rep accompanied Hemingway during a two-day sea journey back to Key West so that he could get his bearings on the new boat.[157] Lovingly Ernest ran his fingers along *Pilar*'s rails and felt the weight of her in the water as he steered her through the current. Emerging from the recesses of boyhood fantasies and an overripe imagination, Ernest noted how her every detail had been fashioned from his precise instructions, and, new, she smelled of mahogany, fresh paint, Italian leather, and gasoline.[158] Equipped with berthing space for eight, ample storage, a modern galley, a roller bar, and a lowered transom (making it easier to bring the big ones aboard), she had been made for Ernest Hemingway to fish the Gulf Stream.

Though he could have asked Uncle Gus, who had purchased Ernest's home and funded his safari, or any other Pfeiffer, for money, he deliberately bought this boat with his earnings from writing, or at least on credit from Gingrich, so that she would belong to him alone.[159] He could hardly believe he had pulled it off, but she was real and she was his. At a time when literary success and growing fame threatened his peace, privacy, and craft even on an island at the end of the world, his new boat offered a floating home, a mobile island granting exhilarating and unprecedented degrees of freedom and power.

Ernest wrote Gingrich to assure him he would honor their agreement, thank him, and gush—during a moment that he seemed completely happy: "The boat is marvelous. Wheeler, 38 footer, cut down to my design. 75 horse Chrysler and a 40 h. Lycoming. Low stern for fishing. Fish well, 300 gal gas tanks. 100 gal water. Sleeps six in cabin and two in cockpit. Can turn on its own tail burns less than three gals an hour trolling and four at cruising speed with the big engine. Will do sixteen with the two motors. The little one will do five hooked up."[160]

While the smooth-talking sales rep demonstrated the boat's innumerable features, listening to him intently, Ernest ordered final adjustments executed without delay. When he returned from this test run, the limitless potential of his sea cruiser was gleaming for a crowd of friends and neighbors at the Key West docks, including his adoring apprentice, Arnold Samuelson, awaiting pearls of wisdom from a true master.[161] Filing a manifest with the maritime authorities in Key West port for his first crossing to Cuba aboard the *Pilar*, Hemingway listed Samuelson as his "engineer" and Charles Lund, a junior seaman with P&O steamship line, as his navigator.[162]

Ernest's wisdom was much better received by aspirants than experienced friends, even those who sought it out. Besieged by Zelda's mental health and by dipsomania, F. Scott Fitzgerald had written his friend, fast becoming the most famous writer in America, eager for his approval on his freshly completed manuscript of *Tender Is the Night*. Fitzgerald had been working on his fourth novel for eight years, and he was desperate to know if it was any good. Though they had grown apart, Scott respected Ernest and his recent accomplishments. When Ernest's response was delayed by several weeks, Scott fired off a follow-up letter: "Did you like the book? For God's sake drop me a line and tell me one way or the other."[163] In the interim, Ernest had written Max Perkins criticizing Scott and his manuscript: the manuscript was poorly written, and Scott was wasting his potential.[164] Yes, Scott's talent was tremendous, wrote Ernest, but he had to be a man: he needed to grow up.

With his father-in-law in tow, Archibald MacLeish dropped down to Key West to visit his friend. Ernest wanted to help his friend to hook the sailfish, which were plentiful then, but after nine days of trying, the poet would not listen to the writer's perhaps well-intentioned but overbearing instructions to slack off the line and insisted on striking instead: "He's after you, Archie! Slack to him! *Slack to him!!!* Shit! Why the hell didn't you slack to him? He's spooked now and he never will come back." According to Samuelson, "The E.H.-MacLeish friendship was never the same after that."[165]

As Ernest's stature increased during the 1930s, his behavior with friends became "erratic, combative, and sometimes intolerable."[166] Passion, energy, arrogance, intellect, and large quantities of booze could make minor disagreements fester into irreconcilable arguments as he said precisely what he thought of those who got in his way. While he apologized profusely afterward, often recognizing his errors, words and deeds in the heat of the moment could scald to the bone, and his inner sensitivity could result in grudges that he or others were unable to let go. "Papa can be more severe than God on a rough day when the whole human race is misbehaving," said his friend Robert Capa.[167] These troubles and his fame resulted in a steady stream of new relationships, yet acts of generosity mark the mystery of a complex and brightly burning man who will never be fully condemnable or completely understood.

A few days after the blowout with MacLeish, Ernest wrote Scott a response concerning *Tender Is the Night*. It began, "I liked it and I didn't like it."[168] The characters were artificial, "faked case histories," rather than real people, and, in his estimation, Scott was allowing his drinking, his worries, and Zelda to distort his powers of perception and to wreak havoc with his writing discipline. He continued, "All you need to do is write truly and not care about what the fate of it is."[169] At the end of a tough letter, Ernest invited Scott down to fish with him in the fall, perhaps intending to set him straight. But hurt perhaps by his friend's reproaches, possibly feeling like too much of a failure relative to his success, Scott dodged the invitation with a story, made up, about an ailing mother.[170] Ernest was right, for, befuddling its reviewers and slumping in sales, the novel would not fare well. To be right about the faults of one's friends was easy, to know how to help them was not, nor was avoiding similar failures.

• • • • •

Twenty minutes from Havana, Hemingway and his devoted crew noticed a burning smell, and after searching the galley and the engine pit, they discovered that *Pilar*'s main motor was so hot that it was melting the paint from the cylinder.[171] The cooling pump had ceased to function, so they turned off the large engine and puttered slowly into port on the smaller Lycoming engine, which the author had installed for trolling and for such emergencies. Against the current, *Pilar* took another two hours to arrive, but they had been lucky the trouble started close to port.

As they entered the harbor beside the Morro, a patrol boat approached, and three soldiers in khaki carrying rifles announced their intention to search the boat for contraband weapons intended for the Communists.[172] When Ernest explained that he was an American coming to fish marlin, the soldiers laughed, saying it was a good story. They would still have to search the boat. As they prepared to board, another boat approached with a man on it who was shouting, "*¡El Hemingway!* "*¡El Hemingway!*"[173]

In the newspapers, the name "Hemingway" belonged famously to the American millionaire who had caught dozens of marlins last season and gave the meat to all who would care to partake of it along the docks. "*¡Hola*, Carlos!" Ernest responded as his employee leaped aboard, "his black eyes glistening with emotion."[174] When soldiers heard the name Hemingway, their faces shrank with embarrassment, and apologizing, they explained that they had not recognized him in this new boat, for which they congratulated him, wished him *suerte en la pesca*, and sent him on his way.[175] Fastening the *Pilar* to the San Francisco dock, Lund, Samuelson, and Hemingway slept their first night in Havana aboard the ship until they could clear customs and a health inspection first thing in the morning. Due to Hemingway's celebrity status, the inspection was a mere formality, for they did not bother to look beneath the bunks and below deck in lockers where hidden ammunition and illegal rifles were stored.

Upon Ernest's orders, Carlos sent for an associate who walked on his heels, whom they called "Cojo," so that he could rebuild their broken pump.[176] While Ernest was ashore sending a telegram to Pauline, a man in rags rowed up alongside the *Pilar* to peddle pineapples. Arnold negotiated with him in broken English and bought a few, but fearing it might be against the law, he refused his offer to trade a jug of wine for American cigarettes. His boss confirmed, "Don't trust anybody. That fellow might have been a government spy trying to get you in a bind. You can never tell who they are."[177]

Intending to entertain heavily that summer, Ernest asked Carlos if he knew a good cook. Carlos presented a skilled but uncouth Spaniard named Juan. He was hungry looking, fiery talking, and proud, and Ernest hired the young man directly. Expecting his wife by P&O ferry, the author went ashore and booked a room at the Ambos Mundos. Pauline's four-day visit would celebrate two birthdays—his thirty-fifth and her thirty-ninth.[178]

The many policemen and soldiers they passed on the streets of Havana did not bother them or spoil their fun. "They nodded their heads at us because we were Americans and they knew Americans never throw bombs or start revolutions but think only of having a good time spending American dollars."[179] As the Hemingways treated Samuelson to a fresh Hatuey beer at a table across from El Capitolio, a reporter approached to snap their picture, and Ernest did not become annoyed; but while they were taking a taxi back, the driver, also knowing they were Americans, charged them double, and "E.H. paid in disgust." After Cojo had performed a first miracle by fashioning metal pieces with a machinist he knew in Havana, and a second by installing a new pump, the crew of the *Pilar* patted his back, named him their saint, and extended an open invitation to fish or "drink himself drunk on good whiskey" aboard, or whenever they were in port.[180]

Acutely conscious of the unusual experiment Ernest had undertaken to convert him from Midwest bumpkin to world-class writer, Arnold seemed as excited as he was terrified. Fretfully, Arnold asked Ernest how many words he wrote a day.

"That varies," he answered. "Sometimes you can write a lot and some days you can't write . . . Have you ever tried any of those exercises we talked about?"

"No. I want to write, but every time I try I have the feeling I can't do it."

Ernest reassured him not to get discouraged: "You've got a chance. Anybody's got a chance if he sets out to be the greatest writer that ever lived . . . The important thing is to keep using your eyes and ears . . ."[181] Dictating daily annotations into the logbook of his new boat, Ernest taught Arnold to observe like a good naturalist protégé and collect life's raw material in service of their literary art. In a manuscript that remained unpublished until after Samuelson's death, he transcribed the action aboard the *Pilar*, the people in Havana, and the places he had lived. That night, the *Pilar* was bustling, and camaraderie aboard was electrified on Sunday by the arrival of an extraordinary trio: Venezuelan painter Luis Lopez Mendez, and Cuban painter Antonio Gattorno and his lively, petite, and adorable wife from France, Lillian.

Out to sea again on the Monday before Pauline's return home to Key West, this time without their friends, the *Pilar* listlessly combed the sea without a marlin to be seen, then witnessed a miracle—a migration of six thousand porpoises in a herd two miles wide and perhaps six miles long, leaping as high as thirty feet in the air when they played in the waves of the boat. Snapping pictures madly with his Kodak, Arnold hollered, "Yi! Yi! Yi! Three of them at a time! Lookit! Oh, boy! Oh boy! Wow! Eeeeyi! Yi!" and Ernest, Pauline, Arnold, Juan, and Carlos bore witness to the wondrous scenes until stunned in a state of silence.[182] The novelist told his trainee that such a scene might never repeat itself, and it certainly could not be written, as nobody could ever do it justice, though a piece of it would appear later in *The Old Man and the Sea*, when Ernest's protagonist near his death dreamed "of a vast sea of porpoises" during their time of mating.[183]

Reading a morning newspaper, they learned that the president of Germany, Paul von Hindenburg, had died, sparking a series of editorials concerned about the path his passing would clear for Adolph Hitler's rise to power. In some Havana news, Ernest read that the home of a fellow ex-Chicagoan in Vedado had been bombed. Dr. M. R. Leeder had practiced law in Havana for twenty years. Amid the rubble of their home, the lawyer and his wife discovered a number of printed circulars chillingly marked the "Terror Squad" and instructing Dr. Leeder to resign as administrator of the property of the former president, Gerardo Machado, at Rancho Boyeros and to leave the island at once.[184] A few lines on the front page would also announce that three Americans had been jailed by the Cuban authorities.[185] Batista cawed that he would be dedicating ten Cuban airplanes and seven warships to hunting down all rumrunners in violation of international law, while strikes, arrests, and bombings continued to complicate the peace.

Dining with the Masons on the eve of a new holiday named "Batista Day" (to honor the Sergeants' Revolt one year before), Ernest was caught unaware as student protesters, incensed by the mysterious deaths of classmates, attacked and succeeded in inciting strikes interrupting tram, telephone, and postal services.[186] Declaring martial law, Colonel Batista posted soldiers at every street corner, reinforced the presidential palace, La Cabaña, and Morro Castle with sandbags and artillery, and ordered searchlights to comb the streets. As student rebels and revolutionaries armed with machine guns attacked city hall and the American-owned Cuban Telephone Company to incite employees to strike, President Mendieta's cabinet did nothing and soon after tendered their resignations: "I never dreamed my cabinet was made up of cowardly persons," the president said. "I no longer trust them." The rebels demanded Mendieta's resignation in turn, suggesting a replacement, and Batista's junta issued a statement: "We want to avoid a repetition of the coup d'état performed by the top sergeants against Carlos Manuel de Céspedes a year ago, tomorrow."[187]

The next day, fifteen bombs exploded across Havana in movie theaters and in the homes of government officials, such as the ones belonging to an army captain and the chief of police. The bombs killed one person and wounded twelve others, including the son of a high government official, when a detonation ripped apart their family home. Among the perpetrators was Humberto Wilfred, an American, and the son of newspaper publisher John T. Wilfred.[188] The Secretary of the Presidency responded with riot squads, attacking the students in Parque Central, and imposing severe conditions of martial law, to attempt to restore order in the streets.[189] As Cuban students fought the army in armed combat, rioting spread to the outer provinces of Santiago and Camaguey; workers across the country were striking in solidarity and under threat from terrorist factions with guns.[190]

The government suspended the constitution and dispersed soldiers to keep the peace. At the end of the first week of October, Hemingway scribbled in the *Pilar* log book: "The town is full of arms, ammunition [sic], dynamite. When the fighting starts will be part of all the factions against Batista and the loyal part of the army and a general dog fight afterward if the revolution is successful." A few days later he added, "Big Bomb last night at 1.45, much promiscuous shooting in town."[191] Undeterred, Ernest continued to fish and to shut himself into the Ambos Mundos to write scenes that would combine to become *Green Hills of Africa*. In the evenings, the Hemingways met the Gattornos in town to have dinner or drinks.[192]

In late September, Ernest met Loló de la Torriente, an attractive female lawyer and respected journalist whom he had met during a previous soirée in the company of her colleague José Antonio Fernández de Castro. Having argued for the release of students imprisoned on the Isle of Pines during Machado's reign, Loló was a lady who was not afraid to go after what she wanted, particularly on behalf of people she cared about or for a cause in which she believed. So it was that she asked Ernest to read the work of a writer she considered to be a prodigy, and she made him promise that once he had read it he would call her to tell her what he thought.[193]

Enrique Serpa had made a reputation for himself in Cuban literature when he published the short story "The Swordfish"—about an old man, his grandson, and an unconquerable fish. Loló was quite sure that Ernest, as a fisherman, would appreciate stories like "The

Marlin" or "Shark Fins," depicting the life of fisherman at sea, in addition to the manuscript *Contraband*, illustrating the dark underworld of piracy and prostitution originating along the wharves and brothels of the docks of San Francisco de Paula at that time. When he had read it, Ernest asked Loló where the author was hiding out and to arrange a meeting with him in the Floridita bar.

The manuscript of Serpa's novel *Contraband* parodied a protagonist who had admired a "well-known American writer who spent his summers marlin fishing in Havana" and who had tacked his picture up to lend himself an air of credibility with his crew. Having caricatured a writer whose reputation for hypersensitivity and temper preceded him, Serpa was apprehensive about the meeting. He saw Hemingway's bulky frame sitting atop a bar stool at the other end of the Floridita and anxiety mounted.

With a hard look on his face, Hemingway led Serpa to a table and asked him: "Listen friend, why are you wasting your time working as a newspaper reporter?"

The Cuban responded, "Because here they don't pay me twenty thousand dollars for a short story to make a movie. You know? And my family and I also eat."

"*Hombre*, you are the best novelist in Latin America," Hemingway countered. "You should forget about everything else and write novels."[194]

Late that night, just after the two writers had said their goodbyes and parted ways, Serpa found himself, notepad in hand, chasing a story on the beat, while Ernest was in the Ambos Mundos getting the rest required to battle marlins aboard his boat for the better part of the next day. Serpa would encounter countless stories at that time that were too dangerous to print in a Havana newspaper. Their friendship, as well as a mutual influence between a Cuban and an American writer, would continue for several years afterward, such that on the shelves of Hemingway's home one can find every one of Serpa's books, with a dedication from his friend.

Amid student demonstrations and growing unrest on September 25, 1934, the police and soldiers raided offices belonging to the opposing party and journalists in order to round up and imprison forty of them who were loyal to the leader of the "Authentic Party" and former president Grau San Martín.[195] This action caused the Secretary of Defense, acting in good conscience, to tender his resignation, though he underlined that he would not turn against President Mendieta or take part in further conflict. Advised that his life was in danger, Grau San Martín and seven members of his family boarded a Pan Am plane two days later and escaped Cuba to Miami, out of the lion's mouth.[196]

Solidifying his position by speaking directly to the American people, Batista got a significant boost in a full-length article by J. D. Phillips appearing in the *New York Times*: "Batista Links His Destiny with Cuba's . . . The ex-sergeant who heads a growing army says that he is guided to do his utmost for the republic."[197] In the interview, Batista would make his case rather compellingly through the favorable descriptions of his significant charms, "I am an idealist, but a practical one. To me all ideals are useless unless they can be put into practice; all theories are without value unless they can be applied. The group who surrounded Dr. Grau San Martín were in the majority earnest, idealistic students who lacked orientation, practicality and knowledge of applying their theories of government."[198] His role, as he saw it, was not dictator, but maintainer of the public order.[199]

What about relations with the United States? Well, due to the size of its northern neighbor and its influence, Cuba was duty bound to maintain amiable relations whether they liked it or not, and it was only natural, normal, and in their interests to do so. One had to recognize that the United States had respected Cuban autonomy, refrained from intervention, and granted many concessions and opportunities, he explained.[200]

• • • • •

A handsome young Cuban gentleman in a white linen suit and a coiling black mustache appeared in the lobby of the Ambos Mundos and presented Ernest Hemingway a letter of introduction from the other "greatest American author" of the day. After a year spent in Louisiana winning some recognition and prizes for his painting, this *caballero cubano* from another time[201] had decamped with an easel to paint along the banks of the Mississippi and called upon William Faulkner at nearby Rowan Oak.[202] Courtly, considerate, and articulate, he had eyes bright with intelligence, and his manners were as gentle as his name, Fernando G. Campoamor.[203] Ernest and Dos Passos liked him at once and invited him to join them for a drink at the Floridita. As time passed, this same kid would become a close friend, particularly as the author's Havana residence became more permanent.

In October 1934, Fernando G. Campoamor was just the sort of fine-looking, serious, and noble young man that Ernest had been at twenty-one years of age. The son of a Spanish merchant from Coaña, Asturias, Spain, Campoamor had been born and raised in Artemisa, a village still in the Havana Province, just to the east of the capital. When Campoamor became involved in student organizations against Machado's dictatorship, the police pursued him and his father. Fearing for his safety, he would arrange for an emergency student exchange visa so that he could spend a year at Lake Charles High School in Louisiana, veiled by the Spanish moss draping serenely in the shade from aging and immutable oaks.

By the end of October, Ernest wrote Perkins that he had finished a seventy-thousand-word manuscript that he was calling "The Highland of Africa," and asked him to visit to retrieve the thing and celebrate with a victory lap aboard his new boat.[204] After the Hemingways had spent Christmas in Piggott, Perkins came down to Key West in January, and writer and editor fixed the title *Green Hills of Africa*.

While "One Trip Across" had included scenes of revolution that were making the news, in *Green Hills of Africa* he was "sick of revolutions" and instead aspired for formal innovation. Drawing on elements specific to his apprenticeship, Ernest painted the country as Cezanne, striving as Ezra Pound's disciple to transcend the styles of his day, by moving through time and space in a stream of consciousness rivaling Joyce's *Ulysses* and hunting what he called "the fifth dimension."[205] Many critics, failing to appreciate as much, reflexively attacked this work, even former allies, such as Edmund Wilson, who said it was the "only book [he] had ever seen that makes Africa and its animals seem dull."[206] History would absolve the work, however; the author known for short sentences and journalism received subsequent praise for his innovation: as Richard Brody wrote in the *New Yorker*, Papa became the "godfather of the long-form" when he fused "fiction and nonfiction" in *Green Hills of Africa*.[207]

Accidentally shooting himself in the leg in April, Ernest wrote about the ordeal for *Esquire* in June. For his carryings-on and for writing about subjects like bullfighting and hunting during a highly political time, Ernest was becoming the author that his critics loved to hate while he pontificated liberally about literature, politics, and many subjects in between. Wilson suggested that his works were "detached from the great social issues of the day."[208] Hicks requested openly that he write about the subjects considered essential at the time: class conflicts, riots, and strikes.[209]

In turn, his articles and full-length nonfiction works became platforms for the author to counterattack a growing crowd of critics attempting to make their careers by taking the big man down. Consequently, in the *Esquire* article, "An Old Newspaperman Writes: A Cuban Letter," Hemingway shot back at the group he now referred to as "the literary revolution boys": "Don't let them suck you in to start writing about the proletariat if you don't come from the proletariat just to please the recently politically enlightened critics . . . if you know and write truly and tell them all where they can place it."[210]

In the pages of *Green Hills of Africa*, he also cast down the gauntlet for any fashionably progressive New York critics whom he did not consider to be writers, but "angleworms in a bottle . . . afraid to be alone in their beliefs . . . lice who crawl on literature."[211] Nine months later, he boiled down the formula in a letter to a friend: "A true work of art endures forever; no matter what its politics."[212] As detractors seemed to spawn and sales on his last two books fell short of his expectations, deeper disillusionment channeled itself into a war against all naysayers, a delight in combat engagements with New York critics, expanding in disproportion until they became a trademark. Though the differences were real enough, Ernest appeared both to become very upset about them and to egg them on.

A deleted passage in his recently completed manuscript of *Green Hills of Africa* exposed the root of his anger: a father who was a "coward" because he had abandoned him "without necessity" by shooting himself.[213] Failing and killing oneself were nonsense. He need not have any part of it, nor wallow, nor lie to himself, like Scott Fitzgerald, "a coward of great charm."[214] In contrast, Dos Passos was "brave as a buffalo" and a true friend. To show his courage, Ernest would get his work done and live life on the grandest terms imaginable.[215] Yet even after these declarations of freedom and integrity, the presence of his critics loomed and pressure to respond to their politics intensified.[216]

CHAPTER 4

An Island like a Ship (1934–1936)

• • • • •

As Cuba seethed with unrest, Key West underwent a transformation as well. Ernest's home was no longer at the edge of the American frontier, for the ruggedness and the seclusion that had drawn the Hemingways there were disappearing while the island tried to become something else.

As Hemingway walked from the port, past the lighthouse, to his Whitehead Street residence, he could see the work parties, rows of men in ragged clothes, bending at the waist to clear the weeds beneath the decrepit shacks, which the city had seized for its restoration initiatives. He saw them in clusters clearing rubbish from the beaches.[1] While he wrote in the early mornings, he could hear their hammers tapping along the house frames of their worksites several blocks away. In Josie's bar, he drank with them and with the veterans who were building bridges for the WPA and who kept their camp on Matecumbe Key.

As he read his newspaper, he could overhear two of them bickering at the other end of the bar. He watched Josie reach for the sawed-off billiard cue he kept behind the cash register and waited to see where it would lead.[2] When one of the men asked Ernest if he was that writer, Ernest looked up expressionless until his face flickered. He glanced at Josie, then responded, "Hemingway . . . ? Sorry, never heard of him," then he stood up, said, "See you later, Josie," and exited the bar—slamming the door behind him with a bang.

As Key West struggled to pull itself out of poverty during the Great Depression, engineers of the New Deal in Washington, DC, hoped that the town could reinvent itself by attracting tourism. Intent on achieving their aims, leaders of the Key West Administration (KWA) shamelessly exploited the writer's celebrity in their attempt to put the city back on the map.[3] *Key West in Transition: A Guidebook for Visitors* ranked Hemingway's home as a tourist attraction and identified its location on maps for tourists.[4] Soon, crowds gathered outside his residence, with sightseers peering in and young boys dancing for dollars to work the tourists over.[5] Enraged, Hemingway fired off a letter to Arnold Gingrich, asking the editor to protest, partly in jest and for his readers' entertainment in *Esquire*. At home, he ordered chauffeur and handyman Toby Bruce to build a six-foot wall around his property.[6]

• • • • •

At that time, Cuba was splashing across the pages of American newspapers, first in January, when a Commission on Cuban Affairs (composed of ten experts from diverse fields, such as economics, politics, education, and agriculture) released their report concluding that future political stabilization and economic prosperity on the island demanded agrarian reform, diversification of agriculture, and a "hands-off" policy by her northern neighbor, including withdrawal from the Guantánamo base.[7] While Roosevelt proposed a "New Deal for Cuba" that would turn the island into the garden spot of the Western Hemisphere, islanders feared such initiatives would result in more of the United States' "finger in their pie."[8]

Fearing for his life after receiving threats, Carlos Hevia, the former interim president of Cuba, fled his homeland in March when civil war broke out anew on the island, as the ABC, Communist Party, Authentic Party, and Joven Cuba group, led by former vice president Guiteras, joined forces in an attempt to topple Batista. They failed. Arriving in Florida via airplane, Hevia, a graduate of the US Naval Academy, reported that the island was in chaos: "Wildest confusion prevails over the island . . . about 200 persons have been massacred since Saturday morning . . . They are finding bodies everywhere and before I left Havana this afternoon I was told of the slaying of six or seven persons that I knew. Men are being taken from their homes presumably destined for prison, and their bodies found later. There is no government in Cuba."[9] A general strike had halted business, interrupted postal and rail service, then erupted into armed conflict. To strengthen his position and squash civil unrest, Batista declared labor unions illegal and summoned military courts to administer the death penalty to "offenders and disturbers."[10]

Meanwhile the kidnapping of a Cuban "capitalist," heir to a sizeable fortune, resulted in the payment of $300,000 in ransom, a manhunt, and the arrest of twenty members of a group calling themselves the "Young Cubans." When police raided Havana's Hotel Park View, suspicions were that Alvin Karpis, an American gangster, had been a coconspirator in the crime.[11] In May, Colonel Batista's forces killed former vice president Guiteras, a patriot and respected leader in the Authentic Party. Inspired by José Martí's exile and triumphant return to his homeland, Guiteras was waiting for a boat in Matanzas Province when he was gunned down by military police.[12]

Ever an art enthusiast, advocate for friends, and entrepreneur, Ernest funded and organized a New York exhibition for Antonio Gattorno's paintings at the Georgette Passedoit Gallery at 22 East Sixtieth Street from January 6 to 25, 1935, and he recruited Dos Passos to collaborate on the show's promotional pamphlet.[13] Once told by Arnold Gingrich to speculate on rare editions of his own books, the author now advised all his business partners to purchase paintings from Gattorno, whom he pitched as a leader of Cuba's vanguard: "Gattorno is a Cuban painter who is also a painter for the world."[14]

When Gattorno seemed to suspect Ernest of profiting at his expense, Ernest protested that his costs greatly exceeded his profits. Salvaging the friendship if not the business partnership, Hemingway advised Gattorno to emigrate to New York where his work could be best represented and he could make a living with dignity.

Helping other artists had never been an easy business; Ernest had tried several times, occasionally receiving compensation for his efforts. Ernest had smuggled Joyce's *Ulysses* into the United States while the book was banned.[15] In the United States, he had encouraged

Prudencio de Pereda, Ned Calmer, and Luis Quintanilla, whose work he invested in and promoted at the Pierre Matisse Gallery in New York. The day after his exhibition opening, Quintanilla was arrested by the Spanish government on charges of conspiracy and held in the Presidio Modelo (the "model prison") in Cuba, so Ernest signed the petition campaigning for his release.[16]

With many causes to take up, some more exasperating than others, he soon received a letter from Arnold Samuelson conveying the good news that one of the young writer's fishing pieces had been accepted for publication in *Outdoor Life*, with Arnold nevertheless admitting that "when you don't look over it, the stuff doesn't seem to go so hot."[17] Bothered by his conscience, Arnold also confessed to Hemingway that he had impregnated an underage Conch girl aboard the *Pilar*, which was the real reason he left town when he did, for, out of loyalty, he had to spare his mentor a scandal.[18] Replying with a few encouraging words and on two occasions with a few bucks, Ernest advised Arnold to keep trying, or accept another career.[19] Arnold moved out to North Dakota and lived in a shack pursuing a monastic life similar to the one lived in upper Michigan by his mentor. Now and again, he did some construction for his brother, or on his own to keep himself fed. Travelling to Mexico on a shoestring budget, he sought experiences that he could write about.

In an *Esquire* "High Seas Letter" called "Monologue to the Maestro," Ernest satirized the failure of the kid he had invited to apprentice as a writer and deckhand in Cuba. Though it was all in good fun, in it he voiced his frustration with mentoring a pupil who seemed doomed to fail. As he told the story, he was "flattered and appalled" when the young man from Minnesota turned up on his doorstep and told him he always wanted to become a writer and go out to sea. Taking pity on him, Hemingway wrote that he tried to give him both: he offered him a job and took him to Cuba, attempting to fulfill the wishes of the young man he nicknamed "the Maestro" for the violin he carried in a beat-up case and played badly aboard—or "Mice," for short. To help another man with so much resolve to become a writer yet so little aptitude was frustrating indeed.[20] Overwhelmed by his time with Hemingway, Arnold was never happy with what he had written.[21] Over his life, Arnold's inner frustrations seemed to express themselves in the domestic abuse and the estrangement of his children as he withdrew, became the county crank, and was ostracized in the town where his family abandoned him and left him to die alone.[22]

• • • • •

Wiring his Cuban skipper, Hemingway told Carlos Gutierrez he would sail south for Havana to fish the marlin that were running as soon as he could fix the *Pilar*'s failing engine, but the weather and ongoing mechanical trouble aboard halted his plans. Rushing out to fasten down his new boat, Hemingway and his family braced for the storm they would later call the "Labor Day Hurricane" of 1935. In a letter to Max Perkins, Hemingway graphically described the hurricane as it tore through the Keys and how he found bloated bodies of veterans that he had personally known floating in the stagnant water afterward.[23]

After the Bonus Army had irritated a conservative government by marching across the nation and camping on the White House lawn to receive their promised "bonus," they had been assigned public works projects, including the revitalization taking place at Matecumbe Key. Leaving the vets endangered in a temporary work camp and failing to come to their aid when the Labor Day Hurricane approached was a negligence that enraged the author when he helped with the eventual clean-up and retrieved their swollen corpses from the surf.

In response, Hemingway launched an article in *New Masses* magazine titled, "Who Remembered the Vets?"[24] In it, he addressed politicians and candidly and graphically presented the reality of the scenes he had witnessed. He insisted that these deaths were preventable and suggested that the public officials did not evacuate the veterans because a hurricane was an expedient and convenient way to dispose of the annoyances of the Bonus Army.[25] Vividly he described the bodies of men abandoned by the feds, drowned, bloated, and blistering in the sun.[26] The bodies of the veterans belonged to men he had known—

they had served in World War I, as he had, and they had drunk at Josie's bar. Remembering and burying them was the least that he could do to honor what he considered to be his band of brothers.

Was he now writing for the journal that he had once called "the most puerile and shitty house organ I've ever seen"?[27] The position he took in *New Masses* was one of the most politically charged he had taken to date, and the "literary revolution boys" seemed to approve of his transformation. Hicks said Hemingway's newfound identification for the working class had a quality "that had been disastrously absent from his previous work," suggesting that "Hemingway was going somewhere."[28] During the same week, Roosevelt aroused the public's admiration with the dedication of the Hoover Dam. Whoever had neglected to protect the veterans of Matecumbe Key at the beginning of the month could be disregarded in the name of progress.

The president had larger geopolitical problems as well. In 1935 the Third Reich's ascension to power, Germany's rearmament and intervention in Spain, Mussolini's invasion of East Africa, and the victory of Nationalist armies in Jiangxi, China, mesmerized America. To the vindication of roaring crowds, Hitler reviled the Treaty of Versailles, assembled his forces, and promised glory *für das Vaterland*. Intellectuals and artists, horrified by these developments, felt it was their duty to do something, and among them there was mounting pressure to take a side and take a stand. As *New Masses* editor Mike Gold proclaimed, "Every poem, every novel and drama, must have a social theme or it is merely confectionary."[29]

At first Ernest Hemingway disagreed: the thing to do was to stay the hell out of it. In "Notes on the Next War: A Serious Topical Letter," written for *Esquire* in September 1935, he defined his position unmistakably against the United States' involvement in the war in Europe: It was a "hell of a broth . . . brewing . . . we have no need to drink . . . We were fools to be sucked in once on a European war and we should never be sucked in again."[30] While lying wounded in the mud on the Italian front during World War I, he had promised himself that he would do everything he could to prevent another war, young men's lives thrown away, because of the fashions and deceits of politics.[31]

In October, Mussolini's troops invaded Ethiopia while the world gasped, too far removed to prevent these acts of conquest. *Esquire* ran Hemingway's article "The Malady of Power: A Serious Second Letter." Recalling his days in Europe as a reporter covering a flawed peace process after World War I, he told readers about his fellow reporter's theory: any politician or patriot, once given the supreme office of the state, deteriorated under the malady of power. "War is coming in Europe as sure as winter follows fall," but President Roosevelt must not succumb to his ambition and serve his countrymen by keeping them out of Europe's never-ending wars.[32] To his credit as a reporter at the *Toronto Star*, Ernest had criticized the Treaty of Versailles and had foreseen the forthcoming consequences of "an unjust, conqueror's peace" in 1922.[33] On the other hand, could he not see the degree that his own ego and ambition were maladies of power affecting his art?

When *Green Hills of Africa* appeared at the end of October, sales were disappointing, and criticism was largely negative. Though the author was sure he had written a good book, several critics condemned it, and his *Esquire* "letters," as a waste of talent. Abner Green called the leisure pieces "potboilers" and asked him directly to give up features about hunting, fishing, or bullfighting. Mike Gold said he was "too bourgeois" and should consider the common man. His friend Edmund Wilson asked him to stop imposing this overblown image of himself and instead write the honest prose he claimed to love about "important themes."[34] Writing for the *New Republic*, T. S. Matthews lamented, "It used to be pretty exciting, sitting down to read a new book by Hemingway, but now it's damn near alarming . . . he thinks he can write about anything and get away with it. He probably can, too. But it isn't the hot stuff he says he knows it is."[35] In a letter to his editor, Ernest complained and blamed Scribner's marketing and pricing of the book, as well as his own bad judgment in arrogantly rubbing certain key critics the wrong way.[36]

• • • • •

Facing continuing civil unrest, bombings, and insurgent intimidation, President Mendieta resigned in December. Colonel Batista remained as head of the military—sparking further controversy and unrest when Cuba appointed José Agripino Barnet (from the National Union party) as its seventh provisional president since Machado's deposition.[37] Without a plan or support from student and paramilitary groups, Barnet was also destined to fail. In a private letter expressing his hope for a type of election that would allow them to continue to work with Batista behind the scenes, Caffery wrote Welles, "The hardest nut to crack is, of course, this matter of elections because it is required and still requires my constant daily hammering."[38]

Contending with Fitzgerald's submission of the first part of *The Crack-Up* in *Esquire*, the second installment of Ernest's novel *To Have and Have Not* appeared in January 1936. Its title, "White Man, Black Man, Alphabet Man," was later changed to "The Tradesman's Return."[39] Unlike Perkins who censored him often, Gingrich would never take issue with an off-color remark, or with racy or risky insinuations about tense alliances between white and black working classes (Conch Captain Morgan and his black shipmate Wesley), enmity against the affluent, or criticism of governmental agencies like FERA and the WPA.

To settle accounts with his friend Antonio Gattorno, Ernest persuaded Gingrich to publish several full color reproductions of his work in May in *Esquire* in a two-page spread along with excerpts from a monograph Ernest had written and published in Havana that year. Gifting him his own fans in North America, Ernest publicly endorsed the Cuban painter: "At thirty-one, he is the youngest person that I know although there is no youth in his painting. There is simply good painting."[40] The Fifteenth International Exhibition at the Art Institute of Chicago soon after selected Gattorno's watercolors for exhibition, resulting in his receiving the Watson F. Blair Purchase Prize. "There now, my boy, did not Daddy do you right?" Hemingway told Gattorno. "Although there was only six years' difference in our age he always called me 'my boy,'" said Gattorno years later, after taking Hemingway's advice and moving to New York. "He was just like a brother to me."[41]

• • • • •

In spite of *A Farewell to Arms*' cinema presence and the writer's unrivaled fame, feelings of failure, anxiety, and depression overtook Ernest as 1936 began. Wherever they travelled throughout the 1930s, inequities were obvious. The sobriety and courage of men, mariners, soldiers, and hunters contrasted with the superiority and effeminacy of privileged imposters, fakers, and would-be artists, never seeming to work in Ernest's midst, filled him with loathing and defined the characteristics of the villains in stories that he was producing in a torrent at that time. As relationships shifted and his deep need for financial independence remained, a cocktail of irritation and intention combusted in the exquisite craft in several stories containing damning descriptions of his family and friends, which he would publish later that year.

Much like in his father, anxiety originating in financial worries grew into recurrent depression as he entered middle age.[42] These matters occupied his mind even while the extraordinary wealth of the Pfeiffer family amply assured their needs. From Pauline's family had come the house, the pool, many cash advances, and most of the trust fund for his mother after his father's suicide.[43] The modest successes of *Death in the Afternoon* and *Green Hills of Africa* had checked his vainglorious ambitions, fueled resentment about his dependence on the Pfeiffers, and put the squeeze on his freedom and pride. Pauline, sensing this displeasure, tried to ease her husband's mind: for the Pfeiffers, money was really nothing to worry about, she reassured. But these assurances backfired on a husband determined to fend for himself and led to a growing animosity with respect to subsequent gifts, such that he increasingly asserted his independence aboard the *Pilar* and during weeks out on the water with Jane Mason.[44]

Continuing to chase Tiamat and Leviathan in Bimini in June and July, he caught a 785-pound mako, nearly a world record, and a 540-pound marlin, his largest ever. To distract him from his worries, Ernest had invited F. Scott Fitzgerald to join him on the island. Whenever fishing lulled, he laced up his boxing gloves and taunted any takers, while literary rival Scott stood by and watched: "Any [Bahamian] Negro who could stay in the ring with him for three-minute rounds" could win a $250 prize.[45]

A letter that Ernest wrote Scott just after the trip reveals the intensity of their friendship and Ernest's competitiveness. In a response to Scott's complaints about his poor health, about Zelda's mental illness, and about his impotence on the page, Ernest expressed sympathy, made suggestions, attempted jokes, and tried to distract him by inviting Scott on another exciting trip, this time to Cuba, where a big-ticket boxing match between Joe Louis and Isidoro Gastanaga was scheduled to take place.[46] Himself a writer prone to insomnia, Ernest suggested Scott just lie in bed even when unable to sleep, so he would still get some rest: "If you can lie still and take it easy and just consider your life and everything else as an outsider and *not give a damn*—it is a hell of a help."[47] Getting some exercise or fresh air might help as well, though Ernest admitted he sometimes lay awake thinking on the boat and looking up in silence at the stars. Perhaps Scott's obsession with youth prevented him from coming of age, Ernest speculated, then cut through his airs of superiority: "You have taken so damned much punishment I have no business trying to tell you anything . . . Would love to see you though."[48] Unable to hold the event in a warzone, promoters feared losing their investment, so Ernest guessed that the fight would be canceled, but he invited Scott anyway to come to Cuba, fish, learn about revolutions (as every writer should), and spend some quality time.[49]

As 1936 began, both writers continued to suffer from writer's block, insomnia, and morose moods that left them on edge. Ernest gained weight, snapped at family and friends, and became difficult to abide.[50] When at a cocktail party, a few months away from his thirty-seventh birthday, Ernest overheard Wallace Stevens speak ill of him to sister Ursula, he stormed out, struck the drunken poet several times in the head, and said he felt much better after giving him "a good beating."[51] To his mother-in-law, he confided that it was his first experience with true sorrow: "Had never had the real old melancholia and [I] am glad to have had it so I know what people go through. It makes me more tolerant of what happened to my father."[52]

While critics belittled him and finances worsened, Ernest told friends, such as Sara Murphy, that he was "going to blow his lousy head off."[53] Whether this despair was family inheritance or writer's curse, it became chronic and conspicuous. In Sara's words, "There were days when he was absolutely a malevolent bastard, full of self-loathing. But the awfulness would leave him after a couple of hours. Generally, before he lost that black mood someone caught hell for it."[54] These periods produced some of his best work, but friends and family often paid a price as he lashed out during the pain of the writing process and in unflattering portrayals of his intimates.

In March, the beautiful and wealthy Masons motored into the Key West yacht basin aboard their cruiser, *Pelican II*, to mingle with the artist, beleaguered at work, and his "Poor Old Momma," who after eight years of marriage had just turned forty years old.

Seemingly recovered from her dive from her bedroom window in 1933, Jane was nevertheless still married to "old stone-face," who sat irritably beside her as they conversed with the Hemingways. Jane had recently become enamored with Richard Cooper, a "white hunter," and had visited his farm at Lake Manyara in Tanzania the year before without Grant, writing the Hemingways to declare that it was "one of the world's most lovely places."[55] The beautiful and damned *matrimonio* of Mr. and Mrs. Mason was swirling in the pot of Hemingway's black temperament, such that it soon engendered acidic portrayals in print.[56]

• • • • •

As Pauline left Key West in April to see her sister in Piggott, her husband, weary of putting fiction on hold for features, sent Gingrich another story instead: "The Horns of the Bull," later published by Scribner's as "The Capital of the World."[57] Published in *Esquire* in June, it told the tale of a waiter, Paco, who fantasizes about becoming a matador but is accidentally killed by coworker Enrique, who pretends with two knives strapped to a chair to be a passing bull.[58] In April, Ernest wrote Perkins with elated news—from the depths of his dolor, he had drudged up five marvels: "Here's the story situation: I have five now." These would later be titled "One Trip Across," "The Tradesman's Return," "The Capital of the World," "The Short Happy Life of Francis Macomber," and "The Snows of Kilimanjaro."[59] Emerging from hell, Ernest also mailed Gingrich "On the Blue Water: A Gulf Stream Letter," an important article for its captivation with the sea and with the Cojímar fishermen whom he would investigate closely for years to come.

"On the Blue Water" holds the "nonfiction seed" of the masterpiece Ernest would pursue during the next fifteen years and later call his "Land, Sea, and Air Trilogy." Growing it first to over one thousand pages, he eventually distilled it into a novella one-tenth that size. At its heart, it was a prosaic poem, an epic about an old man fishing alone at sea, who hooked a great marlin and, after two days' struggle, lost it to sharks.

The core of the stories that Carlos and other fisherman shared with Ernest had happened to an actual fisherman, Anselmo, who was part of the coastal community of Cojímar.[60] Subsequently, Ernest took an active interest in the lives of the fishermen of Cojímar. Reflecting during an interview on his writing process for *The Old Man and the Sea*, Ernest explained that he had at first tried but failed to write the story, so he waited, gathering knowledge as a fisherman, studying the village of Cojímar, and attempting to understand every person in that community before he could begin writing it thirteen years later.[61]

In interviews, many Cojímar fishermen recall drinking with the writer at La Terraza beside the docks and his numerous questions about fishing conditions, the weather, and their experiences in smaller boats.[62] Osvaldo Cernero Piña, "Ova," was a native who had met Hemingway one day in the late 1940s while rowing back to Cojímar after a long day's fishing. From the *Pilar*, Ernest offered him a tow back to his village, and when they got there, the author treated him to a whiskey at the bar. All confirm it was Anselmo, the eldest among them, who had lost his marlin to the sharks, though Ernest's son Patrick pointed out after his father's death that he had so many experiences to draw from: marlin and tuna eaten by sharks, such as the one that, even half-eaten, weighed 468 pounds. Drawing upon the complex brew of reading, relationships, experiences, and conversations overheard, Hemingway showed a unique talent for selection, condensation, and narration.

"The Short Happy Life of Francis Macomber" and "The Snows of Kilimanjaro" were arguably two of the best examples of this technique and the most disparaging to the people he loved. While hunting lions in Africa with a guide and his wife Margot, Francis Macomber acts in cowardly fashion, shirks his duty, and "bolted like a rabbit . . . running wildly," rather than face his lion or conquer the fear within, causing his wife to slip out of their tent in the middle of the night and betray him with their white hunter, Wilson.[63] The three main characters of "Francis Macomber" are almost indistinguishable from Jane Mason, her frequently cuckolded husband, Grant, and the African guide whom both the Hemingways and Masons had used, Philip Percival.[64] One telling description fit the real-life Masons perfectly: "They had a sound basis of union. Margot was too beautiful for Macomber to divorce her and Macomber had too much money for Margot ever to leave him."[65] Like Macomber, Ernest seemed also "on the verge" of a break-up with an aging bride, longing for autonomy but not yet possessing the means to free himself.

Unbreakable dependence in a yellowing marriage reappears as a dominant theme in "The Snows of Kilimanjaro." In that story, Harry is on safari in Africa with his wealthy wife, Helen. Near the summit of Mount Kilimanjaro a leopard's frozen carcass was found, and no one could explain what the animal was seeking at that altitude as it climbed toward the "House of God" ("Kilimanjaro," translated from "Ngàje Naài," the Masai name for the mountain).[66] The metaphor of the summit-seeking leopard symbolizes humankind's aspirations, specifically those belonging to this writer-protagonist Harry, who seeks divinity through his art. Unfortunately, Harry realizes that he will never reach the top because he is held back by his dependence on his wife's wealth.

While trying to photograph a waterbuck, Harry scratches his knee and neglects to apply iodine.[67] The wound becomes infected. Harry slips in and out of hallucinations while reflecting on his fate and mistakes. Due to the remoteness of their camp, they are stuck waiting for transport that will never come, fearing the hyenas and vultures congregating outside the tent, and watching as Harry's infection festers, becoming stinking gangrene. In a stupor, Harry's consciousness free-associates the memories of his expiring life, regretting "all stories he would never write," and blames the "rich bitch," a "kindly caretaker and a destroyer of his talent," ending his ambition with the comforts of "her bloody money," which deadened his sensibilities and destroyed his art.

In addition to his wife, Harry also attacks his friend Scott for worshipping the rich: "The very rich are different from you and me," he wrote, and somebody responded, "Yes, they have more money."[68] To Scott they were a "special glamorous race," but Harry saw clearly how they "wrecked" other people's lives and remained protected always.[69] According to Harry, he was different from Scott in that he could remain detached and thus beat the rich as he beat everyone and everything. Though both writers showed a certain degree of fascination with the rich, Ernest characterized them more often as callous and emasculated, and thus suggested his understanding and solidarity with working people.[70]

When Scott Fitzgerald read the overt attacks in "Kilimanjaro" that summer, he wrote his friend Ernest and asked him to "lay off [of him] in print." He requested that he remove his name from the story when it went to book form, then complimented and corrected: "It's a fine story—one of your best—even though the 'Poor Scott Fitzgerald etc.' rather spoiled it for me. Ever your friend Scott. Riches have never fascinated me, unless combined with the greatest charm or distinction."[71]

The desire to distance himself from the Prince of the Jazz Age was understandable, for he had been associated with Scott and labeled as a spokesperson for the Lost Generation since his Paris days.[72] In later printings, Ernest agreed to change Scott's name to Julian, but he left the rest unchanged. In "Kilimanjaro," Harry confesses his sensation of captivity, feeling like some sort of exotic pet for the rich. As warden of the Pfeiffer family, Hemingway travelled from *la rive gauche* to *la rive droite*, toured first-class through the Côte d'Azur, the Alps, Key West, Spain, and Africa throughout the 1930s, in the company of the Fitzgeralds, Murphys, von Blixens, Straters, and Masons, complicating his alignment with the struggles of the common man. Like his protagonists, Ernest became a man who had betrayed his own principles, seeking extradition, yet trapped and unable to find an escape. "The Snows of Kilimanjaro" and "The Short Happy Life of Francis Macomber" would appear in August and September in *Cosmopolitan* and *Esquire*.

• • • • •

Departing for Havana in the middle of April, Ernest stood at the helm of his fishing boat with Mrs. Mason and Joe Russell beside him as first mates, while Pauline departed in the other direction with Gregory to spend more time with family in Piggott.[73] Pauline, a Catholic who did not believe in birth control, had nearly died while delivering Gregory, and the Hemingways' sex life had suffered subsequently.[74] Careful planning of conjugal encounters was a constraint that Ernest could only tolerate as long as other women offered relief. For a time, the absences and betrayals might have helped to sustain a marriage that was itself founded on an infidelity, and soon the *Havana Post* was announcing the arrival of the famous author and the ever-enchanting Mrs. Jane Mason.[75] In a letter that month to John Dos Passos, Ernest remarked, "Mrs. Mason is almost as apt at going places without her husband as Mr. Josie is without his wife."[76] Since his last visit, American tourists had proliferated in Havana along with more bars, casinos, clubs, horseraces, jai alai matches, soldiers, and brothels. Batista used military power to lock up dissidents, deter bombings, disband opposition, all of which reassured investors and set travellers' minds at ease.[77]

When marlins were scarce and resisted capture, Ernest's reproaches of himself missed their mark and found Carlos Gutierrez, who seemed to him to be "¾ blind and quite deaf" and thereby causing him to lose too many fish.[78] Loyal and hardworking, Carlos was dedicated to his captain, but he had endured one verbal laceration too many from this *patrón* who had accused him and stripped him of his pride by humiliating him in front of guests and his crew. His former employer Jane Mason arbitrated the disagreement, scolding Ernest lightly so that Carlos could save face, then comforted the distressed Cuban captain in private. When they returned to Havana, she offered Carlos his old job, and he took it, leaving his uniform washed and neatly folded on a bench of the *Pilar* the following day.

Pauline joined Ernest for ten days in Havana, before returning via seaplane to Key West. Intending to follow on the *Pilar* that same day, Ernest waited for storms to pass for five days. Wagering that they had cleared, he chanced a crossing and found himself in rough seas and rapidly in grave danger. It was perhaps the most frightening night of his life, alone, fighting gale-force winds, flying over mountainous waves, veering off course to keep the enormous waves from fatally colliding with his boat, and struggling to stay afloat. After cracking the *Pilar's* primary engine block on a nerve-wracking fourteen-hour journey, he spotted Sand Key in front of him and contacted the port authority by radio with his voice caught somewhere between his "ankles and [his] balls." At that moment, said Hemingway, his "balls felt very small," but unlike the protagonist of the story he had just written, "The Snows of Kilimanjaro," he was not destined to die at an early age.[79]

As Ernest departed Cuba, the island democratically elected former mayor of Havana and National Labor Party leader Miguel Mariano Gómez to the office of president during the first election in which women were permitted to vote.[80] Weary of blood, Cubans were hoping the civil government would bring reforms and an end to violence, but there was also widespread fear that a civil government would revert to a police state.[81] Calling for the release of prisoners and the reopening of the University of Havana, groups from the left boycotted the election; however, Batista and his sergeants reassumed their posts at Camp Colombia, now known as "Military City," and renounced power, publicly recognizing President Gómez's quasi-constitutional government.[82] Nonetheless, many perceived powerlessness in Gómez's presidency and expressed concerns about the emergence of a military dictatorship, which would operate behind the scenes. At the center of it, said Russell Porter of the *New York Times*, was Colonel Batista, "the great enigma." If the hopes of the Cuban people went with President Gómez, their fears came from Colonel Batista. Though Batista was an authoritarian, he was also a skillful politician who read his adversaries, maneuvered to survive, and kept the peace in a chaotic democracy struggling to exist.

• • • • •

As soon as he returned to Cuba, Ernest sought out Carlos Gutierrez at Mr. and Mrs. Mason's residence. The sun was rising over the docks of Jaimanitas as the Masons were sleeping in silken sheets, and while Carlos was swabbing the deck of the *Pelican II*. Nearly finished cleaning the boat, Carlos heard someone call his name in a slow and unmistakable baritone. In a practiced motion, Carlos rung the dirty water from his towel into the bucket, flipped his mop, and set it against the dock as he stepped off and extended his gaunt hand to greet his former captain.

Getting to the point, Ernest apologized, telling Carlos he had behaved terribly, he was sorry, and he could really use him aboard. There was no excuse for his behavior, but he said Carlos should understand that he valued his work and that he respected him. If he did not forgive him, he would understand, but Ernest wanted him to know that he was going to take the *Pilar* to Bimini that summer and that he would be very happy if he and Bollo the cook agreed to accompany him. Though the incident nearly destroyed their friendship, so great was Ernest's influence that Carlos nodded his head in agreement. There were knots in their throats, the two men could not speak, but they could break a slight smile. Later, Carlos explained to Mrs. Mason the reason he would forgive the lout: "Don Ernesto understands me as does no one else."[83] During that trip, while friends and family bedded down in the luxurious mansion of Ernest's millionaire-sportsman companion Michael Lerner, in Cat Cay, Ernest and Carlos bunked on the *Pilar*.

Intrigued by Ernest's invitation, Arnold Gingrich came down to visit the party in Alice Town, North Bimini, at the end of June, and one evening in the bar of the Compleat Angler Hotel, Pauline introduced Gingrich to Jane Mason. Although their friendship began there, Jane and Arnold would not marry "until two wives and two husbands later," in November 1955.[84] When Ernest later found out about their sneaking relationship, he blew a fuse, shouting, "That shit! I can't get over it," and he later wrote that he no longer contributed to *Esquire* because of a disagreement with his editor about a blonde.[85]

After two weeks of fishing in Bimini, Ernest was sailing home with his son Jack aboard the *Pilar* when the clashes of the Spanish

Civil War began. Departing from exile in the Canary Islands, Spanish Nationalists orchestrated uprisings in Morocco and Andalusia as General Franco established an outpost on the island of Las Palmas and declared martial law. The fascist coup d'état caused a bloodstained three-year war between the Nationalist right and the Loyalist left. From its outset in July, the war was filled with atrocities from random acts of violence, systematic executions, and *limpieza*, or the cleansing of the nation from the contagious elements of the other side. Between July 1936 and December 1951, some two hundred thousand people were executed by the "white terror" of fascist barbarity and approximately thirty-eight thousand by the "red terror" of the radical left. Imprisonment and murder would often include women, children, and renowned artists like Federico García Lorca. International forces mobilized to stop these assassinations and set captives free.

In August, Dos Passos published *The Big Money*, and Berlin hosted the Olympic Games, where African American athlete Jesse Owens annoyed members of the Aryan "master race" by winning several track and field medals. While the Hemingways were visiting family in Piggott and hunting in Wyoming at the Nordquist ranch in September, dynamiters in Havana set off a bomb in the *El País* newspaper offices, killing four and causing a million dollars in damage. The police foiled a similar attempt at *Diario de la Marina*.[86] Journalists questioned whether the newspaper was sympathetic to the rebels in Spain while Batista's police arrested thirty suspects from a group calling itself the Spanish Socialist Circle.

After working mornings in the corner room overlooking Havana harbor, or the Key West house built like a ship, or the barn behind the Pfeiffer house, or in the backcountry at the ranch, Hemingway amassed a manuscript of 352 pages by October. Based on material from his stories "One Trip Across" and "The Tradesman's Return," it was a story about haves and have-nots, and revolutions "gone badly." In September 1936, Hemingway wrote Max Perkins: "When I finish this book hope to go to Spain if all not over there. Will leave the completed Ms. in a vault so you will be covered on it. I can go over it again when I come back. In case anything should happen to me you would always be covered financially even without this novel by the book of stories."[87]

In October in Europe, Italy and Germany signed the pact known as the Rome-Berlin Axis, and when Franco declared himself head of Spain, the Axis recognized their fellow fascist as the official government of the Iberian Peninsula.

Roosevelt was chosen for a second term during the first week in November while Franco's forces were conducting a lethal siege against the Loyalists in a battle for Madrid that would continue for three years. While the Japanese and Germans spread further angst and fear by signing the Anti-Comintern Pact that solidified the alliances of the Axis powers, the Loyalists' (also called the Republican) government soon had to fall back to Valencia as its base of operations. The strength of the Fifth Regiment, combined with the morale and influx of forty thousand foreign volunteers from the International Brigades, sustained the republic. Cuban volunteers composed approximately one thousand of these troops. American volunteers formed the infamous Lincoln Brigade that would become instrumental to winning the war.

With his Key West handyman Toby Bruce at the wheel, the author stopped in New Orleans with his son Patrick and stayed at the Hotel Monteleone on his way back to Key West from the Nordquist ranch, with a pit stop in Piggott.[88] On November 15, 1936, the New Orleans *Times-Picayune* announced, "Rebels Reported Entering Besieged Capital of Spain: Fascists Declared at the Edge of Madrid After Bombardment from Air Costing 53 Lives" and juxtaposed it with the prodding headline, "Hemingway Stops in City on Way to Key West, Florida: Famous Author Denies Charge He Has Become Soft." Earlier that month, Ernest had received a letter from John Wheeler that invited him to cover the Spanish Civil War for the North American Newspaper Alliance (NANA), and to Pauline's dismay, her husband proudly accepted the position, causing her to fear subsequently for his safety. To assure his wife, Ernest told her he would be in Spain with the Jewish bullfighter she knew, Sidney Franklin, but it was not a great relief.

• • • • •

On Christmas eve, Colonel Batista had President Gómez impeached. When Batista had introduced a bill that called for a nine-cent tax on every bag of sugar to create rural schools under army control, Gómez opposed the bill, so Batista maneuvered by threatening to dissolve the civil government and reinstate military control. To avoid dissolution, the House voted 111 to 45 and the Senate voted 22 to 12 for Gómez's impeachment.[89] Two days later, Cuba named the vice president, Federico Laredo Brú, as Gómez's successor. Brú would support Batista's initiatives and continue in power for nearly four years until Batista himself took over, becoming president, as well as dictator in name and deed.

CHAPTER 5

A Romantic Getaway for Two in Civil-War Spain (1936–1939)

• • • • •

One morning just after Christmas in Joe Russell's Key West bar, Sloppy Joe's, Ernest looked up from his newspaper to encounter two long and shapely legs extending from a bar stool, and then a flash of golden hair tossed back from the pretty head of Martha Gellhorn, a young reporter, purportedly on vacation with her mother and brother in Key West. There has been much speculation among biographers that Gellhorn purposefully engineered the meeting with her future husband.[1] As Pauline's friend from Key West Lorine Thompson later appreciated, "She said she came to see Ernest, she wanted him to read a book she had written, she wanted to know him . . . There was no question about it; you could see she was making a play for him . . . Pauline tried to ignore it. What she felt underneath nobody knew . . . Martha was a very charming girl and if I had known her under other circumstances I would have liked her very much."[2]

After attending private schools, much like Pauline, in native Saint Louis and Philadelphia (John Burroughs School and Bryn Mawr, respectively) the daughter of suffragist Edna Gellhorn had been shrewdly building her career in journalism.[3] While still in her midtwenties, Martha had published articles in the *New Republic*, become a foreign correspondent in France, joined the European pacifist movement, and published a book in 1934 about these experiences called *What Mad Pursuit*. Martha had also managed to cultivate a friendship and feminist alliance with First Lady Eleanor Roosevelt, her mother's friend from Bryn Mawr.[4]

When Martha returned to the United States, the First Lady helped her to obtain a post with Harry Hopkins in the Works Progress Administration as a field investigator for the Federal Emergency Relief Administration. From the disturbing scenes of the Great Depression that she had witnessed, Martha wrote *The Trouble I've Seen*, a title that took its name from the Negro spiritual. With the support of H. G. Wells, the sixty-nine-year-old British author of *The Time Machine* and *The War of the Worlds*, whom she had met at the White House in 1935, Martha published it with Putnam in 1936.[5] This collection of hard-boiled vignettes that she wrote at the age of twenty-eight depicting American poverty in terse and irrefutable prose inspired the *New York Herald Tribune* to compare her style with that of Ernest Hemingway.[6] In fact, she had read and emulated him—his imagination, his gift for dialogue and action, his tenacity and genius.[7]

In December of that year, she took a spur-of-the-moment vacation with her mother and brother to Key West. In the *To Have and Have Not* manuscript in progress when he met Martha Gellhorn, Ernest wrote afterward, "She sat on a high stool with her legs tucked under her and looked out at the street. Freddy looked at her admiringly. He thought she was the prettiest stranger in Key West that winter. Prettier even than the famous beautiful Mrs. Bradley."[8] When he first saw her with her brother, he thought he was her fiancé and resolved to get her alone and away from the "young punk" if given three days to do it.[9]

Martha, or "Marty," spoke about the civil war in beloved Spain and about the fight against fascism in Europe that she had witnessed firsthand as a reporter in France and Germany. Ernest asked patient questions in the presence of her mother and brother about her writing while she applied the brakes to enthrall and not overpower during that first encounter. It might have been one of the first occasions that Ernest Hemingway had been genuinely impressed with the professional accomplishments of a woman he wanted, an element seemingly heightening the thrill of desire as he moved in for the kill.

When her brother and mother left Key West, Martha stayed on at the Colonial Hotel on Duval Street. Stirred by chemistry, exhilarating conversations, and the promise of a relationship that would nourish her development, an affair brewed between the two charismatic and iron-willed writers. Despite all encumbrances, such as civil war and marriage, they found a way to rendezvous and grew ever more intimate in Miami, New York, and Madrid.

Just after her encounter with Ernest, Martha sent Eleanor Roosevelt a full report. The remote and dilapidated island of Key West was "the best thing [she had] found in America."[10] Her first impression of Hemingway reflects a similar perspective; he was falling to pieces, but marvelous in his naturalness, spontaneity, and improbable charms. Defying explanation, he was "an odd bird, very loveable and full of fire and a marvelous story teller."[11] Years later, after marital differences and resentments had taken their toll, Martha's recollection of their first encounter became much less flattering: reading his mail at the bar, he was a frowzy and smelly man, barefooted, and too casual in a wrinkled shirt and soiled Basque shorts held only by a rope belt. She had innocently wandered into the bar without knowing he would be there, and it was he who had approached her party and pursued the conversation.[12] Then he had beguiled her with stories about Cuba, hurricanes, and writing.[13] Though Martha said later that she had not intended to seek Ernest out, it is rather unlikely that this was true since she had read him extensively, admired his work, found inspiration in it, and hoped that the trip to Key West would help her with her writing.[14]

A year before Martha's arrival, Ernest's gentle ribbing of Arnold Samuelson, "Monologue to the Maestro," as it appeared in *Esquire*, specified, "If any more aspirant writers come on board the *Pilar* let them be females, let them be very beautiful, and let them bring champagne," so it is probable Martha read these lines and knew she had an open invitation and a mentor who might help her to break through.[15] It is possible that Martha did not first expect to become romantically involved with Hemingway, or admit to herself that this was among her desires.

What is clear to most observers of this unlikely and volatile couple is the contrast in their appearances. Though both were tall, at thirty-seven years old and two-hundred pounds, massive Hemingway was still as

Joyce described—"a big powerful peasant" as "strong as a buffalo"—but also now showing signs of wear: a receding hairline, a scar across his wrinkled brow, and his large frame burdened by excess weight. In her late twenties, Martha was a knockout. She was tall and thin and had beautiful skin and a "low, husky, eastern-seaboard-accented voice."[16] Youthful, attractive, and stylish, Martha had charm. She was the sort of woman that people noticed as she walked into the room. Beside Martha, Ernest could often appear paternal, talking and acting older than the twenty-eight-year-old with a "fiery, still almost teenage temperament." Skinner, a Sloppy Joe's black bartender, said Martha sitting beside Hemingway that day at the bar reminded him of "beauty and the beast."[17]

While Hadley, Pauline, and Martha were all from Saint Louis and believers in the Hemingway cult, these three women were distinct characters. Martha found Pauline "very grumpy" during their first meeting, much as Hadley had found Pauline to be in the car on the way to the Loire when Pauline was attempting to wrestle her husband away.[18] As Pauline had written Hadley effusive letters after visiting her and Ernest, Martha wrote Pauline a duplicitous thank-you after visiting the Hemingway home at Whitehead Street: "I had a very fine time with Ernestino . . . That man—Ernestino—is a lovely guy as you have no doubt guessed yourself, long before this . . . What I am trying to tell you in my halting way is that you are a fine girl and it was good of you not to mind my becoming a fixture, like a kudu head, in your home."[19]

In her next letter to the Roosevelts, Martha would write that the time in the Caribbean had been good for her, but it felt now that the world was going to hell as Hitler offered his support to Franco with two divisions, and another great war appeared inevitable.[20] Like Ernest, she would conclude that the thing to do was "to work all day and all night and live too, and swim and get the sun in one's hair and laugh and love as many people as one can find around and do all this terribly fast, because the time is getting shorter and shorter every day."[21] If Hemingway represented a pathway to greatness for this brilliant and determined young woman from Saint Louis, heartbreaks experienced together as combat correspondents and in the context of their troubled relationship became an unresolvable reality that shipwrecked their hopes and made their paradise island a living hell.

Nevertheless as Martha departed just after their first meeting in Key West and headed home to Saint Louis via Miami and Jacksonville, Ernest hastened via airplane to catch up with her, meeting her in Miami to dine on steaks with her, as friends, chaperoned by a champion heavyweight fighter (with an uncommonly large head) from New Zealand named Tom Heeney. In the station before Martha departed to Jacksonville and before he departed to New York, Ernest gave her a tender kiss on the forehead and said, "Goodbye, daughter." Knowing Martha's fondness for lost causes, Ernest had given her the manuscript of *To Have and Have Not* to take with her. It contained all the sordid details of a marriage that seemed to be on the ropes.

A correspondence between the two writers began. By mid-January, Ernest officially signed the contract with NANA to cover the Spanish Civil War at one thousand dollars per article and five hundred dollars per cable. Forming Contemporary Historians, Inc., he, Dos Passos, Archibald MacLeish, and Lillian Hellman would collaborate with Dutch director Joris Ivens to produce a film about the war called *The Spanish Earth*. Joining American Friends of Spanish Democracy, he would head a committee to fund the purchase of Loyalist ambulances. Though Martha had not been able to secure an official assignment to report on the war in Spain, she would continue seeking an assignment in Madrid.

While Mr. Hemingway and Martha Gellhorn would soon rendezvous in Spain, Pauline Hemingway passed the time with a young writer named Jack Latimer, who took her up on her offer to edit a manuscript for his mystery novel. Latimer later remembered Pauline as "not pretty, but very winning, very bright. Her face was not beautiful, but so intelligent and alert that she became attractive."[22] While touring Mexico with her friend Esther Chambers in March, Mrs. Hemingway wrote her lost husband to kvetch that she felt misplaced and lonesome, she missed being with him very much, and she missed their secret jokes and "the way we pass the time." Returning home, she wrote more of the same: "[I am] sick and tired of all these people in Key West and I wish you were here sleeping in my bed and using my bathroom and drinking my whiskey."[23] The uncertainty of her sexual relationship with Latimer perhaps gave rise to Pauline's unflattering characterization as an adulteress in *To Have and Have Not*, a "little Mick slut" who became tipsy and smitten with drunken John MacWalsey in her husband's absence.

To Have and Have Not picked up protagonist Harry Morgan's story—that of a fisherman from Key West, fallen on hard times—where "One Trip Across" and "The Tradesman's Return" left off. The characters were so identifiably based on real events and people Ernest knew that it would cause an argument with his editor that could be resolved only with a lawyer's intervention. It also shows an author in transition—trapped somewhere between his modernist detachment and his recognition of the inevitability of World War II and his espousal of the Loyalist cause. While Morgan appeared on the surface to respond to the critics clamoring for Hemingway to adopt a stronger position on the struggles of the oppressed, the novel was apolitical and somewhat nihilistic. While class struggle appeared to be a central theme, the whole corrupt society was ultimately too great for one man to take on and—as in *A Farewell to Arms*—this society kills him. Though the narrative portrays the class struggles, repression, lawlessness, revolution, and betrayals that Ernest had seen, he also abhorred "political systems at least as much as their practitioners," and as the story unfolded, he made his beliefs abundantly clear.[24]

The hero of the novel seemed to be just as adamant as its author about his independence: "Harry Morgan symbolizes the struggle of self-determination."[25] Politics were ephemeral, but he and his art were not. Later in life, Ernest insisted, "If anyone thinks that I am worried about anyone reading political implications in my stories, he is wrong . . . my only concern is that my stories are straight and good."[26]

By 1933, American investors owned 8 percent of Cuban sugar, and creditors held the reins of the sugar industry, tobacco, banks, railroads, streetcar lines, electric plants, telephone systems, and public utilities, but the viewpoint Ernest represented in *To Have and Have Not* was not the one for which fashionable critics clamored.[27] Hemingway never lost his "cynical distaste for all politicians"; after his speech at the Second American Writers Congress on June 4, 1937, he "re-emphasized his abiding lack of faith in governmental solutions to social problems, and reaffirmed his personal and artistic independence from all political parties and ideologies."[28]

To Have and Have Not expresses much irritation with the excesses of the rich and a significant degree of self-loathing from an artist who subsists in their shadows. It resembles "The Snows of Kilimanjaro," except here the writer-protagonist is named Richard Gordon. Richard betrays his rich wife, Helen Gordon, with the even richer and prettier Helène Bradley in a scene strongly resembling Ernest's affair with Jane. The slight variance in the spelling of their names suggests that the two women are nearly interchangeable. Marginalized and disingenuous, Gordon is an inglorious character in this story who appears awkward between two domineering and demanding ladies of means as he attempts to unite with the working people, whom he romanticizes by writing a book about a strike in a textile factory. Riding a bicycle home from Freddy's Bar, he crosses paths with Marie, the wife of the working-class hero Harry Morgan:

> A heavy-set, big, blue-eyed woman, with bleached-blond hair showing under her old man's felt hat, hurrying across the road, her eyes red from crying. Look at that big ox, he thought. What do you suppose a woman like that thinks about? What do you suppose she does in bed? How does her husband feel about her when she gets that size? Who do you suppose he runs around with in this town? Wasn't she an appalling looking woman? Like a battleship. Terrific.[29]

Having seen Marie, not as a person, but as an object, Richard rushes to the typewriter to write about her, but he fumbles the description, creating a caricature rather than a character. Thus Richard's narrative becomes self-conscious and autocritical self-parody of Ernest Hemingway, the author who had created him.

While Richard is having sex with Helène, her husband appears, but she begs Richard not to pay attention to him. When Richard says he does not wish to continue with her husband there, Helène slaps him across the face.[30] Following this scene, Richard Gordon returns home to his wife Helen, who interrogates him: "You have lipstick on your shirt . . . And over your ear. Where have you been?" When Richard explains that he has been at "the Bradleys," Helen answers: "I know. Don't come near me. You reek of that woman." "It's over," declares Helen. "If you weren't so conceited and I weren't so good to you, you'd have seen it was over a long time ago." Richard responds: "You bitch."[31]

While the scene is fiction, the characters' manner of speaking and the resemblance to the Pauline, Ernest, and Jane triangle are so scathing that it must have pained anyone who knew the Hemingways to read. To characterize the wife, Helen, Hemingway references her deep religious convictions, her close relationship with her mother, and her abortion, details all alluding to Pauline.[32] She is also portrayed as a woman who loves her husband more than anything else in the world, just as Pauline was dedicated to her husband, but Ernest was dedicated to his writing.[33]

After reading the manner in which Ernest took aim at all who could have kept him down in the pieces of the manuscript that were scheduled to be released first in *Esquire*, Gingrich insisted that he alter the content to avoid being sued for libel; he flew down personally in January to Bimini to discuss these changes with Ernest, Pauline, and Ernest's lawyer, Moe Speiser. For more than a week, they fought bitterly about the particulars: "It was like those Paris riots, where the rioters and the cops would lay down their brick bats and nightsticks respectively, and adjourn two hours for lunch, then come back and pick them up again . . . Ernest and Pauline and Moe and I would 'riot' all morning, then Ernest and I would go out fishing for the afternoon, then in the evening we would riot again."[34]

While Ernest was in Spain covering the battle against Franco's forces in mid-November, Scribner's cut much of the "Cuban material" out of *To Have and Have Not* to make it more relevant to haves and have-nots in North America. While the cuts made commercial sense, they weakened the narrative, for as readers and critics have often remarked, plot structure in the final draft of *To Have and Have Not* seems incoherent, disjointed, and incomplete.[35]

For a decade before the book's publication, the writer had actively researched revolution in Cuba and had intended to write a book about the subject. He had long been fascinated with the topic of revolutions. Some of his earliest fiction sketched and studied them, such as the short story "The Revolutionist" in 1923, and the full-length novel *A New Slain Knight*, whose protagonist is a professional revolutionist. He worked on the latter for about a year before he abandoned it because he did not know enough about the topic yet to be able to give such a story authenticity.

Later in the dialogues of *Green Hills of Africa*, he confided in his white hunter that he was "studying revolutions." He thought that they were "beautiful . . . for quite a while" until they "[went] bad." When they were with him in Cuba, his sons had witnessed revolution firsthand and became "bloodthirsty" from them, much to Pauline's horror.[36]

Ernest had asked Richard Armstrong, the journalist who had photographed him with the *científicos* in 1933, to provide him with an expert's account of revolutionary activities in Cuba so that his story would ring true, and the reporter responded with a detailed analysis of the cellular organization of the Communist Party and its terrorist derivatives: "The Communist party today is an amorphous group, divided . . . into 22 different groups. The largest group of reds, I'm told are members of the Confederación Nacional Obrera de Cuba of which the notorious Cesar Vilar was the general secretary and boss."[37]

Ernest had integrated the facts from Armstrong's thirteen-page letter, dated August 27, 1936, into an early version of the manuscript of *To Have and Have Not* that included a section titled "The Story of the Dynamite Trip and its Capture."[38] This section of "Cuban material" contained a more radical central character named Tommy Bradley who "justifies terrorism as part of revolutionary activity," but who was cut out entirely—censored before release to American audiences.

The unedited story develops the viewpoint that tyranny imposes upon its sufferers an impenetrable state of silence. Resistance fighters do not seek approval, but only to break the silence with dynamite and irrefutable bodies that will create the "uneasiness that come[s] before conscience." It was an idea that would grow in Hemingway's imagination as his involvement increased in the Spanish Civil War, and he would express it in the plot and characters of *For Whom the Bell Tolls*.

• • • • •

From the third floor of her parents' St. Louis home, Martha was leading the lonesome life of a "Yogi," struggling to eke out uninspiring pages, feeling far removed from the world of action, and longing to return to Paris to get "all the facts tidy once more" for her book. She wrote Ernest about her hope to get "to Spain with the boys." With his departure date also approaching Martha wrote: "I hope we get on the same ark when the real deluge begins. It would be just my luck to survive with the members of the St. Louis Wednesday Club," adding subsequently, "Please don't disappear. Are we not members of the same union? Hemingstein, I am very fond of you."[39]

After a hurried trip to Key West to see family and gather affairs, Ernest returned to New York to embark, in the interim campaigning for Spain, organizing relief efforts, and convincing Max Perkins to buy one of Martha's stories for *Scribner's Magazine*. According to Martha's subsequent accounts, Ernest phoned her often from New York, complained of loneliness, and pleaded with her to come along just before he sailed at the end of February with Evan Shipman and Sidney Franklin aboard the *Paris* to Le Havre as a war correspondent. Passing through Paris, Ernest continued to Valencia via airplane, and onward to Madrid, where he stayed for nearly two months covering the war and working on the film *The Spanish Earth*.

Coached and encouraged by Papa, Martha obtained a letter from *Collier's* that identified her as a member of the press and allowed her to file stories with their weekly review, though they did not offer a salaried post. Her husband off to war, Pauline found herself home alone on the island of Key West and abruptly inutile, or so it seemed, in stopping the momentous forward march of history or her husband's wanderlust. To his Pfeiffer parents, Ernest wrote matter-of-factly before departing, "I hate to go away, but you can't preserve your happiness by trying to take care of it or putting it away in mothballs and for a long time me and my conscience both have known I had to go to Spain."[40]

In March, Martha arrived in Madrid to join the boys and their band of bold reporters, staying at the Hotel Florida. Using terms from ballistics that he had read about, Ernest was able to explain to the others how the architecture of the towers of the hotel prevented projectiles from striking them during the frequent artillery shelling that they heard around them, and he lied so well that they believed him. If there was any doubt whether Martha and Ernest were sleeping together, it was dispelled one evening when, after a bombing raid, all appeared in the lobby in their underwear with the two of them emerging from the same room.

Crossing the border at Andorra on foot with fifty bucks in her pocket and a knapsack full of canned food on her back, Martha had caught a ride to Barcelona, then Valencia. From Valencia, Sidney Franklin took her the rest of the way. By her accounts, she was shocked when Ernest greeted her warmly, then took credit for her determined arrival against all odds: "I knew you'd get here, daughter, because I fixed it that you would."[41] Protectively, he then locked Martha in her room at the Hotel Florida even when she pounded furiously at the door to be released. In retrospect, Martha would see that she should have known then what lay in store.

Despite the Loyalist's esprit, Spanish Nationalists, armed and reinforced by Hitler and Mussolini, had taken Burgos, Segovia, Avila, Saragossa, Teruel, Pamplona, Navarre, and most of Extremadura. They took few prisoners, instead preferring to exterminate civilians, such as in Málaga, in February when they corralled hundreds and opened fire with machine guns, filling the plaza de toros (bullring) with the blood of their own. As women, children, and elderly were fleeing Málaga on the road to Almería, Nationalists chased down five thousand of their former neighbors, and in some cases family members, and murdered them.

By the end of April, German pilots bombed civilians in Guernica, reducing the city to rubble and inspiring Picasso, a Málaga native, to paint these atrocities in his characteristic style. At the end of May, Hemingway passed through New York on the way to Bimini where he would spend a week and return to New York at the end of the month to speak at the League of American Writers Conference where he received a standing ovation for his speech "Fascism Is a Lie."

Spending his time alternatively in Bimini, New York, and Key West, Hemingway completed revisions of *To Have and Have Not* in June. In July, he, Gellhorn, and documentary director Joris Ivens dined with the Roosevelts at the White House and presented *The Spanish Earth.* Then he flew west with Pauline to Hollywood to raise funds among celebrities for *la causa*.

When bulking, hot-tempered, and thin-skinned Ernest Hemingway returned to New York, and Max Perkin's office, in August, Max Eastman, one of his severest critics, had the misfortune to be there. At first uncomfortable yet outwardly polite, Ernest was soon replaying some of the harshest sentences from Eastman's "Bull in the Afternoon" article through in his mind, and with blood inflaming his cheeks and a knot in the gullet, he gnashed his teeth and finally blurted out, "Hey, what do you mean accusing me of impotence?"[42]

Ernest then opened his own shirt to show the chest hair he had on it. "Look false to you, Max?" Gathering steam, he unbuttoned Eastman's shirt to compare: "Why . . . look, it is as smooth as a bald man's head!" Trying to calm the situation, Eastman asked Ernest if he had read the article; bringing a copy of the book that contained it down on Eastman's nose was his response, so Eastman lunged at Ernest, and the two writers were soon in a fracas on Perkins's floor, with the editor attempting to pull them apart. Afterward, Ernest would exploit it as a media opportunity, printing a hilarious interview in the *New York Times*, playing up his side of the scuffle and boasting that he would donate one thousand dollars to the charity of Eastman's choosing for the privilege of spending an hour in a locked room with him with "all legal rights waved."[43]

• • • • •

Churning out phrases like "the great black wings of fascism" that had spread across Europe and "the light against the night," Léon Jouhaux, André Malraux (author of *L'Espoir*), foreign volunteers, and hundreds of other artists and intellectuals found meaning in the struggle against fascism. As Hitler and Mussolini sent food, munitions, and crack troops to support Franco's army as it pushed forward like a shadow to envelop Madrid, the Loyalist battles against dark, relentless, and deadly Nationalists came to signify the struggle against death itself. Amidst them, an impractical and hopelessly romantic esprit grew. It was a cause they could believe in and said they would be proud to die for.[44] In this evocative struggle, volunteers of the era found a form of happiness. As Martha wrote, "Spain was where our adult hope was (the sum total of the remaining hope of youth with a reasoning and logical hope of adults). Spain was a place where you could hope, and Spain was also like a vaccination which would save the rest of mankind from some fearful suffering."[45]

A rift arising from distasteful alliances and ideological differences fractured the Loyalist cause, a luxury it could not afford when fighting the Axis powers, undivided like a malevolent shadow. Some Comintern leaders like André Marty and journalists like Josephine Herbst saw the Soviet Union as their movement's North Star. Others, particularly many Americans, wondered what might result from deals with "red devils." Under Soviet influence, Loyalists purified and policed their ranks and condoned secret executions of their brothers in the International Brigade.

José Robles became one such casualty that troubled John Dos Passos's conscience and made him question the utility of this war. In his other life in America, Robles was a Spanish professor at John Hopkins University who had translated Dos Passos's *The Manhattan Transfer*. When he returned home to war-torn Spain, he soon disappeared, and Dos Passos went looking for him, committing the uncomfortable faux pas of asking about his disappearance. Cauterized Communists insisted that he had been a fascist spy who had gotten what he deserved. Likewise defending intellectual responsibility in reportage, Dos Passos protested, certain the allegations were untrue. If Robles had been murdered, the criminals had to be brought to justice: what good was winning the war if they lost reason along the way and committed such treacheries? However, radicals from the left considered ideological integrity and Soviet alliances critical to defeating Franco, who benefited from Hitler's support.

As far as Ernest was concerned, the truth was not enough: Robles and Dos Passos, and other weak-willed intellectuals who did not know the first thing about winning a war, should focus on the task at hand and keep their outrages and discussions to themselves. Mindful of the odds, Martha and Ernest had committed themselves to winning whatever the cost. After all, these were not normal circumstances. In the face of Hitler, what good was intellectualism? Would the fascists allow dissenters to dilute their intentions? Insisting that the executions were justified, Hemingway expressed impatience with Dos Passos's softness. During war, said Ernest, he should stop asking awkward questions and sentimentally defending rights with "the good-hearted naiveté of a typical American liberal," for he was only endangering lives—his sensibilities were out of place.[46]

The arguments over Robles poisoned their relationship. Writing from Paris at the end of March, Ernest wrote to correct all misconceptions, to ask Dos Passos to pay back all his loans, and to say "so long" in a letter where Ernest was plainly hurting.[47] In an article Ernest wrote for *Ken* three months later, he mentioned the row, and decades later, he continued settling the score through slashing descriptions of his "good old friend" Dos Passos.[48] If during the war Marty and Ernest shared a fervor for the cause, they also shared great disappointment when it seemed all for nothing, and Ernest's novel about the Spanish Civil War depicted divisions between far left and left center as a central theme.

• • • • •

In mid-August, Hemingway again set sail for Paris where he met Martha before continuing to Madrid. By fall, *To Have and Have Not* hit the shelves, and Ernest began a play inspired by his Hotel Florida experiences: *The Fifth Column*. The fifth column, a term originally signifying the people supporting invading forces, came to mean by extension acts of espionage when cited by Nationalist general Emilio Mola. By the end of December, Ernest returned to Pauline, who at last understanding the error of leaving her man alone, had crossed the Atlantic by herself to investigate why "the war had such a hold on her husband."[49] Demanding he meet her in Paris and tolerating his delays, Pauline awaited him just before Christmas.

Travelling with Martha as far as Barcelona, Ernest had Christmas dinner with his mistress and put her on the ocean liner *Normandie*, where she would begin a twenty-two city, two-month lecture circuit in the United States to raise money for medical aid. After cashing a royalty check from *The Trouble I've Seen*, she paid him what she owed him for her expenses while in Spain.

Ernest continued to Paris where he found his better half upset, for she had come to save their marriage and found him distant and unmoved.[50] Though she had gone to great lengths to obtain a visa and braved danger to reach her husband during the war, her disappointment with him was evident. Their reunion degenerated into arguments as she "stormed and raged, promised to get even, to make him pay dearly, threatening to jump off the balcony of their suite at the Hôtel Elysée."[51] Ernest responded that he did not understand why she had come looking for him if she was to be so unpleasant. The fighting continued between them for two weeks during a long cold trip back across the Atlantic. When the Hemingways arrived by liner in Key West, Ernest took the *Pilar* alone to Havana via No Name Key.[52]

At the end of January, Ernest wrote Hadley a nostalgic and somewhat embittered letter detailing his many perilous activities in Spain, enclosing checks from Gus Pfeiffer for Bumby's education and for Christmas, alluding to suicidal urges, and expressing his admiration for the relationship she enjoyed with her new husband, Paul.[53]

After Grace Hemingway attended a Chicago event where Martha spoke passionately against fascism at an Oak Park ladies group meeting, she wrote her son to tell him how impressed she had been. The newspaper account that day described Martha: "With a short black dress setting off her taffy-colored hair hanging childishly about her face in a long bob, Miss Gellhorn looked sixteen but spoke in a luscious, deep, free flowing voice with words of maturity and an emphasis of authority."[54] One witness who saw her speak at the University of Minnesota to three thousand people remembers how she leaped, "spread her legs, threw up her arms like a cheerleader," and shouted "Vive la Republique!"[55]

By mid-February, Ernest wrote his editor from Key West to tell him he was in "an unchristly gigantic jam" such that he might have to go back to "being hungry again," which he appreciated was bound to be good for his writing.[56] Even with the support of one of the wealthiest families in the country, the author was often strapped for cash and in need of a loan. Though Ernest's doctor prohibited alcohol consumption due to a liver condition, he was stubbornly drinking fifteen to seventeen scotch and sodas over the course of the day. At the end of the month until the beginning of March, Ernest and Josie Russell escaped the hoopla in Key West surrounding the completion of the Overseas Highway by taking a brief trip to Havana to fish.[57]

That March, the word was out that Franco's forces had launched a new attack to crush the Catalans by pushing them into the sea: the Aragon Offensive. After Pauline had packed his bag, she accompanied her husband as far as Newark, where he boarded the *Île de France*, and mid-March to mid-May 1938 Ernest returned to the war and to further entangle himself with Martha Gellhorn. Ernest's and Pauline's letters exchanged with friends and family like Virginia, Uncle Gus, and Max Perkins confide a marriage at a crossroads. Writing from Key West at the end of April in a tone reminiscent of that in Hadley's letters, Pauline offered her husband, "If you are happy over there don't come back to be unhappy but hope you can come back and we can both be happy."[58]

In an early draft of Ernest's play, *The Fifth Column*, the character Dorothy, fashioned from Martha, is in a predicament with Phillip, a character that resembles Hemingway, for he can be happy only with her as his mistress. Dorothy wishes to become his wife, despite his many macho idiosyncrasies. While this fantasy seems far-fetched, the reality of Martha's relationship with Ernest is that she was exasperatingly low on his totem pole and had to determine whether to detach, or fully engage; to flee the scene with her autonomy intact, or marry him and become a "kept woman."

In way of a retreat, Martha took Pauline's entrance as her cue to exit, departing on assignment for *Collier's*. She reported from Czechoslovakia during Hitler's Anschluss, or unification, with neighboring Austria, which many felt was a euphemism for annexation, then travelled in England and in France. All the while she remained unsure of the nature of her relationship with Ernest Hemingway, or what the future between them might bring. To her mother, Martha wrote to explain, "Ernest sailed yesterday and I am not exactly happy but am being what the French call '*raisonable*.' There isn't anything left to be,

I have tried everything else. I believe he loves me, and he believes he loves me, but I do not believe much in the way one's personal destiny works out, and I do not believe I can do anything about this. So I am hurrying at last on my *Collier's* job."[59] Strategically speaking, one had to be wise enough to know which battles should not be fought when one hoped to win a war.

• • • • •

Elsewhere in America, Ernest's enterprise and generosity were bearing fruit for a Cuban painter in both significant and peculiar ways as *Esquire* publicity from Hemingway and Dos Passos had led to the acceptance of Gattorno's paintings at the Art Institute of Chicago in 1936 as well as a lucrative commission the following year. *Waiting for Coffee*, a mural for the Bacardi Company headquartered in the Empire State Building, solidified his reputation and career. But a goat named El Señor gave Gattorno more publicity than perhaps he'd hoped for. As the story goes, the Cuban painter brought the goat to the Empire State Building to use as a model. While he was distracted working up in the scaffolds, the goat drank some alcohol-based paint thinner, and in its drunkenness, madly chewed through the rope it was attached to, escaped, and disappeared into offices on the thirty-third floor, where it tried to chew the secretaries. When the artist discovered that the disobedient goat was missing, he chased after him in a rage through a labyrinth of desks and office corridors.

A reporter caught wind of it and printed a story on January 11, 1938, drawing a herd of Bacardi executives and other onlookers, crowding Gattorno at the easel. The painter fumed, remembering his previous invitation to the executives who had not come for him—and who appeared only now . . . *to see a goat?* On a whim, he took up another brush to make a sign: NO SPECTATORS ALLOWED. DO NOT WAIT UNTIL ASKED TO LEAVE.[60] *Hmmph! Take that, imbeciles and El Señor, el goat!* Exasperated with the clown show required of an artist in New York City, Gattorno returned to Cuba to visit family and friends.[61]

Retrieving Bumby for the summer, Ernest headed west. Pursuing the auteur throughout the summer were photographers as he hunted at the Nordquists' L Bar T Ranch in Wyoming, drank at the Stork Club in Manhattan, and fished and put in appearances with Mrs. Hemingway in Key West.[62] The couple was fighting bitterly and seemed quite unhappy to family and friends.[63] Ernest returned from fishing one evening to attend a costume party with Pauline. When he found the door to his studio locked and could not find the missing key, he became cross with his wife, drew a pistol, and shot off the lock. Disheartened, Pauline left for the party without her husband, who later chased her there. When he found her at the party dancing in a hula-girl costume with another man, he punched him and humiliated her by causing a scene.

Scribner's would soon be publishing his newest semifictional short stories along with the play recently completed under fire in Madrid. Remembering the general "gang up" of critics against him for his last novel, *To Have and Have Not*, which he felt was a good novel in several ways, Ernest insisted that the next book be of unquestionable quality, and in a letter to Max Perkins he set the record straight with this disclaimer: "I don't think it is persecution or mania or egotism if I say that there are a lot of critics who really seem to hate me very much and would like to put me out of business. And don't think I mean it conceitedly when I say that a lot of it is jealousy; I do what they would like to do, and I do what they are afraid to do; and they hate you for it . . . Well anyway the hell with it."[64]

At the end of the summer, Ernest returned via Paris with Martha Gellhorn to the war in Spain. After he had departed, Pauline warned in a letter, "I do hope you won't stay away too long. A husband should not stay away from a loving wife too long."[65] A week later she begged him not to humiliate her: "Don't forget I am following rigorously my policy of believing what my husband says in his letters. Also, if you want to keep a contented wife, see to it that she does not hear from strangers where her husband is and with whom."[66] Feeling isolated in Key West without him, she leased an apartment in Midtown Manhattan where she stayed with their son Patrick and could visit family and friends also in the Big Apple.

In Catalonia, Ernest and Martha watched as a fascist army conquered the hearts and bodies of young men, Loyalists who fought to defend the country in vain. Tyranny was winning. When Juan Negrín disbanded the International Brigades in October, Ernest wept—Martha would write in her memoirs that it was the only time she had ever seen him cry.[67]

By the end of the month, Scribner's published the collection *The Fifth Column and the First Forty-Nine Stories*, in which the play appeared. The play depicted the espionage activities of a larger-than-life foreign correspondent, a protagonist resembling Hemingway in civil-war Spain. Ever since he had been a boy in Oak Park, Ernest Hemingway had had a lion-sized imagination captivated by the lives of soldiers, spies, and other adventurers. In World War I, in the Spanish Civil War, in the Caribbean as the captain of his own fishing boat, and later, in France, Belgium, and Germany during World War II, he had romped and frolicked, pretending to be a soldier and a spy, while he was an ambulance driver and a journalist, implicating greater involvement and sporadically crossing the line, but the book drew unfavorable fire from reviewers who regarded the play as an immature, outlandish, and overly sentimental piece, full of fantasy and wartime propaganda.[68]

While walking along a Manhattan avenue, Pauline noted the absence of his new book on Scribner's shelves, so she wrote her errant mate to scold him for his lack of attention to his business: "Perhaps my dear fellow you should be shifting from your mistress—shall we call her War—to your master."[69]

Driven by a fellow reporter and chum-from-the-trenches, Herbert Matthews, across the northeastern boarder to Perpignan, Ernest returned home in November via Paris and New York to winter in Key West with Pauline and his sons. Martha stayed in Barcelona with their friend and fellow journalist Robert Capa to follow the Loyalists' debacle to its ugly end. After a decisive Loyalist defeat in November at the Battle for Ebro, Nationalists forced a Loyalist retreat. Nationalists now outnumbered Loyalists six soldiers to one. When the fascists struck at the heart of Catalonia, bombarding Barcelona and seizing the city at the end of January, defeat became inevitable.

Out of sorts after Spain and no longer happy with his wife in Key West, Ernest returned to New York just after New Year's in 1939 to see Bumby, on holiday from private school, and to attend the theatrical opening of *The Spanish Earth* with Martha and his eldest son. No longer trying to hide the affair, father, son, and girlfriend dined at the trendy Stork Club. Ernest's fifteen-year-old marveled as he beheld the tall, attractive blonde hanging on his father's arm and her husky voice, irresistible while slinging swear words with greater facility than any woman he had ever seen.[70]

Later that year Martha would write to one of her oldest friends, H. G. Wells, to complain of "shabby" Paris and confess her longing to leave the toil of journalism and pursue leisure and writing prospects on a distant beach, which suggested that the conspiracy between "Bug" (Ernest) and "Mook" (Martha) had already begun: "I've written my article on England (just whacking it out, and in such a hurry to be free) and shall soon be going somewhere to swim and sunburn and try to write a book. I won't move or earn money for at least six months, anyhow I hope so."[71]

One of Hemingway's lesser-known stories from that time, "Nobody Ever Dies," is among his first to be set in Cuba, in Jaimanitas, where Grant and Jane Mason lived.[72] Using details from Santería (an Afro-Cuban religion combining elements of Catholicism and Yoruba) and typical scenes like a porch with a caged bird in a swing, the author began to explore Creole culture while combining it with wartime events he had reported on and experienced firsthand. Though this story is somewhat marred by propagandist overtones, it depicts a Loyalist solider, Enrique, who after fighting in the Spanish Civil War flees to the isle where he is killed by reactionaries in the government, tipped off just hours after his arrival. When a policeman guns Enrique down, a heroine, Maria, explains that dying for a cause is impossible, since, uniting with all those who fight for justice, one becomes eternal, lives forever.

In February, *New Masses* published "On the American Dead in Spain," Ernest's tribute to the fallen, evoking lines from *The Sun Also Rises* and his short story "A Natural History of the Dead": in it, he wrote, the winter was blowing through the olive trees of Spain, but when winter became spring, the dead would remain in the Spanish earth—and the fallen American soldiers of the Lincoln Brigade would be immortal. While tyranny in Spain would one day end, the earth would endure forever.[73] Flying out of New York City during a snowstorm, Ernest returned to Key West to find Gus and Louise Pfeiffer on a brief visit to check on the fragile marriage of their favorite niece. Soon after, the Hemingways received Ernest's mother, Grace, who spent a strained six-day visit (at her son's insistence) at the Key West hotel Casa Marina before driving back to Oak Park. It was the last time she would see her son.

Vacationing with her mother in Naples, Florida, Martha Gellhorn waited within striking distance. Making a place for herself in Ernest's life, as perhaps the only woman who would stand up to him, their relationship was now as vital as it would become volatile.[74]

CHAPTER 6

Hemingway's Cuban Family (1939–1941)

• • • • •

The day after Valentine's Day, Ernest boarded his fishing boat and fled from his second failing marriage and his Key West home. He sought refuge, as he often had, on Cuba.[1] This may have been a more or less conscientious attempt to spare his wife from public humiliation, or he might not have yet been entirely at ease with his increasingly public affair.

In a letter to the First Lady, Martha, whose spirits were trodden by the destruction she had recently witnessed in Spain, reaffirmed her intentions to get away from everyone: "Everything that has happened these last six weeks has been so heartbreaking that I cannot endure to think about it."[2] A week before going abroad, Ernest wrote Perkins that he thought he was going to Cuba "to work," so he took inventory of the stories he had written and wanted to write, mentioning one begun in Madrid about an American in the International Brigades soldiering for the beloved Spanish Republic, and another about

> the old commercial fisherman who fought the swordfish all alone in his skiff for 4 days and four nights and the sharks finally eating it after he had it alongside and could not get it into the boat. That's a wonderful story of the Cuban coast. I'm going out with old Carlos in his skiff so as to get it all right. Everything he does and everything he thinks in all that long fight with the boat out of sight

> of all the other boats all alone on the sea. It's a great story if I can get it right.[3]

Though he promised to put it in the forthcoming collection, the story of the Cuban fisherman would not materialize in time.

On Paseo del Prado with Martha at his side and at a desk of a hotel room in Havana, he poured himself into a novel begun as a short story in Madrid—discovering a new happiness. If he were to break from Pauline (and the Pfeiffer family), he would need the money that a new book could bring.[4] It had to be good. Keeping his corner room at the Ambos Mundos, Ernest moved in with Martha at the Sevilla-Biltmore Hotel and had his mail forwarded to that address. In a letter, he let a friend in on the trick: "Tell everyone you live in one hotel and live in another. When they locate you, move to the country. When they locate you in the country move somewhere else. Work everyday till you're so pooped about all the exercise you can face is reading the papers. Then eat, play tennis or swim or something in a work daze just to keep your bowells moveing and (*sic*) the next day write again."[5] Two rooms offered autonomy as well as anonymity, an escape route sometimes unavailable in Key West, and solitude when it was desired in service of his work.

Enamored with baseball and many other things American, hailed among tourists as the Riviera of the Western Hemisphere, and praised by speculators as the "new California," Havana was a thriving and attractive capital in those days, an inebriating cocktail of Old World charm and New World promise. It was an innovative city whose planners had conspired with governors and investors to commission impressive public works projects like waterways, intercity ferries, highways, and the Capitolio dome.[6]

In the central Vedado neighborhood, Art Deco apartment buildings that housed international executives in their upper decks flaunted modern and impertinent architecture, which reached in gleaming style for the radiant skies. In the streets of a historic center, a few blocks from the magnificence of the roaring sea, sun-bronzed beauties strolled beneath white silk parasols, dark hair bouncing behind them, as they passed beside high columns, fanned themselves with

Spanish *abanicos*, and gazed back across their shoulders with interminable brown eyes.[7] The ladies unaccompanied, a man might pursue them beneath the shade of the arched walkways that lined Paseo del Prado, across the grandiose open expanses of the sprawling avenue, and as they ducked into the corners of a more intimate maze of twisting back alleyways.

Street musicians filled those cobbled corridors with song and rumba—rising from fleshy throats bewitchingly, strumming from interiors of guitars vibrantly, intermingling with beats primitive and profound from conga drums, rasping delicate scratches of guiros, and shakes of *shekeres*, and maracas, keeping rhythm amidst the soft humming resonance of a saxophone, awakened by strident wails of trumpets and murmured garbles of trombones, and in low and hallow warbles of muffled tubas from a sonata of improvisation floating though expiring summers, and calming lovers as they sailed along El Malecón, the seawall, watching the crashing waves and immersing themselves in the milk of moonlight. And so, riding the waves of a rare economic boom, of foreign investments at last arriving to bolster her hopes with fruit, sugar, and tobacco trades, Havana blossomed and offered refuge, opportunities, and romance, to exiles, entrepreneurs, and artists, flocking to her shores from Asia, Europe, and North America in need of work, in search of fortune, in obstinate pursuit of paradise.

Among them were many refugees from the Spanish Civil War—including Ernest and Martha in their own way—who treated the writer with great respect and soon became members of his clan. During the war in Spain, these men had been comrades, and in Cuba, they became friends, fishing and drinking, full of raucous laughter, nostalgia, anguish, and a necessity to forget in the blue depths and tawny sunsets of the Caribbean island. Fleeing execution in Iberia, the exiles' revolutionary dreams found new expression on this tropical island in the Americas.

Entranced by his writing and his new social milieu, Ernest was much too busy to attend to finding a permanent house. Routinely excluded from fishing, drinking, or jai alai matches, Gellhorn's irritation with the irregularity and illegitimacy of their situation grew. Taking matters into her own hands, she scoured Havana's classifieds for more suitable quarters. When she stumbled upon an advertisement for a fifteen-acre property located high in Havana's foothills, called Finca Vigía, or "Lookout Farm," for its privileged view of the Cuban capital below, she interrupted his breakfast by slapping the folded newspaper with the ad circled in red across the table. His assignment was clear.

Hemingway took the newspaper gently from her hands. Stretching a pleasant grin across his face, he promised his lover that he would visit the property that very afternoon, just as soon as the day's writing was done. To investigate the house twenty kilometers to the north in the barrio of San Francisco de Paula, Ernest commandeered a taxi from Parque Central and then passing through the zones along the outskirts of Havana would witness a squalor that he had never seen.[8] Arriving at the Finca, Ernest found its front gate closed. He thought some neighborhood children playing out front might help him shimmy the lock.

• • • • •

One of most significant relationships Ernest would develop with a Cuban was with a ten-year-old boy named René Villarreal (two years older than his youngest son, Gregory, and one year younger than his middle child, Patrick), whom he met that morning in front of the place that would soon become his home. On that day in January 1939, Hemingway was thirty-nine years old. René, his brothers, and the other neighborhood children were playing baseball in front of the Finca Vigía when an injured *aura* (a vulture common in Havana) fell from the sky and sought refuge behind the Finca's front gate. The boys had stopped playing to surround and tease the bird when two men in a long dark sedan pulled up. "*¡Muchachos!* What are you doing with that bird?" asked one of the men in American-accented Spanish.[9]

They replied that they were playing, but the men asked the children to leave the bird alone, and they respected his request. According to René's recollection, "El Americano" was a tall, strong man in shorts, leather sandals, long hair, and a thick moustache. They were impressed with him, as not many people could afford cars at that time, and even fewer of such people came to their village.

The men tried the gate a few times before calling the boys back over. El Americano asked if this was the property of Mr. Roger Joseph D'Orn Duchamp de Castaigne, a Frenchman. They replied that it was, and he asked them if they knew how to open the gate. Indeed, the boys had a trick for getting in, and when they showed him, the writer, grinning, gave them each a dollar bill. The boys applauded with joy and thanked the bulky American man. In a day's hard labor, their fathers could not have earned as much.

In polite conversation, Hemingway asked the boys what they had been doing before he came. They had been playing baseball! Kneeling to address them at eye level, he asked them what sort of equipment they used. They showed him a ball made from dingy rags and an old broomstick for a bat and explained that they played "a *manos limpias*," or barehanded. They liked to play baseball in the open fields of the Finca and pick fruit from its many trees, but the owner, D'Orn, did not like them to do so and would send his mean-spirited gardener to chase them off.

If he bought the property, said Ernest to the children, they could play there any time they liked, and he would love for them to meet his sons who were about their age. The children watched the Cuban chauffeur drive the automobile down the dusty gravel driveway and the *americano* disappear into the big house at the top of the hill. After offering *de l'eau fraiche avec du citron* in the salon, the D'Orns relayed the history of Finca Vigía, a hilltop where the Spanish army had maintained a wooden fort during the nineteenth century commanding a privileged view of Havana; the name "vigía" came from *vigilar*, meaning to "keep watch."[10]

"Well, did you see it?" Martha asked, when he returned to their hotel room.

"*Trop chère*," he said, meaning the one hundred dollars per month rent. "Too far from town and it would take months to fix it up." He had tolerated Pauline's overhaul of their Key West home for a decade. Why would he want to go through that again? For two dollars per day, two hotel rooms simplified his life and provided for his every need, such that he could avoid all entanglements and concentrate on his work. Did she expect him to stop writing to renovate a decrepit manor at the precise moment when his next book was going so well? What if he lost it and never got it back? Martha, undeterred, signed the lease with D'Orn. To make the house more habitable, she used her own scarce funds to complete renovations, construct furniture in Spanish style, repair the cracked swimming pool, and resurface the tennis courts. Thus she created a writers' retreat in the middle of the Gulf Stream for this literary duo.[11]

By March 18, a few days after Hitler invaded Czechoslovakia, Martha reported in a letter to the First Lady, "I have taken possession of my Finca . . . what in God's name shall I do with this place now that I have it." After a brief breakdown brought on by overexertion during the renovation, Martha feared becoming entrapped by material possessions and believed herself ill suited for domestic life. She worried that acquiring a house would cause her to "never write again but . . . spend the remainder of my life telling servants to scrub the bathroom floors and buy fresh paper for the shelves," but after sleeping on it she awoke and looked out her window only to see "a saba [ceiba] tree, so beautiful you cannot believe it, and hear the palms rattling in the morning wind, and the sun streaking over the tiled floors, and the house itself, wide and bare and clean and empty, lying quiet all around me."

Simultaneously delighted and ashamed to have so much while she had seen so much suffering in the world, she comforted herself with a resolution to write the book that had haunted her but had not yet been written. Though her money would soon run out and she would have to work hard for it again, she had a "brief breathing spell" now, so she was going to make the most of it. When she was working as a cub reporter at the *Times Union* in a four-dollar-per-week room in Albany, she had never thought that one day through her writing she would be able to live in such a place: "I never dreamed I would write myself into a grove of palms and bamboos and flamboyant trees, nor a terrace covered with bougainvillea, nor a swimming pool: and I can't believe it yet."[12]

• • • • •

Though the Finca was cause for celebration, ten days later, after heavy bombardment, boots and tank tracks crumpled across the cobbled plazas of Madrid when the city fell, and after they had taken Valencia two days later, the flat, metallic voice of the commanding general for Nationalist forces, Francisco Franco, came on the radio and announced the Republican government's surrender: "Today, after having disarmed and captured the Red Army, the Nationalist troops have secured their final military objective. The war is ended. Burgos, April 1, 1939. Year of Victory . . . a totalitarian state will reign in Spain . . . the real power of the Spanish people will be to show their support for the family, the city, the state, and the corporation." As they heard the words, Loyalists were inconsolable, and Franco's forces began executions. At the end of March, the Vatican, the United Kingdom, France, and the United States, weary of the war, recognized Franco's government, but the following week, Mussolini annexed Albania, and the world shuddered, for they knew that it was only the beginning.

In Spain, Hemingway had become fluent in Spanish, had experiences, and developed friendships that opened his understanding of Latin American culture and events. He brought to Cuba a unique vantage point as an American who had been on the front lines of the war in Spain, and an appreciation not only for the complexities of Latin American politics but also for their language, literature, culture, and art.

Betting on jai alai matches and fishing in the afternoons, he was writing by morning, making acquaintance of Basque jai alai players in exile (such as the Ibarlucea brothers, Félix Ermua, Salsamendi y Cazalis), and amassing the pages of a manuscript. Its sprawling cinematic passages reminded him of *A Farewell to Arms*, and the feeling he had while writing that novel returned. Ernest wrote Perkins that he was "down to 198 pounds" and feeling the good "hollowness" when the writing was going well.[13] After a brief trip to Key West at the end of March to see his sons, Ernest returned at the end of the first week of April to Martha and to marlin season with both Carlos Gutierrez and Gregorio Fuentes now employed aboard the *Pilar*.[14]

By the middle of May, Martha's hired hands completed renovations, and vacating his room at the Ambos Mundos, Ernest began to pay his share of the rent at the Finca Vigía. When filmmaker Joris

Ivens met with Ernest in Havana at the end of the month, two hundred pages of his novel about Spain had been completed. Leaving her boys at Camp Te Whanga in Connecticut, Pauline departed for a trip to Europe without her husband to consider her fate.

At summer's end Ernest and Martha stopped in Key West, while Pauline was away, to retrieve his Buick and drive it westward to deliver Martha to her mother in Saint Louis, and Ernest continued farther west in the car to meet Hadley and Paul Mowrer, who had been fishing in Cody, Wyoming, and retrieve his son Jack so that father and sons could hunt together at the L Bar T Ranch, the boy's half brothers having been delivered by driver Tony Bruce from their Connecticut campgrounds.[15] Having stepped out from behind a tree to surprise Hadley and Paul, Ernest wrote them afterward recalling how marvelous they looked at first sight as they returned along the trail from the woods to their lodge after a long hike: "You and Paul were certainly a swell looking pair of people on that trail. I was as proud of you guys as though I had invented you." Not having seen him in years, happily married, and getting along well without him and his fame, the Mowrers on the other hand noticed that Ernest's presence had deteriorated; he appeared anxious and fatigued.[16] On the day that hunting began at the ranch, September 1, the Germans invaded Poland; Great Britain, France, Australia, and New Zealand declared war on Germany. World War II had begun, though two days later the United States declared its neutrality in what it considered to be Europe's war.

Pauline hurried to join the boys at the ranch, perhaps hopeful that the reunion of the family would resuscitate a marriage. After a series of flights and trains from Paris to London to New York to Wyoming, complicated by the grounding of airplanes and evacuations coinciding with the outbreak of war, Pauline arrived afflicted with a severe cold, and Ernest was obliged to care for her and wait for her recovery before breaking the bad news: he needed a divorce. Directing Toby Bruce to take the family home, and arranging for Martha to meet him in the Billings airport, Ernest left to join his mistress in the new Sun Valley Lodge resort in Idaho, where all their expenses would be paid by the owners hoping the writer's visit would give their publicity a boost. There, they befriended Lloyd and Tillie, a resort photographer and his wife who became their longtime friends.

When Virginia spilled the beans to the family that Ernest and Pauline's marriage was ending because Ernest had changed, "Mother Pfeiffer" wrote her son-in-law to ask if it was true. In response, Ernest tried to defend himself, asserting that he had changed less than Pauline and her sister, Virginia, who had "spread" enough lies "at the right time to break up [his] home," but apologized for having to write such a letter at Christmas nevertheless.[17] In reply, his mother-in-law expressed regret: "This is the saddest Christmas I have ever known. A broken family is a tragic thing, particularly so when there are children," but she promised to pray for him.[18]

The long trip home to Key West gave Pauline some time to think, perhaps enough to notice that her husband Ernest, no longer dependent upon Pfeiffer funds and doing exactly as he pleased, was completely in control. When *Collier's* magazine mobilized Martha into action—on a combat assignment to Finland to cover an impending invasion by the neighboring Soviet Union—Pauline asked Toby Bruce to relay a message to her soon-to-be-ex-husband: he was no longer welcome in Key West during the holidays if it be his intention to return to Martha after that.[19] Ernest appeared bullheadedly at the house anyway only to find Pauline had left to spend the holidays in New York with her sister, Virginia, and had taken the boys with her. For good measure, she had gifted the house staff a paid vacation so that Ernest would find himself entirely alone at Christmas on an island unto himself. He inventoried and packed up all belongings (suitcases, books, boxes, and animal heads), leaving what he could not take with him in the storeroom of a building behind Sloppy Joe's bar with the intention of taking it during a subsequent voyage. He loaded what he could into his Buick and boarded a P&O ferry to another life in Cuba, leaving a marriage in the churning wake, and his years with his second wife, Pauline, behind.[20]

• • • • •

Outnumbered 180 to 3 million, the Finns used guerrilla tactics to frustrate the Soviets' attack, then retreated to the forest. Having beheld their heroic yet futile efforts in the field, Martha took refuge in a Helsinki hotel. Just as the Soviets threatened to bomb Helsinki into oblivion unless the Finns met their demands, Martha crossed paths with an American military attaché in her hotel restaurant. "Did she want to be evacuated to Sweden?" he asked. "Christ, yes!" she replied with the mouth that shocked many men of that era. Five minutes later, she returned in a pair of pajamas and with a bottle of whiskey in her hand—for it was not her first evacuation.[21]

Though her reporting trip produced "Slow Boat to War," "Bombs from a Low Sky," "Blood on the Snow," "Bombs on Helsinki," and "Fear Comes to Sweden" for *Collier's*, Hemingway waited for her night after night, believing her time away to be a betrayal of her commitment to him. She was pursuing a narrative with herself as a writing protagonist, a heroine bearing stubborn witness to expose this foul business of war. It was arguably a narrative that she had acquired from him. When air travel was suspended due to inclement weather, Martha got stuck in Lisbon with no option but to take a slow boat. Caught between her career and Ernest's expectations, she wired her apologies across the ocean: "CLIPPERS STOPPED, NO CHOICE EXCEPT REX ARRIVING 11TH POSSIBLE TO KEEP PROMISE BE HOME FIRST STOP ASHAMED DISAPPOINT YOU STOP MISERABLY UNHAPPY."[22] Martha did not arrive in Havana until January 16.

The Sunday before Martha's return, the author wrote his editor, "Have a terrific hangover and can't write this morning (won't write rather as don't want to turn out any hungover pages so write you instead). Make allowances for that in reading. Have been working steady and went on big drunk with some boys down here night before last . . . Am in the stretch on the book now."[23] He enclosed a large portion of it. The experiences and anger of the previous year, focused by a necessity for financial independence, expanded the Spanish epic to fifteen thousand words. Although they were soon to be divorced and not yet fully cured of their wounds, Ernest, who had always respected Pauline's opinion about his writing, had shown her what he had written so far. She encouraged him by calling it some of the best fiction he had ever written.[24]

From Cuba, Hemingway wrote Perkins about the fine hunting, his new home, his intention to stay there away from the war, and his desire to have a daughter.[25] Perkins replied with a cable to the Ambos Mundos: He was "extremely impressed" with the "opening pages" that were "beautiful," and chapter eight was "tremendous"; it "had the old magic."[26] It was all so "perfectly simple," wrote Max, that one could make the mistake of thinking that anyone could do it that way, but, of course, only Ernest could.

• • • • •

When Martha returned, Ernest was hurt that she had made him wait, so he asked her to sign a humorous agreement. With Judge R. R. Rabbit and Judge P. O. Pig as their witnesses, he signed as Mr. Warm Dimpy Gellhorn Bongie Hemmy and she as Mrs. Warm Fathouse Pig D. Bongie Hemingstein, and in it, she promised never to leave him alone again. "I will not leave my present and future husband not for nothing no matter what or anything . . . I, the undersigned, further guaranty not to divorce my husband (previously named, see other page) not for nobody, only he has to be a good boy too and not love nobody but me. But he will not love nobody but me. This is an unnecessary guaranty."[27]

Laughs diffused the tension in this explosive relationship between two fiercely independent writers, but these represented the first shots fired in their personality war. Martha carefully navigated the ebbs and flows of Ernest's moods, allowing him the freedom to romp, while attempting to pursue her career. His message was clear: He had missed her and did not wish to be left alone. He needed to be able to trust her. She must not put him through such a long separation again.

During the first week of March, Sidney Glazer's adaptation of Ernest's play, *The Fifth Column*, opened in New York, but the critics were not amused. Finding inspiration in her experiences in Czechoslovakia, Martha's novel *A Stricken Field* was published by Deull, Sloan, and Pearce during the same month; afterward, Ernest wrote Max that he had not pitched the book to Scribner's because he did not think that it was good policy for writers in the same family to share publishers. While reviewers spoke of the novel respectfully, it did not garner quite the same enthusiasm as *The Trouble I've Seen*.

As a boon to the author's happiness, Ernest was finally visited by his three estranged sons, whose mothers insisted that they spend time in the summer with their father: Jack, "Bumby," age sixteen; Patrick, "Mouse," age eleven; and Gregory, "Gigi," age eight. Making up for lost time, the boys inhaled their Bunyanesque father's life force, imagination, and healthy appetite for playful adventures. They were handsome and intelligent boys who had missed their father; he loved and missed them dearly in return. Ernest took them fishing aboard his boat, to the *frontón* for jai alai matches, to baseball games in a Havana arena, and to the Cerro Hunting Club to shoot clay pigeons. As Hemingway had promised, they became playmates with the baseball-playing children of San Francisco de Paula.[28]

Their father's new girlfriend was blonde, tall, young, and attractive. All too aware of her awkward juxtaposition as stepmother to three boys, Martha focused on winning them over one by one. As a testament to her charisma, she succeeded, and they spoke fondly of her thereafter, particularly the eldest. Jack seemed to have a crush on his stepmother, or at least fondness for the woman he later referred to as his "favorite other mother."[29] In a letter to Jack's mother Hadley, Martha wrote that she had "talked and talked" with Bumby about "any number of things," listened dutifully to his stories about school and trout fishing, felt "unbelievably lucky" to have him as her friend, and concluded, "I don't see how a woman could produce a better or more beautiful boy than you did . . . I think they will accept me as a part of their gang. Ernest's gang, another one of the large families that dashes about obeying Poppa and having a fine time."[30]

By the end of April, Ernest had sent Perkins thirty-two more chapters of his manuscript, was working on the thirty-fifth chapter, was combing the Bible, Shakespeare, and more literary sources for a title, and had worked up a list of more than twenty-four possibilities. None were quite right, but by the end of the following month, he had sent Max a 512-page manuscript and had found his title: "Dear Max: How about this for a title *For Whom the Bell Tolls*. A Novel By Ernest Hemingway?"

While suffering from an illness that nearly killed him, John Donne reflected in "Meditation XVII," from *Devotions upon Emergent*

Occasions, on the toll of a funeral bell, a passage Ernest quoted in its entirety in the same letter to Max:

> No man is an Iland, intire of it selfe; every man is a peece of the Continent, a part of the maine; if a Clod bee washed away by the Sea, Europe is the lesse, as well as if a Promontorie were, as well as if a Mannor of thy friends or of thine owne were; any mans death diminishes me, because I am involved in Mankinde; And therefore never send to know for whom the bell tolls; It tolls for thee.[31]

The phrase borrowed from Donne suggested that fascism's sinister rise was not just a Spanish problem but one that concerned humanity. The events that followed seemed to prove this title to be right, yet for the foreseeable future, Ernest intended to stay far from that struggle.

Congratulating him on the title, Perkins gushed over the book. It was absolutely "magnificent, strange, new . . . I think this book has greater power, and larger dimensions, greater emotional force, than anything you have done, and I would not have supposed you could exceed what you had done before. It is a surprising book."[32] Ernest explained, "I am so damned happy with Marty that everything has gone better."[33] The passages he was writing seemed to express a character who was one part Spanish and another part American: "Every time Robert Jordan looked at her he could feel a thickness in his throat . . . She had high cheekbones, merry eyes and a straight mouth with full lips. Her hair was the golden brown of a grain field . . . Her legs slanted long and clean from the open cuffs of the trousers . . . She moved awkwardly as a colt moved, but with that same grace as of a young animal."[34]

Ernest's mother, Grace, returned to Key West in late April 1940, within ninety miles of her son, but she did not visit him at his Finca Vigía retreat—and he would not have wanted her to.[35] Though Grace appeared to be an extremely influential and significant woman in Ernest's life, the ill feelings he harbored against her snowballed after his father's suicide.[36] In the decades that followed this traumatic event, the ties between Ernest and Grace were a complex net entangled and knotted with hurt and blame, or as Ernest wrote a biographer in the late forties, "I hated my mother as soon as I knew the score and loved my father until he embarrassed me with his cowardice. My mother is an all-time all-American bitch and she would make a pack mule shoot himself; let alone my poor bloody father."[37]

• • • • •

The *americano* told the children of San Francisco de Paula that they could play baseball on the Finca's grounds, and he let them pick mangoes from his trees. Soon, he put bats, balls, and gloves in their hands and fitted their scrawny bodies for new uniforms. "Las Estrellas de Gigi"—Gigi's All-Stars—had been inscribed across the backs, for the team of his design would be made up of the children of San Francisco de Paula and his sons, Jack, Patrick, and Gregory. Among the Cuban children were René Villarreal, his brother Popito, and his friend Fico. Nine-year-old Gregory had taken special liking to Popito (Rodolfo Villarreal) and Fico (Alberto Ramos). Ernest invented errands for the children, like running a letter to the mailbox or taking care of the dogs and cats, so that he could compensate them with money for their families who were noticeably hungry and in need.

As a favor to the previous owner, Ernest had promised D'Orn that he would retain the staff who had worked at the Finca for many years: a Jamaican majordomo named Luis, a heavyset Spanish woman, Maria, and an old Catalan gardener named Don Pedro. For years the children had been chased off the grounds by Don Pedro, who tried to kill them with a machete as he shouted, "Filthy bastards! I am going to cut off your ugly little heads!"—so they were shocked when "Papa" invited them inside the Finca gates.[38] Ernest forbade Don Pedro to chase the children away or to keep any birds on the property in a cage, and the old Catalan left work one day and never returned. When the former gardener's distraught wife came looking for him, nobody knew what to say. Some days later the children smelled a foul odor and were frightened when they discovered Don Pedro's bloated body, swarming with flies, at the bottom of the Finca Vigía's well. The memory of Don Pedro's body disturbed young René for some time afterward, filling him with fear whenever he walked the Finca's grounds until Papa had a talk with him, teaching him that it was natural for him to feel afraid of death; he should not feel ashamed, but only try to confront his fears.

Putting distance between herself and her marriage with Ernest Hemingway in Key West, Pauline moved to San Francisco, where she rented an apartment for herself and her two boys when they returned from their summer in Cuba. With Jack, Patrick, and Gregory, Ernest found a separate peace, fishing in June with Gregorio Fuentes, his new first mate, aboard the *Pilar,* while Martha, stir crazy at the Finca, went to New York for a breath of urban air.

In Havana at the Cerro Hunting Club, the adults drank, talked, and blasted shotguns with gusto while the children chased fly balls on the field opposite the range. Now sixteen, on the threshold of manhood, Jack, still often called Bumby, had been the first to call Papa *Papá*, just as any child brought up in Paris would, with his younger brothers always following his lead. Hemingway was a long and difficult name for the Cuban children to say, so they imitated their teammates, Bumby, Mouse, and Gigi, and called him "Papa," too. While imbibing whiskey and testosterone at the hunting club, Winston Guest heard a dozen children shrieking "Papa! Papa!" and was greatly amused, and soon he joined the chorus to tease his friend. The nickname always carried a dark shade, given Ernest's overbearing tendencies, his paternal personality struggling to reassert control in a life it could not entirely control.

Acknowledging that he did not enjoy babies, "Papa" struggled to play the role of father until the boys were old enough to hunt and fish. After his father's suicide, Ernest asserted his new role as "Papa" not only with his mother and the siblings that remained, but also with women, acquaintances, and friends, causing estrangement and ruptures in numerous relationships. To reinforce this role, "Papa" played expert on matters from sports, to travel, to combat.[39] Having known him since childhood, Katy Smith attested to Papa's rapidly expanding ego at this time. He was "irascible and truculent. . . had a tendency to be an Oracle, I thought, and needs some best pal and severe critic to tear off those long white whiskers which he is wearing."[40]

At the Cerro Hunting Club, "Papa" encouraged the Cuban children to have as many Coca-Colas as they wanted, but when they drank so many that they were spending more time in the bathroom than on the field, he amended, stimulating heroic play by offering a Coke for each home run.[41] To demonstrate how to swing the bat, Ernest would take pitches and let the children run around the bases. Ernest stepped to the plate with René's brother Oscar beside him. The crack of the bat sent the pelota high into the air, dropping it in deep against the wall between right and center field.[42] As Oscar rounded third base, coach Papa called for him to come home. Trying to slide into home, Oscar collided with the ground as the catcher, a much bigger boy than him, pushed him out of the way. Oscar screamed out as he broke his arm. Scooping up the kid and rushing him to the car seconds later was Coach Hemingway, already much sobered as they drove to the center of Havana where he delivered him to the nurses at Calixto García General.

Returning the boy to his parents afterward with his arm in a cast, Ernest apologized to his mother, who told him not to worry: it was just part of growing up. The day they had seen their boys come home with their pockets stuffed full of mangoes and their shirt fronts overflowing, they had understood the kind person Ernest was. When the summer ended and Ernest's sons returned to their mothers and to their private schools, Papa told the children of San Francisco de Paula that they were still welcome to play on the open spaces of the Finca Vigía, but just to please be sure to put the baseball bats and boxing gloves away after they had finished using them for the day. Ernesto treated the neighborhood children with *cariño* and nostalgia while missing his own sons.[43]

One day a laborer was passing along the road in his oxcart. Everyone in the village called him Seboruco (or "large rock"), for his dense disposition. When the children asked him for a ride, he grunted dismally at first, but they were all piling on already so the old farmer gave in. Without enough room in the cart, René's brother Popito sat on the crossbar and the wobbly cart, pulled by two large oxen, made for an exciting ride. Then the cart hit a bump in the road, and eight-year-old Popito fell to the ground with the wagon wheel rolling over top of him before anybody realized or intervened. Though he was clearly in pain, little Popito insisted on walking home by himself like a man. When his mother saw him, she told the boys to hurry to fetch the *americano* and to ask to take her boy to the clinic in his automobile. When the clinic could do nothing for them, they took Popito to a hospital, but the injuries were too serious, and he soon died of irreparable damage to his internal organs. The writer insisted on paying for Popito's funeral expenses.

While the family was mourning, the boys did not return to the Finca, so Ernesto went to check on them and tell them how empty his house felt without the sounds of baseball outside. Like his own boys, he missed them, and attempting to help the distraught family, he suggested that their eldest come to help him around the house to keep him company and to earn some much-needed money for his family. It was a way for Hemingway to share their sorrow and offer them a small comfort during a dark moment. The mother nodded, sending René up the hill with the American. René was a responsible and intelligent boy, but he was only eleven at the time.[44]

• • • • •

Of course, Ernest could also attract the devotion of people his own age—particularly affluent Cuban sportsmen. The jai alai matches, fishing tournaments, and cockfights introduced Hemingway to several new acquaintances and friends. Offering an insider's view of Cuban politics, Mario García Menocal Seva was the son of Mario García Menocal Deop. Educated at prestigious schools in the United States, the Menocals owned sugar plantations, rice mills, and dairy farms in Camagüey Province. Having met Hemingway in Bimini in 1935, "Mayito" became one of the writer's closest male friends in Cuba, and a part of the group of wealthy, cultivated, English-speaking Cuban sportsmen, man-sized children who shared Hemingway's passion for yachting, fishing, hunting, boxing, cockfighting, jai alai, partying, and pranks.[45] Mayito was a trusted friend, a father to Hemingway's children, a member of his inner circle, one of the Cubans who would over the years become like family.[46] Mayito Menocal's cousin, Elicio

Argüelles Pozo, owned the Frontón in Havana, where the three of them went to watch Basque friends play jai alai. A lawyer, ranch and sugar farm owner, shop proprietor, tourism promoter, and sports nut, Elicio also became Hemingway's close friend.[47]

Another of Hemingway's best friends in Cuba was the boxer from Holguín, Evelio Mustelier, more commonly known as "Kid Tunero." Kid Tunero was a Holguín native, a bricklayer, who came to Havana as a boxer in the 1930s. Hemingway and many of his friends were his fans. Following his fights religiously in Arena Cristal, Hemingway sponsored Kid Tunero, sent him to Saragossa to train, and saw him box in Paris where he had a couple of fights. In Paris, Tunero had met Yolette Yolle, a well-to-do tennis player, whom Kid would marry and with whom he had two children. When the Hemingways left the Finca for Europe and Africa in 1953, Kid Tunero and his wife would stay in the Finca as their honored guests.[48]

When interviewed by the *Prensa Libre* (the *Free Press*), Hemingway indicated that his respect for Tunero was inspired as much by his boxing skills as his character. In the article titled "The Gentleman of the Ring," he said, "It shouldn't shock you to discover that one of the men I love most is Kid Tunero . . . the most complete athlete in Cuba . . . if there are still any gentlemen left on Earth, Tunero is one of them . . . he speaks little, but it isn't necessary for him to speak more because his spirit can be seen on his face. It's simple and pure like bread, or like gold."[49] Coming from a white man, this public declaration of admiration and respect was ahead of its time.

Also in his milieu were the Spanish Loyalists like José Luis and Roberto Herrera Sotolongo. Born in Spain, José Luis and Roberto fought against Franco during the Civil War. When fascists took over their homeland, they had fled, immigrating to Cuba just before Ernest established his residence there, later becoming Cuban citizens. Dr. José Luis and Roberto's friendship with Ernesto blossomed when the author became a resident and ended only with the author's death. Estranged on the Cuban island, they shared a language from Spain, culture, history, cause, and a sense of humor. The Herrera Sotolongos were a regular fixture at the Finca for twenty years. They were "bosom friends, not just one of the many individuals who attached themselves to his entourage," and they became trusted and beloved members of his immediate family.[50]

A student of revolutions and regular contributor to the Cuban Communist Party, Hemingway also maintained political relationships on the island. Trade union leader and member of the Central Committee of the Cuban Communist Party, Roman Nicolau was introduced to Hemingway and Martha Gellhorn at the Majestic Hotel in Barcelona by Cuban poet and fellow activist in Spain Nicolás Guillén. Years later, Nicolau visited Hemingway regularly at the Finca Vigía to request contributions for the Cuban Communist Party: "I never asked Hemingway for much money. But he was very generous and used to give me more than I requested. He gave us a total of twenty thousand dollars. It gave him pleasure that we were doing *something* against the government."[51] However, Nicolau did recall that he addressed Hemingway as a *compañero* (friend, companion), but Hemingway responded with *camarada* (comrade), a habit developed during his experiences in civil-war Spain. Of all the foreigners living in Cuba, Nicolau was certain that Ernest Hemingway contributed the most to the Communist Party, and during a separate interview with Cuban biographer Norberto Fuentes, Guillén confirmed this detail to be true.[52]

CHAPTER 7

Don Quixote vs. the Wolf Pack (1940–1944)[1]

• • • • •

In September 1940, Martha rejoined Ernest and his sons for a hunting trip in Idaho. Rubbing elbows among them at Sun Valley Lodge was writer Dorothy Parker and movie star Gary Cooper. On October 21, Scribner's published *For Whom the Bell Tolls*. With his divorce obtained from Pauline on the fourth of November, Martha and Ernest were married by a justice of the peace on the twenty-first at a modest ceremony in the Union Pacific dining room in Cheyenne. Pouring the entirety of its resources into the promotion of their star author's novel, which had been much anticipated and years in the making, Scribner's sold over a million copies of *For Whom the Bell Tolls* in the first six months.

In *Life* magazine on January 6, 1941, appeared "The Hemingways in Sun Valley: The Novelist Takes a Wife," an article punch-drunk with purple prose declaring his "prime physical vigor" and virtues as a writer, boxer, and a hunter before announcing that Paramount Pictures would pay $150,000 for the movie rights, the highest amount ever paid to a novelist by Hollywood. "At 41 Ernest Hemingway has reconfirmed his place in American literature among its greatest living writers."[2] The ten-page spread followed, containing several photographs by his comrade Robert Capa: writing, shooting fowl at the ranch, and celebrating a new literary triumph and a new marriage. Martha Gellhorn also bloomed as she reclined along the logs that bordered their lodge suite's veranda and dangled her hair between the camera and the rough country ever in the background. Wincing as her new husband squeezed her lithe figure tightly against his barrel chest, Martha danced with him cheek to cheek at a rough local watering hole, visibly very inebriated.

Though he had first been against living at the Finca Vigía, now, as a famous writer with a hundred-thousand-dollar movie deal from Hollywood, he had more than enough dough. To keep his own name out of the papers and acquire the mansion with views of Havana, tennis courts, and a pool for the lowest possible price, Ernest asked Toby Bruce to negotiate with D'Orn about buying it outright. They settled on 18,500 pesos in January 1941, which Ernest paid as a belated wedding present to his bride.[3]

Ordering Bruce to bring more of Ernest's books in crates from Key West and to carry out more renovations on their new property in their absence, the Hemingways departed on a working honeymoon with a brief stopover in Hawaii, then onward to the Pacific theater where they would cover the second Sino-Japanese War. As a journalist attuned to world events and her career, Martha had been preparing a trip with *Collier's* magazine to cover Japan's expansionism, ongoing and every day more disconcerting. Not wishing his new wife to go it alone, Ernest arranged to go also as a journalist for *PM* magazine. With involvement from the United States, the Soviet Union, and Germany, China and other Asian nations had resisted Japanese expansionism in China, on the Korean peninsula, and in the Pacific islands.

Travelling from Los Angeles to San Francisco on the way to Hawaii, the happy couple was entertained by movie stars Gary Cooper (and his wife Rocky) and Ingrid Bergman, courting him for the hot roles of Robert Jordan and Maria that they would soon play in the movie version of *For Whom the Bell Tolls*. The new couple's fame was growing to colossal proportions; they were followed by press and pretenders along every single beach stroll, mountain trek, and tiki bar that they would visit on the islands.[4] When their greeters put eighteen leis on his neck and photographers and drunken fans accosted him at the airport, Ernest protested that it was too much: "I had never had no filthy Christed flowers around my neck before and the next son of a bitch who touches me I am going to cool him and what a dung heap we came to and by Christ if anybody else says aloha to me I am going to spit back in his mouth."[5] After touring Oahu and the Big Island, the Hemingways caught the island-hopping Pan Am plane *China Clipper* to Midway, Wake Island, Guam, Manila, and Hong Kong.

For three months Martha plunged herself into the mad pursuit of the news on the front lines while Ernest conducted his own kind of "research," cavorting and carousing with other journalists, diplomats, officers, and businessmen at the hotel bar. The bedlam and debaucheries of these days reappeared in semi-autobiographical form in the novel *Islands in the Stream* when protagonist Thomas Hudson boasts to the Cuban courtesan Honest Lil of his days in China mingling with Chinese millionaires, yet he was feeling very *frustrado*, "mean and disgusted" with the gross inequities and destructive path of war, until one of the millionaires took pity on him and sent him a present: three tall, smooth, and beautiful Chinese prostitutes whom he enjoyed one evening in a foursome in his hotel room in Hong Kong.[6]

Following the war across China and as far west as Lashio, Burma, Martha and Ernest endured grueling conditions while meeting with generals, officials, diplomats, and dignitaries in between, including legendary general Chiang Kai-shek and his wife Madame Chiang. Meanwhile in April, Hitler's forces invaded Yugoslavia and Greece, reinforcing those of Mussolini, who had been beaten back by the Greeks. Returning the way they came in mid-May by plane, train, and motorcar, Ernest and Martha crossed the Pacific and the United States, laying over in San Francisco, New York, and Washington, and stopping in Key West to collect the *Pilar*, Patrick, and Gregory, whom Martha would escort to Havana via Miami by plane while Ernest met Joe Russell to make the crossing by sea to Cuba at the end of the first week of June.

As the Hemingways descended from New York to Havana, they stopped in at the Office of Naval Intelligence for debriefing and advised Secretary of the Treasury Henry Morgenthau that among other things the United States had to keep an eye on the tensions between Communists and Nationalists in Beijing. The Washington visit led some to speculate that the Hemingways had been gathering intelligence for America in a more official capacity.[7] In articles appearing subsequently in *Collier's*, Martha wrote beautifully about the anger and helplessness she had felt in China: "I felt it was pure doom to be Chinese. I longed to escape from what I escaped into: the age of old misery, filth, hopelessness, and my own claustrophobia inside that enormous country," and to a friend, she confessed her indignation for the British Empire's actions in China.[8]

• • • • •

World War II spread its appendages around all facets of human affairs. With everything at stake, war powers amped up to collect every shard and crumb in mobilization against the enemy, insisting it would take every father, mother, daughter, and son to achieve victory against the Nazis. When the United States declared war on the Axis powers, Batista's government pledged Cuban allegiance to the cause. Yet among the thousands that had fled to Cuba from the Spanish Civil War were many fascist Falangist elements that had triumphed over the Loyalists due to Hitler's and Mussolini's support.[9] So American and Cuban officials were justifiably concerned that these elements loyal to the Axis could sabotage Allied interests.

Ernest had recently written the introduction to an anthology of short stories, *Men at War.* Eager to participate in the conflicts he had just been touting in the anthology, the author assured American ambassador to Cuba, Spruille Braden, that he could assemble his network of contacts from the Spanish Civil War to weed out Falangists on the island, frustrate Axis missions, and arrest any Nazis operating in their hemisphere. Enjoying the support of both American and Cuban governments, the writer "enlisted a bizarre combination of Spaniards: some bar tenders; a few wharf rats; some priests; assorted exiled counts and dukes; several Loyalists and Francistas. He built up an excellent organization and did an A-One job."[10] Ernest expressively dubbed the spy cell the "Crook Factory," but whether its informants were behind any of the numerous round-ups and convictions of suspected Axis agents in America and Cuba that year remains classified.

Observing his anti-fascist campaigns in Spain and speculating on his Communist sympathies, Soviet agents approached Ernest in

Havana at the Floridita at least twice in September 1942, but nothing, other than inebriation, resulted from these meetings.[11] Yet the author's "premature fascism" with Loyalist Spain, the Soviet "friends" and spies who pursued him, his recent travels to Communist China, and his rather unconventional involvement in a renegade intelligence ring raised eyebrows among several agents of the FBI in Havana, toward whom the writer had friskily expressed his disgust.[12] These agents opened a case on the author and reported his every move to the director of "the Bureau" at that time, J. Edgar Hoover.

Hoover read these reports with indulgent good humor. But in his own handwriting, at the bottom of the report, the director concluded that Ernest had been an impassioned author with a grand imagination, not a traitor to his country.[13] Hoover advised his agents to stand down, for it was only natural for a courageous and inventive artist like Ernest Hemingway to loathe their dull and dutiful kind.[14] Thus clearing his name as a loyal American, the director nonetheless advised his agents "to discuss diplomatically with Ambassador Braden the disadvantages" of allowing a civilian, outside the purview of government authority and with a wild imagination, to head up such a mission.[15] Though Ernest had hoped to be a spy, the Soviet NKVD (precursor of the KGB), the Office of Strategic Services, and the Federal Bureau of Investigation all seemed to conclude that he never lived up to his full potential.

• • • • •

Understanding that supply lines would determine the outcome of the war, German high officials, studying Allied sources of fuel and metal, seized momentum and took to the offensive to cut them off. Admiral Doenitz sent German U-boats to attack key fuel sources in the Caribbean during Operation Drumbeat: mines in Guyana, refineries in Aruba, New Orleans, and Houston, oil tankers as they emerged from Venezuela. From February to November of 1942, the Germans sank over 400 ships worldwide, and 263 of these were in the Caribbean.[16] At the entryway to the Caribbean Sea and Gulf Stream leading to the Panama Canal, Cuba occupied a strategic position for controlling naval traffic. On March 12, a German submarine sent tremors across the skins of island residents when it sank the *Olga*, a freighter, and the *Texan*, an oil tanker, in the narrows between Wolf Lighthouse and Cayo Confites, very near Cayo Romano.[17] With much of its fleet destroyed by the Japanese Pearl Harbor bombing or engaged in the aftermath in the Pacific, the United States Navy found itself outgunned and ill prepared to defend against the imminent threat of German torpedo boats in Caribbean waters, so it called for yachtsmen and small boat owners to arm themselves as auxiliaries in the fight, offering federal funds for those who joined up.[18]

As one of the first yachtsmen to respond, Ernest received five hundred dollars per month from the US Navy for his reconnaissance. The money equipped the *Pilar* with depth charges and machine guns (and bait and alcohol), transforming his boat into an emergency defense vessel that would patrol the Cuban coast.[19] He named this mission "Operation Friendless," after his favorite cat. Just after the operation began, his sons, released from school for summer vacation, rushed down to Cuba to join their father and his crew of friends, a band of rag-tag sailors and would-be warriors on a real war mission against the Nazis: pursuing U-boats in the *cayos* while fishing, swimming, and sunning in the endangered straits of tropical paradise. During the war when gasoline was in short supply and strictly rationed to others, Ernest received tanks of gasoline, discreetly delivered from the US embassy to his home where they were routinely buried by drunken Basques in his backyard.[20] The month that Ernest began his mission, the first gas chamber was operational at Auschwitz-Birkenau in order to exterminate Gypsies, Sinti, Jews, resistance fighters, and other prisoners of war en masse.

Along for the ride were beefy British polo champion Winston Guest; wild-eyed, balding Spanish Loyalist Roberto Herrera Sotolongo; Basque pelota player Francisco Ibarlucia, or "Paxchi"; such seamen as marine-gunner Don Saxon, "Sinbad" Juan Duñabeitia, ribald priest Don Andrés, Cuban first mate Gregorio Fuentes, communication specialist (from the American embassy) John Saxon, Catalan barkeep Fernando Mesa; and others, like José Regidor and Félix Ermúa, aboard a few weeks but not possessing the stamina to stay with Captain Hemingway until the end.[21]

Armed with machine guns, anti-tank guns, bazookas, hand grenades, and a communication tower, a crack team of Ernesto's closest friends headed directly to the source of the torpedo attack in the crystalline waters between Cayo Guillermo and Santa Maria, between the palms, beneath the sun, and guided by boat captain and tavern owner Augustín Tuerto, "Guincho," who knew the terrain and took the author through the mangroves in the straights near Cayo Francés to the exit point near Nuevitas.[22]

Ernest considered mounting heavy machine guns to the *Pilar* but later recognized this idea as impractical. Instead, his crew would have to lure the "Krauts" to the surface, direct fire at the U-boat's steel hull (to suppress use of their 88 mm deck guns), and move in just close enough for one of his jai alai players to lob a grenade in the conning tower with his special skills.[23] An insane plan, which he pursued with the same wild imagination and delight as he did his childhood adventures in the Walloon woods with his father. Now the son hunted the bad guys with his own children and a passion resembling obsession.

At first praising her husband's bravery, Martha avoided inconvenient questions and accepted an assignment with *Collier's* that summer, taking a two-month hiatus to study the effects of the war on several Caribbean islands. When she returned and found Operation Friendless continuing, Martha departed to New York and Washington, DC. When she was away, he complained of loneliness—he might "die of sadness" without her and without sex: "[Mr. Scrooby] probably will be permanently ruined for disuse."[24] Countering her husband's grumbles, Martha reaffirmed a necessity for fulfillment and invited him to celebrate advancements of her career: "Will you be able to come back and celebrate with me? You must be nearly nuts now, in your floating sardine box, with all those souls and all those bodies so close to you. I admire your patience more than I can ever say. You are a disciplined man. I love you Picklepot. Are the childies having fun?"[25]

While Ernest and Martha Hemingway's letters continued to profess their mutual longing, periods of self-imposed exile grew ever more frequent, on assignment, or at sea, with conflict kindling each time they reunited. In their relationship there was intimacy, love, gratitude for their good fortune and the moments they shared together, as well as acute sensibility to each other's personalities, nostalgia, neglect, frustration, and bitterness. Writing him at their home, Martha entreated her husband, who had exiled himself from her on a mission in the *cayos*: he had been married so much and so long that she could not affect him and longed to become like they once were in Madrid or in Milan, unmarried, and happy together.[26] Immersing herself in writing during Ernest's absences at the edge of the sea, Martha finished a novel called *Liana* in June.

Hunkered down near Cayo Confites hunting German submarines with his "crew," Ernest received Martha's manuscript, and between mission reports, mosquito attacks, pig roasts, and poker games, he read by oil lamp and edited it assiduously.[27] Returning it to her, he offered reconciliation: "Let's be friends again. 'Lest we be friends there is nothing. It is not such a long way to go.' Rilke wrote, 'Love consists in this: that two solitudes protect and touch and greet each other.' I haven't protected you good, and touched you little and have been greeting you scoffingly. But I truly respect and admire you very much. And of this date and hour have stopped scoffing, which is the worst of all."[28]

She would integrate his feedback and responded to his note with appreciation and affection: "Bug my dearest, how I long for you now . . . Oh my I love you and oh my I am homesick for you. I want to fix up your beard in beautiful braids like my Assyrian."[29]

When Martha learned during prepublication from her publisher, Charles Scribner, that the Book of the Month Club and Paramount had passed on *Liana*, she wrote her husband defiantly, "In my heart, I always knew it was not destined to be a best-seller."[30] Yet the novel was positively reviewed by the *Washington Post*, the *Nation*, the *New Republic*, the *New Yorker*, and the *New York Herald Tribune*, who respectfully said that Gellhorn was an artist with "splendid sultry grace," who had "come of age" and written a simple story with sensitive reverberations. Its 27,000-copy first printing sold quickly, making it a bestseller despite Martha's misgivings.[31]

Her production and literary victories contrasted roughly with her husband's frustration at his typewriter at this time, one of the least productive of his career, sowing ill feelings between them. He clucked, "You're the writer in the family now, Marty. Let's give Marty a chance. She deserves one." When she responded that it disgusted her to see that he was giving up at the age of forty-four, he fired back bluntly, "So you don't think I can write anymore? . . . Conceited bitch."[32]

Unable to stand the strangling silence of those tropical flowers encircling their Finca that seemed they could swallow cows whole, Martha departed for Europe at the end of September 1943 to follow the war while he stayed on his boat to fulfill his "true mission" of chasing German U-boats.[33] Having seen too many wars up close, he said, he was in no hurry to return to Europe. Martha accused him of being a slob and a phony as well as a drunken scold; in return, he rebuked her ambition, her preference for war, nobility, and history to an idyllic life together in paradise. While Martha chased stories and churned out copy, in addition to the manuscript that she had recently knocked out, she had had enough of his drinking, carousing, his ambivalence to his talent, and his not writing. Soon after she departed during one of countless trips to clear the air, he wrote her during a moment of clarity and sobriety to apologize. "I love you truly, love you always, and never love and never will love anyone else. I know from what you said how thoughtless, egoistic, mean-spirited and unhelpful I have been." He reassured her that, no matter what, he would never be "uncooperative, selfish, or depreciatory about [her] work," which he respected.[34]

"Beloved Bug . . . It happened like a whirlwind; I heard I had a place for Saturday morning at ten . . . I have $2000 expense money in my purse and a wide open field ahead and I will have a very interesting and instructive time." She wrote him after her first flight, "It's great fun to see the world from 250 miles per hour," and reported that during her layover, she had amused herself with the captain, copilot, a young radio engineer, and a scientist from Montana, who were "all solid drinkers and good dancers and very attentive to your wife so I am having a fine, brainless time."[35]

To this he protested that she was "selfish and ambitious" and did "exactly as she wants to do willfully as any spoiled child, always for the noblest motives," while he "had not done a damn thing [he] wanted to do now for well over two years . . . except shoot live pigeons occasionally."[36] To his mother-in-law, he complained of a gut-wrenching loneliness, which felt like he was dying a little every day. His suffragist mother-in-law observed that "men generally can't manage loneliness. Women are better at it, perhaps because traditionally men have gone and women have waited, so we learn from being left from our fairy story times straight throughout lives."[37]

Urging her husband to join her in Europe in a letter dated December 12, 1943, Martha opened up her back hatch and let the remaining bombs fall. If he did not come at once, he would regret it.[38] The following day, she wrote again declaring a "national holiday," for she had received four of his letters in one day, and because these letters outlined his "absolute opposition to leaving Cuba," she promised to respect his decision, but refused to accept his criticism of journalism as a profession.[39]

While Mrs. Hemingway lamented the squandering of his talent, he *was* writing at this time—passages that would become *Islands in the Stream* and *The Old Man and the Sea*. Perhaps contributing most to his unhappiness was the realization that they did not yet meet the murderously exacting standards that he had set for himself and maintained from the beginning.

• • • • •

In his wife's absence, Ernest had begun spending more and more time in the company of an attractive Cuban woman, closer to his age, named Leopoldina Rodríguez. In anticipation of his commissioning as an officer of the US Army in February, Bumby requested papers from his father to certify his citizenship. Promising he would attend to it, Ernest invited his son to Finca Vigía and offered Leopoldina as Martha's replacement, a "favorite other mother" and personal chaperone.[40]

Subsequently assigned to special command of a unit of black soldiers during the war, Jack would become an intelligence officer working for the Office of Strategic Services, a precursor to the Central Intelligence Agency. After parachuting with a rod, reel, and flies into occupied France, Lieutenant Bumby crossed paths with Martha Gellhorn in Algiers, while he was on leave and while she was on her way to cover the war in Italy.

Perhaps because of limited access to Cuban sources, caused by strained US-Cuban relations or the difficulty of obtaining certain key interviews in English, none of Hemingway's major American biographers mentions Leopoldina Rodriguez, Carlos Baker being the sole exception. Cuban and Russian biographers, on the other hand, have explored the topic in depth. Interviews with Leopoldina's niece, the Cuban journalist Ilse Bulit, as well as translations of interviews from Spanish-language sources, analyses of Cuban scholars' works, and original documents at the Finca Vigía Museum reveal that Leopoldina Rodriguez was not only Hemingway's longtime friend, confidant, and—in all likelihood—lover, but she was also an important influence in his life and on *Islands in the Stream* and even *The Old Man and the Sea*.

Close Cuban friends of Hemingway's, such as journalist Fernando G. Campoamor, writer Enrique Serpa, doctor José Luis Herrera Sotolongo, accountant Roberto Herrera Sotolongo, and his majordomo René Villarreal remember Leopoldina Rodriguez as a regular presence at the Floridita bar and in Hemingway's life.[41] They describe "Leo" as having had ivory-smooth, olive-colored skin, black hair, a "ship-like" body, and an aversion to unkind words and actions; for this reason they often called her "Leopoldina la Honesta."

In *Islands in the Stream*, Hemingway's character Lil would make "her stately progress to the far end of the bar, speaking to many of the men she passed and smiling at others." She had "a beautiful smile and wonderful dark eyes and lovely black hair," and Floridita regulars "treated her with respect" because "nearly everyone she spoke to had loved her at some time in the last twenty-five years"; they called her "Honest Lil" for her aversion to unkind words and obscene actions.

Lil is the same age as protagonist Thomas Hudson, whose attentive gestures and loving descriptions show his enduring fondness for her. When Lil's hair turns gray at the roots, Hudson buys her hair dye: "When it would begin to show white at the roots along the line of her forehead and along the line of the part, she would ask Thomas Hudson for money to have it fixed and when she came back from having it dyed, it was glossy and natural-looking and lovely as a young girl's hair." Hudson bought the coat Lil wears and adores, which causes her to declare with pride that she could have sold it a "half dozen times," but would not have dreamed of doing so.

Cuban biographer Norberto Fuentes also reports that those who frequented the Floridita remember Leopoldina as a "very elegant, refined, well-educated mulatto" who started going to the bar when "the walls of the place were made of marble." The Floridita's marble walls date such memories to before the 1930s and correspond with Hemingway's description in *Islands in the Stream* of Leo's having frequented the bar for more than twenty-five years. According to Campoamor, Leopoldina often spoke with Hemingway alone for long hours at the Floridita or read his tarot cards there, but their relationship was not limited to the bar; she frequently accompanied Hemingway to sports clubs, stadiums, and boxing rings, as on the occasion when they went to the Palacio de Deportes to see mutual friend Kid Tunero fight against Joe Légon, a Havana favorite, in the company of the Cuban writer Enrique Serpa. Serpa recalled Hemingway attending the event in a state of "deep drunkenness."

Cuban researcher Osmar Mariño Rodríguez interviewed Campoamor on several occasions between 1993 and Campoamor's death in 2001. During one interview, Campoamor took out a picture from his personal collection, where Hemingway appeared with Leopoldina, and remembered attending a baseball game with Hemingway at the Tropical between Almendares and Havana. Afterward they went to Floridita and to the Donoban to see a few friends. Sometimes they visited the avenue along the port and the adjoining neighborhoods where the writer liked to mix with common people. "We always had a hell of a good time on these outings," said Campoamor. "We went to see cockfights, to the Montmartre Casino, to Sloppy Joe's, to the Plaza Hotel, to the Sevilla Hotel, to the Sans Souci Casino, and other places around town."[42]

Hemingway's friend and a Floridita regular, Fernando Campoamor, and bartender, Antonio Meilán, both describe Leopoldina as poor, a "prostitute through need," whom Ernest would often invite either to accompany him on the town or back to his home. Apparently, he also gave her gifts, for "sentimental reasons." In an interview with Russian biographer Yuri Páporov, Serpa affirms that Leopoldina was "one of the easy, attractive luxury women in Havana" at the end of the 1930s and 1940s, who suddenly lacked the means of earning a living another way. Serpa acknowledges that in order to support herself and her son, she was known to accept money from the rich and powerful men of Havana who frequented the Floridita. But he also underlines that it would have been difficult to find another woman with "such a pure and tender spirit as Leopoldina."[43] Hemingway and Leopoldina were kindred spirits, Serpa emphasizes, who had both been unlucky in love, found each other, and formed a pact that gave them reciprocal comfort, affection, and loyalty. It would be misleading to reduce their lasting friendship to a business transaction: "Leopoldina could never attain happiness, but more than with any other, with Hemingway she had known friendship, a comforting, tender, and attentive, and often paternal relationship. She was the only woman allowed to enter the Floridita without an escort, and this small privilege she owed to her friendship with Hemingway."[44]

Ilse Bulit, who lived with her aunt Leopoldina in an apartment that Hemingway rented for them in the 1940s and 1950s, confirms the duration and depth of their relationship, documenting its similarity to the one described in *Islands in the Stream*. In a series of articles she published in the Cuban press and in my own recent interview with her, Bulit describes her memories of this relationship in vivid detail. She reports that Hemingway visited her aunt regularly, gave Leo a regular allowance, and for more than a decade paid the rent of her apartment in the Astral building on Old Havana's Calle Infanta. Born in 1941, Bulit remembers Hemingway's constant presence during her childhood: "Leopoldina, a fine-featured, dark-skinned young lady, became Hemingway's lover for many years. The truth is that he never left her for another woman. Hemingway loved Leopoldina, held her very dear to his heart. He paid for her apartment on Calle Infanta and never abandoned her."

Of course, Leopoldina Rodríguez was not simply a Floridita barfly nor Hemingway's would-be mistress, but a complex woman with her own history, experiences, and desires. Her mother was a maid to a powerful and prosperous Havana family, the Pedrosos, who lived near the Plaza de la Catedral, so Leopoldina enjoyed an education unavailable for most Cubans at that time. Bulit affirms, "Like my grandmother María Ignacia, she knew how to use the cutlery, serve wine for meat or fish, and carry some books on the head at home to show good posture in public." Throughout her life, these advantages were useful to Leopoldina in attracting cultured, financially secure men of influence. Hemingway was but one of these men.

As a young woman in Cuba at the turn of the twentieth century, Leopoldina resourcefully attempted to build a life for herself using the means available to her. At that time, one opportunity for a mixed-race woman graced with beauty was to "try her luck" with a wealthy man of good standing, preferably a Spaniard or a Chinaman. As fate would have it, she became involved with a Cuban of Spanish descent, Alberto Baraqué, who would father her only son, Alberto, Jr. But perhaps because of her race, Leopoldina's lover never legitimized their relationship with a marriage proposal. He did, however, invite her to accompany him to Europe.[45] Although Alberto and Leopoldina had their differences and separated there, Leopoldina did not yet retreat to her native land. Instead, she became the mistress to the famed Falangist leader José Antonio Primo de Rivera, executed by Franco in 1936 as a traitor to the Spanish Republic. José Antonio provided Leopoldina with the means to return to Havana and open her own dress boutique in the center of town, although this business, attempted during the tough economic times of the Great Depression, would later fail. In this context Leopoldina began to frequent the Floridita.

Much like Martha Gellhorn, "Leopoldina la Honesta" was not afraid to tell Ernest what she thought. In addition, they offered each other company and friendship during some of the most difficult days of their later years. They taught each other about the cultures of their origins. They became close friends. They looked after and cared for each other in ways that others did not. Ernest, in his middle age—suffering from writer's block and depression, not seeing eye to eye with his wives—frequented the Floridita, drinking heavily, became Leopoldina's loyal confidant, and gained her perspective.

Leopoldina appears to have influenced the writer's religious practices as well as helped him to understand and appreciate Santería, popular folklore, and other elements of Cuban culture. Campoamor confirms, "Hemingway made himself a part of that world easily enough. Leopoldina and others led him to it. Or perhaps it was a natural affinity since those humble, simple people shared a world of illusions and hopes with Hemingway." He routinely visited the Port, Regla, and Guanabacoa [located between the Finca Vigía and Cojímar], and the Church of Regla, the temple of Yemayá, the goddess of the sea, who is known popularly in Cuba as the "Virgen de Regla."[46] For sailors, the Virgin is a savior who guards their ships after she miraculously appeared on September 8, 1696. Campoamor remembered also that with Hemingway, Leopoldina, and Serpa, he visited El Rincón, where one finds the image of Saint Lazarus.

The long conversations at the Floridita with Leopoldina concerning Santería, like those that occur with Lil in *Islands in the Stream*, might certainly have helped Hemingway to acquire a multicultural view of Afro-Cuban religious practices. In *Islands*, Lil, like her real-life counterpart Leopoldina, has "absolutely blind faith" in the Afro-Cuban religion, and in the Saint of Mariners, La Virgen de Regla, as well as Our Lady of Charity, the Virgen del Cobre. Thomas Hudson admires this faith and tells Lil that she "must keep it." In response, Lil reassures Hudson that the Virgin del Cobre is "looking after" his son Tom "day and night."

In *The Old Man and the Sea*, Santiago respectfully keeps his late wife's pictures of the sacred heart of Jesus and the Virgen del Cobre. He also promises to "say ten Our Fathers and ten Hail Marys" and "make a pilgrimage to the Virgin of Cobre," a typical Cuban tradition, if he catches his fish, a promise foreshadowing the writer's own donation of his Nobel Prize medal to the Virgen del Cobre.

Although one must not confuse fiction with reality, the colorful descriptions in *Islands* might provide scholars with a rare window to the past, an illustration of Leopoldina as seen directly from Hemingway's perspective: "There was this lovely face looking down the bar at him, lovelier all the time as he came closer. Then he was beside her and there was the big body and the rose color was artificial now and there was no mystery about any of it, although it was still a lovely face." When Hudson assures Honest Lil that she looks beautiful, she blushes. "Oh, Tom, I am so big now. I am ashamed." He puts his hand on her great haunches and says, "You're a nice big." She confesses her shame at walking down the bar, but Tom insists, "You do it beautifully. Like a ship." Honest Lil inquires, "How is our friend?" to which Tom reports, "He's fine." When will she be able to see him? Lil asks. Tom exclaims, "Any time. Now?" In this familiar scene at the Floridita, Hudson and Lil seem to be on intimate terms, in a sexual friendship that very probably resembles Hemingway's relationship with Leopoldina. Hemingway underlines their familiarity and intimacy with comedy; the mutual friend to whom they jokingly refer is none other than the protagonist's penis.

Written at a time when Hemingway was struggling with separation from his three sons and the failure of three consecutive marriages, *Islands in the Stream* dramatizes its author's sense of isolation and loss. Protagonist Thomas Hudson, having experienced the tragic deaths of all three of his sons, is comforted by Honest Lil's bringing her Afro-Cuban faith to bear.

To raise Hudson's spirits and to break down his stoic heartache, Lil gently goads Hudson to "break the house record" for most daiquiris consumed in one sitting at El Floridita. After building Hudson's morale with sexual innuendo, happy stories, and alcohol, she transitions to the role of therapist. After drinking and talking for a little while with his confidant, Hudson feels a "little less sad" about *"el mundo entero."* In real life, their lasting relationship appears to have been one of meaningful confidences and sincere friendship as well as emotional and possibly physical affection.

• • • • •

By February 2, 1943, the Sixth German Army surrendered to the Soviets at Stalingrad. Having met with English Prime Minister Winston Churchill, French generals Charles de Gaulle and Henri Giraud in Casablanca, Morocco, President Roosevelt delivered on February 12, 1943, a radio address announcing the Allies' policy of "unconditional surrender," borrowing the phrase from American Civil War general Ulysses S. Grant. On May 15, 1943, the Cuban navy's sub-hunting boat, CS-13, sunk German U-boat 197 off the Muriel

Coast.[47] By the middle of May, the Allies defeated the Germans and Italians in North Africa: a perceptible demonstration of the Allies' ability to topple the Axis war machine, halt plans for world domination, and shift momentum in the war.

By July 25, the Grand Council of Fascism voted out Mussolini, the king ordered his arrest, and the Germans invaded northern and central Italy. In July, American workers completed the Big Inch, a twenty-four-inch-wide pipeline transporting oil from Texas to New York and greatly reducing the need for Caribbean oil during the remainder of the war. In September, SS commandos raided Alpine Campo Imperatore and rescued Mussolini, installing him as the head of state in the "Italian Social Republic," consisting of German-occupied Italian territory.

By the time Italy turned tables to declare war on Germany in mid-October, blood was in the water, and correspondents flooded into London in search of the stories that would define their careers. There, Martha constructed a narrative of Nazi atrocities from interviews with Polish and Dutch refugees in London and stroked faraway Ernest's confidence: "Everyone asks after you; everyone speaks with passion of *The Bell*. Everyone admires you. You are a big hero in England & I only profiteer on the glory & power of your name." She pleaded that there he would be "the darling of all. I so wish you would come . . . I restrain myself from sending you cables saying my dearest Bug please come at once, for fear you'd think I was sick or something and that would be a dirty trick on you. But that is what I would like to do."[48] She pleaded with him to leave the "shaming and silly life" of accepting five hundred dollars a month from the US war fund for bait and alcohol and to join her at the real war.[49] Relenting, he promised to pack up the operation and to join her: "Will organize the house, close down boat, go to N.Y., eat shit, get a journalism job, which I hate more than Joyce would, and be over. Excuse bitterness."[50]

But Ernest's bitterness also hinted at his insincerity, and instead of joining Marty and the war in Europe, he stayed in Cuba to continue hunting submarines. Like Don Quixote, supreme hero of Spanish literature, he had been chasing German U-boats for weeks at a time, always on the verge of capturing a monster across the open sea. For

Jack, Patrick, and Gregory, at twenty, fifteen, and twelve years of age, being invited to this adventure with their father was arguably the best of time of their lives, a golden moment of their childhood, a cherished stretch of time with an exceptionally famous and often absent father, an incomparable and unforgettable expedition that might make up for lost time.

Ernest's exploits hunting submarines with his sons inspired a slightly fictionalized account of similar pursuits in *Islands in the Stream*, depicting similar themes and scenes from the point of view of the protagonist, Thomas Hudson, who has three sons: Tom, David, and Andrew. While one must be careful not to equate fiction with reality, a defining characteristic of Ernest Hemingway's personality and literary production was to do exactly that.

In three acts, the novel unfurls in Bimini, in Cuba, and at sea. In the first act, during a spear-fishing expedition snorkeling along the reef, a hammerhead shark attacks David while his father watches, powerless, the "great height of the fin, the way it turned and swung like a hound on a scent, and the way it knifed forward and still seemed to wobble."[51] Though they save the boy just in time, killing the "son of a bitching" shark with a machine gun, the incident leaves Hudson and his three sons shaken, hearts aching with the realization that they could have lost Davy, their brother and son, so rapidly.

Later, when David hooks a thousand-pound swordfish, he shows courage by battling the beast for hours, only to lose him at the end of the fight. The son accepts his loss and discovers his character in a way that makes father Hudson marvel at him, proud.

Throughout the forties and fifties, Ernest Hemingway had written and rewritten a passage in *Islands* reflecting on the temperaments of his three sons.[52] In the passage, their father, like an oracle, had looked at each one and read his fate. The first son was a happy boy, but in repose, the face betrayed a great sadness. During World War II, this son, who said he was good at fly-fishing but not much else, had parachuted into occupied France with a rod and reel, returned home, and sold fishing supplies, then struggling to find his way, worked as a stockbroker for a time, before returning to the army to support his family.[53] "I think," said Jack, "he saw me as a kind of, well, blah, a nice kid, smart enough, but, let's face it, never going to be a world beater."[54]

Though he was strong as a bear, the father wrote curiously in *Islands* that his second son looked just like an otter. With his small animal quality, he was affectionate, good company, and had a life of his own. This middle son had a Cartesian mind and a sense of justice. "I think in Patrick," said the eldest son, "[father] saw the tremendous intellectual potential."[55] After attending Harvard, Patrick moved to Tanzania, became a big game hunter, a safari organizer, and a conservationist. His wife dying just after his father, Patrick would also later move close to his father's grave in the "wild, open country" of Bozeman, Montana.

Like his father in miniature, wrote Ernest in *Islands*, his third son was a "devil." His volatility and darkness merged and became a deceptive meanness, of which his father and brothers were wary—he was bitched from the very start. Wrote Hemingway: "He was a boy born to be quite wicked who was being very good and he carried his wickedness around with him transmuted into a sort of teasing gaiety. But he was a bad boy and the others knew it and he knew it. He was just being good while his badness grew inside him."[56] The signs he read in his youngest son foretold the roller coaster that lie ahead. "I think," said Jack, "[father] recognized in Gregory so much more of himself, the capacity for good and evil."[57] Initially showing greater promise as an athlete, a hunter, and competitor, the third son turned out to be the biggest disappointment of all. He was "a better boy all the time," his father hoped in a letter when eleven-year-old Gigi had outperformed him, his brothers, and the other competitors at a pigeon shooting tournament at the Cerro Hunting Club. They were all proud when Havana newspapers marveled at "*el popularísimo Gigi . . . el joven fenómeno americano*," and Ernest's buddies had a medal engraved.[58] As a teenager, the third son had typed up a short story on his father's typewriter and entered it in a competition at his private school. He won, but it was later discovered that he had plagiarized it from Turgenev.[59] Ernest Hemingway would eventually depict these events in the story, "I Guess Everything Reminds You of Something."

After attending Saint John's College in Annapolis for a year, Greg dropped out and moved to California where he became a mechanic for Douglas Aircraft, followed Scientologist guru L. Ron Hubbard, and married Shirley Jane Rhodes against his father's wishes. Contributing to the instability in his life were his problems with alcoholism, drug abuse, manic depression, and an increasingly conflicted relationship with his parents. Since he was ten, he had struggled with gender dysphoria, experiencing excitement and liberation while dressing in the undergarments of his father's wives. According to Greg, he never wanted to be a woman, but the desire was inescapable, somehow connected to Pauline and Ernest's abandonment of him, their wish that he be a daughter instead of a son, and his father's adamant quest to establish his virility, without question, at every turn. Signing up for the Eighty-Second Airborne, Greg was soon discharged in shame and checked into an asylum where he received shock therapy. After his father's death, Greg ran off to Africa where he would shoot animals as a form of therapy for three years: "I shot eighteen elephants one month, God save my soul," he wrote in *Papa*. Finally graduating from medical school, Greg would later lose his license due to his alcoholism. Growing rich through the marketing of his father's estate, Greg became Gloria and soon after died in the Miami-Dade Women's Detention Center from cardiac arrest and high blood pressure, complications from a gender reassignment operation, bipolar disorder, and his struggles with addiction.[60]

In *Islands in the Stream*, Hemingway also explored the imagined, or eventual, loss of these sons. Soon after his sons leave Bimini to return to their mother and private schools, Hudson receives the unendurable news that David and Andrew have been killed in an auto accident with their mother near Biarritz (a fictional moment likely inspired by Jane Mason's real accident in Havana with Ernest's sons). This is the first tragedy of *Islands*, whose deep, dark currents explore the mind of a middle-aged artist who has witnessed mass destruction in World War I and Loyalist defeat in Spain, who lost his own father to suicide, who just lost several friends (Joyce, Anderson, and Fitzgerald), and whose family was not far from the horrors of World War II.

The second act of *Islands* opens at the Finca Vigía, where Hudson lies on the floor of his living room where he has made a bed of straw mats to better recover from his forty-four days at sea with his cat Boise and his "desperate hopeless love" offering him his only company.[61] Like Ernest, Thomas has grown a beard and is gaining weight. In his drunken moodiness, he has sent the other servants away, so there is not much food in the house except for some eggs and bananas, which his servant Mario (fictional equivalent of René Villarreal) frets superstitiously might be fatal when eaten with alcohol.[62] "I know that you care a lot for me *muchacho*. Gracias," Ernest assures the "Cuban son."[63]

Having recently learned that firstborn son, Tom, was killed in combat, Hudson drinks whiskey and water and converses with his cat while he reads letters crossly from Tom's mother, Ginny Watson, his first wife, whom he still deeply loves. Ginny is no longer with him, for she is at the war, volunteering for the USO. Recruited to hunt subs in a "Hooligan Navy," Hudson is exhausted by his own obsessive pursuit of German U-boats during the interminable patrols he imposes upon himself, running with his crew as far as his failing body will allow, all along the Cuban coast. Between missions, Hudson collapses and convalesces at his Finca and in the Floridita bar, finding some consolation in his exchanges with cats, servants, and the other drunks who make jokes and pull pranks along the bar, and in the company of a courtesan whom everyone knew as "Honest Lil."

Still in uniform, Hudson's first wife, Ginny, flies into Havana at the end of the second act of the novel and steals the thunder of Honesta and her man, or mark, for the evening. Though Hudson is quite drunk, he and his wife make love, and afterward, she drops a depth charge on his heart: his last remaining son has been killed in the war.

• • • • •

At this time, the Finca Vigía was full of servants, a chauffeur, a butler, and a gardener, even though most of the Cubans occupying surrounding houses had trouble simply putting food on the table. As an affluent foreigner living in Cuba, Hemingway was also aware of the radical disparity between the island's classes. In one excerpt of *Islands in the Stream*, the author, between sub patrols, describes his habitual drive from his house to the Cojímar port when he passed through Havana's slums with Cuba "close on either side":

> This was the part he did not like on the road into town. This was really the part he carried the drink for. I drink against poverty, dirt, four-hundred-year-old dust, the nose-snot of children, cracked palm fronts, roofs made from hammered tins, the shuffle of untreated syphilis, sewage in the old beds of brooks, lice on the bare necks of infested poultry, scale on the backs of old men's necks, the smell of old women, and the full-blast radio, he thought. It is a hell of a thing to do. I ought to look at it closely and do something about it. Instead you have your drink the way they carried smelling salts in the old days.[64]

Rather than do something about it, Hudson drinks to make it go away, and in a chapter of *Hemingway à Cuba*, French literary critic Gérard de Cortanze cites the passage above to emphasize the gap between Ernest's luxury and *une démi-siècle de la réalité de la misère cubaine.*[65] Citing Robert Harling's 1950s *London Sunday Times* article that describes the squalor of Hemingway's Cuba, Cortanze notes that fifty years later, nothing has changed about these neighborhoods below the Finca Vigía: the same distress, sadness, dirtiness, hammered tin roofs, sickness, emaciated dogs, lack of food and water, complete nakedness, stranded like one of Hemingway's islands in the stream.

During more than half of a century of US blockade, Democrats and Republicans alike supported the prohibition of basic materials, food, and medicine, for adults and for children. "But back to the Finca," quips Cortanze. Tranquility reigned on the Finca . . . where there was no hint of this noise and unpleasantness, only palm trees, flowers, orchids, hibiscus, jasmine, lovingly chosen by American writers turned housewives.

The real story is perhaps not Cortanze's author-as-careless-gringo-tourist, or the counterpoint that Hemingway sought to lift up the common Cuban man, but a complex combination of the two. In navigating that situation for itself, Hemingway's work from this time asks an important question: Are people bound by their roots, or can they venture to understand and connect with others, regardless of the mores and mandates stipulated by their origins, customs, governments, stereotypes, races, and creeds? Hemingway's relevance today owes much to his attempts to answer that question through his innovatively empirical and intuitive writing, through intrepid and intriguing travels, and through his intoxicating spirit of curiosity and *fraternité*, which is just as fitting as it ever was.

While wife Martha repeatedly and exasperatedly questioned the utility of expeditions resulting only in an absent husband, endless goose chases, bronzed faces, and rum hangovers, Fidel Castro seemed remarkably to have believed in the effort. At a surreal ceremony at the Finca Vigía in 2003, which included American senators and Cuban generals attempting to use Ernest Hemingway as the scissors that might cut the ribbon on Cold War itself, an aging Fidel surprised everyone by appearing out of nowhere and insisting that one "should not believe that the attempt to catch the submarine was fiction. Anyone who is familiar with the psychology of the writer, his history and his life knows that it is not fiction he writes." Roberto Herrera Sotolongo provided another point of view: "Included in the crew, I was receiving seventy-eight dollars per month. There were no German submarines. We fished the straits but didn't find anything. We fished, studied the coral reefs, played dominos and poker. Papa didn't like playing. Instead he read, sometimes wrote, and told us about the stories he was working on."[66]

As the Germans were preparing to invade Hungary, Martha returned in March 1944 from the European theater, determined to "blast [Ernest] loose from Cuba" and persuade him to join her in covering the war. She discovered that he had put on weight and grown a long salt-and-pepper submariner's beard, protruding like an anvil from his chin. Reunited at long last, they were ecstatic at first, but emotional wounds left too long unattended soon festered.

A long-simmering bouillabaisse of injury and resentment bubbled over, resulting in numerous scoldings.[67] During their reunion, there were public humiliations and occasional blows, such as the evening that

Ernest attacked his wife for cutting corners with their servants' Christmas presents and left her stranded on the side of the road. Another evening pickled with alcohol, Ernest backhanded Martha when she was trying to drive him home—so she responded to the affront by driving his Lincoln through a ditch and into a tree, leaving him to think about what he had done while she continued home on foot.[68]

Soon after they arrived together in New York, and Ernest announced to his wife that he had indeed decided to cover the war—but rather than accompanying her so she could build her career, he would be serving as her replacement at *Collier's*.[69] Spite, said Martha later, had inspired him to steal her assignment and a job at a magazine that had been hers alone since 1937. Bumping her from the manifest of a Royal Air Force plane that would have taken her back across the Atlantic to the war, he had effectively blocked her from reporting on it in any capacity. He crossed the ocean on this airplane without her and arrived in London, leaping headlong back into his celebrity status. He produced a scene wherever he went, where hangers-on became his entourage, including would-be writers and adventurers, like kid brother Leicester, who on a crew that included Irvin Shaw had come to create a documentary on the war, trying to become a reporter just like brother Ernie.[70]

During the transatlantic flight, Ernest discovered a new perspective concerning his marriage. In October, he wrote to Max: "I got sort of cured of Marty [by] flying. Everything sort of took on its proper proportion. Then after we were on the ground I never thought of her at all. Funny how it should take one war [Spanish Civil War] to start a woman in your damn heart and another to finish her. Bad luck. But you find good people in a war. Never fails."[71]

Furious with her husband for stealing her assignment with *Collier's* and her means of transport, Martha resolved to find a way across the Atlantic and return to the war as soon as she could. Two weeks later, she was able only to secure passage on a Norweigian freighter loaded with dynamite—a harrowing voyage in seas teeming with German U-boats—as her anger and humiliation attained new heights.

CHAPTER 8

Hemingway Liberates the Ritz Hotel Bar and Pursues the Third Reich (1944)

• • • • •

Like Martha Gellhorn, Mary Welsh Monks was a lady as well as a war correspondent who wore her femininity and good looks conspicuously in the male-dominated profession. The daughter of a lumberjack from Minnesota, Mary was based in London, reporting regularly for the *Daily Mail* and writing features for *Time* magazine. One day in the press cafeteria, she appeared in a skintight sweater that accentuated her breasts and aroused the boys. It had gotten so hot in there, she explained in her tell-all memoir, *How It Was*, that she had been obliged to remove the jacket of her press uniform.[1] Ever since her mother had tried to "harness" her into one at the age of twelve or thirteen, she had not owned a bra.[2] "God Bless the machine that knit that sweater," announced friend Irvin Shaw when he saw Mary's nipples protruding, and he predicted that she would soon attract a swarm of admirers. Sure enough, as the fellows trickled into lunch, they complimented, "Nice sweater!" "The warmth does bring things out, doesn't it?" and so on, as they passed their table. Amidst this herd of horny stags appeared bright-eyed Ernest Hemingway, nudging Shaw to introduce him to his lady friend.

"Above the great, bushy, brindled beard, his eyes were beautiful," Mary thought, "lively and perceiving and friendly." His voice struck her as "younger and more eager than he looked," yet she sensed an "air of solitude about him, loneliness perhaps."[3] The pair made a date for lunch. Later inviting himself into the room Welsh shared with Connie Ernst, Ernest subsequently disenchanted Mary when he demonstrated to them that he was not nearly as interesting to converse with as he was to read or read about. Though Welsh hinted that he take leave by indicating that she had to get up early the next day, Ernest sprawled across their twin beds and whined about his overbearing mother who had never forgiven him for not getting killed during World War I, had never cooked, had bought fifty-dollar hats at Marshall Field's, and had forced him to accompany his prudish sister, Marcelline, when she could not had get a date to the prom on her own.[4]

Although she was still married to her second husband, Noel Monks, an Australian reporter, inspiredly following conflicts to Ethiopia, Spain, France, England, Italy, Egypt, Papua New Guinea, Korea, and Malaysia, their marriage was perhaps already on the rocks as she seemed to be dating several other men. During their third encounter, Ernest shocked her with the declaration of his intention to marry her, and Welsh was repelled initially by his personality and his premature declarations of matrimony.[5] Mary's roommate wondered how she could be so "tough on him" and encouraged Mary to give him a chance: he seemed so lonely, she said, and after all, a gal did not get a chance to marry a guy like that every day. "He's too big," replied Mary, "thinking both stature and status."[6]

• • • • •

When the photographer Robert Capa heard that his buddy from the Spanish Civil War was in London, he decided to celebrate with a party at his flat in Belgrave Square: "I bought a fish bowl, a case of champagne, some brandy, and a half-dozen fresh peaches. I soaked the peaches in the brandy, poured the champagne over them, and everything was ready. At four in the morning, we reached the peaches. The bottles were empty, the fish bowl dry."[7] Returning from Capa's party, Ernest's automobile hit a water tank. When the call came just before dawn, Capa and his girlfriend rushed to the hospital.

"After forty-eight little stitches, Papa's head looked better than new," Capa remembered fondly, years later.[8] When Papa turned his back to the merry couple to submit to a weigh-in from an attendant nurse, Capa's girlfriend, Pinkie, lifted his surgical gown while Capa snapped a photograph and snickered at the writer's glorious buttocks.[9] Receiving visits from his gang, he disobeyed doctor's orders, drinking in the hospital and hiding bottles beneath his bed. Papa would be required, all kidding aside, to stay in the Saint George's hospital for several days and would complain of severe headaches for months after. Sensationalizing the event, the news mistakenly reported him dead.

When at last Martha arrived distressed but alive in London, she checked into the Dorchester Hotel where her husband was staying. Hearing that he had been in an accident, she tracked him to his hospital room where she found him with his stitched head wrapped in a turban and emptied bottles of whiskey and champagne beneath his bed. Infuriated by his enjoyment and indifference to her ordeal, Martha informed him that they were "through, absolutely finished" and walked out.[10] Walking out on Ernest Hemingway was the one thing that a woman, particularly a wife, should not do. Spurred by his feud with Martha, Ernest neglected his health and put himself in harm's way, following the war with frenzied energy while pursuing his romance with Mary Welsh from June to December of 1944.

To cover the invasion of Normandy, Ernest boarded a transport ship, *Dorothea L. Dix*, on June 6, then a landing craft, *Empire Anvil*, but awash amidst the waves while artillery blasts shook the smoldering earth, he was not permitted to go ashore, allegedly, so he returned instead to Mary Welsh's bed in the Dorchester Hotel, causing Martha to fume as she left for the front: "I'm leaving for Italy . . . I came to see the war, not live at the Dorchester."[11] In contrast with her soon-to-be ex-husband, Martha came ashore with the troops to cover the Allied invasion of occupied France as well as report on the liberation of concentration camps like Dachau and Auschwitz. Not to be outdone, Ernest exploited his celebrity status at the end of June to procure invitations from Royal Air Force crews flying missions over the English Channel to repel German V-1s, the "buzz bombs" that had been attacking Portsmouth and London since the middle of the month; he also appeared in boxing gear, shirtless, and with a full beard, shadow boxing in a feature for *Look* magazine.

Meanwhile, the Polish Resistance was putting up an inspiring fight against Hitler's forces and calling for Soviet and American intervention. While Allied forces air-dropped supplies during house-to-house fighting, the Soviet army (only twenty miles away from the battle) abandoned the Poles in their hour of need. It was to become one of the great ignominies of the war. During the uprising, Hitler ordered the complete destruction of Warsaw: thus 80–90 percent of its buildings, artworks, and books were destroyed or stolen by German troops. By the beginning of September, the last of the resistance fighters were killed or captured and sent to concentration camps.

During the liberation of France, Ernest took command of a ragtag band of ten resistance fighters from the village of Rambouillet (just outside of Paris). Present on August 19 during the liberation of Paris, he had "liberated" a German motorcycle and sidecar for his personal use (and reopened his still-healing skull by crashing it into an anti-tank gun) and also "liberated" the Ritz Hotel—and bar—where he requisitioned a large room and proceeded to *faire la fête*, allegedly ordering sixty dry martinis for his rowdy company of adventurers.[12] One reviewer, David Hendricks, put it well: "During the war, Hemingway was good at being Hemingway."[13]

For violating the Geneva Convention's rules for noncombatant journalists, Ernest would have to face a military tribunal in October.[14] Lying under oath, he "beat the rap" to protect himself and Colonel David Bruce by swearing to Colonel Park, who convened the hearing, that he only acted in an advisory capacity.[15] In August, Ernest arranged a transfer from General Patton's Third Army to the First and attached to the Fourth Infantry Division's Twenty-Second Infantry Regiment, commanded by Colonel Charles "Buck" Lanham, who became a lifetime friend. In September the Germans began to launch their long-range missile, the V-2, at targets in London, continuing bombardments there, in Liège, and in Antwerp until March 27, 1945.

• • • • •

On October 17 and 18, a category-four hurricane, with gusts up to 160 miles per hour, struck Pinar del Río, Havana, and Miami, killing three hundred people and causing $10 million in damage. Luckily, René Villarreal was on hand at the Finca Vigía to protect valuable works of art, to place empty buckets about the house when the roof sprang leaks, and to attend to the clean-up after the storm. Miraculously, Gregorio Fuentes defended the *Pilar* in Cojímar harbor, though the hurricane had thrown many from the Cuban navy, merchant marine, and private ships into the streets of Havana, or to the bottom of the harbor.[16]

Prevented by the constitution from running for reelection, Batista emptied the coffers of the treasury when his party lost and went into self-imposed exile. So friendly was the general with American interests that he was welcomed in the United States and spent eight years between his home in Daytona Beach, Florida, and his room at the Waldorf-Astoria Hotel in New York. Divorcing his first wife, Elisa, in 1945, he married his mistress, Marta Fernández, in another changing of the guard.[17] His political career was far from finished: not only would his influence continue behind the scenes, but he would also return to Cuba and the forefront of its politics, running again in the general election and staging a coup in 1952. When a reporter asked him as he returned to power why he had spent so much time in the United States, Batista would respond: "I just felt safer there."[18]

• • • • •

Jack Hemingway was wounded and captured by the German army in the Vosges Mountains on October 28 and interned in a POW camp till the end of the war, where he would lose seventy pounds.[19] By November 7, 1944, Franklin D. Roosevelt, the president in a wheelchair, had been elected to an unprecedented fourth term. That same year, Fidel Castro was named Cuba's best high school athlete. He had been born the illegitimate son of an immigrant from Galicia who owned a sugar plantation in Holguín of 23,000 acres.

During the war, Hemingway produced several articles for *Collier's* that propagated his fame, such as "London Fights Robots," "Voyage to Victory," "Battle for Paris," and "How We Came to Paris." "Surfing" the highs and lows of undiagnosed mania and depression, Ernest was "by turns brave, gentle, obsessive, foolhardy, loving and brutal," pushing his body to the limit to prove to his ex-wife, his mother, himself, and newspapers what he could do—despite being in his mid-forties and suffering from pneumonia, memory loss, and severe headaches in freezing temperatures, harsh conditions, and recurring accidents resulting in several concussions.[20]

After reattaching himself to the Twenty-Second Regiment, Ernest accompanied Colonel Lanham during the action called Hürtgenwald, which bore witness to some of the deadliest battles of war, such as the Battle of Hürtgen Forest, where Allied troops chased the German retreat, pounding heavily fortified defensive positions in the woods, and suffering heavy losses when Axis powers seized the element of surprise and launched the infamous counterattack at the end of December that drove a stake between the First and Third Armies, known as the Battle of the Bulge, in the Forest of the Ardennes. Approximately 140,000 Allied troops were killed during these operations. During these campaigns, it seems likely that Ernest again violated the Geneva Convention—on numerous occasions—by firing upon and killing enemy soldiers, though the exact number is a matter of controversy.[21] In a letter to Charles Scribner, the author asserted that he killed 122, including "a very snotting SS kraut," whom he first interrogated: "And how do you like it *now*, Gentlemen?"[22]

Ernest acquired several souvenirs from the German soldiers, such as his collection of Nazi daggers, on display at the Finca Vigía Museum today.[23] One was a battle trophy appearing in many photographs afterward: a standard-issue leather belt whose buckle bore the inscription *"Gott Mit Uns"* ("God With Us"), referencing Isaiah 7:14 and the battle cry of the Roman Empire, taken up by the Teutonic Order, by Gustavus Adolphus, and made a part of Frederick I's coat of arms in the Kingdom of Prussia, the bedrock of the German Empire.[24] Though the dead German's belt was too big for his waist, the writer wore it above his belt loops throughout his postwar years.

Evidencing Hemingway's obsessive study of war are the shelves at the Finca Vigía, full of books on strategy and military history. He also had a 16 mm projector and would hold private screenings of movies and documentaries (mostly boxing). Once Hemingway managed to get the complete *Victory at Sea* series, which recorded the actions of the US Navy during the victories in the Pacific against the Japanese. He ran them repeatedly, telling the projectionist to stop the film at certain frames. "I doubt this scene will appear in all the prints of *Victory at Sea*," Hemingway said.

"Boys," asked Father Andrés once, "why do you keep stopping the film at that wretched scene?"

"Because we have sworn to kill that guy whenever we find him," explained Dr. Herrera Sotolongo, "and Ernest wants to remember his face well."[25]

In the favored scene, on one of the small barren islands of the Pacific the Marines have just won a victory and Japanese resistance is almost nil. The Japanese are forced to come out of their blockhouse. Outside, an American marine sergeant holding a flame thrower calmly waits for the Japanese soldiers. One by one as they come out he executes them, burning them alive. Their bodies swell as they burn. The film was shot behind the sergeant; every so often he turns around and smiles at the camera.

In a barrage of gushy, forlorn letters from the front of World War II, Papa courted his newest conquest, "beloved" Mary Welsh, promising to take her to a Cuban paradise when the fighting was through, and he returned intermittently to visit her in their room at the Ritz Hotel in Paris: "My Dearest Small Friend, I am just happy and purring like an old jungle beast because I love you and you love me . . . I loved you in the night when I was awake and early in the morning when I was not quite awake and remembered you and how lovely you are . . . and how much fun jokeing [*sic*] and being together. Pickle I miss you very much. I love you as you well know."[26]

From the Netherlands, Martha had written in November petitioning him for a divorce: "We are honest people, Bug, and this is a no-good silly arrangement. It is not our style . . . I think it would be best for you to get this finished with me."[27] Before returning from the Siegfried Line to Mary at the Ritz, Ernest phoned Martha at the Lincoln Hotel to invite her to a "friendly" dinner on Christmas eve at the Twenty-Second command post in Rodenbourg—the opposite of neutral ground. Hoping that Ernest might finally confront the subject of their separation, Martha accepted but did not find her husband alone. Instead, they dined surrounded by buddies from "his" regiment, a band that melted quickly away when drunkenness led to heated scoldings and tears.[28] Six days later, Ernest invited himself to a dinner Martha had planned with William Walton in Luxembourg. Returning from a poker game, Robert Capa found Martha crying. Capa comforted her, inquiring how Ernest could carry on so while in a relationship with another woman.

It was the first time she had heard of Mary Welsh, said Martha, "and I was overjoyed. It meant he *had* to give me a divorce."[29]

"Phone the Ritz and ask for Mary Welsh," Capa belted out while crouching on the floor to count his poker winnings. "I'll tell you what to say." When Ernest came to the phone and "began to vituperate," Capa told Martha to hang up the receiver. "It will be alright now."

To explain the sudden change of heart and his reasons for leaving the front, Ernest wrote his son Patrick to tell him he had been suffering from pneumonia and to complain that Martha had shown great selfishness and disregard for his well-being while he was in the hospital. He was sick and tired of her "Prima-Donna-ism."[30]

In January 1945, the Soviets liberated Warsaw and Auschwitz. From a failed marriage and human atrocities witnessed firsthand, Martha expressed a growing sadness and dejection in her letters during this period, but she began a relationship with a dashing high-ranking officer, James Gavin, and took him to bed as she did several others throughout the war. At thirty-seven years of age, "Slim Jim" was the youngest general to ever command the Eighty-Second Airborne Regiment. "A man must be a very great genius to make up for being such a loathsome human being," wrote Martha to her mother about Ernest with bitterness: she did not wish to hear his name.[31]

Also feeling disappointed and betrayed by his lover was Mary Welsh Monk's husband, Noel, who wrote his wife on February 8, 1945, to bid her farewell and congratulations in a sarcastic letter: "I don't know whether to congratulate you or be sorry for you. I'm sure you must be one of the most envied women in the world. You threw a sprat into the sea and caught yourself a whale. I knew of course there was someone who had caused you to 'lose confidence' in our marriage. But Mister Hemingway . . . I couldn't even match his beard."[32]

From February 13 to 15, Royal and United States Air Forces bombed the city of Dresden, inflicting approximately 25,000 civilian casualties. Bidding farewell to his "Dearest beloved Pickle" in Paris, Ernest left Mary a note before he departed on March 6, 1945. In the letter, he told "Kitten" he loved her and "always will . . . now go to get our life started. Don't let anything bother you. I'm sorry to be so sticky getting off. Will be wonderful when I see you and will be truly faithful to you every minute I am away. In my head and in my body. Your loving husband. Mountain." Was he concerned that she, like Agnes von Kurowsky from the first war, would not follow him home? Or that she would discover he had been unfaithful in her absence? On February 23, following the fourth day of the Battle of Iwo Jima, six marines planted the American flag atop Mount Suribachi, causing Secretary of the Navy James Forrestal to remark that "the raising of that flag . . . means a Marine Corps for the next 500 years," but the battle raged on. By March 26, they had taken the tiny island at the cost of nearly 7,000 American casualties and nearly 20,000 wounded. The Japanese had lost approximately 19,000 of their original force of 21,000.

• • • • •

Hemingway hitched a ride on a bomber bound for New York so that he could do business with his editor and pick up his sons on the way home to Havana. When the plane stopped in London, he deboarded to drop in on Martha, who was laid up with the grippe at the Dorchester Hotel. He informed her that he would grant her divorce but sue her for desertion. Writing wistfully to first wife Hadley, who was now Mrs. Mowrer, he evoked times of old: "Always dearest Katherine Kat get through everything as well as you can and then go to Paris and have a fine life and we will all meet there and eat at some fine restaurant and laugh and make good jokes. All the things wrong with me are getting better."[33]

CHAPTER 9

The Return to the Isle of Paradise with Mrs. Mary Welsh Hemingway (1945–1948)

• • • • •

When Ernest's sons went back to school, their father fell into "black ass" depression and loneliness. With severe headaches continuing, speech slowed and slurred, and memory shot, the effects of the concussion and subsequent neglect of health in the execution of "duty" took their toll. Although he had returned to Cuba determined to get back into writing shape while awaiting Mary's arrival, he was soon carousing with the boys to combat his lonesomeness as well as reigniting his relationship with Leopoldina. On April 28, Mussolini and his mistress Clara Petacci were captured and executed by Italian partisans in Duongo village (near Lake Duomo) while trying to escape to Spain via Switzerland—and strung up on display in Piazzale Loreto in Milan.[1] Two days later, on May 1, 1945, Adolph Hitler and his new bride, Eva Braun, committed suicide in their bunker, as did Reich Minister of Propaganda Paul Joseph Goebbels and his wife, Magda, after distributing cyanide to their six darling children. "Hemingway's Son Is Liberated," the *New York Times* article would declare on May 2, 1945.

The day after Hitler died, Ernest rose early in his villa above Havana and looked over himself in the bathroom mirror. Looking somewhat worse for wear after two world wars, he shaved his sallowing visage as clean as could be, buttoned the fresh-pressed guayabera around a widening midsection, placed his thumb and index finger in his mouth corners, whistled for his driver, Juan, and in the Lincoln Continental convertible headed to the Rancho-Boyeros airport for the much-anticipated arrival of Mary Welsh, a fourth fiancée—pending divorces. He hoped he could succeed in getting her to settle in.[2] Arriving as Ernest had instructed in a thick green press corps uniform, Mary noted the tropical heat, stronger than any summer in her home town of Walker, Minnesota, and, wilting as Ernest gathered her bags, she presented a smile to show her resolve. Mary described her arrival and reunion that day as sweaty, awkward, and out of sorts.[3]

"Sounding like a real-estate agent," he stiffly showed her around the Finca Vigía, explaining how the recent hurricane had stripped the house of its foliage. When he came to one tree, he said, "That's a tamarind" and began to relax. "Exotic tree. Romantic name, don't you think?" But Mary was tense too.

"We could use a little romance," she said brusquely, and "Ernest's face stiffened as though I had slapped it. I could have bitten off my tongue."[4] The awkwardness of their recoupling was amplified when Mary encountered photographs and other mementos of Martha's presence about the house, a reminder that she was number four. From the beginning, Mary expressed uncertainty about giving up her freedom and marrying a husband whose neediness could be oppressive, but she did her best to adapt to the many challenges of her new life in Cuba: new language, new climate, new world of trees, vines, shrubs, and stalks, a new manner of living, with new skills—like fishing and shooting—to learn, and a one leader boss of operations instead of a complex hierarchy like a *Time* magazine, a new focus and activity, yet with no office for herself. Curtailing all correspondence with her former friends and lovers, she decided to make a clean break—"a sharp break, but neat"—and to immerse herself in the universe of Hemingway sons, of aristocrats and insipid wives, and of territorial cats, like Boise.[5]

Though the Finca was expensive to maintain at three thousand dollars per month, battlefield articles and other escapades followed the enormous success of *For Whom the Bell Tolls* on the silver screen and had kept the Hemingway stock high. Ernest reassured his wife that the finances were good, for a producer named Mark Hellinger had just sealed a deal with his lawyer, Speiser, that paid him for the rights to film four short stories at seventy-five thousand dollars apiece and promised him a percentage of the profits.[6] From the short story "The Killers," Hellinger would create a fine film for Universal Pictures starring Ava Gardner and Burt Lancaster, and director Zoltan Korda, who had directed *The Macomber Affair*, a film version of "The Short Happy Life of Francis Macomber," starring Gregory Peck, Joan Bennett, and Robert Preston, and distributed by United Artists.[7] Although he would not publish anything new until 1950, the war reports on Ernest Hemingway would seem to inspire not only Hollywood's investment in his work but also biographical, scholarly, and literary interest. Several studies, such as Edmund Wilson's "The Wound and the Bow," would begin appearing and continue until the present day.

At the Hemingway estate, Mary's first assignment was to learn Spanish, and insisting that she learn the proper continental, Castilian, kind so that she could be understood not only by their Cuban servants but also in other countries, Ernest "wasted no time" finding her a private tutor, named "Pilar."[8] To practice, Ernest introduced Mary to his swankiest friends, "Spanish grandees" like Peps Merito, the Marqués de Valparaíso, Cuban gentry like Mayito Menocal and Elicio Arguelles, and Dr. "Cuco" Kohly and his pretty blonde American wife, Joy.[9] The lunch visits filled with vapid conversation backfired by making Mary miss the stimulating and engaging life of a reporter in the European theater.

Almost a week after her arrival, a celebration erupted in the neighborhood of San Francisco de Paula when the Germans signed an unconditional surrender. While the world declared victory and the war in Europe over, Mary felt nostalgia for her purposeful life in London and the financial independence she once knew there. Ernest's well-intentioned promises to support Mary and her parents made her doubly indebted and dependent. To reciprocate, Mary took command of the author's health and home. She surveyed the villa, noting all that necessitated her attention. In July she wrote enthusiastically to Buck and Pete Lanham: "Stomach flat, headaches gone, appetite healthy."[10]

That summer, as was their custom, Hemingway's sons soon dropped in, with Jack returning rather recently from a POW camp and the two younger half brothers coming shortly after. Though Mary made a gargantuan effort to pack lunches they would appreciate, cheer their exploits, shoot clay pigeons at the Cerro Hunting Club and live birds as they sailed across a bluff, enjoy cockfighting, catch marlin, and tag along on their frenzied adventures, the boys' reactions to their new stepmother took a common theme: while Jack, old enough to drink, was a courteous, generous, and sociable companion at the Floridita and on the tennis court, he did not confuse his relationship with Mary with the affection he felt for Martha, Pauline, or his mother. Gregory confessed that Mary had displaced his "one true love," Marty, and Patrick put it in perspective with the matter-of-fact observation that it was just becoming tiresome for them to adjust to yet another of their father's wives.[11] "They were a boys' club and they did not need me," Mary wrote, feeling estranged when Ernest's sons and "men friends also appeared and turned the house into what seemed to me raucous, rowdy, affectionate boys' dormitory."[12]

"That Ernest was to blame for her troubles," she never questioned, but what made her pause and procrastinate about removing herself was the question of the gravity of her fits and revolt: Were they serious enough to warrant her "busting up a generally good alliance"? Before she could answer that question, there was Papa, "gentle, or thoughtful and loving, and a lilt in the breeze."[13] Into a journal she scribbled these feelings every day, an inner torment that Papa derided by calling them her "Horror Diary."[14] Though, unavoidably, Mary annoyed Ernest when, during her first fishing trip, she made a newbie's mistake of breaking one of his irreplaceable wooden fishing rods; he kept his feelings in check as best he could, and she learned to make herself useful aboard in her auxiliary role.[15]

Relief to the mounting tension in their relationship seemed to come whenever the betrothed couple boarded the *Pilar* and chased their liberty and happiness in the velvety blue waters of a tropical Eden amidst coconut-shaded *cayos*, cool lagoons, and across the sparkling and splendidly untamable sea. The height and seclusion of the *Pilar*'s flying bridge provided Mary with her favorite spot. During one "joyous starlit night" while the sea was only "slightly ruffled, the east breeze cool and gentle," she grabbed her blanket, dragged it up top, and held it there with her feet, standing with their skipper as he steered, murmuring a song that someone had been teaching her to sing along with the *conjunto* of guitars and maracas at the bar.[16]

Soon it would be decided that it was time for "Pickle" to return to

Chicago to obtain her divorce from Noel Monks. In the poor weather, Ernest decided that it would be more prudent for him to drive, but on the old high road to the airport, many trucks had been carrying clay and spilling it onto the asphalt, which when combined with the new rain made the road "greasier than a pancake skillet," such that their Lincoln slid off into an embankment face-first. That impact on June 20 smashed Ernest's tender skull into the rearview mirror, his knee into the dashboard, and his midsection into the steering wheel, breaking four of his ribs. Mary on the other hand went right through the windshield, badly cutting her face. Horrified, the unhappy couple rushed themselves to a nearby clinic and later Dr. Cuco transferred Mary to the hospital where Ernest would finance plastic surgery to decrease her disfigurement. Remaining still under her bandages in an attempt to reduce her scars, she tried to be brave and hide her misery as Vedado mosquitos bred around the clinic that were not only immune to Mercurochrome but had seemingly also developed a taste for it, swarming in hungry schools to feast on her antiseptic.[17] When she recovered, Mary flew home to see her parents and obtain her divorce.

With greater assurance in her position, Mary made a few requests of her own. In her opinion, there were several home improvements that needed to be made (water storage gutters, a cathouse, bigger windows, and better storage for ice). Of importance was his hiring a carpenter so that she could replace pieces that belonged to Martha Gellhorn. Keeping him company in her absence, Buck and Pete Lanham visited the Finca Vigía. Also, while she was away, and to please her upon her return with divorce in hand, Ernest put the staff to work on the improvements his fiancée had ordered. After a joyous return and day of fishing, flourishes, and frozen daiquiris, she and Ernest conducted a top-level conference on programs and projects, and it was determined that Mary's role would be to do the shopping for their food, check the servants' expenditures, supervise the gardeners, but most importantly, keep Ernest's privacy "absolutely intact" when he worked each day "and let nobody get at him."[18]

Once Mary had settled in, Ernest took her for an unsettling luncheon at the Floridita bar and restaurant with his longtime occasional girlfriend and friend Leopoldina Rodriguez, the Cuban courtesan. In her memoirs, Mary recalled that, having seated them, Ernest drifted back to the bar, and Leopoldina said, "You can't appreciate what a wonderful man he is. *Simpático y generoso.*"

"No, but I'll try."

"Everybody loves him. *Todo el mundo.*"

"That's a lot of people."

"Everybody hopes you will be good and sweet to him. Everybody."

"That's nice of them."[19]

Their "catty dialogue" shows the competitive energy produced when Mary and Leopoldina and Ernest were in the room. In it, both women underline their sophistication through the proclamations of their familiarity with French weather—"'No, not as hot as Paris.' 'No. Not as hot as Paris'"[20] In *Islands in the Stream* Ernest also seems to depict Leopoldina's worldliness when the character Lil employs "*au fond,*" a French term unknown to most Cubans, but known to Leopoldina since she had travelled to France.[21]

• • • • •

When James Gavin had been given command of US forces in Berlin in August 1945, Martha Gellhorn joined him there, living in a room on base while covering events in Germany like the Nuremberg trials. She had now become, by her own admission, "*la fille du regiment.*"[22] But learning of Gavin's affair with "that cobra, Marlene Dietrich," Martha departed for the Pacific theater, far from him and other males who prefer "tarts" to women of grit and integrity. "MARTHA GELLHORN SUED FOR DIVORCE," printed the newspapers in Saint Louis on November 22, 1945—the day after their fifth wedding anniversary.[23] For expediency's sake, Ernest had filed it in Cuba where both were still residents, and just in time for Christmas, it came through on December 21 when Martha read in *Time* magazine that her divorce had been granted by Cuban courts.[24]

Earlier that year, Mary had written a letter to her former editors at *Time* to inquire if her old job was still available. Their erratic and volatile relationship caused Mary to waver concerning her decision to marry and to list the reasons why she might leave in her diary: "I wish the hell I were out of here and running my own household and my own life—with no dictatorship . . . This is like being a high-priced whore."[25] On the other hand, there was the villa she commanded, the position beside America's famed writer, and her feelings for him. When her *Time* editors responded and asked if she planned to pursue her earlier inquiry, she telegraphed back: "With much nostalgia for Time . . . I [am] nonetheless eager [to] continue current career of loafer fisherwoman housewife . . . so strike me off the rolls."[26]

After signing an agreement in the morning in a Cuban lawyer's office concerning property rights written in a language she barely understood, seeming to entitle her to "almost nothing" (not even the little antique engagement ring purchased for herself shortly before their wedding day in a Havana shop), Mary accompanied her husband, joking of "drinking hemlock," to the ceremony and to a reception in Vedado where they would toast the union with Ernest's two youngest sons and two dozen friends. "The bride wore a dark scowl," observed Ernest, and she replied that she felt "more like a middle-aged sparring partner than a bride."[27] She was thirty-seven, and Ernest was forty-six years old.

After toasts and countertoasts, all lost themselves in an "increasingly spirited few hours," but returning home Mary and Ernest entangled themselves in an argument in "some misunderstanding of a phrase and a sudden surfacing of underground tensions" that became a "furious earthquake of incrimination and abuse," before Ernest retreated into a deep sleep.[28] In the morning, all was forgiven when Ernest awakened as cheerful and refreshed as ever, and seeing the bags half-packed, he suggested that they never get married again.

Shortly after their wedding, Mary got pregnant; since they had met in London, they had often fantasized about having a daughter, whom Mary fancied calling Bridget, or "Birdie," for Ernest had no girls.

Throughout the spring, Ernest was working hard on a story about the sea. It was emerging organically, and he was allowing it to come. When seventeen-year-old René Villarreal realized that the unexpected exit of the majordomo, Justo, was a golden opportunity, he suddenly became very nervous. René had been running errands for the author ever since he was a boy. "Papa and I spoke about this while we were swimming. I'd feel very happy if you took the majordomo position, but Papa thinks you're very young and doesn't want to give you too much responsibility too soon," Mary told him. "Don't worry, I can give you some pointers."[29] Recently, the Finca Vigía had become home figuratively as well as literally to "Hemingway's Cuban son," whom the author trained to box and nicknamed "Kid Vigía."[30]

During a trial period, René excelled by demonstrating his table-setting, champagne-bucket-icing, and martini-mixing skills; by assuming a boxing stance and ducking when Papa threw a punch; by defending the house from invaders while the Hemingways were away; and during impromptu cat-and-mouse games between the trees at night when Papa, who sent him to lock the front gate, pretended to be an intruder, but in a white-glowing guayabera, failed to sneak up on the boy; so it was decided that René would be the new majordomo—a position he would hold for fourteen years.

Papa called him into his office. "This check is for you. From now on you earn a man's wages," Papa said smiling and looking into the boy's eyes. "Congratulations, René. I expect you will never let me down. It's settled then."[31] With René's help, Mary would be able to see to every detail so that her husband could focus completely on his writing and realize his full potential. Before he left for Ketchum, Idaho, that summer, he had amassed nearly one thousand pages of his Sea book that he was now calling *Islands in the Stream*.[32] On July 27, Gertrude Stein died of cancer at seventy-two years of age, and Alice Toklas subsequently paid for a tomb for her in division 94 of Père Lachaise cemetery in the city of Paris where she had resided for forty-three years; the *New York Times* article reporting her death mentioned Hemingway as an important author who had been influenced by her work.[33]

In anticipation of their upcoming trip, Mary was ignoring Dr. Cuco's orders to cut down on exercise, swimming daily at the Finca Vigía pool, and putting herself into the best shape of her life so that she could dazzle during a grand tour of the West. It would be her last months for a long while in that nimble body, she mused with bittersweet joy for the life inside of her and with eagerness to discover "God's country," beside her husband as he hunted wild animals, and while dining afterward in new dresses confectioned by her village dressmaker from San Francisco de Paula: Joséfa really had to hurry so that her dresses would be finished in time.

Loading up the Lincoln at the Havana docks, they crossed the Gulf Stream and drove "out West" from Miami to Sun Valley Lodge in Ketchum, Idaho, via New Orleans. In New Orleans, they stayed in the French Quarter on Royal Street at a regal hotel of "frayed glories," the Monteleone, lunched extravagantly at Galatoires, and strolled by antique shops, where Ernest spotted a square-cut Brazilian diamond ring.[34] After he purchased it, slid it on her finger, and avowed, "With this ring I pledge my troth," Mary giggled with delight, hugged him, and kissed him behind the counter.

Leaving behind the world of waiters and jackets in black ties, Mrs. Mary Hemingway and her husband "slummed it" in short-order diners and dilapidated motels along the weather-beaten roads of post-war America, and checking into the Mission Motor Court, they bedded down for the evening in Casper, Wyoming, on August 18. In the middle of a dream about the glorious sport of Indian "pig-sticking," which someone in London had told her about, where riders on horseback stabbed wild hogs with beribboned lances, she joined a boisterous hunt but was gored, and writhing on the ground, she began to bleed and to scream.[35] Bloodcurdling screams real and imagined shot her husband out of bed to scour the town for a doctor, only to find that the only one was on a fishing trip hours away. When the ambulance finally arrived, Mary, who was in debilitating pain, was lifted onto a stretcher. Eight or ten hours later, Mary remembered the operating table, her husband's voice beside her, and his rubber-gloved hand milking plasma into her arm. She had suffered a miscarriage during a tubular pregnancy that had caused the tube to burst.

In the morning, Mary awoke, peering through the window of her oxygen tent, and found her husband reading calmly on the other side. Learning from doctors and nurses that he had saved her life, she thanked the angels that he had been with her in her time of trouble, for it seemed that he alone could have saved her, though she had lost the baby. In a letter to Buck Lanham, Ernest explained how he had used surgical skills learned from his father to keep her alive when her tube had burst.[36]

Leaving Mary under the care of devoted nurses in the hospital, Ernest hunted and fished in the prairies, hills, and streams with his three sons. When Mary recovered, she joined the boys in Ketchum. In tribute to the author and to promote their film, Mark Hellinger put on a director's cut premiere at Sun Valley Theater of his "film noir" version of "The Killers." Of all the films produced from Hemingway's literary works, it was the most redeeming, and he told Hellinger so.[37] In December, the Hemingways met with son Patrick, Buck and "Pete" Lanham, and others in New York City, staying at the Sherry-Netherland Hotel for business, then on Gardiners Island, at the eastern tip of Long Island, for hunting, before returning home to Havana. In an interview with the *New York Herald*, he would declare that he had twelve hundred pages of a manuscript written and would need another nine months to finish it. In Cuba for the holidays, Mary pleaded with her husband to allow her to build a tower whose ground floor would be designated as a cat living area and whose upper floor could be a space for Ernest to write and for them to enjoy the sunsets. Giving ground to make her happy, he agreed.

In Key West, Patrick Hemingway suffered a car accident resulting in an undiagnosed concussion. Under duress in Havana preparing for college board examinations, he had a nervous breakdown, sleeping on the lawn after the accident and insulting the staff at the Finca. When the boy collapsed in April 1947, his father stopped writing his Sea book on page 997 to administer twenty-four-hour care and recruited Roberto Herrera Sotolongo, Juan Duñabeitia, and René Villarreal working in shifts to help him. In a fever, Patrick referred to Mary as "Tin Kid," which soon after became the name of the fishing auxiliary boat that his father ordered made for his fourth bride. In the stupor of his illness, Patrick shouted "Black Priest" at Don Andrés when he appeared in his black robes (a name that also stuck thereafter), called René Villarreal his "African brother," and spoke to him only in Spanish.[38] Even Pauline flew down to the Finca Vigía to see and care for her son, whose condition improved under the watchful care of doctors Cuco Kohly and José Luis Herrera Sotolongo, Hemingway's personal physicians and dear friends.

In the United States, Mary had been attending to her own father, who was battling prostate cancer, but she soon returned to find Ernest's second wife in her home. When Pauline stayed throughout the summer, Ernest's second and fourth wives unexpectedly became close friends, and for this Ernest seemed relieved. This unusual situation would nourish Ernest's creative energies and provide inspiration for his fiction, particularly the ménage à trois in the one-thousand-page manuscript he could not return to.[39]

During that same month, May 1947, the ambassador contacted Ernest Hemingway to inform him that the US Army was awarding him a Bronze Star. During a small ceremony at the US embassy on June 14 including a handful of his closest friends, the medal was pinned onto the author's chest to recognize him for acts of valor as a combat correspondent during World War II.[40]

The tacit implication was that he had gone "above and beyond" what would have been generally expected from a journalist, crimes for which his name had already been cleared. Roberto Herrera Sotolongo was present at the ceremony. When Hemingway received the medal, he told Sotolongo that he had invited him not only because he was his friend but also because he felt that as a member of the sub-hunting crew aboard the *Pilar* he deserved to share in the recognition. Receiving the medal, he protested that members of his crew should have also received awards.

Three days after being recognized for his wartime accomplishments, Ernest's "most trusted friend" and editor, Max Perkins, died suddenly of pneumonia.[41] Recent years having brought the loss of mentors and friends, like Sherwood Anderson, James Joyce, F. Scott Fitzgerald, Gertrude Stein, and Perkins, Ernest's weight increased noticeably that summer, and he complained frequently of headaches, a buzzing in his ears, and memory loss. Marital ails continued as his relationship with his fourth wife became increasingly defined by conflict and disillusionment. The joy of the summer was to receive his sons who would be reunited with the Cuban family of Oscar and René Villarreal—handsome photographs depict the boys all sitting on the Capitolio steps sharply dressed and nearly all grown up. Juan the driver would drive them all over the city and out to the country streams to fish for trout and of course to Cojímar and to the hunting club.

The Hemingways pose for a family portrait beside their home in Oak Park, Illinois. The back row from left to right: father Clarence, mother Grace, Ernest, sister Ursula, sister Madelaine ("Sunny"), and sister Marcelline. The front row from left to right: sister Carol and brother Leicester. (Courtesy of Ernest Hemingway Collection. John F. Kennedy Presidential Library and Museum, Boston)

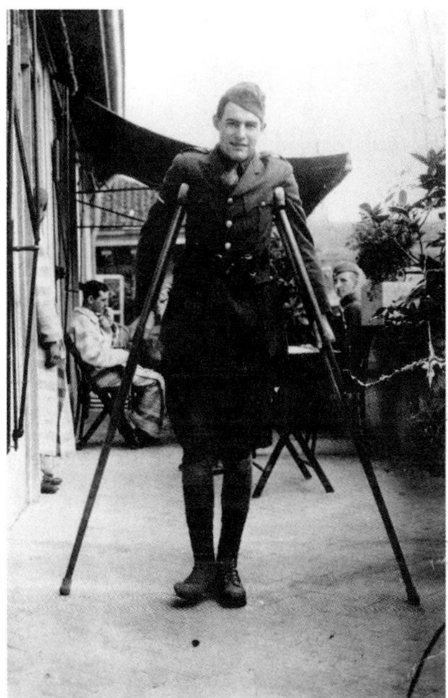

Hemingway walks on crutches at a hospital in Milan after his wounding at the Italian Front. (Courtesy of Ernest Hemingway Collection. John F. Kennedy Presidential Library and Museum, Boston)

Ernest, Hadley, and son "Bumby" (Jack) ski in Schruns, Switzerland. (Courtesy of Ernest Hemingway Collection. John F. Kennedy Presidential Library and Museum, Boston)

Ernest and Pauline Pfeiffer horsing around on their patio in Key West. (Courtesy of Ernest Hemingway Collection. John F. Kennedy Presidential Library and Museum, Boston)

Painter Antonio Gattorno and his wife, Lillian, aboard the *Pilar* with Ernest Hemingway. (Courtesy of Ernest Hemingway Collection. John F. Kennedy Presidential Library and Museum, Boston)

Jane Mason marvels at Hemingway's first mate, Carlos Gutierrez, pictured in a rare moment of repose. (Courtesy of Ernest Hemingway Collection. John F. Kennedy Presidential Library and Museum, Boston)

Ernest and Martha Gellhorn toast each other at the Stork Club in Manhattan. (Courtesy of Ernest Hemingway Collection. John F. Kennedy Presidential Library and Museum, Boston)

Papa stands with his arms around his sons at the Cerro Hunters Club in Boyeros, Cuba. From left to right: Patrick, Jack, Ernest, and Gregory. (Courtesy of Ernest Hemingway Collection. John F. Kennedy Presidential Library and Museum, Boston and Finca Vigía Collection)

Leopoldina Rodríguez and Ernest Hemingway drinking daiquiris at El Floridita Bar. (Courtesy of the Fernando G. Campoamor Collection)

Juan the driver and Mary Hemingway in her yellow Chrysler convertible. (Courtesy of Finca Vigía Collection)

Ernest consults with marlin-fishing experts, Anselmo Hernandez and Gregorio Fuentes, during the filming of *The Old Man and the Sea*. (Courtesy of Ernest Hemingway Collection. John F. Kennedy Presidential Library and Museum, Boston and Finca Vigía Collection)

Adriana Ivancich and Ernest at the Finca Vigía before a party in honor of his Venetian guests. (Courtesy of Finca Vigía Collection)

Hemingway's writing tower and Finca Vigía residence. (Photo by the author)

Ernest shares a happy moment at the Finca Vigía with Cuban writer Fernando G. Campoamor. (Courtesy of Finca Vigía Collection)

At a luncheon sponsored by Hatuey Brewery, an ecstatic Hemingway celebrates with close friends. At this event, he donated his Nobel Prize medal to the *Virgen del Cobre* to underline his debt to the Cuban people. Numbered in the back row are 1) organizer and host, Fernando G. Campoamor; 2) admired boxer, "Kid Tunero"; 3) famed entertainer, *"Bola de Nieve"* (Snowball). (Courtesy of Finca Vigía Collection)

Mary and Ernest enjoy an evening at El Floridita Bar with friends. On the left side of the bar, Roberto Herrera is smoking and speaking. Immediately next to Hemingway, actor Spencer Tracey sits listening in a jacket and tie. (Courtesy of Ernest Hemingway Collection. John F. Kennedy Presidential Library and Museum, Boston and Finca Vigía Collection)

Ernest attends "America" Fuentes's wedding. America was one of the daughters of his first mate, Gregorio Fuentes. (Courtesy of the America Fuentes Collection)

Hemingway casts a dragnet with Cojímar children. (Courtesy of Ernest Hemingway Collection. John F. Kennedy Presidential Library and Museum, Boston and Finca Vigía Collection)

Mary Hemingway took this picture of their Majordomo, René Villarreal, in 1957, when he introduced his fiancée, Elpidia "Fanny" Rodríguez to Ernest at the Finca Vigía. Even though it was a chilly day, Hemingway was wearing shorts, so Mary took the photo from the waist up. (Courtesy of the Villarreal Family Collection)

To promote tourism on the island and meet the author, Fidel Castro and Che Guevarra participate in Hemingway's Marlin-fishing tournament. (Courtesy of Finca Vigía Collection)

Ernest and the Director of the Cuban Institute of Sports, Physical Education, and Recreation present Fidel Castro with trophies after the author's fishing tournament. (Courtesy of Finca Vigía Collection)

A bartender prepares a daiquiri in front of Hemingway's statue at El Floridita Bar. (Franklin Reyes / *Associated Press*)

• • • • •

The Dominican Republic's president and military strongman Rafael Trujillo ruled as dictator from February 1930 to May 1961. "El Jefe" or "El Benefactor," Trujillo was mixed race, like Batista, yet made a reputation through violence against blacks, playing to fear, suspicion, and hatred against Haitian immigrants, accused of stealing crops and cattle from Dominican citizens.[42] Though most every Dominican has some African heritage, identity is often defined through a *blanqueamiento*, a lightening, or self-hatred that denies this very part of their origins. Thus, to gain popularity in October 1937, Trujillo directed his troops to seize all suspicious persons and remedy their "border problem" by murdering approximately 15,000 thousand Haitians with machetes and guns. It was known as the Parsley Massacre, for the people said that Trujillo's men held up a sprig of parsley and asked the accused men to say the name of the plant they held. If the poor sods pronounced the word with the Spanish trill or tap, the soldiers would know they were native Dominicans rather than French-speaking Haitians who pronounced it strangely and deserved thus to be executed on the spot.

By the Spring of 1947, the Caribbean Legion had assembled a small army in Cuba, plotting the overthrow of President Trujillo, preparing to launch their invasion from Cayos Confites and Romano, and benefiting from the open support of the Cuban government under the progressive leadership of Grau San Martín. Though estimates vary, the force was approximately 1,500 strong, composed of Cubans, Spanish Loyalists, American Veterans from World War II, and Dominican exiles, but they did not go to great efforts to dissimulate their intentions and soon attracted international attention.[43] One of the members of the Legion was writer and future president of the Dominican Republic, Juan Bosch, and another was twenty-one-year-old Fidel Castro, and others were Hemingway's friends, Paco Garay and Manolo del Campo Castro.[44]

President Trujillo protested the openness with which money was being contributed to the cause of this invading force assembling near his shores, so he convened an "International Justice Tribunal" to protect his state's sovereignty. A newspaper report from *Diario de la*

Marina implicated Hemingway specifically for his involvement in the plot, implying that he might be a target for the tribunal.[45]

Knowing many Legion members, like former Loyalists Roberto and Dr. José Luis Herrera Sotolongo (who knew Fidel Castro, the university student, at the time), Hemingway supported their cause, contributed money, and attempted to give advice, but felt frustrated by the group's security, logistics, and priorities: "Hemingway gave some money for the Confites thing," said Dr. Herrera Sotolongo, "But we heard he was going to be arrested, so I . . . got him a ticket for Miami . . . We got to the airport just a few minutes before the plane's departure."[46]

It was best for Ernest to take an impromptu trip via Miami to see family on Walloon Lake and to hunt in Sun Valley, without Mary, until the "Confites Affair," as it would later be known, blew over and the cloud of accusations surrounding him dissipated like flurries across the Gulf. Shortly after his name appeared in the newspaper and his plane departed, the arrests began, and police came to the Finca and confiscated his hunting rifles. From afar, Hemingway ordered Gregorio Fuentes to dump the machine guns he kept aboard the *Pilar* into the sea under the cover of night.[47] If Ernest had not had influential friends, such as Paco Garay, a former customs employee, he might not have escaped the affair unscathed.

When Trujillo threatened to attack Cuba to disperse the army and defend his interests, the American government pressured President Grau San Martín to arrest and detain Legion members before the conflict came to a head. Grau San Martín's detractors suggested that his government saw the action in cynically opportunistic terms, for its purposes were impure: if he had started his career as a radical, he had become merely an opportunist in collaboration with Batista, and the invasion of Dominican Republic represented an opportunity to get rid of real radicals. His intention had always been leaving the Legion in the lurch: stranded on Cayo Confites awaiting promised armament or dying in an invasion without adequate support. The coup d'état failed, and President Trujillo ruled the Republic until 1961.

Laying low in a lodge in Ketchum, Idaho, to avoid arrest by authorities back in Havana, Ernest continued writing *Islands in the Stream* in

November and December. With Mary joining, the couple would not return to Cuba until February. For Thanksgiving, Mary travelled to San Francisco to celebrate with her new friend, Pauline Pfeiffer, and two new stepsons, Patrick and Gregory. When his movie producer Mark Hellinger died in December, Ernest sent his condolences and half of his advance, returned to the deceased's family in their time of loss and need, but requested a loan from Scribner's to pay his taxes at the end of the year to the tune of $12,000.[48] Thus, 1947 ended and 1948 began: bittersweetly in the company of good friends, Gary Cooper and Ingrid Bergman, at a New Year's Eve celebration in Trail Creek Cabin.

That winter, Ernest hosted other visitors in Idaho, like Juan Duñabeitia and Roberto Herrera as repayment for their loyalty with Patrick during his sickness. In March, Malcolm Cowley and his son stayed as guests for two weeks while interviewing Hemingway and preparing the article for *Life* magazine and another about Zelda Fitzgerald who died at the age of 48 when a fire engulfed her asylum in Ashville, North Carolina. As spring arrived, it was safe for Ernest to return to Cuba.

One Sunday in April, Papa was reading and relaxing in his favorite chair in a white guayabera, shorts, and moccasins, with René Villarreal, also in casual attire, hanging around the Finca on his day off. To receive the Duke of Windsor, Edward VIII, Ernest's neighbor Frank Steinhart was throwing an extravagant black-tie party, which Mary was attending alone. Steinhart and Mary had both tried to get Papa to attend, but not wishing to waste his Sunday afternoon suffering in formal clothes in the sweltering tropical heat, he refused. The shrill ring of Mary and Steinhart's calls broke the calm of his afternoon several times as they asked Papa to reconsider—yet he politely and firmly declined. When the Duke himself requested an audience with the famous writer, Papa finally surrendered, but he went just as he was, bringing René and his own martini bar, so that he would be able to have a decent drink during the ordeal. Soon the Duke of Winsor and his friends were rolling up their shirtsleeves and asking for martinis "like the one Hemingway was drinking."[49]

During the same month, a twenty-one-year-old young man by the name of Fidel Castro was in Bogotá, Colómbia, to protest against the government of Mariano Ospina Pérez that had assassinated the liberal candidate for president, Jorge Eliécer Gaitán. The protest became a violent riot. At one point, the mob stormed police headquarters and destroyed much of downtown Bogotá. It would later be known as the "Bogotazo," and was said to have given Castro a firsthand education in the power of an angry mob.

In June, the American editor and writer A. E. Hotchner (also known as "Ed" or "Hotch") met Ernest Hemingway in El Floridita after phoning him to arrange a meeting for his article with the dubious title, "The Future of Literature": from that moment, he would become a protégé and a friend helping Ernest to confront his deteriorating health. Hotch also profited significantly from this relationship in numerous articles and books.

In honor of his second son who had recovered and received an acceptance letter to Harvard University in the fall, Ernest organized a ten-day fishing trip in June 1948 to Cay Sal Anguillas and the Bahamas with Patrick, Gregory, Elicio Arguelles, and Mayito Menocal aboard Menocal's large yacht, *Delicias*. That summer, after an extended sea trip with their father for his birthday, Patrick would travel to Europe before starting school. Accompanying them was the young son of a restaurant owner in Cojímar, Manolito, who impressed him by never becoming seasick and who would later serve as inspiration (along with his own sons) for the character of Manolin in *The Old Man and the Sea*.[50]

In August, Ernest's lawyer, Maurice Speiser, would pass away suddenly. Following World War II came the Marshall Plan, the protection of an Israeli state and the resulting tensions, and the Cold War—where Ernest was identified with the code name "Argo" as a potential ally of the Soviets, sympathetic and willing to help their cause. At the end of the summer, he conscripted Roberto Herrera Sotolongo's support to take up a "birthday purse" for his barroom pal and lover, Leopoldina Rodríguez.[51]

CHAPTER 10

A Middle-Aged Author's Obsession with a Young Italian Aristocrat (1947–1951)

• • • • •

Arriving late and fatigued to the port of Havana, Enrique Serpa held the hand of Clara Elena, his twelve-year-old daughter, as he crossed from the road between the parking lot and the docks. Though he was not entirely sure where his group would be, he soon heard the clinking glasses, the gags, and the guffaws, a few yards away. There was then the heavy belly-chuckle and singing of his literary counterpart. Departing for Italy on September 7, Hemingway had organized an impromptu "departure party" for himself before setting sail, and he had invited Serpa. Ernest hugged Enrique so tightly as he arrived to the party that he thought he heard his bones being crushed.[1]

The name of the ship was *Jagiello*, built in Germany, but now manned by a Polish crew. Serpa's daughter, Clara Elena, remembered a folkloric display aboard, including a doll with a Polish dress that she had been admiring. When Hemingway saw her eyeing it, he announced that he would buy it for her. Because the doll was part of the boat's display, it was not for sale. Seeking out his "old friend 'the Commissioner,'" Hemingway insisted that he be allowed to buy it for Serpa's daughter; "for religious reasons," they could not float across the ocean with such a totem aboard. Hemingway's friend, Cuban bureaucrat Paco Garay, offered the captain's assistant "special permission" to sell the doll without tax imposed.[2] In due course, the merry band again got its way, and Hemingway purchased the doll. In their enthusiasm, all the members of the party signed the doll and gave it to Clara Elena. Nearly an adolescent at the time and ambivalent to the fact that there were famous writers in the group, Clara Elena related later that she despised the doll whose charm the group desecrated, its face and limbs marred with the signatures of drunken strangers.[3]

The Hemingways disembarked at Genoa at the end of September. Met by Italian writer, journalist, translator, and critic Fernanda Pivano, who had been translating the manuscript of *Adio alle armi* in 1943, the Hemingways were welcomed in Italy where they made themselves at home for a season in another land.[4] At the beginning of November, the Hemingways moved from the Venice Hotel Gritti to the Locando Cipriani on Tocello Island, quiet, picturesque, yet only a half hour by speedboat from the action. Celebrities in their "*bella macchina americana*," they enjoyed *la dolce vita* as they stayed in Venice, visited Stresa, Como, Bergamo, and retreated into the mountains of Cortina d'Ampezzo to ski.[5] Though Mary had the misfortune of breaking her ankle on the slopes, the Hemingways became friends with four noble families during that trip to Italy (Franchetti, Di Robilant, Kechler, and Ivancich), with whom they would cultivate relationships in succeeding years.[6]

Back in Cuba, on October 10, Carlos Prío Socarrás became the nation's president when Grau San Martín turned over the reins to his protégé, a fellow member of the "Authentic Party," which was by then widely mistrusted due to the era's rampant corruption and gangsterism. Under Prío's administration, Cuba would create the National Bank of Cuba (1948) as well as the Agricultural and Industrial Development Bank (1951) as the government passed several initiatives designed to decentralize Cuba's economy and diversify its agricultural production.[7] Remaining in power until 1952, Prío would come to be known as *el presidente cordial*,[8] for in the midst of criticism, he advocated civility over harsh words and violent protests, but his administration, like that of Grau San Martín, would be clouded by discontent and allegations of corruption.

• • • • •

As the invited guest of the Franchettis one weekend at the beginning of December 1948, Ernest Hemingway was hunting at their lodge near Latisana, to the northeast of Venice. And he met Adriana Ivancich. Apologizing for the Allied bombing of her family home, he offered her a swig of whiskey from his flask.[9] Later, after a rainy day of hunting, he came across her again while she was drying her long dark hair beside an open fire and went barmy as she revealed her beauty, breeding, and other charms. Hemingway wrote afterward that "something like lightning struck at the crossroads in Latisana in the rain," so he met the girl he nicknamed "Black Horse" for lunch at the Gritti Palace soon after his return to Venice.[10] Her dark, long, and luxurious hair, her smooth, olive-brown skin, her intense green eyes, her sharp aquiline nose, her grace, her elegance, her innocence, and her intelligence, came together in the form of a charming girl of just eighteen years of age who bewitched Hemingway, and soon turning fifty, would cause him to behave like a lovestruck buffoon.

F. Scott Fitzgerald had superbly and rather evilly prognosticated that each major work by his friend Ernest Hemingway would require a new wife, as a muse to excite his creative fires. In fact, Ernest pursued a new love, and a new marriage, during each of his novels: Hadley, *A Sun Also Rises*; Pauline, *A Farewell to Arms*; Martha, *For Whom the Bell Tolls*; and Mary, *The Old Man and the Sea*. This time, however, the girl he would fall for and pursue would ultimately reject, perplex, pervert, and hurt him, resulting in a novel expressing his physical and literary impotence.[11]

Although Dora Ivancich cordially received the Hemingways and their offer of friendship, instinct, convention, and perhaps revulsion prohibited her from permitting her daughter to be left alone with that randy old man.[12] Whereas Hemingway's powers of enchantment were significant, they were unable to overcome the societal structure of "*La Torre Bianca*" that engendered and protected such a Venetian jewel. *La torre bianca* (*The White Tower*) became the title of Adriana's memoirs, the focus of which was a fond and sorrowful reflection on her time with Hemingway.

Observing her husband and Adriana, "busily launching a flirtation," Mary wrote later that she was more concerned for Ernest's feelings than her own, for he was weaving a mesh in which he might entangle himself and cause himself pain. In the interim, in the mountains near Cortina, Ernest began a short story about duck hunting in Venice that grew into the novel *Across the River and into the Trees*. While in Italy, he also wrote a nostalgic article about Cuba for *Holiday* magazine called "The Great Blue River."

When Ernest unexpectedly contracted a severe eye infection, doctors feared it would cause damage to his brain and evacuated him to a hospital in Padua where he would spend ten days before returning to Venice. There, they would meet Adriana Ivancich's brother, Gianfranco. Gianfranco had already received an offer of employment in Havana with Sidharma Shipping Agency.[13] Enamored with his sister, Ernest became fond of the boy—who had seen combat during the war—befriended him, and offered him a place to live in their beloved Cuban home.[14]

• • • • •

The article "The Great Blue River" recalled his encounter with *Cosmopolitan* magazine reporter Ed Hotchner, who apologized for being sent down to Havana "on the ridiculous mission of interviewing [him] regarding 'The Future of Literature.'" If he could just send a few words of refusal, he said, "it would be enormously helpful to 'The Future of Hotchner,'" and he would be on his way.[15] Early the next morning, the phone rang in the young reporter's hotel room:

"This Hotchner?"

"Yes."

"Dr. Hemingway here. Got your note. Can't let you abort your mission or you'll lose face with the Hearst organization, which is about like getting bounced from a leper colony. You want to have a drink around five? There's a bar called La Florida [*sic*]. Just tell the taxi."[16]

Arriving on time, Ed Hotchner stood inside the famed Floridita bar, beside the slab of mahogany that ran the length of the room, peering at the photographs of the author and his wife on the wall. Soon the man himself burst through the double doors of the entryway, and as Ernest Hemingway stopped to talk to one of the musicians in fluent Spanish, something about the man hit the twenty-seven-year-old reporter: "*Enjoyment*: God, I thought, how he's *enjoying* himself! I had never seen anyone with such an aura of fun and well-being. He radiated it and everyone in the place responded."[17] It was a portrait of the man in a moment in time, yet it was the genius that seemed to defy portrait, or time, itself: "He had so much more in his face than the photographs."[18]

While Hemingway and Hotchner "chain-drank" daiquiris, their conversation turned soon to the author's selection of Cuba as a place to live and write. Ernest attempted to explain: "Character like me, the whole world to choose from, they naturally want to know why here. Usually don't try to explain. Too complicated. The clear, cool mornings when you can work good with just Black Dog awake and the fighting cocks sending out their first bulletins."[19] During the conversation, Hemingway seemed to get "lost in a maze of diverse and contradictory reasons"—cockfights, lizards . . . black dog?—for as fellow Nobel Prize winner Gabriel García Márquez appreciated, "the reason for the choice of the place where one writes is one of the insoluble mysteries of literary creation."[20]

Like previous articles about Cuba, "The Great Blue River," written in 1949, paid tribute to both mentors Carlos Gutierrez and Gregorio Fuentes.[21] In its careful sentences were water and weather, the other boats arriving and departing in an evangelical rhythm, the squids they used as baitfish, the reels, the lines, the other fishermen, the Spanish fort of the Morro, the background buildings of Old Havana, and all the people he knew walking along the Malecón.[22]

From the flying bridge of his boat we are made to experience Havana harbor and to feel the enjoyment doing what he loved most, the masterful descriptions becoming a dimension unto itself. As the sun sets upon Mr. and Mrs. Hemingway, and "The Great Blue River," first mate Gregorio sees, zigzagging amidst the lines, a wake slicing through the dark water, a gorgeous dark purple body, and wings spread wide like an aquatic bird.[23] "Feesh, Papa! Feesh!" he shouts. Papa tells readers, "If you are ever flying across between Havana and Miami and looking down on the blue sea, and you see something making splashes such as a horse dropped off a cliff might make, and behind these splashes a black boat with green topside and decks is chasing, leaving white wake behind her—that will be us."

• • • • •

Departing out of Genoa, the Hemingways set sail again on the *Jagiello* at the end of April 1949, and after a brief stop at Cristóbal on the Caribbean side of the Panama Canal, arrived at the Finca Vigía at the end of May.

Upon their return, Mary finished the labor of love, which she had been perfecting since construction had begun in 1947: her husband's new workroom at the top of a writing tower. With the acquisition of a woven reed chaise longue as its final touch and a bell so that he could ring for René, Mary declared her masterpiece "ready for his inspection and occupancy."[24] At last, Ernest would have an airy workspace of his own where he could find solace to write, and Mary would not have to worry about the telephone's ringing and disturbing him or have to hush "the more strident conversations in the kitchen."[25] A week later, Mary found her husband standing again before his typewriter propped atop the bookshelf of his bedroom, rather than in the white tower she had built for him. Caught in the act, he thanked her, but told her that it felt too lonely up there: he missed the sounds of the house.[26] Though it had been intended to give him an office much like the one he had worked in in Key West, connected to the main house yet separated by a bridge, the white tower would stand mostly empty after that—except for its feline inhabitants.

Missing Adriana a few days following his return from Italy, Ernest "acquired a pretty, pleasant secretary to take dictation," moonlighting after her day job at the American embassy.[27] Her name was Juanita Jensen, though he preferred calling the shapely thirty-two-year-old with the peachy complexion "Miss Nita" or "daughter."[28] Miss Mary could be as prickly, high-strung, and territorial as her writer-husband, so the "acquisition" of a young secretary (on the heels of his flirtation with the Venetian girl) appeared quickly on Miss Mary's radar, flared feathers, and provoked a discussion. After confirming Nita did not have plans to take her place, Mary classified her as a "non-threat," and seeing that the secretary freed her from several tedious duties, she allowed her to settle in.

Convincing Miss Nita to dye her hair blond, then to cut it short, Ernest indulged erotic fantasies, despite Mary's protests, and invited the girl to accompany him aboard the *Pilar* where he made a pass at her that she nervously refused.[29] Under the pretext of visiting her parents, Mary departed at the end of the summer. Mollifying his wife in frequent letters, Ernest assured that his first mate Gregorio was his only company aboard his yacht.[30]

Enclosing checks, he swore Mary was the only one (who mattered) and announced the good news: *Cosmopolitan* was agreeing to serialize his new novel, "for a comfortable sum," so she could "proceed with Operation Mink Coat." Then from Charles Scribner he borrowed ten thousand dollars "to make up to [Mary] for how shitty I have been when jamming in the stretch."[31] Returning soon after by plane from Chicago, her "luggage bulging with presents," Mary was feeling "enchanted" again with "the sweet smell" of flowers, with the warmth of Cuba, with her "new mink riding grandly on [her] arm," and by her husband who so thoughtfully met her at the airport with frozen daiquiris from the Floridita for the couple to sip on the way to their home—when it pleased the missus, Ernest made it a tradition.[32]

In addition to Miss Nita, Adriana, and Leopoldina, Ernest conciliated the pangs of his aging appetite by contracting the services of a "younger, more beautiful new whore," a seventeen-year-old whom Leopoldina had arranged and whom he jokingly nicknamed Xenophobia for her aversion to foreigners.Thus continued Papa's *viejo verde* ("green old man") period.[33] In addition, two days before Mrs. Hemingway returned, Ernest bragged to Scribner about a date with Leopoldina, a reliable lover and a tolerant friend.[34] According to her niece, Hemingway's presence at Leopoldina's apartment in central Havana, where he was paying the rent at that time, was routine.[35]

That month, *The Viking Portable Hemingway*, first edited by Malcolm Cowley in 1944, would go into its second printing. At the end of October, Gianfranco Ivancich arrived in Cuba without a visa, so Papa called Paco Garay to leverage his connections to help this likeable, nice-looking young man—an "unexpected guest" who appeared at the Finca like an orphan enticed by Mr. Hemingway's welcoming invitation. At first, he told them that he planned to stay "a couple of weeks," but his visit "would stretch, with intervals, to seven years."[36]

In November, Mr. and Mrs. Hemingway flew to New York and rented a suite at the Sherry-Netherland Hotel (at the southernmost corner of Central Park, six blocks from the Museum of Modern Art, and ten blocks from Charles Scribner & Sons), where Ernest told journalist Lillian Ross that he wanted to avoid "news people" and "publicity."[37] In their suite, he feasted on caviar and champagne with actress Marlene Dietrich (who had just broken up with Martha Gellhorn's post-Hemingway beau) and received Charles Scribner, boxing trainer George Brown, actress Virginia "Jigee" Viertel (the wife of screenwriter Peter Viertel), Lillian Ross, and son Patrick, who had come "down from Harvard" to see his father and to "look at pictures" at the Met while Papa drew long sips of whisky from his flask. From her close encounters and correspondence with Hemingway, Lillian Ross would sketch in a *New Yorker* article, "How Do You Like It Now, Gentlemen?" a satirical portrait of the ill-groomed author in his taped-up glasses, with his battered briefcase in hand, hugging an unfortunate businessman whom he had forced to read his new manuscript on the plane, accompanied by his subservient wife and several other beautiful women to mollify his ego, and talking in his own peculiar terminology.[38]

On the other side of the Atlantic, the Hemingways stayed in Mary's old war room at the Ritz in November and December, attended horseraces at Auteuil near Bois de Bologne with Peter, Jigee Viertel, and Hotchner (in town to retrieve the last three chapters of his master's manuscript). There, the old man, unfulfilled by his wife alone, cultivated another "friendship," flirtation, or affair with Peter Viertel's wife, with whom he spent an hour and a half alone in her Ritz Hotel room while Mary waited angry and alone in their marital bed. Afterward, Jigee accepted a "strings-free" gift of two thousand dollars from Ernest, to spend on herself shopping in Paris—among other unusual goings-on that aroused both spouses' suspicions and jealousies.[39]

Influenced by his "toe-curling" enthrallment with a girl thirty years younger than himself, Papa's sappy prose was gracing the pages of *Cosmopolitan* magazine in the painful first installments of *Across the River and into the Trees* in February 1950, while Mary again broke her ankle—the left one this time—skiing.[40] In New York, Mary met with a doctor and confirmed her fears: after her near-death experience in Casper, Wyoming, an "occluded" fallopian tube would make her chances of death during pregnancy nearly certain. Feeling like a "failed member of the human race," she conveyed the news to her husband: she would never be able to give birth to human life or deliver the daughter he had hoped for.[41]

Adriana happened to be staying in Paris with a school friend to study art. To celebrate the selection of Adriana's drawings for the book cover of *Across the River and into the Trees*, the Hemingways held a luncheon in her honor a few days before their planned return to Cuba. Afterward, Ernest invited Adriana to escort him for a walk alone along the Seine, and, over gin and tonics at Les Deux Magots, he proposed. Averting his advances, Adriana reminded him about his wife, Mary, and maintained their friendship.[42]

After a transatlantic crossing, the Hemingways arrived back in Cuba, and Mary watched in dismay as Ernest staked his hopes in an intense correspondence with the Venetian girl, at last convincing her to come to Havana.[43] Why did she accept? Did Adriana enjoy the power she held over this grand old man who had worked himself into a state of desperate frustration on her behalf?[44] To Scribner, Ernest complained that he could buy a mink coat for his dependents but could not spend one dime on the girl he loved. Overcome by feelings, he had written a novel about a girl "loved more than anyone in the world," and he was the "character with a broken heart."[45]

Immersed frequently in a vapor of alcohol, Ernest's "bad-boy behavior" intensified. When Mary's cousin Bea came to visit in May, her husband invited the ladies to meet him for lunch at the yacht club, Club Náutico. After leaving the ladies to bake in the sun, he turned up very late and drunk in the company of the "young whore" he called Xenophobia. Angered and offended, Mary was unable to speak, but she wrote her husband a letter two days later: she had decided to leave him, for their marriage had failed. Receiving the news soberly that morning, he came into her room, read a couplet from Shakespeare, and stated, "Stick with me, kitten. I hope you will decide to stick with me."[46]

Distracting her subsequently with encouragement to renovate the villa as she had often dreamed and with the announcement of his intention that he would soon be holding the first marlin fishing tournament bearing his name—an annual tradition that began that year, which continues in Havana till this day—Hemingway somehow made her stay. In her memoir, Mary explains that she felt closest to her husband when they were at sea, and during this competition, she said she took pride in competing from her own boat, the *Tin Kid*, which her husband had ordered made for her.

In June, while Ernest revised the galleys of *Across the River and into the Trees*, seventy-five thousand Northern troops crossed the thirty-eighth parallel and took Seoul by June 28, but the Democratic People's Republic of Korea, backed by the Soviet Union, found itself face-to-face with the US-backed Republic of Korea to the south in a gruesome war that would kill 2.5 million people, continue until July 1953, and remain unresolved even today, a Cold War consuming countless lives and resources.

Then as the author awaited the publication of his novel, and the arrival of Adriana, his drinking, meanness, and depravity picked up steam. In one dispute, he called his wife "a camp-follower and a scavenger," and a couple of days later, "You have the face of *Torquemada*" (an evil priest and torturer during the Spanish Inquisition). Such pronouncements caused her to run to the rose garden, sit in the shade of the lychee tree, and have conversations with herself.[47] That season, there were several ranting and raving letters, apparently written in a state of drunkenness, such as those where he chewed out Charlie Scribner for his disorganized publishing house that set a "new record" for delays in delivering his "fucking page proofs . . . Jesus Christ I'd like to put your [Publishing House] in order."[48] In May, he had challenged Senator Joseph McCarthy to come to Cuba and fight him man to man, rather than continue to waste his time with Communist witch hunts, which "bored the bejeesus out of the tax-payers."[49]

References to Leopoldina and Xenophobia routinely seasoned his letters that summer, both while Mary was in Havana and when she took leave. On the anniversary of his 1918 wounding at Fossalta di Piave, he "commemorated" with a double-date with Gianfranco, Xenophobia, and Leopoldina, or so he told Charles Scribner in a letter: "Yesterday was the 8th July. Fossalta di Piave. So I told Gianfranco we ought to make an act of celebration. So we went into town and found Leopoldina and Xenophobia, after work done, and a couple or eight drinks and ran off *The Killers*, which is quite a good motion picture until the very last."[50]

When he returned from Italy, said Dr. José Luis Herrera Sotolongo, "He started to drink heavily. If you keep on drinking this way, I told him, you won't be able to write your own name," but averaging four to six bottles of whiskey per week and two to three cases of wine, he was always drunk.[51] "One day I said, 'Look kid, you have turned into a drunkard and I hate that. If you don't change, we'll have to stop being friends. I've tried to help you the best way I know, but I have failed, so perhaps it is better that we go our own way!'"[52] On the afternoon of November 17, 1955, José Luis went to meet with his friend Ernest and saw that his face and eyes had turned yellow.[53] Calling in a specialist, they determined that Hemingway had contracted hepatitis. José Luis prescribed bedrest and firmly restricted his friend's drinking. Hemingway obeyed his doctor's orders. Over time, his condition improved, and the danger was averted.

José Luis was a man he respected, a doctor like his father, and a longtime friend whom Ernest could not lose. Limiting his consumption of alcohol, he tried and failed to maintain a strict regimen and get back on the right track. On the first of July, attempting to anchor the *Pilar* behind the reef at Rincón, he misjudged the distance, cracked his head open, and severed an artery. Dr. José Luis administered several stitches, sewn with a silk thread while the author braced himself in Mary's leather office chair with only gin for anesthetic, causing his headaches to reappear. When Miss Nita walked into the room the following week, she found her boss without any pants on: "Forgive me for exposing myself, but I wanted you to see what happened to me. Look here at my right thigh . . ."[54]

• • • • •

"With the final galley proofs of *Across the River* corrected and sent north and the pressure of work lifted," wrote Mary, then "Ernest floundered in the void and the need to wait for the arrival of Adriana and her mother."[55] Rather than allow herself to be sucked into the tornado of "fluctuating tempters," Mary, returning to the "warm Cuban earth and the grasses beneath the liche tree," resolved to stabilize her marriage with understanding and patience as best she could.[56]

On September 7, Scribner published *Across the River and into the Trees*. Incongruously he had dedicated his novel about his infatuation with the young girl to his wife, Mary, who had had doubts early on about the plot and structure that she did not dare articulate.[57] The day the reviews were to appear, Mary departed Cuba to help her parents resettle in Gulfport, Mississippi. After finding them a suitable residence, she returned to Chicago to move them down.

Left alone on Finca Vigía, Hemingway had read an advance copy of one review of his novel by John O'Hara that would appear in the *New York Times Book Review* and in *Time*. It was a full-page spread with an illustrated caricature of Hemingway looking like a worn-out boxer titled "On the Ropes." Taking his lead from the writer's bragging and boxing talk recently appearing in Lillian Ross's "How Do You Like Me Now, Gentlemen?" O'Hara wrote, "Hemingway was the champ all right. He was past 50, but still the champ, and he was ready to take on all comers," but in his new novel he "never wins a round" and was merely a "bore who forfits the reader's sympathy."[58] These jabs were tough to take, even with the distraction of the whores and the booze to dull the blows, particularly for an exacting writer who believed he knew his craft and a thing or two about the world he was writing about.

Blame and denial rose like black bile in his throat as he read this. He fired back at O'Hara, "A man without education nor culture nor military experience naturally can't understand the book nor the girl, nor the Colonel, nor Venice."[59] He sent Juan the driver to town to pick up reviews from *Newsweek*, *Times Daily*, and *Times Sunday*. Confounded as O'Hara's words sank in, he attempted to let it go: "I'm going to take a dry martini now and the hell with it," his mind drifting to Venice and to Adriana's visit.

On the following day, the battle at Inchon began. Supported by advisors from the Soviet Union, the army of the Democratic People's Republic of Korea drove UN forces back as far south as the Pusan perimeter where they held their position from August 4 until mid-September. Launching a risky counteroffensive, Douglas MacArthur landed an amphibious assault at Inchon, and UN forces seized control of the Korean capital two days later. Cutting the North Korean force in half, UN forces swept the peninsula, capturing all enemies, pushing north, and forcing their retreat.

Alfred Kazin's review, entitled "The Indignant Flesh," appeared in the *New Yorker.* It concluded that Hemingway's latest novel would "only distress anyone who admires Hemingway": "It is hard to say what one feels most in reading this book—pity, embarrassment, that so fine and honest a writer can make such a travesty of himself, or amazement that a man can render so marvelously the beauty of the natural world and yet be so vulgar." Kazin concluded that it was full of self-loathing rather than hope: "A rage that is deflected into one of the most confused and vituperatively revealing self-portrayals by an American I have ever seen."[60]

Right before his eyes, his imaginative mind, which had always served him so well, snowballed into obsessive delirium and caused him to commit the monumental blunder of his career. Unable to attain Adriana or to become a valiant Buck Lanham, he had imagined a story where protagonist Richard Cantwell would do both. What the author wished was occurring between him and Adriana appeared a bit too plainly on the page, such that readers found themselves suddenly voyeurs to the love games of an aging wolf and his latest little lamb, a sad prospect for most. Whatever he had attempted, the critics handed him his head, no longer excusing errors or indulgences, dismissing him and his novel as a total failure, and pronouncing his writing career complete. After all, who deserved it more than the man who had droned for years how important it was to be tough?

"Oh well. It is all horse-shit anyway," chuffed the writer in a letter to Buck Lanham; but then he defended himself, pointing out that although the novel had sold 130,000 from the first printing, after reading these first hostile reviews sellers had ordered only 25,000 more copies. What did they know anyway? They were old ladies, like Henry James, angleworms in a bottle, who had not seen a day of combat.[61] When his novel hit number one on the bestseller list the following week, the writer took to the pulpit in the *New York Times Book Review* to emphasize his "combat experience" that his critics, weak-kneed as they were, clearly knew nothing about. They were incapable of comprehension. He was light-years ahead of them. They were expecting arithmetic while he was doing advanced trigonometry. Why would he need their approval? He needed only to write.[62]

• • • • •

Upon being invited to Cuba, Dora Ivancich first responded cautiously that she would consider the matter. She then perplexed Mary by accepting the illogical invitation. Later her daughter would explain that in the face of greatness, the "Venetian tendency" was to float. Enjoying a drink on the terrace with a journalist from *People* magazine and basking in the afterglow of Hemingway fame, Adriana later allowed, "Being a Venetian is a psychological handicap. Nothing is ever good enough, and floating is one's favorite way of facing life."[63]

At the age of nineteen Adriana had been herself unsure what lay in store. A trip to Cuba, and to America along the route, promised to increase the young *italiana*'s perspective and show her the way. Possibly she and Hemingway could help each other, she reasoned. While not "in love" with the aging and married man, she was genuinely in awe of his work and fond of him, and she expressed concern about him.[64]

Facing the Ivanciches' upcoming visit with the renewal of her own optimism (perhaps resembling insanity), Mary went shopping, as ordered, to pick up new guayaberas, shoes, and shorts for her husband at the department store El Encanto.[65] Busying her staff to ensure their estate was prepared for the imminent arrival of these very important guests, she commanded workers to tear down and rebuild each room until she was certain that the Finca was in impeccable condition, and her husband was thoroughly annoyed with the disturbance.[66] So thrilled was he that Dora and Adriana were arriving by the end of October that he would take the *Pilar* to meet their ship, the *Luciano Manara*, before it had even arrived. While Gregorio, Gianfranco, Roberto, and Mary waited outside Morro Castle for the ship to dock, they waved endlessly to all aboard, Adriana pretty in her lavender dress and her mother as usual in gray.[67]

It had long been his practice to play the role of generous host, but for the Ivanciches, he would become triply so, for he said the Venetian family had shown him a great kindness and hospitality abroad, and Adriana's affections might depend on it. As they boarded his ship, Ernest's eyes misted over when he clasped Adriana finally in his arms. Paco Garay fast-tracked mother and daughter through customs and immigration. Loading their luggage into their yellow Buick, the Hemingways smiled as they showed their guests to the newly remodeled "Venetian room" (once belonging to the kitties, but now renamed). So that Ernest could show Adriana all that he loved about Cuba, the household subsequently embarked on a frenetic agenda of "social festivities, both given and received, such as they never undertook before or since": they fished from the *Pilar,* lunched at Club Náutico, shot pigeons at the Cerro Hunting Club, and paraded the freshly picked Italian flower before his friends at the El Floridita.[68]

As soon as his muse arrived in Cuba, Ernest presented her a copy of the novel she had inspired. One week later, he asked her for her opinion: "I hesitated but then I spoke up. 'The girl is boring. How could your colonel love a girl who is so boring? A girl like that does not exist, if she is lovely and from a good family and goes to Mass every morning. Such a girl would not drink all day like a sponge and be in bed at the hotel.'" She did exist, he protested. Girls like her do exist; he had known many of them. Backing off, she said how much she had liked his other books, and he promised, "For you I will write a good book, better than I have ever written before. Wait and see."[69]

Leading Adriana into his writing tower, he encouraged her to work on her drawings while he wrote. Although she was terrified that her work showed little talent, he told her that in that tower they were anonymous, a secret society with the freedom to create and be, away from everyone else in the world who might pronounce judgment on their actions and on their works in progress. The name of their "private organization" was "White Tower Inc," he said, or "WTI" for short. "Here we can work with discipline and honesty, independently yet united," said Papa, setting her down at his desk in his room at the top of the tower, and setting up a desk for himself to work on the first floor.[70] With Adriana inciting his imagination, a new story had begun to flow out of him: "Adriana is so lovely to dream of, and when I wake I'm stronger than the day before and the words pour out of me."[71]

Bursting and imploding during Adriana's visit, Ernest struggled to rein in his emotions. After rejections, he fell into depression, then regrouped his forces for another attempt. Bearing the brunt of his frustrations, Mary did her best to ride out this difficult period in their marriage by sympathizing with her husband's predicament, but she also eventually broke down. The lowest point came one evening when Dr. Herrera Sotolongo was dining with the Hemingways and the Ivanciches. In February, Adriana and Dora were planning to travel to the United States with Mary as their guide for part of the way so they could discover Key West, Miami (while she visited her parents in Gulfport), a night of Mardi Gras in New Orleans, and on to the museums and Broadway shows of New York.

In preparation for this trip, Mary had agreed, after dinner, to help Gianfranco type up a visa request to accompany them. "Taking umbrage with the scene" unfolding, Ernest seized her typewriter and chucked it onto the floor. A remark from Mary later upset Ernest and caused him to throw wine in her face and stain the whitewashed wall behind her. Mary, in shock, shouted that Ernest should take care to show some respect for their guests, and all sat without a word. Looking "grim-faced," José Luis retreated to the other room while Dora and Adriana sat like monkeys on a branch on the sofa, seeing no evil, and Gianfranco stood nervously nearby.[72]

Mary decided to approach her husband while he was peacefully working one day, typing on the bookshelf in his room, the moment when he should never be disturbed. Asking him to come into her room so they could talk, Mary told him she understood his feelings for this girl but that she loved him and their life in Cuba, and that she would not leave until the morning he came to her sober and asked her to, which he never did.[73]

Meanwhile Adriana had begun to date a Cuban boy from a good family, attending several social gatherings with people her own age, and inspiring jealous outbreaks from the author during one of the grimmest New Year's Eves that Mrs. Hemingway could remember.[74]

"Before the holidays and again as we hurtled into 1951 none of us had time to squander brooding," Mary wrote. "We were forever going places."[75] They went to Vedado to hear Rubinstein play Chopin, to the casino and nightclub Montmartre, with the palm tree growing up through the grandstand where they met all their friends and danced through the night, to the Barnum and Bailey Holiday Circus, to the Floridita for "Papa Dobles," to Puerto Escondido aboard *Pilar.* Afterward, they organized a huge party at the Finca Vigía in honor of the Ivanciches, with signs and posters made by Adriana and Gianfranco, extra servants, live music, fresh flowers, and drinks. After their automobiles had been parked by Juan the driver, a small international crowd of eighty guests descended, following candles to the pool shimmering in the moonlight and to a bar under a pergola where bartenders from the Floridita filled their glasses with champagne and whiskey. A *conjunto* of guitars and maracas filled the air with music, and migrating to the house, they dined on a buffet on the terrace and admired the distant lights in the valley of Havana.

The end of Ivanciches' time in Cuba loomed with Juan Verano accompanying Mary, Adriana, and her mother on part of their return trip across the States. The fruitlessness of their visit made Ernest increasingly depressed and angry as he came face-to-face with his own delusions concerning not only Adriana but also the novel he had written, his own limitations, and the fool he had been.

Whatever happened in the dance of their relationship, the myth that they invented, its mystery and mystique, outlasted them, for whether passionate or platonic, Ernest and Adriana had a connection, complex and evolving feelings. Inspiring and enraging the boy from Oak Park, Adriana gave Ernest reason to "float" when he was starting to drown.[76] Like Ernest and his brother, Leicester, Adriana would later fail to live up to the grandeur of her own imaginings. After two troubled marriages and the book *La torre bianca*, which she published in 1980, Adriana hanged herself from a tree in her front yard in 1983, making her story as ill-fated as the one belonging to the talented writer who, through the strangest of circumstances, became her friend, and whom later she could not seem to forget.

In her book, Adriana struggles and succeeds at describing these complex feelings and her relationship with Hemingway. Some believed her to have a father-figure relationship with him. It wasn't that. Her father was morally correct, punctual, disciplined, comprehensive, and loving. Hemingway came from another culture, and although courageous like her father, he often behaved like a little child whom she wanted to protect. In his presence, she felt like the older one, she said.[77]

CHAPTER 11

A Citizen of Cojímar and a Cuban Nobel Prize (1951–1956)

• • • • •

In January of the New Year, Hemingway's first biographers—Carlos Baker and Charles Fenton, professors at Princeton and Yale—courted him by letter to ask for his cooperation in summarizing the story of his life. Resenting their prematurity and the absurdity of the request, Hemingway refused: "I am resolved not to aid, and to impede in every way, including legal, anyone who wishes to write a story of my life while I am alive. That would include my wife, my brother or my best friend."[1] When Baker adeptly kept in contact by shifting gears to what he suggested would be aggrandizing literary-study about Hemingway's work rather than his life, the writer was pleased, softened, and assisted him in completing *Hemingway: The Writer as Artist* (1952).[2]

When Fenton insisted on pursuing the biographical study, *The Apprenticeship of Ernest Hemingway, The Early Years* (1954), the writer got gruff and told him to "cease and desist" immediately: "Nobody likes to be tailed . . . I think you ought to drop the entire project."[3]

What kind of business was it to pick at a man's bones while he was still alive? His career and his life were not over, and he would show literature's bean-counters, vultures "making quick-moving shadows as they sailed overhead," and Adriana just how much life he had left.[4]

From Mrs. Hemingway's memoir, an incident just before Adriana's departure illustrates the power of Ernest's imagination, his superstitious nature in interpreting the signs, and a fear of death's proximity:

> Ernest's enthrallment with his house guests did not appear to redeem me [Mary] from whatever sins I was supposed to be committing. His internal turbulence continued to explode, mostly in my direction, for unsuspected, unexpected reasons. Soon after the Ivancich mother and daughter arrived he disapproved of a dark dress I had chosen to wear for dinner at home and to a film to which we were all going, a dress of which he had never before proclaimed dislike. Now he regarded it with distaste and commented, "Your hangman's suit. Your executioner's suit." As we were embarking in the car for the film, he announced, "You've sabotaged it."[5]

The proximity of Adriana and Mary in her dark dress appeared to spook the writer, for it sharpened his already acute sensibility, and heightening his awareness of his passion for living, his steep decline, and his approaching demise.

While Adriana's visit had caused frustration, marital strife, and pain, it also ignited creative fires and spurred artistic growth, evidenced on the fifth day of the new year of 1951 when Ernest Hemingway wrote Hotch to announce the good news: he had been writing steadily during the last two months, such that he had finished the Sea part of his envisioned "Land, Sea, and Air" trilogy on "Xmas Eve."[6] Having returned from World War II in 1945, Hemingway had begun an ambitious "Proustian Land, Sea and Air Trilogy" and, drawing upon a lifetime of experiences spent fishing the Gulf Stream, had worked on the Sea part sporadically since then. In his lifetime, he never published the whole Sea book, which was over one thousand pages long, but nine years after her husband's death, Mary, controlling the Hemingway estate, would edit and publish parts of it as *Islands in the Stream*. Ernest had never published this part because he was not satisfied with his results, but the final chapter, or coda, was very promising indeed.

Making forward progress on this last chapter, he had written Mary that he was plowing through a black-ass mood by exceeding his projected word count on the story of a Cuban fisherman.[7] As he was reading it back to himself before writing new prose each morning, he was realizing that the third part was so well written that it had to become the end, so he made it the fourth part and began to rewrite the middle, expanding part three to improve the whole. He told himself that he would use the story about the Cuban fishermen as a coda at the end of the larger book even if the character and plot of this story were unique. When he showed it to family, friends, and editors, they responded with the same enthusiasm, for he had been saving this story—about "an old man fishing alone in a skiff out of Cabañas hooked a great marlin"—for more than fifteen years.[8]

After Mardi Gras, Dora, Adriana, and Juan picked up Mary in Gulfport heading toward Jacksonville. In another letter to Mary, Ernest, purified by the prose he was achieving, wrote these romantic words to his legal wife, "Christ how I miss you being here to read it. Also miss you for several other reasons . . ."[9] By February 14, the Ivanciches departed Jacksonville bound for New York while Mary returned to Cuba. By the time she unpacked, Ernest had completed the first draft of a 26,531-word manuscript that would be titled first "The Sea in Being," then "The Dignity of Man," then *The Old Man and the Sea.*

Why had he failed so miserably with *Across the River and into the Trees* and throughout much of the Sea book, yet was now succeeding in the coda? As he would admit to a half-dozen interviewers afterward, this time he was writing honestly about something he knew well. He knew about fishing the Gulf because he had been doing it for twenty years in the company of Cuban fishermen. Thus details like the flying fish, the terns, and the robber birds, flowed naturally into his prose and made his narration authentic. He had written it true. He knew his characters, basing them on real people he had spent years with, admired, and respected. He knew about Cuba and about the village of Cojímar where he kept his boat. On mining material in the Spanish language, he had noted in *Green Hills of Africa*: "You can only really follow anything in places where you speak the language. That limits you of course. That's why I would never go to Russia. When you can't overhear it's no good. All you get are handouts and sightseeing . . . You get your good dope always from the people and when you can't talk with people and can't overhear you don't get anything that's of anything but journalistic value."[10] The linguistic and cultural proficiency allowed him to bring messages from another world—writing convincingly about a Cuban setting and characters for English-speaking readers.

His new Cojímar hero committed himself humbly, earnestly, and to the present task rather than reposing disingenuously on past achievements or complaining bitterly about the odds or the forces conspiring against him: "The thousand times that he had proved it meant nothing. Now he was proving it again. Each time was a new time and he never thought about the past when he was doing it."[11] As Mary read the fruits of each day's work, he could see goose-pimples on her arms, difficult to manufacture and a sign that the story was good: "I did okay today, mmmm?" Mary, sensing that Ernest was about to kill his protagonist, campaigned and begged him not to: "Everybody would be happier if you let him live." A few nights later she would read a more ambiguous ending: "Up the road, in the shack, the old man was sleeping again. He was still sleeping on his face and the boy was sitting by him watching him. The old man was dreaming about the lions."[12]

Though he had employed a stream of consciousness technique in other novels, it had perhaps not yet permitted readers to empathize to the same degree. For the first time in his career, Hemingway's novel had nothing to do with "the war." Instead he had written about an old man, a boy, their village, a fish, and the sea. A far cry from impotent Jake Barnes, disillusioned Frederic Henry, self-serving Harry Morgan, martyrish Robert Jordan, or embittered Colonel Cantwell, his hero Santiago, "with eyes the color of the sea," was unassuming and undaunted despite his age, his poverty, and his terrible luck. The narrative was compelling, credible, and simple. It assimilated details from decades spent fishing the Gulf to create a character, ethos, and universe.[13]

While reading it, Americans could forget that on the other side of the world their nation was engaged in the fourth bloodiest conflict in its history, later known as "the Forgotten War," locked in a stalemate as the Chinese and North Koreans continued their offensive, pushing United Nations troops back and retaking Seoul while General MacArthur considered the use of nuclear weapons.[14]

Visitors, sister Ursula and Charles Scribner, read the "coda" manuscript about an old man and the sea. With bronchitis and a fever, Ernest fell ill during Scribner's stay and missed a lot of the fishing, and afterward Ernest wrote Charlie, "I was very happy you liked what you read of the book. (The end.) But I would have thought you a certifiable fool if you had not (he says cheerfully). There is never any doubt when something is right. But it makes you very happy to have someone you like and respect say so. I had been getting good opinions only from my family."[15] In the same letter and in subsequent letters, Ernest revealed his cagey inner core by launching into vehement attacks of James Jones, a fellow Scribner's author for whom Charlie had asked Ernest for a blurb in anticipation of the publication of his novel, *From Here to Eternity*. He could not offer his support for a book he despised: he and Colonel Jones were a "different breed of cats," for Jones was a "psycho and not a real soldier" like him.[16]

In March, *Holiday* magazine published two Hemingway fables, "The Good Lion" and "The Faithful Bull," and in April *True* magazine published "The Shot," a nonfiction story about an antelope hunt. In April, he finished a first draft of the final section of the Sea book—the sub-chasing part, and dissatisfied with it, he spent April to October revising and chopping down *Islands in the Stream*. When he had done so, he wrote Scribner about the final section that was "*exactly* 26,531 words": "This is the prose that I have been working for all my life that should read easily and simply and seem short and yet have all the dimensions of the visible world and the world of a man's spirit. It is as good prose as I can write now."[17] He had to be patient, he told his editor, as the entire trilogy was 182,231 words counted to date: "The same people are in books 1, 2, 3. In the end, there is only the old man and the boy = (Book 4). I have many titles for it. But will get one finally."

A week after his fiftieth birthday, Ernest's mother Grace died. In the final years of their relationship, Ernest and his mother had settled into ceasefire whereby he provided and exchanged polite letters in a slow boil of anger beneath the veneer of their civility. "I hate her guts, and she hates mine," he told Charlie Scribner in a letter. "She forced my father to suicide." He would not attend the funeral.

• • • • •

In round reading glasses and disheveled necktie, Eduardo "Eddy" Chibás was working himself into a sweat while denouncing corruption in Cuban politics. His "Vergüenza Contra Dinero" ("Shame Against Money") campaign resonated with the general public, as did his integrity, reasoned argument, and facts. Insisting on a peaceful revolution through honest and legal means, Chibás stood as one of the few alternatives to the gangsterism epidemic in Cuban politics. Forming the Orthodox Party in 1947 and critiquing former president Grau San Martín and President Prío, Chibás used his popular radio show as a platform and had gained an unprecedented degree of notoriety and support as an Independent, but amidst controversy he lost to Prío during the 1948 presidential elections.

Bidding his followers farewell, apologizing to them for failing to produce evidence that the Minister of Education had been misappropriating public funds, and warning of an impending coup attempt by Batista, Eddy Chibás shot himself in the stomach with a .38 caliber pistol at the end of his radio show on August 5, 1951.[18] Though he had intended to kill himself on the air, he did not succeed, for the shot was muffled by an advertisement for Café Pilón, and he was rushed to intensive care at a hospital nearby where he lay for eleven days while the whole country awaited bulletins on his condition. When he died, hundreds of thousands of people came to Colón Cemetery to mourn him at his funeral. He became a martyr, justifying outright rejection of the government. Many of his admirers speculated that he had been well positioned for the election of 1952—among them was the outspoken twenty-five-year-old activist Fidel Castro.

Receiving a call at the end of September that her son Gregory had been incarcerated for entering a woman's bathroom in Los Angeles, Pauline flew down from San Francisco to post his bail. From the home of her sister, Virginia, Pauline telephoned Ernest to report the incident; accusations and embittered shouting ensued. Later that evening, Pauline had to be rushed to the hospital where she abruptly died of shock before doctors could operate. Ernest wrote Charles Scribner, "The first wave of remembering has finally risen so that it has broken over the jetty that I built to protect the open roadstead of my heart. And I have full sorrow of Pauline's death with all the habour scum that caused it. I loved her very much for many years and the hell with her faults."[19]

During the following month while Gregory and his wife, Jane, were visiting the Finca Vigía, Gregory would comment a bit too casually on his arrest, "It wasn't so bad, really, Papa."

"No?" his father responded. "Well, it killed Mother."[20] The relationship with his third son was deteriorating into resentment, anger, and threatening letters, but it would infuse new purpose into his creation of a manuscript of new fiction, the following year, exploring the source of evil, *The Garden of Eden*.

"People are dying that never died before," mumbled Ernest as he read in the newspaper in December 1951 that his longtime friend Harold Ross, co-founder of the *New Yorker* magazine, had died.[21] In November, his dear friend and outwardly indestructible ship captain Juan Duñabeitia had suffered a third heart attack while returning from sea and been taken in and cared for at the Finca while he recovered.[22] Death looming, losing loved ones, clashing with family, and at odds with his critics, Ernest Hemingway had been having trouble sleeping and was taking sedatives. At the beginning of the New Year, the Hemingways, wanting very much to get away, departed for a few days to the Mariel Coast.

Ernest and Mary asked Gregorio and Felipe to prepare the *Pilar* and Mary's auxiliary, the *Tin Kid*, departing west along the coast toward Pinar del Río and Paraíso Key and secluding themselves, to fish outside the reef, out beyond Punta Purgatorio, between sea and sky, and in the shadows of the mangroves, from January 10 to February 20. Aboard, he had the manuscript that he tinkered with from time to time: "The old man knew he was going far out and he left the smell of land behind and rowed out into the clean early morning smell of the ocean."[23]

For ice and other provisions, the Hemingways came ashore at La Mulatta on February 16. When they called the Finca to check in, René read a telegraph informing them that Charlie Scribner had died of a heart attack. Heartbroken himself, Ernest wrote with his condolences to Mrs. Scribner two days later, "Now my dear and good friend is gone and there is no one to confide in nor trust nor make rough jokes with and I feel so terribly about Charlie being gone that I can't write anymore."[24]

The Hemingways made a brief stop back in Cuba to meet the Haywards who, hopeful that they could collaborate with Ernest on a script, had taken leave of Tinseltown. Then, with their bags packed, they settled into the front seat of the Buick and began driving down their "hibiscus-splashed driveway" toward the front gate. Juan asked "*¿Has oído qué pasa en la Habana?*" ("Have you heard what's happening in Havana?") No, they had not heard anything on Radio Reloj, the Cuban news that announced itself punctually with the ticking of a clock. Had they not heard about the company of Cuban soldiers that had surrounded the presidential palace and a crowd amassing in the streets? "Let us go as usual to the Club Náutico," insisted Ernest.[25]

After the Haywards' visit, the Hemingways again exiled themselves on an extended cruise past Purgatory Point, where the Gulf Stream hit the end of a wide reef and offered a secret alcove; they were "living in a world of twenty shades of blue," alone except for their steward and the dolphins they saw playing in the waves.[26] With his manuscript in the Haywards' hands, Ernest began new fiction during that Edenic spring. By revisiting past lives and describing present utopia, the writer employed a favorite technique of creating immediacy and depth in his fiction. In scenes as utopic as those he was experiencing in Cayo Paraíso, Ernest Hemingway explored memories from his early adolescence in upper Michigan, from his twenties in Hendaye and Le Grau-du-Roi, and the root of evil in incest and androgyny. He would never allow this fiction to be published during his lifetime, but it did appear posthumously as "The Last Good Country" and *The Garden of Eden*.

In "The Last Good Country," game wardens pursue Nick Adams for poaching as he escapes to the northern forests of upper Michigan in the company of his admiring kid sister, "Littless," whom Nick calls a "Devil" when she toys with gender by cutting her hair like a boy to please him.[27] The story appeared to draw inspiration from a real-life incident when he was seventeen, impulsively shot a blue heron, and fled with his sister Ursula.[28] Then when they are alone together in the virgin forests where the trees rose sixty feet, making it seem like a sacred place, like a cathedral, where "no sun came through . . . His sister put her hand in his and walked close to him," and though they both felt "strange," they were not afraid because they were together. Later when his sister woke, she would tell her brother that she wanted to become his "Common-law wife," to go with him to Europe, and to have his children.

In *The Garden of Eden*, an American writer, David Bourne, and his wife, Catherine, are happily honeymooning on the French Riviera and travelling to Spain and back again while David is attempting to work. The trouble arises when Catherine begins to change at the same age as Gregory Hemingway was that summer: twenty-one.[29] The transgender experiments between David and Catherine are the beginning of evil in the garden, leading them to allow Marita, an intruder, into their Edenic existence. Trying to cure their sickness, both husband and wife made love to her, but the destruction was already done.

Mary and her "sweet and happy" husband were alone on the sea, yielding to a world of physical pleasure, while Ernest created new fictional tales of David, Catherine, Marita, Littless, and Nick Adams: "As I had noticed other times when we were alone together on the sea, my husband did not often invite me into his bigger bed, and I thought I understood why. In our mutual sensory delights, we were smoothly interlocking parts of a single entity, the big cogwheel and the smaller cogwheel, I felt, with no need for asserting togetherness. Maybe we were androgynous."[30] The unsavory threesome of Catherine, David, and Marita travelling together in the French Riviera and Spain found clear inspiration in the ménage-à-trois between Hadley, Ernest, and Pauline, which had broken up his first Eden in Paris. These works were the first to explore this time where paradise had been lost. Later, he would write about it again in *A Moveable Feast*.

• • • • •

At the same time, paradise was being lost in Cuba. "It is my destiny to make bloodless revolutions," announced Colonel Batista on the television and on radio. "The only blood spilled will be that of those who oppose us. We are the law."[31] During his six years in exile in Daytona, Florida, Batista had remained active in Cuban politics, surveying the situation from a distance, until his election to the Senate *in absentia* demonstrated that the time might be right for him to return to the forefront. The Prío administration had become exceedingly corrupt, and the opposition had been clamoring for change. Returning to Cuba, Batista entered the presidential election of 1952. When an opinion poll in *Bohemia* (Cuba's leading national magazine) showed him far behind the other two candidates—Roberto Agramonte from the Orthodox Party and Carlos Hevia from the Authentic Party—Batista returned to his previous ways.[32] Three months before the presidential election in June, he staged on March 10, 1952, a bloodless coup, like the Sergeant's Revolt of 1933, this time recruiting disaffected junior officers to organize and turn against their superiors.[33]

The facility with which Batista returned evidenced the excesses of his Partido Auténtico-Revolucionario; it was said that President Prío fled in such a hurry that he forgot his cocaine stash in the presidential palace while his brother continued to dance the night away in the Sans Souci.[34] In the words of historian Hugh Thomas, "The Auténtico-Revolutionary Movement was neither authentic nor revolutionary. It was a democratic party but most of the leaders were anxious to enjoy the fruits of power more than to press through such reforms as needed by Cuban society. Their program turned out to be words."[35] Prío went into exile in Miami and Puerto Rico where he worked as a developer and an entrepreneur, met with Carlos Ochoa in Montreal, and attempted to rally opposition to return to Cuba, but he killed himself in Miami in 1977, a week after the US House Select Committee on Assassinations had called him for questioning. "They say that I was a terrible president of Cuba," Prío had once pointed out. "That may be true. But I was the best president Cuba ever had."[36]

Suspending the constitution to reestablish provisory martial law, Batista canceled elections, suspended congress, deployed tanks into the streets, and published a new constitutional code to support a more "disciplined democracy."[37] In a radio broadcast, the Cuban strongman announced that he had returned and taken these measures "to save the country from chaotic conditions." The 275 articles would conserve the constitution's "democratic essence" while taking certain measures to ensure order and progress.[38] Demonstrating vision and his skills as a tactician during the escalation of the Cold War, Batista upheld a discourse that was anti-Communist and pro-investment. Consequently, Secretary of State Dean Acheson wrote President Truman that the State Department "naturally deplores the way that the Batista coup was brought about. . ." yet offered his support for a Cuban presidential administration that promised to stabilize the country, "curtail international communist activities in Cuba," and support the American investment of "private capital."[39] A friend against "the Reds" in Latin America, Batista would become one of the Eisenhower administration's closest allies in weeding out "subversive communist elements." Seventeen days after Batista's coup, the United States recognized his government arriving to the seat of power by military coup. Preparing a campaign to run for the Cuban Congress during the June elections was young lawyer Fidel Castro, graduate of the Law School of the University of Havana. When Batista illegally seized power in Cuba for the second time, Fidel brought several lawsuits against him that produced zero results.

Escaping the turnover of power in Cuba and people once again, Mary and Ernest Hemingway departed and, enjoying an idyll in their marriage, did not return from Médano de Casigua, a secluded alcove of Cayo Paraíso, protected by the barrier reef, amidst turquoise waters, white sand beaches, and green lagoons, until the end of March. There, Gregorio dropped anchor, prepared cocktails, and cooked, while they fished, drank, bathed naked, and walked along the shore with Ernest finding moments in the shade and putting the finishing touches on his coda story.

• • • • •

When they returned, they received a visit from Walter Houk and Miss Rita who announced their engagement. Upon Mary and Ernest's insistence, they held the reception at the Finca Vigía on April 20 with Ernest in the absurd position of giving the bride away. On the marriage certificate Ernest's profession was listed correctly: *"ocupación escritor."* In June, Alfred Eisenstaedt arrived to take color photographs of the author and eighty-year old Anselmo, a model for Santiago in Cojímar, in the exhausting heat until Ernest called for them to stop.

On Labor Day, September 1, 1952, 5,318,650 million copies of a special issue of *Life* featuring *The Old Man and the Sea* hit the stands . . . and sold within the first forty-eight hours.[40] A week later Scribner's released 57,700 copies, sold out in advance. It was picked up for the Book of the Month Club the following day. Along with a "whispering campaign" that preceded its release, the three-pronged publishing assault gave the book unprecedented momentum as it leaped into view.[41] Just after in October, Carlos Baker released his own volume, *Hemingway: The Writer as Artist*, a literary exaltation of his works that clearly benefited his cause. In America, Scribner's sold 3,000 per week after the first 50,000, and in the United Kingdom, advanced sales reached 20,000, then continued afterward at 2,000 per week. From *Life*, the author brought in $137,000, and $38,000 from Scribner and Sons.

Several of the critics and competitors who had condemned him for Colonel Cantwell and *Across the River and into the Trees* were now jumping over one another to be first in line to praise him for Santiago and *The Old Man and the Sea*. Nearly all the same voices who had called his career kaput were again singing his praises while admiring the simple and sad story of an elderly Cojímar fisherman, catching the fish of his life, and losing it to sharks.

In a short advance review for *Shenandoah* magazine in August, his literary nemesis William Faulkner hailed it as one of literature's highest achievements.[42] In the *New York Times*, Orville Prescott praised his discipline and skill as a "master technician once more at the top of his form."[43] In the *New York Herald Tribune Review of Books*, Malcolm Cowley called the novella "nearly faultless . . . the essence of classical prose."[44] Across the pond in London, Cyril Connolly smothered him with praise in the *Sunday Times*: "I believe this is the best story Hemingway has ever written. Get at it at once, read it, wait a few days, read it again, and you will find . . . that no page of this beautiful master-work could have been done better or differently."[45]

The Cuban Tourist Institute was the first organization to recognize him for *The Old Man and the Sea* with the Medalla de Honor (Medal of Honor) on September 24. The next day Mary flew to New York to shop and to bask in her husband's success.[46] Weary of the spotlight and of the sort of "heckler" fans he would cross in the streets of New York, Ernest stayed in Cuba aboard the *Pilar* to pursue the running marlins. Reading perhaps of Ernest's successes in the newspapers, thieves came to call on the Finca Vigía more than once that year, evading booby traps and dogs (Blackie and Negrita), breaking furniture, rummaging drawers, and stealing Ernest's knives, war trophies, gold cufflinks, ties, silver picture frames, and nearly all of Gianfranco's wardrobe.[47] Reporting it to the police, but not wanting to post a guard for fear he might be equally corrupt, Ernest and Mary slept with loaded pistols atop their night tables.

In October, more critics like Mark Schorer of the *New Republic* and Joyce Cary of the *New York Times Book Review* maintained that *The Old Man and the Sea* was a success, while dissenting voices suggested that *Life*'s publicity, Hemingway's fame, and his reader's affection for their hero explained the novel's popularity and the exaggerated enthusiasm.[48] In *Commentary*, Philip Rhav dumped cold water on the fire of runaway praise: even tough the artist had appeared to reestablish control over an ego that had been declining into morbid irritability, self-love, and self-pity, the novella was "by no means a masterpiece which the nationwide publicity set off by its publication in *Life* magazine has made it out to be . . . Hemingway's big marlin is no Moby Dick, and his fisherman is not Captain Ahab."[49] If some passages could be moving, the artistry was marred overall by unnatural moments superimposing Christian symbols or intruding into the voice of a narrative that did not belong to Santiago but to Hemingway himself—self-pitying, at odds with the world around him, and blaming his critics, "the sharks," for the failures of his creations and his career.

Blood in the water, and it would not be long before the other sharks would come in for the kill. As they circled, Hemingway impatiently wrote his old friend, and critic, Edmund Wilson, "You know I was thinking about actual sharks when I wrote the book and had nothing to do with the theory that they represented critics. I don't know who thought that up . . . I have always hoped for sound, intelligent criticism all my life as writing is the loneliest of all trades."[50]

Harvard educated and insightful in his eighties, Bernard Berenson was an art historian whom Mary had met and befriended while sightseeing in Florence four years previously while Ernest was hunting ducks (and Adriana Ivancich). Initiating an intellectual exchange with Ernest Hemingway via letter, Berenson, whom the writer had called a "wise old man," would come in handy when critical wind started to shift against *The Old Man and the Sea*.[51] Catching wind of these developments weeks after his novel's release, Hemingway wrote awkwardly to Berenson to ask him to write an intellectual's endorsement of the book in a blurb that Scribner's could use to market the book.[52]

It was only normal that his public should confuse his Homeric novella with Melville, wrote Hemingway, but as *conoscitori*, he and Berenson knew better. "Then there is the other secret. There isn't any symbolism. The sea is the sea. The old man is the old man. The boy is a boy and the fish is a fish. The sharks are sharks, no better, no worse. All the symbolism that people say is shit. What goes beyond is what you see when you know. A writer should know too much." As requested, Berenson sent Scribner's the ammunition—a blurb that could pad subsequent advertisements and book jackets: "Hemingway's 'The Old Man and the Sea' is an idyll of the sea as sea, as un-Byronic and un-Melvillian as Homer himself, and communicated in a prose as calm and compelling as Homer's verse. No real artist symbolizes or allegorizes—and Hemingway is a real artist—but every real work of art exhales symbols and allegories. So does this short but not small masterpiece."[53] However, some critics like Schwartz and Aldrige insisted, relentlessly, that the work's overwrought and sentimental passages were not great and only reminded readers of what Hemingway had once been.[54]

Just after, another selachian would read the corrosive words appearing in newspapers and academic reviews and repeat them in his father's ear. Having lost his mother that year, Gregory Hemingway was under pressure to pass pre-med exams and enter UCLA medical school, and he was seeing a therapist for the feelings he just could not seem to shake. On July 3, he wrote his father and his wife to apologize to Mary for stealing her French underpants from her room six years ago: "Give my love to Miss Mary and tell her if I see her I sure as hell would like to be forgiven. I did a terrible thing in lying about that clothes business and I make no excuses for it."[55] Intoxicated and very probably resenting the resurgence of an incident he would have preferred to forget, Ernest replied angrily in a letter to the undisciplined son whose unchecked perversion had killed his mother.

On November 3, Greg replied to his father: "If you ever write another letter like that I'll beat the shit out of you." Ten days later, when Gregory turned twenty-one, he sent his father another letter, calling him a "gin-soaked abusive monster," naming Mary as a shameless hireling, and asking God for mercy on his soul for the misery he had caused him by accusing him of killing his mother. "You accused me of killing her—said it was my arrest that killed her . . . If I ever meet you again, and you start pulling the ruthless, illogical, and destructive shit on me, I will beat your head into the ground and mix it with cement to make outhouses . . . I suppose you wonder what has happened to all my filial respect for you. Well, it's gone *Ernestine*, dear, it's gone."[56]

Father responded with the request that his son stand down: "Your threats to beat up your father are comic enough . . . Right now I could use a good flash of your old charm and decency. I cannot use any more obscene or threatening letters. Mary can do without your thefts and insults. Your father, E. Hemingway."[57] However, when his son reopened the subject of cross-dressing—"Please understand . . . please understand . . . please understand . . . This clothes business is something I have never been able to control"—his father would refuse to continue the dialogue even though all indications suggest he himself had been exploring transgender yearnings at that time, not only in the fictional scenes with Littless and "Devilish" Catherine, discussed previously in "The Last Good Country" and *The Garden of Eden*, but also in recent real-life sexual encounters with Mary in Cayo Paraiso and in Africa where he wrote in his wife's journal:

> Mary is an espece [species] (sort of) prince of devils . . .
> She has always wanted to be a boy and thinks as a boy

> without ever losing femininity. . . Mary has never had one lesbian impulse but has always wanted to be a boy. Since I have never cared for any man and dislike any tactile contact between men . . . I loved feeling the embrace of Mary which came to me as something quite new and outside tribal law. On the night of December 19th, we worked out these things and have never been happier.[58]

During the three weeks following the release of *The Old Man and the Sea*, eighty to ninety letters a day arrived at the Finca Vigía from high school kids, soldiers, sailors, columnists, professors, old pals from Italy, Montana, and Bimini, and many strangers praising him and wishing him well.[59] While the letters continued, the Finca Vigía and the Floridita had become a zoo with an endless stream of visitors, house-guests, fans, friends, solicitors, and hangers-on.

• • • • •

When Senator Estes Kefauver sought to eradicate organized crime and tightened gambling regulations in Las Vegas, the Mob looked to Cuba for friendlier business territory. As *Variety* magazine reported in 1953: "It was the chill of the Kefauver hearings which to a large measure induced the Americans to seek warmer and more hospitable grounds to the south."[60] Thus in Francis Ford Coppola's *The Godfather II*, character Hyman Roth (played by Lee Strasberg and representing Meyer Lansky) would declare with glee, "These are wonderful things that we've achieved in Havana, and there's no limit to where we can go from here . . . We have now what we have always needed: real partnership with a government. Here we are, protected, free to make our profits, without Kefauver, the God-damned Justice Department and the FBI—90 miles away, partnership with a government."[61] Cultivating long-established business relationships with American investors and organized crime, President Batista provided incentives and protection in exchange for a percentage of the profits.[62] Supported by Batista's government, Santo Trafficante, Jr., expanded operations in casinos, hotels, cabarets like the Sevilla-Biltmore, Havana-Hilton, the Capri (the largest and most extravagant hotel casino outside of Las Vegas, with actor George Raft as its famed greeter, until it was outdone by the Riviera, and until the Havana Hilton outdid the Riviera), the Sans-Souci, El Comodoro, and the Deaville, with Mrs. Batista's "bagman" depositing nightly 10 percent of their cut.[63] Concurrently, brothels, burlesques, drag shows, and peepshows under Mafia purview, such as Casa Marina, Aunt Nena Club, the 212 Club, the Mambo Club, the Palette Club, the Bohemian Club, and the Shanghai Theater (a world depicted by Graham Greene) multiplied and made millions.[64]

With the inheritance from his mother, Ernest's middle son, Patrick, had acquired a 2,300-acre homestead in Tanganyika and a house with several servants and twenty-two rooms. Benefiting from letters of introduction from his father to Philip Percival, the young man became a professional hunter and would live in Africa shooting wild animals during the next twenty-five years. By the middle of October, Ernest and Mary Hemingway were preparing a return trip to Africa so that he could write a series of articles (at ten thousand dollars per article with fifteen thousand dollars in expenses) for *Look* magazine that would take his readers on a photo safari through the camera of Earl Theisen, with stops in Paris, Spain, and Italy en route. In November, former general Dwight D. Eisenhower beat a progressive candidate, Adlai Stevenson, during a landslide election.

In December, Ernest attended the burial of Floridita bartender Constantino Ribalaigua and hosted Slim and Leland Hayward who flew into Havana to discuss the details of their deal with Warner Brothers for a film version of *The Old Man and the Sea*. For the rights, and agreeing to serve as consultant to the film, Ernest would receive $150,000. "In search of suitable fish footage" in Peru, the film's $2 million budget grew to $5 million, and the author, catching the largest fish of his life to assure the realism of the movie, had the last laugh.[65] "We'll never make it to Africa before the long rains," said Ernest to Mary, wishing to free himself from a life of obligations: he told her that he felt like a juggler with one hand tied behind his back.[66]

One day in 1953, the Hemingways suffered a great loss when Ramón Wong, their cook, died of a heart attack. When the author offered to take care of funeral expenses and provide for his family, his widow declined; it turned out that the cook had been a shrewd businessman who had made a small fortune as a partner in a restaurant in Havana's Chinatown.[67] In January when thieves returned for the third time since July, Ernest chased them off with a .22 rifle, shooting at the last one escaping through the window, and drawing blood that they would find on the terrace and track down the hill, over the fence, and into the village below.[68]

From dying friends, persistent thieves, financial anxieties, and familial disagreements, Mary and Ernest again sought sanctuary aboard the *Pilar.* While they were anchored off Cayo Paraíso and fishing from Purgatory Point, the infamous "razzle-dazzle" scandal broke in Havana smearing the reputation of the city's gambling joints and potentially discouraging the future business of American tourists. The cover of the *Saturday Evening Post* read, "Suckers in Paradise: How Americans Lose Their Shirts in Caribbean Gambling Joints," and was followed by a "crack down" two days later entailing the arrest of thirteen "cardsharps" and the deportation of eleven of them.[69]

Duty compelled the Hemingways to return to Havana at the beginning of April to receive the Haywards, to discuss the details of the film with them, and Spencer Tracy, the actor who would play Santiago, and to receive the writer's first son, Jack, his wife, Puck, and their daughter, Muffet. During his visit, Tracy was able to "catch a glimpse" of Anselmo Hernandez in his natural element exhaustedly sleeping in his shack after fishing all night, and he spoke with Gregorio and Felipe at length about the specifics of fishing marlin from a one-man boat.[70]

Fishing and hiding off Cayo Paraíso again, the Hemingways heard the announcement on the radio that *The Old Man and the Sea* had won the Pulitzer Prize on May 4, 1953. Two days later, Ernest wrote a letter to Wallace Meyer fondly thinking of Leopoldina and wondering how she would react to the news: "Am sure my old whore Leopoldina whose favorite book is the one she calls Too Many Short Stories by Ernest Hemingway celebrated the award with my other friends at the Floridita. It was on the Cuban radio too at fifteen minute intervals all day. Leopoldina and Co. probably think it is the Nobel Prize and they are waiting for me to come back and spend that money."[71] In his hard-boiled style, Hemingway seems to employ the epithet "my old whore" ironically. It was one of his habits to employ disparaging nicknames for people he loved dearly: "Feo" ("Ugly") for Dr. José Luis Herrera Sotolongo, "Mousie" for his son Patrick, or even "Mr. and Mrs. Fathouse-Pig" for himself and Martha Gellhorn.

Departing from Havana at the end of June for Africa via New York and Europe, they boarded the transatlantic vessel *Flandre*, docked in Le Havre, then drove to Paris, reaching Spain by July, for the feria of Pamplona—then onward to Madrid, Paris, and Aix-en-Provence.

That same June, a student named Ernesto "Che" Guevara, having returned from a five-thousand-mile trek through South America, completed his studies and graduated from medical school in Buenos Aires, Argentina, while insurgent leader Fidel Castro organized 165 men and women to attack the Moncada Barracks. Inspired by Batista's illegal coup d'état, twelve hundred of Castro's men had been training at the university and at firing ranges in Havana, and disguising themselves as businessmen and hunters shooting clay pigeons.[72] Their plan was to take the garrison, use its transmitters to confuse the Cuban military, then take control of Santiago's radio station, in order to broadcast the speeches of Eduardo Chibás, and by this means incite the general populace to revolt. Before the attack, Fidel told his men that their victory was part of an irrepressible Cuban movement: "This movement will be victorious . . . from the people will arise fresh new men willing to die for Cuba. They will pick up our banner and move forward . . . The people will back us in Oriente and in the whole island. As in '68 and '92, here in Oriente we will give the first cry of Liberty or Death!"[73]

The attack on July 26, 1953, failed and killed most of Castro's men. Most of the captured were executed, and many were tortured by police. Among those involved but who escaped were former president Carlos Prío Socarrás and his minister of education and foreign affairs, Aureliano Sánchez Arango, whom Chibás had so often criticized for embezzlement on his radio show. A few of the rebels managed to escape and retreat into the highlands. Lying in a shack on the first of

August in the backcountry near Santiago de Cuba, Fidel Castro was awakened in the middle of the night by the police. Arresting him and other rebels, they took them to the local jail in Boniato.[74]

Five days after Fidel's arrest, the Hemingways boarded the *Dunnottar Castle* in Marseilles and sailed for Mombasa. Ernest and Mary spent August to December on safari in Tanganyika, in Kenya, and in Uganda with Philip Percival (and with invited guest from Cuba, Mayito Menocal), and on the vast new property with son Patrick. In September, Scribner's published *The Hemingway Reader.*

Of the 122 Cuban rebels indicted, 99 were detained and tried from September 21 to October 6, 1953.[75] Fifty-five were convicted and given sentences ranging from seven months to thirteen years in the prison on the Isle of Pines.[76] During a separate trial, Fidel, a licensed attorney, confessed, accepted full responsibility, and delivered a historic defense that appealed to his judges as human beings and concluded with, *"Condenadme, no importa, la historia me absolverá."* ("Condemn me. It doesn't matter. History will absolve me.") Throughout the trial, he referred to the Moncada attack as "the 26th of July Movement," transforming himself into a legend and defining a platform for future action. Evoking José Martí as the father of Cuban independence, Castro openly attacked Batista for selling the country's resources for personal profit while unemployment soared among his people who did not have access to health care or education. Calling for a return to the constitution of 1940, Castro insisted upon agricultural reform, profit-sharing among Cuban workers in industry and on sugar plantations, and seizure of assets deceitfully acquired. The court sentenced him to fifteen years.

Castro was sent to the Presidio Modelo on the Cuban islet to the southwest. Batista announced that elections would be held the following November 1954, but that the Communist Party would continue to be prohibited and its adherents systematically deported.[77] In Mexico City the following month, a group of influential exiles signed the "Pact of Montreal," declaring their unity against Batista.

On January 21, the Hemingways ended their safari. During the return, their plane en route to Murchison Falls struck a telegraph wire.

"HEMINGWAY, WIFE: KILLED IN AIR CRASH" declared the *Daily Mirror,* with pictures of the author posing beside a leopard with a rifle, and another of Mary. "No Sign of Life at Wreck . . . Mrs. Mary Hemingway, fourth wife of Pulitzer Prize winning author Ernest Hemingway, is believed to have perished with him in the crash of a charter plane in the East African jungle where they had been on safari."[78] Picked up by a passing riverboat, the couple was taken to Butiaba along Lake Albert, then to Entebbe on Lake Victoria where, the next afternoon, they hired another rickety plane that caught on fire as it took off. The newspapers again declared the Hemingways dead; they would have to telegram their families and inform them that they were alive.

Recovering in Nairobi, Ernest wrote "The Christmas Gift," recounting his escape from the burning aircraft for his readers in *Look* magazine. Aboard the return ship, he would write a letter to Hotchner, who was coming to join him in Italy: "Today's check up shows—rupture of kidneys, collapse of intestine, severe injuries liver, major concussion, severe burns legs, belly, right forearm, left hand, head, lips, paralysis of sphincter, large blood clot left shin outside above ankle, dislocated right arm and shoulder etc." Yet, discretion not getting the better part of valor, he joined in for sea fishing off Mombasa.[79]

By the middle of March, the Hemingways had boarded SS *Africa* for their return trip to Italy through the Red Sea. In Venice they stayed at the Gritti Palace, where Ernest needed to recover. Though they had planned to go duck hunting, he really was not well. "His face was emaciated, his hands nearly transparent and without energy, the body broken by his inner injuries and fractured bones. But he did not yet renounce the fight for life. He did not want pictures taken of him. He said, 'You should not photograph a beaten man,'" his translator, Fernanda Pivano, recalled.[80]

Adriana Ivancich, whose cover illustration had recently appeared on *The Old Man and the Sea,* came to visit Ernest at the Gritti. Having believed what the newspapers had reported, Adriana was ecstatic to see her friend alive, but also heartbroken by his condition, such that she broke into tears as soon as she saw him, and Ernest responded in kind. "Watch me, now you can say you saw Hemingway crying," he said.[81] At the Gritti, he received the news that he had been accepted for a Merit Medal and a thousand-dollar prize from the Academy of Arts and Letters, which he accepted.

Her injuries only slightly less severe, Mary caught a plane to Paris, then travelled to London, Seville, and Ronda with friends. In the Lancia with Adamo Simon as their driver, Papa and Hotch visited Adriana at her palazzo, then departed Venice, ultimately headed for Madrid, with stops in Milan, Nice, Aix-en-Provence, Nîmes, Arles, Montpellier, Carcassonne, Biarritz, San Sebastián (picking up Juan Quintana), Burgos, and attending the San Isidro feria in *la capital*. On a side trip to El Escorial, they watched Luis Miguel Dominguín practice with the bulls and take photographs for publicity. In May, Robert Capa, his dear friend, died in Indochina after stepping on a landmine while covering the conflict raging between the French and the Vietnamese. By the beginning of June, the Hemingways boarded the *Francesco Morosini* in Genoa for their return voyage to Havana. No sooner had they arrived home than Mary would have to repack her bags and depart to attend to her dying father in July.

In Gulfport, Mary found her father looking as sickly as a man in an El Greco painting. Having endured much as a companion and friend, Ernest's fourth wife received a letter while she was helping her parents in Gulfport: "Honestly Kittner, he should go to a hospital. Cost means nothing. He can have what I have. But he is going to die and he should die with some dignity and some regard for other people."[82] With her husband complaining of feelings of loneliness and depression, Mary returned the day before his birthday. The following day Ernest received the Order of Carlos Manuel Céspedes, Cuba's highest honor.

When Batista's regime suggested that they hold the ceremony at the presidential palace, Ernest tactfully declined, sensing it might send the wrong signal to "appear to support a dictator." Instead, he agreed to accept the award at their "little yacht club on the bay," where Batista's undersecretary of state delivered a "pleasant, not-too pretentious speech." In the company of a dozen of their closest friends congregating at the bar, Ernest thanked all for the honor and emphasized his esteem for "the Cuban pueblo—the common people—and his best wishes for their welfare."[83] Afterward, the Hemingways celebrated in grander style, for Mary's sake—after a difficult week in Gulfport—with a big, boisterous lunch at the Floridita.

On July 26, with their movement gathering stream, Haydée Santamaría and Melba Hernández organized a protest at Colón Cemetery that commemorated the anniversary of the Moncada attack. That same month of July, Batista enthusiastically announced his presidential candidacy to the disgruntled masses. The Hemingways received visitors at the Finca Vigía, such as Ava Gardner, swimming naked in his pool and fishing aboard the *Pilar* while Gregorio, eyes widening with glee, sloshed pails of sea water across the deck, and later in the Floridita, Ernest's old nodding acquaintances, rich, paunchy sugar growers, politicians, and simple men of business became instant intimates enchanted and jostling for position in an attempt to meet the North American starlet.[84] In the meantime, another guest, Luis Miguel Dominguín had been impressing their chauffeur, Juan, with his stamina as he lurked in Havana's many brothels: "Señora," said the bullfighter to Mrs. Hemingway afterward, "[Juan] knew places I never even heard of. And such beautiful girls. So friendly."[85] Hemingway took Dominguín to cockfights in Cotorro and to Guanabacoa to see high priests of Santería.[86] In October, the rebels published Fidel's "History Will Absolve Me" speech and spread it across the island.

• • • • •

On October 28, Ernest, having heard rumors from friend and man of letters Harvey Breit, had not yet heard definitive news about the long-coveted Nobel Prize. They must have figured it was now or never, he thought, when they phoned and told him. At dawn, he tiptoed into his wife's bedroom, tapped her arm softly as she slept, and said, "My kitten, my kitten, I've got *that thing*. Maybe you better get up." His smile was hesitant, his voice soft and happy.

"Huh?"

"You know. The Swedish thing."

"Hell's bells. You mean the Prize, the Nobel Prize?" his wife asked, already all over him, clinging and hugging and smooching.[87]

They had to get going, realized Mrs. Hemingway, slipping into her shorts and shirt and hurrying into the kitchen to prepare to host press and visitors. There she found her staff, who had heard the announcement on the servants' radio, already abuzz, polishing silver trays, and Mary joined in, arranging *bocaditos* of fresh pineapple, Spanish and English ham, and cheeses, and opening bottles of Marqués de Riscal wine in anticipation of the flash-flood party that she had somehow neglected to anticipate.[88] The old-fashioned wall phone was soon ringing continuously while Ernest penciled a wry little speech in Spanish to read to the three US wire services, correspondents from Stockholm, Havana newspapers, movie photographers, American and Cuban television, and other "friendly spongers" in attendance.[89]

Getting his start as a cub reporter at the *Kansas City Star*, Ernest had always been somewhat of an anomaly in the literary world. He had never attended university. Self-taught, he was the embodiment of American individualism and self-realization. Travelling to the source to witness places and events, he had prided himself on being a man of action rather than letters.[90] All the years fishing in Cuba had given him a story of a humble fisherman that had caused the European committee to recognize him and Cuba as a part of the civilized world.

When Harvey Breit phoned from the *New York Times* to interview him that day, he could not believe it. "I do not know what Man (with a capital M) means. I do know what a man (small m) is. I do know what man (with a small m) means and I hope I have learned something about men (small m) and something about women and about animals . . . I have learned very much from criticism."[91] Humbled, he said he would have been happier if the prize had been awarded to greater living writers, like Isak Dinesen, Bernard Berenson, and Carl Sandburg: "As a Nobel Prize winner I cannot but regret that the award was never given to Mark Twain, nor to Henry James, speaking only of my countrymen. Greater writers than these also did not receive the prize."[92] Then, he said, "What a writer must try to do is to write as truly as one can . . . to invent out of what he knows . . . to make something . . . that . . . will become part of the experience of those who read him."[93]

In a clean gray suit and dark sunglasses, a handsome and joyful young man from Cuban television soon appeared on the front steps of the Finca Vigía asking to speak with the author of *The Old Man and the Sea*. At fifty-five years of age, corpulent Papa had a full white beard, although his hair was still gray on top. As was his habit, he wore a white guayabera. In contrast to the journalist's pomp and fanfare, the writer was noticeably shy in front of the camera throughout the interview. He stood stiff, fingers fumbling for his shirttails in front of him. Sheepishly avoiding the eyes of his viewers on the other side of the camera, the author's gaze drifted to the floor as the interviewer presented him.

Although his contentment was clear, he seemed embarrassed by the spotlight. During the interview, Hemingway spoke in slow, measured, American-accented Spanish. He made a few mistakes—but through his simple declarative sentences, the author reached across cultures and moved diverse listeners with the terse sincerity of his message and his determination to accept this honor with humility and to dedicate it to his second homeland.

"I am very happy to be the first *Cubano sato* to have won this prize, and happy because it's been said that it is based on a Cuban landscape, which is Cojímar, more or less my town."[94]

Hemingway said he was donating his prize to Cuba to demonstrate his appreciation. Cojímar was a "very serious thing" to him, something sacred. He felt at home in Cuba, among family and friends, so he expressed his desire to receive the prize as "just one more Cuban." He had been fishing Cuba's waters for two decades and considered himself one of Cojímar's fishermen. Fishing with Cubans over the years, Hemingway had learned to share their respect for the power of the sea, their solidarity, and their humility. These are the values he expressed in *The Old Man and the Sea*, which resounded the world over and bestowed him with enduring international fame. After all his wretchedness and in spite of his pride, Ernest Hemingway had found Cuba, the story of Santiago's simplicity and strength, and a sincere gesture that offered him some redemption.

Hurricanes having just grazed the island during the stormy month of October, this day was calm and dry with sunlight pouring in the open windows. While Papa fielded questions from reporter after reporter on the front steps, revelers streamed in, sipping drinks, lunching on *bocaditos*, and clamoring to a steady rumble as they gathered in the sitting room. At three o'clock, the author squeezed into the sitting room to read a slightly more inebriated speech in Spanish: "Lacking are those types by which one can see the good which is humanity and those who manage to eat their failures. So, these are many words. I don't wish to abuse the word and let us now go to acts. I wish to give this Swedish medal to Our Señora the Virgen de Cobre."[95] His guests whistled and cheered. Still jabbing, he informed them that there was no point in breaking into the house to hunt for the prize money, for it had not yet arrived.

Having delivered his "discourse," he set words aside. Noting the happy fiesta catching fire in the heart of his home, drifting out his doors, and spilling onto the terrace that bordered a jungle, the writer joined the celebration of his victory, fanning its flames with good cheer and alcohol and by insisting that "his Cuban family," eleven employees in all, be included. By the time they had finished drinking, said gardener Publio Enriquez, they could not find the door.[96] Hemingway was realizing perhaps that he had enjoyed a unique friendship from the Cuban people since 1928 that not only enabled him to win the Nobel Prize but also stood out in stark contrast to political tensions between an America that supported Cuban dictators and his adopted country, offering hope for a more peaceful future. "This is one prize that belongs to Cuba, because my work was conceived and created in Cuba, with my people of Cojímar, where I'm a citizen. Throughout all the translations, this, my adopted country is present, and here I have my books and my home," he told one reporter.[97]

Having learned the power and importance of good publicity from the disaster of *Across the River and into the Trees* and from several failed Cuban leaders, Hemingway requested that Campoamor, a journalist and one of his best-connected friends in Cuba, organize a ceremony so that he could underscore his donation as a sign of his gratitude to Cuba and friendship with her people.[98] According to Campoamor, Leopoldina had influenced the writer's decision to donate his Nobel Prize to the Cuban people.[99] Although Hemingway pretended otherwise, said Campoamor, his close friends understood that he had dreamed of the

Nobel Prize. "During one of our visits to the Avenue along the Port," he recalled, "Leopoldina read [Hemingway's] cards, and predicted that he would win the greatest prize of his life for his writings that had to do with Cuba."[100] Skeptically, Ernest retorted that he would donate his prize to the shrine of the Virgen del Cobre in Santiago (in accordance with the Cuban tradition) if her prediction ever came true. Cubans often ask the Virgin for favors and promise to make a pilgrimage when their wishes are fulfilled.

Dr. José Herrera Sotolongo joked that the donation was also pragmatic, since at the time the church was one of the few places in Cuba that Hemingway felt he could be sure the medal would not be stolen. José Luis also offers interesting insights concerning Hemingway's observation of Afro-Cuban religious practices and superstitions: Hemingway was unusually superstitious in a characteristically Cuban manner (carrying lucky stones, lucky rocks, insisting on the number 13 in his license plate number, etc.).

His back still too badly injured from two plane crashes to travel to Stockholm, Hemingway appeared at the American embassy in Havana at the end of November to deliver an acceptance speech that Ambassador John Cabot read December 10 when he accepted the medal on the author's behalf in Stockholm: "Writing, at its best, is a lonely life. Organizations for writers palliate the writer's loneliness but I doubt if they improve his writing. He grows in public stature as he sheds his loneliness and often his work deteriorates. For he does his work alone and if he is a good enough writer he must face eternity, or the lack of it, each day."[101]

On December 13, Hemingway's face appeared on the cover of *Time* magazine: "An American Storyteller." When Cabot returned, he delivered the author's Nobel Medal to the Finca Vigía himself, not wanting to miss it for all the world. The prize stimulated a resurgence of interest in all his works, establishing him as a legend.[102]

• • • • •

Later that winter, smiling as he shook hands at President Batista's inauguration was Richard Nixon. Vice President Nixon flew down to meet with Cuba's leader and represent American interests, nineteen years before "Tricky Dick" resigned as president of the United States. Before departing to Havana, Nixon held a briefing with his corps of US diplomatic officers: most Cubans were against Batista, but the army was "the key to the situation." Batista is "friendly to the U.S., admires the American way of life, and believes in private enterprise." In Cuba, there were "25,000 hard core commies," but Batista, "master politician" had these "under control."[103] After his return to Washington, Nixon reported to President Eisenhower and his cabinet that the new president of Cuba was a "remarkable" man, "strong, vigorous," and "desirous of doing a job more for Cuba than doing a job [for] Batista."[104] By April, Allen Dulles, the director of the CIA, visited and organized the Bureau for the Repression of Communist Activities (BRAC) with Batista and self-proclaimed "father of the BRAC," US ambassador, former banker, and industrialist Arthur Gardner.[105]

Following Batista's second coup in 1952, the US government had been steadily increasing aid for weapons and military goods to Cuba from $400,000 in fiscal year 1953, to $1.1 million in 1954—as Batista's officers filled out requisition orders for submachine guns, recoilless rifles, hand grenades, incendiary bombs, rocket launchers, armored cars, T-33 jet-trainer aircraft, radio equipment, trucks, and more. When resistance mounted, Washington spent more: $1.6 million in 1955 and $1.7 million in 1956. When the revolution came to a head in 1957 and 1958, the Pentagon sent $2 million and $3 million respectively so that Batista could keep the world safe (from Communism) and suppress his domestic enemies.[106]

Since the rebels had been imprisoned for attacking the Moncada Barracks on July 26, 1953, their families, their comrades, journalists, and politicians had been petitioning and campaigning for their release. On May 15, the Cuban congress passed a bill granting amnesty to thirty rebels. They had served twenty-two months of their sentence when the bill was ratified by President Batista's signature. Among them was Fidel Castro. Facing the impossibility of organizing his revolution in Cuba, Fidel boarded a small tourist prop plane departing for Merida, Mexico, on July 7, and continued to Mexico City.[107]

There he met the Argentinian doctor and activist Che Guevara, who soon after joined their cause. In Mexico, Castro and Guevara sought out General Alberto Bayo. Cuban-born Bayo had fought Moorish rebels in Morocco and against Franco's forces during the Spanish Civil War.[108] He was a seasoned combat veteran, serving both as a pilot and an infantry officer, and as an instructor at military academies. By 1956, he was a sixty-four-year-old exile who liked to write poetry and owned a furniture factory. But he had trained other rebel groups, understood warfare and guerrilla tactics, and, agreeing to administer a crash course in insurgency training, proved himself as a skilled teacher and mentor to the architects of the Cuban Revolution.

In July, more pressing matters of business disrupted Ernest Hemingway's progress on an African manuscript. He and Mary had to travel to Key West to prepare the Whitehead Street property for rental. There they met Ed Hotchner, who returned with them to Havana. When *The Old Man and the Sea* film crew arrived from Hollywood at the end of August, Hemingway set his writing aside to collaborate on the script and filming during the first half of September. He insisted on employing as many of Cojímar's fishermen as possible.

During the shoot, Leland and Slim Hayward stayed at the Finca, as did Spencer Tracy, who would play Santiago, and actress Katharine Hepburn, all pickling themselves in alcohol with the author. Tracy's appearance, out of shape and refusing to exercise, irritated Hemingway: he "looked more like a rich, overweight actor than an old starving fisherman," he complained to René.[109] To create the most "authentic" set for the film, the Warner Brothers crew planted new palm trees and built new huts in the village of Boca de Jaruco. Sneaking across the border at Reynosa, Mexico, to meet with former president Prío on September 1 in a hotel room in McAllen, Texas, was Fidel Castro. It was humiliating, said the rebel leader much later in an interview, to ask Prío for funds he knew were stolen from the Cuban treasury, but he needed to finance his revolution by the means that were available to him at that time.[110] After Castro outlined his plan, Prío promised him fifty thousand dollars and assisted him in making contact with others in the United States.

That month, Hemingway received the Order of San Cristóbal at Havana Sports Palace and made a will that gave his entire estate to

Mary in the event of his death. The duty of bearing witness fell upon his staff. During the last two weeks of September, he fell ill with a kidney infection, kidney inflammation, and liver inflammation, and, bedridden, would not be able to leave his house until January.[111]

Still sick in bed in November, Ernest caught wind of the news that "two wives and two husbands later," Arnold Gingrich, his former editor, had married his old flame Jane Mason. "I can't get over it," the author exclaimed. "I can't believe she married that little turd."[112] In October and November, he had been working on his African manuscript and, by the end of December 1955, had 748 pages complete.

In November—as Castro returned to the US with Manuel Márquez to request financial support from exiles in New York, Tampa, Key West, and Miami for his revolution—Batista ran for reelection as a member of the National Progressive Coalition. Protesting the election that he believed to be rigged, former president Grau San Martín from the Authentic Party withdrew his candidacy.

On April 4 in Cuba, Colonel Ramón Barquín López led a failed conspiracy of officers, the Conspiracy of the Pure, and was sentenced to six years on the Isle of Pines. At his court-martial, he was defended by José Miró Cardona.

Meanwhile in Mexico, on June 24, Castro's group of twenty-eight revolutionaries was detained when authorities discovered a stockpile of their weapons. Arguing with police and "shouting fervent Marxist-Leninist statements," Che Guevara was kept for five weeks while his friend, Fidel, was kept for only four.[113] Later, Fidel remembered that he, too, would have been released earlier had it not been for Che's lapse of self-control. In September, an armed revolt toppled Argentina's president Juan Perón, providing an example to the young revolutionaries. While the Castro brothers were in Mexico, their father in Cuba died.

• • • • •

In September, the Hemingways boarded the *Île de France* bound for Paris to travel to Spain in the middle of the month. They stayed until the end of October to attend Feria del Pilar in Saragossa.

Leaving their drunken entourage behind them after the feria, Ernest Hemingway, feeling his internal organs rebel, heeded advice from an old friend in Madrid, Dr. Juan Manuel Madinaveitia, to reduce his alcohol to no more than six ounces of whiskey and two glasses of wine per day. As they came up from Spain, Ernest and his wife stopped off along the splendid coast for a night in Biarritz, strolled along the Charente River in Angoulême as the leaves of autumn fell and the poplar trees burned, and admired the spires of the grand gothic cathedral at Chartres as they made their way to the City of Lights. Arriving in Paris, Charles Ritz showed them to rooms 56 and 57, where they would stay in late November, throughout December, and for most of January. Due to the fighting over the Suez Canal that year, their route to Africa was closed, so they had to cancel their travel plans and spend the holidays in Paris.

CHAPTER 12

A North American Writer and a Cuban Revolution (1956–1959)

• • • • •

On November 25, the salvaged and refurbished yacht *El Granma* left Tuxpan, Mexico, with a group of Cubans aboard who had received intensive revolutionary training during several months of exile. The old and decrepit boat had been built to accommodate twelve people, yet they overloaded her with eighty-two revolutionaries, two thousand gallons of gasoline, weapons, and gear, straining her till they split her hull. To distract Batista's forces and cover Fidel's impending landing, an underground army, wearing hand-sewn emblems on their arms and organized by Frank País (a former student-teacher), attacked police and maritime headquarters and raided weapons depots.[1] When the people of Santiago de Cuba awoke, they found that the rebels had painted "M-26-7! Down with Batista!" on every block.[2] In Guantánamo and Holguín, other cells of M-26-7 had staged similar attacks.

The rebels survived their hellish sea journey of twelve hundred miles through rough seas. As Fidel Castro described it: "When the men weren't throwing up over the side, they were bailing water out of the hull."[3] When they were spotted by a Cuban helicopter on December 2, the guerrillas urgently disembarked in a swamp. Unexpectedly, they found themselves chest-high in mud, bitten by mosquitos, pinched by crabs, and unable to cut their way through the mangroves. Cuban airplanes strafed them as they ran for cover and left weapons and supplies sinking in the muck. "It was less of a 'landing' and more of a 'shipwreck,'" one of the expedition's members recalled.[4]

When they sat down to rest beside a sugarcane field at Alegría de Pío, they were ambushed—and believed they were betrayed by their guide. As Che Guevara later described with literary flair reminiscent of *A Farewell to Arms*, "We reached solid ground, lost, stumbling along like so many shadows or ghosts marching in response to some obscure psychic impulse. [After] seven days of constant hunger and sickness [at] sea . . . three still more terrible days on land . . . a night-long march interrupted by fainting and frequent rest periods, we reached a spot paradoxically known as Alegría de Pío."[5] Unfortunately, the spot they chose was one hundred yards from an army post.[6] "Everything seemed lost," thought Che Guevara as he lay on the ground with blood gushing out of his swelling neck after taking a bullet.[7] Two weeks later, forty-two fighters had been confirmed dead and seventeen had been captured.[8] On December 3, the United Press headlines announced President Batista's successful defense of the Cuban nation and the death of the rebel leader Fidel Castro: "CUBA WIPES OUT INVADERS; LEADER IS AMONG 40 DEAD."[9]

Relieved just to find each other breathing, the survivors of the *Granma* expedition reassembled and reorganized in the foothills of Purial on December 18. Of the *Granma* expedition, only twelve remained—the Castro brothers (Fidel and Raúl), Che Guevara (who was wounded and bleeding), Camilo Cienfuegos, Juan Almeida, Efigenio Amejeiras, Ciro Redondo, Julio Díaz, Calixto García, Luis Crespo, Jose Ponce, and Universo Sanchez—so they sought cover and respite in the Sierra Maestra mountains on December 21, with just seven weapons on hand.[10]

Incensed by the rebels' flight, Batista declared "suspension of Constitutional guarantees," giving absolute authority to police to suppress subversive activity and restore public order.[11] However, the move backfired. Given free rein, soldiers and police abused their authority, forcing their way into people's homes, interrogating suspects, torturing prisoners, extorting merchants, raping daughters, and murdering sons, such that the 26th of July Movement gained popularity and a more organized network of committed young leaders emerged.

In January, Ambassador Gardner enlisted embassy and CIA officials to extend full support to President Batista and to Major General

Diaz Tamayo, his chief of army operations. To attend to BRAC business, Batista's defense minister, Santiago Rey, travelled to Washington that month on a McCarthyesque mission of "erasing the red scourge" as an invited guest of the US government.[12]

In countries of Spanish descent, Christmas is a much-cherished holiday, and it typically lasts the two weeks from December 24 to January 6, beginning with "Nochebuena" (a traditional dinner on Christmas eve) and ending with "Reyes Magos" (Epiphany, the manifestation of Christ to the Gentiles, represented by the visit from the Magi, the three kings, or wise men, from the East). This holiday season had already begun in December. The people of eastern Cuba were decorating their houses with trees, tinsel, and presents for their families, and lighting candles in churches where caroling seeped from open windows into the cooling island breeze.[13] Then, after a night of bombs, sirens, and gunfire, the people of Santiago awoke to find the bodies of sons tortured by police and scattered like rubbish along the road during what came to be known as the "Bloody Christmas Massacre."

During Operación Regalo de Navidad (Operation Christmas Present), Lieutenant Colonel Fermín Cowley, military commander of a regiment in Description Holguín, had given the order to execute twenty-three dissident organizers: the executions had to occur before twelve o'clock on December 24, for no one was to be killed on Christmas eve. In practice, killing everyone that they had to kill in a single day proved impractical, so the assassinations carried over from December 23 to 25. Those killed were not detained or tried but dragged from their homes and murdered in front of their families on the eve of Christ's birth.[14]

While travelling on a recruitment mission in Havana, Frank País gave the order to the militants of M-26-7 to respond to the Bloody Christmas with acts of sabotage in Santiago de Cuba commencing December 30—exploding bombs between the hours of seven and eight, taking over the CMKC radio station to address the public, scattering nails to stop the flow of traffic, and disrupting the electric grid. Three boys were apprehended near a baseball field where the police suspected them of planting a bomb: William Soler Ledea, Froilán

Guerra Ramírez, and Hugo Alejandro de Dios. Alejandro de Díos, age twenty, was shot trying to escape while the other two were apprehended by the police amidst frantic pleas by neighbors on their behalf. They were tortured and killed over the next three days.[15]

In another part of the city, the bodies of two young Santiagueros were discovered on the side of the road: Nínive Gross Bataille, a twenty-year-old mechanic, and José de la Luz Díaz Ruiz, former sales manager of Anderson Trading Company. After dozens of young men had been murdered by the police, grieving, sadness, fury, and frustration mounted.

After attending mass in the Dolores School chapel on the morning of Epiphany, Soler Ledea's mother walked out of the church along with forty other women, dressed in black, and they began to march up Enramada Street in silence carrying a banner that said, "STOP THE MURDER OF OUR SONS. CUBAN MOTHERS."[16] Others spontaneously joined them until their numbers grew from forty to two hundred to eight hundred to one thousand women. Men stood on both sides of the streets in solidarity.

When a jeep full of soldiers screeched to a stop beside the crowd and with machine guns told them to disperse, the ladies at the head of the procession held the hands of the women beside them. Her sadness within turning to despair, then to recklessness, Soler's mother looked up, with tears welling in her eyes, at the soldier who looked so young to her and who, unlike her son, still lived: "Would you not allow me to protest the killing of my own son?"[17] she said with such intensity that the soldier responded, "Go ahead, señora," allowing the women to pass through them like water between the rocks. At the end of the procession the mothers delivered a declaration to the offices of the city newspaper, *Diario de Cuba*: they protested the crimes committed against their sons and demanded that they immediately stop. The "Mothers' Protest March" produced an uncanny effect on the rest of the Cuban population, stirring sympathies and frustrations that had been long suppressed and empowering others to act. By the end of January, six disgruntled peasants had joined Fidel's band—which had by then grown to fifteen men—making them an army of twenty-one.

With reports of human rights violations filing the newspapers, lower-level officials in the State Department started to express concern and recommend that Batista be reined in. In February, his supporter US Secretary John Foster Dulles stifled these recommendations with the observation that doing so might be "interpreted as U.S. intervention [in] internal Cuban affairs." But as power shifted and violence increased, covered diligently by the American press, the State Department was forced to ease back its support for the dictatorship in the middle of 1957, fearing that it might result in "serious criticism from Congress and the United States public."[18]

• • • • •

Surrendering to her husband's lust for younger women and concerned about his health and happiness, or perhaps no longer threatened by them, Mary allowed Ernest his "flirtations" more and more during the later years of their marriage, such as with the beautiful girl she had spotted for him in the gym during ocean their crossing whom Mary recommended he take to lunch "as a possible diversion."[19] When he returned from his date at Le Berkley, a fashionable restaurant in the eighth arrondissement, he was glum. *"On s'ennuyait à mourrir."* ("We were bored to death.") Wishing him farewell at her front door, she had not allowed him into her apartment after lunch. Did it matter? Wasn't he on a "love-making diet" anyway (under doctor's orders)? his wife asked.

One day while they were still in Paris, Charles Ritz called Ernest over at lunch. Would the "Monsieur" be willing to take the large trunk and another small one that had been stored in the hotel's luggage room since 1928?[20] What trunks? asked Ernest, not remembering storing them but recalling a trunk made for him by Louis Vuitton. When the hotel owner had the bellboy bring them up after lunch, Ernest discovered a treasure trove of newspaper clippings, Parisian ephemera, and two stacks of notebooks of his writing inside. "The notebooks! So that's where they were! *Enfin!*" exclaimed the author as he sat down afterward on the floor reading them spellbound.[21]

Far from the bloodstained Christmas in revolutionary Cuba and the aggressions of the Suez Canal crisis blocking another safari in

Africa, the Hemingways stayed at the Ritz for two months, aside from the week of vacation Mary took away from Ernest to see friends in London and to shop a bit beyond her means. While wifey was away, Ernest bet on the horses nearly every day at Auteuil and poured over the rediscovered "little blue and yellow Notebooks." Mary instructed Cartier's of London to address the bill discreetly and only to her, so when it arrived at the Ritz addressed to Ernest, and his blood pressure spiked, Mary muttered, "Those bastards!" and made amends by producing her gift, a fancy whisky flask from among the many items she had bought.[22]

The two stacks of notebooks were far greater treasures than any trinket they might have picked up. Rather than risk damage to the notebooks found in the decaying trunks in the Ritz's basement, Ernest visited the Louis Vuitton shop before his departure to buy "a battery of luggage big and varied enough for a troupe of chorus girls."[23] On January 22, they loaded thirty-three pieces of luggage on the *Île de France* before departure across the Atlantic.

• • • • •

By 1954, Ernest had sustained five major concussions—at least—the last one, produced by head-butting the door of a burning airplane to save his and Mary's life, had caused cerebrospinal fluid to leak out of his ear.[24] Complaining frequently in his letters of memory loss and frequent headaches during the last seven years of his life, Ernest Hemingway was a doctor's son who regularly consulted several physicians; he knew what was happening as he suffered from post-concussive syndrome (exacerbated by his alcoholism, hypertension, and diabetes).[25] It became increasingly difficult for him to manage the manic-depression apparently prevalent in his family, and the mood swings he had reined in during most of his life through sheer guts. In the last years, his temper became increasingly unstable.

Luckily, the notebooks linked him to the past. The younger Hemingway was now in direct communication with the aging man. Goddamnit if the notebooks did not show him what he loved, what he could do, the "hunger" of Paris—the mojo that defined him.

Taking better care of himself, Ernest was sleeping better, and his blood pressure was down. During their return trip on the *Île de France*, he befriended the ship's doctor, Dr. Jean Monnier, who had been treating him successfully by prescribing him remedies for his varied illnesses. Though he missed "Black Dog" who had passed a way while he was gone, Ernest looked enthused as he spent mornings organizing piles of papers from Paris on his library floor and picking through them as he matched them with the memories they awakened.[26]

In the mid-1950s, Leopoldina Rodríguez had also been suffering as she got on in age and was diagnosed with cancer. Throughout her terminal illness, Hemingway had been paying her hospital bills.[27] In 1956, Leopoldina died in that same Calle Infanta apartment that Hemingway had rented for her all those years. Her niece Ilse Bulit remembers the way Leopoldina would look at her—a young, plain-looking mulatto girl wearing thick glasses—and tell her that her intelligence was her only way to escape poverty. Leopoldina frequently gave her money for her studies, money that may have come from Hemingway. Ilse also remembers that, in her awkward adolescence, she harbored an aversion to Hemingway for his constant sweating, his odor of alcohol, his frequent failure to acknowledge her grandmother, Maria Ignacía Pedroso, when they saw him in public, and for an occasion when he slammed the door in Ilse's face so that he could be alone with her aunt. But recalls Ilse, Leopoldina's illness brought Hemingway much closer to their family, and particularly to Leopoldina's mother.[28]

When Leopoldina passed away that summer, Hemingway paid for and attended her funeral. "A solitary man who accompanied her remains to the cemetery paid for her funeral," wrote Cuban biographer Norberto Fuentes in the 1980s. "He was gray haired and bearded, an American wearing a short-sleeved guayabera, large moccasins and a pair of very wide baggy pants."[29] Bulit suggests that witnessing the senseless suffering of friends like Leopoldina and finally losing them may have contributed in part to Hemingway's own feelings of hopelessness and possibly his 1961 suicide.[30] One afternoon after making love, they had argued about the authenticity of his protagonist, and the old man's dreams, and she had screamed at him that he had no idea what it was truly like to come face-to-face with his own mortality. Now, Leopoldina was gone.

While somewhat worse for the wear, Ernest reconstructed his past from the Paris notebooks meticulously arranged across his Finca's floor, straining to assign order to the details of a world where reality and fiction collided. Outside of his gates, Cuba was at full-scale war again, stubbornly and foolishly flirting with hope, its people killing one another on the brink of change.

• • • • •

Following Fidel's orders, Frank País and Faustino Pérez travelled with fake identification papers to Havana to establish alliances with other factions that could advance the movement's objectives in the capital. Coming out of the tree line at the mouth of the Plata River on January 15, Castro's band of twenty-one guerrillas with twenty-three weapons approached a small army garrison, and after observing its fifteen men from a distance for a day, ambushed them, killing two soldiers and wounding five fatally. Taking three prisoners, they took control of the garrison.[31] It was their first victory, but the rebels were also aware that they had just thrown a pebble at Goliath. Indeed, twenty-one guerrillas had just picked a fight with thirty to fifty thousand army regulars (*ejército permanente*), the navy, and the air force—which benefited from aircraft, armored tanks, artillery, and heavy weaponry—seven thousand police, and the national guard (*Guardia Rural*).[32]

In response to the attack, General Batista's army ordered two of its best officers to hunt the rebels down and knock them from their mountain perch: Lieutenant Ángel Sánchez Mosquera, leading a crack platoon, and Major Joaquín Casillas, at the head of a column. Understanding that their attack on the garrison would draw Batista's army in large numbers, Fidel's insurgents looked around them at the dark forests and narrow clearings that were the natural ways of approach and decided to prepare an ambush. Having studied guerrilla tactics in Mexico, they applied their training, setting up positions around a natural clearing at Arroyo del Infierno to surprise the enemy. From miles away, the rebels could hear Lieutenant Sánchez Mosquera's frontline platoon arriving and skittishly shooting at rustling in the trees. Waiting patiently for them to come, the rebels at last opened fire—killing five and causing the rest to take flight.[33]

Applying General Boyo's teachings, Fidel's men did not pursue the attack, but pulled back into the mountains. Shooting his first enemy soldier with a single bullet through the heart, Che's gun whetted his appetite for blood; while adrenaline was still coursing through his veins, he wrote his wife, Hilda Gadea, a letter: "From the woods of Cuba, alive and thirsting for blood, I write these fiery lines in the spirit of Martí. Just when they think we're in their grasp, they see us disappear like soap through their fingers. Naturally, the fight is not completely won and many battles lie ahead, but things now lean in our favor, as they will increasingly."[34] The rebels had not only something to fight for but also effective tactics in their favor. "Guerrilla warfare resembles a boxing match in which there is no Knockout for round after round, but one of the fighters is winning on points and a time comes when the K.O. can be delivered," Herbert Matthews later wrote.[35]

After two armed clashes, it was no longer possible to deny the rebels' existence in the Sierra Maestra. General Batista deployed fourteen hundred troops to the region under the command of Colonel Pedro Barrera Pérez. Surrounding the insurgents to cut off their supply lines and prevent additional members from joining their ranks, the colonel rattled their bones with airstrikes on their positions at Caracas Peak with five of the American planes acquired from World War II: B-26 Invaders and P-47 Thunderbolts.[36] Under cover and on the move, the rebels avoided three bombardments largely through a streak of luck, missing a direct hit by two hundred yards. If the airpower had been better coordinated, the revolution might have ended by February 8.

On the morning of the ninth, forward scouts informed Fidel that 140 men to their north, from Major Casillas's column, were advancing into attack position. Before they struck them at Altos de Espinosa, Fidel dispersed his men into three units and ordered them to fall back and reassemble three days later at a predetermined position. Leading one unit, Fidel gave the other two to Che Guevara and Camilo Cienfuegos. Their guerrilla tactics were working against an enemy that appeared poorly trained in counterinsurgency techniques. As Che predicted, they were slipping like "soapy water" through the fingers of Batista's commanders just when they thought they had them in their grasp. When it was discovered that a peasant, Eutímio Guerra, had betrayed them by informing the enemy of their position and had plotted to assassinate Fidel (in exchange for ten thousand dollars and a farm promised by Batista), "El Che" stepped forward to execute him when the others avoided the unpleasant task. Establishing a reputation as a man willing to take life or give his own for the cause, he would later be feared for this ruthlessness. If both men were able soldiers, clever, and articulate, followers gravitated to Fidel as a more level-headed, judicious, and political leader.

An essential element of the movement's noncombatant strategy was to win the favor of the foreign press, particularly that of North America.[37] To assure his mission's success, Fidel sent two of "the Twelve" *Granma* survivors, Faustino Pérez and René Rodríguez, to establish contact with Felipe Pazos, former president of the Cuban National Bank, and his son Javier, a student activist at the University of Havana. Felipe knew Ruby Hart Philips, the *New York Times*' resident correspondent personally. When Felipe walked into her office that morning to whisper in her ear that Fidel was alive, Ruby nearly dribbled her morning coffee down her chin.[38] As the island's most visible American journalist, she had to rule herself out from making direct contact with Fidel.[39] After she racked the brains of her officemate Ted Scott, he said, "Ding dong. Got a letter yesterday from a guy who'd be perfect for it."

Having reported for the *New York Times* since the Spanish Civil War, Herbert Matthews had been as inspired with the Loyalist cause and the International Brigades as Martha Gellhorn and Ernest Hemingway, and as heartbroken when they had been crushed by Franco's fascist army. Ernest called him "as brave as a badger," and Martha said he had most likely been Ernest's model for Robert Jordan, the hero of *For Whom the Bell Tolls*.

Slipping past enemy positions, the rebels brought Matthews undetected to Fidel's hideout.[40] At dawn, the master of ceremonies appeared like a black-bearded wizard on the scene. The other *barbudos*, as they were called because of their beards, had laid out a blankie for them and served tomato juice, and ham-cracker sandwiches, and hot coffee in tins. Ever observant, Fidel noticed Matthews checking out his sniper scope, so he informed the journalist that his men had more than fifty of the sort, infinitely useful for killing Batista's soldiers from a thousand meters away: "They never know where we are, but we already know where they are." Like a gracious host at the end of a business luncheon, the guerrilla broke open a box of good cigars, which he had commandeered for this special occasion, and during a three-hour interview, the two men smoked and whispered in Spanish and English. Throughout their talk, soldiers ran here and there, taking orders from Fidel and bringing the report from the "second column," which did not exist, as they wanted Matthews to believe they were more numerous and better organized than they might have been.[41] As the interview was ending, Fidel called one of his men over to show him "the cash" used to pay the *guajiros* (peasants). Unwrapping a stack of pesos one foot high (the equivalent of four thousand dollars), Fidel assured the reporter of his financing that would assure his victory: "He had all the money he needed and could get more." The coinage he had obtained from displaced previous governors who had raided the coffers was a powerful weapon against poorly paid and resentful troops. The morale of Batista's soldiers was too low, and they would not fight: "Why should soldiers die for Batista for $72 per month? When we win, we will pay them $100, and they will serve a free and democratic Cuba."[42]

"You have taken quite a risk in coming here, but . . . we will get you out safely," promised the rebel leader as Matthews left; in truth, both men had taken a risk, well worth it in the end. Having attended to the *gringo del periódico*, Fidel, the "great talker" whose personality, said Matthews, was "overwhelming," turned to the deadly business of revolt during the first National Directorate of M-26-7, meeting with Frank País, Raúl Castro, Armando Hart, Haydée Santamaría, Celia Sánchez, Faustino Pérez, and Wilma Espín in the mountains. When a guard stopped Herbert Matthews and his wife on their way back into Havana, then let them go, Mrs. Matthews, exhaling in relief, appreciated that the private could have been promoted to general if he had only searched them and found the notes containing Fidel's signature.

Even though the rebels remained alive in the sierra, a thorn in Batista's side, they were not likely to succeed without recruiting more soldiers. Many new recruits had been urban rebels who became suspects due to their subversive activities, and, hunted by homicidal police, fled town to the relative safety of the mountains. During the first meeting, the National Directorate worked out a system for recruiting new guerrillas, equipping and resupplying themselves, and communicating with each other. A month after the meeting, the police arrested and jailed M-26-7 leaders Frank País, Armando Hart, Carlos Franqui, and Faustino Pérez for their subversive activities.

On February 24, the *New York Times* reported, "Cuban Rebel is Visited in Hideout: Castro [Leader of Revolt] Is Alive and Still Fighting in the Mountains. First Reporter to Talk with Fidel Castro Is Informed that the Movement Is Gaining," and published an interview that won Fidel's rebels much support in America and around the world.[43] The article exposed the lies concealed by the Cuban dictatorship and Batista's army, and made a laughing stock of Herbert Matthews's rivals at his own paper, who had previously declared Fidel dead. Apparently enthralled with Fidel's "overpowering personality," wild beard, and glowing cigar, Matthews confirmed that Fidel was indeed full of life and described him in the most glowing terms—idealizing the revolutionary and solidifying his position as the leader of the movement: "This was quite a man—a powerful six-footer, olive-skinned, full-faced, with a straggly beard . . . educated, dedicated, fanatic, a man of ideals, of courage, and of remarkable qualities of leadership. It was easy to see that his men adored him and also to see why he has caught the imagination of the youth of Cuba all over the island." By Fidel's own profession, he was committed to "democracy, social justice, the need to restore the Constitution."[44]

Possibly equating Castro with the International Brigades that he still adored and could not let go, Matthews had written from the heart, and his article had transformed Fidel Castro from "hot-headed communist to youthful face of the future."[45]

Batista's administration initially censored the *New York Times* interviews and reports about Fidel Castro from the island's news, so Matthews and Ruby Hart Phillips ran articles about its censorship, causing his administration to look worse, forcing him to shift gears, and to respond. His defense minister, Santiago Verdeja, said the story was a "chapter in a fantastic novel."[46] His military chief in the eastern provinces, General Martín Díaz Tamayo, said that the "imaginary interview" could not have taken place, for it would be "impossible for anyone to get through the lines of troops surrounding the section in which Señor Castro is operating without being stopped by Government patrols." When the *New York Times* answered these pronouncements with a photograph of Fidel Castro and Herbert Matthews smoking cigars during their interview in the sierra, they caused further embarrassment and hilarity to ensue.[47]

Batista's administration was not the only one caught with its pants down, for the American embassy, headed by Arthur Gardner, had been closely allied with the Cuban dictator, regardless of his violence, suppression, and corruption, because he supported the BRAC and the CIA's war on Communism. Regretting Matthews's "unbalanced" and "overzealous" portrayal of the rebels, the US embassy contacted the reporter to tell him off the record that several officials were "seething" about the article and to inquire if he could begin pitching for the home team.[48]

• • • • •

In addition to Fidel, there were many other revolutionary leaders, such as the president of the Federation of University Students (Federación Estudiantil Universitaria, or FEU) and founding member of the Directorio Revolucionario Estudiantil (DRE) José Antonio Echeverría, who had participated in military actions in Costa Rica, campaigned for the Castros' release from the Isle of Pines, and had visited their group in Mexico to sign a pact pledging the DRE's support in overthrowing Batista. Echeverría had many supporters, and some argued he was a better leader for the movement than Fidel. When Echeverría was reelected unanimously to the FEU, he told those who elected him: "The History book is awaiting us. We shall write in it actions worthy of our ancestors. Ahead us on our shoulders we representatives of Cuban youth must accomplish a serious task." There was two-time former congressman from the Authentic Party and DRE member Menelao Mora Morales, who had fought against Machado as an Abecedario. There was Frank País Pesqueira, leader of the Santiago de Cuba group, Revolutionary National Action, and urban coordinator of M-26-7. Some felt that the *New York Times* fathered Fidel Castro by thrusting him into the limelight and to the top of the movement, yet one must too appreciate that many leaders became martyrs in 1957, dying in the fighting, as did Echeverría, Mora, and País, leaving a vacuum of power and one man at the forefront. Fidel survived when others, including Che and Camilo, died.

On a clear day of spring, a bright red truck, with "FAST DELIVERY, *ENTREGA RÁPIDA DE PAQUETES. EXPRESO HABANA*" ("Havana Express Package Service") written in white across the side, sped down San Lázaro Street toward the center of Havana. When it reached the southern entrance of the presidential palace, the truck and two cars beside it screeched to a halt. Fifty men with submachine guns and grenades poured out the back, shot a private at the gate, then the sergeant behind him, and a colonel in the interior on the first floor, forcing their way into the southern entrance of the palace. On the rooftops of neighboring buildings (Museo Nacional de Bellas Artes, Hotel Sevilla, and a tobacco factory), snipers had taken positions to support the attack. They succeeded in entering the first floor of the palace, hoping the dictator would be in the offices there.

Having received a tip-off from an informant that an attack was imminent, President Batista barricaded himself and his family on the top floors, awaiting the perpetrators with a "loaded .45," and took up the telephone to bark orders to his aides as they defended the citadel. The only way to reach the third floor was by elevator. Finding themselves trapped on the second floor without a way to get through, the attackers were cut down by machine guns. For forty minutes gunfire rang out in the presidential palace, and for three hours more when a line of ten tanks, several thousand troops, and antiaircraft guns fired at a neighboring building to dislodge a sniper. "Witnesses said the palace steps and patio ran with blood."[49] Thirty-five insurgents and five palace guards were killed that day in March. Among them was a former congressman and an important leader in "the movement," Menelao Mora Morales, and Peter Korinda, an American tourist who had stepped out on the Parkview Hotel's balcony to survey the action and taken a stray bullet to the neck.

Meanwhile, another group of fifteen militants, led by José Antonio Echeverría, simultaneously attacked the radio station Radio Reloj in Vedado while the famed news program was in progress to shout an announcement into the microphone: Batista had been assassinated, rebel forces had taken control, and a general strike was already underway.[50] Leaving several bullet holes on the recording booth glass and delivering their message, the attackers fell back toward the safety of Havana University, but as their aquamarine-and-cream Ford '57 turned the corner of L Street to University Avenue, José Antonio Echeverría encountered a patrol car full of policemen who gunned down "the Manzanita" (the twenty-four-year-old was affectionately nicknamed "Little Apple" by his friends for his chubby, rose-colored cheeks) in plain view. Two hours later, General Tabernilla's voice came on the airwaves to deliver the ominous message that the rebellion had been put down and that Batista had survived. Had the attack succeeded that day, Echeverría's supporters have theorized, it might have given more importance to the anti-Communist DRE and "saved" Cuba from the Castros.[51]

Beaming on the front page of the *New York Times* in a picture where he is surrounded by his soldiers cheering, Batista emerged as a survivor from the attack and emphasized prophetically to the press:

> It is not important whether or not Fidel Castro is alive, but it is important that Mr. [Herbert] Matthews has stated that he heads an "anti-Communist and pro-democratic group." This is entirely erroneous . . . Unemployment in Cuba is today much less than in previous regimes. Since the population is increasing as rapidly in Cuba as in the rest of the world there is bound to be a considerable number of unemployed. However, the economic conditions of Cuba have never been better.[52]

After the assassination attempt, Batista's men locked down the capital city, suspending the usual twelve flights per day between Havana and Miami, curbing television and radio broadcasts, and imposing a 6:00 p.m. curfew as Batista's men searched vehicles and hunted down assailants in a backlash of violence that continued throughout the night with gun battles erupting across the city. Some victims had improbable connections with the attack and appeared to have been killed gratuitously by Batista's police as collateral damage, or simply for being members of the opposition, such as distinguished attorney and former senator Pelayo Cuervo Navarro. Carlos Márquez-Sterling, another vocal opponent of Batista, attorney, and professor of law at Havana University, was also detained and later released.

From the end of March until the middle of May, Anselmo Alliegro, a senator and president of the Cuban Congress, called for a compromise, appointing a bicameral commission to engage in discussions with members of the opposition to overcome the nation's current impasse. Skeptical of the commission's capacity to guarantee a fair election, M-26-7 and the Orthodox Party rejected these initiatives. At the end of March, Batista, heavily guarded, attended the opening of a new refinery for Shell Oil, insisting that the mountain guerrillas had been eradicated, and attended a glitzy party with his wife in a sequined dress, his cabinet in tails, and several leading members of the Mob smirking as they shook his hand at the grand opening of the $24 million, 572-room, 25-floor Havana Hilton on March 22 at the corner of Twenty-Three and L, also known as La Rampa, because it towers over the rest of Vedado.

• • • • •

As Havana glued itself to the radio, rumors buzzed, and speculation simmered among the staff of the kitchen at the Finca Vigía. But like many Cubans, Ernest Hemingway had been trying to get on with his own life. Fighting through the consequences of concussions, and the medicinal haze to treat them and other illnesses, he filed his taxes, answered four hundred letters, and growled at visitors whenever they unexpectedly appeared. That spring Ernest attempted something new and difficult: giving up hard alcohol for his writing, for his health, and for his wife. Off the sauce, Papa wrote to "Hotchenroll," Ed Hotchner, that he had his weight down to 210 pounds and blood pressure to 140 over 68: "The reason before I didn't write and Mary did was that was working over the ears and writing has been difficult. Had last drink of hard liquor on March 5th. Will not bore you with the details. It is about as much fun as driving a racing motor car without lubrification for a while. A good car that you know well and just what it takes to lubricate and just what it can do with lubrification."[53]

When a Miss Phoebe Adams, a flirtatious editor in a floppy red straw hat turned up at the Finca requesting fiction for the *Atlantic Monthly*'s hundred-year anniversary, he granted her godforsaken wish by churning out "Get a Seeing-Eyed Dog" and "Man of the World"—two stories that would have benefited from further revision and seemed to express a growing fear that his injuries and ailments were causing him to go blind—for one thousand dollars apiece.[54] In the first story, a man sullenly insisting on spelling the title term with a *d* sends his wife away so that he can get used to a "Seeing-eye[d] dog" on his own. In "Man of the World," an old man who haunts gambling joints in Nevada loses his eyesight in a brawl, then routinely insists on taking a twenty-five-cent cut from whomever he hears winning at slots.

When majordomo René Villarreal brought the girl he would marry, Elpidia, or "Fanny," to the Finca, Ernest took a break from struggling with sentences in his bedroom to ogle the pretty young lady with black hair and a beautiful smile, and to congratulate them. "*Cuida bien de mi hijo Cubano*" ("Take care of my Cuban son"), he told Fanny, and the next day when René brought in his mail, he said, "Your fiancée seems like a wonderful girl. You know you can move to the bungalow if you want. That way, you'll always be close to her."

"Thank you, Papa, but we already rented an apartment very close. It's just outside the Finca. I can see the pine tree path from our window."

"You can take the bungalow and save on the rent. Miss Mary and I always want you to be close. You can always move into the house when we're away."[55]

It was a generous offer that the couple politely refused. Fanny got pregnant, and they lost their firstborn before the end of that year. When René came to work as usual that week, Ernest ordered him to go home and be with his wife. His first responsibility was to his wife and family, said Papa; time would heal their wounds, but they had to console and take care of each other.

Ernest's first son, Jack, had also moved down to Havana that year with his wife, Puck, and their two daughters to work for a brokerage firm. Unintentionally, wrote Mary, she and Ernest had given them less attention than planned, though she had babysat the girls, their animals, and plants when Jack fell ill with hepatitis.[56]

• • • • •

For the attack on the presidential palace and Radio Reloj, reprisals continued the following month. On April 20, Colonel Esteban Ventura Novo and his men from Batista's secret service burst into apartment 201 of 7 Humboldt Street and slayed four youths for their suspected involvement: Fructuoso Rodríguez (who succeeded Echeverría as the president of the FEU and one of the founders of the DRE), Joe Westbrook Rosales (founding member of the DRE), José Machado Rodríguez, and Juan Pedro Carbó Serviá (also wanted for the killing of Colonel Antonio Blanco Rico). On April 23, Robert Taber from CBS News became the second American journalist to interview Fidel Castro in the Sierra Maestra for a television broadcast.

In May, the urban rebels responded to the Humboldt Street massacre with a bombing campaign in and around Havana—with eighteen exploding in one evening—on May 5. Five days later, the Urgency Court of Santiago tried 115 suspects en masse for participation in the *Granma* expedition, or the November 30 uprising; 40 rebels were sentenced to one to eight years, including 22 who had landed with the *Granma*, and the other 75 were acquitted and released—among them was key M-26-7 organizer, Frank País.[57] During the verdict, a dissenting judge, Manuel Urrutia Lleó, defended the insurgents. He would later become the first provisional president under the revolutionary government. On May 19, Taber's documentary, "Rebels of the Sierra Maestra: The Story of Cuba's Jungle Fighters" aired on CBS, building on Herbert Matthew's flattering portrayal of Fidel. On May 27, Taber published the same material in an illustrated article in *Life* Magazine, one day later in *Bohemia*, and two days later in *Life en Español*. These articles and news programs, in which Castro reiterated that he was not a Communist, were viewed by millions of people.

Under pressure from American press and displeased with the American ambassador's mismanagement of Cuban affairs, the State Department retired Ambassador Gardner on May 14 and sent in Earl E. T. Smith as a replacement in June. Smith was a war hero, an Eisenhower intimate, and a former businessman who did not speak a lick of Spanish; his ability to stop a long-accumulating rebellion in progress would prove limited.[58]

At the time, the Cuban economy was not raising the standard of living for Cubans while foreign profit and corruption were running rampant. On May 26, 1957, *Carteles*, a Cuban magazine reported that twenty members of Batista's government had bank accounts in Switzerland with deposits of more than $1 million apiece. In addition, American investors were making a profit of $77 million annually from Cuban holdings, but only employing a little over 1 percent of the Cuban population. On the day the article appeared, rebels crippled the massive Tinguaro Sugar Mill in Matanzas with a bomb.[59]

Two days later, a force of twenty-seven *Ortodoxo* insurgents financed by former president Prío and led by Calixto Sánchez White, the former president of the Cuban Pilots' Association and suspect in the presidential palace attack, left the Bay of Biscayne aboard an eighty-foot yacht, the *Corinthia*, and landed at Cabonico. Their fate became a subject of controversy as the government, under the direction of Colonel Cowley, reported capturing 5 and killing 16 while the invaders said they landed 150 men who split into three groups that later incorporated themselves with Fidel's men.[60]

Conscripted by Frank País's 26th of July Movement in Santiago, fifty fresh recruits had been incorporated into Fidel's guerrilla force in the Sierra Maestra in March. Under the rigors of training, foraging, and constantly moving through the jungle, some of the new recruits quit, but those who stayed on grew lean and hungry for action. To distract Batista's attention away from the Corinthian landing to the North, Fidel and Che plotted what to attack next. Che had been hankering to pounce on the convoys full of soldiers whom they had been observing passing regularly on a nearby road, but with reliable intelligence from an ally in the government, Fidel thought it shrewder to take El Uvero garrison.[61]

Pitting eighty rebels against fifty-three Rural Guard soldiers, the surprise attack, lasting three hours on May 28, marked a significant win for the rebels. From the perspective of "El Che," it was a turning point: "For us, it was a victory that meant our guerrillas had reached full maturity. From this moment on, our morale increased enormously, our determination and hope for victory also increased, and though the months that followed were a hard test, we now had the key to the secret of how to beat the enemy."[62] Subsequent to the attack, Fidel promoted Che to comandante and gave him control of a column of guerrilla troops. That same day, urban terrorists detonated a bomb, shut down the grid of Havana Electric Company, and left the capital without power for two days.

• • • • •

In the eye of a revolutionary storm striking Cuba once again, Ernest, standing in his bedroom beside the bookshelf, and sitting barefoot at the table beneath the thatched arbor beside the swimming pool, had begun to put Paris to paper. In the days when "there was no money to buy books," you borrowed them from Shakespeare and Company, "the library and bookstore of Sylvia Beach at 12 rue de l'Odéon. On a cold windswept street, this was a lovely, warm, cheerful place with a big stove in winter, tables and shelves of books, new books in the window, and photographs on the wall of famous writers both dead and living."[63]

It was in Paris that he had discovered he could write about a place better when in another: he called it "transplanting" (a gardening technique) and supposed it could be "as necessary with people as it is with other sorts of growing things."[64] And now he was in Cuba, writing the story of Paris, of his own awakening in the cafés along the Seine where he had learned to do what he loved—writing stories like "Big Two-Hearted River" and "Up in Michigan."

Looking up, then at the farm in front of him in Cuba, there was the swimming pool, the quail drinking in the pool, the lizards living and hunting in the arbor overhead, and the strange and lovely birds always living on the farm, the smell of jasmine and the blossoms of the *framboyan*, and the eighteen kinds of mangoes, the boy who had started transplanting in Oak Park in books, who found his father on Walloon Lake, who put pen to paper in upper Michigan without success, who had seen Cézannes in the Musée du Luxembourg, the horrors of war in Italy and Spain, the heights of life and death in Kilimanjaro, what a man could endure in Cojímar, and the Stream, and then he had returned to his island to paint his Paris with incomparable clarity.[65] The confessions of the narrative ached with nostalgia. As he aged—far too rapidly—Hemingway reflected on his origins, and painfully remembered the sins he had committed as a young man, because of ambition: betrayals of first wife, Hadley, and of himself for pride; the loss of his first family; Paris, and the magic . . . it was gone now, but there was a part of it he could hold onto, forever, if he could just get the words right. Could he still see how good it was as he wrote it? Or as he read it back the next day?

While a writer who had just turned fifty-eight chased eternity in the hills above Havana, eternity was also chasing a twenty-three-year-old rebel leader, Frank País. Having just been informed that he was being followed, País had fled with Raúl Pujol Arencibia to a "safe-house" that was not safe. Betrayed by an informant, they were shot in the back of the head by Colonel José Salas Cañizares, chief of police in Santiago de Cuba. Joining many other young men like José Antonio Echeverría who had hoped for freedom and fair play, they became martyrs *para siempre*.[66] His brother had met the same fate a month before. It is estimated that sixty thousand *santiagueros* attended the funeral the following day and continued to protest his murder in a general strike that shut Santiago down for three days during the US ambassador's first trip to the city. The following month, the Cuban secret service made dozens of arrests.

On August 20, a column of fifty men led by Fidel Castro took an outpost manned by one hundred Cuban soldiers at Palma Mocha in the Las Cuevas region. Three days later, the film version of *The Sun Also Rises* was released. The rights had been purchased by producer Darryl Zanuck. It was directed by Henry King with screenplay by Peter Viertel, starring Ava Gardner, Tyrone Power, Errol Flynn, Mel Ferrer, and Robert Evans. Much to the producer's disappointment before the picture's release, Hemingway had disparaged it to the press by telling them that the film was "so disappointing" that he walked out twenty-five minutes into it. Mr. Zanuck, who made $1,500,000 in revenue during the film's first year, fired back: "I tell you what happened . . . He was paid $15,000 by a third party for the book, and [we] bought it from that party for $150,000 . . . Maybe that's one of the reasons Mr. Hemingway is sore. That's not my fault . . . I don't think he saw the picture. I think someone told him about it. He doesn't have the right to destroy us publicly for something he's been paid money for."[67] Having given all rights to his first novel and film to his first wife, the writer did not stand to benefit financially from its success.

In a constant state of fear and revulsion, Cubans were weary of the dictator who was ruling their island and in favor of any alternative. Bringing the reality of the situation home, René Villarreal's childhood friend from San Francisco de Paula, Guido Pérez, had been found tortured and murdered. In another instance, René's brother, Luis, came home from his job at the mineral water company during the middle of the day with his cap in his hand, so René knew something was wrong. Their sister-in-law, Chela, had told him that her husband (their brother), Helio, had not been home all night. Their mother became very anxious when a body matching Helio's description was found in an abandoned lot in Havana. Papa saw the troubled faces and asked what was wrong. Then he instructed Juan to take René and Luis to the morgue to see if it was their brother's body. The person lying on the table had been tortured—he had broken fingers, stab wounds to the chest, and a *quemarropa* [clothes-burner] .22 caliber police-pistol shot through his chest at point-blank range. It was said that the police placed a burner beneath a chair to burn their victims slowly when they wanted to extract a confession, and the genitals of the man they saw were badly burned—but it was not their brother. When Helio, who had a reputation as a womanizer, turned up late the next day after a night of drinking, his relieved family gave him a thorough scolding.

Even closer to home, one dark night, Mary, Ernest, and René were awakened by the frantic barking of their dogs. Parking one jeep in front of the Finca Vigía and another in front of the Steinharts' house, about nine Cuban soldiers in khaki uniforms were approaching the house. Upset by the intrusion, Hemingway, meeting them at the stairs, asked, "What are you looking for?! What are you doing on my property?!" The soldiers, looking tired and reeking of alcohol, responded that they were looking for "*jóvenes revolucionarios*." "There are no *revolucionarios*," said the author. "Leave my property immediately."[68] Skulking off, the soldiers were followed by barking dogs to the entrance. "*Esos hijos de puta*—probably wanted money to get more drunk!" said Hemingway, beside himself.[69] The following day, one of the Hemingways' dogs, Muchakos, did not show up to breakfast, and René found his body hidden behind the trees with his skull crushed by the butt of a rifle. "Those animals!" Hemingway said, and tried to report them to their superiors, requesting support from the US embassy to bring the soldiers to justice, but nothing came of it.

As September turned to October 1957, the Hemingways travelled to New York City, staying at the Westbury Hotel, in the company of African game warden Denis Zaphiro, for four months. There, Ernest would join Ed Hotchner to watch Carmine Basilio win the middleweight championship against Sugar Ray Robinson and the first two games of the World Series between the Braves and the Yankees at Yankee Stadium. When the Soviet Union launched Sputnik I and II into the stratosphere in October and November, many Americans fretted that the Russians were winning the "space race," but Ernest was not perturbed. It might motivate the United States to spend more dough on science, he said.

At the end of the preceding summer, Gregory had been admitted into Miami Medical Center, diagnosed with schizophrenia and administered electric shock treatments. When his son wrote him on August 20, "Sorry that I got into this shape, but I will be out of here soon," his father called the hospital, spoke with his son's doctors, and arranged to take care of the bill as his son had requested. "They say that treatment cannot possibly do your brain any harm . . . We want to do everything that can be done to make you well, Gig. Do you have a good radio?"[70] In the middle of October when he was released, Ernest flew up to Miami to retrieve him from the hospital, driving with him as far as Key West in a rented car and giving him a ticket to Cuba. Instead of taking the flight, Greg cashed the ticket in and never saw his father again.

• • • • •

In the middle of October, leaders of vying factions like the Authentic Party, Orthodox Party, Revolutionary Directorate, M-26-7, Revolutionary Workers Directorate, and Democrats announced the formation of the Cuban Liberation Junta, setting aside differences to bring about the overthrow of Fulgencio Batista. There was a growing tension between members of the Miami Pact devised by the junta and the Sierra Maestra Pact that Castro had worked out with Raúl Chibás and Felipe Pazos in July. (Coincidentally, Pazos's eleven-year-old son, Felipe, Jr., played mandolin alongside Spencer Tracy in *The Old Man and the Sea.*) Feeling that ex-president Prío's endgame was to return himself to power, Castro would renounce any obligations to the junta in December and inform them that he had already designated Manuel Urrutia Lleó as provisional president.

In November, the opulent Hotel Capri and Casino, owned by mobster Santos Trafficante Jr., opened two blocks down the street from the Hotel Nacional, and Che Guevara began publishing an illicit newspaper to run counterculture to the national press: "As for the dissemination of our ideas, first we started a small newspaper, *El Cubano Libre* [The Free Cuban] . . . We had a mimeograph machine brought up to us from the cities, on which the paper was printed."[71] On November 10, Ed Hotchner's television adaptation of Hemingway's short stories, *The World of Nick Adams*, premiered on CBS and received mostly positive reviews.

From October until December, Ernest alternated between revisions of *A Moveable Feast* (300 pages that Mary retyped), *The Garden of Eden* (still rough, repetitious, and somewhat condescending, but with brilliant passages showing potential), and the chronicles of Africa (843 pages).[72] From New York, the Hemingways travelled to Washington, DC, on the way back to Cuba. On the first day of 1958 while Mrs. Hemingway was making a key lime pie for New Year's Day, her mother's sanatorium cabled her to tell her she had "expired" after twenty-four hours of sickness the day before. Phoning in the funeral arrangements for flowers, a singer, and a Christian Science reader, she flew home dutifully to Minnesota to attend alone: "My mother rested among flowers in one of her favorite rose-red dresses, her skin made up unobtrusively with rouge, her thin old hands crossed on her stomach. But no artistry could erase the look of permanent distress on her features."[73]

Although their health had been on the mend with Papa's liver, kidneys, and blood cholesterol, and Mary's anemia improving, it had been a trying year with the burden of financial problems from Jack, Ernest's first son, the ongoing shock therapy of his third son, Gregory, the bombings and poverty in Cuba, the fishless barrenness of the Gulf Stream, their dog killed by Batista's soldiers, and the death of Mary's mother.[74] At the end of December, Gregory Hemingway returned to Miami Medical Center to continue treatment.

While Castro's revolution had been gaining popularity by pushing government forces from positions, massive hotels were rising along the skyline of Havana with mafia-run casinos filled with tourists and night clubs in every alley and recess. Having established contacts in the thirties and strengthened them residing in the United States, Batista had returned ready to do business in Cuba on an unprecedented scale—providing protection and incentives that promised to make himself, Meyer Lansky, Santo Trafficante, and their associates a great deal of money.[75] Consequently from 1956 to 1958, the Capri, the Riviera, then the Hilton, would compete to become the most attractive, luxurious, and lucrative casinos in the world as the president dispensed public funds and his friends and relatives profited from building and operation contracts. In December, a photojournalist from *Paris Match*, Enrique Meneses, liaised with Fidel's forces in the sierra, and stayed with them for four months, publishing humanizing photos of them that endeared their cause.

Accompanying the hotel and casino boom in this unparalleled "sin city" was a boom in the sex industry. Rivaling those of Paris's Montmartre, chorus line cabarets opened in all of the major hotels, such as Tropicana, Parisien in the Hotel Nacional, Salón Rojo in the Hotel Capri, and El Caribe in the Habana Hilton. There was a profusion of nightclubs with names that were welcoming for American boys: Pennsylvania, Johnny's Dream Club, Tally-Ho, Dirty Dick's, Hollywood Cabaret, High Seas, Skippy's Hideaway, Surf Club, Zombie Club, Pachin, Rumba, Las Vegas, 21, 212, Sans Souci, Ali Bar, Johnny's 88 Club, Club Bambu, Topeka, 1900 Club, and Turf Club. On the corner of every street there seemed to be a Cuban pimp leading a gang of young men into an alley where bar-brothels had been stocked with Cuban "B-girls" (bargirls) dressed in blue jean shorts and ponytails, speaking good English, and looking "just like the little blond girls they were afraid to fuck back home."[76]

The Hemingways were weary of gangsters and revolutions, but not yet sure where would be better: "The tunnel is finished and will be opened in February they say. They are talking of filling in the bar from the Maine Monument to the Castillo de La Punta to make more land to build Hotels on. The present Malecón to be an inside street . . . Havana is more like Miami Beach all the time. I don't know where to go. Do you?"[77] The fish seemed to have disappeared from the ocean, leaving Cojímar's fishermen more desperate than ever.[78] Nonetheless, the Finca Vigía still offered a refuge where most days it was possible to focus on one's work, to recover one's health, and live a comfortable life.[79]

Through the narrative of his manuscript of *A Moveable Feast*, Hemingway was studying regret, hunger, memory, evil, and the ephemerality of human paradise—clearly inspired by the paradise disappearing around him. Alternately in another manuscript, *The Garden of Eden*, he was chasing similar themes, concurrently developing similar characters, sunning, swimming, and riding three bicycles in Le Grau-du-Roi, Aigues-Mortes, Camargue, and Hendaye—drinking aperitifs in the Gulf of Lions—romantic settings as incorruptible as the steep blue slopes of Cayo Paraíso or the unending sky of mighty Africa. As dusk descended on his life and confusion blurred his genius, he painted the world in Impressionist watercolors as natural and enchanting and bewildering as his youth. The themes of the story were insatiable hunger, androgyny, adultery, his writing, and the destruction of paradise.[80]

• • • • •

All of Cuba's arms, aircraft, tanks, ships, and military supplies had come from the United States, such that Cuba depended upon its ally for parts. The three branches of the Cuban military had been trained by advisors from the US armed forces. By January 1958, Castro's rebels advanced on Manzanillo, an important sugar refinery port in the east of Cuba. Under pressure from the rebels, the US embassy, and the press, President Batista restored the guarantees of the Cuban constitution and its bill of rights in the middle of February.[81]

The rebels raided the Boniato jail on January 26 to break out Felipe Pazos and Armando Hart, who had been arrested by Batista's police.[82] In addition, Fidel explained during a February 4 interview for *Look* magazine that his rebel army would be using a tactic that had been a part of Cuban warfare since generals Máximo Gómez and Antonio Maceo had discovered its effectiveness during the one of the three wars for Cuban independence: crop burning, specifically sugar. It was effective because it impacted the businessmen who controlled the country and understood only business.[83]

Eloy Gutiérrez Menoyo was a Spaniard whose family had fought for the Loyalists and fled to Cuba after the Spanish Civil War. His brother was killed in the assault on Batista's presidential palace in March 1957. When he identified the body at the morgue, Menoyo vowed to honor his brother by continuing the fight. In November, he began to organize a force of three hundred men from the DRE to open a front in the Sierra Escambray, intending to stick a second thorn in Batista's side.

In December 1957, a red-headed, overweight, pasty-faced kid from Toledo, Ohio, had turned up in an all-white leisure suit in Havana, looking like one more tourist on the prowl. When he began asking around for someone to take him to Fidel, it became clear that the chain-smoking twenty-nine-year-old was not looking for a prostitute. William Alexander Morgan had read about the Cuban revolution in the newspapers, including Fidel's interview in the *New York Times*. When his friend Jack Turner had been caught smuggling arms to Cuba, then "tortured and tossed to the sharks by Batista," Morgan had heard the "bell that tolled in the jungles of the Sierra Maestra."[84]

Making contact with potential allies in Old Havana, Morgan met a radicalized student named Roger Rodríguez. Conversing in hushed tones with Rodríguez, Morgan explained that he was not intimidated by the danger and wanted to fight for good: "The most important thing for free men to do is to protect the freedom of others." Yes, said Rodríguez, distrustful of the gringo and his story, suspecting him to be a CIA agent.

The rebels who escorted Morgan also suspected that he was a spy, so they took him to Menoyo's group in the Sierra Escambray rather than endangering their leader by bringing him to Fidel. He was so fat, joked one rebel soldier, that he had to be CIA. There, they ran Morgan ragged over the hills and walked him through poisonous shrubs until his fair skin swelled up and turned red. *"No soy mulo!"* ("I am not a mule!") he protested but continued to march, proving himself in the process.[85]

Afterward, they began to feel sorry for the gringo who had lost thirty-five pounds and whose appearance had changed dramatically. They began to believe him. When their rebel band was attacked, Morgan showed bravery during the battle and earned their respect. Having served in the US Army, he had more experience than most of the student rebels, was adept at judo and knife fighting, and soon became a favorite among the men. When the group was later interviewed by the *New York Times*, the American was a curiosity and so was asked what he was doing there fighting with the rebels. "Here are men who are fighting for liberty and justice in their land and I am here to fight with them," he replied.[86]

Morgan was afterward promoted to the rank of comandante by Fidel Castro. He, Menoyo, and Che were the only foreigners to earn that honor. When US-Cuban relations soured, Morgan had his American citizenship revoked in September 1959, yet many in Cuba regarded him as a hero, including his wife, Olga, who had met him fighting for freedom in the Cuban revolution. Regretfully, after the war ended, Morgan would witness the autocratic tendencies of the revolutionary government firsthand—being imprisoned and executed for treason despite his service to its cause.

Taking the offensive, Fidel Castro gave his brother Raúl command of fifty to eighty riflemen and ordered him to create a second front in the Sierra Cristal. He gave command of another column to Juan Almeida to create a third front in Santiago de Cuba. Taking up positions in the mountains within striking distance of the northeastern plantations of the Oriente, Raúl Castro at first had the mission of applying economic pressure burning fields of sugarcane, but as rebels witnessed the United States continue to prop up Batista's Army and US rockets raining on the houses of Cuban peasants who were supporting them in the mountains, Fidel wrote Celia Sánchez about other options: "When I saw the [US-supplied] rockets being fired at Mario's house, I swore to myself that the Americans would pay dearly for what they are doing. When this war is over a much wider and bigger war will begin for me: the war that I am going to wage against them. I know that this is my real destiny."[87]

Staging a protest off on Pier 16 within sight of the Brooklyn Bridge, a group of Castro supporters picketed the *Villanueva*, a ship that had been reported to contain rifles and machine guns destined for Batista. Raúl Castro's men began to observe and photograph Guantánamo Bay, gathering intelligence, with Che Guevara as his second in command.[88] When one hundred rebels ambushed at Pinto del Agua on February 18, Batista's forces withdrew. On February 24, Guevara assembled an antenna and transmitted his first broadcast of Radio Rebelde, sentimentally selecting that day, for it was the anniversary of the beginning of José Martí's War of Independence. Using mobile transmitters, the rebels would continue to broadcast "from the free territory of Cuba" to the island's people in a powerful message of propaganda that inspired further subversion and hope.[89]

At the end of the month, the 26th of July Movement received an open letter signed by forty-five civic associations and guilds—

architects, public accountants, dentists, electrical engineers, social workers, professors, and veterinarians—announcing their support. Fidel himself had received a visit in the Sierra Maestra from an influential delegate from the Communist Party and a former member of Batista's government, Carlos Rafael Rodríguez, who had formerly expressed reservations, told Fidel not to attack Moncada Barracks, and refused his support; however, a new alliance formed between these two men that day in the hills.[90] Returning toward the end of July to the mountains with a dozen men, Rafael Rodríguez would allegedly donate eight hundred thousand dollars to El Comandante's cause. Hugging Rodríguez, Fidel supposedly shouted, "Now we're ready to win the war."[91]

"Batista Insisting on Holding Vote: Determined on June Election Despite Spreading Revolt and Forecasts of Fraud," declared the *New York Times* on March 1. Prevented by the constitution of 1940 from seeking a second consecutive term and planning to take over supreme command of the Cuban armed forces to avoid going into exile, Batista propped up Andrés Rivero Agüero, his "obedient and colorless" prime minister whose face had already been plastered on campaign posters everywhere.

Promising "ballots not bullets," former president Grau San Martín seemed favored to win, though his previous reign of eight years had caused most Cubans to view his administration as both corrupt and incompetent. The other opposition candidate from the new "Free People's Party" was Dr. Carlos Marquez Sterling, a former provisional president, lawyer, and Economics professor at the University of Havana. "This is Batista's dilemma," he pitched, "If the election is honest, he will have to yield the government to the political opposition; if it is a fraud, he will have to yield the government to the rebels."[92] In a now-familiar refrain, Márquez Sterling vowed to return to the 1940 constitution, promised amnesty for all offenders, and warned a victory for Castro would result in the death of democracy for Cuba.[93] Later jailed by Castro's government and exiled in Miami, Márquez Sterling would assert that he had been cajoled by Fidel and Herbert Matthews to abandon the elections and support Fidel in exchange for a high position in the revolutionary government.

• • • • •

In April, George Plimpton's "The Art of Fiction" interview with Ernest appeared in the *Paris Review,* allowing the readers to peer in on the writer at work in San Francisco de Paula. It documented the ritual of rising at dawn, standing in front of a bedroom bookshelf, shifting weight from one foot to the other, scribbling on the onionskin paper on his clipboard—"excited as a boy, fretful, miserable" during the ecstasy and agony of the process—and the chart on a piece of cardboard, set up against the wall beneath the stuffed head of a gazelle, tallying the daily word-output so that he would not feel guilty about a day off to fish the Gulf. Before knocking off work at noon to stroll down to the pool with his knotted walking stick to take his daily half-mile swim, Hemingway enlightened readers with words of wisdom. George Plimpton asked him if the actual process of writing was pleasurable. He responded, "Very." Pressed by Plimpton to "say something of this process," Hemingway reiterated his mantra for would-be voyeurs: "When . . . working on a book or a story I write every morning as soon after first light . . . There is no one to disturb you and it is cool or cold and you come to your work and warm as you write. You read what you have written and, as you always stop when you know what is going to happen next, you go on from there. You write until you come to a place where you still have your juice."[94]

In April, Mary and Ernest received his old friends and former Chicago roommates Bunny and Bill Horne at the Finca Vigía. The group had driven together to Folly Ranch near Sheridan, Wyoming in July 1928, and their visit evoked memories of the old days in the Old West that arguably, combined with wistful reports from Mary's recent trip, would tempt the writer to return there again.[95]

After a prolonged letter campaign by Arnold MacLeish, Ernest Hemingway, Robert Frost, and T. S. Elliot, the US government dismissed treason charges against Ezra Pound—brought on by his pro-Mussolini tirades—and in May, set him free from Saint Elizabeth's Hospital. In June, Ezra was photographed as he arrived in Italy giving America the fascist version of flipping the bird. *Heil!* Ezra said he had never been released from the insane asylum in America because the entire country was an asylum. Pound, although outwardly insane, seemed to remember lucidly that the US Army had locked him in a steel cage during three summer weeks of 1945 at the Disciplinary Training Center north of Pisa. To his most patient mentor and friend from Paris, Hemingway had sent a check for one thousand dollars, the "end of the Nobel Prize money," while he was still in the asylum in July 1956, and another fifteen hundred dollars upon his release to help his *"Muy Querido Maestro Ex Lunacy"* continue what remained of his days with his daughter at Schloss Brunnenburg in Merano, Italy, in July 1958.[96]

• • • • •

While the US government had officially committed to a policy of strict noninterference in Cuba's internal conflict, the rebels suspected that they were not strictly following through. Operating in mountains above Guantánamo, Raúl Castro was now the comandante of Column Six. Taking heavy bombardments from Batista's planes, Raúl believed the dictator's aircraft were being repaired and refueled at the American air base of Guantánamo. Base workers in communication with Raúl furnished photographic evidence of this and of a delivery of three hundred missiles to Batista's forces on May 18. This counterintelligence justified Raúl's enactment of Military Order no. 30, Operación Antiaérea (Operation Anti-Aircraft) on June 22.[97]

On June 27, two hundred rebels surrounded a Nickel Mining Project at Moa Bay to kidnap ten Americans and two Canadians (a mixed bag of construction superintendents, engineers, a chemist, and a geologist) working for the company investing $79 million in development of nickel mining there. It was the kind of money that the United States would not wish to see jeopardized. The following day, a busload full of sailors and marines were returning to Guantánamo base after a night of drinking and womanizing in Caimanera, the town just north of base. Suddenly, a rebel with a rifle appeared on the road and fired a warning shot into the air. So sedated were the marines by their Cuban shore leave that they stopped the bus and surrendered on the spot. At the end of these insurgent operations, the rebels counted fifty total hostages in their care. They were clear in their communication: they had taken the hostages to retaliate against the United States' financial and tactical support for a dictator—interference in a civil war.

At pains to let his captives know that "he meant no offense," Raúl let five who professed medical problems go, then three more, then five more the following week. Feeding and housing the others, he "drafted an apology note to their parents, wives, and sweethearts." Received with such graciousness and consideration, quite a few of the kidnapped men became "equally gallant," sympathetic to the rebels' cause, and all in all, rather "amused" to be involved in a revolution they had previously only read about in newspapers or heard about on the radio. *Time* correspondent Jay Mallin reported on the scene: "'A swell guy, that Raúl Castro,' said Edward Cannon, a builder from Cornwall, Ontario, as he stepped off a helicopter at the base upon being freed. 'We had good food and plenty of it, and beds with clean sheets,' chimed in Henry Salmonson of Portland, Oregon."[98] Keeping tabs on these events, Ernest wrote Bill and Bunny on July 1 to thank them for their visit in April, relaying the Cuban news where "kidnappings are the latest local sport. They now have mining engineers, sugar mill technicians, consular officials, seamen (all ratings) and Marines—I called the Embassy to ask when they were going to start picking up the F.B.I.—the latest gag is that F[idel] Castro will entertain more Americans on July 4 than Ambassador Smith."[99] And indeed, to celebrate America's independence on the fourth of July, the rebels prepared a roast pig for their guests, attempting to sway the press and the American public to their cause.

In the letter, Ernest offered apologies for not writing earlier, "but was racing with this book," not yet making definite plans for future travel, blocking out the world around him, immersed in the Finca and in his fiction. At this time, Mrs. Hemingway also felt her husband's absence, and perhaps the darkest hours of their marriage: "You try all your life to merge. Falling in love is building the beautiful deception of two in one. But it is a dream. You are always alone. There are thousands of contented [people] who are never bothered by this. Who knows it and . . . can live with it . . . is strong . . . 'Togetherness' is not a cup of Lipton tea. It is wordless desperation."[100] Like the Mrs. Hemingways before her, Mary found it hard to sustain a loving relationship with a man who put writing first.

• • • • •

Before their release, Raúl Castro had taken the hostages to see a three-year-old boy "with a big hole in his head" from a Batista air raid and reiterated the reason he had captured them: to protest the May 18 delivery of three hundred rocket warheads to Batista's air force when a ban on arms was supposed to be in force. These were corrections to orders made before the ban, explained US officials, because they had mistakenly delivered practice warheads to Batista instead of live ones. In view of the three-year-old boy and the three thousand other Cuban deaths that the rebels estimated the missiles had caused, the distinction was irrelevant.

Responding to rebel requests that the United States truly suspend the shipment of arms to Batista and maintain a noninterventionist policy as promised, Ambassador Smith assured that "in compliance with the United States policy of nonintervention in Cuban internal affairs, the base has not—and will not—refuel or in other ways service the Cuban military aircraft engaged in combat activity."[101] After being treated like honored guests and shown peasants' homes destroyed by Batista's bombs, the last hostages were freed by their "rebel hosts" on July 28, "because of the Lebanese situation" that demanded the deployment of US Marines. "If the admiral wants to send you into battle in Lebanon," said Raúl Castro, clearly milking the publicity for all it was worth, "we don't want to hold you back."[102]

Although the kidnappings were a gamble that turned some Americans against the rebel cause, they appeared for the most part to be a success. They enhanced the rebels' worldwide prowess by demonstrating Batista's ineffectiveness, highlighted the guerrillas' cordiality, and significantly reduced Batista's ability to project airpower and drop napalm on their positions during the Operación Verano, or the Summer Offensive. Visiting not only the hostages but also Fidel and Raúl's rebel headquarters in Sierra Maestra and Cristal, the *Time* reporter estimated that the rebels had amassed approximately two thousand men (in all likelihood they had as few as half or a fourth of that number), noted the numerous trucks and jeeps stolen from the Cuban army, ammunition "plentiful enough to be wasted on potshots at coconuts," and an operating airstrip where arms were delivered from "some mysterious supplier."[103] Although the revolution was gaining ground, decisive moments still lay ahead.

From June 28 to August 8, Operación Verano finally initiated the full-blown offensive that half the world had been waiting for to crush the rebels and their "big-mouthed" leader, Fidel. Under the joint command of Generals Eulogio Cantillo and Alberto del Río Chaviano, ten to fifteen thousand troops took up positions around the Sierra Maestra mountains. While the rebels were concerned, they were also confident, for they now knew the terrain, had the cooperation of the local population, and had set many mines and booby traps. They reportedly wired loudspeakers throughout the jungle to blast the enemy with music, jingles, and songs—to spook their attackers and to make themselves seem ubiquitous.

Two-thirds of the men in the attacking force were new recruits, badly paid, and terrified of the fate that awaited them in the mountains. Other than a meager paycheck and fear of the disciplinary consequences if they refused, the soldiers had little reason to fight.[104] Though they had far superior numbers and armament, these army regulars proved themselves unresponsive, disloyal to the regime, and too poorly trained to meet the rigors of counterinsurgent combat ahead. In contrast, the rebels were well trained and committed to their cause.

While the rebels were doing battle with Batista's army in the Sierra Maestra, the people of Havana and San Francisco de Paula were still anxiously awaiting liberation. Even though the Hemingways, keeping a low profile within the Finca Vigía walls, were by and large insulated from these events, they began to feel that the life they had known in Cuba was in jeopardy. There were public "explosions of human violence and covert brutalities," old friends disappearing, young men from their village imprisoned and tortured by Batista's men, or left for dead in a ditch along the road.[105]

One afternoon, Ernest, Mary, and Gregorio departed from Cojímar on a "fishing trip." Mary was surprised when Gregorio began to open hidden compartments and dump an "arsenal of weapons" (heavy rifles, sawed-off shotguns, hand grenades, and canisters and belts of ammunition for automatic rifles) into the sea. What was going on, asked Mary, figuring that he must have plopped two thousand dollars' worth of weapons into the deep. "Stuff left over from the old days. Nobody's going to use it now," her husband responded. Then he added, "My contribution to the revolution. Maybe we've saved a few lives."[106]

• • • • •

The first battle of Batista's Summer Offensive took place on June 28 as two battalions of Batista's troops that were camped at Estrada Palma Sugar Mill advanced with armored cars along the road, ran into mines, and were subsequently ambushed by Che Guevara's men. Attempting to fall back, they found themselves taking heavy fire from rebel sharpshooters advancing on both flanks, cutting them to pieces, and killing eighty-six of them. The rebels lost only three and captured much armament and ammunition.

The second encounter that summer was the Battle of La Plata, which took place at the intersection of the rivers La Plata and El Jigüe on the downward slope of Turquino Peak. Intending to surround and decapitate Fidel's command center at the base of peak, General Cantillo ordered Major José Quevedo Pérez to land Battalion Eighteen ten kilometers to the southeast at the mouth of La Plata River (Silver River). As soldiers were advancing up the tunnel formed by the *v*-shaped narrows of the river rising toward Fidel's headquarters, they were ambushed by perfectly positioned guerrillas who were expecting them.[107] Caught in the death trap by interlocking fields of fire, each time Battalion Eighteen attempted to advance, rebel bullets beat them back. After seventy-two hours, Quevedo's men were out of food and getting hungry.

To come to their aid, General Cantillo landed two hundred reinforcements on a beach to the west. Finding 50-caliber machine guns aimed at the beach, the reinforcements were unable to land, so instead landed at the mouth of La Plata River, behind Battalion Eighteen. In another attempt to come to Battalion Eighteen's aid, General Cantillo sent Battalion Seventeen in through the mountains, but they were met with determined resistance from Che Guevara's men. In a last-ditch effort, Cantillo called in airstrikes, unleashing bombs, strafe, and napalm on Fidel's position, shaking and scorching the earth while the rebels took cover.[108] After the thunder had passed, the rebels emerged like rabbits from their holes and, sighting in on Battalion Eighteen, reassumed control.

When Fidel heard that his old school chum José Quevedo Pérez was leading the battalion, he released one of his prisoners to deliver a gentlemanly note. It was with "great sorrow" that he came to know that Quevedo was in command of the troops who were surrounded: "We know that you are a learned and honorable military officer of the Academy, with a law degree. You know that the cause for which your soldiers, as well as yourself, sacrifice and die is an unjust cause."[109] The major should know that he would be guaranteed "a dignified and honorable surrender," and that it would not be to an enemy, but to "a sincere revolutionary fight[ing] for the welfare of all Cubans, including that of the soldiers who fight us. You will surrender to a university classmate who wants the same things that you want for Cuba." Ignoring the letters, Quevedo held out for four more days hoping that reinforcements would arrive.

On the morning of July 20, Fidel again asked Quevédo politely if it would be all right to cease fire. Emerging from their foxholes, the men of Battalion Eighteen were offered food, water, and cigarettes. They accepted the provisions with gratitude. Unexpectedly the two sides were embracing each other and weeping with emotion.[110] The battle killed forty-one of Batista's soldiers, and wounded thirty, while the rebels had lost only three. The victors took two hundred forty prisoners, turned over to the Red Cross, and 249 weapons (including bazookas, mortars, heavy machine guns, 31,000 rounds of ammunition, and a heap of grenades).[111] Fidel was able to convince Quevedo to join his rebels and to get others to do the same.

Having scored a major victory, Fidel imprudently pursued Battalion Seventeen, which seemed to be retreating. Rebel major René Ramos Latour spearheaded the attack and killed approximately thirty regulars. But stealing a page from the guerrilla handbook, General Cantillo drew the rebels in, and they soon found themselves surrounded by more than fifteen hundred of Batista's men and under heavy fire. Coming forward to reinforce Major Latour's column, Fidel's men, too, were drawn into the trap, suffering seventy casualties. When Che brought his unit forward to offer some relief, Fidel Castro ordered his men to retreat and sent a note on August 1 to Cantillo, requesting a ceasefire. Overrun, Fidel was ready to negotiate: "It is necessary to open a dialogue so that we can put an end to the conflict."[112] While Cantillo was consulting with his advisors and Batista about how to proceed, Fidel withdrew his forces. By the time Cantillo realized what was happening, there was no enemy left to fight: the rebels had once again slipped from their grasp.

Feeling that a moment of opportunity had been lost and the deaths of their comrades had been in vain, the troops were wholly demoralized. At the end of the count, the government had lost 519 troops and a mountain of weapons while the rebels had lost 73. Though the tactical gains were significant, the political and psychological victories expanded one hundredfold. Taking to the airwaves of Radio Rebelde, Fidel used his exceptional oratory skills to exploit the event for all it was worth. Declaring victory, he called for an immediate end to the caudillo pitting Cuban against Cuban, and Batista's supporters soon flocked to Fidel Castro as liberator for a much-beleaguered nation. Having sent representatives to Caracas to solidify alliances with the revolutionary and abstentionist factions of the *junta de liberación*, he read the signatures from the Caracas Pact (establishing a unified front composed of all factions against Batista), calling for armed insurrection, requesting the United States to cease all military support for the dictatorship, and demanding a provisional government and a new democracy.[113]

• • • • •

While war was waging in the sierra, Ernest declared war on *Esquire*—at least that's how the story appeared. The magazine with first publication rights to his stories published there had expressed their intention to republish his Spanish War stories, and Ernest, objecting, instructed his lawyer, Alfred Rice, to forbid them to do any such thing. Ernest's request ended up becoming *New York Times* literary gossip when his attorney blabbed to a reporter. The attention irritated the author. In July, Ernest had turned fifty-nine years old. That year in the isolation of the Finca Vigía, he had thrived by living a more disciplined life, getting himself back into shape, advancing in his work, and he was feeling much better. But as the summer ended and the revolution draggedon, the Hemingways continued to explore the idea of a second residence out west.[114]

In August, Ernest asked Lloyd and Tillie Arnold's assistance in finding them a house near Sun Valley to rent for a season. When they wrote back about the Heiss House in Ketchum for $175 per month, the Hemingways instantly agreed.[115] After more than a year of disciplined writing, Ernest was revising and arranging eighteen sketches of a Parisian memoir, and his book was nearly complete. Intermittently, he had also been revising *The Garden of Eden* and would have twenty-eight chapters by the end of June. In July, he predicted it would be finished the following month, but he did not know how to finish it in mid-September when the word count reached two hundred thousand words, forty-eight chapters.[116] An inability to conclude projects was a snowballing problem that haunted his final years and resulted in five unpublished manuscripts: *Islands in the Stream*, *The Dangerous Summer*, *A Moveable Feast*, *The Garden of Eden*, and *True at First Light*.

Seeking refuge from militaries, burglars, tropical storms, revolutionary terrorism, and unwelcomed visitors, Ernest and Mary flew out of Havana bound for Key West on September 30. Catching another flight, Betty Bruce and Mary went to Chicago for an impromptu shopping trip while Toby Bruce and Ernest drove the Bruces' "big comfortable station wagon" to pick up their wives on October 4, and they continued westward together to Ketchum, Idaho.[117] Cocktail hour began at six o'clock in the car, with Toby drinking rum on ice, Ernest fresh lime juice with Pinch whiskey (Haig & Haig), and the ladies dry martinis, the "speedometer ticking off the miles" as they spotted antelope grazing near Casper and stopped to see black and brown bears up on their haunches in Yellowstone.

On October 7, the film of *The Old Man and the Sea* opened to mediocre (and even poor) reviews. The *New York Times* praised the thunder, emotional color, and poignancy of Dimitri Tiomkin's musical scores, Tracy's courage in the role, and Felipe Pazos, Jr.'s evocative casting as Manolin, but the reviewer felt the film had not been rendered with enough imagination, and with the exception of rosy dawn in Cojímar, too many scenes had been shot in a studio tank to express the power of the sea. The voiceover, too, was a poor substitute for the poetry and eloquence expressed in the original work[118]—a hat-tipping compliment to the author's artistry with which he would have likely agreed.

Settling in, the foursome established a routine in Ketchum fishing the Big Wood River, hunting Sawtooth Forest and along Snake River Plain, and cavorting in the lodge. As suns set over Boyle Mountain, splashing amber over the ripples of Sun Valley Lake, the weather cooled, and the Hemingways and Bruces warmed their hands and faces by a fire. Ernest was writing four days a week and hunting three, sometimes going out in the afternoons if the writing went well.[119] Shooting and drinking at the Silver Creek Rod and Gun Club, they received visits from Gary Cooper and Ed Hotchner.

While uncertainties of Cuba haunted and Mrs. Hemingway queried softly about future plans, Ernest preferred to concentrate on finding the ending to *The Garden of Eden* or, alternatively, revising the typed manuscript that his wife had prepared of *A Moveable Feast*. Nonetheless, four adjoining lots on the slope adjacent from the Arnolds' home were for sale, so the Hemingways purchased them with Pappy Arnold standing in to keep prices low. Having acquired the land, Mrs. Hemingway set to work designing the house of their dreams. When the decisions of home creation disturbed writing and fun, Ernest sniped and procrastinated.

At the end of November while living in a cabin near the creek, Papa wrote his second son to tell of his intentions to return to Cuba once he had finished his book in Idaho. Then he would go to Spain for San Isidro, stay the summer there, and go to Africa in the fall: "Cuba is really bad now, Mouse. I am not a big fear danger pussy but living in a country where no one is right—both sides atrocious—knowing what sort of stuff and murder will go on when the new ones come in—seeing the abuses of those in now . . . We are always treated OK as in all countries and have fine good friends. But things aren't good and the overhead is murder." If politics and fishing continued as bad as they had been in Cuba during the last two years, he confided in his son, he might pull out.[120]

Deciding it better not to take on a project, the Hemingways looked at houses already built and available in the area. The best belonged to Bob Topping, a wealthy socialite who had moved to the Arizona desert for his health. Its architect combined rough-cut lumber in the traditional log-cabin style and poured concrete molds to create a functional and attractive bunker-like home with a view of the aspens and cottonwood trees of the Sawtooth Forest and the "tent-shaped mountains" beyond, with unparalleled protection against Idaho weather and time, lush wood-paneled interiors, seventeen acres of land, and access to the Big Wood River and the Sun Valley Lodge.[121] At fifty thousand dollars, half its original construction cost, the house was a steal even if it became a vacation home, such that by April they committed to the deal.

• • • • •

To get to Las Villas, Che, Camilo, and their 210 guerrillas would have to cross the plains of central Cuba where sugar plantations made the population prosperous and generally unsympathetic to their cause. With few places to hide as they marched six hundred kilometers on foot, they would be pursued by hostile army regulars vowing to punish them for their arrogance in strolling so brazenly across their terrain: "They shall not pass! We shall serve the corpses of their chiefs on a silver platter, because they have had the audacity to think that they can conduct a military parade throughout Camagüey," declared a commander of the Rural Guard.[122]

Rather than attackers, they resembled fugitives on the run, hungry, overheated, and fatigued as they took fire, split up (into two columns—under Cienfuegos and Guevara's respective commands), hid in the woods, and agreed to reassemble once they reached the Escambray Mountains, their objective. Making their own luck like the fishermen Hemingway admired, the rebels marched forward toward the Escambray proving themselves with each forward step, no matter how many steps they had already taken, that meant nothing.[123] By mid-October, Che and Camilo took up positions in the Escambray Mountains, and Fidel was poised to take control of the East.[124]

At the end of October and in Early November, insurgents hijacked three airplanes carrying hostages, supplies, and weapons. The most notorious was Cubana Airlines flight 495, a Vickers Viscount 755D, taking off from Miami, Florida, destined for Varadero but never landing due to the insurgents' ill-conceived plan. It instead splashed into Nipe Bay drowning seventeen out of twenty passengers. Attributing the disastrous mission to overzealous M-26-7 members acting on their own initiative, Fidel Castro emphasized that he had not ordered the attack.[125]

On November 8, Cuba held a controversial election that many believed to be either rigged, or impossible to hold under insurgent threats and duress, and declared Andrés Rivero Agüero—Batista's puppet candidate—to be the new president of Cuba, the day after the rebel army seized Alto Songo Garrison in the East of Cuba.[126] With dissension in the ranks, Batista's army suppressed a military conspiracy on November 27 and arrested several top officials including much-respected General Martín Díaz Tamayo, for a plot to overthrow the government.[127]

On the fourteenth of December, Che Guevara's column seized the town of Fomento in Sancti Spíritus, and the rebels now closed in on the stronghold of Santa Clara to the northwest. The threat so unnerved US officials that Ambassador Smith paid a visit to Batista in his swank private residence in Kuquine, to inform the dictator that Washington had decided it was time for him to go.[128] What if Uncle Sam assisted him to install a provisional military junta, Batista inquired, he . . . he could lay low for a while, then once things cooled down, return to power?[129] No, they answered, at this point that was not in the cards. After that, said Batista, "There was not much to talk about," so Smith got up, shook hands, and left. After this meeting, General Cantillo was chosen by military brass to be the one who would negotiate with Fidel Castro. By December 19, the rebel army was taking cities rapidly in shocking succession: Jiguaní, Caimanera, and Mayajigua, then Guayos, Cabaiguán, Placetas, Manicaragua, Cumanayagua, Camarones, Cruces, Lajas, Sagua de Tánamo, Puerto Padre, and Sancti Spíritus, and a few days later Caibarién, Remedios, Palma Soriano, and Cienfuegos.

By taking Santa Clara, Fidel Castro had reasoned, he could cut the island in half, stop counteroffensives, suffocate supply lines, and cover the rebels' advance upon Santiago de Cuba in the east. If the rebels took Santiago, and its notorious Moncada Barracks, they could acquire the sort of armament, tanks, and artillery that they would need to emerge victorious in subsequent battles for key strongholds, like Agramonte in Camagüey, in Pinar del Río, and in Havana. By the end of December, rebel forces had swelled with sympathizers, defectors, and peasants to approximately two thousand troops in the east under the Castros' tactical control, and a thousand in Las Villas under Guevara, Vega, and Cienfuego's command.[130]

On January 1, 1959, Che Guevara's rebel forces took the city of Santa Clara, defended by approximately sixty-five hundred heavily armed men, ten tanks, B-26 bombers, and "*un tren blindado*" ("an armored train"), which was neutralized by bribery or by Molotov cocktails, depending upon one's source, thwarted Batista's last attempt to reinforce the linchpin city.

While most of Batista's men snivellingly surrendered, Colonel Cornelio Rojas, the chief of police, and his men put up a fight. Rojas was taken prisoner.

At first sending a note of *salvo conducto* (safe conduct) to Rojas's family to assure them that his life was in good hands, Comandante Guevara then decreed instead that Rojas would be executed, filmed the execution, and televised it across Cuba as a warning to others. During the first moments they saw Rojas on television, his daughter, wife, and grand daughter thanked God that he was alive. When they realized he was standing with other prisoners in front of a brick wall, they gripped each other tightly and screamed.[131]

Refusing the blindfold, Cornelio Rojas waved and said his last stoic words: *"Muchachos, ya tienen su tu revolución. Cuídenla."* ("Boys, now you have your revolution. Take care of it.") Then he faced the line of rifles sighting in on him head on and gave the order himself: *"Apunten, listos, ¡fuego!"* ("Ready, aim, fire!") Disseminated in world news, the graphic murder was perhaps the first ever witnessed on television.

CHAPTER 13

New Year, New Government (1959–1960)

• • • • •

In the Idaho mountains, three inches of snow were finally falling and making it look like Christmas, delighting skiers and the Hemingways alike as they warmed their bodies by an open fire in Trail Creek Cabin on a Saturday night, sang Austrian mountain songs, dined beneath a bower of spicy pine, and danced to "Jelly Roll Blues."[1]

After Spanish grape eating on New Year's Eve, a sweetly aging couple went early to bed but awakened cheerfully at midnight to exchange a kiss, to wish each other happy New Year, and to think good thoughts for family and friends in Cuba.

In the grand open windows of Old Havana, Cuban high society and vacationers could be seen sipping at flutes of champagne. Ringing in "Nochevieja" in ballrooms of the last soirées, lovers fell endlessly into each other's arms to the tempo of clave clacks, the maracas' scratch, the hum of bass strings, and the warble of trumpets and trombones.[2] In the casino cabarets of towering new hotels that shined before the sea, revelers munched *las doce uvas de la suerte*, twelve grapes for twelve new months of luck, one for each clock strike at the Puerta del Sol, to ward away the witches, for superstition, and for hope.

At a hushed gathering at dawn, Batista announced his resignation to "prevent further bloodshed." He appointed Carlos Manuel Piedra as provisional president with General Cantillo supporting him as commander of the army. General Cantillo had met with Castro previously in the Sierra Maestra, established a secret alliance, and promised to help him bring Batista to justice. The general then double-crossed Castro by helping Batista escape and attempting to seize control of Cuba with a military junta backed by the United States.

At 2:00 a.m., Batista, his family, and his top military aides departed aboard five airplanes bound for the Dominican Republic (where dictator Rafael Trujillo offered Batista the asylum that the United States deemed too prickly politically), New York, Jacksonville, Miami, and New Orleans. The provisional president that Batista had supported, Andrés Rivero Agüero, fled with him to the Dominican Republic and later settled in Miami. In their entourage were approximately 225 people and millions in assets, national treasures, art, and jewels, to add to those already amassed in Swiss banks. Some valued the heist as high as $700 million, but others said it was closer to $300 million.[3] Hemingway wrote, "Batista looted [Cuba] naked when he left. He must have 600 to 800 millions and that will buy a lot of newspapermen—and has."[4] When the *batistianos* arrived in Miami, they were met by a mob of two thousand Fidelistas who had to be beaten back with riot gear.[5]

During the same year, Batista would find refuge in Madeira, Portugal, in 1959, then in Estoril in 1963, and would migrate later with his family to Costa del Sol, Guadalmina, Spain, where he would die in 1973 of a heart attack at the age of seventy-two. His widow, Marta Fernández de Batista, died in 2006 at the age of eighty-two in West Palm Beach, Florida. During the seven years of his last presidency, Fulgencio Batista was estimated to have murdered twenty thousand people.[6] Under the revolutionary government, Cantillo was arrested and sentenced to fifteen years in prison on the Isle of Pines.

While the hollow shell of Batista's power was crumbling at the end of 1958, Ernest Hemingway had received an invitation from Bill Davis and wife at Villa la Consula in Málaga, Spain, and uncertain of his next move, he had been imagining a mano a mano of six magnificent bulls and two valiant matadors: Antonio Ordóñez and Luis Miguel Dominguín, Antonio's brother-in-law.

• • • • •

When the people of Cuba learned that their tyrannical ruler had fled, they roared into the streets on New Year's Day to loot casinos, banks, department stores, and hotels.[7] Cruise ships set sail and American tourists fled Cuba en masse to escape the chaos. At Moncada, five thousand army regulars laid down their arms for Huber Matos's Ninth Column, and Fidel took Santiago de Cuba without firing a single shot.[8]

From the heart of the Oriente after a victory at Santiago, Fidel proclaimed to a cheering crowd, "This time the revolution will not be frustrated! This time, fortunately for Cuba, the revolution will achieve its true objective. It will not be like 1898, when the Americans came and made themselves masters of the country."[9] He was referring to the moment of the Spanish-American War when General Calixto García and his men, after fighting fiercely alongside Americans to liberate Cuba from Spain, were prohibited from entering Santiago. It was a moment that Cubans remembered, but America did not. Castro appeared expertly aware that the American press was not present that day in Santiago to cover the speech.

Many Americans would have been baffled to hear such ingratitude from Cuba's new leader, including Eisenhower, who would say, "Here is a country that, you would believe on the basis of our history would be one of our real friends. The whole history . . . would seem to make it a puzzling matter to figure out just exactly why the Cubans and the Cuban government would be so unhappy when, after all, their principal market is here, their best market. You would think they would want good relationships. I don't know exactly what the difficulty is."[10] Hemingway perhaps understanding this history, but perhaps not hearing the speech, wrote a friend in a letter then: "The Cuban people now have a decent chance for the first time ever. I wish Castro all the luck."[11]

While Mr. and Mrs. Hemingway were watching the Rose Bowl game on New Year's Day in Ketchum, the news services phoned to ask Ernest to comment on the change of power in Cuba. Ernest said, "I believe in the historical necessity for the Cuban revolution and I believe in its long range aims. I do not wish to discuss personalities or day to day problems." When asked specifically about Fidel Castro's rebels, Ernest told them he was "delighted" with the news. Mary told her husband, not knowing what excesses Castro would commit or if the firing squads were lining up that very moment, that the comment seemed imprudent: "'delighted' was too strong a word." "One bloody word," he grumbled, not wanting to retract what he said. When she insisted that he made his living with words and that the distinction was important, he called them back and changed his word to "hopeful," which the *New York Times* changed just minutes before the article went to press.

Calling for a general strike, Fidel demanded the appointment of Manuel Urrutia Lleó, a judge sympathetic to the revolution, as provisional president in Piedra's place, and on the evening of January 1, the Supreme Court followed this order, installing Urrutia the following day. Under pressure from the United States, who sought an alternative to the Castros, Batista's colonel Ramón Barquín was released from prison and appointed by the Cuban Supreme Court to the command of the Cuban army on January 1.[12]

On January 2, Che Guevara and Camilo Cienfuegos marched their rebel columns into Havana victorious. Founding a new government, José Miró Cardona took the reins as prime minister on January 3. Both Cardona and Urrutia were liberal, but not Communist. Supported for the moment by the Supreme Court and by Fidel Castro as commander in chief of the rebel army, Miró and Urrutia were officially recognized by the United States on January 5, and Fidel Castro was recognized two days later.[13] The following day, the first issue of the first rebel newspaper, *Hoy*, published the news.

From the far reaches of Oriente, Fidel Castro's much-anticipated troops arrived triumphantly in the capital city of Havana on January 8. Despite the fact that he was not yet officially connected to the provisional government, he was a popular and articulate commander of a winning army, and like Caesar, the conqueror returning with his legions to Rome, Castro had influence and made a huge impact. A natural orator and showman, and a "good talker," Castro was very skilled at managing his image and the press. The young *barbudo* soldiers that accompanied him, piled atop Sherman tanks, looked as tickled as they were confused in their tangled beards, muddled green uniforms, ingenuous eyes, and rifles roughly slung. Looking like amateurs was part of their allure. Fate had chosen them to defend, to become martyrs, and like Maccabees or samurai, soldiers for a sacred Cuban cause, they had listened to the call. Or at least that is how these mountain men seemed as they descended from the sierra, and compared to Batista, they looked marvelous.

Establishing his headquarters in the penthouse of the Havana Hilton hotel along with his men who used its fancy restaurant like their chow hall, Fidel met with reporters and government officials there, creating an appealing contrast made for television only a decade after NBC, CBS, ABC, and DuMont had begun broadcasting full schedules. The rebel stumbled through English while his bearded buddies became a bit too jubilant in the background. The reporter, hamming it up at the end of the interview, asked if Fidel might shave his beard: "Now that the revolution is over, American 'touristas' will come here, and you will be the main attraction. Will you shave off your beard?" Thoughtfully stroking his whiskers, Fidel kept calm and searched for the unknown phrase in English, asking one of the *barbudos* behind him for help. "I am . . . ," then a light came suddenly to his eyes, "used to it . . . the beard. It does not bother me at all! I have asked the people if they want that we cut. [He then pointed both index fingers into the air.] Ev-ery-body say no, no."[14]

Years later Fidel, the old man, would elaborate, "The story of our beards is very simple: it arose out of the difficult conditions we were living and fighting under as guerrillas. We didn't have any razor blades. Everybody just let their beards and hair grow, and that turned into a kind of badge of identity. For the campesinos and everybody else, for the press, for the reporters we were '*los barbudos*'–the bearded ones."[15] Sometimes they did not even have soap. As attached as Fidel became to his facial hair, he would tell Barbara Walters in an interview in 1977 that he would shave it if the US lifted the embargo. Members of the press, historians, and biographers have repeatedly described Fidel Castro as a "Christ-like" liberator or "redeemer" who suffered on his people's behalf.[16] For a moment, the next generation was taking over, and the truth was as simple as this description.

Some remained skeptical. With twenty-five years as a foreign correspondent for the *Guardian*, Alistair Cooke had seen dictators come and go, and watching "the hero himself" enjoy his slow approach into Havana while thousands cheered, the reporter found it difficult to accept his renunciations of ambition for power while retaining his position as chief of staff of the armed forces. For the moment, Fidel was "the living symbol of release from an interminably brutal and corrupt dictatorship," perhaps because he looked "so young and modern, and talks so gallantly," yet one could also recall at that moment that, as a young soldier, Fulgencio Batista had also once been hailed as a "poor audacious rebel" before becoming "just another bigshot" ensconced in an office downtown, with brutal secret police at his disposal.[17] While some still remember *barbudos* arriving to deliver Havana and grandmothers jostling just to touch Fidel or pass him a rosary, others recall widespread disorder and rough bearded men barking at people in the streets ordering them to get into their homes and stay there, or be killed. With the assistance of the urban civil leagues they implemented, soon the rebels had the anarchy somewhat under control.

• • • • •

Ambassador Smith resigned on January 1 but continued to work until his replacement, Philip Bonsal, arrived. Hemingway knew Bonsal from the 1930s in Spain with Pauline. Shortly after Batista left and Fidel came to power in 1959, Hemingway wrote a letter from Ketchum to his new editor at Scribner's, Harry Brague, in which he would make some of his most explicit comments about the United States' role in the changing political situation in Cuba: Things were "ok" in Cuba. They had friends in the new government, like Phil Bonsal, who had been with them at the feria in Salamanca, and the officer commanding the Havana garrison, who was an old San Francisco de Paula boy who played baseball on their local team. "Castro is up against a hell a lot of money. The island is so rich and has always been stolen blind. If he could run a straight government, it would be wonderful."[18]

Keeping close tabs on the situation and his property in Cuba, Ernest was receiving news from Herbert Matthews's ongoing dispatches, from United and Associated Press, from friends still in Cuba like the Herrera brothers, Mario Menocal, and Jaime Bofill, and from his majordomo, René Villarreal. From Idaho, Ernest wrote Gianfranco Ivancich that he heard from René Villarreal that there had been a general strike and a shortage of food, so he told him to butcher one of the calves and loan the station wagon to any revolutionaries should they need it. He heard the bittersweet news that the policemen who had killed his dog had been executed "with the usual mutilation." The newspapers were announcing the retreat of Batista to the Dominican Republic and the cruise ships fleeing with him. He wrote to Gianfranco: "They all sailed as soon as they could round up the revelers. Wish we had been there together. Very funny. You and Liugino saw him come in, remember. I wish we might have seen him go. Remember we went to Cayo Paraíso on that 10th of March—Mary and Gregorio and I—Sic transit hijo de puta [so passes the son of a whore]."[19]

Hemingway appeared to believe sincerely that the Cuban Revolution would represent positive changes for most Cuban citizens and for the nation's future. Papa was invited several times to meet Batista, and he always turned him down. He seemed to take particular delight not only in the dictator's passage, but also the irony of his casino customers running with fear from an island at last in revolt. As far as his interests were concerned, the author, trying not to worry, took consolation in a phone call from Jaime Bofill, a Loyalist friend from civil-war Spain, who had been appointed to the provisional government and who said he would ensure personally that the Finca was protected.[20]

In January, 30,000 "jeering spectators" crowded into the Havana Sports Arena to see the first of the Cuban "purge trials." Among 600 Batista henchmen accused of horrendous war crimes were Major Jesús Sosa Blanco, Major Pedro Morejón, and Lieutenant Colonel Ricardo Luis Grau. Thirty witnesses attested to the fact that former Holguín army detachment commander Major Jesús Sosa Blanco had murdered 108 people. Among his crimes were his execution of 11 nickel mine workers and the cremation of a man by leaving him tied up in a burning house.

"I'm not here to justify myself or to ask for clemency," said Sosa, who also stated he had no respect for anyone in the crowd. "I do not know whether I am on trial in the Roman Coliseum or whether I am standing before our Lord Jesus Christ. I have nothing to say except that I only carried out orders. I am a man of honor." Hearing that remark, the crowd broke "into even wilder hoots" and the tribunal president Humberto Sorí Marín threatened to have everyone thrown out of "the Coliseum." A bearded judge of the rebel court then informed Sosa and his attorney that he had every right to defend himself, but that describing the court as a Coliseum did seem to amount to an adequate defense. Unremorsefully, he responded, "I would do it again under the same circumstances." Just then, a woman who said she had eleven children came forward and accused Sosa of killing her husband, saying, "What of my children?" When Sosa responded that the rebels would raise them, the woman went berserk, started attacking the accused, and had to be carried away. Sentencing the men to death, the rebel courts subsequently announced that the trials would continue behind closed doors.

Though he once hated it, said Herrera Sotolongo, Ernest started watching television, listening to the radio, and reading the daily newspapers, particularly when Fidel was involved or speaking. At one of those rallies, Fidel addressed the controversial executions: "The hired killers must be shot, for even the Bible says, 'he who lives by the sword shall die by the sword.'"[21] If, said Fidel, Americans who felt more tolerance for the mass slaughter of innocents at Hiroshima and Nagasaki, felt discomfort when seeing Cuba's executions, it was because they had never experienced Batista's repression and torture firsthand. Was it any wonder that the "student of revolutions" Ernest Hemingway, who had supported extreme measures in Spain, was glued to the television during these events?

The following day, Fidel flew to Venezuela where a coup d'état had just ousted General Marcos Pérez Jiménez to spread his revolution before a crowd of 300,000 fans and to ask for their "sister nation's" support.[22] The visit would inaugurate a lasting and obstinate connection between the two countries. Upon returning from Venezuela, Fidel would discover that President Urrutia had outlawed casinos and brothels. In an uproar, Fidel questioned the decision made in his absence, which drastically reduced revenues for a country sorely in need.

On February 13, José Miró resigned from the post of prime minister "to avoid a duality of government" and suggested Fidel Castro was the most appropriate choice for the position. Embracing Miró, Castro accepted it, about the swellest valentine that any rebel could receive, and after advising President Urrutia, the deal was as good as a done.[23] In March, Cuba nationalized the International Telephone and Telegraph, which had infamously given Batista a golden telephone, so that they could raise rates and continue to extract excessive profit from Cuban callers.[24] In the Havana Hilton, when a BBC journalist asked Fidel how long it would be until Cuba held elections, he responded that his country would be ready in eighteen months to two years.

• • • • •

Still lying low in Idaho, Ernest had negotiated a contract with *Life* magazine to cover the bullfights that summer in Spain. Spending the summer in Málaga, perhaps he could get down to see Patrick too. By the end of February, he was on chapter 45 of *The Garden of Eden*, did not have an ending, and was nearly finished revising *A Moveable Feast*. According to Emmet Watson, a small-time reporter from the *Seattle Post-Intelligencer*, he was on a pleasure trip with a friend to Sun Valley Lodge, in the right place at the right time, when he chanced upon white-bearded Hemingway sipping Haig & Haig with a twist of lime on a Saturday evening just before dinner and "exchanging banter" with locals and visiting skiers.

Invited to Watson's table, Ernest came over and entered amicably into a conversation, talking with him for a half hour or so. When Emmett offered to buy him another drink, the writer apologized for not being able to stay longer, "I'm supposed to be home soon or I'll get in trouble," but he stayed anyway, talking freely, regaling jokes and stories, and laughing often as they talked, and after a half hour of conversation about boxing and writing and so on, got up to leave, then said, "Oh well, just once more. I can loaf a while longer." When they had lost track of time, a man came over and whispered in Ernest's ear, and tossing back his drink, the author said, "Mary just called. Looks like I'm in trouble. After all, I'm supposed to be working up here. I just went out for a walk and now I'm in trouble."[25]

Two days later, the high sun of early afternoon was turning the snow into slush along the sidewalk of the ski village. Emmett Watson and company were leaving the Challenger Inn to give the slopes a go when they ran into a tall, white-bearded man with steel-rimmed spectacles, carrying a stack of papers wrapped in a brown sack, who invited them for another drink at a place called The Ram. There Hemingway spoke freely with Watson whom he knew to be a reporter, "Look I'm all through working. And I don't mind talking. Anything you want to talk about is fine." So, Watson asked him about Cuba, and the conversation took a more serious turn.

He seemed, said Watson, to have some things that he wanted to get off his chest about Castro's uprising against Batista:

> I believe in the cause of the Cuban people. They have had changes in government before in Cuba. But these were just changes of the guard. When the new ones got in, they went right on stealing from the people. Some of Batista's officials and police were good honest men, but a lot of them were thieves, sadists and torturers. They tortured kids, sometimes so badly they would have to kill them.

This, however, "is the first revolution in Cuba that really is a revolution," he noted. Cataloguing the unprintable horrors of torture and mutilated bodies discovered, he described the graft and corruption, a high official who had stolen $6 million in the last six years, and how teachers could not find jobs unless they paid bribes to these officials. Said the Nobel Prize winner speaking intently about a country he loved, "Cuban kids have a right to an education," He described the case of a father who sent his girls to a school to become teachers, but who could not get a job because they did not have $2,000 to pay the graft money to be given the position.

The labor laws under Batista were good, Hemingway believed, "but the unions were closed to a lot of workers. Others couldn't get in. They were closed and a lot of people couldn't work. They were actually going hungry." He described the plantations that denied its workers the right to plant gardens on the land they lived on during the off season, who were forced to buy food in company stores. "American companies have some 800 million dollars invested in Cuba. Some of them behaved well. United Fruit and the Hershey Sugar Co. were good. Others were not so good, and others were drawn into the pattern before they realized what was going on. They came to Cuba and thought this was the accepted way of doing things."

Citing a story from the daily news about a man who had been executed a few days prior, Hemingway said, "I know him. If they shot him a hundred times it wouldn't be enough punishment for the terrible things he has done." Concerning the tribunals of secret police, he said,

> The government has to carry out its promises. There was a lot of criticism over the shooting of Batista officials. So the Castro government began conducting public trials and executions. People abroad began to yell, 'Circus!' But the government had to do this to show it was in control, to give people a respect for law and order. The Castro movement promised the Cuban people that Batista's men would be punished. The new government has to carry out its promises. The trials are necessary."

Having finished his work for the day, Hemingway sipped his Scotch slowly. Across the table, his ruddy face conveyed warmth, and he seemed very happy. He spoke about returning soon to Cuba to live. "Cuba has been good to Americans. It's a wonderful place to live. I lived there and worked there. *The Old Man and the Sea* was about a

Cuban fisherman, and it was written in Cuba." Then lowering his voice shyly, "It was kind of a good book." He reiterated, "I have great hope for the Castro revolution, because it has the support of the Cuban people. I believe in their cause. I only wonder if Castro has the strength to carry it out."

Toward the end of their interview, Watson noticed that his writing hand was marked by several deep scratches, and Hemingway, chuckling, explained,

> My pet owl. I've been training him. He didn't mean to scratch me. He was just trying to stay on my hand. I was going to train him as a decoy for crows. . . But I got too fond of him. I like the way he sits on my hand. [Then holding out his hand to show him. . .] He sits there and stares right back at you. I like owls. They look you right in the eye. They don't take any guff from anybody. I guess I'll turn him loose when the weather warms. [Then with his face brightening] He had a better winter than any owl around here.

When Watson tried to show him the article the following day to ensure there were no errors in it, Papa joked that it "would probably get him killed," but said he did not need to see it: "I think you probably got it right."[26]

Watson's story was picked up by the major papers and rebranded as "Trials in Cuba Defended by Hemingway." When the press asked Castro how long the trials would continue, he responded until all war criminals were brought to justice. In response to the journalists' objections, Fidel said, "We are not executing innocent people or political opponents. We are executing murderers and they deserve it."[27] When Fidel appeared later on the popular American television show, *This Is Your Life*, he was again pressed about the tribunals that were executing his former enemies: "Let me tell you what Ernest Hemingway, winner of the Nobel Prize for Literature, defender of the rights of humanity, thinks about that: the executions in Cuba are a necessary phenomena. The military criminals executed by the revolutionary government received what they deserved."[28] How had the bearded Cuban rebel, formerly imprisoned, become a star of prime-time entertainment for American audiences?

• • • • •

In the middle of March with A. E. Hotchner joining them, Ernest and Mary left Ketchum for Havana. Stopping in a Phoenix hotel, they watched the second half of Hotch's adaptation of *For Whom the Bell Tolls* air on CBS, and, passing through Tucson, they visited Ernest's enchanting, childlike friend, the painter, Waldo Peirce at his home. They headed east and dropped Hotch in New Orleans, continued to Fort Myers, and on to Key West, where they flew the next afternoon to Havana and received a warm welcome from their Cuban family.

Behind the immigration counter at Boyeros Airport on March 29, they first found Juan and Roberto Herrera's welcoming faces waiting for them. Pausing at the Floridita, they were reunited with friends, and arriving home, they hugged René, Lola, and Ana on the front steps beneath the ceiba tree. "People were sweet and cheerful, the pool deliciously clean and cool, the house fresh and airy, beasts healthy, vines, shrubs, flowers, and trees flourishing," wrote Mrs. Hemingway in a state of bliss.[29] Pulling fish caught in the *cayos* out of the deep freeze, they lunched with Mayito Menocal, Elicio Arguelles, and other Cuban friends. Though most appeared hopeful about Castro's revolution, said Mary, the economy showed signs of slumping. In the airport, Ernest clutched Dr. José Luis Herrera Sotolongo close to tell him he wanted to arrange a meeting as soon as possible with Fidel and help him in any way he could.[30] At the end of March, after 483 executions, the trials were suspended for Easter.

On March 26, the police arrested and charged five men for a conspiracy to kill President Fidel Castro: Roberto Corral Miramón, Roberto López Paz, Roberto Pérez Merens, José Sosa Mojena, and Andrés Arango Chacón.[31] Lethal pro-Batista exiles, Rolando Masferrer and Ernesto de la Fe were implicated in the plot. The press and the pubic became increasingly apprehensive about the new government as it continued to purge henchmen from the previous regime.

The radicalization of Castro's regime was mirrored by radicalism of its northern neighbors whose interests allied themselves with those of Cuban refugees. Investigating the abuses of the CIA, NSA, FBI, and IRS a decade and a half later, the Church Committee excluded assassination as a tool for foreign policy—specifying that it was "incompatible with American principle, international order, and morality," yet according to CIA Director Richard Helms, the executive branch had long pressed the CIA to "get rid of Castro."[32] "If surviving assassination attempts were an Olympic event," said Fidel later, "I would win the gold medal."[33] Former head of Cuban intelligence and the Cuban Department of State, author Fábian Escalante counted 638 attempts on Castro's life (from Kennedy's to Clinton's, when Escalante wrote his book in 1996): thirty-eight occurring during the Eisenhower administration and forty-two during the Kennedy years.[34]

Seeking to improve his image, Fidel accepted an invitation in April to hand deliver the truth to the American people.[35] Hearing this announcement, Hemingway asked Dr. José Luis Herrera Sotolongo to request a meeting with El Comandante in advance of his trip so that he could prepare him to deal with the American press. As the head of the Cuban delegation, Castro would be going to the United Nations in New York, and Hemingway wanted the new leader to be briefed on American politicians and the idiosyncrasies of his people, so Castro assigned Vázquez Candela, assistant editor of the newspaper *Revolución*, to go to Hemingway's house. Late at night at Finca Vigía, Ernest opened the door with a pistol in his pocket.

While Vazquez was sure the trip would be a waste of time, after two hours of drinking white wine and conversing with the American novelist while Bach and Ravel played softly on the record player, he changed his mind. The Cuban journalist was impressed that Hemingway was so concerned about Fidel's well-being before the vultures of the *Miami Herald* and *Time*. He had to emphasize the current stability in Cuba, not respond to hecklers, not lose his temper, promise to oppose Communism, give clear answers, and keep his cool. When Vazquez left the Finca, Ernest told him to tell his comrades that he supported them and their cause.[36] On April 14, Hemingway heard a few minutes too late that Fidel and Camilo were playing baseball for their "Barbudo" baseball team.[37] To go down to the El Cerro Stadium, he ordered the car brought 'round so that he could meet them personally and exchange ideas but he missed them, and Fidel began his American tour the next day.

From April 15 to 26, Fidel Castro travelled as a guest of the American Society of Newspaper Editors and as a keen emissary of goodwill to the United States. Hiring a public relations firm, Fidel attempted to conquer public opinion in America during an eventful eleven-day tour. The Cuban rebel laid a wreath on George Washington's grave, delivered a speech in Central Park to thirty-five thousand fans, stared starry-eyed at Yankee Stadium, spoke with students at Harvard, pet a Bengali tiger at the Bronx Zoo, as well as fed the elephants, and met the classmates of his eight-year-old son who had been quietly attending Public School no. 20 in Queens while his father was overthrowing the government back home.[38] At his son's school, the children were given real rebel army caps and pretend beards, and while they touched Fidel's real beard, a Spanish-speaking New York City cop named Seymour Schimler had stepped in to play the role of his interpreter.

Young, tall, and intelligent, Castro made an impression that did not disappoint his American hosts. He still wore the combat boots and fatigues that would become his trademark. When he spoke in broken English with effusive emotion and astonishing eloquence, a smile often escaped from beneath his bushy beard. With a hopeful heart perhaps, he waved to crowds, and sat down for lengthy interviews in which he submitted himself to American scrutiny and answered rough questions. He carried babies and signed autographs for awestruck beauty queens, while the flashbulbs of photographers crackled around him like popcorn, or fire.

Of course, not everybody was as charmed by Fidel. The painter who Hemingway had convinced to leave Cuba to advance his career in the States, Antonio Gattorno, had become an accomplished and influential Cuban-American émigré, so he maneuvered a meeting with the visiting Cuban leader. Thirty-three-year-old Castro offended fifty-five-year-old Gattorno when he arrived late and advised, "You should return home to Cuba where you belong. I can help you to become a famous painter there." Gattorno responded that he was "already famous" and would return to his island "When you [Fidel] are no longer there."

On *Face the Nation*, Castro was asked if political parties would be allowed to run candidates in the elections, and he responded movingly in broken English, "Yes, of course! If we don't give free[dom] to all parties to organize, then we are not a democratic country."[39] Why was it necessary to wait eighteen months before free elections could be held? Castro responded that what his people wanted now was peace rather than more conflict. Would the Communist Party be allowed to participate in these elections? Castro answered, "What I think about that . . . all the rights before tyranny will return, free speech . . . are you afraid of an idea? Do you believe that a democratic man ought to be afraid of any idea? I am a man of faith."[40]

Leaving dozens of fans and a cloud of cigar smoke in America, Fidel Castro returned home. Although he had made many friends, his perceived impertinence had also made him many enemies. When one considers that Fidel emphasized with the best of intentions that he was not visiting America to beg the "yanquis" for money, one wonders if a meeting with a wordsmith could have helped to refine his rhetoric.[41]

Absconding to a golf course, Eisenhower, with no intention of meeting with Fidel Castro, shunned him during his visit. He sent lackey Vice President Nixon in his place. After their meeting, Nixon emerged with a "somewhat mixed" impression: he possessed qualities that made him a leader of men, and whatever they thought of him, he seemed destined to be "a great factor in the development of Cuba and very possibly in Latin American affairs generally." He seemed sincere but was "either incredibly naive about Communism or under Communist discipline." Nixon's guess was the former, and his ideas on how to run a government or economy were "less developed than those of almost any world figure I have met in fifty countries." Still they had no choice but to try to educate and guide him.[42]

Perhaps put off by Castro's effusive nature, Nixon emerged from their meeting stiffly concerned about the leftist leanings of Fidel's brother, Raúl, and those of his intimate associate, Che Guevara. Dulles's replacement as secretary of state, Christian Herter, seconded Nixon's reservations. Should we attribute Nixon and Castro's missed connection and opportunity to innocence, arrogance, or misunderstanding? Whatever was lost in translation might have been intentional or accidental.[43]

Shortly after his return, Fidel Castro fulfilled the promises of his Moncada agenda by signing the Agrarian Reform Act on May 17—limiting the size of land holdings to one thousand acres, divesting foreigners of the right to own land, expropriating thousands of acres of farmland, and redistributing it to the Cuban people like Robin Hood.

CHAPTER 14

El Comandante Meets His Favorite Author (1960)

• • • • •

The Hemingways departed on April 22 on a plane for New York City, then boarded the *Constitution* for Algeciras, Spain. For the second consecutive summer, Ernest would be reporting on the bull fights, this time for *Life* magazine. Mrs. Hemingway noted that they had left the Finca "fully staffed, expecting to return in the autumn or winter" and with "all its silver, Venetian glassware, eight thousand books, a number of them autographed first editions, and Ernest's small collection of paintings, one Paul Klee, two Juan Gris, five André Masson, one Braque and several good lively paintings of bulls by Robert Domingo. At my bank in Havana we have left reams of unpublished manuscript."[1]

That summer at the home of Bill and Annie Davis in La Consula, Ernest wrote "The Art of Short Story" as an introduction to a student edition of his short stories for Scribner's. At the Hotel Suecia in Madrid during San Isidro, the Hemingways met nineteen-year-old Valerie Danby-Smith, "purportedly" there, wrote Mary, to interview Ernest for the Irish press. With a "creamy complexion, pink cheeks, and tangled dark hair" (reminding some of Goya's Duchess of Alba), she was "seldom far from Ernest's side" after that.[2]

From June to September, Ernest followed the Ordóñez-Dominguín corridas. During the Pamplona Feria from July 7 to 14, young Valerie Danby-Smith rejoined their party, irritating Mrs. Hemingway. Ernest was planning a "little country fiesta" for his sixtieth birthday party at La Consula, including Chinese vegetables from London, champagne from France, a long table by the pool with Japanese lanterns, an orchestra, a procession of guitarists and flamenco dancers, a shooting gallery, silly hats for people to put on, a burro for them to ride, photographers, and fireworks. As one of many enchanting guests, friends old and new, travelling over land and over sea to attend, the matador Antonio Ordóñez remembered: "The Consula party was only a party, but it was a very good one."[3]

• • • • •

Enticed by high returns for sugar, Cuban agriculture became increasingly dependent on the crop. When the sugar market yo-yoed, only those who were well-insulated and well-positioned could ride out the storms and influence the market to their advantage—for the majority, the economy proved unsustainable. Faced with a period of austerity caused by civil strife, the falling price of sugar, the flight of tourism, and rising unemployment, the people demanded the promised revolution now.[4] Public perception was that President Urrutia, living now in the presidential palace, was an anti-Communist, while Prime Minister Fidel Castro was determined to represent the people, and it had been rumored that a rift had been growing between them. When Castro resigned from his Prime Minister position in protest, a ground swell of public opinion asked him to reconsider during a demonstration with signs painted "With Fidel to the Death! We are with you Fidel!" ending at the presidential palace with union leaders like Conrado Bécquer calling for Urrutia's resignation instead.[5]

On the evening of July 17, Castro took to the air waves to set himself apart from Urrutia, distinguishing himself as a man of the people. His differences with Urrutia had, he said, led to his resignation. He never wanted the post in the first place. "I had never wanted to be prime minister, but in the first month of government I saw no moves in the council of ministers toward any measures of social character . . . When I became prime minister, I proposed the reduction of government salaries beginning with my own." But while sugar workers' salaries were being cut, Urrutia had insisted that his remain at

$100,000 annually and purchased an expensive villa, an excess in Castro's opinion that betrayed the revolution's ideals.[6] Repulsed, Urrutia sought asylum in the Venezuelan embassy, then fled to New York. In his place, Fidel Castro named the pliable Osvaldo Dorticós Torrado president and reinstated himself as prime minister.

• • • • •

Throughout his "Dangerous Summer" for *Life* magazine, Hemingway had been following two dueling vedette toreros with Bill Smith, Hotchner, Valerie, Mary, and Annie Smith in Málaga, Valencia, Madrid, Saragossa, Bilbao, and other cities in Spain.[7] The season resulted in brutal gorings for both the talented newcomer, Luis Miguel Dominguín, and his brother-in-law, a more established veteran, Antonio Ordóñez (their fathers were also legends in the sport). One fight in Bilbao ended the competition and nearly took Dominguín's life. Maintaining an exhausting pace throughout the summer, Hemingway, a true aficionado of the bloodsport, called the last match the greatest bit of bullfighting he had ever seen, favoring Ordóñez as the sport's true master and comparing him to Pedro Romero.[8]

Tired of corrida after corrida in the summer heat, of eating and drinking in excess without sleep, and in the company of flattering fans like Slim Hayward or Valerie Danby-Smith, Mrs. Hemingway wrote that she felt "inaudible and invisible," underappreciated if not outright ignored, and told her husband that she was leaving him for good. "Neglect, rudeness, thoughtlessness, abusive language, unjust criticism, false accusations, failures of courtesy and friendliness" were among the reasons she cited in a letter, the last straw being when Ernest invited the Ordóñezes to Cuba without first consulting her, the matron of the house.[9] "Most hurtful of all," Mary wrote her husband, "were your compliments and attentions and interest and kisses for many girls and women, nothing for me. Nothing spontaneous toward me on your part, not even on the night of your birthday party . . . if I went to ask you a simple question . . . your face took on a look of irritation and impatience and you would say, 'I haven't got time. I have to go shit now. I have to go swim now.'"[10]

In New York, she resolved to rent an apartment for herself first, then return to put the Finca Vigía and the Ketchum house in order in advance of his guests' arrival, then return to New York to begin a new life alone.[11] Expressing regrets, but by and large ignoring the drama, Ernest allowed his wife to withdraw while he travelled from September 27 to October 27 with Valerie and Bill Davis to Nîmes, Aigues-Mortes, and Le Grau-du-Roi, "to ensure the accuracy" of scenes in *The Garden of Eden*.

While Hemingway was on this tour, Havana was strafed on October 21 by two private planes from Miami that also dropped bales of anti-Castro propaganda. Two people were killed by strafing from the aircraft and fifty were injured as Fidel Castro denounced the attack as terrorism. Uncomfortable with the rising influence of Communism in Cuba, evidenced by the displacement of President Urrutia, Huber Matos, a comandante who played a pivotal role in the revolution, resigned his post as military commander of Camagüey Province on October 19.[12] Dispatched by Castro to attend to Matos's acts of treason, General Camilo Cienfuegos, a much-loved popular hero, disappeared mysteriously in an airplane crash and joined the list of martyrs, dying in service of *la Revolución*.

Just a few days later, Ernest Hemingway boarded the transatlantic liner *Liberté* with Antonio and Carmen Ordóñez on the return trip to Cuba via New York. Of course, given America's anti-Communist anxieties, Hemingway's support for the revolution generated some publicity, which the press relished as news-generating scandal. Arriving in the United State, Hemingway was accosted by a group of gossip columnists as he descended the gangplank. After patiently waiting for the disparaging insinuations about Cuba and the revolution to subside, he snapped, "Are you through, gentlemen? I think everything is fine there." Then he precised: "We, the people of honor, believe in the Cuban Revolution." A longtime inhabitant of Havana, Hemingway had seen dictatorships come and go—as they conspired with American investors and organized crime to rob the island blind—in addition to the violent uprisings and reprisals. Because of what he had seen and what he understood, he remained firm in his opposition of continued injustice, made several financial contributions to the cause, putting his reputation and his property at risk as tensions intensified, and finally, speaking out in support of the people's revolution. In New York, he delivered a copy of his Paris memoir to Scribner and Sons.

Three days later, when the group landed in the Havana airport, they were again greeted by reporters. When asked to comment on the revolution, Ernest reiterated: "We, the people of honor, believe in the Cuban Revolution, I am happy to be here again, because I consider myself one more Cuban . . . I haven't believed any of the reports published against Cuba in the foreign press. My sympathies are with the Cuban government and with all *our* difficulties . . . I don't want to be considered a yanqui." He kissed the Cuban flag, but too quickly for reporters to capture it on film. When they asked him to do it again so that they could photograph it, the author responded: "I kissed it with all my heart, not as an actor."[13] Appreciating his style, they applauded.

Flying ahead via Chicago with her servant, Lola, Mary travelled in advance of her husband's arrival to make the Ketchum house presentable for his matador guests. On November 19, Ernest, Roberto Herrera Sotolongo, and Carmen and Antonio Ordóñez arrived. During a hunting expedition, eight days into their visit, Mary tripped on a root on the slippery frozen ground and shattered her elbow. Scolding her for her inattention, Ernest complained that she had ruined their plans and that he had to do the servants' work in her absence. The injury became a pretext to delay her threat of leaving him.[14] In Cuba, the administration of death sentences was suspended for the holiday season.

During the icy December after the bullfighter and his wife departed from Ketchum, Ernest was becoming more paranoid and withdrawn. What was causing him to behave that way? Did Hemingway's sudden mental breakdown have anything to do with Cuba? Is it possible that the precariousness of his longtime residence was somehow contributing to Hemingway's instability and eventual destruction?

Suffering from a broken elbow, insomnia, and hypertension between them, Ernest and Mary took the train to Chicago, then returned to Havana by plane at the end of January 1960. Setting forty-five chapters of *The Garden of Eden* aside, Ernest forged ahead with his "Dangerous Summer" pieces. Receiving a ticket from the Hemingways, young Valerie Danby-Smith travelled to Cuba to serve as Ernest's "last secretary."

• • • • •

In February, First Deputy Premier of Russia, Anastas I. Mikoyan, visited Cuba with an offer of $100 million in trade credit with 2.5 percent interest. Over the course of the next five years, the Soviets agreed to buy 5 million tons of sugar and to supply Cuba with crude oil, wheat, machinery, fertilizers, and petroleum products. During his stay, Mikoyan paid a special visit to the Finca Vigía bearing gifts of wooden dolls, caviar, and a collection of Hemingway's works translated into Russian. In addition to Papa's declaration that vodka was good to gargle for sore throats and colds, the writer made sure to communicate sentiments that would keep him out of trouble during tense times: "As a result of the revolution, I can say one thing for sure: for the first time in Cuba, there is a clean government."[15]

In February and March, Hotchner's adaptations of *The Fifth Column* and "The Snows of Kilimanjaro" aired on CBS, continuing to enhance the income and prestige of Ernest Hemingway through the medium of television. Fearing libel and doubting his work, Ernest wrote Scribner in March to ask him to return his Parisian memoirs and to suspend its publication until further notice. By the end of March, Ernest had written sixty-three thousand words of *The Dangerous Summer.*

• • • • •

On March 4, the French freighter *La Coubre,* delivering Belgian arms to Havana harbor, exploded, killing 101 people. Fidel Castro immediately denounced the United States for "sabotage."[16] To protest the "heinous act," commanders Che Guevara, Ramiro Valdés, Camilo Cienfuegos, William Morgan, Eloy Gutiérrez Menoyo, Osvaldo Dorticós (who would remain the president of Cuba until 1976), and Fidel Castro walked arm in arm down Calle Neptuno, forming a dramatic contrast between the street's garish neon signs and the plain green of their uniforms and the sobriety of their mission.

In a photo taken on March 5, 1960, by Alberto Korda at a ceremony for the victims of the tragedy, Che appears full of sorrow, anger, and determination. That image would become ubiquitous across the world, a trademark, appearing on T-shirts and countless other commodities. Che transcended his personhood and became both a symbol for the struggle against tyranny and of tyranny itself. His spirit seemed to impress even nihilist philosophers like Jean-Paul Sartre who, with Simone de Beauvoir, was there that mournful day when Che's picture was taken.

One of Che's first questions in taking over as president of the Banco Nacional de Cuba in November was where Cuba had deposited its gold reserves and dollars. When he was told Fort Knox, he said that the gold would have to be sold and converted into currency in Canadian and Swiss accounts. During a speaking engagement at the bank two months later, Che apologized "because my talk has been much more fiery than you would expect for the post I occupy; I ask once more for forgiveness, but I am still much more of a guerrilla than President of the National Bank," and as if to prove it, he signed banknotes with his nom de guerre, "Che."[17] The agenda was the struggle, and so it would remain, and *La Coubre* only confirmed the necessity of his resolve and commitment to the bitter end.

• • • • •

Most every Thursday evening that season, Ambassador Phil Bonsal dined with Ernest Hemingway. One evening he came also to deliver an upsetting message. The US government was going to break off relations with Cuba. As the island's most conspicuous, high-profile expatriate, Washington decreed that Hemingway should leave Cuba as soon as possible and publicly proclaim his disapproval of Castro's government. If he did not, he could be sure that he would face serious and unpleasant consequences.[18] Hemingway protested: his business was not politics, but writing, and for twenty-two years Cuba had been his home. Be that as it may, Bonsal replied that high officials maintained a different view, had used the word "traitor," and saw his collaboration as a nonnegotiable.

That was the message he had to deliver, said the ambassador, and he believed that Ernest should take it quite seriously. As the course of dinner conversation drifted to other subjects, the Hemingways and their dinner guests tried to think about happier things but found it difficult to forget what had just been said. Hemingway was not one to take orders, and one can imagine that this news and the imminent loss of his cherished home would have been very unsettling. From Bonsal's warning, it is also difficult to know the severity of the "consequences" that might have come as a response to Hemingway's acts of "treason." A letter of reprimand, loss of citizenship, a fine, imprisonment, or something much more sinister?

On his next visit, Phil told them that he had been recalled, and diplomatic relations between the United States and Cuba had officially been broken. He was leaving the next day. They tried to be cheerful, saying it was just temporary, that it would pass. Before leaving, however, Phil softly reminded Ernest of the warning he had made on his previous visit. From her unique vantage point as Hemingway's "last secretary," Valerie Danby-Smith witnessed these scenes firsthand: "He felt now more than ever that Ernest would have to make an open choice between his country and his home—loudly and clearly, so that the world would know where he stood. We all embraced, promising to meet again before too long, believing things could only improve. While we waved to Phil from the steps as he left, I noted the sadness in Ernest's eyes. None of us would see Phil again." It was time for Ernest to "review his narrowing options. The noose was tightening."[19]

Although Ernest prided himself on being loyal to his own country, a good American—as a longtime resident of the island, he had also forged deep bonds with Cuban people, family and friends, to whom he was unable to remain indifferent at a time when they were finally attaining what he felt was their "decent moment in history." Consequently, Hemingway did not abandon his residence or speak out against Fidel Castro, but instead invited him and Che Guevara to go fishing. The annual Hemingway Marlin Fishing Tournament scheduled for May 16 would attract sports enthusiasts from across the world during one of the first international events since the Cuban Revolution. Disregarding Ambassador Bonsal's disturbing warning, Hemingway fraternized with the young revolutionaries and allowed reporters to photograph him by Castro's side.

Deep sea fishing is a skill learned with years of practice. Fidel was not a fisherman, but he would enjoy a stroke of beginner's luck: following the rules and not cheating, he managed to hook two marlins the first day and another the second. Watching through their binoculars from the *Pilar* as Fidel fished and Che read Stendhal's *Le rouge et le noir*, Mary and Ernest could hardly believe their eyes when Fidel brought the two marlins in and stopped his assistant from gaffing them until Fidel could grasp the leader himself (rather than the line—just as the rules specified).

Despite his busy schedule during the fragile first months of the revolution, Fidel would make a point of attending the competition all week. When asked if he planned to continue until the end of the contest, Fidel responded that the competition was organized by the National Institute of Tourism, so he participated to show his support and to promote tourism on the island: "The tournaments are very good, very well organized and many foreign fishermen have come to the international competition. I don't presume to be a great fisherman, but I was invited and told that Hemingway would take part as well, I believe tomorrow, and as you know, he has always defended Cuba and the Revolution. He is a writer whose presence here is of great satisfaction for us."[20]

Fidel managed to win numerous individual prizes. Moreover, the comandante met one of his heroes eye to eye at the awards ceremony: Ernest Hemingway, the Nobel Prize winner, who had been gallant enough to support his cause. Castro took the silver trophy cup, which the writer presented him that evening at the dock.

"I am a novice at fishing," said Fidel, unexpectedly shy in the company of the white-bearded writer, looking thinner than in any picture he had ever seen.

"You are a lucky novice," Hemingway replied. "I congratulate you *Comandante*. On the other hand, I am rarely as fortunate. I never have any luck during competitions. In general, I am very unlucky!"

They chuckled. Afterward, Hemingway and Castro conversed for about thirty minutes somewhat separated from the rest of the crowd.

"He said he'd read *The Bell* in Spanish and used its ideas in the Sierra Maestra," Ernest mumbled uneasily to his wife on the way home, possibly doubting Castro's sincerity after meeting him in person. Having optimistically proclaimed his support for Castro in public, Hemingway now perhaps found himself over his head in Cuban politics and uncertain how the revolution and his role in it would turn out.[21]

During the tournament, Ernest Hemingway and the other fishermen would have had ample opportunity to look back from the water at the Havana skyline, at the harbor and the peninsula where the fortress, El Morro, and the prison, *La Cabaña*, still stood. *La Cabaña*'s prison cells now swelled with dissidents, people who opposed Fidel Castro's Revolution. Behind the fortress and the prison stood a new addition carved in Carrera Marble in Rome, blessed by Pope Pius XII, and inaugurated on Christmas Day in 1958 by President Batista and his wife, only one week before they fled the island in haste and two weeks before the last liberator, or conqueror, of Cuba, Castro, arrived triumphantly home, in the capital city of Havana.[22]

After her family—and her husband's presidency—survived the attack on the Presidential Palace on March 13, 1957, Fulgencio Batista's wife, Martha Fernández Miranda, vowed to erect a statue of Christ that could be seen by the entire city of Havana, so she initiated a competition. Presenting her terrestrial sketch of the Christ figure, artist Gilma Madera won the competition and the statue's commission. As popular legend remembers today, Mrs. Batista vowed to complete the statue even if it required using her own funds. Thereafter perched on the spine of the peninsula and towering over La Cabana stands a gigantic statue of Christ, *El Cristo de la Habana*, watching and presiding over the old city, *Habana Vieja*, and raising a stone hand to bless new arrivals, even if his wrinkled brow appears to express also an appropriate measure of hesitation. Madera said that she attempted to depict a figure full of "vigor and human firmness with a face of integrity and serenity, certain in his ideas, not a little angel flying in the clouds, but someone with his feet firmly on the ground."[23] In an interview, the sculptor also explained that she attempted to create a Christ with distinctively Cuban features, originating in the blend of African and indigenous traits, inspired not by a specific model, but by her ideals of male beauty—oblique eyes, fleshy lips—the perfect harmony of a racial mix in her part of the world.[24] Given the skyrocketing fame of Cuba's Nobel Prize winner, Ernest Hemingway, and his recent depiction of an earthly, Christ-like, protagonist, Santiago, in *The Old Man and the Sea*, one cannot help but wonder if Mr. and Mrs. Batista, who were very unpopular at the time, were influenced by Hemingway's work in their decision to also offer an earthly Christ to *el pueblo cubano*[25] by selecting an artist who would portray him in their own likeness.

Having converted to Catholicism more than thirty years earlier to marry Pauline, Ernest would have surely appreciated the Divine Trinity expressed by the statue's extended index finger, middle finger, and folded thumb. Even before the time of Christ, this gesture had evoked a trinity in a supernatural family—a mother, a son, and a spirit of light—in Aphrodite, Zeus, and Chronos—in Venus, Jupiter, and Saturn—terrestrial beings and celestial sources, mystical origins for falling stars, their state of purgatory, and aspirations to return. As he ascended in his literary universe, Ernest included an epitaph which also served as title for his first novel, *The Sun Also Rises*: "One generation passeth away, and another generation cometh: but the earth abideth forever. The sun also ariseth, and the sun goeth down, and hasteth to his place where he arose" (Ecclesiastes 1:4–7).[26] Fishing from her coastal water and gazing back at El Cristo as he watches over the grand old city of Havana, one can only reflect upon his epitaph, and wonder about Cuba's future.

CHAPTER 15

Hemingway Never Left Cuba: A Lion's Suicide (1960–1961)

• • • • •

Complaining of an inability to write and struggling to cut down and finish his article for *Life* magazine, Ernest, unable to focus, appeared so perceptibly anti social and withdrawn that Mary asked George Saviers, her husband's doctor from Idaho, to come down to Havana. The author's eyesight was deteriorating quickly, and his weight was dropping at an alarming rate.[1] To Charles Scribner, his editor, Ernest confided as he eased off the pursuit of the memoirs that would become *A Moveable Feast*, "Feel terrible about post-poning book but if I do not rest a little as I work the Dr. says I will blow a gasket. Haven't been able to sleep more than 2 ½ to 3 hrs at a time. Get about 4 a night—five at most. Weigh 200 this morning."[2]

In television interviews, Fidel Castro had been repeating that the Americans who had not exploited the Cuban people would not be touched by his regime, but bearded revolutionaries seemed often outside his control, appropriating the businesses of North Americans, rich Spaniards, and rich Cubans, under the radar or outside his purview. As the Hemingways pulled up in their American automobile, San Francisco de Paula villagers still yelled out "Mismary, Mismary" in a neighborly way, but everywhere the couple went, there were signs declaring "*¡Cuba sí! ¡Yanqui no!*"[3] Nonetheless in the quiet of their village and at the Finca, the aging Hemingways led a monastic life, including sunset walks around the grounds with Valerie, writing, reading, gardening, tending their cats and dogs, swimming, fishing, and dining with friends.

Even though they had contributed, by Mary's count, close to $750,000 to Cuba's economy by employing their staff and living there, they were "beginning to feel unwelcome" as North Americans in the middle of a revolution that had an ever more antagonistic relationship with the United States. Faced with the problem of remaining as foreigners in Cuba, Ernest would still not entertain Mary's suggestions that they abandon the Finca and their servants there or remove some easily portable paintings and the more valuable possessions.[4]

Seemingly rebounding after Dr. George Saviers's departure as spring ended and marlin season continued, Hemingway would have over 100,000 words of his mano a mano for *Life* who had asked for only 10,000 words. Mary's arm, which had had to be reset, had not yet fully healed, but she was working hard on it and showing much progress. In a letter to Hotch, Ernest said he thought it would be "perfectly safe for [Mary] to take fish like dolphin or bonito with it now," and "Val had caught 2 white marlin."[5] His fair-faced young secretary was handling the rod very well, said Ernest, and swam one hundred round trips in the pool on her birthday.

On June 27, Hotch flew down to help Papa cut 60,000 out of 120,000 words from the manuscript. While Ernest grumbled throughout theprocess, eventually he would agree to the changes. The magazine paid him ninety thousand dollars for the article but printed only part of what "Pecas"—as Ernest called Hotchner for his freckles—sent in.[6] By June, other worries crept into the author's mind: "Been doing Income Tax-copying and re-writing since Mary is in a big bind with the Income Tax."[7]

• • • • •

By June 16, Cuban police had arrested two American diplomats, Edwin L. Sweet and William G. Friedman, at a meeting of counter-revolutionaries—and charged them with encouraging terrorism, granting asylum, financing subversive publications, and smuggling weapons. Under pressure from Eisenhower's administration, Shell, Esso, and Texaco refused to refine Soviet oil, and US companies stopped selling fuel to Cuba. Thus Castro's government confiscated the refineries on June 29 and July 11. Retaliating on July 3, the US Congress, after an all-night session, passed the "Sugar Act," empowering the president to cut the quota of sugar bought from Cuba as he saw fit—to slap the island on the wrist—so he cut it by seven hundred thousand tons.[8] Two days later, Castro thumbed his nose at the "economic aggression" by nationalizing all American businesses and commercial property on the island, a "decision justified by the necessity to indemnify the nation for the damages caused to the economy and to affirm the consolidation of the economic independence of the country."[9] Two days after that, the Soviet Union announced that it would buy the sugar that the United States did not, and China followed with a similar pronouncement by the end of the month.[10]

Taking leave of trade-war tensions, Mary, Ernest, and Valerie departed Havana for Key West and New York. When summer came, and a new bullfighting season began, the writer returned to Spain—leaving Mary and Valerie behind in New York—to complete an additional installment covering *tauromachia* for *Life* magazine. If he could see a few more bullfights, he thought, perhaps then he could set the words down on paper convincingly once again. But there Hemingway began to unravel at the seams, suffering headaches, paranoia, and delusions, complaining frequently of the IRS, the FBI, and the CIA, who he believed were following him—and who were, in reality, investigating him at that time. Perhaps attributable to a history of mental illness in his family, numerous concussions, or other health problems, Ernest would seem to be losing his sanity.

Planning to go to Cuba to check on their affairs as soon as she had made her New York "nest livable," Mary encountered daunting new hurdles for "foreign residents regardless of nationality to secure military permits for departure."[11] When Mary called René, he informed her that thieves had broken into their property, that the pool and other renovations needed money and attention, and that all letters were being opened and reviewed. She asked him what he thought of her coming down to help him for a week or two: "No, no, Miss Mary," he warned. "Much better to stay there. Much."[12]

From Spain, Ernest wrote his wife, "Honey I miss you so and our old lovely life," but "would *not* go to Cuba in September."[13] He was "sick of the whole [bullfighting] racket," "fearing a complete physical and nervous crack up" with a "worn out head—not to mention body," and pursued by nightmares: "I wish you were here to look after me and help me out and keep me from cracking up. Feel terrible and am just going to lie quiet now and try to rest . . . Lots of problems . . . Not sleeping, tricky memory etc. bad—any drinking bad for me except lightest claret. Plenty others [problems] but we will work them out and I'll get healthy and write fine."[14]

Concerned about her husband's well-being, Mary answered, "I wish I could give you something wonderful and refreshing and renewing—3 weeks of our old-style holidays at Paraíso." She sent Valerie to help him in Spain.

While the FBI kept tabs on Ernest Hemingway—indeed J. Edgar Hoover kept the Hemingway file open until the author's death—the CIA was attempting to assassinate Fidel Castro. The agency staged hundreds of failed attempts, such as the exploding cigar they planned to give him when he visited the United Nations in New York in 1960.[15] Another cigar was laced with botulinum toxin, and another with LSD to confuse him during the speech. They also tried to give him thallium salts with a depilatory effect so powerful it would cause his iconic beard to fall out—like Samson's hair in the Bible.[16]

• • • • •

In early September, tensions between Cuba and the United States escalated sharply when Castro nationalized the tobacco factories, plants, and warehouses, including H. Upmann and Partagas, and all the US banks on the island: First National City Bank of New York, First National Bank of Boston, and Chase Manhattan Bank. Then, later in the month, he led a Cuban delegation on a trip to New York to address the United Nations General Assembly. Like his first visit, it was a media blitz, but tensions had increased significantly with his northern neighbor since then. Now the public relations grandstanding looked more like a warpath.

When Castro's entourage was barred from the elitist hotels of Midtown Manhattan and from attending President Eisenhower's Latin American leaders' luncheon, they stayed in Harlem at the Hotel Theresa; lunched with working-class African Americans; met with Soviet Premier Nikita Khrushchev, Egyptian President Gamal Abdel Nasser, Indian Prime Minister Jawaharlal Nehru, Langston Hughes, Allen Ginsberg, and Malcolm X. Astutely, Fidel brought with him Comandante Juan Almeida, a black man who was one of his highest ranking officers, to underline the opportunities in Cuba for Negroes that did not yet seem to exist in America. His landmark speech at the United

Nations first pointed out how expensive it was for a third-world delegation to come to New York to have its voice heard. He promised to be brief yet spoke for four and a half hours (after all, he had paid for it), narrating history from Cuba's perspective, denouncing American imperialism and exploitation, and refusing to be marginalized or silenced.[17]

Fidel cited from the "Declaration of Havana." Ratified on September 2, the Declaration of Havana was Cuba's response to the Declaration of San José, when Latin American ministers, gathering in Costa Rica, yielded to financial pressure from the United States (who refused loans to countries favoring Cuban autonomy) and opposed Cuba's self-determination.[18]

Although these Latin American ministers had voted against him and in favor of the United States, said Fidel, over 1 million Cubans had gathered to approve his Declaration, in a National General Assembly at the José Martí Revolution Square, and he was confident that Latin American oppressed peoples of the world would also vote in its favor. To protect themselves, oppressed nations had the right to arm and defend themselves against their oppressors. After his address, Fidel Castro received a standing ovation.

On the same day Fidel spoke at the UN, four boats left Miami carrying two hundred men poised to invade Cuba. The mission—funded by the CIA and led by Rolando Masferrer Rojas—failed miserably.[19] After only one of the boats made it across and landed in Cuba, twenty-eight men were captured: eighteen were sent to Cuban prison, and ten were executed by firing squad. Three of them, Allan D. Thompson, Anthony Zarba, and Robert O. Fuller, were Americans. When Castro returned to Cuba, he continued to nationalize banks, sugar mills, farms, and industry supported by Urban Reform Law no. 890, and the United States responded by levying a partial embargo on all imports except medicines and food.

Campaigning for president in October 1960 at the Democratic dinner in Cincinnati, Ohio, Senator John F. Kennedy rebuked his opponent, Vice President Nixon, for his misreading and mishandling of foreign policy regarding Cuba, specifically his confidence in Batista's regime and his alienation of Castro's government that caused one of America's closest neighbors and former allies to slip behind the Iron Curtain: "And Fidel Castro seized on this rising anti-American feeling, and exploited it, to persuade the Cuban people that America was the enemy of democracy—until the slogan of the revolution became *'Cuba, sí, Yanqui, no'*—and Soviet imperialism had captured a movement which had originally sprung from the ideals of our own American Revolution."[20]

• • • • •

From Spain, Papa wrote Hotch that he was sorry he had not written: he had "been in really lousy shape but feeling better . . . Never was so dead in the head in my life but it is starting to bull out of it. The head I mean."[21] Worried, Hotchner flew to Spain in October to check in on his buddy and business partner. Discovering the extent of the writer's paranoia, Hotch brought Papa immediately back to New York.

Mary and George Brown drove out to meet them, smiling and waving at Hemingway, despondent and gray, at Idlewild Airport. Fretting about Valerie's Irish passport, Ernest was sure that he would be interrogated by the authorities.[22] In the little Sixty-Second Street apartment Mary had been fixing up, he seemed out of place: outwardly polite, yet adrift in its rooms, distracted, lost in a quagmire of hidden difficulties within, and afraid to communicate them.

When his wife tried to take him to the Central Park Zoo to get some air, he was afraid to leave the apartment. "Somebody's waiting out there," he said. Summoned by Mary, Dr. George Saviers once again travelled a great distance to meet the Hemingways in their hour of need. When his wife lost patience with her husband's paranoia, he "retreated into silence."

With the assistance of George Brown in New York, Bea Guck in Chicago, and Dr. George Saviers ushering the couple back to the Shoshone station platform, the Hemingways and their luggage made their way west to Ketchum. Briefing Dr. Saviers on his kidney trouble and blood pressure, Hemingway installed himself at his writing table that looked upon the Big Wood River Valley. His "spirits seemed to rally," said Mary. "He was remembering more and more of Paris when he was an ebullient young man there, and getting words on paper." Betty Bell, local champion skier and efficient secretary, assisted him every step of the way.[23]

Alas, Papa's demons, "doubts, suspicions, and unreasonable fears" would not leave him alone. When two men in topcoats came out of a restaurant, Ernest was certain that they were government men "tailing me out here already." When a windstorm blew a cottonwood tree across the river near their home, he was wrought with worry: "Anybody could get over here from there." His wife tried to convince him that they were surrounded by friends who wished them well, but she could no longer break through. To reassure his numerous financial worries, Mary had the vice president of their bank phone and tell them how much they were ahead financially in hard, irrefutable numbers, while Ernest listened in on the other line scribbling the numbers on a notepad and not believing a single number he heard. They were hiding something, he insisted; they were covering something up. What reason could they possibly have to cover something up, Papa? "I don't know," said Ernest digging in, "but I know."[24]

When they discovered Hoover's investigation into Ernest's connection with Communism, with Cuba, and with Fidel Castro, when they understood that they were tapping his phones and following him around, his loved ones would have to come to terms with the influence of FBI surveillance on Ernest's mental health. Hotchner later realized that he had "regretfully misjudged" his friend's fears of the organization and the subsequent treatment that used electric shock therapy to eradicate delusions that were actually facts.[25]

When Dr. Saviers suggested that he check into the Menninger Clinic, Ernest protested that "they'll say I'm losing my marbles," but the thirty-nine sessions of electric shock treatment were already causing him to do just that.[26] They finally decided to check Hemingway into the Mayo Clinic in Minnesota, where he was strapped down to receive numerous electroconvulsive shock treatments as traumatic as his previous concussions, leaving him shattered, unable to write, never the same again. Moods became unpredictable, despondent, or paranoid, worsening from week to week. The treatments alleviated his depression for a time but wiped out the author's ability to create, stripping him of all purpose in the new year.

In early 1961—as the United States threatened to invade Cuba and Castro responded with a military parade of Soviet-made rocket launchers, artillery, tanks, antiaircraft, and anti-tank guns—the press revealed that Ernest Hemingway had been in the Mayo Clinic receiving treatment: "The white-bearded, 61-year-old novelist is in St. Mary's hospital in Rochester for 'medical treatment'" a brief statement from the clinic said. A clinic spokesman would not reveal the nature of Hemingway's illness nor say how long he had been under the care of doctors at the diagnostic center. But it was unofficially reported that Hemingway's ailment was not considered serious."[27] On the door of his room Ernest had hung a bizarre sign: "FORMER WRITER ENGAGED IN PREPARATION OF SCHEDULED FULL-SCALE NEWS CONFERENCE AS PROMISED IN THE P-D BY OUR SPOKESMAN. PLEASE DO NOT DISTURB UNLESS ABSOLUTELY NECESSARY TO OBTAIN PHOTOGRAPHS OR CONFIRMATION OF TREATMENT GIVEN EXCLUSIVELY TO THE P-D."[28]

• • • • •

When photographs from round two of *The Dangerous Summer* appeared unflattering to a rapidly deteriorating Ernest, the writer accused *Life* of betraying the bullfighters and exposing him as a "double-crosser" and a fool. Asked to write something for President Kennedy's inauguration, he sat for several hours before a blank page, and unable to compose a single sentence, he broke down. "It just won't come anymore," he told Hotchner and wept.[29]

The Kennedys telegrammed Hemingway to invite him to the inauguration, and he responded the following day to express gratitude for the invitation and to apologize for not being able to attend due to his health. At the ceremony, Kennedy asked, "Can we forge against these enemies a grand and global alliance, North and South, East and West, that can assure a more fruitful life for all mankind? Will you join in that historic effort? . . . My fellow citizens of the world, ask not what America will do for you, but what together we can do for the freedom of man."[30] After watching the speech on the television with his wife, Hemingway wrote the president a thank-you letter: "[Dear Mr. President] Watching the inauguration from Rochester there was the happiness and the hope and the pride how beautifully we thought Mrs. Kennedy was and then how deeply moving the inaugural address was. Watching on the screen I was sure our President would stand any of the heat to come as he had taken the cold of that day."[31]

Released from the Mayo Clinic, Ernest returned to Ketchum on January 22. There, he saw Gary Cooper, who had once played leading roles in *A Farewell to Arms* and *For Whom the Bell Tolls*, but who was now dying of cancer. They had been friends now for twenty years: "Coop is a fine man; as honest and straight and friendly and unspoiled as he looks. If you made up a character like Coop, nobody would believe it. He's just too good to be true."[32] It was the last time they would see each other before Coop died in May.

Getting on track, Ernest wrote Harry Brague at Scribner's on February 6, 1961, with the page count of each of the eighteen chapters of his Paris memoirs. Figuring the average number of words with and without conversation, he crunched numbers and applied complex operations of long division to deduce that he had about 42,000 to 45,000 words. He said he was still working on the nineteenth chapter and his title by making his usual long list, but something was wrong with all the titles on his list, specifically because Paris was generally cliché and wrecked as a subject.

Not wanting "to bitch," but imagining Brague might appreciate a "situation report," Hemingway allowed: Estranged from Cuba, he did not have access to his library, good food, or a secretary, though Mary had been interviewing candidates according to her criteria.[33] At a minimum for "title-ing," he needed a copy of the Oxford Book of English Verse and a Bible (King James Version): "This is the minimum and there is nothing here." The letter shows the extent that Ernest's displacement from the Finca Vigía disrupted his routine, affected his mental stability, and impeded his writing at this moment when his health was on a sharp decline.

That spring, on the Caribbean island that Ernest increasingly missed, the United States launched two airstrikes that knocked out 27 percent of the Cuban air force in anticipation of an amphibious and airborne landing, now known as the debacle of the Bay of Pigs. Made wise to the operation both by loose lips in Miami and the KGB, Castro was ready to receive and personally led the counteroffensive with Soviet T-34 and IS-2 tanks, SU-100 tank destroyers, 122 and 105 mm howitzers, B-26 bombers, Hawker Sea Fury fighters, and T-33 jets.

The Cuban foreign minister, Raúl Roa, who had refused the offer to defect to the United States just days before, denounced the American attacks to the United Nations, and President Kennedy responded, "On that unhappy island, as in so many other arenas of the contest for freedom, the news has grown worse instead of better. I have emphasized before that this was a struggle of Cuban patriots against a Cuban dictator. While we could not be expected to hide our sympathies, we made it repeatedly clear that the armed forces of this country would not intervene in any way."[34] When it became clear that the ground operation was destined for failure while the whole world watched, the fledgling president opted not to proceed with a second sortie of air support.

The repelled attack made the United States, and President Kennedy, look weak, and it solidified Castro's alliance with the USSR and the cohesion of his new country. Spurred by the monumental failure of the operation, Kennedy sought to step up assassination attempts to topple Castro. For Ernest Hemingway, the failure of the Bay of Pigs perhaps signified the loss of his beloved Finca, the place where he had felt most at home. As an American, he was not likely to be regarded any longer as a friend.

On April 21, Mary awoke and found her husband "in front of the vestibule of the house with his shotgun, two shells and a note he had written me. For an hour I talked to him—courage, his bravery, faith, love—managed to delay any decisive action until George [Saviers] arrived, perceived the situation and managed to take Papa to the Sun Valley hospital where they put him to bed and gave him sedatives."[35] Convincing George Saviers that he had to return to the house on April 24, Hemingway again grabbed his rifle and had to be subdued by his hunting buddy Don Anderson and George Saviers, who escorted him by plane to Rochester, Minnesota. When the plane stopped to refuel in Rapid City, South Dakota, Ernest ran off, looking in parked cars for ways to kill himself and attempting to walk into a moving propeller of a plane, but the motor cut off just in the nick of time. On April 26, the newspapers reported, "Hemingway Back at Mayo Clinic . . . A spokesman said the Nobel Prize–winning author was in satisfactory condition but that 'rest and quiet are absolutely essential.'"[36]

Though he was obviously dangerous to himself, Ernest's friends and family found flashes of hope in the old intellect, such as his cocksure challenge to psychiatrists: pick any sentence of *The Old Man and the Sea* at random and try to rewrite it in fewer words. It was impossible. Having used considerable charm to play the part of a patient in recovery, Hemingway diluted the objective judgment of his doctors at the Mayo

Clinic. Dr. Rome soon recommended him for release to his wife, who had come for a visit and had been "dumbfounded to see Ernest there, dressed in his street clothes, grinning like a Cheshire cat," appearing upbeat and ready to go.[37] No sooner had he arrived in Ketchum than he began to pursue his demise like a determined hunter stepping intently through the grim woods of his darkening mind.

When Hotchner visited his friend in June after a fresh round of electroshock therapy, he had not improved. "Very gently," Hotchner asked him why he wanted to kill himself. The man who had faced charging rhinos, howling hurricanes, and the terrifying "nada" of an empty page every dawn of his life interrogated: "What do you think happens to a man going on 62 when he realizes that he can never write the books and stories he promised himself? Or do any of the other things he promised himself in the good days?" How could he say that, protested Hotchner, when he had already written as beautiful a book about Paris as anybody could have ever hoped to write. Hemingway responded that he had written the best of it before and now could not finish it. Well, Hotchner advised, why not retire, or just relax. He'd earned it, hadn't he?

"Retire?" scoffed Hemingway. A writer could not retire like a baseball player or a prizefighter when his legs or reflexes were shot. Everywhere he went people would ask him what he was working on.

To hell with those people, said Hotchner; after all, he never cared what they said about him.

"What does a man care about? Staying healthy. Working good. Eating and drinking with his friends. Enjoying himself in bed. I haven't any of them. You understand, goddamn it? None of them." He then turned on Hotchner, attacking him and accusing him of being in on it, conspiring with "the Feds," merely pumping him for information that would later be used against him. It was the last time that they would see each other. Hemingway without writing was not Hemingway, but a man stripped of all identity and determined to die.[38]

• • • • •

Early on the morning of July 2, 1961, the author rose as full of intention as on any day of his writing life, drew his favorite shotgun from his storage room in Ketchum, Idaho, and took it to the entrance of his home. Timing his death to occur at precisely 7:00 a.m., he pressed the double barrels to his forehead and ended his own life.

When his wife of fifteen years heard the shot, she came rushing in and, distraught, insisted for several months that it had been an accident. Enamored with an idol, perplexed by his act, and advancing a career, Emmett Watson, the minor reporter from the *Seattle Post-Intelligencer* who had tapped Papa's views on Castro, now returned for another scoop, speaking with the officers cordoning the crime scene and becoming the first to "break the story" that it had not been an accident, but a suicide, despite his widow's insistence that he had unintentionally shot himself while cleaning his weapon.[39]

"I'll let the Maestro end this," wrote Arnold Gingrich, editor, in *Esquire,* then allowed Hemingway's almost forgotten former writer-in-training, Arnold Samuelson, to contribute a few lines in memoriam, for they seemed to be exceptionally well written. Marrying and buying a ranch in Robert Lee in west-central Texas, Samuelson sank into domestic oblivion, incessantly tortured by the heavy expectations created by a summer spent in the presence of a literary god.[40] Samuelson had never once forgotten his time with Hemingway and just after the writer's death had written Gingrich to express his grief in writing: "Ernest lived as long as he could. His last act was the most deliberate of his life. He had never written about his own suffering. He said it all without words in the language any man can understand."[41]

Among the countless tributes to Hemingway after his death, the Cuban painter Antonio Gattorno remembered in an interview for the *New Bedford Standard Times* in Acushnet, Massachusetts, "He was just like a brother. His loss to me is the same as if I had lost a brother."

Several analysts have subsequently speculated that Hemingway's strange and sudden decline (much like several family members who exhibited many of the same symptoms) might well have been a genetic disease known as hemochromatosis, in which the inability to metabolize iron results in a rapid mental and physical deterioration.[42] Many readers and loved ones were unaware that he had lost his mind, suffering for a year with dementia from concussions, genetics, and electroshock treatment, before finally taking matters into his own hands.

CHAPTER 16

Finca Vigía Becomes the Finca Vigía Museum (1960–Present)

• • • • •

Nineteen days after the shotgun blast that resonated across the world, Cuban Revolution leader Fidel Castro appeared at the North American writer's estate to drink in the ambiance, to pay his respects, to stroke his beard, to ponder the scene, to smoke a *habano*, and to take accounts. There, Castro would find René Villarreal, guarding the home of his former employer from would-be interlopers, a loyal employee who would not quit his post. "Do you know who I am?" asked Fidel Castro with a smirk when he saw Villarreal, who had lived there for most of his life.

"Yes, of course. Fidel Castro, accompanied by his officers."

"Where can I find René Villarreal?"

"I am René Villarreal."

"Calm down, there is no need to be nervous. You're the man the newspapers say lived next to Ernest Hemingway since childhood? *Su hombre de confianza* . . . his right-hand man. Can we come in and talk? We would like to see how he lived."[1] Upon parting, Fidel suggested that Villarreal should consider curating a museum dedicated to his former employer. Uncertain about the offer and about Castro, Hemingway's majordomo said nothing.

Not yet completely accepting that her husband's death had been intentional, Mrs. Hemingway had been busying herself with the project of organizing his estate. One of her first priorities was to return to Cuba to recover the unfinished manuscripts of *The Garden of Eden*, *A Moveable Feast*, *Islands in the Stream*, *The Dangerous Summer*, and *True at First Light*, and to salvage all else in the house that she believed was valuable and could be safely transported to the United States, without unduly alerting the revolutionary administration, which was nationalizing property more zealously than ever.

Following Papa's instructions, his fourth wife and "his last secretary" reduced to ashes in a barrel of flames all the letters he had written in anger and not mailed.[2] He had marked the letters "burn in case of death" and tied them with a string. Now the two ladies carried out the ritual of tossing them into the fire along with bales of rotting magazines that he had kept for many years. After a month of collecting, burning, and resolving debts, Mary, aware that Castro admired her husband and his work, and eager for his support, invited El Comandante one day in August of 1961 to coffee at the Finca Vigía, and put the servants at attention in a double-rowed receiving line. His ego flattered, he took another VIP tour of the house.

Mary told Castro that it was her intention to donate the Finca Vigía. Though Fidel was pleased, he told her that she could take whatever she wanted and that he would always keep a place for her to stay at the Finca in the guest house. She asked Castro for his assistance in securing authorization from customs to transport some of her personal belongings to the United States, including valuable Impressionist paintings from Paris. When she had tried to get that clearance for herself, she had been blocked by corrosive bureaucrats.

His regard softening, he nodded, then suggested, "Why don't you stay here with us in Cuba?"[3] "Oh, señor, that would be interesting. But there is much work to be done about the estate, and it cannot be done here." Pledging his support to Mrs. Hemingway, Fidel continued to look about the room, fascinated by Hemingway's hunting trophies, particularly the heads of the African animals. When Castro looked up to admire the weapons on the wall, Mary offered him her husband's .256 Mannlicher-Schoenauer, and although Fidel thanked her, he responded that he preferred that the gun become part of a Finca Vigía museum that would honor her husband as a longtime resident writer of their land.

Fidel paused in front of one hunting trophy, the head of an eland;

Mary, making conversation, remembered that eland was the best producer of meat among Africa's wild beasts. In turn, visionary Fidel wondered aloud if these meat-producing animals could not be imported and domesticated on his island. "Who knows?" said Mary, unnerved in the presence of the young revolutionary's wild ideas, and politely yet coyly replied, "It could be possible. But their natural habit is at an altitude of two thousand meters." Inspecting Ernest's bedroom with his wife, then climbing to the top of his writing tower with his view over the field of royal palms and the distant hills of Havana, Fidel let out a long sigh and said, "I imagine señor Hemingway enjoyed this view."

"It's the truth. Every day," Mary lied.

"I will help you with your pictures," pronounced the prime minister, looking slyly into Mrs. Hemingway's eyes as he descended the steps in front of her former home.

Mary hurriedly boxed up jewelry, paintings, fine china, silverware, and linens and secured its passage in the holds of a fishing boat bound for Florida, which would forego a load of fish to carry more precious cargo. Dropping Fidel's name when necessary and benefiting from his support, she sidestepped officials and roadblocks as they occurred to ship as many of her belongings as the boat could take in one trip.

The rest she gave away: the *Pilar* to Gregorio, the car to driver Juan, and the other car to the Herrera Sotolongo brothers. To each of their employees, she distributed final payments. Pedro Buscarón, who had worked for eight years at the farm, was given the right to continue to graze his horse on the property, along with José Herrera, the head gardener, who received the Finca's cattle and the right to graze them there. On July 21, 1962, Finca Vigía was renamed Museo Hemingway.

Today the Finca Vigía remains otherwise just as Hemingway left it, containing his full library of phonograph records and nine thousand books, his clothes, African trophies, and hundreds of other possessions, including the yacht *Pilar*, which Gregorio, soon after he was gifted it, decided to donate back. By former employees and friends who turned guides under a new regime (Villarreal, Campoamor, and Roberto Herrera Sotolongo), then by Cuban conservationists, the *Finca Vigía* has been lovingly cared for and preserved and remains one of the world's best living literary museums. In Havana today, aside from Hemingway's perfectly preserved home, one can still discover La Terraza bar where Santiago and Manolin shared a beer in Cojímar port, Hemingway's typewriter that still sits before the window of room 511 in the Hotel Ambos Mundos, the Barlovento Yacht Club where he held his fishing competitions, which was renamed "Marina Hemingway" shortly after his death, and even a bronze statue of the author—leaning across El Floridita bar—immortal.

When asked why, during a fifty-year Cold War and economic blockade, Cuba's revolutionary government had conserved the home and the memory of this North American writer, Fidel Castro responded that he did it out of "admiration": a great author had honored his country by choosing to live and write some of his major works there. Fidel said he felt "grateful to him for the great pleasure" he experienced reading his books: "I think we would have been savages if we did not recognize the importance of preserving this place. We do not deserve the recognition; we simply behaved in a civilized fashion."[4] While Hemingway's first mate, Gregorio Fuentes, stayed in Cuba until he died, a fixture for the tourists to admire and converse with at the La Terraza (provided that a small honorarium was paid), the other living embodiment of the old man in *The Old Man and the Sea*, Anselmo Hernández, fled the island at the age of ninety-two, crossing the Florida straits with two hundred and fifty other refugees of the Castro Regime in 1965, and lived the remainder of his life as a dissident in Miami, estranged.[5]

• • • • •

Throughout his life, Fidel remembered and referred to Hemingway, often at moments that were decisive to his career. In 1967, defending Hemingway, Fidel declared, "All the work of Hemingway is a defense of human rights."[6] Much later in 1975—twenty years after the revolution—when two journalists interviewed Castro, he again cited Hemingway's *For Whom the Bell Tolls*, noting its influence on his thinking at a critical moment in Cuba's history.[7] To appreciate the influence of Hemingway's writing on the Cuban leader's thinking and character, we might also cite the famous speech Castro made before the United Nations in 1979 while urging world governments to work toward peace and growth. There to underline his commitment to peace and civilization, Fidel invoked a Hemingway title: "We say farewell to arms and shall consecrate ourselves in a civilized manner to the most pressing problems of our time . . . This is, moreover, the essential premise for human survival."[8]

Before Fidel's death, in his office there hung a large poster of Hemingway beside an enormous swordfish that the writer sent him shortly after their meeting at the fishing competition. Read in Cuban high schools as part of the curriculum, Hemingway has had more influence on Cuban literature than any other writer, except for José Martí.[9] Despite political tension between the United States and Cuba, North American writer Ernest Hemingway has remained one of the most esteemed writers in Cuba to this day. Fidel Castro declared that Hemingway was his favorite author on numerous occasions, and Fidel's friend Gabriel García Márquez vouched for the sincerity of this affirmation.[10]

Hemingway's first mate Gregorio Fuentes shares an interesting anecdote. He reports that during the Cuban Revolution, Hemingway knew his first mate was hiding arms on the *Pilar* to support the movement. Ernest did not interfere. Then, one day, when he saw him wearing the militia uniform, he hugged him and proclaimed enthusiastically, "I love you more each day."[11] Phil Bonsal, understanding the historical necessity of Fidel's rise to power, said, "The Castro regime seems to have sprung from a deep and widespread dissatisfaction with social and economic conditions as they have been heretofore in Cuba and to respond to an overwhelming demand for change and reform."[12]

When Castro forced Batista into exile, Hemingway remarked to his friend Ed Hotchner, "I just hope to Christ the United States doesn't cut the sugar quota. That would really tear it. It will make Cuba a gift to the Russians. You'd be amazed at the changes. Good and bad. A hell of a lot of good. After Batista any change would almost have to be an improvement."[13] Hemingway was a man of intelligence and shrewd observation who witnessed events in Cuba at close range. As an American and a patriot, he hoped his country would see events with clarity and do the right thing.

In his eighties in 2008 during his interview with Ignacio Ramonet, Fidel Castro would again openly affirm that he would have liked to have known Hemingway better.

> He liked Cuba. He loved this island. He lived here and left many things, his library, his home, which is a museum today. During the first year following the revolution, I spoke with him on two occasions, relatively briefly. Had Hemingway lived a few more years, I would have liked to have talked more with him, more intimately. I have read several of his novels more than once. In many of them, like *For Whom the Bell Tolls* or *A Farewell to Arms*, his main character has inner dialogues with himself. This is what I like most in Hemingway, the monologues, when his characters talk to themselves. As in *The Old Man and the Sea*, the book which earned him the Nobel Prize. In my brief encounters with him, his habits, his work, his general dealings gave me the impression of a very humane person. I always liked his work very much. He portrayed himself in his books, the adventures he lived and those he wanted to live and couldn't. I felt sincere admiration for his thirst of adventure.[14]

When relations with the United States went from poor to worse, Fidel, and his brother Raúl after him, remained loyal supporters of all things Hemingway, ensuring the museum was well cared for by René Villarreal and well administered. Despite the scarcity of the country's resources, Cuba's government has consistently funded the museum—$4 million during 2005's renovation alone—and employed fifty-five of its citizens to work there, full-time, at the task of protecting the memory of a North American author. The restoration of the *Pilar*, too, was complicated and costly. Approximately 164 tourists per day or (73,000 tourists annually) from the world over can look through the open windows he left behind, know how he lived, and feel his presence in the spaces, in his books, in objects he endeared, and in the fading photographs. The museum has become an indispensable stop for diplomats and celebrities passing through Cuba.

On his desks are dozens of bullets, casings, artillery shells, talismans, hunting spears, walking sticks, rabbits' feet, and other totems that he picked up along the way and kept for good luck. One curator spent weeks dusting a wall to reveal the place where he recorded his weight beside the bathroom scale. Beside his bed on a bookshelf sits the same typewriter where, often sweating profusely, Hemingway wrote *The Old Man and the Sea*, *Islands in the Stream*, *Across the River and into the Trees*, *A Moveable Feast*, *The Dangerous Summer*, and *The Garden of Eden*.

• • • • •

On December 2, 1961, Castro allied with the Soviet Union, reversing his early positions to declare "I am a Marxist Leninist and I will be one until the last day of my life." While Herbert Matthews continued to defend Castro's government as "free, honest, and democratic," Cuban exiles blamed the *New York Times* for fathering Fidel's fame.[15] According to Matthews, Hemingway's support for Fidel mirrored his own, and despite the rumors to the contrary, it had not wavered, "Now that he is dead, I can divulge that one who stood by me at all times was Ernest Hemingway, as did his wife, Mary. My last letter from Ernest, written in the late summer of 1960 while he was in Spain, was to assure me that the reports saying he had 'gone sour' on Fidel and the Cuban Revolution were false."[16]

Amping up the embargo against Cuba, Kennedy imposed a full naval sequester in February 1962. Shortly after, Mary Hemingway and Ernest's three sons heard Hemingway's last will and testament read to them by the executor of his estate. Then, on March 9, 1962, an article appeared in the *New York Times:* "Manuscripts Hemingway Left May Yield Four More Novels."[17] The piece focuses on Mary: "It's always the same," she said, referring to the unpublished batch. "It's his work—you could tell. I loved them, I'm mad about them," said his widow in her apartment the day before but added that she was still undecided as to when, or if, they would be published. "I am *bajo sus órdenes*—I am under Papa's order," she said, "I must do my utmost to know what he would want done about his work."

On April 10, the first sections of *A Moveable Feast* appeared as a teaser in *Life* magazine, and by May 23 Scribner's published a full-length book with masterful editing from Mary and editor Harry Brague. In October, the world had held its breath while President Kennedy and Soviet Premier Nikita Khrushchev brought the human race to the brink of a nuclear holocaust during the Cuban missile crisis. And on November 22, 1963, the nation wept when Kennedy was assassinated; two days later, Mob-connected Jack Ruby killed Kennedy's suspected assassin, Lee Harvey Oswald.

In October 1967, Che Guevara was killed in Bolivia where he had travelled to stir up a revolution as he had previously done in the Congo. Later, Richard Borne would call Che the "Apostle of the Immaculate Revolution"; Frantz Fanon described him as "the world symbol of the possibilities of one man"; and French philosopher Jean-Paul Sartre would write, "Che was the most complete human being of his age. He lived his words, spoke his own actions, and his story and the story of the world ran parallel."[18]

When Che was martyrized like Camilo Cienfuegos before him, Fidel Castro also wrote beautifully but hauntingly: "[Che] distinguished himself in so many ways, through so many fine qualities . . . As a man, as an extraordinary human being. He was also a person of great culture, a person of great intelligence. And with military qualities as well. Che was a doctor who became a soldier without ceasing for a single minute to be a doctor."[19]

When Castro's regime turned Communist, Spaniard-turned-Cuban-rebel Eloy Gutiérrez Menoyo would find himself marginalized and flee the island in 1961. He returned as a member of Alpha 66, a paramilitary organization whose intent was to overthrow Castro and bring real democracy to Cuba. When Castro caught Menoyo, he spared his life but imprisoned him for twenty-two years.

• • • • •

After months of preparation and talks between Cuban and American government officials, scholars, curators, and the Hemingway family, a ceremony was held in November 2002 to commemorate a historical agreement to collaborate to preserve and protect the structures and the contents of the Hemingway Museum and to grant world scholars access to the Finca Vigía papers. Congressman Jim McGovern, present at the ceremony, would emphasize the extraordinary importance of this moment. While all shared a love for Ernest Hemingway, McGovern confessed another passion: "I believe that the Cuban and the American people have been kept apart for far too long by politics, rhetoric and mistrust. I have a passion for tearing down those unnecessary walls and for building a new relationship based on communication, exchange, trust and mutual respect. And even today, forty years after his death, Ernest Hemingway can help us achieve that goal."[20]

After Congressman McGovern called for a change in relations between the two countries, Hemingway's and Max Perkins's grandchildren spoke, thanking Cuba for its creation of the Hemingway Museum and heartfelt protection of his works. Last, an aging Castro took the stand and expressed his admiration of his works and his gratitude to Hemingway for honoring his country by residing and for writing his masterpieces there. Fidel then shared more specific ruminations on Hemingway's submarine hunts during World War II, referencing parts of *Islands in the Stream* and *For Whom the Bell Tolls*.[21] Concluding his remarks, President Castro moved his hands along the microphone and cable. He paused before continuing, and gathering his thoughts, he endeavored to explain: "What is man without history? Without history we would not even have an idea of how limited the work of the human species is. The human species continues to make mistakes all the time."[22]

One of the most famous series of photographs in Cuba captures the moment when these two men met at Hemingway's fishing tournament. Prints of Ernest and Castro are everywhere in Cuba—hanging above the hotel bars, on walls in offices and lobbies, proudly displayed in private homes, the two most famous beards of their time, chin to chin, grinning at each other.

AFTERWORD

When Your Neighbor Is Ernest Hemingway: Cojímar and San Francisco de Paula Today

• • • • •

Part of the reason Hemingway's memory endures in Cuba is that he consistently treated his Cuban neighbors with kindness and generosity. Hemingway had a close relationship with the people of Cuba, and he lived in a very good neighborhood. I do not mean the neighborhood had pretty houses, nor that it had well paved roads, but that good people inhabited it, possessing next to nothing, and still today they have very little. But one gets the sense that if somebody were in need, these would be the kind of neighbors who would give all they could spare. One finds here not dog-eat-dog, sink-or-swim, fear of dangerous strangers, but rather neighborly solidarity.

Most of Hemingway's neighbors, now in their sixties or older, still live here in Havana and very clearly remember El Americano walking in their neighborhood or driving by in his Buick, and most have at least one small story to tell. The village of San Francisco de Paula lies about twenty minutes by car to the southwest of Havana.

After weeks hunched over the documents at the Finca Vigía's extensive library and documentation center, one afternoon I slipped out the back door of the museum to seek out some of Hemingway's neighbors. It was a pleasantly sunny day in San Francisco de Paula. A gentle breeze was blowing through the leaves of the palm and mango trees above me. I walked along the dirt road between the aging wooden houses, each with its sagging porch, cast-iron rocking chairs, caged parakeets, and vegetable gardens. In the yards, hens patrolled their well-travelled lawns, their heads darting left and right, scanning for edible kernels. Neighborhood children were returning from school in their starched white-cotton and red-polyester uniforms. In the road, dogs socialized, their tails wagging in a cheerful greeting.

I crossed paths with a lean old man, in his late seventies, perhaps early eighties, who was also walking along the road. He noticed me, clearly not a neighbor, not by a long shot, in the small town. He shyly grinned, waved, slowed his pace to say "hello" and perhaps offer help to a stranger.

"*Buenas tardes,*" I said. "I am a researcher from the United States studying Hemingway in the museum. I wonder if I might ask you a few questions."

"*Claro, con placer.*" ("Surely, my pleasure.") Wearing a flannel shirt, he was a very thin old man, with a white mustache and intelligent, friendly eyes. "Name's Ortho," he said, extending his hand.

"*Mucho gusto,*" I said, shaking his hand. "I would like to talk to anybody who might have known him. If I might ask, how long have you lived in San Francisco de Paula? Did you know him?"

"I have been here since 1955, but my wife has been here longer. I knew him all right, or in any case, he was my neighbor. This is my house to your left. Would you like to come in?" I had the weird and wonderful sensation of suddenly stepping fifty years into the past.

"Oh . . . yes. Thanks very much."

"No trouble," he said, showing me the path that led along his garden to the front door. "Please, this way."

"You have a lovely garden. How do you keep it so nice?"

"Ah, a little toil. I am a bit older now, but it is a small garden. I have always done it. Anyway, I enjoy it."

"You still work in the garden at your age."

"Sure. I am not as old as I look," he said, laughing. "And my nephew helps me with the heavy stuff."

The house was modest and creaking with its age but kept clean and orderly. Motioning for me to sit down on the sofa, Ortho went into the kitchen, and in a moment, his wife came out with glasses of cold water. She was in her eighties. The glasses were trembling on the tray. Ortho and I helped her before she had an accident! A little embarrassed, I thanked her for the water. She smiled bashfully.

"This is my wife, Dolores," said Ortho.

"*Encantado,*" I said. ("Enchanted, nice to meet you.")

"*Igualmente,*" she responded. ("Likewise.") She motioned for me to sit down, and she and her husband did the same.

I noticed photographs, which seemed to be of their children and grandchildren on the wall, clearly taken at Disney World. The photos must have been at least twenty years old.

Seeing my interest, Ortho said, "Our daughter. They live in Orlando. From which part are you?"

"From Washington. From the capital," I said.

"Ah, really. Well . . ." he paused, thinking, then exclaimed, "you are welcome in Cuba! My last name is Durand. My grandfather was French," he explained. Then, with his index finger resting on his chin and his eyes rolling back, he paused to remember. "I saw El Americano on many occasions. He would pass by here, in his Buick with his wife. What was her name . . ." (I learned that Hemingway's neighbors did not know he was a famous writer until he won the Nobel Prize; they just knew him as El Americano.)

"Mary! Lovely woman," interjected Ortho's wife, who, while slow-moving in her eighties, was apparently still quick-thinking and in full possession of her memory.

"Ah yes, Mary," Ortho said. "Anyway, he would pass here in front of our house to get to his house there, on the hill, and we would see them occasionally in church where they had a bench reserved, or in the bodega, in front of our house, over there."[1]

"My sister used to sell rum and beer in the bodega," offered Dolores, "and he used to buy it there. He was a big man. And always he walked everywhere very quickly, with large steps."

"Yes, that's it!" said Ortho. "We would see them occasionally in the neighborhood, at the horse races that they had in the streets of the town, or just strolling around with his walking stick with Mary, or in the Parque de Niño, the park and a little café where they sold drinks and snacks." Then smiling at the memory, he added, "That was where we used to go on dates, Dolores and I. I courted her for five years." He pointed sharply in the air to punctuate his sentence, gazing fondly at his eighty-year-old wife, rosy-eyed with the memory. "We just held hands, and would go to the Parto, and talk, every Friday, always chaperoned. That was the way it was in those days," he explained, smiling.

"Sometimes we would see them there, during the town festivals, seated in chairs they brought from their garden," he continued. "But the only real one-to-one contact I had with Mister Way"—his neighbors sometimes shortened his name to make it easier to pronounce—"was one day when I was cutting the hedges in my garden here in front of the house. He drove by while I was pruning them, and having seen me, he stopped his car."

"'Those scissors aren't the right ones to do that job,' he said.

"'I know,' I said, 'But, I don't have the right ones.'

"So he nodded, and he left. Then, in a little while, he returned with his cutting shears and gave them to me," said Ortho. "He insisted that I keep them. That was the only contact I had with Hemingway."

"You should really talk to Luisito who has lived here longer than anyone. He is San Francisco's historian," said Mrs. Durand. She pulled out her address book. "Let me call him for you."

"All right," I said. "Thank you."

"I just hope he is home," she said, looking up from the black book full of loose cards and pages, falling apart in her frail, wrinkled hands. "It's ringing!" she announced merrily.

That day walking around Hemingway's neighborhood, I met the Durands' neighbor Irgan, also in her eighties, sitting on a rocking chair on her front porch, who would confirm the Durands' stories. She told us that, at the time, before the revolutionary government established the museum, the walls of the Finca were not as high as they are now, built to protect the museum, so the neighbors could once see into his yard, and he could see the other neighbors. One could walk onto the property simply by moving a wire out of the way.

I met his neighbor Orlando de Armas who lived just behind the Finca, and whose father trained his fighting cocks with Hemingway's birds. Hemingway enjoyed this Cuban tradition and kept some twenty fighting cocks, charging his gardener, José Herrero, with the task of maintaining them.

So many of the neighborhood residents offered me a glass of water, retrieved their parents and grandparents from the house, and set chairs out on the front porch or in their living rooms so that we could chat, think, remember, and just enjoy each other's company. I wondered why they were so friendly. It shocked me. Maybe they were pre-information-age peoples, somehow sealed in a time capsule? Maybe without raises and bonuses keeping them at the office, they simply had more time to talk to me? Or maybe it was that "tropical warmth in their blood," in their hearts as an idiosyncrasy of the Cuban character, which Hemingway once light-heartedly referred to as "the sunlight in their eyes" over drinks at the Floridita with his biographer Ed Hotchner. Whatever the reason, Cubans do still treat one another, even foreigners, as family. It makes even the large city of Havana feel like a small town.

Today, despite a legacy of tension, Cubans are very happy and curious to speak to Americans. They typically told me that they do not confuse the American people with American foreign policy or politics. The trickle of a few American visitors is a recent phenomenon. As one of those people, I can report that Cubans look at us as if to say, "How wonderful to see an American. Maybe he is only the first. Maybe more will come. Maybe this is the sign of change we have been waiting for. Maybe this war between us is about to end."

• • • • •

Since Hemingway spent so much time on his yacht, he had a second neighborhood in Cojímar, the fishing village to the east of Havana where Hemingway's first mate Gregorio Fuentes lived, made famous in *The Old Man and the Sea*. Hemingway's Finca was nine miles to the south of the fishing village, a distance that meant about thirty minutes by automobile at that time. The author praised its proximity in an article for *Esquire*, "The Great Blue River": "The biggest reason you live in Cuba is the great, deep blue river, three quarters of a mile to a mile deep and sixty to eighty miles across, that you can reach in *thirty minutes from the door of your farmhouse*, riding through beautiful country to get to it, that is when the river is right, the finest fishing I have ever known."[2] I knew that I had to make an expedition out to Cojímar village, so I invited the *directora* of the Finca Vigía Museum, Ada Rosa Rosales. I needed her to help me locate the residents who knew Hemingway, and to accompany me to lunch at La Terraza, where I had heard they did a good paella.

Among the people I met that day was Gregorio Fuentes's daughter, named América, who still lives in Cojímar. She remembered Hemingway very well since her father worked as the writer's first mate for twenty-three years, from 1938 until 1961. She told us that her father and Hemingway respected each other and that they were close. She remembered clearly when Hemingway came to her wedding on August 8, 1954, at the Guanabacoa Church (La Iglesia de Guanabacoa). "He also came when my sister was married. For us, Hemingway was El Americano. We didn't think of him as a famous author at that time. Nobody was to go on his boat, only my father, but the entire town watched after it so that nothing would happen to it. Cojímar is a very small town.

"He had a strong character," América remembered. "He was respected, but also sensitive to the people of Cojímar. He spoke to them humbly, a bit shyly at first, and then only later opened up. With time though, he walked very comfortably through our streets, or sat at La Terraza drinking with the fishermen. He was friendly with most all of them, and invited them to his house several times, and then of course, during the filming of the movie, *The Old Man and the Sea*, and to the party to celebrate his Nobel Prize. Mainly though, when he was not on the yacht, he would sit at La Terraza with my father and the other fishermen. If he came into the village proper, it was mostly to see my father in this very house.

"I can remember once, when Hemingway was going to travel to Europe, he left my father a blank check, signed, in case he needed to fix the boat, or anything. 'If my father needed it to eat,' he said. 'For whatever he needed.' He trusted him immensely.

"When my father gave the boat to Cuba, he said to Fidel, 'I am giving this boat, on one condition: that it go to the museum. This is the boat, which he gave me to do with what I wish, and it must go to the museum.' That is what he said to Fidel," América recalled.

The *directora* said to América, "Any time. Any time you want to come to the museum, just call me at this number. Or if you need anything . . . a doctor, medicine. Or if you want to visit. Just call me, and I will send someone to pick you up. I don't have money, but I can give you what I have, and it comes from here," she said touching her heart.

As we said goodbye, América looked up at me and asked, "Well, did I give you . . . something? Something you could use?" And we walked down the hill toward the sea while América stood watching us. Her eyes still bright, she was living evidence of a lifelong friendship between a North American writer and a Cuban fisherman.

"She is still a sharp one," I said, "Very alert, for her age . . . How old do you figure she is?" I asked Ada Rosa.

"Oh, I don't know." She turned back to América. *"América, cuantos años tiene, señora?"*Ada Rosa yelled in her unabashed, neighborly Cubanness.

A wry grin crept across América's lips. *"¡Ochenta y cuatro!* Eighty-four!" she yelled back to us, holding up first eight aging fingers, and then four more. She would have been fourteen years old when Hemingway moved to Cuba.

At the bottom of the slope, arriving from the Gulf Stream, the breeze rippled across the waters of the sleepy port. It blew through narrow streets of the small village of Cojímar where Cuban fishermen had once built their houses on this hill beside the sea. On a pedestal behind the old fort, Hemingway's bust seemed to look out across the harbor as if contemplating the two men in a small wooden boat who were casting a small fishing net to catch baitfish in the middle of the cove.

• • • • •

Among Hemingway's personal effects, museum curators found a collection by the only writer in Cuba who is more recognized and celebrated than Ernest Hemingway: José Martí, Cuba's "national poet," of prophet-like importance. Referring to him as "General Martí," Hemingway owned a complete set of his works and cited them often. After twenty-two years on the island, it would have been next to impossible not to have been familiar with Martí, a poet who was wise beyond his years.

Among the many beautiful things that José Martí wrote during his lifetime is this: "*Patria es humanidad.*" ("Our homeland is humanity.") The three words signify that our loyalty as human beings should be to one another first. Charging in to parts unknown to experience new places and mores, Hemingway reported back from other worlds, from people with new perspectives and wisdom to convey.

In Cuba, Hemingway became a friend to a people that he had come to know and to admire. Rejecting the dominant political narrative of the day, he strove to understand and to express his solidarity. Today, children still read *The Old Man and the Sea* in Cuban schools and think highly of Hemingway, appreciating the beauty and universal values that he expressed. In contemporary Cuban vernacular, to say "*Eso es Hemingway*" ("*That* is Hemingway") means that the thing being referred to is magnanimous, great, or fantastic. In other words, in Cuba, Hemingway's name has become synonymous with grandeur.

Beyond his art, the Cuban people also elevate Hemingway as a symbol for the lost understanding and friendship with his native United States. They remain hopeful that this friendship will someday be renewed. As Hemingway's hero Santiago says, "It is silly not to hope."[3]

NOTES

• • • • •

INTRODUCTION

1 News agencies reported Hemingway dead after a jeep accident while chasing Nazis as a foreign correspondent in Europe during World War II, then again after a plane crash while on safari in Africa. "Report from Africa: Hemingway, Wife Killed in Air Crash," *Daily Mirror*, January 25, 1954.

2 Author interview with América, Gregorio Fuentes's daughter, in Cojímar, 2011.

3 Literally translated as "a mixed breed, a mutt; a stray street-dog Cuban." Figuratively it means a "garden-variety Cuban."

4 The faithful believe that La Virgen de la Caridad del Cobre, or the Merciful Virgin of the Copper Church, once appeared when three fishermen from Santiago were about to be engulfed by a violent storm at sea, protected them, and assured their safe passage back to shore. Today, thousands believe the Virgin to possess divine powers; they ask her favors, then make pilgrimages to Santiago when their wishes are fulfilled. The coffers of the Church are lined with Olympic medals from Cuban athletes, trophies, offerings from family members who have requested help for dying relatives, and Hemingway's Nobel Prize medal.

5 Jividen, "Cinema and Adaptations," 83.

6 "Hemingway Dead of Shotgun Wound; Wife Says He Was Cleaning Weapon," *The New York Times*, July 3, 1961.

7 Fuentes, *Hemingway in Cuba*, 237.

CHAPTER 1

1 The ship travelled at 14 knots per hour, or 16 miles per hour. "Ship Descriptions," TheShipsList, Swiggum, accessed October 30, 2011, http://www.theshipslist.com/ships/descriptions/ShipsO.shtml.

2 Baker, *Ernest Hemingway: A Life Story*, 191.

3 After a brief refueling and cargo stop in Bermuda aboard RMS *Orita*, the Hemingways arrived in Havana late Sunday evening at 10:50 p.m. on April 1, 1928. *Official records of dockings, Morro Castle*, July 31, 1927–May 2, 1928 (Havana: National Archives, 1928), 436.

4 Hawkins, *Unbelievable Happiness and Final Sorrow*, 54; Ernest Hemingway to Pauline Hemingway. March 28, 1928, in Hemingway, *Ernest Hemingway: Selected Letters*, 275.

5 Cristoforo Colombo in Genoese, Cristóbal Colón in Spanish, Christopher Columbus in English. To this day, the names of plazas and cities bear his name, such as the District of Columbia. Much like Columbus, Ernest would have first seen the shores of the Bahamas as they passed. See excerpts from Christopher Columbus's 1492 travelogue at the Franciscan Archive, http://www.franciscan-archive.org/columbus/opera/excerpts.html. Consensus among historians is that Christopher Columbus first landed in America at a place he named San Salvador. He noticed gold pendants in the natives' noses and was determined to find the source. When the natives told him about a large island called "Colba," he set sail to find it. While the expedition did not find gold, they did "discover" the natives smoking an unusual herb that they called "tabaccos." Smith, "Routes of Columbus's Second, Third, and Fourth Voyages, 1493–1504," in Bowman and Isserman, *Discovery of the Americas: 1492–1800*, 28–29.

6 Hemingway, *A Moveable Feast*, 175.

7 Zinn, *A People's History of the United States*, 6.

8 "They offer to share with everyone. They would make fine servants . . . With fifty men we could subjugate them all and make them do whatever we want." Christopher Columbus, "Journal of the First Voyage of Columbus,"quoted in *The Northmen, Columbus and Cabot*, 114.

9 "As soon as I arrived in the Indies, on the first Island which I found, I took some of the natives by force in order that they might learn and might give me information of whatever there is in these parts." Zinn, *A People's History of the United States*, 7.

10 Christopher Columbus, "Columbus reports on his first voyage, 1493," The Gilder Lehrman Institute of American History, accessed April 11, 2015, https://www.gilderlehrman.org/content/columbus-reports-his-first-voyage-1493.

See also José Barreiro, "A Note on the Tainos," in Yewell, Dodge, DeSirey, eds., *Confronting Columbus*, 30; Todorov, *The Conquest of America*, 25–27.

11 Finding only traces of gold, Columbus condemned 8 million natives to death, or to lives of slavery, dismemberment, and disease, which spread quickly in the abysmal conditions imposed in search of precious metal. 85 percent of the Taíno, Guanajatabey, and Ciboney peoples were killed. Those who resisted slavery or failed to produce gold every three months were burned alive, had their noses, ears, and hands cut off, and were left to bleed to death. Those who attempted to escape were hunted down, hacked to pieces, and fed to dogs while Bartolomé de las Casas, a missionary on their expedition, bore witness. See Zinn, *A People's History of the United States*, 10; Columbus, *The Four Voyages*, 139. De las Casas, *A Brief Account of the Destruction of the Indies*; "Estimates of Haiti's pre-Columbian population range as high as 8,000,000 people . . . a census of Indian adults in 1496 . . . came up with 1,100,000." Loewen, *Lies My Teacher Told Me*, 63.

12 Also known as El Castillo de los Tres Reyes Magos del Morro. On April 1, 1928, the moon in Havana was waxing gibbous, which is to say nearly full.

13 Columbus was ultimately betrayed by his own men, imprisoned, and expelled from the Americas in chains. Although he was later pardoned and allowed to return, he was stripped of his governorship and his promised percentage of the profits. Loewen, *Lies My Teacher Told Me*, 50.

14 They were now Taíno, Guanajatabey, and Ciboney; Gallego, Canario, Andaluz, Castellaño, and Catalan; Bantu, Yoruba, Ibo, Ibibio, Ijaws, Ewe, and Fon; Canton, Hakka, Mandarin, Japanese, American, English, French, Italian, and German.

15 Habaneros are people from Havana. Their full names are *El Castillo San Felipe del Morro* and *La Fortaleza de San Carlos de la Cabaña*.

16 The ramparts of El Castillo de Tres Reyes Magos del Morro and El Castillo de San Salvador de la Punta.

17 "I'll have little Pilar kick for them (if they don't mind playing with a girl)," Pauline had written her husband in a note while in transit over the Atlantic Ocean. Pauline Pfeiffer to Ernest Hemingway, March 21, 1928, Ernest Hemingway Personal Papers. During Hemingway's separation from Pauline that Hadley had requested as a condition for a consensual divorce, Ernest took a bachelor trip with Archibald MacLeish to see a late season bullfight and feria in Saragossa, Spain. Originally, "the name Pilar refers to the image of the Blessed Virgin on a pillar or porphyry in the shrine and church at Saragossa held on 12 or 13 October." Raymond S. Willis, quoted in Baker, *Ernest Hemingway*, 177, 593.

18 Eby, *Hemingway's Fetishism*, 18. For Hemingwayesque descriptions that suggest the author's strong attraction to this hairstyle, see Hemingway, "Cat in the Rain," in *The Complete Short Stories of Ernest Hemingway*, 131, and Hemingway, *The Garden of Eden*, 45. See also Bennett, "The Poor Kitty and the Padrone and the Tortoise-shell Cat in 'Cat in the Rain,'' in Benson, ed. *New Critical Approaches to the Short Stories of Ernest Hemingway*, 248.

19 Leaving a love note for Ernest in their cabin, on ship's stationery during the trip, Pauline would lament, "*Cher Ami*, No one would think from the magnificence of this paper that I was writing this note in squallar [*sic*] . . . but here I am four days out on an English boat and not yet even the offer of a bath." On return trips, the ship was routinely loaded to capacity with sugar, and her frequent stops combined with tropical heat would often cause the cane to rot along the way. As the Hemingways exited, passing once more through those foul-smelling passageways, they felt grateful to be arriving in Havana and leaving *Orita* behind. Pauline Pfeiffer to Ernest Hemingway, March 21, 1928, Ernest Hemingway Personal Papers.

20 For date and location of arrival see Baker, *Ernest Hemingway*, 191. For ship's manifest and route see "The Pacific Steam Navigation Company: R.M.S. Orita," The British Presence in Southern Patagonia, accessed June 4, 2012, https://patbrit.org/bil/social/orita.htm.

21 "She reminded me more than anything of Helen Hayes," said Jack Latimer in an interview with Bernice Kert in April 1979. Kert, *The Hemingway Women*, 293.

22 Havana residents, Pigeons' Square, Lions' Fountain, and bathtub.

23 Fuentes, *Hemingway in Cuba*, 10, 21; Author interview with historian at Ambos Mundos Hotel, June 2010; Author interview with Finca Vigía historian Gladys Rodríguez, June 2010.

24 Hemingway, "Marlin off the Morro," *By-Line: Ernest Hemingway.*

25 In her "bankruptcy letter," Hemingway's mother, Grace, tallied his numerous transgressions through which he had depleted the emotional account between mother and son: "There is nothing before you but bankruptcy: *You have overdrawn* . . . Come to yourself; cease your lazy loafing and pleasure seeking . . . stop trying to graft a living off anybody and everybody; spending all your earnings lavishly and wastefully on luxuries for yourself; stop trading your handsome face to fool little gullible girls, and neglecting your duties to God and your Savior . . . there is nothing before you but [moral] bankruptcy . . . Do not come back until your tongue has learned not to insult and shame your mother. Grace Hemingway to Ernest Hemingway, July 24, 1920, Ernest Hemingway Personal Papers. His father, Clarence Hemingway, supported his mother and seconded that his son was to stay away from the lake house until they invited him to

return. If he did not get a job and start behaving responsibly, "the Great Creator will cause him to suffer a whole lot more than he ever has so far." Hemingway, *My Brother, Ernest Hemingway*, 57. When disenchanted young Hemingway holed up with PTSD in the family cabin in Michigan but without ambition or source of livelihood, his parents were not pleased. Grace Hemingway to Ernest Hemingway, July 27, 1920, Hemingway Personal Papers. This experience resulted in the story "Soldier's Home." In the story, parents confront their son's PTSD and apathetic attitude after returning from World War I.

26 "It was, in fact the Ryerson Collection of Homer that drew Ernest and Hadley to the Art Institute that week. There, for the first time, he saw Homer's brilliant watercolors from his Gulf Stream period: 'Tornado, Bahamas,' 'Breaking Storm,' 'Gulf Stream' and 'Stowing Sail,' among others." Reynolds, *Young Hemingway*, 187. In 1928, Hemingway would write his painter friend Waldo Peirce about the exhibition, "But by Christ they have some Winslow Homers that give me the same feeling I get from the Monsters or a faena de Belmonte." His son Patrick, who had oft been praised by his father for his interest in painting, would suggest that *To Have and Have Not* strongly resembled Winslow's painting *The Gulf Stream*. Charlene M. Murphy, "A Shared Palette: Hemingway and Winslow Homer, Painters of the Gulf Stream," in *Hemingway, Cuba, and the Cuban Works*, ed. Grimes and Sylvester, 123–32.

27 "Your head, your heart, and your very lovely hands." Ernest Hemingway to Hadley Hemingway, November 18, 1926, in *Ernest Hemingway: Selected Letters*, 228.

28 "The moment she entered the room an intense feeling came over me. I knew she was the girl I was going to marry." Ernest Hemingway, quoted in Hemingway, *My Brother, Ernest Hemingway*, 71.

29 After the death of her second husband, Hadley remembered, "[Ernest] was a beautiful physical specimen." Ruth Bradfield described him at that time: "You wouldn't believe what a beautiful youth Ernest was. He was slender and moved well. His face had the symmetry of fine bony structure and he had a small elastic mouth that stretched from ear to ear when he laughed. He laughed aloud a lot from quick humor and from sheer joy in being alive. I have never been able to see him in photographs of 'Papa.'" Baker, *Ernest Hemingway*, 78. See also Hadley Richardson in conversation Alice Sokoloff, in Diliberto, *Hadley*, 37, 52.

30 "He was the best looking one in the room and his disarming smile stretched from ear to ear . . . His flattering habit of focusing his entire attention on a person, gazing out from watchful brown eyes, was not a pose for he was an alert listener. And on this particular night he concentrated on Hadley . . . he gave no sign that he was interested in anyone but her." Kert, *The Heming-*

way Women, 86. A good listener was how many, like Gertrude Stein, Dorothy Parker, Lillian Ross, Valerie Hemingway, and A. E. Hotchner, would later describe him: extremely charming when he wanted to be. Joseph Dyer: "It was also the way he listened to you, attentively, smiling encouragingly, asking questions . . . If you knew all about roses, he would talk to you about roses until he knew everything you knew . . . it was very flattering to be listened to like that." Valerie Hemingway: "When he met those people, it wasn't that they took [his] writing in isolation; they took the writing in combination with this person himself. Hemingway was a charmer, [but] he wasn't an idle charmer. He was a charmer when he had a goal." Blume, *Everybody Behaves Badly*, xiii, xiv; Reynolds, *Hemingway: The American Homecoming*, 172; Larsen, *Stein and Hemingway*, 28.

31 Diliberto, *Hadley*, 42.

32 Nesto, Hemingstein, Oinbones, Tattie, Tiny, Hemmy, Wemedge, Wax Puppy, Binny, Hash, Hasovich, Feather Kitty, and Wicky Poo were aided by the postal service, offering two daily deliveries between Saint Louis and Chicago. Hadley Richardson to Ernest Hemingway, Ernest Hemingway Personal Papers.

33 Hadley Richardson to Ernest Hemingway, May 6–7, 1921, in Diliberto, *Hadley*, 41.

34 Donning her overcoat and slippers to walk to the corner of Cates and Goodfellow avenues, she dropped the letters in a mailbox hanging on a lamppost and spent an extra ten cents to have them delivered special delivery. "She had poured so much feeling into the pages, she told Ernest, 'It's so hard to mail them—like putting myself in the box.'" Hadley Richardson, in Diliberto, *Hadley*, 42.

35 She had $30,000 and was about to inherit another $20,000. Sokoloff, *The First Mrs. Hemingway*, 32–33; Kert, *The Hemingway Women*, 95; Diliberto, *Hadley*, 42.

36 Hadley Richardson to Ernest Hemingway, April 30, 1921. Sokoloff, *The First Mrs. Hemingway*, 26–27, cited in Kert, *The Hemingway Women*, 93–94.

37 Bumby's babysitters had been F. Puss the Cat, Marie Cocotte, and Gertrude Stein. Hemingway, *A Moveable Feast: The Restored Edition*, 145.

38 Quoted in Diliberto, *Hadley*, 159, 161.

39 "You—who are the best and truest and loveliest person that I have ever known." Hemingway, "To Hadley Hemingway, Paris, 18 November 1926," in *Ernest Hemingway: Selected Letters*, 228.

40 Coffee with bread and butter and jam.

41 Ernest Hemingway to Hadley Hemingway, March 26, 1928, Hemingway Personal Papers.

42 Hotchner, *Hemingway in Love*, 31; Hawkins, *Unbelievable Happiness and Final Sorrow*, 44.

43 Hemingway, *A Moveable Feast*, 129.

44 Hemingway, *A Moveable Feast*, 133.

45 Ernest developed a competitive relationship with Harold Loeb, a Jewish Princeton graduate, a fellow writer, and a boxer. Ernest later challenged Loeb to a fight when the two locked horns over Duff Twysden's affections during San Fermín. Later, he would depict the incident and Loeb as Robert Cohn in *The Sun Also Rises*. Hawkins, *Unbelievable Happiness and Final Sorrow*, 43.

46 Cline, *Zelda Fitzgerald*, 174; Hotchner, *Hemingway in Love*, 33.

47 Baker, *Ernest Hemingway*, 180.

48 Cannell, "Scenes with a Hero," in Sarason, *Hemingway and the Sun Set*, 146.

49 Hawkins, *Unbelievable Happiness and Final Sorrow*, 4.

50 Cannell, "Scenes with a Hero," in Sarason, *Hemingway and the Sun Set*, 146. Based on her interviews with Pfeiffer family friends, Kenneth Wells, Ayleene Spence, and Pauline's sister-in-law Matilda Hawkins, Pauline's biographer suggests that Ernest was attracted to Virginia for her family's money.

51 Baker, *Ernest Hemingway*, 144.

52 Hotchner, *Hemingway in Love*, 31.

53 Not only was Pauline younger, better dressed, and quicker-witted than Hadley, she also had a $60,000 trust fund, which would have guaranteed Ernest the sort of financial security that was indispensable to his literary production. While Ernest's perspective is developed in *A Moveable Feast*, Pauline's is not. Translated from Latin: fertile ground. Item 845, Hemingway Personal Papers; Bruccoli, *Conversations with Ernest Hemingway*, ix.

54 "'Pauline was nice to me. She wanted to be friends. She didn't go straight for my husband. But once she made up her mind that he was what she wanted, she was very aggressive and [brave]. She had the guts to spend a lot of violent energy on Ernest. He couldn't help himself . . . Pauline fell madly in love with him. And Ernest was weak in the sense that if someone wanted him very much, he was tremendously touched by it.' More importantly, Pauline worshipped Ernest and seemed oblivious to his faults." Hadley Hemingway, in Diliberto, *Hadley*, 204–06.

55 From Norberto Fuentes's interviews with Francisco Castro, cabinetmaker at the Ambos Mundos Hotel who became Hemingway's carpenter at Finca Vigía, and Manuel Asper, the owner of the Ambos Mundos Hotel during Hemingway's stays. Fuentes, *Hemingway in Cuba*, 7. See also Rodríguez, *Hemingway*, 23, 26.

56 Taxi drivers.

57 Beegel, "Eye and Heart," in Wagner-Martin , ed., *A Historical Guide to Ernest Hemingway.* As his fellow Nobel Laureate Gabriel García Márquez perceptively appreciated later, it is not likely that a man like that would have remained indifferent to the details he observed or unaware of the upheavals and transformations occurring in Havana at that time. Fuentes, *Hemingway in Cuba*, 7.

58 Martí had been endangering his life by speaking out for Cuban independence since the age of sixteen, when he had created his newspaper *Patria Libre,* and by seventeen he had already been sentenced to six years of hard labor by the Spanish government. For his resistance during the first and second wars for independence, Martí was twice banished from his homeland and compelled to live most of his life abroad, in Spain, in Latin America, and in the United States, where he studied law, worked as a teacher and a journalist, and became a determined advocate and key organizer of the third war for Cuban independence.

59 Hemingway "saved" four books of Conrad, then "used up" the four books in two months in Toronto, reading them when he "needed them badly, when the disgust with writing, writers and everything written of and to write would be too much." Ernest Hemingway, "Conrad: Optimist and Moralist," *Transatlantic Review* (October 1924): 134.

60 "As if it were too great, too mighty for common virtues, the ocean has no compassion, no faith, no law, no memory." Conrad, *The Mirror of the Sea*, 372.

61 "Remorse was a fine good thing and with a little luck and if I'd been a better man it might have saved me for something worse probably instead of being my true and constant companion for the next three years." Hemingway, *A Moveable Feast*, 176.

62 Baker, *Ernest Hemingway*, 211.

63 Hemingway, *A Moveable Feast*, 174.

64 Diliberto, *Hadley*, 203. "When the husband is a writer and doing difficult work on a book so that he is occupied much of the time and is not a good companion or partner to his wife for a big part of the day, the arrangement has advantages until you know how it works out." Hemingway, *A Moveable Feast*, 174.

65 Although *A Moveable Feast* depicts Pauline as a predator, Ernest was perhaps not quite innocent in the affair. *"El amor y la guerra son una misma cosa, y así como en la guerra es cosa lícita y acostumbrada usar de ardides y estratagemas para vencer al enemigo, así en las contiendas y competencias amorosas se tienen por buenos los embustes y marañas que se hacen para conseguir el fin que se desea."* Translation: "All is fair in love and war. In love as in war, it is lawful to use strategy to attain the desired end." Miguel Cervantes, part 2, chap. 21 in *Don Quixote.* While

biographers often depict Pauline negatively, for a traditionally Catholic girl of good upbringing and a family of high reputation, a married man seems the least likely choice. It is very possible that due to Pauline's considerable abilities as an editor as well as her financial resources, Ernest was much more pursuer than pursued. Hawkins underlines that Ernest's affections for Pauline developed not coincidentally at the time that Hadley's trust fund was diminishing to nothing and that Uncle Gus increased Pauline's trust fund to $60,000 with a yield of $250 per month. Hawkins, *Unbelievable Happiness and Final Sorrow*, 46–47.

66 Hemingway, *A Moveable Feast*, 174.

67 The incongruence of high praise and low sales caused Ernest later to question Boni and Liveright's mismanagement of the marketing of his book. By writing the parody of his mentor Sherwood Anderson, *The Torrents of Spring*, which Boni and Liveright would not publish as it criticized their much-esteemed author, he hatched a scheme to wiggle out of his contract and move to Fitzgerald's publishing house, Scribner and Sons. Mellow, *Hemingway*, 314, 317–18. *The New York Times* called *Torrents* "fibrous and athletic, colloquial and fresh, hard and clean, his prose seems to have an organic being of its own." *Time* wrote: "Ernest Hemingway is somebody; a new honest un-'literary' transcriber of life—a Writer." Comparing his war and bullfighting scenes to those of Francisco Goya, critic Edmund Wilson specified in "Mr. Hemingway's Dry Points" in the literary magazine *The Dial*: "I am inclined to think that this little book has more artistic dignity than anything else about the period of the war that has yet been written by an American. His prose is of the first distinction . . . he is . . . strikingly original, and in the dry compressed little vignettes of *In Our Time* [*sic*], has almost invented a form of his own." *Dial* 77, October 1924, 340–41.

68 Diliberto, *Hadley*, 159.

69 Meyers, *Hemingway*, 168; Hemingway, *Selected Letters*, 495.

70 "It was necessary that I leave Schruns and go to New York to straighten out who I was publishing with after the first book of stories. It was a bitter winter on the North Atlantic and there was snow knee deep in New York and when I got back to Paris I should have caught the first train from the Gare de l'Est that would take me down to Austria. But the girl I was in love with was in Paris now, still writing to my wife, and where we went and what we did and the unbelievable wrenching, kicking happiness, selfishness and treachery of everything we did, gave me such happiness and un-killable dreadful happiness so that the black remorse came and hatred of the sin and no contrition, only a terrible

remorse." From Hemingway, *A Moveable Feast: The Restored Edition*, excerpted in *The New York Times*, June 26, 2009, www.nytimes.com/2009/06/28/books/excerpt-moveable-feast-restored-edition.html.

71 Both Stein and Anderson were offended and appalled by the attacks coming from the upstart that they had so cordially mentored. Later, Anderson wrote his friend to express his disbelief and disappointment: "Damn it, man, you are so final—so patronizing. You always speak to me like a master to a pupil. It must be Paris—the literary life. You didn't seem like that when I knew you . . . Come out of it, man. I pack a little wallop myself." Sherwood Anderson to Ernest Hemingway, June 14, 1926, in Anderson, *Selected Letters*, 80. See also Stein, *The Autobiography of Alice B. Toklas*, http://gutenberg.net.au/ebooks06/0608711.txt.

72 Hemingway, *A Moveable Feast*, 176.

73 Diliberto, *Hadley*, 205; Hawkins, *Unbelievable Happiness and Final Sorrow*, 64.

74 Hawkins, *Unbelievable Happiness and Final Sorrow*, 66.

75 Diliberto, *Hadley*, 86. See also Mellow, *Hemingway*, 329.

76 Diliberto, *Hadley*, 216. See also Hawkins, *Unbelievable Happiness and Final Sorrow*, 52.

77 "What he seemed to be saying to me was that it was my fault for forcing the issue." Hadley, in Kert, *The Hemingway Women*, 178–79.

78 Cannell, "Scenes with a Hero," 146.

79 Reynolds, *Hemingway*, 31.

80 Hawkins, *Unbelievable Happiness and Final Sorrow*, 66.

81 Blume, *Everybody Behaves Badly*, 170. Because both having a baby out of wedlock and having an abortion would have been disgraceful alternatives for Pauline, discreetly having the abortion in another country might well have proven the lesser of two evils. Later, during a "self-imposed exile," Pauline would write Ernest: "I thought very hard and what I think is four months . . . is a lot tighter than nine." Pauline Pfeiffer to Ernest Hemingway, October 2, 1926, Ernest Hemingway Personal Papers.

82 The scenes of their encounter arguably served as inspiration, not only for the story "Hills Like White Elephants" (presented to Pauline on their honeymoon) about an abortion, "a simple operation . . . all perfectly natural . . . just to let the air in" (Hemingway, "Hills Like White Elephants," in *The Complete Short Stories of Ernest Hemingway*, 217), but also for the monologues of *To Have and Have Not*: "Love is that dirty aborting horror that you took me to. Love is my insides all messed up," uttered by a character resembling Pauline (110). Hemingway, *To Have and Have Not*.

83 The term "white elephant" denotes a troublesome gift that is difficult to dispose of, and refers to the custom of the kings of Siam giving a white elephant,

a holy animal that was expensive to maintain and could not be used for anything functional, to a courtier they despised, hoping the gift would lead to their ruin. "White Elephant," *Oxford Living Dictionaries*, s.v. "white elephant," accessed June 24, 2016, https://en.oxforddictionaries.com/definition/us/white_elephant; Hemingway, *Selected Letters*, 207.

84 Hemingway, *Selected Letters*, 207.

85 Hadley Hemingway to Ernest Hemingway, May 1926, Hemingway Personal Papers.

86 "Pfeiffer is stopping off here Wednesday." Hadley Hemingway to Ernest Hemingway, May 1926, Hemingway Personal Papers.

87 Everyone. Together.

88 Baker, *Ernest Hemingway*, 171. See also Lynn, *Hemingway*, 345.

89 Reviewing *In Our Time*, Paul Rosenfeld of *The New Republic* had written: "There is something of Sherwood Anderson, of his fine bare effects and values coined from simplest words, in Hemingway's clear medium . . . There is Gertrude Stein equally obvious." *The Torrents of Spring*, "My Own Life," *The Autobiography of Alice B. Toklas*, "The Sun Also Sets," "Men without Rabbits," "A Farewell to Val," "For Whom the Bull Flows," "Bull in the Afternoon," "The Shop-Happy Wife of Ernie Macomber," "Death in the Rumble Seat," "For Whom the Gong Sounds," "Across the Potomac and Into Her Pants," and, inevitably, "The Old Man and the Seafood." Hemingway, *Selected Letters*, 62; Daniel Pollack-Pelzner, "Swiping Stein: The Ambivalence of Hemingway Parodies," *The Hemingway Review* 30, no. 1 (Fall 2010): 69–82.

90 Hemingway, *The Sun Also Rises*, 57.

91 F. Scott Fitzgerald to Ernest Hemingway, June 1926, in Fitzgerald, *A Life in Letters*, 142.

92 Ernest Hemingway to F. Scott Fitzgerald, November 24, 1926, in Hemingway, *The Letters of Ernest Hemingway: Volume 3, 1926–1929*, 164.

93 He said he would be cutting the first two chapters, yet insinuated that this was his idea rather than that of Scott: "I think it will move much faster from the start that way . . . Scott agrees with me." Ernest Hemingway to Maxwell Perkins, June 3, 1926, Ernest Hemingway Collection; Blume, *Everybody Behaves Badly*, 178.

94 "The only effect I ever had on Ernest was to get him in a receptive mood and say let's cut out everything that goes before this. And so he published it without that and later we agreed that it was a very wise cut. This is not literally true and I don't want it established as part of the Hemingway legend." F. Scott Fitzgerald to John O'Hara, July 25, 1936, in Fitzgerald, *A Life in Letters*, 303.

95 Donnelly and Billings, *Sara & Gerald*, 25; Gerald Murphy to Ernest Hemingway, September 6, 1926, Hemingway Personal Papers; Miller, *Letters from the Lost Generation*, 21. The tense train ride back to Paris was depicted in Hemingway's short story "A Canary for One," which ends, "We were returning to Paris to set up separate residences." Hemingway, "Canary for One," *The Complete Short Stories of Ernest Hemingway*, 261.

96 In *A Moveable Feast*, Hemingway later criticizes the Murphys bitterly for their role in the breakup, but he was thankful at the time.

97 Putnam and Moss reported after seeing Ernest during this year: "It did not take me long to discover that the somewhat shy and youthful reporter whom I had met in Chicago had vanished." "In his place was a literary celebrity," a "tarzan of [the] printed page." Putnam, *Paris Was Our Mistress*, 128; Arthur Moss, "Time of the Expatriates: A Reporter's Recollections of the Lost Generation," Carlos Baker Collection of Ernest Hemingway.

98 Hadley Hemingway to Ernest Hemingway, October 16, 1926, Hemingway Personal Papers.

99 John Dos Passos to Ernest Hemingway, November 19, 1926, Hemingway Personal Papers; Diliberto, *Hadley*, 235.

100 "I love you, Dad. Life is beautiful with Dad." French was the only language Bumby spoke at the time. Hotchner, *Hemingway in Love*, part 5.

101 Hadley Hemingway to Ernest Hemingway, November 16, 1926, Hemingway Personal Papers. See also her letter of November 19.

102 THREE MONTHS TERMINATED AT HADLEY'S REQUEST SHE STARTING IMMEDIATELY OWN REASONS STOP COMMUNICATION RESUMED STOP SUGGEST YOU SAIL AFTER CHRISTMAS WHAT ABOUT ME. Virginia to Pauline Pfeiffer, November 17, 1926, Hemingway Personal Papers; Reynolds, *Hemingway*, 80.

103 They refused to play a part in such hypocrisy. Hawkins, *Unbelievable Happiness and Final Sorrow*, 74; Reynolds, *Hemingway*, 124.

104 The mayor's office. Pauline's sister, Virginia, and Ernest's banker, Mike Ward, witnessed the ceremony.

105 Fashionable hairdo. Hotchner, *Hemingway in Love*, 79.

106 Imagining her daughter and new son-in-law on the day of their marriage across the sea, she wrote them from Piggott: "My dear Children: God bless you and keep you always in his care. I hope your wedding garments this morning are bright and shining as the sun, befitting those who have come through great tribulations. For many months I have been asking our Heavenly Father to make the crooked ways straight and your life's pathway one of peace and

happiness, and this morning I feel a quiet assurance that my prayers have not been in vain." Mary Pfeiffer to Ernest and Pauline Hemingway, May 10, 1927, Patrick Hemingway Papers.

107 Mellow, *Hemingway*, 346.

108 "I think that perhaps the luckiest thing Bumby will ever have is to have you for a mother." Hemingway, *Selected Letters*, 228. "I complimented her brave and generous reaction and told her I was now informing Scribner that all of my royalties from *The Sun Also Rises* should go to her. I admitted that if I hadn't married her I would never have written this book, helped as I was by her loyal and loving backing and her actual cash support. I told her that Bumby was certainly lucky to have her as his mother. That I had great admiration for her head, her heart and lovely hands, and prayed that God would take care of her to make up for the hurt I had inflicted on her. That she was the best and honest and loveliest person I had ever known. I folded the letter, put it in an envelope that had Murphy's return address, consciously ran the glue of the envelope's flap across my tongue and carefully sealed the flap. I had achieved the moment I had tenaciously sought, but I wasn't elated, nor did I send a cable to Pauline. What I felt was the sorrow of loss. I had contrived this moment, but I felt like the victim." Hotchner, *Hemingway in Love*, 28, 47, 74.

109 Hemingway, *Selected Letters*, 228.

110 Without a fixed residence.

111 "Dos Passos had first mentioned Key West to the Hemingways as a place to live." Carol Hemingway, "907 Whitehead Street," in Curnutt and Sinclair, *Key West Hemingway*, 37. "Ernest's attention was drawn to Key West, Florida, by Dos Passos, who described it as tropical, maritime, and unspoiled." Kert, *The Hemingway Women*, 207; Dos Passos, *The Best Times*, 198–99.

112 *John Dos Passos*, directed by Knapp Hubert (Éditions Montparnasse, 2000), DVD.

113 Carr, *Dos Passos*, 231, quoted in Hawkins, *Unbelievable Happiness and Final Sorrow*, 87.

114 Baker, *Ernest Hemingway*, 191. In the 1920s, tobacco dominated the island's industry, bringing the Cuban companies and workers, making the island seem much more Creole than American. In the streets one found a mix of Creoles, Cubans, black Bahamians, and white Bahamian "Conchs." Dos Passos, The *Best Times*, 198–99; Fuentes, *Hemingway in Cuba*, 97.

115 "We were truly poor." Hemingway, *A Moveable Feast*, 102. Hemingway later described the influence of money as degrading and cancerous to his character; later, in "The Snows of Kilimanjaro," he would compare it to gangrene

(Hemingway, "The Snows of Kilimanjaro," in *The Complete Short Stories of Ernest Hemingway*, 58).

116 Gott, *Cuba*, 32.

117 The British returned Havana to Spain in the Treaty of Paris. The cannon blast was only suspended once, during World War II, for fear of German U-boats; the tradition continues every evening at nine o'clock.

118 A national hero.

119 Historians estimate that approximately 2 million of the 10–15 million slaves that were taken from Africa died en route. Approximately 779,000 of those landed in Cuba while others came from other sources such as Haiti, the Dominican Republic (also known as Hispaniola), and Jamaica. The number of slaves increased steadily with the demands of the agricultural economy, which included fruit, tobacco, and, predominantly, sugar. Estimated number of Africans landing alive in Cuba per year: from 1521 to 1762, about 500; 1763 to 1789, 600; 1790 to 1820, 8,300; 1821 to the 1870s, 16,700. The origins of these slaves changed over the years, but we know that they came from four major groups: approximately 400,000 Bantu (from northern Angola, southern Zaire, and southern Congo); 275,000 Yoruba (from southwestern Nigeria); 200,000 Ibo/Ibibio/Ijaw (from southeastern Nigeria); 200,000 Ewe/Fon (from Benin); and approximately 185,000 from other areas. As early as 1526, royal decrees permitted slaves to purchase their freedom. They brought their religions, which mixed with one another and with Catholicism. The most prevalent African religion practiced in Cuba today is Santería, which is mainly the assimilation of Yoruba and Catholic rituals and beliefs as well as the some of the traditions from the Regla Arará and Palo Monte religions. In Cuba, the slaves reorganized themselves into cabildos, ethnic associations of Abakuá, Mandinga, Ganga, Mina, Lucumí, Carabal'í, Macaua, and Congo, which partially resisted Spanish hegemony and preserved their religions and culture. Gott, *Cuba*, 47–48; Eltis and Richardson, *Atlas of the Transatlantic Slave Trade*; Lopes Valdez, "Slavery in Cuba" (lecture), Cuban Academy of Sciences, May 1992. See also Aimes, *A History of Slavery in Cuba*; Ortíz, *Hampa Africana*; Bergad, García, and del Carmen Barcia, *The Cuban Slave Market*; Stephen D. Behrendt, David Richardson, David Eltis, & W.E.B. Du Bois Institute for African and African-American Research, Harvard University, Transatlantic Slave Trade (database); Gates and Appiah, *Africana*.

120 This figure does exclude increased mortality rates among subsequent generations. Owen 'Alik Shahadah, "African Holocaust: Dark Voyage" (audio CD), http://www.africanholocaust.net/news_ah/african%20holocaust.htm; Meltzer, *Slavery*.

121 Yes!

122 *"¡Al combate, corred, Bayameses!, Que la patria os contempla orgullosa. No temáis una muerte gloriosa, Que morir por la patria es vivir. En cadenas vivir es vivir. En afrenta y oprobio sumidos. Del clarín escuchad el sonido; ¡A las armas, valientes, corred!"*

123 García and Alberto, quoted in Pérez, *To Die in Cuba*, 18.

124 Miller, *Voice of the Leopard*, 172.

125 Desperate to influence a war that he was losing, the Spanish king proclaimed all slaves fighting on the side of Spain to be free, but it was already too late. By 1873, the last known slave ship had already arrived in Cuba, and by that time, 83 percent of Cuba's exports, such as sugar, tobacco, and coffee, were going to the United States, with only 6 percent going to Spain. Exiled in the United States, José Martí organized the Cuban War of Independence from abroad and founded the Cuban Revolutionary Party in 1892. In 1895, the Cuban sugar industry had produced a million long tons of sugar, valued at $62 million.

126 Ernest Hemingway to Janet Flanner, April 8, 1933, in Hemingway, *Selected Letters*, 386.

127 "You shall not covet your neighbor's house," says the tenth commandment.

128 Jefferson's ambassador, General Wilkinson, communicated the offer to Spain. Carmen Diana Deere, "Here Come the Yankees! The Rise and Decline of United States Colonies in Cuba, 1898–1930," *Hispanic American Historical Review* 78, no. 4 (November 1998): 729–65.

129 Thomas Jefferson, quoted in Schlesinger, *The Cycles of American History*, 150.

130 "These islands (Cuba and Puerto Rico) are natural appendages of the North American continent, and one of them (Cuba) almost within sight of our shores, from a multitude of considerations has become an object of transcendent importance to the commercial and political interests of our Union . . . But there are laws of political as well as of physical gravitation; and if an apple severed by the tempest from its native tree cannot choose but fall to the ground, Cuba, forcibly disjoined from its own unnatural connection with Spain, and incapable of self-support, can gravitate only towards the North American Union, which by the same law of nature cannot cast her off from its bosom." John Quincy Adams, quoted in Pérez, *Cuba in the American Imagination*, 30.

131 Deere, "Here Come the Yankees!"

132 Jones, *Crucible of Power*, 195.

133 Richard L. Kagan, "Prescott's Paradigm: American Historical Scholarship and the Decline of Spain," *American Historical Review* 101, no. 2 (April 1996): 423–46.

With "Remember the *Maine*" as its battle cry, along with other imaginative headlines, the yellow press of William Randolph Hearst's *New York Journal* and Joseph Pulitzer's *New York World* enjoyed commercial success as it whipped the American public into a fervor and rallied public opinion in favor of military intervention in Cuba, Puerto Rico, and the Philippines. Popular songs and newspaper narratives of the "Cuba Libre" movement described a vigorous, Protestant, democratic, and hard-working America that had the chance to come to the aid of a fledgling democracy to stop the aristocratic, tyrannical, and enslaving corruption of a colonial monarchy, which had accumulated its riches from the gold it had stolen and extracted from the Americas.

134 *"Viví en el monstruo y le conozco las entrañas, y mi honda es la de David."* José Martí, "An unfinished letter to Manuel Mercado," in Abel and Torrents ed., *José Martí*, 14.

135 Retiring at the age of forty-nine, Irénée du Pont had architects Covarrocas and Govantes design the four-story, eleven-bedroom mansion for him in July 1927 and later added a golf course designed by architects Herbert Strong and Sim Cuthrie, which was completed in September 1931. The $1.3 million estate, comprising five miles of pristine private beach, was named Xanadú after the legendary palace of Kublai Khan. The estate eventually expanded to 1,328 acres in the municipality of Cárdenas, purchased at a bargain rate of four cents per acre. In 1932 he installed an 11,000-pipe organ, the largest in Latin America.

136 The USS *Maine* monument was inaugurated in 1925 by President Zayas, with American general Pershing in attendance.

137 Much like Havana's Capitol Dome, the USS *Maine* memorial had a sister shrine that preceded it in the United States, in New York's Central Park, a decade before.

138 "Protected" nations like Cuba and the Philippines, seized during the Spanish-American War, did not take well to American occupation, and resisted neocolonial intervention as they had resisted colonial rule until real independence from the United States was finally achieved.

139 "Cuba cannot have true moral peace, which is what the people need for their happiness and good fortune—under the transitional government. This transitional government was imposed by force by a foreign power and, therefore, is illegitimate and incompatible with the principles that the entire country has been upholding for so long and in the defense of which half of its sons have given their lives and all of its wealth has been consumed." Bethell, *The Cambridge History of Latin America*, 246.

140 "A century ago, the United States jumped into the world by going to war with

Spain. The Americas, and the world, are still feeling the consequences." "The War of 1898: Forget the Maine!" *The Economist*, January 1, 1998, https://www.economist.com/special/1998/01/01/forget-the-maine.

141 Leonard Wood to William McKinley, April 12, 1900, Wood Papers, Library of Congress, cited in Pérez, *On Becoming Cuban*, 158.

142 "The Spaniards, we are told, are to go by December 1, or soon after. Then is to come an American "army of occupation," some saying it is to be 50,000 strong. It is but natural that we should ask, Why is this great army sent to Cuba? When the Spaniards are gone, who is it going to fight?" Bartolomé Masó, *San Francisco Call* 84, no. 159 (November 1898).

143 *New York Journal*, August 16, 1898, 2; Hyatt and Hyatt, *Cuba*, 115–16; *The New York Times*, August 3, 1898, 10; "Developing Oriente," *Cuba Magazine*, September 1909, 4–7; George Reno, "Oriente, the California of Cuba," *Cuba Review* (August 1927): 14–20; George Fortune, "What's Doing in Cuba for the Younger American," *Cuba Magazine*, February 1912, 336–40; Vivian and Smith, *Everything about Our New Possessions*, 112–19; Forbes-Lindsay, "Cuba Land of Promise," *World To-Day*, February 1908, 141–50, in Pérez, *On Becoming Cuban*, 190.

144 *McClure's Magazine*, April 1899, 66.

145 A Latin term, for the they were similar to the ranches of Ancient Rome that colonized Magna Graecia and Sicily, Egypt, Northwest Africa, and Hispania Baetica for the production of grain, wine, and olive oil.

146 In 1906, *Commercial and Financial World* called it both "a poor man's paradise and the rich man's mecca." *Commercial and Financial World*, April 7, 1906, 10. Writer George Reno called eastern Cuba "the new frontier," declaring that "Oriente [Province] is the California of Cuba." Reno, "Oriente," *Cuba Review*, August 1927, in Perez, *On Becoming Cuban*, 191.

147 "For almost four years contending forces had laid siege to the largesse of the land, preying upon the bounty of its resources, and practicing pillage of every kind as the normal method of warfare. And when it was over, in 1898, the toll of Cuban independence reached frightful proportions. The fields were blighted; the pastures, barren; and the fruit trees, bare. Agriculture was in desperate crisis in an economy predominantly agricultural. The rich sugar provinces of Havana and Matanzas were each cultivating fully less than one-half of the area in 1899 than they had before the war. Of the 1,400,000 total acres under cultivation in 1895, only some 900,000 acres returned to production after the war . . . Foreign lenders in particular and especially United States creditors, were anxious to claim Cuban properties." After the passage of Military Order 139 granting debt collectors the authority to seize holdings, investors like United Fruit

were able to purchase land at rock-bottom prices: 200,000 acres at $1 per acre in 1902 and another 180,000 acres in 1904. They were financed at high interest rates by banks like Chase National Bank of New York, the First National City Bank of New York, and the Royal Bank of Canada, using the mills as collateral and with rates closely connected to the sugar market. Louis A. Pérez, Jr., "Insurrection, Intervention, and the Transformation of Land Tenure Systems in Cuba, 1895–1902," *The Hispanic American Historical Review* 65, no. 2 (May 1985): 229–54.

148 The loan started at $10 from Chase Manhattan, owned by the Rockefeller Family, but grew due to their fear that not loaning greater and greater sums might cause the dictator to slip from power and consequently to default. Benjamin, *The United States and Cuba*, 41.

149 Gabriel García Márquez, "Hemingway—Our Own" (Introduction), Fuentes, *Hemingway in Cuba*, 8.

150 A Cuban *solar* is a single-room tenement residence, often with a dirt floor, where an entire family would live. A *barrio marginal* is a marginal neighborhood, or a slum.

151 "The bank that underwrites the cutting of the cane is foreign, the cutting of the cane is foreign, the consumers' market is foreign, the administrative staff set up in Cuba, the machinery that is installed, the capital that is invested, the very land of Cuba held by foreign ownership . . . all are foreign, as are, logically enough, the profits that flow out of the country to enrich others." Ortíz, *Cuban Counterpoint*, 63.

152 The destruction of beet sugar farms in Belgium and France during World War I caused a boom for Cuban sugar as the European market shrank, the supply fell, and the price of sugar leaped from 2.11 cents to 4 cents per pound. The European sugar market shrank from 9,088,000 tons in 1913 to 1,801,000 in 1920. This deficit created a great opportunity for Cuban producers, and output increased from 2,719,961 tons in 1913 to 4,448,389 tons in 1919. Wright, *The Cuban Situation and Our Treaty Relations*, 8.

153 Cited in Pérez, *On Becoming Cuban*, 281.

154 *Zafra*, or harvest; *colonia*, or colony (a large unit of land). From 1900 to 1959, Cuban sugar production increased dramatically: 700,000 tons in 1900 to 6 million tons in 1930, or a quarter of the world's total. By the 1960s, Cuba was nearing a production output of 10 million tons. By 1910, 75 percent of Cuban lands belonged to American or Spanish residents, with only 25 percent belonging to Cubans. The increase of American investment from

$204 million in 1914 to $1.360 billion by 1924, and the expansion of the central railroad system, shifted the center of Cuban sugar production from the West to the East where American mills were rapidly expanding. Instead of diversifying its agriculture and developing its industry for the long term, Cuba focused on sugar production in the short term and became dependent on satisfying this demand. US control of sugar production surged from twenty-nine mills in 1905 (21 percent of the total production) to sixty-four mills in 1916 (53 percent) to seventy-five mills in 1926 (63 percent). Juan Carlos Santamarina, "The Cuba Company and Eastern Cuba's Economic Development, 1900–1959," *Essays in Business and Economic History* (Spring 2001), http://ebhsoc.org/journal/index.php/journal/article/viewFile/134/129; Jenks, *Our Cuban Colony*, 183.

155 Ayala, *American Sugar Kingdom*, 81, 201; Palmié and Scarano, *The Caribbean*, 463.

156 Palmié and Scarano, *The Caribbean*, 463.

157 *Discurso leído, el 31 de mayo de 1926* (Havana: Rambla Press, 1926); *Declarations of General Gerardo Machado y Morales regarding his electoral platform as presidential candidate in the elections which will take place on this first of November 1928* (Havana: Rambla Press, 1928); McGillivray, *Blazing Cane*, 152.

158 Machado, *Ocho años de lucha*; Machado, *Por la patria libre*; Benjamin, *The United States and the Origins of the Cuban Revolution*, 81.

159 Benito Mussolini to Edwin L. James, *The New York Times*, 1928.

160 Maurer, *The Empire Trap*, 224.

161 Jules Benjamin, "The 'Machadato' and Cuban Nationalism, 1928–1932," *Hispanic American Historical Review* 55 (February 1975): 66–91.

162 Benjamin, "The 'Machadato' and Cuban Nationalism."

163 The child whose name was destined to become Patrick instead of *Pilar* would later state: "There are two versions of life: one is to turn the other cheek, the other is to destroy the enemy," his was from the latter camp while Hadley had been from the former. As a Harvard grad and a professional game hunter, Patrick would attempt to follow in the footsteps of both mother and father spending most of his life in Tanganyika shooting animals and running his safari expedition company. His younger brother, Gregory, later known as "Gloria," finished medical school, but spent much of his life battling with alcoholism, drug addition, manic depression, grief, dishonesty, and transgender issues. Patrick Hemingway, interview on September 26, 2014, in Blume, *Everybody Behaves Badly*, 331.

CHAPTER 2

1 Reynolds, *Hemingway*, 167.

2 They were staying in a modest apartment above the Trevor and Morris Ford agency. Baker, *Ernest Hemingway*, 192.

3 Volunteering as an ambulance driver for the American Red Cross at the age of seventeen, Hemingway witnessed horrifying scenes of war that destroyed his romantic notions regarding the "adventure of combat." During the Battle of Caporetto, Italian forces suffered one of the worst defeats during World War I. Exploring and exploiting his war wound experiences along the Italian Front in *A Farewell to Arms*, Hemingway depicted the humiliating defeat that they suffered as well as their retreat to neutral ground that came to define the attitude of his generation, lost and coming of age in an ideal-shattering modernist age. At Caporetto, the Italians suffered a brutal loss to Austrian forces, perhaps the greatest defeat in Italian history. Still today, the word *Caporetto* in Italian denotes a humiliating loss. Hemingway, *A Farewell to Arms*.

4 He began a manuscript titled "A New Slain Knight" in September 1927 and abandoned it in March 1928 to begin a short story that grew into *A Farewell to Arms*. Hemingway Personal Papers.

5 In *A Farewell to Arms*, Frederic Henry's story of betrayal by love and war has intimate roots in the writer's biography. Eager to get closer to the action on the Italian front, young Ernest volunteered to deliver chocolate and cigarettes by bicycle to the men in the trenches. He was struck by a mortar and machine gun bullet at *Fossalta di Piave* then transported to a hospital in Milan. Recovering, he initiated a romantic relationship with an American nurse Agnes von Krurowsky. At 26 years old, Agnes was seven years older than Ernest. When he returned home to North America, he asked Agnes to join him and to marry him, but Agnes rejected him for his immaturity. Agnes encouraged Hemingway when he was young, injured, and vulnerable to accept a woman's protection and love, then betrayed him with another man. Freshly wounded and perhaps still traumatized by his wartime experiences, Hemingway took his first major love story and rejection rather badly and remained in the bed of his childhood home for several weeks thereafter. Meyers, *Hemingway*, 41; Kert, *The Hemingway Women*, 70. The trauma of Agnes von Kurowsky, and perhaps his deteriorating relationship with his mother, seemed to have lasting consequences on his subsequent relationships. Lynn, *Hemingway*, 99. He returned to the injury in four separate works, including "Soldier's Home," "The Snows of Kilimanjaro," "A Very Short Story," and *A Farewell to Arms*. Lynn, *Hemingway*, 98–99. For the rest of his life, he left women before they could leave him; he

established the security of a new relationship before ending a previous one, and created the conditions for a new marriage before ending a previous one. As late as 1936, he wrote of Agnes' traumatic rejection in "The Snows of Kilimanjaro": "He had written her, the first one, the one who left him, a letter telling her how he had never been able to kill it . . . How everyone he had slept with only made him miss her more. How what she had done could never matter since he known he could not cure himself of loving her." "The Snows of Kilimanjaro," Hemingway, *The Complete Short Stories of Ernest Hemingway*, 71. Writing also appeared to provide significant refuge from the fear that seemed to accompany loving and depending upon others. In 1919, just after Agnes and the war, Ernest purchased a new typewriter and withdrew to the northern wilderness of Michigan to isolate himself and commit himself to writing. Wounded at war and at love, he would now bet on himself instead; alone in the silence of the woods, he was again autonomous and free. Whatever would subsequently occur in his life, he could create and control what appeared on the empty pages of his Royal Portable Corona. Thereafter, the story he created would depend upon no one else. Ernest Hemingway to Clarence Hemingway, October 28, 1919, 209; Ernest Hemingway to Grace Hemingway, November 11, 1919, 211; Ernest Hemingway to Ursula Hemingway, mid-December, in Hemingway, *Letters of Ernest Hemingway: Volume 1, 1907–1922*, 219. Copping a callous attitude, young Hemingway would write his male friend about Agnes, whose letter he was clearly working over in his mind. "Had a very sad letter from Ag from Rome yesterday. She has fallen out with her Major. She is in a hell of a way mentally and says I should feel revenged for what she did to me. Poor damned kid I'm sorry as hell for her. But there's nothing I can do. I loved her once and then she gyped me. And I don't blame her. But I set out to cauterize out her memory and I burnt it out with a course of booze and other women and now it's gone. She's all broken up and I wish there was something I could do for her thou. But that's all shut behind me—Long ago and far away. And there aint no busses runnin' from the Bank to Mandalay." Ernest Hemingway to Howell G. Jenkins, June 15, 1919, in Hemingway, *Letters of Ernest Hemingway: Volume 1, 1907–1922*, 193. Hemingway cites a poem by Rudyard Kipling, "Mandalay," about a British soldier in London who was beckoned to return to Mandalay by a Burmese girl.

6 As Reynolds puts beautifully, "Hemingway was making a war up in his head more real than any war he had known. It was all there, the country, the people, the weather always . . . Every day went like that, the snow falling in his fiction and the sweat running from his brow." Reynolds, *Homecoming*, 170.

7 "That is what we are supposed to do when we are at our best—make it all up—

but make it up so truly that later it will happen that way." Ernest Hemingway to F. Scott Fitzgerald, May 28, 1934, in Hemingway, *Ernest Hemingway: Selected Letters*, 407.

8 Bruccoli, *The Only Thing That Counts*, 139.

9 As fate would have it, Carlos Gutierrez eventually became the first first-mate of Hemingway's boat, the *Pilar*, and years later, Gregorio Fuentes became the second.

10 Fuentes, *Hemingway in Cuba*, 99.

11 McLendon, *Papa*, 52, quoted in Michael J. Crowley, "Reexamining the Origins of 'After the Storm,'" in Curnutt and Sinclair, *Key West Hemingway*, 196; Mark P. Ott, "The *Anita* Logs and *To Have and Have Not*," in Curnutt and Sinclair, *Key West Hemingway*.

12 McLendon, Papa, 52, quoted in Crowley, "Reexamining the Origins of 'After the Storm,'" in Curnutt and Sinclair, *Key West Hemingway*, 196; Ott, "The *Anita* Logs and *To Have and Have Not*" in Curnutt and Sinclair, *Key West Hemingway*. Baker, *Ernest Hemingway*, 228.

13 McLendon, Papa, 52, quoted in Crowley, "Reexamining the Origins of 'After the Storm,'" in Curnutt and Sinclair, *Key West Hemingway*, 196; Ott, "The *Anita* Logs and *To Have and Have Not*" in Curnutt and Sinclair, *Key West Hemingway*. Baker, *Ernest Hemingway*, 228.

14 Hemingway, "Marlin off the Morro," in *By-Line: Ernest Hemingway*, 180.

15 Hemingway, "On the Blue Water," in *By-Line: Ernest Hemingway*.

16 Clarence Hemingway to Ernest Hemingway, April 11 and 13, 1928, Ernest Hemingway Personal Papers; Grace Hemingway to Ernest Hemingway, March 11, 1928, Hemingway Personal Papers; Sanford, *At the Hemingways*, 227, cited in Reynolds, *Hemingway*, 171. See also Hemingway, *My Brother, Ernest Hemingway*, 94–95.

17 Hemingway, "Fathers and Sons," in *The Complete Short Stories of Ernest Hemingway*, 372.

18 Clarence Hemingway to Ernest Hemingway, April 27, June 4, and June 17, 1928, Ernest Hemingway Personal Papers, in Reynolds, *Hemingway*, 104, 171.

19 Lynn, *Hemingway*, 25. In addition to the abundant comic books and dime store adventure stories that he read, stories from his Uncle Willoughby, a missionary who had travelled to the Far East and met the Dalai Lama in Mongolia, nourished this young man's appetite for adventure and his opened worldview. Baker, *Ernest Hemingway*, 13.

20 Crime rose steadily as the town lamented the risqué dances of its youth. Horse and buggies disappeared as many more families obtained an automobile. At one point, Oak Park boasted more automobiles per capita than any other vil-

lage in the United States. It is significant that Hemingway's conservative father held on to his horse and buggy much longer than was necessary. Reynolds, *Young Hemingway*, 6.

21 Griffin, *Along with Youth*, 25.

22 Kert, *The Hemingway Women*, 35.

23 *The Kansas City Style Book*, 1, Miscellaneous Publications, Other Materials, Hemingway Collection, John F. Kennedy Library.

24 George Plimpton, "The Art of Fiction XXI: Ernest Hemingway," *Paris Review*, Spring 1958, Newspaper Clippings, Hemingway Reference Collection.

25 Mellow, *Hemingway*, 7. As he came of age and Oak Park veterans of the Civil War died, young Hemingway would have heard their glories sung at community gatherings and inscribed in the obituaries of local newspapers. Michael Reynolds, "The Hemingway's Revisited: Back to the Future" (forward), Sanford, *At the Hemingways*, xiv. See also Meyers, *Hemingway*, 17.

26 Baker, *Ernest Hemingway*, 9, Meyers, *Hemingway*, 17.

27 Villard and Nagel, *Hemingway in Love and War*, 1, cited in Megan Floyd Desnoyers, *Ernest Hemingway: A Storyteller's Legacy*, JFK Exhibit, accessed May 18, 2016, https://jfklibrary.org/Research/The-Ernest-Hemingway-Collection/Online-Resources/Storytellers-Legacy.

28 There is a controversy surrounding Hemingway's attempt to join the regular Army. He led his family to believe that he had attempted to enlist but had been rejected for poor eyesight in his left eye, yet there exists no record of his rejection. "We all have that bad eye like Mothers, but I'll make it to Europe some way in spite of this optic," he told his sister Marcelline. Biographer Kenneth Lynn asserts that he never attempted to enlist, for he wished to take part in the event of the war, but did not necessarily wish to serve and die in the trenches. Lynn, *Hemingway*, 73.

29 Mellow, *Hemingway*, 56–57; Reynolds, *Young Hemingway*, 14.

30 The Armistice was signed on November 11, 1918, the bulk of American troops would return in January 1919. The Nineteenth Amendment for women's suffrage passed on May 20, 1919.

31 "First Lieutenant Hemingway Comes Back Riddled with Bullets and Decorated with Two Medals," *Oak Parker*; "Newspaper Man Survives 200 Battle Wounds," "Wounded 227 Times," "Oak Park Boy Shot to Pieces Jokes about It," "Yankee Punctured by 227 pieces of Austrian Shrapnel," and "Hero Back Loaded with Medals," Grandparents' Scrapbook, Hemingway Personal Papers. He did not disclose that he was merely an ambulance driver on a bicycle, delivering mail, chocolate, and cigarettes to the regular infantry troops when he was wounded.

32 Roselle Dean, "First Lieutenant Hemingway," *The Oak Parker*, February 1, 1991, Newspaper Clippings, Hemingway Reference Collection. Later, Hemingway would give insight into how he felt about exaggerating his combat role in the story "A Soldier's Home": "Krebs found that to be listened to at all he had to lie and after he had done this twice he, too, had a reaction against the war and against talking about it. A distaste for everything that had happened to him in the war set in because of the lies he had told." Hemingway, "Soldier's Home," *The Complete Short Stories of Ernest Hemingway*, 125.

33 "I am writing this late at night after a long think by myself, & I am afraid it is going to hurt you, but, I'm sure it won't harm you permanently . . . I realize it was my fault in the beginning that you cared for me, & regret it from the bottom of my heart. But, I am now & always will be too old, & that's the truth, & I can't get away from the fact that you're just a boy—a kid . . . I expect to be married soon. And I hope & pray that after you have thought things out, you'll be able to forgive me & start a wonderful career & show what a man you really are." Agnes von Kurowsky to Ernest Hemingway, March 7, 1919, Hemingway Personal Papers.

34 He did not publish any stories from this period, but the experiences later became the material for "Out of Season," "Up in Michigan," "My Old Man," "The Big Two-Hearted River, Parts I and II," "The Undefeated," "Indian Camp," "The Killers," "Cat in the Rain," "The Battler," and "Three Day Blow" and for magazines and collections like *Three Stories and Ten Poems* and *In Our Time*.

35 Meyers, *Hemingway*, 49.

36 Two unpublished stories emerge from 1919 and 1920: "The Mercenaries" (previously titled "Wolves and Donuts") and "The Woppian Way" (previously titled "The Passing of Pickles McArty"), about an Italian Boxer who cannot, after serving on the Italian front, return to an unexciting career in boxing. Items 572 and 834, Hemingway Personal Papers.

37 Meyers, *Hemingway*, 50–51.

38 In a subsequent article, Clark gave this colorful one-line assessment of Ernest: "A more weird combination of quivering sensitiveness and preoccupation with violence never walked the earth." Gregory Clark, "Hemingway Slept Here," *Montreal Standard*, November 4, 1950, 13.

39 The style was dynamic, humorous, and instructive from an insider's point of view, and concerned such subjects as painting rentals, free shaves, critiques of the major, store thieves, fox ranching, whiskey smuggling, and wedding gifts. Hemingway, *By-Line: Ernest Hemingway*, cited in Meyers, *Hemingway*, 52.

40 "Come to yourself; cease your lazy loafing and pleasure seeking . . . stop trying

to graft a living off anybody and everybody; spending all your earnings lavishly and wastefully on luxuries for yourself; stop trading your handsome face to fool little gullible girls, and neglecting your duties to God and your Savior . . . there is nothing before you but [moral] bankruptcy . . . Do not come back until your tongue has learned not to insult and shame your mother." Grace Hemingway to Ernest Hemingway, July 24, 1920, Hemingway Personal Papers. His father, Clarence Hemingway, supported his mother and seconded that his son was to stay away from the lake house until they invited him to return. If he did not get a job and start behaving responsibly, "the Great Creator will cause him to suffer a whole lot more than he ever has so far." Cited in Hemingway, *My Brother, Ernest Hemingway*, 57.

41 When disenchanted-young-PTSD Hemingway holed up in the family cabin in Michigan without ambition or source of livelihood, his parents were not pleased. As evidence, there as the famous bankruptcy letter from Grace Hemingway to Ernest Hemingway during the summer of 1920, "Interest in Mother's ideas and affairs. Little Comforts provided for the home; a desire to favor any of Mother's particular prejudices, on no account to outrage her ideals. Flowers, fruit, candy or something pretty to war, brought home to Mother, with a kiss and a squeeze. The unfailing desire to make much of her feeble efforts, to praise her cooking, back up her little schemes; a real interest in hearing her sing, or play the piano, or tell the stories that she loves to tell—A surreptitious paying of bills, just to get them off Mother's mind; Thoughtful remembrances and celebration of her birthday and Mother's day (the sweet letter accompanying the gift of flowers, she treasures most of all). These are merely a few of the deposits which keep the account in good standing." Grace Hemingway to Ernest Hemingway, July 27, 1920, Hemingway Personal Papers. There was the story that resulted called "Soldier's Home." In the story, parents confront their son's PTSD and apathetic attitude while returning from World War I. Hemingway, "Soldier's Home," *The Complete Short Stories of Ernest Hemingway*, 130. See also Muriel Hemingway, *Running from Crazy*, dir. Barbara Kopple, New York: Virgil Films, (2014), DVD.

42 Mellow, *Hemingway*, 118.

43 In addition to his publishing company editors, these exceptional literary mentors provided Hemingway not only with examples but also with direct feedback, coaching, encouragement, and editing. Close friends and relatives provided the sort of dedication and patience required for such work.

44 He also rented a room at 39 rue Descartes to escape the noise and get his writing done. His correspondence with Ezra Pound attests to his affinity for

French and "Rooshians" writers during this period, and recollections of his sister, Hadley, and his subsequent declarations to the press substantiate his voracious and omnivorous reading habits. In addition to the books were the music and paintings that he and his circle consumed. In a 1958 interview, George Plimpton asked Hemingway to sum up his literary influences, and he replied: "Mark Twain, Flaubert, Stendhal, Bach, Turgenev, Tolstoy, Dostoevsky, Chekov, Andrew Marvell, John Donne, Maupassant the good Kipling, Thoreau, Captain Marryat, Shakespeare, Mozart, Quevedo, Dante, Virgil, Tintoretto, Hieronymus Bosch, Breughel, Patinier, Goya, Giotto, Cezanne, Van Gogh, Gauguin, San Juan de la Cruz, Góngora—it would take a day to remember everyone." Brasch and Sigman, *Hemingway's Library*, 16. See also Reynolds, *Hemingway's Reading 1910–1940.*

45 Later, they would vacation in Schruns, Austria, along the *côte d'Azur,* and at the Running of the Bulls of San Fermín.

46 Incredibly, William Carlos Williams, a medical doctor as well as a poet, would also circumcise Ernest and Hadley's son in the kitchen of their apartment in Paris.

47 Greenberg, *Calvin Coolidge*, 78–79. Several songs were written in support of the campaign for the veterans Rus Collier and Ben Siegel, *Give A Bonus to Our Men*, 1922. One example, written by Lew Hatton, is "I've Got These Bonus Blues," from 1922. "When I lay me down to sleep / I pray the Lord to keep that pay / comin' in on its way to me / When I start to sing or hum/those blues get me / Better days are sure to come / That's plain to see / Uncle Sam will surely send it / And I know just how I will spend it / That will cure those Bonus Blues."

48 Hemingway, *A Moveable Feast*, 69.

49 By 1932, he was calling it the "iceberg technique" or "art of omission." If a writer of prose knows enough about what he is writing about, he may omit things that he knows and the reader, if the writer is writing truly enough, will have a feeling of those things as strongly as though the writer had stated them. The dignity of movement of an iceberg is due to only one-eighth of it being above water. A writer who omits things because he does not know them only makes hollow places in his writing. He also shared his early struggles as a writer and the reason behind his morbid fascination with violence and death: "I was trying to write then and I found the greatest difficulty, aside from knowing what you really felt, rather that what you were supposed to feel, and had been taught to feel, was to put down what really happened in action; what the actual things which produced the emotion that you experienced . . . I was trying to learn to

write, commencing with the simplest things, and one of the simplest things of all and the most fundamental is violent death." He chalenged himself and his fellow writers to use words precisely and creatively: "All our words from loose using have lost their edge." Hemingway, *Death in the Afternoon*, 6, 34, 83. The iceberg theory, or theory of omission, has often been cited by writers familiar with Hemingway's work, such as George R. R. Martin in recent days, who has often spoken about the universe a fantasy writer like he or J.R.R. Tolkien creates as the underwater part of the "iceberg." "Tolkien made more than a story or history in that book, Martin says: Tolkien's 'secondary world' of languages, mythology and appendices was the bulk of the proverbial iceberg, and the Lord of the Rings just the tip. Martin admits he's doing a bit of 'a magician's trick,' saying that he enjoys the world-building as it comes rather than as a goal." "George RR Martin: 'Drogon could never beat Smaug in a fight,'" *The Guardian*, October 27, 2014, https://www.theguardian.com/books/booksblog/2014/oct/27/george-rr-martin-world-ice-and-fire.

50 Hemingway, *A Moveable Feast*, 62.

51 Hemingway, *A Moveable Feast*.

52 *The Sun Also Rises* illustrated the disillusioning effects of World War I on a group of cynical and rather self-indulgent young expatriates in Paris and Pamplona. American journalist, Jake Barnes, is the novel's narrator. Lady Brett Ashley is the story's enchantingly overripe heroine, a twice-divorced flapper whose sexual freedom embodies 1920s libertarianism. When their young group journeys to Spain to participate in the drunken festival of San Fermín, tension mounts between four men who desire Lady Brett. Even though Brett is engaged to Mike Campbell, she has a brief and sordid affair with Jake's friend from college, Robert Cohn. Although Jake loves Brett, his war wound has left him impotent, such that he must bitterly accept becoming her confidant and friend. Taunted as an imposter and a Jew by several members of the group, Robert Cohn, a former Princeton boxing champion, challenges and brawls, like an enraged bull, with Brett's numerous pretenders. Weary of Cohn and unfaithful to anyone, Brett sleeps instead with Pedro Romero, a bullfighter. Hemingway, *The Sun Also Rises*, 247–51; Baker, *Ernest Hemingway*, 155; F. Scott Fitzgerald, "Preface," *This Side of Paradise*; Hemingway, *A Moveable Feast*, 29–31, 38–39.

53 He also received high praise for his dialogue and characters from Conrad Aiken of the *New York Herald Tribune*, Bruce Barton of *The Atlantic*, and Ernest Boyd of *The Independent*.

54 Ernest Hemingway to Grace Hemingway, February 5, 1927, *Selected Letters*, 244–45.

55 Hemingway's father, Ed, shared similar concerns in the letters he and his son exchanged. He was annoyed to have learned about the divorce from newspaper clippings forwarded by his friends rather than from his own son. Was he merely depicting a Lost Generation, or as his personal life would seem to indicate, was he also "lost"? "Oh Ernest how could you leave Hadley and Bumby? . . . Our family has never had such an incident before and trust you may still make your get-away from that individual who split your home." Clarence Hemingway to Ernest Hemingway, August 8, 1927, Hemingway Personal Papers.

56 Operated by Florida East Coast Railway, the *Havana Special* was the *chef-d'œuvre* of industrialist Henry Flagler, an eccentric whose dream was an oversea railway, running north to south, offering daily departures from Havana (via seaplane and train) to New York via Key West, and a trip duration of just forty-two hours.

57 Reynolds, *Hemingway: The 1930s*, 42.

58 Kert, *The Hemingway Women*, 199.

59 During his final months, Clarence's daughters, Carol and Marceline, remember their father's frequent headaches, his failing health and irritability, and his mounting paranoia from his financial problems. Clarence, who had been strong and intelligent in his youth, was a healer by profession. It came as a shock to this able-bodied doctor, patriarch, and provider to a large and prosperous family, to fall ill, to lose faculties, and face the fact that he was unable to cure himself. Cited in Mellow, *Hemingway*, 371.

60 In his autobiographical novel, he remembers. Hemingway, *The Sound of the Trumpet*, 182–83.

61 Cited in Meyers, *Hemingway*, 208–09.

62 Ernest Hemingway to Max Perkins, December 6, 1928, Archives of Charles Scribner's Sons.

63 Ernest Hemingway to F. Scott Fitzgerald, December 9, 1928, *Selected Letters*, 291; Henry Strater to Ernest Hemingway, December 8, 1928, Hemingway Personal Papers; Ernest Hemingway to Max Perkins, December 6, 1928, Archives of Charles Scribner's Sons.

64 Hemingway, *My Brother, Ernest Hemingway*, 111.

65 Berman, *Surviving Literary Suicides*, 110; Sanford, *At the Hemingways*, cited in Lynn, *Hemingway*, 379.

66 Ernest Hemingway to Maxwell Perkins, December 16, 1928, *Selected Letters*, 291.

67 Concerning George, Ernest would write his mother, "He did more than any-

one to kill Dad and he had better do something in reparation." He would write Perkins concerning his mother's financial situation: "There are my mother and two kids Boy 12 girl 16 still at home—$25,000 insurance—a $15,000 mortgage on the house (house should bring 10 to 15 thousand over the mortgage but sale difficult). Various worthless land in Michigan, Florida, etc. with taxes to pay on all of it. No other capital—all gone—my father carried a 20–20 yr. Endowment insurance which was paid and lost in Florida. He had angina pectoris and diabetes preventing him from getting any more insurance." Hemingway, *Selected Letters*, 292.

68 Ernest Hemingway to F. Scott Fitzgerald, December 9, 1928, *Selected Letters*, 291.

69 Grace Hall Hemingway to Ernest Hemingway, February 24, 1929, Hemingway Personal Papers, cited in Mellow, *Hemingway*, 375.

70 Baker, *Ernest Hemingway*, 200.

71 Hemingway, *My Brother, Ernest Hemingway*, 110–11.

72 Reynolds, *The American Homecoming*, 211–13.

73 Note found in the Baker files, dated October 1931. A sentiment that bears resemblance to Nobel Prize speech, delivered more than two decades later, every man faces his deliverance or his annihilation, his "eternity or the lack of it," alone. Carlos Baker Collection of Ernest Hemingway.

74 Maxwell Perkins to Ernest Hemingway, February 9, 1929, Museum Ernest Hemingway Collection, cited in Bruccoli, *The Only Thing That Counts*, 86.

75 Historical records at *El Morro* and *Ambos Mundos*, interview with Historian at Ambos Mundos Hotel, June 2010, interview with Finca Vigía historian and Gladys Rodríguez, June 2010. See also *The New York Times*, April 5, 1929, cited in Reynolds, *The American Homecoming*, 258.

76 Wagner-Martin, *Ernest Hemingway: A Literary Life*, 86.

77 McParland, *Beyond Gatsby*, 22.

78 Palmié and Scarano, *The Caribbean*, 463.

79 Pérez, *Cuba*, 257.

80 Pérez, *Cuba*, 257.

81 Max Perkins to Ernest Hemingway, August 1, 1930, in Bruccoli, *The Only Thing That Counts*, 144.

82 Max Perkins to Ernest Hemingway, August 12, 1930, in Bruccoli, *The Only Thing That Counts*, 146.

83 Max Perkins to Ernest Hemingway, September 3, 1930, in Bruccoli, *The Only Thing That Counts*, 147.

84 "Please don't under any circumstances give Scott our Paris home address—Last

time he was in Paris he got us kicked out of one apt. and in trouble all the time. (Insulted the landlord—pee-ed on the front porch—tried to break down the door at 3–4 and 5 a.m. etc.) will meet him in public places but have this apt where we're quiet and comfortable and found it with great difficulty and he would get us ousted by only one performance." Bruccoli, *The Only Thing That Counts*, 96.

85 Lawrence and Olive Nordquist, Henry Slater, Max Perkins, Arnold MacLeish, Josephine Herbst, John Herrmann, Gus, Louise, and Virginia Pfeiffer, and Carol Hemingway. Reynolds, *An Annotated Chronology*, 61. Mellow, *Without Consequences*, 390.

86 Confederación Nacional Obrera de Cuba (CNOC). August, *Democracy in Cuba and the 1997–98 Elections*, 127.

87 Pérez, *Cuba*, 255.

88 Hemingway, *Selected Letters*, 323.

89 Hemingway, *Selected Letters*, 333–34.

90 University Student Directorate.

91 Cited in Moruzzi, *Havana Before Castro*, 44.

92 Maurer, *The Empire Trap*, 224, 223; "Two Cuban Editors Protest Government Ban on Nine Papers," *Chicago Daily Tribune* (January 23, 1931), 8.

93 Henry Guggenheim and Henry Stimson, cited in Maurer, *The Empire Trap*, 224.

94 Argote-Freyre, *Fulgencio Batista*, 38.

95 "Havana Unrest Fails to Disturb Sugarfield Calm. Cane Being Burned? Just a Spanish Custom," *Chicago Daily Tribune*, January 23, 1931, 8.

96 "Cuba's Mussolini," *Time Magazine*, January 19, 1931.

97 Jules Benjamin, "The 'Machadato' and Cuban Nationalism, 1928–1932," *Hispanic American Historical Review* 55 (February 1975): 78. See also Bonachea and Martín, *The Cuban Insurrection*, 9.

98 Its founder was Joaquín Martínez Saenz. Pérez, *Cuba*, 257.

99 On January 22, 1931, a reporter from the *Chicago Daily Tribune* described the scene in Matanzas where Milton Hershey owned a sugar mill and his own railroad leading to a northern port. "This old Cuban City, capital of a province which is given over almost exclusively to the production of sugar, does not appear to be much worried over the complexities of government that are so upsetting the calm of Havana. The natives are as complacent as the oxen in the cane fields. Many are very, very poor and there is evidence of financial distress along each other narrow streets. The natives are hungry but they are too tired to get stirred up over the political unrest that is a source of conversation every place in Havana." "Havana Unrest Fails to Disturb Sugarfield Calm. Cane Being Burned? Just a Spanish Custom," *Chicago Daily Tribune*, January 23, 1931, 8.

100 E. E. Allen, Jr., "Hershey Chocolate's Success: Turning Smaller Volume into Increasing Profits," *Barron's*, May 9, 1932, 22.

101 The contractors of Associated Cuban Contractors and Warren Brothers of Boston were awarded the contract by the Cuban government. The country's length from east to west is 780 miles. Edwin J. Foscue, "The Central Highway of Cuba," *Economic Geography* 9, no. 4 (October 1933): 406–12.

102 Benjamin, *The United States and Cuba*, 41; Maurer, *The Empire Trap*, 189.

103 With Max Perkins, John Herrmann, Gus Pfeiffer, Charles Thompson, Chub Weaver, Happy, W. D. Sidley, Bra Saunders, Berge Saunders, and Albert Pinder.

104 Kert, *The Hemingway Women*, 232; Hawkins, *Unbelievable Happiness and Final Sorrow*, 130.

105 McIver, *Hemingway's Key West*, 106.

106 Ernest Hemingway to Max Perkins, April 27, 1931, in Bruccoli, *The Only Thing That Counts*, 156–57.

107 Mellow, *Hemingway*, 404.

108 Baker, *Ernest Hemingway*, 222.

109 Luís E. Aguilar, "Cuba, c.1860–c.1930," in Bethell, *Cuba*, 21–55; "Cuban Leader Gets Refuge in Legation: Ex. President Menocal Obtains Protection of Brazil After Arrest of Associated. Police Surroud Building Mendieza, Mendez Penate and Other Oppositionists Are Sent to Isle of Pines. Cuba Leader Gets Legation Asylum," *The New York Times*, May 25, 1932, 1; "Cuba Seizes Chiefs of 1931 Rebellion," *The New York Times*, May 24, 1932, 9.

110 Pérez, *Cuba Under the Platt Amendment, 1902–1934*, 289; Munro, *The United States and the Caribbean Republics, 1921–1933*, 366.

111 "Cuba Revolts Again," *The Nation*, August 26, 1931.

112 Ernest Hemingway to Guy Hickok, October 14, 1932, *Selected Letters*, 372.

113 Meyers, *Hemingway*, 224.

114 The saga of Gregory Hemingway's neglect and psychological breakdown is well explored/documented in Valerie Hemingway's *Running with the Bulls*, John Hemingway's *Strange Tribe*, and Lorian Hemingway's *Walk on Water*.

115 Ernest Hemingway to Mrs. Paul Pfeiffer, January 5, 1932, *Selected Letters*, 350.

116 Ernest Hemingway, "Paris Is a Mecca of Fakers," *Toronto Star*, March 25, 1922. "It was never enough to simply bask in the wonders of Paris and become part of the scenery . . . God help any well-wisher who 'bitched' his writing sessions on the terrace of his home café, La *Closerie des Lilas*. He reviled creative poseurs who squandered hours drinking and gossiping at cafés like *La Rotonde*. He appeared to prioritize writing above all else—including Hadley and the little son they had two years into their Paris adventure." Blume, *Everybody Behaves Badly*, xiii.

117 Eighty-two years later, middle son, Patrick, would recall the sentiment he had often heard his father repeat: "Family life [was] the enemy of accomplishment . . . on several occasions he said being a good husband, a good father . . . all of [these things were] not recognized by a reviewer when he reviewed your book," yet when not writing, there might have been little left of him for his family who could often play third fiddle to other pursuits: "he really loved the mountains and getting away and fishing. There's no question about which he preferred." Patrick Hemingway, interview on July 30, 2014, cited in Blume, *Everybody Behaves Badly*, 11–12.

118 "Default on public debt cannot be postponed much longer." Harry F. Guggenheim to Henry L, Stimson, January 25, 1932, Nuermberfer et al., eds., *Foreign Relations of the United States, The American Republics* vol. 5, 1932, 536, cited in Maurer, *The Empire Trap*, 190.

119 "Cuban Bombings Resumed," *The New York Times*, January 1932, 2; Davis, *Buda's Wagon*, 16; Benjamin, "The Machadato and Cuban Nationalism, 1928–1932." Munro, *The United States and the Caribbean Republics, 1921–1933*, 368; Thomas, *Cuba*, 595; "3 Hurt by Bomb in Havana," *The New York Times*, February 20, 1932, 9; "Two Dead in Cuba in Bitter Election," *The New York Times*, February 29, 1932, 36.

120 Dickson and Allen, *The Bonus Army*, 50.

CHAPTER 3

1 Key West as described by Samuelson, *With Hemingway*, 9.

2 Samuelson, *With Hemingway.*

3 Man of letters and adventure.

4 Hawkins, *Unbelievable Happiness and Final Sorrow*, 138, Baker, *Ernest Hemingway*, 221.

5 *Anita* Logs, Hemingway Personal Papers.

6 Grits and grunts (grunts are a fish commonly found in Florida's waters) is a famous dish in Florida composed of the grunt fish, so named for the sound it makes, and grits, made from coarsely ground corn kernels, hominy, boiled with water or milk. Johnson, *Highways and Byways of Florida*, 99. "Glad too, to have my fill of sea food, Florida lobsters, shrimps, pompano, red snapper, and the famous dish of grits and grunts, mighty tasty withal, though I do not like the sad noise with which the little grunts quit this life," *Life* (October 1932), 26.

7 "It was a full moon." *Anita* Logs, box 88, Hemingway Personal Papers.

8 Ernest Hemingway to John Dos Passos, May 30, 1932, *Selected Letters*, 359.

9 Hemingway, "Marlin off the Morro," in *By-Line: Ernest Hemingway*, 148.

10 "I used to be co-owner of [The Blind Pig] Sloppy Joe's. Silent partner, they call it. We had gambling in the back, and that's where the real money was. But getting good dice-changers was difficult because if he was so good, you couldn't detect it yourself, you knew he would steal from you. The only big expense in a gambling operation, ours included, is police protection. We paid $7,500 to elect a sheriff who, in his second year in office, went God-happy on us and closed us down, so we closed down the sheriff." Ernest Hemingway to A. E. Hotchner, cited in McIver, *Hemingway's Key West*, 53, 116.

11 Shakespeare, *Henry IV*, 1.5.4. 115–21.

12 Hemingway, *My Brother, Ernest Hemingway*, 118; Ernest Hemingway to John Dos Passos, May 30, 1932, *Selected Letters*, 359.

13 Ernest Hemingway to John Dos Passos, May 30, 1932, *Selected Letters*, 359.

14 "Carlos Gutierrez, Ernest Hemingway, Joe 'Sloppy Joe/Josie' Russell, and others aboard the Anita." Access number EH01148N, Hemingway Personal Papers.

15 *Anita* Logs, Hemingway Personal Papers. He arrived April 24, 1932. Baker, *Ernest Hemingway*, 228; Reynolds, *Hemingway: The 1930s*, 91. After three days of fishing he would give an interview to the *Havana Post*, and the story would appear on April 28, 1932.

16 Fuentes, *Hemingway in Cuba*, 98.

17 Ernest Hemingway to John Dos Passos, May 30, 1929, *Selected Letters*, 359.

18 Hemingway, "Marlin off the Morro," in *By-Line: Ernest Hemingway*, 460; Hemingway, *My Brother, Ernest Hemingway*, 118.

19 Hemingway, "Marlin off the Morro," in *By-Line: Ernest Hemingway*, 148.

20 Ernest Hemingway to John Dos Passos, May 30, 1932. *Selected Letters*, 359.

21 *Anita* Logs, April 24, 1932, Hemingway Personal Papers.

22 Hemingway, "Marlin off the Morro," in *By-Line: Ernest Hemingway*, 148.

23 Hemingway, *Islands in the Stream*, 98.

24 Hemingway, *Islands in the Stream*, 96.

25 Hemingway, *Islands in the Stream*, 97.

26 Hemingway, *Islands in the Stream*, 88–109.

27 Ernest Hemingway to John Dos Passos, May 30, 1932, *Selected Letters*. 359.

28 Says José Abeal, another legend—apparently untrue—is that a newspaper man had once been evicted from the joint because he refused to pay his bill and had vindictively written about the substandard conditions of the establishment in the newspaper. Abeal y Otero, *Sloppy Joe's Bar Cocktail Manual*. Sloppy Joe's owner, José Garcia Abeal, cited in Moruzzi, *Havana Before Castro*, 73; Andrea Strong, "Ode to Sloppy Joe, a Delicious Mess," *The New York Times* (October 9, 2002), https:

//www.nytimes.com/2002/10/09/dining/an-ode-to-sloppy-joe-a-delicious-mess.html?mtrref=undefined.

29 *La Zaragozana* is literally a woman from Zaragoza, but it is also the symbolic seat of the Basilica de Nuestra Señora de Pilar, the church belonging to Spain's patron saint of the same name. It is also the name of a Spanish beer founded in 1900. Fernando G. Campoamor, Manuscript, Memoir, 1999. Journalist, author, and friend of Hemingway in Havana for twenty-five years.

30 The names of streets are revealing: Street of the Soul, Mercy, Cheap, and so on. Interviews and Manuscript Notes, Fernando G. Campoamor, 1993–1999, Loló De la Torriente, "La prosa de Enrique Serpa," *Bohemia*, May 28, 1971, 6–7; Loló De la Torriente, "Reedition of *Contraband*," *Instituto del Libro Cubano*, cited in Leonard Depestre Catony, *Cubaliteraria* (2005), http://www.cubaliteraria.cu/articulo.php?idarticulo=10345&idseccion=35; Campoamor, "Enrique Serpa," *Bohemia*, 4. See also Páporov, *Hemingway en Cuba*; Moruzzi, *Havana Before Castro*, 118.

31 Terry, *Terry's Guide to Cuba*, cited in Moruzzi, *Havana Before Castro*, 126–29.

32 Skwiot, *The Purposes of Paradise*, 123.

33 John Rybovich, cited in Miller, *Trading with the Enemy*, 168.

34 Perez, "Image and Identity," 129.

35 Davis, *Buda's Wagon*, 17, cited in Maurer, *The Empire Trap*, 190.

36 Baker, *Ernest Hemingway*, 228; Ernest Hemingway to Pauline Pfeiffer, April 25, 1932, Museum Ernest Hemingway Collection; Ernest Hemingway to Waldo Peirce, April 15, 1932, and Ernest Hemingway to John Dos Passos, May 30, 1932, *Selected Letters*, 357–61; *Official records of dockings, Morro Castle, 1931–1932*, 440; *Official records of dockings, Morro Castle, 11 August 1931 to 30 July 1932* (Havana: National Achives, 1928), 436.

37 Meyers, *Hemingway*, 435; Hawkins, *Unbelievable Happiness and Final Sorrow*, 152.

38 In the most recently published version of *A Moveable Feast*, Hemingway described the early years with Pauline as a time of "unbelievable happiness" followed by later years of "final sorrow" (186). *Unbelievable Happiness and Final Sorrow* was the title Ruth Hawkins choose for a biography of Pauline Pfeiffer. Originally, this line was omitted from Hemingway's memoirs, edited and published posthumously by Mary Hemingway, who had been attempting to gain favor at the time she edited the book with Hadley Richardson and negotiate the transfer of an expensive work of art: *The Farm*, by Juan Miró.

39 "I really shouldn't be telling this because as soon as fishermen learn the possibilities here and Havana prepares to care for fishermen, it will become famous and crowded. And when it does, we'll find some other fishing ground." Ernest

Hemingway, *Havana Post*, April 28, 1932, quoted in Reynolds, *Hemingway: The 1930s*, 94.

40 Ernest Hemingway to Max Perkins, May 14, 1932, Ernest Hemingway Collection.

41 Kert, *The Hemingway Women*, 240.

42 *Anita* Logs, Hemingway Personal Papers; Hawkins, *Unbelievable Happiness and Final Sorrow*, 140.

43 Kert, *The Hemingway Women*, 235.

44 Hemingway, *My Brother, Ernest Hemingway*, 119.

45 Hemingway, *My Brother, Ernest Hemingway*.

46 Alane Salierno Mason, "To Love and Love Not," *Vanity Fair*, July 1999.

47 Hawkins, *Unbelievable Happiness and Final Sorrow*, 140.

48 Pauline Hemingway to Ernest Hemingway, four letters from May to June 1932, Hemingway Personal Papers, quoted in Reynolds, *Hemingway: The 1930s*, 96.

49 Hemingway, "Marlin off the Morro," in *By-Line: Ernest Hemingway*, 148.

50 Jane Mason to Pauline Hemingway, May 10, 1932, and *Anita* Logs, Hemingway Personal Papers.

51 *Anita* Logs and correspondence between Jane Mason and Ernest Hemingway, 1932, Jane Mason Personal Papers and Hemingway Personal Papers.

52 "Ernest resisted falling in love with women who had emotional problems. He liked to describe his women as 'happy, health, hard as a rock.'" Kert, *The Hemingway Women*, 243, 250.

53 "He came to think of Jane Mason as his very own Zelda, except that he proposed to make her well by giving her lessons in marlin fishing, and by telling her over and over again that she wasn't crazy, even as he had always responded to his own problems by publically denying their existence." ("I know what I am doing and have never felt a 'malajust,'" he would reassure one of his correspondents on August 9, 1932.) Lynn, *Hemingway*, 404; Christopher Martin, "Ernest Hemingway: A Psychological Autopsy of a Suicide," *Psychiatry* 69 (Winter 2006): 4.

54 "When questioned about the enigmatic title of his short story, 'A Way You'll Never Be,' he said it was an effort to cheer up a hell of a nice girl going crazy from day to day." In the story, Nick Adams, suffering from a head injury, was much nuttier than this girl was ever going to be. The girl he referred to was Jane Mason. Kert, *The Hemingway Women*, 250.

55 Brian, *The True Gen*, in McIver, *Hemingway's Key West*, 50.

56 Once they had returned to Whitehead Street, the argument continued until Archie decided to board the train home. Brian, *The True Gen*, 91.

57 Soft-spoken Charlie Thompson was another important exception to the rule. Archibald MacLeish to Ernest Hemingway, April 7, 1932, in MacLeish, *Letters of Archibald MacLeish*, 247.

58 Kert, *The Hemingway Women*, 243.

59 *Anita* Logs, Hemingway Personal Papers.

60 On May 5, a tornado struck Havana and the party had a close call in heavy seas. "Tornado Strikes Havana," *Chicago Daily Tribune*, May 5, 1932; *Anita* Logs, Hemingway Personal Papers.

61 *Anita* Logs, Hemingway Personal Papers.

62 *Chigaco Daily Tribune*, May 20, 1932, 11.

63 *Chigaco Daily Tribune*, May 20, 1932, 11.

64 *Chigaco Daily Tribune*, May 20, 1932, 11

65 "Bombs Delivered to Cuba Leaders: One Hurled at Residence of Maj. Rasco; Plot Is Laid to Terrorists," *The Washington Post*, May 23, 1932, 1; "Other Officers Get Bombs," *The New York Times*, May 23, 1932, 5.

66 Max Perkins to Ernest Hemingway, April 19, 1932, and Ernest Hemingway to Max Perkins, June 2, 1932, cited in Bruccoli, *The Only Thing That Counts*, 166–67.

67 "*Can't* get a son of a bitch down here—am feeling alone now with Joe holding the other rod and an insane night life jig to steer—goes to sleep while steering—goes to sleep minute he hits the boat. Spends the dough he makes every night on night life. At this hotel—*Ambos Mundos*—you can get a good clean room with bath right overlooking the harbor and the cathedral—see all the neck of the harbor and the sea for $2.00–2.50 for two people. Write the name down . . . Have gone over book 7 times and cut all you objected to (seemed like the best to me God damn you if it really was) cut 4 ½ galleys of philosophy and telling the boys—cut all of last chapter except the part about Spain . . . Left Old Lady in . . . wish you luck with yours." Ernest Hemingway to John Dos Passos, May 30, 1932, *Selected Letters*, 360.

68 Ernest Hemingway to John Dos Passos, May 30, 1932, *Selected Letters*, 360.

69 "I do not follow the fashions in politics, letters, religion etc . . . If the boys swing to the left in literature you may make a small bet the next swing will be to the right and some of the same yellow bastards will swing both ways. There is no left and right in writing. There is only good and bad writing. These little punks who have never seen men street fighting, let alone revolution, I am no goddamned patriot nor will I swing to left or right. Would as soon machine gun left, right, or center any political bastards." Ernest Hemingway to Paul Romaine, July 6, 1932, *Selected Letters*, 363.

70 The poem "Dulce et Decorum Est" by Wilfred Owen, one of the best known

about the subject of war, was written by a solider from Ernest Hemingway's experiential context of World War I. The Latin comes from an Ode by Horace, an old lie, often retold.

71 In the book, he wrote, "Bullfighting is the only art in which the artist is in danger of death and in which the degree of brilliance in the performance is left to the fighter's honor." About Spaniards, he wrote, "Honor to a Spaniard, no matter how dishonest, is as real a thing as water, wine, or olive oil. There is honor among pickpockets and honor among whores. It is simply that the standards differ." Hemingway, *Death in the Afternoon*, 77–78.

72 Ernest Hemingway to Scott Fitzgerald, April 20, 1926, *Selected Letters*, 200.

73 "Three Bombs Explode in Havana Schools: Beginning of New Terroristic Campaign," *The New York Times*, June 1, 1932, 4, cited in Maurer, *The Empire Trap*, 186.

74 "Cuba Starts Drive on Foes of Regime: Hundreds Are Seized or Sought on Charges," *The New York Times*, June 15, 1932, 4, cited in Maurer, *The Empire Trap*, 186.

75 "Secret Police Head Is Slain in Havana," *The New York Times*, July 10, 1932, 1. "Cuba Guards Our Embassy Against Bombing by Reds," *The New York Times*, August 1, 1932, 15; Guggenheim to Stimson, July 25, 1932.

76 Hemingway, "Old Newsman Writes" in *By-Line: Ernest Hemingway*, 187.

77 "Last week William Hushka's Bonus for $528 suddenly became payable in full when a police bullet drilled him dead in the worst public disorder the capital has known in years." "Heroes: Battle of Washington," *Time*, August 8, 1932.

78 Later, Eisenhower, who became president, said famously that he had told that "dumb son-of-a-bitch" General MacArthur "not to go down there," for it was "no place for a Chief of Staff." Major Patton commanded the unit that attacked the veterans' camp and set fire to their shelters. A highly decorated soldier, Joe Angelo, a man who saved Eisenhower's life at the Meuse-Aragon Offensive, was also present and attempted to confront Patton. Wukovits, *Eisenhower*, 43; D'Este, *Eisenhower*, 223; Dickson and Allen, *The Bonus Army*, 50, 254, 325.

79 "Cuba Will Continue Martial Law Rule," *The New York Times*, June 22, 1932, 3.

80 Max Perkins to Ernest Hemingway, July 22, 1932, in Bruccoli, *The Only Thing That Counts*, 174.

81 Ernest Hemingway to Max Perkins, July 27, 1932, in Bruccoli, *The Only Thing That Counts*, 175.

82 Hemingway, "Fathers and Sons," *The Complete Short Stories of Ernest Hemingway*, 377.

83 Hemingway, "A Clean Well-Lighted Place," *The Complete Short Stories of Ernest Hemingway*, 290–91.

84 Hemingway later confessed in an interview with Lillian Ross that his analyst was "Portable Corona No.3," his typewriter. Ross, *Portrait of Hemingway*, 36. He also counseled Scott Fitzgerald on May 28, 1934: "You especially have to hurt like hell before you can write seriously. But when you get the damned hurt use it—don't cheat with it. Be as faithful to it as a scientist." Hemingway, *Selected Letters*, 408.

85 Maxwell Perkins to Ann Chidester, July 15, 1943, in Perkins, *Editor to Author*, 151.

86 Wilson, *The Bit Between My Teeth*, 522.

87 Ernest Hemingway to Arnold Gingrich, December 4, 1932, *Selected Letters*, 378.

88 Arnold Gingrich to Ernest Hemingway, February 24, April 24, and May 26, 1933, private collection, cited in Reynolds, *Hemingway: The 1930s*, 331, and Hemingway Personal Papers. See also Stephen Marche,"Down in Havana, Searching for the Ghost of Hemingway," *Esquire*, September 30, 2015, https://www.esquire.com/entertainment/a37859/havana-ghost-of-hemingway/.

89 Ernest Hemingway to Arnold Gingrich, December 4, 1932, and March 13 and April 3, 1933, *Selected Letters*, 378, 383–85.

90 Russell Porter, "Revolt by Terror Going on in Cuba," *The New York Times*, February 4, 1933, 1.

91 The article insinuated that Machado's daughter was a lesbian. Thomas, *Cuba or Pursuit of Freedom*, 574.

92 "Called the office just after you left (the day I left) and then wired you at the house. Haven't written because I started a novel . . . have 3 ½ chapters done and 2 stories finished. Going well . . . What the hell about our Cuban trip? Or will you be coming down in May or June? Any time you want to come is fine. Let me know though." Ernest Hemingway to Arnold Gingrich, February 27, 1932, *Selected Letters*, 381.

93 "Our Relations with Cuba," *The Atlanta Constitution*, April 30, 1933, 1; "Cuba Glad Welles Becomes Ambassador," *Christian Science Monitor*, April 22, 1933, 1.

94 "Welles Is Welcomed by Havana Authorities," *The Washington Post*, May 8, 1933, 1.

95 Pauline Pfeiffer to Ernest Hemingway, May 18, 1933, Bernice Kert Personal Papers, cited in Kert, *The Hemingway Women*, 247.

96 "The Protest of 13." Bueno, "José Antonio Fernández de Castro."

97 José Antonio Fernández de Castro, "Fishing for Marlin with Hemingway:

Interview with the U.S. novelist," *Diario de la Marina*, May, 28 1933. Later José Antonio became the editor of *Orbe*, a weekly pictorial magazine.

98 "José Antonio was the best person to know in Havana if you had never been there before," said Langston Hughes when he met him in Havana three years before. A native with open accounts with all the drivers, José Antonio knew how to wine and dine foreigners, but it was his openness and connections with all kinds that most impressed the "jazz poet" and harbinger of the Harlem Renaissance: "Painters, writers, newsboys, poets, fighters, politicians and rumba dancers were all José's friends . . . That is why I liked José Antonio. He lived in Vedado, but he knew all of Havana. Although he was a white Cuban of aristocratic background, he knew and loved Negro Cuba . . . He was a human dynamo who set things in motion. That first night we went straight to Marianao." In Marianao, he showed Hughes "those fabulous drum beaters who use their bare hands to beat out rhythm, those clave knockers and maraca shakers who somehow have saved—out of all the centuries of slavery and all the miles from Guinea—the heartbeat and song beat of Africa. This ancient heartbeat they pour out into the Cuban night from a little row of café hovels at Marianao. Or else they flood with song those smoky low-roofed dance halls where the poor of Havana go for entertainment after dark. Most Cubans who lived in Vedado, Havana's fashionable section, had no idea where these dance halls were." Hughes, *I Wonder as I Wander*, 7.

99 "I have some pictures tonight, and will have more tomorrow. Also I will change my mind and take a loan of ten or fifteen dollars if you still feel like that," said the note written on Western Union stationary from the Western Union Office in Havana addressed from Walker Evans to Ernest Hemingway at the Ambos Mundos Hotel. On the back of the envelope, in Ernest's handwriting, the words "loaned $25" are written. Toby Bruce later discovered the forty-six prints and letters in the basement of Sloppy Joe's in 2002. Later in his diary, Walker Evans would remember guiltily that he still owed Hemingway "a small amount of money." Mellow, *Walker Evans*, 199.

100 *Anita* Logs, May 31, 1933, Hemingway Personal Papers; Ernest Hemingway to Harvey Breit, July 4 and 20, 1952, Ernest Hemingway Collection, cited in Mellow, *Walker Evans*, 180, 587.

101 "Two Sons of Hemingway Safe After Auto Plunge," *The Washington Post*, May 25, 1933, 1.

102 Mellow, *Hemingway*, 425; McIver, *Hemingway's Key West*, 131.

103 Mellow, *Hemingway*, 425; McIver, *Hemingway's Key West*, 131.

104 Alane Salierno Mason, "To Love and Love Not," *Vanity Fair*, July 1999.

105 Mason, "To Love and Love Not." Over a decade later, Hemingway would remember the accident and make use of it while writing about the imagined death of his two sons in *Islands in the Stream.*

106 *Anita* Logs, Hemingway Personal Papers; Ernest Hemingway to Archibald MacLeish, 1933, Archibald MacLeish Personal Papers; interviews of Jack Hemingway, Patrick Hemingway, and Anton Mason; and Hemingway, *Islands in the Stream*, 183, cited in Meyers, *Hemingway*, 245.

107 *Anita* Logs, Hemingway Personal Papers; *Havana Post*, June 4, 1933.

108 Jane Mason to Ernest and Pauline Hemingway, September 2, 1933, and Dr. K.P.A. Taylor to Ernest Hemingway, July 19, 1933, Hemingway Personal Papers.

109 Significant evidence exists to support the diagnoses of bipolar disorder, alcohol dependence, traumatic brain injury, and probable borderline and narcissistic personality traits. "Ernest Hemingway: A Psychological Autopsy of a Suicide," *Psychiatry* 69, no. 4 (Winter 2006): 351–61. See also Lawrence S. Kubie, "Principles of Psycho-Analysis as Applied to the Modern Literature of Neuroticism," unpublished, both cited in Kert, *The Hemingway Women*, 270–71. Jane Mason to Lawrence Kubie, July 13, 1935. See also Susan Beegel, "Editor's Note," Safari Edition, *Hemingway Review* 21, no. 2 (Spring 2002).

110 Interview with Michael Reynolds, in Reynolds, *Hemingway: The 1930s*, 126; Reynolds, *Hemingway: The 1930s Through the Final Years*, 118.

111 J. D. Phillips, "Machado Offers Reforms for Cuba," *The New York Times*, June 8, 1933, 1.

112 J. D. Phillips, "Machado Denies He Plans to Quit," *The New York Times*, June 2, 1933, 1; "Machado Will Quit; Tells Plan to Pacify Cuba," *Chicago Daily Tribune*, June 8, 1933, 1.

113 "There is an unconscionable quantity of bull—to put it as decorously as possible—poured and plastered all over what he writes about bullfights. It is of course a commonplace that anyone who too much protests his manhood lacks the serene confidence that he is made out of iron. Most of us too delicately organized babies who grow up to be artists suffer at times from that small inward doubt. But some circumstance seems to have laid upon Hemingway a continual sense of the obligation to put forth evidences of red-blooded masculinity." Max Eastman, "Bull in the Afternoon," *The New Republic*, June 1933, 94–97.

114 "It is certainly damned fine to have friends—They hear you are out in the country and they open up. Good. Bring on some more friends. I'll be a long way out

of the country and they will all get very brave and say everything they wish were true—Then I'll be back and we will see what will happen. You see what they can't get over is (1) that I am a man (2) that I can beat the shit out any of them. (3) that I can write. The last hurts them the worst. But they don't like any of it. But Papa will make them like it." Ernest Hemingway to Max Perkins, June 13, 1933, in Bruccoli, *The Only Thing That Counts*, 190–91.

115 Reynolds, *Hemingway: The 1930s*, 141.

116 Ernest Hemingway to Max Perkins, August 10, 1933, in Bruccoli, *The Only Thing That Counts*, 196.

117 "Machado to Invoke Rule by Military as Strikes Spread," *The New York Times*, August 7, 1933, 3; Gustavo Reno, "Riots in Havana; 26 Killed: Troops Fire on Mob; Machado Refuses to Quit," *Chicago Daily Tribune*, August 8, 1933, 1; *Havana Post*, August 13, 1933; Anthony Mason, interview by Michael Reynolds, cited in Reynolds, *Hemingway: The 1930s*, 142. See also "Machado's Overthrow in Cuba Climaxes Nine Years of Political Turmoil," *Lodi-News Sentinel*, August 26, 1933, 2.

118 Gustavo Reno, "Cuba Lashed By Hurricane; 3 Looters Shot," *Chicago Daily Tribune*, September 1, 1933, 1.

119 "U.S. Destroyers to Cuba. Roosevelt Acts as Mobs Renew Killing, Looting. Three Warships Are Sent to Protect Americans," *Chicago Tribune*, August 14, 1933, 1.

120 Argote-Freyre, *Fulgencio Batista*, 58, 61.

121 "Rioters in Havana Shoot *Porristas*," *Chicago Tribune*, August 14, 1933, 1.

122 Telegrams 191–95, the Ambassador in Cuba (Wells) to the Secretary of State, September 5, 1933, *Foreign Relations Series* V, US Department of State; "Ships Carry 50 Men Each," *The New York Times*, August 14, 1933.

123 "The five were: Dr Ramon Grau San Martin (medical Dean and a known radical); editor, Sergio Carbó; banker, Porfirio Franca; lawyer José Maria Irissari; and a law professor, Guillermo Portela." The Ambassador in Cuba (Wells) to the Secretary of State, telegrams 191–95, September 5, 1933, *Foreign Relations Series* V, US Department of State; Antoni Kapcia, "The Siege of the Hotel Nacional, Cuba 1933: A Reassessment," *Journal of Latin American Studies* 34, (2002): 283–309.

124 Acronym denoting Directorio Estudiantil Universitario.

125 Argote-Freyre, *Fulgencio Batista*, 58, 84.

126 The Ambassador in Cuba (Wells) to the Secretary of State, telegrams 191–95, September 5, 1933, *Foreign Relations Series* V, US Department of State; Benjamin, *The United States and Cuba*, 139.

127 Hemingway, "Marlin off the Morro," in *By-Line: Ernest Hemingway*, 148.

128 Raeburn, *Fame Became Him*, 45–50.

129 "Marlin off the Morro," Hemingway, in *By-Line: Ernest Hemingway*, 148.

130 Ernest Hemingway to Patrick Hemingway, December 2, 1933, *Selected Letters*, 402.

131 "Batista was the only individual in Cuba today who represented authority . . . due in part to the fact that he appeared to have the loyal support of a large part of his troops." The Ambassador in Cuba (Wells) to the Secretary of State, telegram 340, October 4, 1933, 7 pm, 837.00/4131, *Foreign Relations Series* V, US Department of State.

132 "Cubans Loot American Consulate: Army Officers Face Guns of Troops," *Chicago Tribune*, September 9, 1933, 1; the Ambassador in Cuba (Wells) to the Secretary of State, telegrams 220–22, September 5, 1933, *Foreign Relations Series* V, US Department of State; Kapcia, "The Siege of the Hotel Nacional, Cuba 1933."

133 Kapcia, "The Siege of the Hotel Nacional."

134 English, *Havana Nocturne.*

135 Quoted in English, *Havana Nocturne*, 33–34.

136 Quoted in English, *Havana Nocturne*, 32.

137 "Lansky and I flew to Havana with the money in the suitcases . . . Lansky took Batista straight back to our hotel, opened the suitcases and pointed at the cash. Batista just stared at the money without saying a word." Quoted in English, *Havana Nocturne*, 37.

138 Caffery had gained some notoriety for his diplomacy during the United Fruit workers' strike known as the Banana Massacre: the Army had fired into a crowd killing forty-seven fruit-pickers, women, and children. The incident was later depicted by Gabriel Garcia Marquez in *One Hundred Years of Solitude*.

139 Jefferson Caffery, *Diario de la Marina*, December 19, 1933, 1; the Personal Representative of the President (Caffery) to the Acting Secretary of State, telegram 837:00. 4558; *Foreign Relations Series* V, US Department of State, 544.

140 "Caffery belonged to the same school of suave diplomats as Sumner Welles. A political conservative of elegant manners, Caffery was once described as a 'somewhat frostbitten diplomat of the old school, who holds to the Hamilton belief that those who have should rule.'" Spaulding, *Ambassadors Ordinary and Extraordinary*, 262, cited in Aguilar, *From Cuba 1933*.

141 Hemingway, *Green Hills of Africa*, 36.

142 Hemingway, *Green Hills of Africa*, 167.

143 Fitch, *Sylvia Beach and the Lost Generation*, 343–44.

144 Hemingway, "Shootism vs. Sport," in *By-Line: Ernest Hemingway.*

145 "1934 Wheeler Catalogue," cited in Hendrickson, *Hemingway's Boat*, 58–59.

146 Ernest Hemingway to Arnold Gingrich, March 24, 1934, Hemingway Personal Papers.

147 Samuelson, *With Hemingway*, 76.

148 Pablo De la Torriente Brau, *Bohemia*, April 1934, 3.

149 "While the government is taking extreme precautions against disorders, labor is preparing the greatest demonstration ever held in Havana to celebrate International Labor Day," *The New York Times*, April 30, 1934; "Labor Day in Cuba to Be Legal Holiday: Workers Arranging for Greatest Demonstrating Ever Held—Authorities on Guard," *The New York Times*, May 1, 1934, 2.

150 "Labor Day in Cuba to Be Legal Holiday," *The New York Times*.

151 "Am going to Havana tomorrow to see May Day—Back in a couple days." Ernest Hemingway to Max Perkins, April, 30, 1934, in Bruccoli, *The Only Thing That Counts*, 210.

152 *Havana Post*, May 2–May 5, 1934.

153 Ernest Hemingway to Max Perkins, April 16, 1934, Ernest Hemingway to Lester Ziffren, May 18, 1934, and Ernest Hemingway to Arnold Gingrich, May 25 1934, in Baker, *Ernest Hemingway*, 260

154 Samuelson, *With Hemingway*, 7–8.

155 Hemingway, *My Brother, Ernest Hemingway*, 146–47.

156 Samuelson, *With Hemingway*, 26.

157 Hendrickson, *Hemingway's Boat*, 84.

158 Hemingway and Brennen, *Hemingway in Cuba*, 27.

159 Pauline's rich Uncle Gus had purchased a new home for the couple for $8,000 in Key West, just after they had returned from the African safari, which had also been financed by Uncle Gus for the sum of $25,000 during a time when most of the country was suffering the consequences of the Great Depression. Hemingway would meet his lifelong friend and editor Arnold Gingrich shortly before, and for *Esquire* magazine, he would write frequent articles from 1933 to 1935 under the title "Letters." Although Hemingway often eschewed journalism as a distraction from more serious writing, Gingrich left Hemingway free to write about subjects and themes that interested him; writing for the magazine, he would thus greatly increase his fame as an editorial writer, adventurer, traveler, and sportsman. Many Americans followed the column and lived his adventures by proxy. The *Pilar* cost $7,455. Gingrich advanced Hemingway $3,000 against ten stories to place the order. Kert, *The Hemingway Women*, 232, 250.

160 Ernest Hemingway to Arnold Gingrich, May 25, 1934, Hemingway Personal Papers.

161 Samuelson, *With Hemingway*, 24.

162 *Pilar* Logs, Hemingway Personal Papers.

163 F. Scott Fitzgerald to Ernest Hemingway, May 10, 1934, in Bruccoli, ed., *The Sons of Maxwell Perkins*, 179.

164 Ernest Hemingway to Max Perkins, April 30, 1934, Ernest Hemingway Collection.

165 Samuelson, *With Hemingway*, 34.

166 Reynolds, *Hemingway: The 1930s*, 273.

167 Cited in Hemingway, *My Brother, Ernest Hemingway* 192.

168 Ernest Hemingway to F. Scott Fitzgerald, May 28, 1934, *Selected Letters*, 407.

169 Ernest Hemingway to Max Perkins, April, 30, 1934, in Bruccoli, *The Only Thing That Counts*, 207–210. "You're a rummy and Zelda does not help." Ernest Hemingway to F. Scott Fitzgerald, May 28, 1934, *Selected Letters*, 407–09.

170 Hawkins, *Unbelieveable Happiness and Final Sorrow*, 168.

171 Samuelson, *With Hemingway*, 67.

172 Samuelson, *With Hemingway*, 68

173 Samuelson, *With Hemingway*.

174 Samuelson, *With Hemingway*.

175 Good luck fishing.

176 "Cojo" means lame. An affectionate nickname due to the accident that cut off all his toes.

177 Samuelson, *With Hemingway*, 71.

178 Reynolds, *Hemingway: The 1930s*, 178.

179 Samuelson, *With Hemingway*, 74.

180 Samuelson, *With Hemingway*, 71.

181 Samuelson, *With Hemingway*, 59–61, 95, 176, 178.

182 Samuelson, *With Hemingway*, 92.

183 Hemingway, *The Old Man and the Sea*, 43.

184 "Terrorists Bomb Ex-Chicagoan's Home in Havana," *Chicago Daily Tribune*, August 6, 1934, 1.

185 Suspecting Frederick H. Wilcox, Basil A. Needham, and Arthur W. Hoffman of smuggling arms and agitating rebels, the secretary of the interior deported the vigilantes and stepped up security searches on all vessels subsequently entering Cuban waters. Due to increasing evidence against them and rumors circulating that a large shipment of arms had arrived near Havana's coast, the cuban secretary decided to deport them as a precaution, for Hoffman was a known rebel sympathizer who had been involved in another incident the week before. "Cuba to Deport 3 Americans," *Wall Street Journal*, August 9, 1934, 3. See also *Havana Post*, August 9, 1934, 1.

186 *Havana Post*, August 28, 1934, 1; "10 Planes, 7 Warships Hunt Rum Runners

Near Cuba," *Chicago Daily*, August 6, 1934, 14; "Cubans to Strike over Two Killings: Employees of 5 Departments, All Students and Others Prepare for Protest Today, Leftist Bury Youth, Supposed Informer Is Missing—Former Strikers Are Expected to Fight for Jobs," *The New York Times*, September 3, 1934, 5.

187 "Cuba Swept by Riots: Martial Law Declared. 19 Wounded in Havana; Cabinet Quits," *Chicago Daily Tribune*, September 5, 1934, 3.

188 "Cuba Drafts a Law to Check Terrorism: Severe Measures Are Expected Soon—Fifteen Bombs Are Exploded in Havana," *The New York Times*, September 6, 1934, 12.

189 "United Cuba Faces Rioting Demonstrators," *The Christian Science Monitor*, September 7, 1934, 3.

190 "Cuban Students Fight Soldier; Rioting Spreads," *Chicago Daily Tribune*, September 7, 1934, 3.

191 *Pilar* Logs, October 7 and 11, 1934, Hemingway Personal Papers.

192 *Pilar* Logs, Hemingway Personal Papers.

193 Loló de la Torriente, "La prosa de Enrique Serpa," *Bohemia*, May 28, 1971, 6–7.

194 Author translation. Loló de la Torriente, "Reedition of *Contraband*," *Instituto del Libro Cubano*, cited in Catony, Cubaliteraria.

195 "40 Grau Adherents Arrested in Cuba," *The New York Times*, September 26, 1934, 1.

196 "Grau Leaves Cuba to Escape Injury: Former President Flees with Family to Miami," *The New York Times*, September 28, 1934, 3.

197 *The New York Times*, October 14, 1934, 3.

198 *The New York Times*, October 14, 1934.

199 *The New York Times*, October 14, 1934.

200 "The American Government has treated Cuba with every consideration and has done everything in its power to aid us, as is witnessed by the abrogation of the Platt Amendment, by the sugar quota and by the new reciprocity treaty. Many times during the past two years the United States has had the right to intervene but has refrained from doing so, and I think it is up to the Cubans to work out their own problems." *The New York Times*, October 14, 1934.

201 Cuban gentleman.

202 Rodríguez, *The Havana of Hemingway and Campoamor*, 14.

203 Miller, *Trading with the Enemy*, 166–67.

204 Ernest Hemingway to Max Perkins, November 20, 1934, in Bruccoli, *The Only Thing That Counts*, 215–16.

205 Hemingway, *Green Hills of Africa*, 115; Frederic I Carpenter, "Hemingway Achieves the Fifth Dimension," *PMLA* 69, no. 4 (September 1954): 711–718.

206 *New Republic*, cited in Mellow, *Hemingway*, 441.

207 "Precisely because of what it left out, Hemingway seems to have considered that literary revolution to have been incomplete and unresolved. In *Green Hills of Africa*, Hemingway put in what Joyce left out—the presence of physical danger and the sense of memory arising in real time. The stream of consciousness that Hemingway aspired to capture in writing was the one in which he was living in the present tense, which is why the higher dimensions of prose that he envisioned were built from nonfiction—from the existential reclamation of his own thoughts and actions at a given moment. Unlike Joyce's innovations, Hemingway's experimental fusion of fiction and nonfiction remained largely at the level of theory—but it has proven to be even more enduringly influential. Hemingway's stream has become hard to recognize and to distinguish, because it has become the mainstream." Richard Brody, "Hemingway as the Godfather of the Long-Form," *The New Yorker*, July 29, 1935, https://www.newyorker.com/culture/cultural-comment/hemingway-as-the-godfather-of-long-form.

208 Meyers, *Ernest Hemingway*, 163, cited in Milton Cohen, "Beleaguered Modernists," in Curnutt and Sinclair, *Key West Hemingway*, 78.

209 Meyers, *Ernest Hemingway*, 163.

210 "Of course the boys are all wishing you luck and that helps a lot. (Watch how they wish you luck after the first one.) . . . They are all really very newly converted and very frightened, really, and when Moscow tells them what I am telling you, then they will believe it. Books should be about the people you know, that you love and hate, not about the people you study about. If you write them truly they will have all the economic implications a book can hold." Hemingway, "Old Newsman Writes: A Letter from Cuba," in *By-Line: Ernest Hemingway*, 183–84, 188.

211 Hemingway, *Green Hills of Africa*, 67.

212 Ernest Hemingway to Ivan Kashkin, August 19, 1935, in *Selected Letters*, 419.

213 "My father was a coward. He shot himself without necessity. At least I thought so. I had gone through it myself until I figured it in my head. I knew what it was to be a coward and what it was to cease being a coward. Now, truly, in actual danger I felt a clean feeling as in a shower. Of course, it was easy now. That was because I no longer cared what happened. I knew it was better to live it so that if you died you had done everything that you could do about your work and your enjoyment of life up to that minute, reconciling the two, which is very difficult." Baker, *Ernest Hemingway*, 609.

214 Hemingway, *Green Hills of Africa*, 275.

215 Lynn, *Hemingway*, 415; Mellow, *Hemingway*, 372.

216 He had long been working on a book about revolutionaries before he wrote *A Farewell to Arms*. In early 1936, he wrote leftist critic John Weaver that he wanted to write a book studying "the mechanics of revolution" just a week before he declared to Maxwell Perkins in a letter that he would never again "notice [the New York bunch], mention them, pay attention to them, nor read them. Nor will I kiss their asses . . . make friends with them, nor truckle to them." Reynolds, *Hemingway: The 1930s*, 225; Bruccoli, *The Only Thing That Counts*, 243.

CHAPTER 4

1 Hemingway, "The Sights of Whitehead Street," in *By-Line: Ernest Hemingway*, 199.

2 "'My jaw's broken,' the cooled one said thickly. Blood was running out of his mouth and down over his chin. 'You're lucky you aren't killed, that wallop he hit you,' the thick-set young man said. 'You run along now.'" Hemingway, *To Have and Have Not*, 121.

3 E. Stone Shiftlet and Kirk Curnutt, "Letters and Literary Tourism: Your Key West Correspondent in 'The Sights of Whitehead Street,'" in Curnutt and Sinclair, *Key West Hemingway*, 224.

4 Hemingway, "The Sights of Whitehead Street," in *By-Line: Ernest Hemingway*, 460.

5 Picture from State Archives of Florida. Cited in Shiftlet and Curnutt, "Letters and Literary Tourism," in Curnutt and Sinclair, *Key West Hemingway*, 237.

6 Hawkins, *Unbelievable Happiness and Final Sorrow*, 174; Hemingway, "The Sights of Whitehead Street," in *By-Line: Ernest Hemingway*, 460.

7 Nonintervention was a misnomer. Intervention had produced destructive effects on Cuban solvency. "Program of Reform for Cuba Urged: Rockefeller-Financed Commission of Ten Releases Report," *Los Angeles Times*, January 27, 1935, A4; "Hands Off Cuba U.S. Is Urged in Survey Report: Study of Conditions Finds Suspicion of Meddling by Washington," *Christian Science Monitor*, January 28, 1935, [illegible].

8 *The Washington Post*, January 27, 1935, B1.

9 "Cuba Death Orgy Told: Former President, Escaping to Florida, Declares Hundreds Slain," Associated Press, March 12, 1935, 1.

10 "Cuba Death Orgy Told," Associated Press.

11 United Press, "Cuba Rounds up 20 Suspects in $300,000 Kidnaping Case," *The Washington Post*, April 11, 1935, 1.

12 Paul Vanorden Shaw, "Victory in Cuba? Death of Antonio Guiteras at the

Hands of Batista Forces Marks Passing of Respected and Feared Liberal from Cuban Scene," *The Washington Post*, March 13, 1935, 6.

13 Hemingway, *Gattorno*, cited in Carr, *Dos Passos*, 33.

14 Hemingway, *Gattorno*, quoted in Poole, *Gattorno*, 35–36.

15 Birmingham, *The Most Dangerous Book*, 11; J. Beall, "Ernest Hemingway's Reading of James Joyce's *Ulysses*," *James Joyce Quarterly* 51, no. 4 (2016): 661–72.

16 Baker, *Ernest Hemingway: A Life Story*, 267.

17 Arnold Samuelson, fragment, circa late 1950s–early 1960s, Arnold Samuelson Papers, cited in Hendrickson, *Hemingway's Boat*, 140.

18 Hendrickson also discovers a letter "buried in an archive" from Arnold to Ernest: "I let her on board. The rubber was irritating, a lousy brand sold downtown, and she asked me to throw it away . . . It was the first time I'd ever been involved in that sort of trouble, she was only seventeen and, not knowing a damned thing about what they can do to fellows who knock up young girls, I imagined the worst, I was afraid of having my folks find out about it and what bothered me the most was the fear there would be a scandal on your boat. The only thing I could give you was absolute loyalty and I hadn't even given you that. I wanted to tell you about it but I didn't have the courage. I knew I would have to quit and go up north." Arnold Samuelson to Ernest Hemingway, cited in Hendrickson, *Hemingway's Boat*, 581.

19 As time went by Arnold kept in contact with Ernest, who threw him some encouragement and an infrequent favor, such as possibly brokering the sale of one of Arnold's *Esquire* articles, "Mexico for Tramps," behind the scenes. Arnold Samuelson to Ernest Hemingway, May 1936, Hemingway Personal Papers.

20 Mice: "What do you mean by good writing as opposed to bad writing? Your correspondent: Good writing is true writing. Mice: How can a writer train himself? Y.C.: Watch what happens today. If we get into a fish see exactly what it is that everyone does. If you get a kick out of it while he is jumping remember back until you see exactly what the action was that gave you the emotion. Hemingway, "Monologue to the Maestro," in *By-Line: Ernest Hemingway*, 1967.

21 Hendrickson, *Hemingway's Student*, 137–39.

22 Robert Lacy, "Icarus," *North Dakota Quarterly* 70, no. 4 (Fall 2013): 214, cited in Hendrickson, *Hemingway's Student*, 36.

23 "The wind was coming very high and in gusts of great strength tearing down trees, branches, etc. . . . the wind was too high to get out and there was no communication with the keys. Telephone, cable, and telegraph all down, too rough for boats to leave. The next day we got across [to Lower Matecumbe

Key] and found things in a terrible shape. Imagine you have read in the papers but nothing could give you an idea of the destruction. Between 700 and 1000 dead . . . Over thirty miles of railway washed and blown away . . . Saw more dead than I'd seen in one place since the lower Piave in June of 1918. Max, you can't imagine it, two women, naked tossed up into the trees by the water, swollen and sinking, their breasts as big as balloons, flies between their legs. Then, by figuring, you locate where it is and recognize them as the two very nice girls who ran a sandwich place and a filling-station three miles from the ferry." Ernest Hemingway to Maxwell Perkins, September 7, 1935, in *Selected Letters*, 421.

24 Ernest Hemingway, "Who Murdered the Vets?" *New Masses*, September 17, 1935, 9–10.

25 During the Great Depression, the veterans were out of work and demonstrated for their war bonus, which was only redeemable after 1945. Responding to their first march, President Herbert Hoover had ordered the army commanded by General Douglas MacArthur to disperse the demonstrators' camps in Washington, DC, in 1932. In 1933, President Roosevelt had defused a second march by promising the veterans jobs in the Civilian Conversation Corps. After this hurricane and widespread criticism, the Congress would finally override Roosevelt's veto and grant the veterans their early bonus in 1936.

26 "They are only human beings; unsuccessful human beings, and all they have to lose is their lives. They are doing coolie labor for a top wage of $45 per month and they have been put down on the Florida Keys where they can't make trouble. If it is hurricane months, sure, but if anything comes up, you can always evacuate them, can't you? . . . when we reached Lower Matacumbe there were bodies floating in the ferry slip." Ernest Hemingway, "Who Murdered the Vets?"

27 Hemingway, *Selected Letters*, 216.

28 Later, Herbert Solo even wrote an article called "Substitution at Left Tackle: Hemingway for Dos Passos" in the *Partisan Review* that asserted that Dos Passos's role at *New Masses* was diminishing while Hemingway's favor with leftist critics like Gold, Hicks, and Cowley was gaining traction. Meyers, *Ernest Hemingway*, 213.

29 Mike Gold, quoted in Dan Monroe, "Hemingway, the Left, and Key West," 93, in Curnutt and Sinclair, *Key West Hemingway*.

30 Hemingway, "Notes on the Next War," in *By-Line: Ernest Hemingway*, 211–13.

31 Hemingway, "The Killers," in *By-Line: Ernest Hemingway*, 215.

32 Hemingway, "The Malady of Power," *By-Line: Ernest Hemingway*, 228.

33 Hemingway, *Dateline: Toronto*, 90.

34 In 1928, Mike Gold called him "too bourgeois to accept the labor world." In 1931 in *The Nation*, Isidor Schneider pointed out that Lenin was opposed to the "baby talk" of the "Hemingway school." Meyers, *Ernest Hemingway*, 163, cited in Milton Cohen, "Beleaguered Modernists," in Curnutt and Sinclair, *Key West Hemingway*, 78. In response to *Green Hills of Africa*, Green called the travelogue boring and suggested that he should abandon the trivial subjects of hunting, fishing, and bullfighting, and instead take up the more important issues in the "contemporary American scene": "I would like to have Hemingway write a novel about a strike . . . because it would do something to Hemingway . . . He is very bitter about the critics and very bold in asserting his independence of them, so bitter and so bold that one detects a sign of bad conscience." Grandville Hicks, quoted in Monroe, "Hemingway, the Left, and Key West," 93.

35 Cited in Lynn, *Hemingway*, 426.

36 Ernest Hemingway to Max Perkins, December 17, 1935, Ernest Hemingway Collection.

37 "Cuba Seeks Reform Without Violence: The Republic, Now Tired of Revolution Wants to Solve Its Many Problems in a Peaceful Atmosphere," *The New York Times*, August 24, 1936, SM5.

38 Jeffrey Caffery to Sumner Welles, October 17, 1935, Welles Papers, "Major Correspondents, 1920–1950," quoted in Argote-Freyre, *Fulgencio Batista*, 187.

39 Ernest Hemingway to Arnold Gingrich, December 8, 1935, quoted in Baker, *Ernest Hemingway: A Life Story*, 616.

40 Hemingway, "Gattorno: Program Note," *Esquire*, May 1936, 111.

41 Poole, *Gattorno*, 34.

42 "I've been working hard. Had a spell when I was pretty gloomy, that was why I didn't write first, and didn't sleep for about three weeks." Ernest Hemingway to Pauline Pfeiffer, January 26, 1936, *Selected Letters*, 436. See also Michael Reynolds, "Hemingway's Home: Depression and Suicide," *American Literature* 57, no. 4 (1985), 600–10.

43 Kert, *The Hemingway Women*, 230, 250; Hawkins, *Unbelievable Happiness and Final Sorrow*, 178.

44 "It was Papa's idea to take the savings. Nobody to pay back and can bring along some more if you wish. Pay yourself a *good* salary. To hell with the bill. Can bring along some more if you wish. Have no end of this filthy money. Just leave me know [if you wish me to bring more money] and don't get another woman, your loving Pauline. Poor Papa, rich papa." Pauline to Ernest Hemingway, May 31, 1934, cited in Kert, *The Hemingway Women*, 263. "Happy birthdays have

come again . . . Please accept our congratulations and the enclosed checks. Make merry with the latter and don't forget to count your blessings. They are many and great. A happy union, lovely children, a fairy godfather, etc." "As usual when I am writing a novel I am making nothing and am probably regarded by the family intelligence service as a loafer. On the other hand when I am all through with the novel I make plenty of money and then, when I am loafing, am regarded with respect as a Money maker." Ernest Hemingway to Mary Pfeiffer, July 18, 1934, cited in Hawkins, *Unbelievable Happines and Final Sorrow*, 174.

45 June–July 1935. Baker, *Ernest Hemingway: A Life Story*, 274–75.

46 The fight had been postponed due to a terrorist attack. "The fight is put off until Feb 2. So come on down then if that's all right to leave Zelda. I'm terribly sorry she was so ill again. And you with a bad liver, lung, and heart. That's damned awful. How are you doing now? We all get those livers. Mine was in a hell of a state about six or seven years ago but got it all cleared up. What is the matter with your heart? And your lung?" Ernest Hemingway to Scott Fitzgerald, December 21, 1935, in *Selected Letters*, 427–29.

47 "I go to sleep wake and hear the clock strike either one or two then lie wide awake and hear three, four, and five. But since I have stopped giving a good goddamn about anything in the past it doesn't bother much and I just lie there and keep perfectly still and rest through it and you seem together almost as much repose as though you slept. This may be no use to you but it works for me." Hemingway, *Selected Letters*.

48 Hemingway, *Selected Letters*.

49 "He is too valuable a piece of property to risk so far away as Havana where there is shooting, etc. It's damned strange the violence that is bred from violence and what a lot of those kids have turned into. Cuba is a hell of an interesting place now and has been for the last five years. Probably before too you say. But only know what I've seen. Anyway am writing a story about this next revolution. Come on down any time and I'll take you over there in the boat and you've get a good story out of it anyway." His instincts were right, for the fight was later canceled. Hemingway, *Selected Letters*.

50 Baker, *Ernest Hemingway: A Life Story*, 283.

51 "Nice Mr. Stevens. This year he came again pleasant like the cholera and first I knew of it my nice sister Ura was coming into the house crying because she had been at a cocktail party at which Mr. Stevens had made her cry by telling her forcefully what a sap I was, no man . . . So headed out into the rainy past twilight and met Mr. Stevens who was just issuing from the door haveing [*sic*]

just said, I learned later, 'By God I wish I had that Hemingway here now I'd knock him out with a single punch.' So who should show up but poor old Papa and Mr. Stevens swung that same fabled punch but fertunatly [*sic*] missed and I knocked all of him down several times and gave him a good beating." Ernest Hemingway to Sara Murphy, February 27, 1936, in *Selected Letters*, 438–39.

52 Ernest Hemingway to Mary Pfeiffer, January 26, 1936, in *Selected Letters*, 435.

53 Ernest Hemingway to Sara Murphy, February 11, 1936, cited in Miller, *Letters from the Lost Generation*, 156.

54 Sara Murphy to Pauline Hemingway, May 11, 1936, cited in Miller, *Letters from the Lost Generation*, 164–65; Brian, *The True Gen*, 98, cited in Reynolds, *Hemingway: The 1930s*, 228.

55 Jane Mason to the Hemingways, May 17, 1935, quoted in A. S. Mason, "An Introduction to Jane Mason's Safari," *The Hemingway Review* 21, no. 2 (2002): 13–21; Kert, *The Hemingway Women*, 270. The term "White Hunter" refers to the professional big game hunters of American or European origin who made their living hosting African safaris for affluent clientel during the first half of the twentieth century.

56 Translation from Spanish: *matrimonio*.

57 Hawkins, *Unbelievable Happiness and Final Sorrow*, 186.

58 When Scribners republished it in 1938 in the collection *The Fifth Column and the First Forty-Nine Stories*, he renamed it "The Capital of the World."

59 Their plan was to publish a collection of his best short stories called *The First Forty-Nine*, which would ultimately appear, along with *The Fifth Column*, in 1938. Ernest Hemingway to Max Perkins, April 9, 1936, *Selected Letters*, 442.

60 A *Cojímar* native and village historian, Joaquín Hernandez Mora authored *Cojímar, pueblo de pescadores* (*Cojímar, village of fishermen*), which contains interviews with many of the fishermen Hemingway knew and reports that Hemingway went out of his way to build friendships with the fishermen of Cojímar: towing them to port as they rowed to shore, buying them a drink at La Terraza, and interrogating them about every detail of their existence. Osvaldo Osvaldo Cernero Piña, "Ova," quoted in Mora, *Cojímar, pueblo de pescadores*, 53.

61 "I decided to write a story. After that, I understood that I wasn't ready. Not because I didn't know everything I needed to know about fishing. I was already an experienced fisherman. I needed another kind of knowledge. So I started studying a village . . . Thirteen years later, when I sat down to write the book, I knew everything there was to know about its people: how they made their living, what they loved, what they hated, what they didn't give a damn about. I knew each family and the life story of each of its members." Conversation with

Genrij Borovik, 1960, cited in Páporov, *Hemingway en Cuba*, 121. Borovik is a Russian journalist who accompanied Vice Minister of the Soviet Union Anastase Mikoyan during his visit with Hemingway at the Finca Vigía on February 8, 1960.

62 "*Preguntaba de todo!* [He asked about everything!] We had many stories to share. He came often, weekends, during the week. Often he was there with Chago, Comema, Mario, '*el bobito*,' [lil' dizzy] Billín, Figurín, El Sordo, Anselmo, Arsenio, and Paco." One day he said to us, '*Estoy escribiendo una novella. Se llamará* El viejo y el mar. *El protagonist es Anselmo.*' [I am writing a novel. It will be called *The Old Man and the Sea*. The protagonist is Anselmo.] He also told us that he would be making a movie and that all the Cojímar fishermen could work in it. They paid us twenty dollars a day. We first fished in the sea. Then we did the land scenes. After we finished the movie, they had a party for us at the Hatuey beer company." Mora, *Cojímar, pueblo de pescadores*, 53.

63 Hemingway, "The Short and Happy Life of Francis Macomber," in *The Complete Short Stories of Ernest Hemingway*, 24.

64 "'Clear cut as a cameo is her Botticelli beauty of pale gold hair and wide set eyes like purple pansies. Her flawless skin is delicate as a wood anemone,' gushed an advertisement for Pond's Extract creams that featured photos of the celebrated beauty." Alane Salierno Mason, "To Love and Love Not," *Vanity Fair*, July 1999.

65 Hemingway, "The Short and Happy Life of Francis Macomber," in *The Complete Short Stories of Ernest Hemingway*, 34.

66 Hemingway, "The Snows of Kilimanjaro," in *The Complete Short Stories of Ernest Hemingway*, 57.

67 Hemingway, *The Complete Short Stories of Ernest Hemingway*, 39.

68 Hemingway, "Snows of Kilimanjaro," in *The Complete Short Stories of Ernest Hemingway*.

69 "Snows of Kilimanjaro," *Esquire*. See also "Snows of Kilimanjaro," Manuscript, Hemingway Personal Papers.

70 Susan J. Wolfe, "The Poor Are Different from You and Me, Masculinity and Class in *To Have and Have Not*," in Curnutt and Sinclair, *Key West Hemingway*, 158–71.

71 Scott Fitzgerald to Ernest Hemingway, July 16, 1936, in Fitzgerald, *A Life in Letters*, 302.

72 Hemingway, *A Moveable Feast*, 62.

73 On this trip, Hemingway spent nearly six weeks in Cuba, returning on May 27. Baker, *Ernest Hemingway*, 285; Hawkins, *Unbelievable Happiness and Final Sorrow*, 188.

74 "If I hadn't been such a bloody fool practicing Catholic, I wouldn't have lost my husband . . . 'Coitus interruptus? I wondered but never asked.'" Pauline Pfeiffer to Mary Welsh, cited in Hemingway, *How It Was*, 266.

75 *Havana Post*, May 10, 1936.

76 Ernest Hemingway to John Dos Passos, April 12, 1936, in *Selected Letters*, 446; Baker, *Ernest Hemingway*, 285–86.

77 "Cuba Orders Inquiry into Wave of Killings: Army Officials Will Investigate Mysterious Deaths of Several Persons in Police Custody," *The New York Times*, May 3, 1936, 38.

78 Kert, *The Hemingway Women*, 274; Ernest Hemingway to Mike Strater, August 11, 1936, Hemingway Personal Papers. See also Hemingway, *My Brother, Ernest Hemingway*, 192–93; Ernest Hemingway to Margaret and Nonie Briggs, July 7, 1936, Hemingway Personal Papers.

79 In the end of it, he was "coming out of a blind squall [and] had Sand Key dead ahead." He had the "recurrence of the old difficulty of keeping voice sounding somewhere between your ankles and your balls. My balls felt very small. When the Capt. of the Cuba heard we'd left to cross that night he told Sully they'd have to give us up." *Key West Citizen*, May 23–28, 1936; Ernest Hemingway to John Dos Passos, June 10, 1936, Ernest Hemingway Collection; Ernest Hemingway to Archibald MacLeish, May 30, 1936, Archibald Macleish Personal Papers, cited in Reynolds, *Hemingway: The 1930s*, 229–30.

80 "Cuba Seeks Reform Without Violence: The Republic, Now Tired of Revolution Wants to Solve Its Many Problems in a Peaceful Atmosphere," *The New York Times*, August 24, 1936, SM5.

81 Russell Porter, "Gomez Promises Freedom in Cuba: A Constitutional Government with Civil Guarantees for All Assured by President," *The New York Times*, July 4, 1936, 1.

82 Farber, *Revolution and Reaction in Cuba, 1933–1960*, 81–82.

83 Carlos Gutierrez, quoted in Hemingway, *My Brother, Ernest Hemingway*, 192–93.

84 Bernice Kert, "First Perspectives on Safari," *Hemingway Review* 21, no 2 (Spring 2002): 21.

85 Antony Mason, quoted in Meyers, *Hemingway*, 256.

86 "Dynamiters Destroy Havana Paper, Killing Four; Truck of explosives discovered at nearby plant. Church wrecked and 500 buildings damaged in blast. 20 are wounded. Loss placed at $1,000,000. Guards stationed at other papers. Traffic is barred near them. Twenty leftists nabbed by police. Rased *El País* is strong supporter of Spanish rebels. Other backs Col. Fulgencio Batista." *The Atlanta Constitution*, September 21, 1936, 1.

87 Ernest Hemingway to Max Perkins, September 26, 1936, in *Selected Letters*, 454.

88 *The Times-Picayune*, November 15, 1936, 1.

89 Hargrove, *Fulgencio Batista*, 53–54; Elections and Events 1935–1951, Latin American Election Statistics, University of San Diego, https://library.ucsd.edu/research-and-collections/collections/notable-collections/latin-american-elections-statistics/Cuba/elections-and-events-19351951.html.

CHAPTER 5

1 Kert, *The Hemingway Women*, 289.

2 "Pauline always tried to be very tolerant of Ernest and any of the girls that sort of made a play for him, or that he seemed entranced with. I don't think he fell in love with other women. He was nice and maybe a lot of women thought he was giving them more attention than what there was; his was in a kidding way." Lorine Thompson, quoted in Bryan, *The True Gen*, 101–02.

3 Rollyson, *Beautiful Exile*, 5.

4 Moorehead, *Gellhorn*, 98.

5 Of Wells, a former lover had said that "he smelled of walnuts and that frisked like a nice animal." Moorehead, *Gellhorn*, 113.

6 "Who is this Martha Gellhorn? . . . her writing burns . . . Hemingway does not write more authentic American speech. Nor can Ernest Hemingway teach Gellhorn anything about the economy of language." Louis Gannett, "Who Is This Martha?" *New York Herald Tribune*, September 25, 1936, quoted in Kert, *The Hemingway Women*, 289.

7 If her review of *The Sun Also Rises*, written on December 8, 1926, in *College News* during her freshman year at Bryn Mawr is any indication. Rollyson, *Beautiful Exile*, 23; Gellhorn, *Selected Letters of Martha Gellhorn*, 45.

8 Hemingway, *To Have and Have Not*, 82.

9 Moorehead, *Gellhorn*, 124.

10 "It's hot falling to pieces and people seem happy. Nothing much goes on languidly a sponge or a turtle gets fished, people live on relief cozily, steal coconuts off the municipal streets, amble out and catch a foul local fish called the grunt, gossip, maunder, sunburn and wait for the lazy easy years to pass. Me, I think all that is very fine indeed and if all the world were sunny I daresay there'd be much less trouble as well as much less of that deplorable thing called officially progress." Gellhorn, *Selected Letters of Martha Gellhorn*, 44–45.

11 Gellhorn, *Selected Letters of Martha Gellhorn*.

12 Gellhorn, *Selected Letters of Martha Gellhorn*.

13 Gellhorn, *Selected Letters of Martha Gellhorn*, 45.

14 Rollyson, *Beautiful Exile*, 61.
15 Hemingway, *By-Line: Ernest Hemingway*, 221.
16 Rollyson, *Beautiful Exile*, 62.
17 Rollyson, *Beautiful Exile.*
18 Kert, *The Hemingway Women*, 290.
19 Martha Gellhorn to Pauline Hemingway, January 14, 1937, Hemingway Personal Papers.
20 Gellhorn, *Selected Letters of Martha Gellhorn*, 45.
21 Gellhorn, *Selected Letters of Martha Gellhorn.*
22 Jack Latimer, interview with Bernice Kert, April 5, 1937, in Kert, *The Hemingway Women*, 293.
23 Pauline Hemingway to Ernest Hemingway, March 15, April 20, and April 27, 1937, Hemingway Personal Papers, cited in Hawkins, *Unbelievable Happiness and Final Sorrow*, 199–200.
24 Steve Paul, "Tropical Iceberg: Cuban Turmoil in the 1930s and Hemingway's *To Have and Have Not*," in Curnutt and Sinclair, *Key West Hemingway*, 129; Scott Donaldson, *By Force of Will*, 94.
25 Paul, "Tropical Iceberg," in Curnutt and Sinclair, *Key West Hemingway*, 142.
26 Cited in Theodore M. O'Leary, "Hemingway-*Esquire* Controversy Involves Rights of Republication," *Kansas City Star*, August 26, 1958; Paul, "Tropical Iceberg" in Curnutt and Sinclair, *Key West Hemingway*, 141–42.
27 "Sugar, the Great White Specter That Fills Cuba with Idleness and Unrest," *Kansas City Star* (September 19, 1933), cited in Paul, "Tropical Iceberg," in Curnutt and Sinclair, *Key West Hemingway*, 131.
28 Donaldson, *By Force of Will*, 121–22, cited in Paul, "Tropical Iceberg," in Curnutt and Sinclair, *Key West Hemingway*, 141–42.
29 Hemingway, *To Have and Have Not*, 102.
30 Hemingway, *To Have and Have Not*, 111.
31 Hemingway, *To Have and Have Not*, 108.
32 "You wouldn't marry me in the church and it broke my mother's heart." Hemingway, *To Have and Have Not.*
33 "Pauline, who had everything she wanted in her husband, sacrificed all else for love. She loved him after seven years of marriage as much as when they first fell in love in Paris. For Ernest, however, both love and truth seemed secondary to his art, and often he appeared to need neither." Hawkins, *Unbelieveable Happiness and Final Sorrow*, 173.
34 Arnold Gingrich, "Scott, Ernest, and Whoever," *Esquire*, October 1973, 374.
35 As scholars Rena Sanderson and Frank Ryan affirmed, the "two loosely inter-

woven plots" of *To Have and Have Not* (1937) were not well received. "Almost all of the critics thought it signaled a decline. There was scattered applause for some features: the style, dialogue, and some of the narrative action; and concerted cheering for others: the bar-room scene; the main character, Harry Morgan; the bedroom scene involving Harry and his wife. However, the most serious and extensive concern of the critics was with two elements in the novel which were inter-related, the social theme and the structure . . . On the whole, the adverse criticism was accurate in pinpointing the faults of the novel: the confusing shifts in point of view, the eagerness to destroy the rich and the powerful, the irrelevant attacks on literature through Richard Gordon, the writer in the novel." Ryan, *The Immediate Critical Reception of Ernest Hemingway*, 25, 27. See also Grimes and Bickford, *Hemingway, Cuba, and the Cuban Works*.

36 Hemingway, *Green Hills of Africa*, 133.

37 Larry Grimes, "Introduction," Armstrong, *The State of Things in Cuba*, xi. See also Ernest Hemingway, "Outline of *To Have and Have Not*," item 212, Hemingway Personal Papers.

38 Larry Grimes, "Introduction," Armstrong, *The State of Things in Cuba*, xi. See also Hemingway, "Outline of *To Have and Have Not*," item 212, Hemingway Personal Papers.

39 Moorehead, *Gellhorn*, 128.

40 Ernest Hemingway to Mr. and Mrs. Pfeiffer, cited in Moorehead, *Gellhorn*, 126.

41 Quoted in Kert, *The Hemingway Women*, 236.

42 Berg, *Max Perkins*, 326.

43 "Hemingway Slaps Eastman in Face," *The New York Times*, August 14, 1937, https://archive.nytimes.com/www.nytimes.com/books/99/07/04/specials/hemingway-slaps.html.

44 Martha Gellhorn to Bill and Annie Davis (Hemingway's old friends with a house near Málaga, Spain), June 1942, in Gellhorn, *Selected Letters of Martha Gellhorn*, 125.

45 Martha Gellhorn to Bill and Annie Davis, June 1942, in Gellhorn, *Selected Letters of Martha Gellhorn*, 130.

46 Koch, *The Breaking Point*, 283.

47 "I want to speak to you about something that seems to me to be serious. A war is still being fought in Spain between people whose side you used to be on and the fascists. If with your hatred of communists you feel justified in attacking for money, the people who are still fighting that war I think you should at least get your facts straight . . . So this is the end of the letter if you ever make any money and want to pay me any on what you owe (not the Uncle Gus money

when you were ill. I mean others, just small ones, afterwards) why not send thirty dollars if you make three hundred or twenty or ten or any damn thing, I've got uses for it now. Now I won't send the letter because of why. Because of old friends. Good old friends you know. Knife you in the back for a quarter. Anybody else charge fifty cents. So long, Dos. Hope you're always happy. I imagine you always will be. Must be a dandy life. Used to be happy myself. Will be again. Good old friends. Always happy with the good old friends." Ernest Hemingway to John Dos Passos, circa March 26, 1938, in *Selected Letters*, 463–64.

48 Bookish, balding, tall and ungainly, sunny in temperament, too trusting of others' good will, Dos Passos was the sort of man who aroused Hemingway's sadistic appetite. "White as the under half of an unsold flounder at 11 o'clock in the morning just before the fish market shuts" was one of Hemingway's fictionalized descriptions of his old friend. Hemingway seems to have needed to destroy a friendship or a marriage every few years just to keep functioning. In Madrid he did both." George Packer, "The Spanish Prisoner," *The New Yorker*, October 31, 2005, https://www.newyorker.com/magazine/2005/10/31/the-spanish-prisoner; Ernest Hemingway, "Treachery at Aragon," *Ken*, June 1938.

49 Hawkins, *Unbelieveable Happiness and Final Sorrow*, 204.

50 Hawkins, *Unbelieveable Happiness and Final Sorrow.*

51 Kert, *The Hemingway Women*, 312.

52 Kert, *The Hemingway Women.*

53 "Probably feel cheerful as hell tomorrow. Mr. H. has great elasticity. Excuse lousy gloomy letter. Look at beautiful checks and rejoice. Much love to you and all my best to Paul. I admire you both very much." Ernest Hemingway to Hadley Mowrer, January 31, 1938, in *Selected Letters*, 462.

54 Martha Gellhorn, "Spain and Her Lesson of War," speaking tour, Oak Park's Ninetieth Century Club, *Oak Leaves* (February 3, 1938) on meeting taking place January 31; Grace Hemingway to Ernest Hemingway, February 3, 1938, quoted in Reynolds, *Hemingway: The 1930s*, 283.

55 Dan Brennean, quoted in Rollyson, *Beautiful Exile*, 87.

56 Ernest Hemingway to Max Perkins, mid-February 1938, in Bruccoli, *The Only Thing That Counts*, 256.

57 Baker, *Ernest Hemingway: Life Story* 324; Hemingway, *My Brother, Ernest Hemingway*, 213.

58 Pauline Pfeiffer to Ernest Hemingway, April 19, 1938, Hemingway Personal Papers.

59 Martha Gellhorn to Edna Gellhorn, May 26, 1938, in Gellhorn, *Selected Letters of Martha Gellhorn*, 62.

60 Quoted in Poole, *Gattorno*, 35, 41.

61 Poole, *Gattorno*, 40.

62 The author.

63 Hawkins, *Unbelieveable Happiness and Final Sorrow*, 209.

64 Ernest Hemingway to Max Perkins, July 12, 1938, in *Selected Letters*, 471.

65 Pauline Pfeiffer to Ernest Hemingway, September 2, 1938, Hemingway Personal Papers, quoted in Hawkins, *Unbelieveable Happiness and Final Sorrow*, 211.

66 Pauline to Ernest Hemingway, September 17, 1938, Hemingway Personal Papers, quoted in Hawkins, *Unbelieveable Happiness and Final Sorrow*, 211.

67 Martha Gellhorn to David Gurewitsch, 1950, in Gellhorn, *Selected Letters of Martha Gellhorn*, 222.

68 Verna Kale, "*The Fifth Column*: A Play by Ernest Hemingway (Review)," *The Hemingway Review* 27, no. 2 (Spring 2008): 131–34.

69 Pauline Pfeiffer to Ernest Hemingway, October 18, 1938, Hemingway Personal Papers.

70 Hemingway, *Misadventures of a Fly Fisherman*, 30–31.

71 Gellhorn, *Selected Letters of Martha Gellhorn*, 66.

72 Fuentes, *Hemingway in Cuba*, 132.

73 "The Spanish people will rise again as they have always risen before against tyranny. The dead do not need to rise. They are a part of the earth now and the earth can never be conquered. For the earth endureth forever. It will outlive all systems of tyranny. Those who have entered it honorably, and no men ever entered earth more honorably than those who died in Spain, already have achieved immortality."

74 Bernice Kert, quoted in Aaron Latham, "Papa's Mother and Wives," Book Review Desk, *The New York Times*, July 17, 1983, 8.

CHAPTER 6

1 Reynolds, *Hemingway: The 1930s*, 318, Moorehead, *Gellhorn*, 157.

2 Martha Gellhorn to Eleanor Roosevelt, March 18, 1939, in Gellhorn, *Selected Letters of Martha Gellhorn*, 87–88.

3 Hemingway, *Selected Letters*, 479.

4 What began as the short story "Under the Ridge" later expanded to become *For Whom the Bell Tolls*. Ernest Hemingway to Max Perkins, March 25, 1939, and Max Perkins to Ernest Hemingway, November 21, 1939, in Bruccoli, *The Only Thing That Counts*, 274–75.

5 Ernest Hemingway to Tommy Shevlin, April 4, 1939, in *Selected Letters*, 484.

6 R. Ybarra, "Influence of U.S. Strongest in Cuba," *The New York Times*, March 7, 1939, 10.

7 Fans.

8 In the San Francisco de Paula neighborhood.

9 While visiting San Francisco de Paula, I first heard the story of Hemingway befriending the neighborhood children during an interview with Óscar Blas Fernández, who was seven years old when Hemingway arrived that first day, but was seventy-seven at the time of the interview. Villarreal and Villarreal, *Hemingway's Cuban Son*, 24; Fuentes, *Hemingway in Cuba*, 26.

10 Some fresh water with lemon. When Miguel Oasua Pascual y Berguer, a Catalan from Gerona whose wife, Teresa Serra, was a Cuban of Catalonian origin, purchased "Lookout Hill" in 1886, he was hopeful that the change of scenery some distance from the city would help his wife to recover from the loss of two children. It was the same year that the Spanish, under pressure from Creole landowners and slaves of mixed blood, abolished slavery on the island. Once they had built the villa, the Catalan couple moved in the following year, and lived there for sixteen years with their surviving son, Pedro, abiding the Spanish soldiers who came to occupy that strategic hill during the unending War of Independence. When the Americans intervened and the Spanish lost the Spanish-American War in 1898, the Spaniards set fire to the hill, forcing the Pascual family to rebuild. Luckily, much of the original structure remained intact, and so the home could be restored. When Pedro married in 1903, he left the bitterness of the Finca behind him, moving his wife and aging parents, *los viejos*, into the city center, looking for opportunity. Though they originally intended to maintain the villa as a retreat, postwar necessity dictated that they sell it to a foreigner named D'Orn two years later, whose business was real estate. Joseph D'Orn Duchamp de Castaigne had lived in the property, but unable to maintain it, he moved into the city and advertised it in a newspaper. Interview with Sara Pascual Canosa, conducted by Maximo Gomez Noda, Havana, October 1, 1985, quoted in G. R. Ferrero, "Museo Finca Vigía Celebrates Its 45th Birthday," *The Hemingway Review* 27, no. 2 (Spring 2008): 16–34.

11 Ferrero, "Museo Finca Vigía Celebrates Its 45th Birthday."

12 "I have taken possession of my Finca. I had a moment of acute depression bordering on despair yesterday, which was produced by protracted housecleaning and shopping at the ten cent store for kitchen ware. I'm not much of a house woman (*femme d'intérieur*, as the French so sweetly say) and the week's work of getting a place habitable seems to me far more trying than a week at the front

line, or a week working myself to the bone getting an article in shape. I got very gloomy, thinking now I am caught, now at last I have possessions (and I have feared them and fled them all my life), and what in God's name shall I do with this place now that I have it. So I felt that the world was at an end, I had a house and would never write again but would spend the remainder of my life telling servants to scrub the bathroom floors and buy fresh paper for the shelves . . . When I was living in a $4 per week room in Albany, just after I left Bryn Mawr, working as a cub reporter on the *Times Union*, I never dreamed I would write myself into a grove of palms and bamboos and flamboyant trees, nor a terrace covered with bougainvillea, nor a swimming pool: and I can't believe it yet." Martha Gellhorn to Eleanor Roosevelt, March 18, 1939, in Gellhorn, *Selected Letters of Martha Gellhorn*, 74.

13 "Am down to 198 pounds. Have place where can play tennis and win and happy and healthy although always that hollow in the middle of yourself daily emptied out feeling you get when working well on a long book. Wish me luck Max. I find I know a lot more than when I used to write and think that is maybe what makes it easier in the end but it is still a very tough business, but working the way I do now I feel as happy and as good as when I was going good on A Farewell to Arms." Ernest Hemingway to Max Perkins, March 25, 1939, in Bruccoli, *The Only Thing That Counts*, 274.

14 *Pilar* Logs, Hemingway Personal Papers.

15 Hemingway, *Misadventures of a Fly Fisherman*, 35.

16 Diliberto, *Hadley*, 264,

17 Ernest Hemingway to Mrs. Paul Pfeiffer, December 12, 1939, *Selected Letters*, 499.

18 Hemingway, *Selected Letters*, 500.

19 Hawkins, *Unbelieveable Happiness and Final Sorrow*, 222.

20 He would not bring the *Pilar* down until the end of March. Ernest Hemingway to Maxwell Perkins, circa February 4–11, 1940, "Will have the boat over here at the end of March," *Selected Letters*, 502.

21 Rollyson, *Beautiful Exile*, 108–09.

22 Martha Gellhorn to Ernest Hemingway, January 2, 1940, quoted in Kert, *The Hemingway Women*, 334.

23 Ernest Hemingway to Maxwell Perkins, January 14, 1940, in Bruccoli, *The Only Thing That Counts*, 277. "Well here is your regular Sunday hangover letter. We won again at the pelota last night and stayed up till three a.m. So today will have to take Marty to the movies as a present for being drunk Saturday night I guess. Started on absinthe, drank a bottle of good red wine with dinner, shifted

to vodka in town before pelota game and then battened it down with whiskys and sodas until 3 a.m. Feel good today. But not like working." Ernest Hemingway to Maxwell Perkins, circa February 4–11, 1940, *Selected Letters*, 502.

24 Ernest Hemingway to Max Perkins, March 25, 1939, in Bruccoli, *The Only Thing That Counts*, 274.

25 "It's fine out here in the country. There are quite a lot of quail on the place and lots of doves. Patrick and Gregory were over for the holidays and they had a fine time. I wish you could see this joint. Hope can renew the lease in June. I don't care about going to war now. Would like to live a while and have fun after this book and write some stories. Also like the kids very much and we have good fun together. Also would like to have a daughter. I guess that sounds funny to a man with five of them but I would like to have one very much." Ernest Hemingway to Maxwell Perkins, circa February 4–11, 1940, *Selected Letters*, 502.

26 Max Perkins to Ernest Hemingway, January 18 and 19, 1940, in Bruccoli, *The Only Thing That Counts*, 279.

27 Martha Gellhorn to To Whom It May Concern, January 19, 1940, in Gellhorn, *Selected Letters of Martha Gellhorn*, 81.

28 Villarreal and Villarreal, *Hemingway's Cuban Son*, 37.

29 Villarreal and Villarreal, *Hemingway's Cuban Son*.

30 Martha Gellhorn to Hadley Richardson Mowrer, April 10, 1940, in Kert, *The Hemingway Women*, 341. See also Hemingway, *Misadventures of a Fly Fisherman*; Hadley Richardson Mowrer, interview, quoted in Allie Baker, "Luck, Pluck, and Serendipity: Bumby's Wartime Experience," The Hemingway Project, February 13, 2014, http://www.thehemingwayproject.com/2018/08/17/luck-pluck-and-serendipity-bumbys-wartime-experience-with-hadley-audio/.

31 Ernest Hemingway to Maxwell Perkins, April 21, 1940, *Selected Letters*, 504.

32 Maxwell Perkins to Ernest Hemingway, April 22 and 24, 1940, in Bruccoli, *The Only Thing That Counts*, 283.

33 Ernest Hemingway to Max Perkins, April 21, 1940, quoted in Kert, *The Hemingway Women*, 342.

34 Hemingway, *For Whom the Bell Tolls*, 305, 322, 325.

35 Pauline Hemingway to Gerald and Sara Murphy, April 23, 1940, in Miller, *Letters from the Lost Generation*, 249–50.

36 Ernest Hemingway to Carlos Baker, 1951, quoted in Reynolds, *Hemingway: The Final Years*, 242.

37 Ernest Hemingway to Malcolm Cowley, May 14, 1944, and July 15, 1948, the Maurice F. Nelville Collection of Modern Literature, Pt II.

38 Villarreal and Villarreal, *Hemingway's Cuban Son*, 40.

39 As biographer Kenneth Lynn puts it, Hemingway had now become "an overbearing know-it-all" whose deteriorating literary production "testified" to the invasion of Hemingway's serious writing by his myth." Lynn, *Hemingway*, 396, cited in Gail Sinclair, "The End of Some Things: A Decade of Loss," in Curnutt and Sinclair, *Key West Hemingway*, 66.

40 Miller, *Letters from the Lost Generation*, 100.

41 Miller, *Letters from the Lost Generation*.

42 The ball.

43 Affection.

44 Fuentes, *Hemingway in Cuba*, 36.

45 Mayito Menocal, cited in Páporov, *Hemingway en Cuba*, 21.

46 Ernesto trusted Mayito enough to leave him alone with youngest son, Gregory, to go to the Pan American to listen to the baseball game on the radio, as he mentions in a letter to his second son, Patrick. Hemingway, *Selected Letters*, 542.

47 Interview in Coral Gables, Florida, 1983, in Meyers, *Hemingway*, 331–32.

48 Villarreal and Villarreal, *Hemingway's Cuban Son*, 94.

49 *Prensa Libre*, June 1945, cited in Rodríguez, *Hemingway*, 32.

50 Fuentes, *Hemingway in Cuba*, 58.

51 Quoted in Fuentes, *Hemingway in Cuba*, 187–88.

52 Fuentes, *Hemingway in Cuba*, 187.

CHAPTER 7

1 The title phrase from Gregory Hemingway's sardonic memoire, *Papa*.

2 "It culminates a writing career of 19 years . . . Today, in prime physical vigor, 210 lb. in weight, a good boxer, a crack wing shot and an excellent solder, he is an acknowledged master of his art. His style, so terse and clean, yet vivid and rich, has been imitated by many, but matched by none." *Life*, January 6, 1941.

3 They would later buy two more parcels of neighboring land from the previous owner and in March 1956 acquire a third parcel from a neighbor named Roberto Salmón. *Notary of Guanabacoa* 239, 41, quoted in Páporov, *Hemingway en Cuba*, 8.

4 Mark Ott, "Hemingway's Hawaiian Honeymoon," *The Hemingway Review* (Fall 1997): 58.

5 Gellhorn, *Travels with Myself and Another*, 11.

6 "I was very embarrassed because I had never made love with three girls. Two girls is fun even though *you* do not like it. It's not twice as good as one girl but it is different and it is fun anyway when you are drunk. But three girls is a lot of girls and I was embarrassed." Hemingway, *Islands in the Stream*, 212.

7 Reynolds, *Hemingway: The Final Years*, 44.

8 Spruille Braden, quoted in Moorehead, *Gellhorn*, 210.

9 Latin mutation of the Greek word "phalanx," *falange* refers to the famed battle formation demanding infantry to tightly assemble themselves and advance with shields, armor, helmets, and long spears to make themselves impervious to foreign penetrations. Borrowing its title from this effective battle formation, the Falange Movement became synonymous with the movement of fascism in Spain. José Antonio Primo de Rivera, son of General Primo de Rivera, founded the party, which emphasized Spanish traditions and combined them with Spanish ideology. The Falangists were precursors to the Spanish Nationalists led by the charismatic army leader General Franco. In 1936, José Antonio Primo de Rivera was seized and executed by the Republicans, the opposing army loyal to Spanish communal values at the outset of the Spanish Civil War. But the term "Falangist" continued being used more broadly to refer to Spanish fascists during and after the war.

10 Spruille Braden, quoted in Moorehead, *Gellhorn*, 210.

11 In their reports, they assigned Hemingway the code name "Argo" after Jason and the Argonaut's vessel in Greek mythology. Reynolds, *Writer, Sailor, Soldier, Spy*, 215.

12 Hemingway would later remark irreverently that he had an embarrassing case of "premature[ly ejaculated] fascism." Keneth Kinnamon, "Hemingway and Politicsm," in Donaldson, *The Cambridge Companion to Hemingway*, 149–69.

13 "Chronicling Ernest Hemingway's Relationship with the Soviets," interview with Nicholas Reynolds, *Weekend Edition*, NPR, March 18, 2017.

14 Report from Agent Leddy to J. Edgar Hoover, FBI file, October 8–9, 1942, https://vault.fbi.gov/ernest-miller-hemingway/ernest-hemingway-part-01-of-01/view. See also Mitgang, *Dangerous Dossiers*, 61–71, and Páporov, *Hemingway*, 57.

15 Nicholas Reynolds, "A Spy Who Made His Own Way: Ernest Hemingway, Wartime Spy," *Studies in Intelligence* 56, no. 2 (June 2012): 11.

16 *The New York Times*, June 28, 1942, 21. Commander C. Alphonso Smith, "Battle of the Caribbean," *United States Naval Institute Proceedings* (September 1954): 976–82, quoted in Reynolds, *Hemingway: The Final Years*, 56–57.

17 "Hit 5 Ships in U-Boat Raids: Caribbean Isle Is Attacked by Submarine," *Chicago Daily Tribune*, March 14, 1942, 1.

18 Arthur Krock, "The Program for Simplified Sub-Chasers and Escorts," *The New York Times*, June 19, 1942, C22.

19 Mort, *The Hemingway Patrols*, 114–221.

20 Villarreal and Villarreal, *Hemingway's Cuban Son*, 59.

21 Cirules, *Hemingway the Stranger*, 105.

22 Summer 1943, in Gellhorn, *Selected Letters of Martha Gellhorn*, 145; Rollyson, *Beautiful Exile*, 138.

23 Mort, *The Hemingway Patrols*, 129.

24 Ernest Hemingway, cited in Rollyson, *Beautiful Exile*, 136.

25 Summer 1943, in Gellhorn, *Selected Letters of Martha Gellhorn*, 145.

26 "You have been married so much and so long that I don't believe it can touch you where you live and that is your strength. It would be terrible if it did because you are so much more important than the women you happen to be married to. I would like to be young and poor and in Milan and with you and not married to you. I think that I always wanted to feel in some way like a woman and if I ever did, it was the first winter in Madrid . . . Bug my dearest, how I long for you now. I wish we could stop it all now. The prestige, the possessions, the position, the knowledge, the victory. And by a miracle, return together under the arch at Milan . . . you so brash in your motorcycle sidecar and I badly dressed, fierce, loving. That loud reckless disheveled girl was a better person. I only write to you tonight as I feel or think, because why not?" Martha Gellhorn to Ernest Hemingway, June 28, 1943, Hemingway Personal Papers.

27 Ernest Hemingway to Martha Gellhorn Hemingway, July 10, 1943, Museum Ernest Hemingway Collection; Winston Guest interview with Reynolds, *Hemingway: Final Years*, 78.

28 Ernest Hemingway to Martha Gellhorn, midsummer 1943, Museum Ernest Hemingway Collection.

29 "My dearest beloved Bug . . . I have never seen it so dazzingly beautiful . . . the house is a lovely pink; it was never prettier, around the pool looks like I don't know what, something so fresh and sweet. And Mother's room is really a dream." Martha Gellhorn to Ernest Hemingway, July 9 and July 28, 1943, in Gellhorn, *Selected Letters of Martha Gellhorn*, 145, 148.

30 Martha Gellhorn to Ernest Hemingway, October 13, 1943, quoted in Kert, *The Hemingway Women*, 383.

31 January 22 and February 28, 1944, quoted in Moorehead, *Gellhorn*, 238.

32 Hemingway, *Papa*, cited in Wagner-Martin, *Ernest Hemingway: A Literary Life*, 138.

33 Interview with Bernice Kert, *The Hemingway Women*, 390, quoted in Rollyson, *Beautiful Exile*, 149.

34 Ernest Hemingway to Martha Gellhorn, August 28, 1940, Museum Ernest Hemingway Collection.

35 Martha Gellhorn to Ernest Hemingway, October 29, 1943, Bernice Kert Collection, John F. Kennedy Library, quoted in Kert, *The Hemingway Women*, 385.

36 Ernest Hemingway to Patrick Hemingway, Archibald Macleish, Maxwell Perkins, and Edna Gellhorn, 1943, quoted in Moorehead, *Gellhorn*, 228.

37 Rollyson, *Beautiful Exile*, 149.

38 "You will feel deprived as a writer if this is all over and you have not had a share in it . . . the place is crying out for you, not for immediate stuff but for the record . . . I beg you to think this over very seriously . . . I say this not only because I miss you and want you here, but I hate not sharing it with you . . . It would be a terrible mistake to miss this, for both of us . . . I would never be able to tell you about it because I could never do the things that you can. You would be the one who would see for us." Martha Gellhorn to Ernest Hemingway, December 12, 1943, Bernice Kert Collection, John F. Kennedy Library, cited in Kert, *The Hemingway Women*, 388.

39 Martha Gellhorn to Ernest Hemingway, December 13, 1943, Bernice Kert Collection, John F. Kennedy Library, cited in Kert, *The Hemingway Women*, 389. See also Rollyson, *Beautiful Exile*, 148.

40 Ernest Hemingway to Jack Hemingway, August 2, 1942, Hemingway Personal Papers.

41 Cited in Páporov, *Hemingway*; Fuentes, *Hemingway in Cuba*; and Rodríguez, *Hemingway*.

42 Osmar Mariño Rodríguez interviews with Fernando Campoamor, 1996, in Rodríguez, *Hemingway*, and my subsequent interviews with Rodríguez in Havana, May 2008.

43 Páporov, *Hemingway*, 55–59.

44 Ilse Bulit, "Hemingway, Leopoldina, María Ignacia, y Yo," parts I–V, *SEMlac Cuba*, July-August 2009, redsemlac-cuba.net/Criterios/hemingway-leopoldina-mariaignacia-y-yo-i.html.

45 Leopoldina's lover and the father of her son, Alberto Barraqué, was the scion of an important Cuban political family. His own father, Jesús María Barraqué, had been a member of Gerardo Machado's cabinet. Although Leopoldina and Alfredo Barraqué never married, Leopoldina often employed his last name in order to borrow its legitimacy and aristocracy for herself and their son, Alberto, Jr., quoted in Bulit, "Hemingway, Leopoldina, Maria Ignacia y Yo."

46 Virgin of Regla.

47 F. R. Dodge, Commander-in Chief, Gulf Sea Frontier, US Navy, "Declassified United States Navy Report Regarding the Sinking of U-176," May 24, 1943,

National Archives and Record Administration, in Adelphi Road Washington Ship Yard Record Relating to U-boat Warfare, 1939–1945.

48 Martha Gellhorn to Ernest Hemingway, November 10 and December 9, 1943, in Gellhorn, *Selected Letters of Martha Gellhorn*, 155; Rollyson, *Beautiful Exile*, 146–47.

49 Martha Gellhorn, quoted in Kert, *The Hemingway Women*, 375. The only Cuban national accredited with sinking a German U-Boat, Mario Ramírez Delgado, seemed to think that Ernest was a "playboy who hunted submarines off the Cuban coast as a whim." Lynn, *Hemingway*, 502–03.

50 Edna Gellhorn to Ernest Hemingway, January 9, 1944, and Ernest Hemingway to Martha Gellhorn, January 13 and 31, 1944, Hemingway Personal Papers.

51 Hemingway, *Islands in the Stream*, 75.

52 Hemingway, *Islands in the Stream*, 52–53.

53 See Hemingway, *Misadventures of a Fly Fisherman*, 220–21.

54 Paul Hendrickson, "Papa's Boys," *The Washington Post*, July 30, 1987, washingtonpost.com/archive/lifestyle//07/30/papas-boys/dee92b89-5da5-4dbe-b9f5-4a3f42cf70d8/?utm_term=.4aecdfc2ea63>.

55 Hendrickson, "Papa's Boys."

56 Hemingway, *Islands in the Stream*, 54.

57 Jack Hemingway, quoted in Hemingway, *Islands in the Stream*, 54.

58 Hemingway's buddies at the club had a medal engraved: "To Gigi as a token of admiration from his fellow shooters, *Club de Cazadores del Cerro*." Ernest wrote, "At nine years old [he exaggerated by two years], he beat 24 grown men, all good shots, and many of them very fine shots, shooting live pigeons." In the papers, he was known as "el joven fenómeno americano and day before yesterday an article called him "el popularísimo Gigi," so said his father. "Now we say go down to the post-office and get the mail popularíssimo or time for bed, popularíssimo. But inside himself he is very happy to be the popularísimo and he shoots like a little angel." Ernest Hemingway to Hadley Mowrer, July 23, 1942, in *Selected Letters*, 535–36.

59 "Turgenev should have won the prize. He wrote the story. I merely copied it, changing the setting and the names, from a book I assumed Papa hadn't read because some of the pages were still stuck together." Hemingway, *Papa*, 106.

60 Ian Ball, "Death Stranger Than Fiction for Hemingway's Tormented Son," *The Telegraph*, October 7, 2001. telegraph.co.uk/news/worldnews/northamerica/usa/1358754/Death-stranger-than-fiction-for-Hemingways-tormented-son.html; "Transsexual Son Haunts Hemingway Clan," *The Independent*, Sep-

tember 27, 2003, independent.co.uk/news/world/americas/transsexual-son-haunts-hemingway-clan-88844.html.

61 "Boise continued with his lovemaking . . . Boise was happy . . . Your cat, Boise, loves you . . . We ought to have that cat Boise here. He'd be proud of you." Hemingway, *Islands in the Stream*, 203.

62 Hemingway, *Islands in the Stream*, 179.

63 Villarreal and Villarreal, *Hemingway's Cuban Son*, 58.

64 Hemingway, *Islands in the Stream*, 188.

65 A half-century of misery in the Cuban reality.

66 Páparov, *Hemingway in Cuba*, 40. Author's translation.

67 "I was not received with loving tender care though I was absolutely exhausted; the flight from Tangiers in the freezing aluminum belly of a bomber with a few sick G.I.'s being sent home was bad enough. But Ernest began at once to rave at me. The word is not too strong. He woke me when I was trying to sleep to bully, snarl, mock—my crime really was to have been at war when he had not, but that was not how he put it . . . I was supposedly insane, I only wanted excitement and danger. I had no responsibility to anyone, I was selfish beyond belief . . . it never stopped and believe me, it was fierce and ugly. I put it to him that I was going back, whether he came or not, and through Roald Dahl, he could get a plane seat." Martha Gellhorn, February 15, 1982, cited in Kert, *The Hemingway Women*, 392, and Lynn, *Hemingway*, 505.

68 Wagner-Martin, *Ernest Hemingway: A Literary Life*, 138.

69 Reynolds, *Hemingway: The Final Years*, 92.

70 Hemingway, *My Brother, Ernest Hemingway*, 229–40.

71 Hemingway and Brennen, *Hemingway in Cuba*, 84.

CHAPTER 8

1 Originally published in 1976, fifteen years after her famed husband's passing.

2 Hemingway, *How It Was*, 94.

3 Hemingway, *How It Was*.

4 Hemingway, *How It Was*, 95.

5 "I don't know you, Mary. But I want to marry you. You are very alive. You're beautiful, like a May fly." Silence. "I want to marry you now, and I hope to marry you sometime. Sometime you may want to marry me." A long silence. "Don't be silly," I said finally, "if you're not joking. We're both married and we don't even know each other." "This war may keep us apart for a while," Ernest plowed on softly. "But we must begin our Combined Operations." His voice

was calm, I thought, sad. Resigned, maybe. "You are very premature," I said. Hemingway, *How It Was*, 95–96.

6 Hemingway, *How It Was*, 96.

7 Marie Brenner, "Robert Capa's Longest Day," *Vanity Fair*, June 2014, www.vanityfair.com/culture/2014/06/photographer-robert-capa-d-day.

8 Brenner, "Robert Capa's Longest Day."

9 The picture appeared in Brenner, "Robert Capa's Longest Day."

10 "If he really had a concussion, he could hardly have been drinking with his pals or even receiving them. He did not look the least ill anyway." Martha Gellhorn, quoted in Kert, *The Hemingway Women*, 398.

11 Martha Gellhorn Hemingway to Ernest Hemingway, June 7, 1944, quoted in Kert, *The Hemingway Women*, 406.

12 Have a party.

13 David Hendricks, "During the War Hemingway Was Good at Being Hemingway," *My San Antonio*, January 12, 2017, mysanantonio.com/entertainment/arts-culture/books/article/During-war-Hemingway-was-good-at-being-Hemingway-10850684.php.

14 James H. Meredith, "Hemingway's U.S. 3rd Army Inspector General Interview During World War II," (introduction), *The Hemingway Review* 18, no. 2 (1999): 91–94; Meyers, *Hemingway*; 409–10.

15 William Cote, "Ernest Hemingway's Murky World War II 'Combat' Experience," *The Hemingway Review* (September 22, 2002): 88–104.

16 Hemingway, *How It Was*, 158.

17 DiEugenio, *Destiny Betrayed*, 8.

18 "Cuba: Batista at Work," *Newsweek*, March 24, 1952, 60, 62.

19 Allie Baker, "Luck, Pluck, and Serendipity: Bumby's Wartime Experience," *The Hemingway Project*, February 13, 2014. See also Hemingway, *Misadventures of a Fly Fisherman*.

20 He complained of headaches and colds to Lanham and to Mary Welsh in his letters from this period. Hemingway Personal Papers, cited in Michael Reynolds, "A Brief Biography," in Wagner-Martin, *A Historical Guide to Hemingway*, 42–43.

21 "I got in 8 months, 26 Krauts (armed) sures. No way of counting possibles and did nothing I was ashamed of except when we were athwart their escape route . . . I shot at what looked like a usual kraut with an M-1 and turned out to be a 17-year-old boy when we checked him for papers." Ernest Hemingway to Archibald McLeich, August 27, 1948, box 7, folder 23, Carlos Baker Collection

of Ernest Hemingway, cited in Cote, "Ernest Hemingway's Murky World War II 'Combat' Experience." In interviews, two senior officers from the First Army would tell Ernest Hemingway's first biographer that the writer distinguished himself through acts of bravery repelling German soldiers with a machine gun during an ambush and killing "a few." Cololnel Charles Lanham and General John F. Ruggles, quoted in Baker, *Ernest Hemingway*, 433, 436, 638.

22 "I have 22 wounds that are visible (probably beside the hidden one) and have killed 122 sures besides the possibles. The last, not the last, but the one made me feel the worst, was a soldier in German uniform with helmet rideing [*sic*] on a bicycle along their escape route toward Aachen they [that] we had gotten astride of above St. Quentin." Ernest Hemingway to Arthur Miezner, June 2, 1950, *Selected Letters*, 697–8. The manuscript of the unpublished short story "Black Ass at a Crossroads" (Hemingway Personal Papers) contains a similar story. See also Ernest Hemingway to Charles Scribner, August 27, 1949, *Selected Letters*, 672.

23 Fuentes, *Hemingway in Cuba*, 19.

24 Rodenberg, *The Making of Ernest Hemingway*, 33.

25 Fuentes, *Hemingway in Cuba*, 60.

26 "I am as committed as an armoured column in a narrow defile where no vehicle can turn and without parallel roads . . . Please love me very much and always and take care of me Small Friend the way Small Friends take care of Big Friends—high in the sky and shining and beautiful." Ernest Hemingway to Mary Welsh, September 13, 1944, *Selected Letters*, 558–69. See also Reynolds, *Hemingway: The Final Years*, 127–28.

27 Martha Gellhorn, Mario Menocal, and Patrick Hemingway, quoted in Baker, *Ernest Hemingway*, 635, and Kert, *The Hemingway Women*, 411.

28 "He insisted that I have dinner with him; I did think we could talk about divorce. Instead he had a band of his younger soldier pals from 'his' regiment and in front of them insulted and mocked me throughout dinner. They were miserable and slowly left and when I could, I got up from the banquette seat where I'd been hemmed in and fled." Martha Gellhorn, quoted in Kert, *The Hemingway Women*, 411.

29 Kert, *The Hemingway Women*.

30 "All smashed up with terrible headaches she would not do anything for a man that we would do for a dog . . . I made a great mistake on her—or else she changed very much—I think probably both—But mostly the later. I hate to lose anyone who can look so lovely and who we taught to shoot and write so well. But I have torn up my tickets on her and would be glad to never see her

again . . . Thought I would write you about Marty so that you would know what the score is." Ernest Hemingway to Buck Lanham, September 15, 1944, Museum Ernest Hemingway Collection.

31 Martha Gellhorn to Edna Gellhorn, quoted in Moorehead, *Gellhorn*, 264.

32 Noel Monks to Mary Welsh, February 8, 1945, Mary Hemingway Personal Papers.

33 Ernest Hemingway to Hadley Richardson, April 24, 1945, *Selected Letters*, 592.

CHAPTER 9

1 A year before, facists officials had executed fifteen partisans and displayed their bodies in Milan's Piazzale Loreto, so Partisans retributed by hanging the bodies of Mussolini and his entourage from their boots and later renamed the square Piazza Quindici Martiri to honor those who died there: Fifteen Martyrs' Square.

2 "My thick northern Europe army uniform was much too heavy for those latitudes; but I wore it to Havana as Ernest had instructed me to do. He was shaved, combed, and crisp in a white guayabera." Hemingway, *How It Was*, 154.

3 "Inside the Finca's wooden gate we drove through a bower of scarlet flowers, up a little rise and half around a circular driveway from which rose a prodigious tier of broad old stone steps, with an enormous [Ceiba] tree growing out of one rise. The house seemed to have grown gradually out of its hilltop. Its roof and a projecting terrace were laden with flowers and the air smelled of plants growing. I thought of Jane Austen and Louisa May Alcott and country vicars' manses and fell instantly in love. 'A ruin,' Ernest said. 'It's beautiful. It's wonderful.' Afternoon sunlight was brightening the inside, making the house look hospitable through its open doors and windows. Juan and the butler were bringing my bags into the sitting room. 'You can stay in the Little House if you like,' said Ernest. 'It's where the children stay, but it's ready for you.' He was polite and distant. 'Where you prefer.' Hemingway, *How It Was*, 154–55.

4 Hemingway, *How It Was*, 155.

5 Hemingway, *How It Was*, 200.

6 Hemingway, *How It Was*, 156.

7 Baker, *Ernest Hemingway*, 453.

8 Hemingway, *How It Was*, 157.

9 Hemingway, *How It Was*.

10 Mary Hemingway to Buck and Pete Lanham, July 1945, quoted in Kert, *The Hemingway Women*, 420.

11 Jack, Patrick, and Gregory Hemingway, quoted in Kert, *The Hemingway Women*, 420.

12 Hemingway, *How It Was*, 182.

13 Hemingway, *How It Was*, 162.

14 Hemingway, *How It Was*, 169.

15 Hemingway, *How It Was*.

16 "'*Soy como soy,* / I am as I am. *Y no como Papa quiere,* / And not as Papa wishes, *Qué culpa tengo yo* / What fault have I? *De ser así?* / To be like this? Was it the lament of a local whore?' Mary mused aloud, and Papa, putting his arm around his 'Pickle,' told her that it was 'just the invention of the *conjunto*.'" Hemingway, *How It Was*, 163.

17 Hemingway, *How It Was*, 167.

18 Hemingway, *How It Was*, 177.

19 "Leopoldina claimed that she was a descendant of Maximilian, the Emperor of Mexico, eighty years before, and she had the lovely green-tinted skin of Latins and the large lugubrious dark eyes of the offspring of deposed or murdered potentates. I found her conversation less alluring than her looks [. . .]

'Do you enjoy living in Havana?'

'No. It's an evil city. *Depravada*.'

'What a shame. I haven't yet seen that.'

'It's evil, and it's too hot,' Leopoldina declared.

'But not as hot as Paris.'

'No. Not as hot as Paris,' she agreed. Then she glowered at me, suspicion in her lovely eyes, and told me that her liver was bothering her." This anecdote from Mary's memoirs establishes that Ernest and Leopoldina's "intimate friendship" began long before Mary's 1945 arrival in Havana." Hemingway, *How It Was*, 178.

20 Hemingway, *How It Was*.

21 Hudson remarks that his whipped, frozen daiquiri looks like the wake of a boat doing thirty knots. He wonders how his daiquiri would look if it were phosphorescent, which leads to a discussion of the Cuban custom of eating the phosphorous found in match heads to commit suicide. A morbid discussion of suicide ensues, suggesting Hudson's own dark thoughts and depression after having lost his sons. Honest Lil insists that drinking shoe ink and iodine are "*au fond*" gestures, cries for help and not serious suicide attempts like the *auto da fé*, the classic method of Cuban women in response to betrayed love, pouring alcohol on themselves and setting themselves on fire as a passionate last expression of rage. Hemingway, *Islands in the Stream*, 181.

22 The girl of the regiment. Martha Gellhorn to Allen Grover and the Editors of *Collier's*, December 1945. "When I am alone sorrow drowns me. This is a grief I did not know I could feel and it is very hard to bear." Martha Gellhorn to David Gurewitsch, April 7, 1950, quoted in Moorehead, *Gellhorn*, 266.

23 Quoted in Rollyson, *Beautiful Exile*, 169.

24 Kert, *The Hemingway Women*, 423.

25 "1. On being alone 5 out of 7 mornings. 2. On cultivating sports which bore the shit out of me. 3. One having so little company I don't know why the hell I try to stay here." She reasoned, "Whatever else the critics say about them, they certainly [are] right about him and women—he wants them like Indian girls—completely obedient and sexually loose. That I think I might learn to handle. But the . . . criticism and long intelligent speeches about [the] inadvisability or expense of something—after about 3 samples in one day—I get that smothered feeling." Mary's Journal, October 13, 1945, Mary Hemingway Personal Papers, quoted in Reynolds, *Hemingway: The Final Years*, 133.

26 Reynolds, *Hemingway: The Final Years*.

27 Hemingway, *How It Was*, 183.

28 Hemingway, *How It Was*, 184.

29 Villarreal and Villarreal, *Hemingway's Cuban Son*, 73.

30 Villarreal and Villarreal, *Hemingway's Cuban Son*, 65.

31 Villarreal and Villarreal, *Hemingway's Cuban Son*, 76.

32 Ernest Hemingway to Buck Lanham, June 30, 1946, quoted in Reynolds, *Hemingway: The Final Years*, 144.

33 "Gertrude Stein Dies in France; 72," *The New York Times*, July 28, 1946, 40. "Gertrude Stein Dies in Paris; Tumor Cause," *Los Angeles Times*, July 28, 1946, 1.

34 Hemingway, *How It Was*, 188.

35 Hemingway, *How It Was*, 189.

36 Ernest Hemingway to Buck Lanham, August 1946, quoted in Hemingway, *How It Was*, 189–90.

37 Baker, *Ernest Hemingway*, 453; Reynolds, *Hemingway: The Final Years*, 149.

38 Villarreal and Villarreal, *Hemingway's Cuban Son*, 78.

39 Hemingway, *The Garden of Eden*.

40 The citation read, "Mr. Ernest Hemingway has performed meritorious service as a war correspondent from 20 July to 1 September, and from 6 November to 6 December 1944, in France and Germany. During these periods he displayed a broad familiarity with modern military science, interpreting and evaluating the campaigns and operations of friendly and enemy forces, circulating freely under fire in combat areas to obtain an accurate picture of conditions.

Through his talent of expression, Mr. Hemingway enabled readers to obtain a vivid picture of the difficulties and triumphs of the front-line soldier and his organization in combat." Hemingway Personal Papers.

41 "You are my most trusted friend." Ernest Hemingway to Max Perkins, June 10, 1943, quoted in Bruccoli, *The Only Thing That Counts*, 325.

42 The Boss, the Benefactor.

43 Ameringer, *Caribbean Legion*; Clinton, "The United States and the Caribbean Legion" (dissertation).

44 Villarreal and Villarreal, *Hemingway's Cuban Son*, 78.

45 "Santo Domingo Will Accuse Cuba, Venezuela, and Guatemala Before the International Tribunal," *Diario de la Marina*, October 17, 1947, quoted in Fuentes, *Hemingway in Cuba*, 225–26. See also Cirules, *Hemingway the Stranger*, 127–29.

46 José Luis Herrera Sotolongo, quoted in Fuentes, *Hemingway in Cuba*, 253–54; Ernest Hemingway to Buck Lanham, April 1947, quoted in Reynolds, *The 1930s Through the Final Years*, 444; Hemingway, *Running with the Bulls*, 171.

47 Villarreal and Villarreal, *Hemingway's Cuban Son*, 78.

48 Baker, *Ernest Hemingway*, 463.

49 Villarreal and Villarreal, *Hemingway's Cuban Son*, 83.

50 Baker, *Ernest Hemingway*, 466.

51 Ernest Hemingway to Charles Lanham, July 28 and August 8, 1948, and Ernest Hemingway to Charles Scribner, August 13 and 25. "His mood of euphoria lasted through most of the summer. He helped Roberto make up a birthday purse for 'Leopoldina,' the aging Havana prostitute." Baker, *Ernest Hemingway*, 466, 648.

CHAPTER 10

1 Enrique Serpa, quoted in Páporov, *Hemingway en Cuba*, 9.

2 Páporov, *Hemingway en Cuba*, 10.

3 Author interview with Clara Elena Serpa Aenlle, June 3, 2010.

4 Hemingway, *A Farewell to Arms*.

5 Beautiful American car, the sweet life.

6 Baker, *Ernest Hemingway*, 372.

7 Perez-Lopez, *The Economics of Cuban Sugar*, 7.

8 The cordial president.

9 Ivancich, *La torre bianca*, 9.

10 Ernest Hemingway to Adriana Ivancich, February 15, 1954, in Meyers, *Hemingway*, 440.

11 The intervals listed below, the absence of time spent as a bachelor, and the descriptive pet-names born in the conquest of each new wife provide us with an instructive "tale of the tape": 1. Hadley "Kitten" Richardson (from 1921 to 1927, six-year marriage; marries, leaves mother, Grace Hemingway, moves to Paris); 2. Pauline "*Pilar*" Pfeiffer (from 1927 to 1939, eleven-year marriage; leaves Hadley, marries, moves to Key West, Piggott); 3. Martha "Rabbit," "Bug," "Mrs. Fathouse Pig," Gellhorn (from 1940 to 1945, five-year marriage; affair in Spanish Civil War, marries, moves to Havana, persuades husband to move out of hotel into Finca); 4. Mary "Pickle" Welsh (from 1946 until author's death in 1961, fifteen-year marriage; affair in World War II Paris at Ritz Hotel, Welsh moves to Havana, marries Hemingway).

12 On the island of Capri, Adriana's aunt owned Villa L'Ulivo. Ivancich, *La torre bianca*, 195. The Ivanciches were an old Venetian family though several biographers have suggested that bad investments and postwar years had considerably diminished their holdings if not dulled their character or their façades.

13 Independent of Ernest Hemingway's invitation.

14 Later, Gianfranco perhaps became a "male surrogate" or "vicarious substitute," a "mirror image" of his sister, inspiring the work in progress and distracting his affection for his sister when his desires could not be fulfilled. Meyers, *Hemingway*, 429, 442.

15 Hotchner, *Papa Hemingway*, 4.

16 Hotchner, *Papa Hemingway*, 8.

17 Hotchner, *Papa Hemingway*, 6–7.

18 Hotchner, *Papa Hemingway*.

19 Hotchner, *Papa Hemingway*, 8.

20 Gabriel García Marquez, "Hemingway—Our Own" (introduction), Fuentes, *Hemingway in Cuba*, 11, 12.

21 "We had a great mate before Gregorio, named Carlos Gutierrez, but someone hired him away from me when I was away at the Spanish Civil War. It was wonderful luck to find Gregorio, and his seamanship has saved *Pilar* in three hurricanes." Hemingway, "The Great Blue River," in *By-Line: Ernest Hemingway*, 388–89.

22 Hemingway, "The Great Blue River," in *By-Line: Ernest Hemingway*, 389.

23 Blessed.

24 Hemingway, *How It Was*, 239–40.

25 Hemingway, *How It Was*.

26 "It's lovely up there. It's calm and beautiful, and thank you very much for it." "Something must be wrong with it," she responded. My husband looked sheep-

ish and bemused. "It's too lonely. I'm used to the sounds of the house. Miss them—René sweeping the matting. You clicking around." Hemingway, *How It Was*.

27 Hemingway, *How It Was*, 241.

28 Interview with Wallter Houk, quoted in Hendrickson, *Hemingway's Boat*, 395.

29 *Hemingway's Boat*, 407.

30 Hemingway, *How It Was*, 245.

31 Hemingway, *How It Was*.

32 Hemingway, *How It Was*.

33 In Cuban Spanish a *viejo verde* is literally a "green old man," but it means an older man who is hot for young girls. Ernest Hemingway to A .E. Hotchner, October 3, 1949, in DeFazio, *Dear Papa, Dear Hotch*, 47.

34 On October 4, "This noon I go into town to see the oldest and best whore I ever knew. She is the same age I am and I knew her when she was a kid . . . and we will tell sad stories of the death of Kings and get the local gossip. She tells me everything about everybody and gives me all the handkerchiefs her boyfriends leave. Have initialed handkerchiefs from every sugar king in the Island. That will kill today and Roberto [Herrera] is bringing the young, new, beautiful whore out tonight. Then will work tomorrow morning and Miss Mary comes on the plane in the evening in her coat on Thursday." Ernest Hemingway to Charles Scribner, October 4, 1949, *Selected Letters*, 679.

35 Ilse Bulit, "Hemingway, Leopoldina, María Ignacia, y yo," *SEMlac Cuba*, parts I–II, redsemlac-cuba.net/Criterios/hemingway-leopoldina-mariaignacia-y-yo-i.html.

36 Hemingway, *How It Was*, 246–47.

37 Lillian Ross, "How Do You Like It Now, Gentlemen?" *The New Yorker*, May 13, 1950, newyorker.com/magazine/1950/05/13/how-do-you-like-it-now-gentlemen.

38 Ross, "How Do You like It Now, Gentlemen?"

39 Hemingway, *How It Was*, 249. See also Reynolds, *Hemingway: The Final Years*, 213.

40 Nicholas Shakespeare, "The Old Man and His Muse: Hemingway's Toe-Curling Infatuation with Adriana Ivancich," *The Spectator*, September 1, 2018, www.spectator.co.uk/2018/09/the-old-man-and-his-muse-hemingways-toe-curling-infatuation-with-adriana-ivancich.

41 "Some days later when I told it to Ernest, the cheer drained away from his face. But he rallied himself and me, saying 'That's our lousy luck, my kitten. But we'll share it. It will be our lousy, dark secret which we keep together. No.

You won't have that 'maybe' operation. The hell with it. I wouldn't ask you to jump off a roof with an umbrella for support." Ernest never referred further to that incapacity of mine, but for years I felt myself a failed member of the human race, being unable to contribute a creature to it." Hemingway, *How It Was*, 260–61.

42 Ivancich, *La torre bianca*, 96–101.

43 What he missed most about her was her voice, he wrote Adriana in a lonely letter, "If you were here, Ay as one says in Spanish if you were here . . ." He made her promise to get her immigration papers in order and "carry them as a gift" to him. Adriana Ivancich to Ernest Hemingway, March 21 and March 22, 1950; Ernest Hemingway to Adriana Ivancich, April 1950, quoted in Kert, *The Hemingway Women*, 452–53. In his letters he insisted that there was "no remedy if not in the Calle del Rimedio [Adriana's address]," for he would always love her and could not help it, but he would agree not to write it or say it to her ever again and try only to serve her well and be happy company when they met, but then he added: "Nobody can control what their heart feels if they have any heart." Ernest Hemingway to Adriana Ivancich, June 16 and June 26, 1950, quoted in Ivancich, *La torre bianca*, 192, 316, quoted in Knigge, *Hemingway's Venetian Muse Adriana Ivancich*, 34.

44 Adriana Ivancich, quoted in Kert, *The Hemingway Women*, 457.

45 He complained to Charles Scribner in a letter that he would have to begin another book to keep his wife in a mink coat yet he was not able to give a dime to the woman he adored. Two weeks later he described himself to Lillian Ross as a "character with a broken heart" and told Harvey Breit in June that his novel was about someone he "loved more than anyone in the world." Ernest Hemingway, quoted in Kert, *The Hemingway Women*, 455.

46 "I think we must now both admit that this marriage is a failure. Therefore let us end it." Hemingway, *How It Was*, 264.

47 Hemingway, *How It Was*, 276.

48 "I would never go with any other publishing house; but Jesus Christ I'd like to put yours in order." "My Dear Charlie, Your fucking page proofs (first series) turned up yesterday. That ought to be almost a record . . . The hell with it all . . . I am a bad boy, Charlie, and not proud of it. You are older than me and I should be respectful." Ernest Hemingway to Charlie Scribner, July 10 and 16, 1950, Hemingway Personal Papers.

49 Ernest Hemingway to Senator Joseph McCarthy, May 8, 1950, *Selected Letters*, 693.

50 Hemingway's "running off" or showing the movie, himself, suggests a home projector, and that he and Gianfranco may have brought Leopoldina and Xenophobia to the Finca. Ernest Hemingway to Charles Scribner, July 9, 1950, *Selected Letters*, 703.

51 Rising consumption confirmed by ledger detailing expenditures on alcohol maintained in archives at the Finca Vigía. Fuentes, *Hemingway in Cuba*, 63.

52 Fuentes, *Hemingway in Cuba*.

53 Fuentes, *Hemingway in Cuba*, 65.

54 Juanita Jansen, quoted in Hendrickson, *Hemingway's Boat*, 365.

55 Hendrickson, *Hemingway's Boat*, 270.

56 Hendrickson, *Hemingway's Boat*, 277.

57 Hendrickson, *Hemingway's Boat*, 246.

58 "After reading Ernest Hemingway's new novel, *Across the River and into the Trees*, only the most sentimental referee could raise Hemingway's arm with the old chant: 'The winner and still champion!' Hemingway likes to discuss his writing in prize-ring talk but the fact is that a writer can be licked only by himself. Colonel Cantwell, like his creator, addresses women he likes as 'daughter,' was divorced from a war-correspondent wife, loves art and hunting, talks a carefully arranged language of tough-guy sentimentality." John O'Hara, "On the Ropes," *Time*, September 11, 1950.

59 Ernest Hemingway to Charles Scribner, September 9, 1950, Hemingway, *Selected Letters*, 713–14.

60 "The Colonel is all the Hemingway prizefighters, hunters, drinkers, and soldiers in one. Yet this book is different, for it is held together by blind anger rather than lyric emotion that gives Hemingway's best work its unforgettable poignance. The thing most deeply felt in the book is the Colonel's rage at having to die." Alfred Kazin, "The Indignant Flesh," *The New Yorker*, September 19, 1950, 113–18.

61 "Writers should work alone. They should see each other only after their work is done, and not too often then. Otherwise they become like writers in New York. All angleworms in a bottle, trying to derive knowledge and nourishment from their own contact and from the bottle." Hemingway, *Green Hills of Africa*, 18.

62 "Sure, they can say anything about nothing happening in *Across the River*, but all that happens is the defense of the Lower Piave, the breakthrough in Normandy, the taking of Paris and the destruction of the 22d Inf. Reg. in Hurtgen forest plus a man who loves a girl and dies . . . In writing I have moved past through arithmetic, through plane geometry and algebra, and now I am in calculus. If they don't understand that, to hell with them. I won't be sad and I will

not read what they say. They say? What do they say? Let them say. Who the hell wants fame over a week-end? All I want is to write well." Ernest Hemingway in Harvey Breit, "Talk with Mr. Hemingway," *The New York Times Book Review*, September 17, 1950, 14.

63 Olhina Ivan Di Robilant, "Ernest Hemingway's Long-Ago Crush on a Venetian Girl Is Once Again the Talk of Italy," *People*, December 1, 1980, https://people.com/archive/ernest-hemingways-long-ago-crush-on-a-venetian-girl-is-once-again-the-talk-of-italy-vol-14-no-22. See also Ivancich, *La torre bianca*.

64 "Certainly she was not in love with him." Hemingway, *Papa*, 113.

65 Villarreal and Villarreal, *Hemingway's Cuban Son*, 98.

66 Hemingway, *How It Was*, 271.

67 Baker, *Ernest Hemingway*, 488.

68 Hemingway, *How It Was*, 282.

69 Ivancich, *La torre bianca*, 31, 136–40, quoted in Kert, *The Hemingway Women*, 456–57.

70 Ivancich, *La torre bianca*, 180.

71 Hemingway, *Papa*, 111.

72 Hemingway, *How It Was*, 280.

73 Hemingway, *How It Was*, 280–81.

74 Hemingway, *How It Was*, 282.

75 Hemingway, *How It Was*.

76 Ivancich, *La torre bianca*, 141.

77 "Perhaps some think that I liked Hemingway like a father. It is not like that . . . Often I have the impression of being next to a big child. Sometimes I feel the desire to protect him against himself. Sometimes I have the impression that he is looking for a solution to his inner restlessness in me. If one would say that between us, sometimes, I am the older person, everybody would laugh. But it is true." Ivancich, *La torre bianca*.

CHAPTER 11

1 Ernest Hemingway to Carlos Baker, February 17, 1951, Carlos Baker Collection of Ernest Hemingway, quoted in Mellow, *Hemingway*, 570.

2 When Hemingway died, Carlos Baker began the first full-length biography, and after eight years' preparation and Mary's initial resistance and eventual support, published it in 1969. Needless to say Philip Young's unauthorized biography *Ernest Hemingway* (1952), theorizing that all of Hemingway's fiction had been the result of a need for self-analysis subsequent to the trauma of a war wound in 1918, had not been well received by the writer himself.

3 During his lifetime, Hemingway discouraged biographers like Charles Fenton, Carlos Baker, and Malcolm Cowley. Ernest Hemingway to Charles Fenton, January 12, 1951, and June 18, 1952, quoted in Joan Didion, "Last Words," *The New Yorker,* November 9, 1998, newyorker.com/magazine/1998/11/09/last-words-6; Donaldson, *The Death of a Rebel*; Ernest Hemingway to Malcolm Cowley, June 10 and March 9, 1949, quoted in Mellow, *Hemingway*, 565.

4 Paraphrased from Hemingway, "The Snows of Kilimanjaro," *The Complete Short Stories of Ernest Hemingway.*

5 Hemingway, *How It Was*, 279.

6 He wrote A. E. Hotchner: "Jamming on the [land sea and air] book . . . finished the first volume Xhmas Eve. The sea part. But will do other parts before I publish it. It's a property already. Not just a piece of un-finished business." Ernest Hemingway to A. E. Hotchner, January 5, 1951, in De Fazio, *Dear Papa, Dear Hotch*, 111. It seemed the author intended to write a land, sea, and air trilogy. The sea portion became *Islands in the Stream. The Old Man and the Sea* was originally intended to be a part of the sea portion, but it was later published as its own entity. See also Burwell, *Hemingway*, 51–52.

7 "Couldn't work the first day and had black-ass the second but worked anyway and did 874. [Big for him.] Day before yesterday did 665 and yesterday 62 . . . Don Andrés came out to lunch Thursday and to spend the afternoon because he had black-ass and José Luis had it terribly last night. So maybe it is a seasonal complaint. I can cheer up everybody except me. You better come home and do that . . . Am in the very toughest part of the story to write. He has the fish now and is on the way in and the first shark has shown up." Quoted in Hemingway, *How It Was*, 285.

8 Hemingway, "On the Blue Water," in *By-Line: Ernest Hemingway*, 492.

9 Ernest Hemingway to Mary Hemingway, quoted in Hemingway, *How It Was*, 285.

10 Hemingway, *Green Hills of Africa*, 115.

11 Hemingway, *The Old Man and the Sea*, 36.

12 Hemingway, *How It Was*, 286.

13 A fine example: "In the dark the old man could feel the morning coming as he rowed he heard the trembling sound as flying fish left the water and the hissing that their stiff wings made as they soard away in the darkness. He was very fond of flying fish as they were his principal friends on the ocean. He was sorry for the birds especially the small delicate dark terns that were always flying and looking and almost never finding, and he thought, the birds have a harder life than we do except for the robber birds and the heavy strong ones. Why did

they make birds so delicate and fine as those sea swallows when the ocean can be so cruel? She is kind and very beautiful. But she can be so cruel and it comes so suddenly and such birds that fly, dipping and hunting, with their small sad voices are made too delicately for the sea." Hemingway, *The Old Man and the Sea*, 20.

14 The Korean conflict that was raging on the other side of the globe would later be known as "The Forgotten War"; despite the draft, it did not demand the full mobilization, or enter the American psyche of American youth quite as subversively as Vietnam.

15 Ernest Hemingway to Charles Scribner, March 5, 1951, *Selected Letters*, 720.

16 Ibid, and Ernest Hemingway to Charles Scribner, April 11–12, 1951, *Selected Letters*, 722–23.

17 Ernest Hemingway to Charles Scribner, October 5, 1951, *Selected Letters*, 738.

18 Martín, *Eduardo Chibás in the Time of Orthodoxy*.

19 Ernest Hemingway to Charles Scribner, October 2, 1951, *Selected Letters*, 737, quoted in Hawkins, *Unbelieveable Happiness and Final Sorrow*, 271.

20 Hemingway, *Papa*, 8. See also Robert Clark, "*Papa y el tirador*: Biographical Parallels in Hemingway's 'I Guess Everything Reminds You of Something,'" *The Hemingway Review* 27, no. 1 (September 22, 2007): 89.

21 Hemingway, *How It Was*, 290.

22 Baker, *Ernest Hemingway*, 497.

23 Hemingway, *The Old Man and the Sea*, 20.

24 Ernest Hemingway to Vera Scribner, February 18, 1952, *Selected Letters*, 748–49.

25 Hemingway, *How It Was*, 295.

26 Hemingway, *How It Was*, 294.

27 Hemingway, "The Last Good Country," 525.

28 Baker, *Ernest Hemingway*, 32. See also Godfrey, *Hemingway's Geographies*, 71–73.

29 Hemingway, *The Garden of Eden*, 16–17.

30 Hemingway, *How It Was*, 294.

31 Hemingway, *How It Was*, 296.

32 *Bohemia*, December 16, 1951, 127, 146.

33 Brenner and Eisner, *Cuba Libre*, 62.

34 Calhoun, *Gangsterismo*, 40.

35 Thomas, *The Cuban Revolution*, quoted in Calhoun, *Gangsterismo*, 35.

36 Schlesinger, *A Thousand Days*, 216.

37 "Batista: He's Got Past Democracy's Sentries." *Time*, April 21, 1952.

38 Thomas, *The Cuban Revolution*, 13.

39 "Under these circumstances, I believe it would be detrimental to the special

relations that this country has with Cuba to hold up [diplomatic] recognition any longer [given] our very special position in Cuba which includes heavy capital investment, enormous international trade, the Nicaro nickel plant operation, the Guantánamo Naval Base, three armed services missions and the recent signing of a bilateral military assistance agreement which requires implementation." Quoted in Calhoun, *Gangsterismo*, 41.

40 Baker, *Ernest Hemingway*, 504.

41 Baker, *Ernest Hemingway*.

42 "His best. Time may show it to be the best single piece of any of us, I mean his and my contemporaries. This time, he discovered God, a Creator." William Faulkner, *Shenandoah*, August 1952, quoted in Wagner-Martin, *Ernest Hemingway:*, 5.

43 Orville Prescott, "Books of the Times," *The New York Times*, August 28, 1952, http://movies2.nytimes.com/books/99/07/04/specials/hemingway-oldman.html.

44 Malcom Cowley, "Hemingway's Novel Has the Rich Simplicity of a Classic," *The New York Herald Tribune Review of Books*, September 7, 1952. In *The New York Times Book Review*, Robert Davis, a professor of English from Smith College, observed, "It is a tale superbly told and in the telling Ernest Hemingway uses all the craft his hard, disciplined trying over so many years has given him." Like the young man in "Big Two-Hearted River," with *The Old Man and the Sea*, Hemingway had gotten back to something good and true in himself that had always been there, and in it, there were new indications of humility and maturity, and a deeper sense of being at home in life—which promised well for the novel in the making. "Hemingway is still a great writer," Davis said, "with the strength and craft and courage to go far out, and perhaps even far down, for the truly big ones." Robert Gorham Davis, "Hemingway's Tragic Fisherman," *The New York Times*, September 7, 1952, 20.

45 Connolly continued that a long physical struggle was described with the dynamic right words even as the changing qualities of the static sea were portrayed in their true colours, and the soul of the old man—humble, fearless, aromatic—was described perfectly too. Cyril Connelly, "Review of *The Old Man and the Sea*," *London Sunday Times*, September 7, 1952, 5.

46 Ernest Hemingway to Bernard Berenson, September 26 and October 2, 1952, *Selected Letters*, 782–83.

47 Hemingway, *How It Was*, 308.

48 "Everywhere the book is being called a classic . . . [It] is not only a moral fable, but a parable . . . Hemingway's art, when it is art is absolutely incomparable,

and that he is unquestionably the greatest craftsman in the American novel in this century." In December in *The New York Times Book Review*, Joyce Cary upheld that it was his favorite book of the year: "Hemingway's old man is profoundly original. It deals with the fundamentals, the origins. Its form, so elaborately contrived, is yet perfectly suited to the massive shape of a folk theme." Mark Schroer, "Grace Under Pressure (Review)," *The New Republic*, October 6, 1952, 19, quoted in Meyers, *Ernest Hemingway*. In *Harper's*, Gilbert Highet offered, "A hero undertakes a hard task. He is scarcely equal to it because of ill luck, wounds, treachery, hesitation, or age. With a tremendous effort, he succeeds. But in his success he loses the prize itself, or final victory, or his life." Gilbert Highet, *Harper's*, "Review of *The Old Man and the Sea*," October 6, 1952.

49 Phillip Rahv, "The Old Man and the Sea, by Ernest Hemingway; and *East of* Eden, by John Steinbeck," *Image and Idea*, October 1, 1952, 194–95, quoted in Mellow, *Hemingway*, 582.

50 Ernest Hemingway to Edmund Wilson, November 8, 1952, quoted in Mellow, *Hemingway*, 580.

51 Baker, *Ernest Hemingway*, 505.

52 "Do you think it would be wrong if I asked you if you wanted, or wished to, or would be pleased to, write 2 or 3 sentences or 1 sentence about this book that could be quoted by Scribner's?" Ernest Hemingway to Bernard Berenson, September 13, 1952, *Selected Letters*, 780–81.

53 Quoted in Baker, *Ernest Hemingway*, 505; Mellow, *Hemingway*, 580.

54 Insinuating *The Old Man and the Sea* recycled themes in previous works ("The Undefeated"), poet Delmore Schwartz responded two months later in *Partisan Review* that the praise for Hemingway's latest had gotten out of hand: "There was a note of insistence in the praise and a note of relief, the relief because his previous book was extremely bad in an ominous way, and the insistence, I think, because this new work is not so much good in itself as a virtuoso performance which reminds one of Hemingway at his best." Delmore Schwartz, "Review of *The Old Man and the Sea*," *Partisan Review*, November 1952. Roughly and somewhat unfairly, Schwartz suggested that the novella in itself was not great, but only reminded readers of what Hemingway had once been. But by the spring of 1953, even baby sharks like John Aldridge in the *Virginia Quarterly Review* were daring enough to question the overwrought and sentimental prose: "I confess that I am unable to share in the prevailing wild enthusiasm for . . . *The Old Man and the Sea*," which was "strictly minor Hemingway fiction." John W. Alridge, *Virginia Quarterly* (Spring 1953): 311–20, quoted in Lynn, *Hemingway*, 651. By the spring of 1953, in *Hudson Review*, R.W.B. Lewis praised

Hemingway for depicting "the stimulating and fatal relation between integrity of character and the churning abundance of experience," and noted that "his style catches this perception with a good deal of its old power," but doubted "if the book can bear the amount of critical weight already piled on up on it . . . [It] is not absolutely persuasive . . . Our assent has to be partially withheld." R.W.B. Lewis, "Review of *The Old Man and the Sea*," *Hudson Review* (Spring 1953). Three years later in *New York Herald Tribune Book Week*, John Aldrige's criticism, supported by other mutineers, grew braver: "The action of the novel is . . . to my mind, a façade, a classic parable in stone, terribly picturesque and meaningful, but quite dead. One must question the vitality of a story that becomes a myth too quickly, that is accepted as universal before it has been felt as particular." John W. Alridge, "Two Poor Fish on One Line," *The New York Herald Tribune Book Weekly*, June 20, 1965, 16, 19, quoted in Lynn, *Hemingway*, 651.

55 Gregory Hemingway to Ernest Hemingway, July 3, 1952, quoted in Hendrickson, *Hemingway's Boat*, 471.

56 "Little goody-goody Mary, for instance, who's taken more shit from you than they dump in Havana Harbor. But we know better, don't we, you'll never write that great novel because you are a sick man—sick in the head and too fucking proud to admit it. In spite of the critics, that last one was as sickly a bucket of sentimental slop as was ever scrubbed off a barroom floor. There's nothing I'd rather see than you write a beauty and there's nothing I'd rather see than you act intelligently, but until you do I'm going to give you just what you deserve, and in extra large handfuls to make up for the trouble you've caused me." Gregory Hemingway to Ernest Hemingway, November 13–14, 1952, in Hemingway, *Strange Tribe*, 116–17.

57 Ernest Hemingway to Gregory Hemingway, November 17, 1952, in Hemingway, *Strange Tribe*, 119–20.

58 Ernest Hemingway in Mary's journal, December 20, 1953, quoted in Reynolds, *Hemingway: The Final Years*, 217; cited also in Hemingway, *How It Was*, 370–71.

59 Baker, *Ernest Hemingway*, 505.

60 *Variety*, March 4, 1953, 56, quoted in Perez, *Cuba in the American Imagination*, 196.

61 Foreign investors expanded operations with Cuban officials' tacit support, such that by "the late '50s, U.S. financial interests included 90 percent of Cuban mines, 80 percent of its public utilities, 50 percent of its railways, 40 percent of its sugar production and 25 percent of its bank deposits—some $1 billion in total." Quoted in Natasha Geiling, "Before the Revolution," *Smithsonian Magazine*, July 31, 2007. "Daily life had developed into a relentless degradation

with the complicity of political leaders and public officials who operated at the behest of American interests." Perez, *On Becoming Cuban.*

62 As "the Mob's accountant," Meyer Lansky, running casinos at the Hotel Nacional, Riviera, and Montmartre, deposited upward of 30 percent of the take, or millions of dollars annually, into Swiss accounts. Batista purportedly amassed a fortune upward of $20 million. Díaz-Briquets and Pérez-López, *Corruption in Cuba*, 77.

63 English, *Havana Nocturne*, 206.

64 The new regime extended tax incentives, government loans, and casino licenses to investors who benefited from a favorable relationship, such as the Hotel Law 2074. "Mobsters Move in on Troubled Havana and Split Rich Gambling Profits with Batista," *Life*, March 10, 1958, quoted in Moruzzi, *Havana Before Castro*, 163. A new amusement park called "Coney Island," owned by US businessman Howard Frederick Anderson, had recently opened in Havana, and a greyhound racetrack in Miramar had been opened by Jerry Collins, a developer from Florida. After the revolution, Anderson, having evacuated his family to the United States, came back to Cuba and was executed by a revolutionary firing squad for counter-revolutionary activity in anticipation of the Bay of Pigs invasion. His family sued Castro's government for wrongful debt and won monies frozen by Eisenhower during the early stages of the embargo. Rachel Price, "Coney Island to La Isla del Coco," *Journal of Latin American Cultural Studies* (November 2, 2011): 217–31; Perez, *On Becoming Cuban*, 196.

65 "Cinema: Two with Tracy," *Time*, October 27, 1958.

66 Hemingway, *How It Was*, 312.

67 Villarreal and Villarreal, *Hemingway's Cuban Son*, 112.

68 Hemingway, *How It Was*, 312.

69 Russo and Esperian, *Offshore Vegas*, 63.

70 Hemingway, *How It Was*, 319–20.

71 Hemingway, *Selected Letters*, 821–22.

72 Castro and Ramonet, *My Life*, 106–13.

73 De la Cova, *The Moncada Attack*, 70–73; Coltman, *The Real Fidel Castro*, 79.

74 "Cuban Student Held as Leader of Revolt," *The New York Times*, August 2, 1953, 29.

75 "Cuba Begins Trial of 100 for Revolt," *The New York Times*, September 22, 1953, 19.

76 De la Cova, *The Moncada Attack*, 70–73.

77 "Batista Says Cuba Cleaned Out Reds: On Anniversary of Coup, He Pledges Fall Election and Lists Achievements," *The New York Times*, March 11, 1954, 5.

78 Having survived the wreck, the group took shelter on a nearby ridge. A rescue

plane, spotting their wreckage from the air with no people in sight, reported the accident as resulting in "no survivors." Hemingway Personal Papers.

79 Ernest Hemingway to A. E. Hotchner, March 14, 1954, in DeFazio, *Dear Papa, Dear Hotch*, 169.

80 Pivano, *Hemingway in Venice*, 169.

81 Ivancich, *La torre bianca*, 324.

82 Hemingway, *How It Was*, 403.

83 Hemingway, *How It Was*, 405.

84 Hemingway, *How It Was*, 407.

85 Hemingway, *How It Was*.

86 Villarreal and Villarreal, *Hemingway's Cuban Son*, 117.

87 Hemingway, *How It Was*, 407.

88 Finger sandwiches.

89 Hemingway, *How It Was*, 407.

90 "A life of action is much easier to me than writing. I have a greater facility for action than for writing." *Selected Letters*, 417. Reading Tolstoy, he would thus retain only the "wonderful, penetrating and true descriptions of war and of people" in *War and Peace*, while ignoring the "ponderous and Messianic thinking," which represented exactly what a writer should not do. He aspired to write "what gave you the emotion; what the *action* was that gave you the excitement;" purging himself of sentimentality and pseudo-intellectualism, he wrote instead "as truly, as straightly, as objectively and as humbly as possible." Hemingway, *By-Line: Ernest Hemingway*, 219; Hemingway, "Introduction to *Men at War*," xvii–xviii.

91 Ernest Hemingway, quoted in Harvey Breit, "The Sun Also Rises in Stockholm," *The New York Times*, November 7, 1953, BR1.

92 Breit, "The Sun Also Rises in Stockholm"

93 Breit, "The Sun Also Rises in Stockholm."

94 My translation. From *El Hemingway de Cuba* (Havana: Citmatel y Cuba Literaria, 1999), CD-ROM.

95 *"Señoras y señores, Debo dar las gracias a todos ustedes que han venido . . . [what follows is Mary's translation.]* As you know there are many Cubas. But like Gaul it can be divided in three parts. Those who have hunger, those who endure and those who eat too much. After this *suburbia* [bourgeois] luncheon we are all in the third category, at least for the moment. I am a man without politics. This is a great defect but it is preferable to arteriosclerosis. With this defect of being apolitical, one can appreciate the problems of the Palmolivero [the fellow who sniffs canned heat] and the triumphs of my friend Alfonsito Gomez Mena. I was friend of Manolo Guas who was the uncle of Felo Guas and also

the friend of Manolo Castro [gamblers] I like the [fighting] cocks and the Philharmonic Orchestra. I was a friend of Emilio Lorents and this has not hurt my friendship wih Mayito Menocal who with Elicio Arguelles are my best friends in this country. God grant that it is not a mortal sin to consider Antonio Maceo a better general than Bernard Law Montgomery and to hope for the death of Trujillo, that he dies in bed, naturally. [He] is the only person whom I would like to see finished before I finish. Now excuse some jokes and a legitimate admonition which follows and which one sees every morning in the mirror." Hemingway, *How It Was*, 411.

96 Publio Enruquez, a gardener, remembered that "by the time we were done drinking, I could barely find the door." Quoted in Hemingway and Brennen, *Hemingway in Cuba*, 102.

97 Fuentes, *Hemingway in Cuba*, 238.

98 Rodríguez, *The Havana of Hemingway and Campoamor*, 89. English citations in the text are author translation.

99 Rodríguez, *The Havana of Hemingway and Campoamor*, 75.

100 Rodríguez, *The Havana of Hemingway and Campoamor*.

101 Ernest Hemingway, "Nobel Prize Acceptance Speech," Nobel.org, December 10, 1954, nobelprize.org/nobel_prizes/literature/laureates/1954/hemingway-speech.html.

102 Charles Scribner, "Introduction," Hemingway, *The Old Man and the Sea*.

103 Notes on an oral briefing, February 1955, Nixon Papers, quoted in Paterson, *Contesting Castro*, 26.

104 Richard Nixon, in Diary of James C. Hagerty, March 11, 1955, box 1, James C. Hagerty Papers, quoted in Paterson, *Contesting Castro*, 26.

105 In a letter after his return, Dulles wrote Batista: "May I say, Mr. President, what a great honor and pleasure it has been to meet and talk with you. I trust we will be in a position to assist you and your country in our mutual struggle against the enemies of Freedom." After referencing the BRAC, he continued that he was "honored that your Government has agreed to permit this Agency to assist in training some of the officers in this most important organization." Allen Dulles to Fulgencio Batista, July 15, 1956, quoted in Shoultz, *That Infernal Little Cuban Republic*, 72; Carrozza, *William D. Pawley*, 214.

106 "U.S. Policy Toward Latin America," NSC 5613/1, September 25, 1956, box 18, "Cuba—U.S. Foreign Assistance," box 551, John Sherman Cooper Papers; "Mutual Security Program, Fiscal Year 1958 Estimates, Latin America," box 42, Confidential File; box 3377, 737.5-MSP, Department of State Records, National Archives, quoted in Paterson, *Contesting Castro*, 69.

107 Castro and Ramonet, *My Life*, 635.

108 Graham H. Jr. Turbiville, "Guerrilla Counterintelligence: Insurgent Approaches to Neutralizing Adversary Intelligence Operations," *JSOU Report* (January 2009): 9–1.

109 Villarreal and Villarreal, *Hemingway's Cuban Son*, 142.

110 Fidel Castro, *Guerrillero del tiempo*, 12–13.

111 Meyers, *Hemingway*, 575.

112 Ernest Hemingway, quoted in Alane Salierno Mason, "To Love and Love Not," *Vanity Fair*, July 1999, www.vanityfair.com/culture/features/1999/07/hemingway-199907; Hemingway, *My Brother, Ernest Hemingway*, 119.

113 Castro, *Guerrillero del tiempo*, 15–6

CHAPTER 12

1 Alvarez, *Frank País*, 160.

2 Cannon, *Revolutionary Cuba*, 113.

3 Moore, *Fidel Castro*, 50.

4 Juan Manuel Márquez, in Franqui, *Diary of the Cuban Revolution*, 124.

5 Guevara, *Reminiscences of the Cuban Revolutinary War*, 196.

6 Moore, *Fidel Castro*, 50.

7 Franqui, *Diary of the Cuban Revolution*, 125.

8 Alvarez, *Frank País*, 135.

9 *The New York Times*, December 3, 1956. See also Gadea, *My Life with Che*, quoted in Harris, *Che Guevara*, 72.

10 Moore, *Fidel Castro*, 49. See also Thomas, *Cuba or the Pursuit of Freedom*, and Matthews, *Revolution in Cuba*. The number of *Granma* survivors—somewhere between 12 and 20—is controversial. See Bonachea and Martin, *Cuban Insurrection*, 366; Szulc, *Fidel*, 381.

11 "President Batista of Cuba announced on Tuesday that the suspension of constitutional guarantees would continue for another forty-five days. This is the seventh such renewal since last Dec. 2, the day on which the young rebel, Fidel Castro, landed on the coast of Oriente Province." "Cuba's Iron Curtain," *The New York Times*, October 31, 1957, 30.

12 Kirkpatrick, *The Real CIA*, ch. 7. On "erasing the red scourage" of Communism, see Tomlin, *Murrow's Cold War;* Benson, *Writing JFK*, 32.

13 Alvarez, *Frank País*, 167–69.

14 Hart, *Aldabonazo*, 365.

15 Alvarez, *Frank País*, 168.

16 Desroches, *Allow the Water*, 149.

17 Klouzal, *Women and Rebel Communities in the Cuban Insurgent Movement*, 87–88.

18 Foran, *Taking Power*, 63.

19 Foran, *Taking Power*, 442.

20 Meyers, *Hemingway*, 533. See also A. E. Hotchner, "Don't Touch *A Moveable Feast*," *The New York Times*, July 19, 2009, https://www.nytimes.com/2009/07/20/opinion/20hotchner.html.

21 Afterwards, "for hours on end he sat on the floor beside the trunks reading" them. Hemingway, *How It Was*, 440; Hotchner, "Don't Touch *A Moveable Feast*."

22 Hemingway, *How It Was*, 441–42.

23 Hemingway, *How It Was*.

24 Meyers, *Hemingway*, 575.

25 JFK Library, "Dr. Andrew Farah, Chief of Psychiatry, High Point Division, University of North Carolina Healthcare System, discusses his new book, Hemingway's Brain with Dr. Linda Miller," YouTube video, 1:18:15, from a livestream April 20, 2017, by the John F. Kennedy Library, https://www.youtube.com/watch?v=n5L48qUSr7w.

26 Hemingway, *How It Was*, 444.

27 Bulit, interview with the author, June 9, 2009.

28 Bulit, *SEMlac* Parts I–IV.

29 Fuentes, *Hemingway in Cuba*, 237.

30 Bulit, "Hemingway, Leopoldina, María Ignacia, y Yo," *SEMlac Cuba*, part V, October 12, 2009.

31 Guevara, *Che Guevara Reader*, 26.

32 Batista's forces of 21,000 in 1953 are estimated to have grown to around 30,000 in 1958, and 40,000–50,000 in 1959. Compare that to 12 survivors from the original 82 boarding the *Granma* in Mexico in November 1956, which never rose to higher than 180 men until the summer of 1958 with perhaps as many as 1,000 additional in all other insurgent groups not under Fidel's command, such as José Antonio Echeverría's DRE or *"13 de Marzo,"* Blas Roca's *Partido Socialista Popular*, student groups like Rafael Barcena's *Movimiento Nacionalista Revolucionario* (MNR), *Segundo Frente Nacional del Escambray, Sociedad de los Amigos de la República, Conspiración de los Puros*, and militants from the Authentic, Orthodox, and Workers Parties. When Castro's success was assured after December 31, 1958, it is estimated that as many as 40,000 citizens joined in. However, Castro's army consisted of 803 men and approximately 1,000–1,500 militants from other groups at the height of its fighting strength on victory day. Brennan, Huberman, Sweezy, Draper, Thomas, Sartre, and Goldenberg. Russell, *Rebellion, Revolution, and Armed Force*, 22–33.

33 Dosal, *Comandante Che*, 79–80.

34 Ernesto Guevara to Hilda Gadea, January 28, 1957, in Dosal, *Comandante Che*, 81.

35 Matthews, *Fidel Castro*, quoted in Major Monte H. Callen (USAF), "Analysis of the Military Strategies and Warfare Principles of Che Guevara and Fidel Castro During the Cuban Revolution," Report# 85-0360, Maxwell, AFB: Air Command and Staff College, July 8, 1985, 3.

36 Matthews, *Fidel Castro*, 3.

37 Che Guevara, in Dosal, *Comandante Che*, 85.

38 Ruby Hart Phillips blurted out: "You have contact with Fidel Castro! I cannot believe it!" Felipe Pazos to Herbert L. Matthews, June 10, 1960, box 1, Matthews Papers, quoted in Paterson, *Contesting Castro*, 84.

39 Matthews, *The Cuban Story*, 18–19.

40 Matthews, *The Cuban Story*, 18–19.

41 Raúl Chibás, "La entrevista de Herbert Matthews con Fidel Castro: Memorias de la revolutión cubana," Raúl Chibás Collection; Franqui, *Twelve*, 94–95, 102.

42 Herbert Matthews, "Cuban Rebel Is Visited in His Hideout," *The New York Times*, February 24. 1957, 1.

43 Matthews, "Cuban Rebel Is Visited in His Hideout."

44 Matthews, "Cuban Rebel Is Visited in His Hideout."

45 Jonathan Alter, "Taking Sides: Review of *The Man Who Invented Fidel* by Anthony DePalma," *New York Times Book Review*, April 23, 2006, https://www.nytimes.com/2006/04/23/books/review/taking-sides.html?mcubz=1.

46 Herbert L. Matthews, "Cuban Rebel Only 30; His Men Younger: Stronger than Ever, He Boasts in Interview. Cubans Stirred," *The New York Times*, March 1, 1957, A3; Ruby Hart Phillps, "Cubans Debating Rebel Interview," *The New York Times*, March 1, 1957, 8.

47 Matthews, "Cuban Rebel Only 30; His Men Younger"; Ruby Hart Phillps, "Cubans Debating Rebel Interview."

48 Arthur Gardner, "Joint Weekly," Havana Embassy and Department of State, in Paterson, *Contesting Castro*, 26.

49 "Cuba Suppresses Youths' Uprising; Forty Are Killed," *The New York Times*, March 14, 1957, 1.

50 Jules Dubois, "Revolt in Havana; 50 Slain. Batista Forces Crush Attack on his Palace. President Blames Assalt on 'Pro-Reds,'" *Chicago Daily Tribune*, March 14, 1957, 1.

51 Faria, *Cuba in Revolution*, 416.

52 Ruby Hart Phillips, "Cuba Recovering from Brief Rising," *The New York Times*, March 15, 1957.

53 Ernest Hemingway to A. E. Hotchner, May 28, 1957, in DeFazio, *Dear Papa, Dear Hotch*, 216–17.

54 Dearborn, *Ernest Hemingway*, 584.

55 Villarreal and Villarreal, *Hemingway's Cuban Son*, 147.

56 Hemingway, *How It Was*, 445.

57 Márquez-Sterling, *Cuba 1952–1959*, 107.

58 Smith, *The Fourth Floor*, 94.

59 García-Pérez, *Insurrection & Revolution*, 89.

60 R. Hart Phillips, "Rebel Battles Reported in Cuba; Dynamiters Cut Havana Utilities," *The New York Times*, May 29, 1957, 1, 3.

61 Anderson, *Che Guevara*, 247.

62 Ernesto Guevara, in Harris, *Che Guevara*, 75.

63 Hemingway, *A Moveable Feast*, 40; Hemingway, "The Great Blue River," in *By-Line: Ernest Hemingway*, 338.

64 When writing about a "wild, cold blowing day" in "Up in Michgan," "I had already seen the end of the fall come through boyhood, youth and young manhood, and in one place you could write about it better than another. That was called transplanting yourself, I thought, and it could be as necessary with people as with other sorts of growing things." Hemingway, *A Moveable Feast*, 40.

65 "Christ I wish I could paint," he had written to his most sympathetic critic, Bernard Berenson, four summers ago. Ernest Hemingway to Bernard Berenson, August 11, 1953, *Selected Letters*, 823.

66 For always / Forever. Che's famous saying was "Hasta la victoria siempre / Until victory, always."

67 Art Buchwald, "The Great Feud of Mr. Hemingway and Mr. Zanuck," *Los Angeles Times*, November 29, 1957, B5.

68 Buchwald, "The Great Feud of Mr. Hemingway and Mr. Zanuck."

69 Those bastards.

70 Ernest Hemingway to Gregory Hemingway, August 20, 1957, in Hendrickson, *Hemingway's Boat*, 478.

71 Ernesto "Che" Guevara, quoted in "Articles by Che Guevara from the Sierra Maestra," *The Militant* 10, no. 3 (January 22, 1996).

72 Hemingway, *How It Was*, 453.

73 Hemingway, *How It Was*, 448.

74 Hemingway, *How It Was*, 447.

75 Moruzzi, *Havana Before Castro*, 165.

76 Sayles, *Los Gusanos*, quoted in Perez, *On Becoming Cuban*, 194–95.

77 Ernest Hemingway to Gianfranco Ivancich, January 31, 1958, in Hemingway, *Selected Letters*, 882.

78 Ernest Hemingway to Gianfranco Ivancich, January 31, 1958, *Selected Letters*, 882.

79 Hemingway, *Selected Letters*.

80 Hemingway, *The Garden of Eden*, 4–5.

81 "Cuban Army Uses Tanks in a Clash: 400 Rebels Reported Routed Near Hide-Out of Castro—Election Delay Urged," *The New York Times*, February 18, 1958, 22.

82 "Cuban Rebel Attack Frees Jailed Youths," *The New York Times*, January 27, 1958.

83 "ST. GEORGE: You say you will burn Cuba's entire sugar crop. The island's economic life depends on it. What can you gain by this? CASTRO: Our intent is to burn the harvest to the last stalk, including my own family's large sugar-cane farm here in Oriente Province. It is a *hard* step. But it is a legitimate act of war. From sugar taxes, Batista buys bombs and arms, pays his newly doubled army. Only their bayonets now keep him in power. Once before, Cubans burned their cane, razed their very towns, to wrest freedom from Spain. During your revolution, didn't the American colonists throw tea into Boston Harbor as a legitimate defense measure?" Fidel Castro and Andrew St. George, "Cuban Rebels," *Look*, February 4, 1958, 30; Zanetti and Garcia, *Sugar and Railroads*, 177.

84 David Grann, "The Yankee Comandante: A Story of Love, Revolution, and Betrayal," *The New Yorker*, May 28, 2012, https://www.newyorker.com/magazine/2012/05/28/the-yankee-comandante.

85 Grann, "The Yankee Comandante.

86 Herbert L. Matthews, "Cuban War Aided by Second Front," *The New York Times*, April 3, 1958, 3.

87 Coltman, *The Real Fidel Castro*, 133; Bourne, *Fidel*, 155; Rimonet, *My Life*, 609.

88 "Castro Backers Picket," *The New York Times*, March 15, 1958, 6.

89 Harris, *Che Guevara*, 79.

90 Weyl, *Red Star over Cuba*, 102. See also Draper, *Castro's Cuba*, 18.

91 Weyl, *Red Star over Cuba*.

92 Homer Bigart, "Batista Insisting on Holding Vote: Determined on June Election Despite Spreading Revolt and Forecasts of Fraud," *The New York Times*, March 1, 1958, 1.

93 Márquez-Sterling, *Cuba 1952–1959*, 55.

94 "And know what will happen next and you stop and try to live through until the next day when you hit it again. You have started at six in the morning, say,

and may go on until noon or be through before that. When you stop you are as empty, and at the same time never empty but filling, as when you have made love to someone you love. Nothing can hurt you, nothing can happen, nothing means anything until the next day when you do it again. It is the wait until the next day that is hard to get through." Interview with Georpe Plimpton, "Ernest Hemingway, The Art of Fiction No. 21," *The Paris Review*, Spring 1958, https://www.theparisreview.org/interviews/4825/ernest-hemingway-the-art-of-fiction-no-21-ernest-hemingway.

95 Ernest Hemingway to Mr. and Mrs. William D. Horne, July 1, 1958, *Selected Letters*, 884.

96 Ernest Hemingway to Ezra Pound, July 19, 1956, and June 26, 1958, *Selected Letters*, 864, 883.

97 Lipman, *Guantánamo*, 139.

98 "Caught in a War," *Time*, July 14, 1958, 29.

99 Ernest Hemingway to Mr. and Mrs. William D. Horne, July 1, 1958, *Selected Letters*, 884.

100 Reynolds, *Hemingway: The Final Years*, 310.

101 "Rebels Seek End of Aid to Batista: U.S. Officials Believe That Is Aim of Kidnappings by Cuban Insurgents," *The New York Times*, July 1, 1958, 3.

102 "All Free," *Time*, July 28, 1958, 34.

103 "Caught in a War," *Time*, July 14, 1958, 29.

104 Bockman, *The Spirit of Moncada*.

105 Hemingway, *How It Was*, 448.

106 Hemingway, *How It Was*, 449–50.

107 Bockman, *The Spirit of Moncada*.

108 "'On the morning of the fifteenth, the air force appeared,' Fidel reported over Radio Rebelde. The aerial attack against our positions, with machine-gun strafing and 500-pound explosive bombs as well as napalm, lasted uninterrupted from six in the morning until one in the afternoon. The pasture and forest . . . were left scorched, but not one of the rebel combatants moved from his position." Cannon, *Revolutionary Cuba*, 92.

109 Cannon, *Revolutionary Cuba*.

110 Cannon, *Revolutionary Cuba*.

111 Bockman, *The Spirit of Moncada*.

112 Bonachea and Martin, *The Cuban Insurrection*, 257.

113 It had been signed by Fidel Castro (26th of July Movement); Carlos Prío Socarrás (Organización Auténtica); Enrique Rodríguez Loeches (DRE); Justo Carrillo (Agrupación Montecristi); Manuel A. de Varona (Partido Revolucionario

Cubano Insurreccional); Ángel Santos (Resistencia Cívica); Lincoln Rodón (Partido Demócrata Independiente); David Salvador, Ángel Cofiño, Pascasio Linares, Lauro Blanco and José M. Aguilera (Unidad Obrera); José Puente and Omar Fernández (FEU); and Dr. José Miró Cardona (Coordinador General).

114 Ernest Hemingway to Archibald MacLeish, October 15, 1958, *Selected Letters*, 885.

115 Lloyd and Tillie Arnold to Ernest Hemingway, August 19 and 25, 1958, in Reynolds, *Hemingway: The Final Years*, 402.

116 Baker, *Ernest Hemingway*, 540.

117 Hemingway, *How It Was*, 453.

118 "For the obvious fact is that the achievement of communicating in pictorial form the eloquence of Mr. Hemingway's minor epic of an old man's lonely battle with a fish called for supreme imagination and even luck on the part of the artists on the job. And those are favoring factors that the artists here seem to have lacked." Bosley Crowther, "Hemingway; 'Old Man and the Sea' Stars Spencer Tracy," *The New York Times*, October 8, 1958, https://www.nytimes.com/1958/10/08/archives/hemingway-old-man-and-the-sea-stars-spencer-tracy.html.

119 Ernest Hemingway to Patrick Hemingway, November 24, 1958, *Selected Letters*, 887.

120 Hemingway, *Selected Letters*, 887.

121 Baker, *Ernest Hemingway*, 544.

122 Confidential orders by Colonel Suarez Suquet, commander of the Camaguey Rural Guards Regiment, in Bonachea and Martín, *The Cuban insurrection*, 263.

123 Hemingway, *The Old Man and the Sea*, 36.

124 Franqui, *Diary of the Cuban Revolution*, 418.

125 "Flight 482 Is Missing," *Time*, November 17, 1958, 38. See also Paterson, *Contesting Castro*, 22.

126 Nohlen, *Elections in the Americas*, 217; Karl E. Meyer, "Foes Attack Batista-Called Election," *The Washington Post*, September 18, 1958, A16.

127 "On 27 November considerable numbers of Cuban army officers were arrested for complicity in a military conspiracy against the government or for cowardice in refusing to continue the fight against the Castro rebellion. The respected General Martín Díaz Tamayo was retired for suspected involvement in this plot, and has recently been arrested." "Developments in Cuba Since Mid-November," Glennon, ed. *Foreign Relations of the United States, 1958–1960, Cuba*, vol. VI, 182; *Special National Intelligence Estimate*, Washington, December 16, 1958, SNIE 85/1–58.

128 "Despite his nice manner," Batista later remembered, "Señor Smith could not hide through his smile his deep sorrow." Smith, *The Fourth Floor*, 181.

129 Smith, *The Fourth Floor*, 181.

130 Dispatch from the Embassy in Cuba to the Department of State, no. 1060, Havana, March 23, 1959, drafted for the ambassador, Daniel M. Braddock, Minister-Couselor, Department of State, Central Files, 737.00/3–2359, confidential. *Foreign Relations of the United States, 1958–1963, Cuba*, vol. VI.

131 Barbara Rojas, in Fontova, *Exposing the Real Che Guevara*, 96–97.

CHAPTER 13

1 Hemingway, *How It Was*, 457.

2 New Year's Eve.

3 Ricardo Alarcón de Quesada, "The Long March of the Cuban Revolution," *Monthly Review* 60, no. 8 (January 2009): 14–27; Tim O'Meilia, "Widow of Cuban Dictator Batista Dies in WPB," *The Palm Beach Post* (October 4, 2006). See also Bourne, *Fidel*, 158–59; Quirk, *Fidel Castro*, 203, 207–208; and Coltman, *The Real Fidel Castro*, 137.

4 Hemingway, *Selected Letters*, 892.

5 "Batista Supporters Harassed," *Daily Boston Globe*, January 2, 1959.

6 "More than 20,000 Deaths Counted as the Tragic Bottom Line from the Batista Regime," *Bohemia*, January 11, 1959. John F. Kennedy, "Speech of Senator John F. Kennedy," Cincinnati, OH, Democratic Dinner, October 6, 1960, https://www.presidency.ucsb.edu/documents/speech-senator-john-f-kennedy-cincinnati-ohio-democratic-dinner. Comandante Fidel Castro Ruz, "No decían que estaban siendo sometidos a juicios los criminales de guerra que habían asesinado y torturado a 20 000 compatriotas," speech, Plaza Area del Silencio, Caracas, Venezuela, January 23, 1959.

7 Estrada, *Havana*, 235.

8 Ruby Hart Phillips, "Batista and Regime Flee Cuba; Castro Moving to Take Power; Mobs Riot and Loot in Havana; Army Halts Fire; Rebels Seize Santiago and Santa Clara—March on Capital," *The New York Times*, January 2, 1959), 1.

9 Speech by Fidel Castro to Santiago, January 3, 1959, Latin American Network Information Center, The University of Texas at Austin, http://lanic.utexas.edu/project/castro/db/1959/19590103.html.

10 Speech by Fidel Castro to Santiago.

11 Baker, *Ernest Hemingway*, 543.

12 J. Dubois, "New Cuban Rulers Picked," *Chicago Daily Tribune*, January 2, 1959.

13 Phillips, "Batista and Regime Flee Cuba."

14 BBC News, "Fidel Castro on his Beard, Free Election & Gambling (1959)—BBC News," YouTube video, 1:13, November 26, 2016, from an interview broadcast January 10, 1959, https://www.youtube.com/watch?v=iDZ5GyVDqOc.

15 "It had its positive side: in order for a spy to infiltrate us, he had to start preparing months ahead of time—he'd have had to have six-months' growth of beard, you see . . . Later, with the triumph of the Revolution, we kept our beards to preserve the symbolism." Castro and Ramonet, *My Life*, 195.

16 Geyer, *Guerrilla Prince*, 198.

17 Alistair Cooke, "Castro Is Cuba's Saviour for Now," *The Guardian*, January 8, 1959, https://www.theguardian.com/theguardian/2014/jan/08/fidel-castro-cuba-alistair-cooke.

18 "Returning to Cuba, he would kiss the Cuban flag, and declare, 'I am happy to be here again, because I consider myself one more Cuban . . . My sympathies are with the Cuban Revolution and all our difficulties. I don't want to be considered a yanqui.'" "I have complete faith in the Castro Revolution because it has the support of the Cuban people. I believe in his cause." Hemingway, *Selected Letters*, 892, 899; Fuentes, *Hemingway in Cuba*, 274–75.

19 Ernest Hemingway to Gianfranco Ivancich, Janaury 7, 1959, *Selected Letters*, 890.

20 Ernest Hemingway to L. H. Brague, Jr., January 24, 1959, *Selected Letters*, 890.

21 Speech by Fidel Castro before Havana rally, January 21, 1959, LANIC, The University of Texas at Austin, http://lanic.utexas.edu/project/castro/db/1959/19590121.html.

22 "I came to Venezuela, first, for a sentiment of gratitude, second, for a fundamental duty of reciprocity for all the institutions that have generously invited me to participate in the happiness for Venezuela this glorous day of 23 January (Applause and exclamations), but also for another reason: because the Cuban people need the people of Venezuela's help." Castro and Ramonet, *My Life*, 637. That day, Castro would apparently ask Betancourt if Venezuela could supply Cuba with oil and advance a $300 million loan so that when they became "embroiled in a game of gringos," Cuba would be prepared. Coltman, *The Real Fidel Castro*, 153.

23 Jules Dubois, "Castro Becomes Premier: Cabinet Quits in Plan to End 'Double Rule,' Rebel Chieftain Widens Power," *Chicago Daily Tribune*, February 14, 1959, 1.

24 "The symbol of this shortsighted attitude is now on display in a Havana museum. It is a solid gold telephone presented to Batista by the American-owned Cuban telephone company. It is an expression of gratitude for the

excessive telephone rate increase which the Cuban dictator had granted at the urging of our Government. But visitors to the museum are reminded that America made no expression at all over the other events which occurred on the same day this burdensome rate increase was granted, when 40 Cubans lost their lives in an assault on Batista's palace." Kennedy, "Speech of Senator John F. Kennedy," Cincinnati, OH, Democratic Dinner, October 6, 1960.

25 Emmett Watson, "Hemingway Talks on Cuba," reprinted as "Hemingway Defends Cuban Trials," *Seattle Post-Intelligencer*, March 9, 1959; Watson, *My Life in Print*, 68–75; Emmett Watson, "Hemingway's Writing, At Its Best, Made His Literary Audience Care," *The Seattle Times*, July 6, 1999; Mickelson, "Seattle By and By" (thesis), 5042.

26 Watson, "Hemingway Defends Cuban Trials"; Watson, *My Life in Print*, 68–75; Emmett Watson, "This, Our City: A Drink with Hemingway," *Seattle Post-Intelligencer*, March 4, 1959; Watson, "Hemingway's Writing, At Its Best, Made His Literary Audience Care."

27 Bourne, *Fidel*, 168.

28 Fidel Castro, in Páporov, *Hemingway en Cuba*, 397–99; Reynolds, *Hemingway: The Final Years*, 331–33.

29 Hemingway, *How It Was*, 462.

30 Páporov, *Hemingway en Cuba*, 397.

31 "5 Seized in 'Plot' Opposing Castro," *The Washington Post* and *Times Herald*, March 12, 1959, 1.

32 "Alleged Plots Involving Foreign Leaders," U.S. Senate, Select Committee to Study Governmental Operations with Respect to Intelligence Activities, S. Rep. No. 755, 94th Cong., second session.

33 "Fidel Castro: Dodging Exploding Seashells, Poison Pens and Ex-Lovers," BBC, November 27, 2016, https://www.bbc.com/news/world-latin-america-38121583.

34 Escalante, *CIA Targets Fidel*. See also Duncan Campbell, "638 Ways to Kill Castro," *The Guardian*, August 2, 2006, https://www.theguardian.comworld/2006/aug/03/cuba.duncancampbell2.

35 Paterson, *Contesting Castro*, 18.

36 Candela Vazquez and Dr. José Luis Herrera Sotolongo, in Páporov, *Hemingway en Cuba*, 397–99.

37 Páporov, *Hemingway en Cuba*, 399.

38 Married in 1948, Mirta Diaz-Balart and Fidel Castro, like many Cuban couples at that time, honeymooned in New York City and divorced while Fidel was in Mexico in 1955.

39 *Face the Nation*, "Fidel Castro on *Face the Nation* in 1959," YouTube video, April 19,

2018, 28:30, from an episode airing January 11, 1959, https://www.youtube.com/watch?v=GUeR4c4-6QE.

40 *Face the Nation*, "Fidel Castro on *Face the Nation* in 1959."

41 Ed Cony, "A Chat on a Train: Dr. Castro Describes His Plans for Cuba," *Wall Street Journal*, April 22, 1959.

42 Richard Nixon's summary of his meeting with Fidel Castro on April 19, 1959, Department of State, Central Files, 711.12/4–2459, https://history.state.gov/historicaldocuments/frus1958-60v06/d287.

43 After his visit to Cuba in 1955, Nixon had written that "emotional," "romantic," and "childish" people suffer from "excessive pride." Twelve cubans, North Americans believed, suffered from an "exaggerated nationalism." "Notes from Oral Briefing at Room P-53, on January 31, 1955," box 1, Central American Trip, 1955, series 361, Vice President, Pre-Presidential Papers, Richard M. Nixon Papers, Federal Archives and Records Center, Laguna Niguel, California. As a writer from the *Houston Post* wrote, "One nice thing about Cuba is that she can have a revolution any time hotbloods get in the mood without adding to world tension." To this condescension, Cuban writers responded that America's failed relationships with Latin America could be attributed to this same pride and ignorance: Americans were "brilliant communicators but bad listeners. I will tell you why. It's because you think you are so superior to us that you don't have to know about us." Paterson, *Contesting Castro*, 15.

CHAPTER 14

1 Hemingway, *How It Was*, 485.

2 Kert, *The Hemingway Women*, 490.

3 "Hemingway shot cigarettes out of my mouth with pellets from the kind of air gun you use at a fair stand. There were not real bullets, but they could damage your face. Later on at El Escorial outside Madrid, he shot cigarettes out of my mouth with real bullets. Hemingway respected Davis more than Hotchner because he thought Hotchner was a poor writer. I named him *El Pecas*: Freckles. We dressed him up as a torero. He marched in my opening paseo but didn't take part in the actual fight." In attendance were Bill and Annie Davis, Antonio and Carmen Ordóñez, Buck Lanham, Evangeline and David Bruce, Gianfranco and Christina Ivancich, Valerie Danby Smith, the Maharajah of Cooch, George Behar, Pat Saviers, A. E. Hotchner, and Peter Buckley. Meyers, *Hemingway*, 529.

4 Quirk, *Fidel Castro*, 249.

5 Quirk, *Fidel Castro*, 250–51.

6 Thomas, *Cuba*, 92.

7 Bullfighters.

8 Reynolds, *Hemingway: The Final Years*, 330.

9 Hemingway, *How It Was*, 473.

10 Mary Hemingway to Ernest Hemingway, October 19, 1959, in Reynolds, *Hemingway: The Final Years*, 334.

11 Hemingway, *How It Was*, 477, 450.

12 According to Matos, he had tried to resign as soon as Urrutia did, but Fidel had told him: "Your resignation is not acceptable at this point. We still have too much work to do, I admit that Raúl and Che are flirting with Marxism . . . but you have the situation under control . . . Forget about resigning . . . But if in a while you believe the situation is not changing, you have the right to resign." When he insisted with a second letter of resignation in September—"The Communist influence in the government has continued to grow. I have to leave power as soon as possible. I have to alert the Cuban people as to what is happening"—Fidel sent Camilo to arrest him.

13 Páparov, *Hemingway en Cuba*, 400.

14 Kert, *The Hemingway Women*, 492.

15 Páporov, *Hemingway en Cuba*, 401; Villarreal and Villarreal, *Hemingway's Cuban Son*, 24.

16 Speech by Fidel Castro in Havana, March 7, 1960, LANIC, The University of Texas at Austin, http://lanic.utexas.edu/project/castro/db/1960/19600307-1.html.

17 Yaffe, *Che Guevara*, 26.

18 Hemingway, *Running with the Bulls*, 113.

19 Hemingway, *Running with the Bulls*, 175.

20 Fidel Castro, "Statements in Revolutionary Works," transcription of previous evening's broadcast on television, Havana, July 9, 1960; Fuentes, *Hemingway in Cuba*, 128.

21 *Life*, June 1960, quoted in Jon Michaud, "Hemingway, Castro, and Cuba," *The New Yorker*, May 24, 2012; Páporov, *Hemingway*, 401.

22 Blanco, *Batista, el ídolo del pueblo*, 158.

23 "Seguí mis principios y traté de lograr una estatua llena de vigor y firmeza humana. Al rostro le imprimí serenidad y entereza como para dar alguien que tiene la certidumbre de sus ideas; no lo vi como un angelito entre nubes, sino con los pies firmes en la tierra." [Author's translation] Gilma Madera, cited in "El Cristo de la Habana," Edured.cu, https://www.ecured.cu/El_Cristo_de_La_Habana.

24 "Para esculpirlo no empleó ningún modelo, sino que se inspiró en su ideal de

belleza masculine: ojos oblicuos, labios pulpusos, en sintonía con el mestizaje racial en este pedazo del mundo." [Author's translation] Madera, cited in "El Cristo de la Habana."

25 The Cuban People.

26 This passage from Ecclesiastes, quoted here from the King James Bible, had served Hemingway as inspiration for his novel *The Sun Also Rises*.

CHAPTER 15

1 "Been having bad trouble with my eyes . . . down to 194 lbs. this a.m." Ernest Hemingway to Charles Scribner, July 6, 1960, *Selected Letters*, 906.

2 Ernest Hemingway to Charles Scribner, March 31, 1960, *Selected Letters*, 902.

3 Hemingway, *How It Was*, 484.

4 Hemingway, *How It Was*, 485.

5 Ernest Hemingway to A. E. Hotchner, May 9, 1960, in DeFazio, *Dear Papa, Dear Hotch*, 291.

6 Pecas, the nickname Hemingway had given A. E. Hotchner in Spain that summer, means "freckles," and he subsequently signed his letters "A .E. Pecas." In one letter, he signed "Sen John F. Hotchennedy," in a tip of the hat to the man who would win the nomination for president at the Democratic National Convention. DeFazio, *Dear Papa, Dear Hotch*, 291.

7 Ernest Hemingway to Dr. George Saviers, June 14, 1960, *Selected Letters*, 904.

8 "Congress Passes Sugar Bill," *The New York Times*, July 4, 1960, 1.

9 "Castro Forces Carry Out Seizure of U.S. Properties," *The New York Times*, August 8, 1960, 1.

10 "Red China and Cuba Shaping Barter Pact," *Chicago Daily Tribune*, July 23, 1960, 1-s13.

11 Hemingway, *How It Was*, 488.

12 Hemingway, *How It Was*, 489.

13 Ernest Hemingway to Mary Hemingway, August 15, 1960, in Hemingway, *How It Was*, 489.

14 Ernest Hemingway to Mary Hemingway, September 25, 1960, *Selected Letters*, 907.

15 Readers can still access this report on the FBI's webpage to endeavor to understand the Bureau's interests in this North American author. Although the FBI maintains a link to the Investigation on Ernest Hemingway, half of its 120-plus pages are blotted out to protect the Bureau/in the interests of National Security. See https://vault.fbi.gov/ernest-miller-hemingway/ernest-hemingway-part-01-of-01/view.

16 An agent from the CIA said: "The Agency had a plan to place a box of cigars in a location where they could be smoked by Castro. If and when he lit one, the agent said, the cigar would explode and blow his head off." Escalante Font, *Executive Action*; "CIA Assassination Plots Against Castro," *U.S. History in Context*, Gale.com, http://go.galegroup.com/ps/i.do?p=UHIC&u=wheelerschlib&id=GALE|EJ2165000135&v=2.1&it=r&asid=c4fbc14a.

17 As was appropriate. Speech by Fidel Castro to the United Nations General Assembly, September 26, 1960, LANIC, The University of Texas at Austin, http://lanic.utexas.edu/project/castro/db/1960/19600926.html.

18 Walter Lippmann, scan from original English-language pamphlet, July 3, 2007, http://walterlippmann.com/fc-09-02-1960.html.

19 FBI 100-344127–NR 3.15.60, FBI 2-1622-38, Cover Page 6, Hughes, and FBI File No. 105-3138. FBI 2-1622-45, 46, quoted in Michael Canfield, Gerry Patrick Hemming, and Alan Weberman, "Coup d'Etat in America: The CIA and the Assassination of John F. Kennedy," *Nodule XI*, July 9, 2010, https://the-eye.eu/public/concen.org/JFK%20Kennedy%20Assassination%20Zapruder%20Film%20Hoax%20research%20pack/ebooks/Coup%20D%27Etat%20in%20America%2C%20Vol%201.pdf.

20 Remarks of Senator John F. Kennedy at Democratic Dinner, Cincinnati, Ohio, October 6, 1960, JFK, presidency.ucsb.edu/ws/index.php?pid=25660.

21 Ernest Hemingway to A. E. Hotchner, September 8, 1960, DeFazio, *Dear Papa, Dear Hotch*, 298.

22 Reynolds, *Hemingway: The Final Years*, 348–49.

23 Hemingway, *How It Was*, 492.

24 Hemingway, *How It Was*, 493.

25 Peter Beaumont, "Fresh Claim Over Role the FBI Played in Suicide of Ernest Hemingway," *The Guardian*, July 2, 2011, theguardian.com/books/2011/jul/03/fbi-and-ernest-hemingway.

26 Ernest Hemingway, quoted in Hemingway, *How It Was*, 491.

27 "Hemingway at Mayo Clinic," *Boston Globe*, January 11, 1961, 10.

28 Hemingway's Medical Files, Hemingway Personal Papers.

29 Hotchner, *Papa Hemingway*, 180–82.

30 "In the long history of the world, only a few generations have been granted the role of defending freedom in its hour of maximum danger. I do not shrink from this responsibility—I welcome it. I do not believe that any of us would exchange places with any other people or any other generation. The energy, the faith, the devotion which we bring to this endeavor will light our country and all who serve it—and the glow from that fire can truly light the world.

And so, my fellow Americans, ask not what your country can do for you; ask what you can do for your country." John F. Kennedy, "Inaugural Address," January 20, 1961, ohn F. Kennedy Library, jfklibrary.org/Research/Research-Aids/Ready-Reference/JFK-Quotations/Inaugural-Address.aspx.

31 Ernest Hemingway to John F. Kennedy, January 24, 1961, *Selected Letters*, 916.

32 Ernest. Hemingway, quoted in *Cooper and Hemingway: The True Gen*, dir. John Mulholland (Passion River, 2013).

33 Ernest Hemingway to L. H. Brague, Jr., February 6, 1961, *Selected Letters*, 916–917.

34 John F. Kennedy, "Address Before the American Society of Newspaper Editors," April 20, 1961, John F. Kennedy Library, https://www.jfklibrary.org/asset-viewer/archives/JFKPOF/034/JFKPOF-034-018.

35 Mary Hemingway to Ursula Hemingway Jepson, April 25, 1961, Mary Hemingway Personal Papers.

36 "Hemingway Back at Mayo Clinic," *Boston Globe*, April 27, 1961, 36.

37 Hemingway, *How It Was*, 500–02.

38 A. E. Hotchner, "Hemingway: Hounded by the Feds," *The New York Times*, July 1, 2011, https://www.nytimes.com/2011/07/02/opinion/02hotchner.html.

39 "Hemingway Dead of Shotgun Wound; Wife Says He Was Cleaning Weapon," *The New York Times*, July 3, 1961, 1. Emmett Watson, "Real Story of Death of Hemingway," *Seattle Post-Intelligencer*, July 7, 1961, 1.

40 "My problem is that I have a year of Ernest Hemingway's life [the word is mangled] locked up in my head . . . I have everything to work with . . . the diary, the log dictated by Ernest during the quiet intervals as we fished, a three-hundred-page manuscript outlining the conversations and the action that I wrote when the events were fresh in my mind. But the manuscript was badly written and never worked over. and is in no shape for publication. Much was left out and I am the only one who can put it back in . . . If I do nothing to the Hemingway diary and the 300 page manuscript, when I am dead. It will have not value to anyone. On the other hand, if I can fix it up so that it can be read, who knows, it might be literature . . . I was lucky enough to have that experience, and now I would like to put it out on paper and give it to others. It happened to me. Now let me see if I can make it happen to you." Arnold Samuelson, circa late 1950s–early 1960s, Arnold Samuelson Papers, cited in Hendrickson, *Hemingway's Boat*, 581.

41 Arnold Samuelson and Arnold Gingrich, "E. H: A Code from the Maestro: Publisher's Page," *Esquire*, October 1961, cited in Samuelson, *With Hemingway*, 183.

42 In fact, medical records made available to the public in 1991 confirm that

he was diagnosed with the disease in 1961. Susan Beegel, "Hemingway and Hemochromatosis," *Hemingway Review* (September 1990). Additionally, the suicides of two of Hemingway's siblings, Ursula and Leicester, both committed late in life, might also support this theory.

CHAPTER 16

1 Villarreal and Villarreal, *Hemingway's Cuban Son*, 161.

2 Hemingway, *Running with the Bulls*, 338–40. Mary boasts in her biography that she also managed at the time to smuggle out jewels and monies for a disaffected Cuban in her handbag. Hemingway, *How It Was*, 506–09; Fuentes, *Hemingway in Cuba*, 277–79.

3 Fidel Castro, in Hemingway, *How It Was*, 507–08.

4 Cited in Hemingway and Brennen, *Hemingway in Cuba*, 84.

5 Quoted in Humberto Fontova, "Did Andy Garcia fall for Castro Propaganda?" Babalú Blog,June 24, 2013, https://babalublog.com/2013/06/24/did-andy-garcia-fall-for-castro-propaganda/. See also "Fisherman Among Arrivals at Key West Says He is Model for 'Old Man and Sea,'" *The New York Times*, October 22, 1965.

6 Desnoes, "The Final Summer," *Punto de Vista*, 47; Fuentes, *Hemingway in Cuba*, 428.

7 "J&M: Which authors [do you read]? FIDEL CASTRO: Of the American writers, Hemingway is one of my favorites. He was a friend of ours. J&M: Did you know him personally? FIDEL CASTRO: Yes, I met him after the triumph of the revolution, during the ceremony of the awarding of the Hemingway Prize in a fishing competition. But I knew his work long before the Revolution. For instance, I read *For Whom the Bell Tolls* when I was a student. It was all about a group of guerrillas and I found it very interesting, because Hemingway told about a rear guard that fought against a conventional army. I can tell you now that that Hemingway novel was one of the books that helped me plan the tactics with which to fight Batista's army . . . The methods the men of that other time used to solve their problem helped us considerably to find a way to do it." Mankiewicz and Jones, *With Fidel*, Fuentes, *Hemingway in Cuba*, 428. Castro would mention *For Whom the Bell Tolls* and Hemingway in numerous interviews, for example in Ignacio Ramonet's *Cien horas con Fidel* (Spanish title; in English: *In Conversation with Fidel*). In this lengthy volume, he would remember Hemingway and his books on several occasions: "Castro: In Spain there was war even on the rear-guard; this is what inspired Hemingway to write his novel *For Whom the Bell Tolls.* The history about what happened in the rearguard during the Spanish Civil War was useful to us. We learned about the way in which the Republi-

can guerrillas at the rearguard of Franco's troops seized the weapons from the army. That book helped me to develop the conception of an irregular war in Cuba. Ramonet: You mean Hemingway's novel? Castro: Yes, because I remembered a lot about that book . . . Someday when we talk about it I'll let you know. Ramonet: Why don't you tell me about it now? Castro: Well, as you wish. I first read *For Whom the Bell Tolls* when I was a young student. And I must have read that novel more than three times ever since. I also watched the film that was made later on. I was interested in that book because, among other things, it deals, as I said, with a struggle that is waged at the rearguard and it illustrates the existence of a guerrilla, and the way in which it can operate within a territory which is supposedly under enemy control. I am referring to the very accurate descriptions made by Hemingway in that novel. We had our own idea of what an irregular war would be militarily as well as politically. But *For Whom the Bell Tolls* allowed us to visualize that experience. In all his books, Hemingway's descriptions are very realistic, clear, and unambiguous. Everything there is rational and convincing. You can hardly forget what you have read, because he makes you feel that you have gone through that experience yourself. He had the capacity to transport his readers to the theater where that cruel Spanish Civil War was fought. Later on, we knew about life inside a guerrilla through our own personal experience at the Sierra Maestra Mountains. So the book became something familiar to us. We always went back to it for inspiration, even after becoming guerrilla fighters. Obviously, we read many other books about real-life events, or fiction books which addressed that topic. We tried to introduce an ethics to the struggle waged under the specific circumstances of our country. As I said, I couldn't affirm that we were the only guerrillas with an ethics. Ramonet: But you turned that ethics into a fundamental principle. Castro: Hadn't we implemented that philosophy here, combatants would perhaps have shot prisoners right and left, and would have committed all sorts of reprehensible acts. There was so much hatred against injustice and crimes. Ramonet: Did you resort to terrorism, for example, against Batista's troops, or engage in assassination plots? Castro: Neither terrorism nor assassination."

8 Speech delivered as President of the Movement of Unaligned Countries before the XXXIV Period of Sessions of the General Assembly of the United Nations, New York, October 12, 1979.

9 Ada Rosa Rosales, director of the Finca Vigía Museum, Havana, personal interview, December 2009; Armando Cristoval (Cuban Mystery Writer), personal interview, December 2009; Desnoes, "The Final Summer"; Raúl Mesa (Cuban Poet and Essayist), personal interview, December 2009.

10 "No other writer—with the exception of José Martí—has been the object of so many Cuban tributes at so many different levels. From the first moment, Fidel Castro himself has been the sponsor of the most meaningful of them. It was he who took care of Hemingway's widow—Mary Welsh—on the two occasions in which she visited Havana after her husband's death. It was they who together agreed on the terms under which Finca Vigía would remain intact, as it is today, converted into a museum so true to life that at times one seems to feel the presence of the writer wandering through the rooms with his great dead-man shoes . . . You have to know Fidel Castro to realize that he would never say such a thing as a simple courtesy, since he would have to go beyond some important political considerations to say it with such conviction. The truth is that Fidel Castro has been for many years a constant reader of Hemingway, that he knows his work in depth, that he likes to talk about him, and knows how to defend him convincingly. On his long and frequent trips to the interior of the country, he always takes a confusing pile of government documents to study in his car. Among them one can often see the two volumes with red covers of the selected works of Ernest Hemingway." Gabriel Garcia Marquez, "Hemingway—Our Own" (introduction), Fuentes, *Hemingway in Cuba*, 14.

11 Fuentes, *Hemingway in Cuba*, 273.

12 Carbonell, *And the Russians Stayed*; Perez, *On Becoming Cuban*, 445.

13 Hotchner, *Papa Hemingway*, 320.

14 Ramonet, *In Conversation with Fidel*, 668–69.

15 Matthews, *The Cuban Story*, 14–16.

16 "Ernest Hemingway is still the great hero of the Cuban people. He is staying at his home and working as a deliberate gesture to show his sympathy and support for the Castro revolution. He knows Cuba and the Cuban people as well as any American citizen. I was glad to find that his ideas on Fidel Castro and the Cuban Revolution are the same as mine." Matthews, *The Cuban Story*, 298.

17 Gay Talese, "Manuscripts Hemingway Left May Yield Four More Novels," *The New York Times*, March 9, 1962, https://www.nytimes.com/1962/03/09/archives/manuscripts-hemingway-left-may-yield-four-more-novels.html.

18 Richard Bourne, *Political Leaders of Latin America*, 99.

19 Moore, *Fidel Castro*, 45.

20 Moore, *Fidel Castro*, 45.

21 "I must express my gratitude to Hemingway for many things. First, because a great author bestowed on us the honor of choosing to live in our country and writing some of his major works here. I am also grateful to him for the great

pleasure that I experience reading his books. He is one of the greatest authors that ever lived." Fidel Castro, in Hemingway and Brennen, *Hemingway in Cuba*, 84, 116.

22 Fidel Castro, in Hemingway and Brennen, *Hemingway in Cuba*, 84, 116.

AFTERWORD

1 A *bodega* is a neighborhood grocery store that also typically sells beer and wine.

2 Our italics. Hemingway, "The Great Blue River," in *By-Line: Ernest Hemingway*, 390.

3 Hemingway, *The Old Man and the Sea*, 51.

BIBLIOGRAPHY

• • • • •

WORKS BY ERNEST HEMINGWAY

By-Line: Ernest Hemingway: Selected Articles and Dispatches of Four Decades. New York: Scribner's, 2002. First published 1967.

The Complete Short Stories of Ernest Hemingway: The Finca Vigía Edition. New York: Scribner's, 1987.

Dateline: Toronto: The Complete Toronto Star *Dispatches, 1920–1924*. Edited by William White. New York: Scribner's, 1987.

Death in the Afternoon. New York: Scribner's, 1999. First published 1932.

Ernest Hemingway: Selected Letters, 1917–1961. Edited by Carlos Baker. New York: Scribner, 2003. First published 1981.

A Farewell to Arms. New York: Scribner's, 1929.

For Whom the Bell Tolls. New York: Scribner, 1995. First published 1940.

The Fifth Column and the First Forty-Nine Stories. New York: Scribner's, 1938.

The Garden of Eden. New York: Scribner's, 1986.

The Green Hills of Africa. New York: Scribner, 2016. First Published 1935.

In Our Time. New York: Scribner's, 1925, 1996.

"Introduction," *Men at War: The Best War Stories of All Time*. New York: Crown, 1960. First published 1942.

Islands in the Stream. New York: Scribner's, 2002. First published 1970.

The Letters of Ernest Hemingway: Volume 1, 1907–1922. Edited by Sandra Spanier and Robert W. Trogdon. New York: Cambridge University Press, 2011.

The Letters of Ernest Hemingway: Volume 2, 1923–1925. Edited by Sandra Spanier, Albert J. DeFazio III, and Robert W. Trogdon. New York: Cambridge University Press, 2013.

The Letters of Ernest Hemingway: Volume 3, 1926–1929. Edited by Rena Sanderson, Sandra Spanier, and Robert W. Trogdon. New York: Cambridge University Press, 2015.

The Letters of Ernest Hemingway: Volume 4, 1929–1931. Edited by Sandra Spanier and Mariam B. Mandel. New York: Cambridge University Press, 2017.

A Moveable Feast. New York, Scribner's, 1996. First published 1964.

A Moveable Feast: The Restored Edition. Edited by Seán Hemingway. New York: Scribner's, 2009. First published 1964.

The Old Man and the Sea, New York: Scribner's, 2002. First published 1952.

The Sun Also Rises. New York: Scribner's, 2006. First published 1926.

Three Stories and Ten Poems. Edited by Robert McAlmon. Paris: Contract Publishing, 1923.

To Have and Have Not. New York: Scribner's, 2002. First published 1937.

BOOKS

Abeal y Otero, Jose. *Sloppy Joe's Bar Cocktail Manual*. Havana: Create Space Independent Publishing Platform, 2008.

Abel, Christopher, and Nissa Torrents. *José Martí: Revolutionary Democrat*. London: Bloomsbury, 2015.

Aguilar, Luis E. "Cuba, c.1860–c.1930." In *Cuba: A Short History*, edited by Leslie Bethell, 21–55. *The Cambridge History of Latin America*. New York: Cambridge University Press, 1993.

———. *From Cuba 1933: Prologue to Revolution*. New York: Norton, 1974.

Aimes, Hubert. *A History of Slavery in Cuba: 1511 to 1868*. New York: Octagon Books, 1967.

Alvarez, Jose. *Frank País: Architect of Cuba's Betrayed Revolution*. Boca Raton: Universal Publishers, 2009.

Ameringer, Charles. *Caribbean Legion: Patriots, Politicians, Soldiers of Fortune, 1946–1950*. University Park: Pennsylvania State University Press, 1996.

Anderson, John Lee. *Che Guevara: A Revolutionary Life*. New York: Grove Press, 1997.

Anderson, Sherwood. *Selected Letters*. Edited by Charles E. Modlin. Knoxville: University of Tennessee Press, 1984.

Argote-Freyre, Frank. *Fulgencio Batista: From the Revolutionary to the Strongman*. New Brunswick: Rutgers University Press, 2006.

Armstrong, Richard. *The State of Things in Cuba: A Letter to Hemingway*. Kent: Kent State University Press, 2013.

August, Arnold. *Democracy in Cuba and the 1997–98 Elections*. La Habana, Cuba: Editorial José Martí, 1999.

Ayala, Cesar J. *American Sugar Kingdom: The Plantation Economy of the Spanish Caribbean, 1898–1934*. Chapel Hill: University of North Carolina Press, 2009.

Baker, Carlos. *Ernest Hemingway: A Life Story*. Norwalk: The Easton Press, 1994.

———. *Ernest Hemingway: The Writer as Artist*. Princeton: Princeton University Press, 1998.

Beegel, Susan F. "Eye and Heart: Hemingway's Education as a Naturalist." In *A Historical Guide to Ernest Hemingway*, edited by Linda Wagner-Martin. New York: Oxford University Press, 2000.

Benjamin, Jules Robert. *The United States and Cuba: Hegemony and Dependent Development, 1880–1934*. Pittsburgh: University of Pittsburgh Press, 2009.

———. *The United States and the Origins of the Cuban Revolution: An Empire of Liberty in an Age of National Liberation*. Princeton: Princeton University Press, 1990.

Bennet, Warren. "The Poor Kitty and the Padrone and the Tortoise-shell Cat in 'Cat in the Rain.'" In *New Critical Approaches to the Short Storeis of Ernest Hemingway*. Edited by Jackson J. Benson. Durham: Duke University Press, 1990.

Benson, Jackson J. *New Critical Approaches to the Short Stories of Ernest Hemingway*. Durham: Duke University Press Books, 2009.

Benson, Thomas W. *Writing JFK: Presidential Rhetoric and the Press in the Bay of Pigs Crisis*. College Station: Texas A&M University Press, 2004.

Bergad, Laird W., Fe Iglesias García, and María del Carmen Barcia. *The Cuban Slave Market, 1790–1880*. New York: Cambridge University Press, 1995.

Berg, A. Scott. *Max Perkins: Editor of Genius*. New York: Riverhead, 1997.

Berman, Jeffrey. *Surviving Literary Suicides*. Amherst: University of Massachusetts Press, 1999.

Bethell, Leslie, ed. *Cambridge History of Latin America*, volume 5: 1870-1930. Cambridge: Cambridge University Press, 1980.

Birmingham, Kevin. *The Most Dangerous Book: The Battle for James Joyce's* Ulysses. New York: Penguin, 2014.

Blanco, Alejandro Prieto. *Batista, el ídolo del pueblo*. Sevilla: PUnto Rojo Libros, 2017.

Blume, Lesley M. M. *Everybody Behaves Badly: The True Story Behind Hemingway's Masterpiece* The Sun Also Rises. New York: Houghton Mifflin Harcourt, 2016.

Bockman, Major Larry James. *The Spirit of Moncada: Fidel Castro's Rise to Power, 1953–1959*. Quantico: Marine Corps Command and Staff College, 1984. https://www.globalsecurity.org /military/library/report/1984/BLJ.htm.

Bonachea, Ramon L. and Marta San Martin. *The Cuban Insurrection, 1952–1959*. New Brunswick: Transaction Publishers, 1974.

Bourne, Peter G. *Fidel: A Biography of Fidel Castro*. New York: Dodd Mead, 1986.

Bourne, Richard. *Political Leaders of Latin America*. New York: Knopf, 1970.

Brasch, James D., and Joseph Sigman. *Hemingway's Library: A Composite Record*. New York: Garland, 1981.

Brenner, Philip, and Peter Eisner. *Cuba Libre: A 500-Year Quest for Independence*. Lanham: Rowman & Littlefield, 2018.

Brian, Denis. *The True Gen: An Intimate Portrait of Ernest Hemingway by Those Who Knew Him Best*. New York: Grove Press, 1989.

Bruccoli, Matthew J., ed. *Conversations with Ernest Hemingway*. Jackson: University Press of Mississippi, 1986.

———. *The Only Thing That Counts*. Columbia: University of South Carolin Press, 1996.

———. *The Sons of Maxwell Perkins: Letters of F. Scott Fitzgerald, Ernest Hemingway, Thomas Wolfe, and Their Editor*. Columbia: University of South Carolina Press, 2004.

Bueno, Salvador. "José Antonio Fernández de Castro: periodista e investigador." In *Temas y personajes de la literature cubana*. Havana: Ediciones Unión, UNEAC, 1964.

Burwell, Rose Marie. *Hemingway: The Postwar Years and the Posthumous Novels*. Cambridge: Cambridge University Press, 1999. First published 1996.

Calhoun, Jack. *Gansterismo: The United States, Cuba, and the Mafia, 1933 to 1966*. New York: OR Books, 2015.

Cannell, Kathleen. "Scenes with a Hero." In *Hemingway and the Sun Set*. Edited by Bertram D. Sarason. Washington, DC: NCR Microcard Editions, 1972.

Cannon, Terrence. *Revolutionary Cuba*. New York: Thomas Crowell, 1981.

Carbonell, Néstor T. *And the Russians Stayed*. New York: William Morrow, 1989.

Carrozza, Anthony. *William D. Pawley: The Extraordinary Life of the Adventurer, Entrepreneur, and Diplomat Who Cofounded the Flying Tigers*. Washington DC: Potomac Books, 2012.

Carr, Virginia Spencer. *Dos Passos: A Life*. Evanston: Northwestern University Press, 2004.

Castro, Fidel, interviewed by Ignacio Ramonet. *My Life: A Spoken Autobiography*. New York: Scribner, 2009. First published 2008.

Cirules, Enrique. *Hemingway the stranger*. Havana: Editorial Arte y Literatura, 2015.

Cline, Sally. *Zelda Fitzgerald: Her Voice in Paradise*. London: Faber and Faber, 2013.

Colombus, Christopher. *The Four Voyages*. Translated by J. M. Cohen. New York: Penguin, 1969.

Coltman, Leycester. *The Real Fidel Castro*. New Haven: Yale University Press, 2003.

Conrad, Joseph. *The Mirror of the Sea*. Rockville: Wildside Press, 2003. First published, 1906.

Curnutt, Kirk, and Gail Sinclair, eds. *Key West Hemingway: A Reassessment*. Gainesville: University Press of Florida, 2016.

Davis, Mike. *Buda's Wagon: A Brief History of the Car Bomb*. Brooklyn: Verso, 2007.

Dearborn, Mary. *Ernest Hemingway: A Biography*. New York: Knopf, 2017.

DeFazio, Albert J., III, ed. *Dear Papa, Dear Hotch: The Correspondence of Ernest Hemingway and A. E. Hotchner*. Columbia: University of Missouri Press, 2005.

De las Casas, Bartolomé. *A Brief Account of the Destruction of the Indies*. London: Penguin, 2007. First published 1689.

De la Cova, Antonio. *The Moncada Attack: Birth of the Cuban Revolution*. Columbia: University of South Caroline Press, 2007.

Desnoes, Edmundo. *Punto de Vista*. Havana: Instituto del Libro, 1967.

Desroches, Leonard. *Allow the Water: Anger, Fear, Power, Work, Sexuality and Practice of Non Violence*. Ottawa: Dunamis, 2003. First published 1996.

D'Este, Carlo. *Eisenhower: A Soldier's Life*. New York: Henry Holt and Company, 2015.

Diaz-Briquets, Sergio, and Jorge Pérez-López. *Corruption in Cuba: Castro and Beyond*. Austin: University of Texas Press, 2006.

Dickson, Paul, and Thomas Allen. *The Bonus Army: An American Epic*. New York: Walker Books, 2006.

DiEugenio, James. *Destiny Betrayed: JFK, Cuba, and the Garrison Case*. New York: Skyhorse, 2013.

Diliberto, Gioia. *Hadley*. Boston: Ticknor & Fields, 1992.

Donaldson, Scott. *By Force of Will: The Life and Art of Ernest Hemingway*. Lincoln, NB: iUniverse, 2001. First published in NB: 1978.

———. *The Death of a Rebel: The Charlie Fenton Story*. Lanham: Fairleigh Dickinson University Press, 2012.

——— ed. *The Cambridge Companion to Hemingway*. New York: Cambridge University Press, 2006. First published 1996.

Donnelly, Honoria Murphy, and Richard N. Billings. *Sara & Gerald: Villa American and After*. New York: Holt, Rinehart, and Winston, 1984.

Dosal, Paul J. *Comandante Che: Guerrilla Soldier, Commander, and Strategist, 1956–1967*. University Park: Pennsylvania University Press, 2003.

Dos Passos, John. *The Best Times: An Informal Memoir*. New York: New American Library, 1966.

Draper, Theodore. *Castro's Cuba: A Revolution Betrayed?* New York: The New Leader, 1961.

Eby, Carl P. *Hemingway's Fetishism: Psychoanalysis and the Mirror of Manhood*. New York: SUNY Press, 1998.

Eltis, David, and David Richardson. *Atlas of the Transatlantic Slave Trade*. New Haven: Yale University Press, 2015. First published 2010.

English, T. J. *Havana Nocturne: How the Mob Owned Cuba . . . and Then Lost It to the Revolution*. New York: Harper Collins, 2008. First published 2007.

Escalante Font, Fabián. *CIA Targets Fidel: Secret 1967 CIA Inspector General's Report on Plots to Assassinate Fidel Castro*. Melbourne: Ocean Press, 1996.

———. *Executive Action: 634 Ways to Kill Fidel Castro*. Australia: Ocean Press, 2006.

Estrada, Alfredo José. *Havana: Autobiography of a City*. New York: St. Martin's Griffin, 2008. First published 2007.

Farber, Samuel. *Revolution and Reaction in Cuba, 1933–1960: A Political Sociology from Machado to Castro*. Middletown: Wesleyan University Press, 1976.

Faria, Miguel A. *Cuba in Revolution: Escape from a Lost Paradise*. New York: Hacienda, 2002.

Fitch, Noel Riley. *Sylvia Beach and the Lost Generation*. New York: Norton, 1985.

Fitzgerald, F. Scott. *A Life in Letters*. Edited by Matthew J. Bruccoli. New York: Scribner's, 1994.

Fitzgerald, F. Scott. *This Side of Paradise*. Columbia SC: Bruccoli Clark, 1975.

Fontova, Humberto. *Exposing the Real Che Guevara: And the Useful Idiots Who Idolize Him*. New York: Sentinel, 2008.

Foran, John. *Taking Power: On the Origins of Third World Revolutions*. Cambridge: Cambridge University Press, 2005.

Franqui, Carlos. *Diary of the Cuban Revolution*. New York: Viking, 1980. First published in French in 1976.

———. *Twelve*. Translated by Albert B. Teichne. New York: Lyle Stuart, 1968.

Fuentes, Norberto. *Hemingway in Cuba*. Secaucus: Lyle Stuart, 1984.

Gadea, Hilda. *My Life with Che: The Making of a Revolutionary*. Translated by Ricardo Gadea. New York: Palgrave Macmillan, 2008. First published 1972.

García-Pérez, Gladys Marel. *Insurrection & Revolution: Armed Struggle in Cuba, 1952–1959*. Translated by Juan Ortega. Boulder: Lynne Rienner, 1998.

Gates, Henry Louis, and Kwame Anthony Appiah, eds. *Africana: The Encyclopedia of the African and African American Experience*. New York: Basic Civitas Books, 1999.

Gellhorn, Martha. *Selected Letters of Martha Gellhorn*. Edited by Caroline Moorehead. New York: Henry Holt, 2006.

———. *Travels with Myself and Another*. New York: Penguin Putnam, 2001. First published 1978.

Geyer, Georgie Anne. *Guerrilla Prince: The Untold Story of Fidel Castro*. Kansas City: Andrews McMeel, 1991.

Glennon, John P., ed. *Foreign Relations of the United States, 1958–1960, Cuba*, vol. VI. Washington, DC: US Government Printing Office, 1991.

Godfrey, Laura. *Hemingway's Geographies: Intimacy, Materiality, and Memory*. New York: Palgrave Macmillan, 2016.

Gott, Richard. *Cuba: A New History*. New Haven: Yale University Press, 2004.

Greenberg, David. *Calvin Coolidge*. New York: Henry Holt, 2006.

Griffin, Peter. *Along with Youth: Hemingway, the Early Years*. New York: Oxford University Press, 1985.

Grimes, Larry Edward, and Sylvester Bickford. *Hemingway, Cuba, and the Cuban Works*. Kent: Kent State University Press, 2014.

Guevara, Ernesto "Che." *Che Guevara Reader: Writings on Politics and Revolution*. Edited by David Deutschmann. Melbourne: Ocean Press, 2003.

———. *Reminiscences of the Cuban Revolutionary War*. Melbourne: Ocean Books, 2008. First published in Spanish, 1963.

Harris, Richard Legé. *Che Guevara: A Biography*. Santa Barbara: Greenwood, 2011.

Hart, Armando Davalos. *Aldabonazo: Inside the Cuban Revolutionary Underground, 1952–1958, a Participant's Account*. Edited by Mary Alice Waters. Atlanta: Pathfinder Press, 2004. First published 1997.

Hawkins, Ruth. *Unbelievable Happiness and Final Sorrow: The Hemingway-Pfeiffer Marriage*. Fayetteville: University of Arkansas Press, 2012.

Hemingway, Gregory H. *Papa: A Personal Memoir*. New York: Houghton Mifflin, 1976.

Hemingway, Hilary, and Carlene Brennen. *Hemingway in Cuba*. New York: Rugged Land, 2005.

Hemingway, Jack. *Misadventures of a Fly Fisherman: My Life with and without Papa.* Dallas: Taylor Publications, 1986.

Hemingway, John. *Strange Tribe: A Family Memoir.* Guilford: The Lyons Press, 2007.

Hemingway, Leicester. *My Brother, Ernest Hemingway.* London: Weisenfeld & Nicolson, 1962.

———. *The Sound of the Trumpet.* New York: Holt and Company, 1953.

Hemingway, Lorian. *Walk on Water: A Memoir.* New York: Harcourt Brace and Company, 1998.

Hemingway, Mary. *How It Was.* New York: Knopf, 1976.

Hemingway, Valerie. *Running with the Bulls.* New York: Random House, 2004.

Hendrickson, Paul. *Hemingway's Boat: Everything He Loved in Life, and Lost, 1934–1961.* New York: Vintage, 2011.

———. *Hemingway's Student: The Devotions of Arnold Samuelson, Assistant and Acolyte.* New York: Knop Doubleday, 2011.

Hotchner, A. E. *Hemingway in Love: The Untold Story.* New York: Picador, 2016.

———. *Papa Hemingway.* New York: Random House, 1966.

Hughes, Langston. *I Wonder as I Wander; An Autobiographical Journey.* New York: Hill and Wang, 1956.

Hyatt, Pulaski F., and John T. Hyatt. *Cuba: Its Resources and Opportunities.* New York: J. S. Olgivie, 1898.

Ivancich, Adriana. *La torre bianca* [*The White Tower*]. Milan: Arnoldo Mondadori Editore, 1980.

Jenks, Leland H. *Our Cuban Colony.* New York: Vanguard Press, 1928.

Jividen, Jill. "Cinema and Adaptations." In *Ernest Hemingway in Context.* Edited by Debra A. Moddelmog and Suzanne del Gizzo. New York: Cambridge University Press, 2013. First published 2012.

Johnson, Clifton. *Highways and Byways of Florida.* New York: Macmillan Company, 1918.

Jones, Howard. *Crucible of Power: A History of American Foreign Relations to 1913.* Lanham: Rowan & Littlefield, 2009.

Kert, Bernice. *The Hemingway Women.* New York: W. W. Norton, 1998.

Kirkpatrick, Lyman B., Jr. *The Real CIA.* New York: The Macmillan Company, 1968.

Klouzal, Linda A. *Women and Rebel Communities in the Cuban Insurgent Movement, 1952–1959.* Cambria: Amherst, 2008.

Knigge, Jobst C. *Hemingway's Venetian Muse Adriana Ivancich: A Contribution to the Biography of Ernest Hemingway.* Berlin: Humboldt University, 2011.

Koch, Stephen. *The Breaking Point: Hemingway, Dos Passos, and the Murder of Jose Robles.* New York: Counterpoint, 2005.

Larsen, Lyle. *Stein and Hemingway: The Story of a Turbulent Friendship.* Jefferson: Mcfarland, 2011.

Lipman, Jana. *Guantánamo: A Working-Class History between Empire and Revolution.* Berkley: University of California Press, 2009.

Loewen, James. *Lies My Teacher Told Me.* New York: New Press, 1995.

Lynn, Kenneth. *Hemingway.* Cambridge: Harvard University Press, 1987.

Machado, Gerardo. *Ocho años de lucha.* Miami: Ediciones Históricas Cubanas, 1982.

———. *Por la patria libre.* Havana: F. Verdugo Press, 1926.

MacLeish, Archibald. *Letters of Archibald MacLeish.* Edited by R. H. Minnick. Boston: Houghton Mifflin, 1983.

Mankiewicz, Frank, and Kirby Jones. *With Fidel. A Portrait of Castro and Cuba.*Chicago: Playboy Press, 1975.

Márquez-Sterling, Manuel. *Cuba 1952–1959: The True Story of Castro's Rise to Power.* Wintergreen: Kleiopatria, 2009.

Martín, Elena Alavez. *Eduardo Chibás en la hora de ortodoxia* [*Eduardo Chibás in the Time of Orthodoxy*]. Havana: Editorial de Ciencias Sociales, 1994.

Matthews, Herbert. *The Cuban Story.* New York: Brazillier, 1961.

———. *Fidel Castro.* New York: Simon and Schuster, 1969.

———. *Revolution in Cuba.* New York: Scribner's, 1975.

Maurer, Noel. *The Empire Trap: The Rise and Fall of U.S. Intervention to Protect American Property Overseas, 1893–2013.* Princeton: Princeton University Press, 2013.

McGillivray, Gillian. *Blazing Cane: Sugar Communities, Class, and State Formation in Cuba, 1868–1959.* Durham: Duke University Press, 2009.

McIver, Stuart. *Hemingway's Key West.* Sarasota: Pineapple Press, 2002.

McLendon, James. *Papa: Hemingway in Key West.* Key West: Ketch and Yawl, 1972.

McParland, Robert. *Beyond Gatsby: How Fitzgerald, Hemingway, and Writers of the 1920s Shaped American Culture.* Lanham: Rowman & Littlefield, 2015.

Mellow, James. *Hemingway: A Life Without Consequences.* Boston: Da Capo Press, 1993.

———. *Walker Evans.* New York: Basic Books, 1999.

Meltzer, Milton. *Slavery: A World History.* Cambridge, MA: Da Capo Press, 1993.

Meyers, Jeffrey. *Hemingway.* Boston: Da Capo Press, 1999.

———, ed. *Ernest Hemingway: The Critical Heritage.* New York: Routledge, 1982.

Miller, Ivor. *Voice of the Leopard: African Secret Societies and Cuba.* Jackson: University Press of Mississippi, 2009.

Miller, Linda Patterson. *Letters from the Lost Generation: Gerald and Sara Murphy and Friends.* Gainesville: University Press of Florida, 2002.

Miller, Tom. *Trading with the Enemy: A Yankee Travels Through Castro's Cuba.* New York: Basic Books, 1992.

Mitgang, Herbert. *Dangerous Dossiers: Exposing the Secret War Against America's Greatest Authors.* New York: Random House, 1988.

Mora, Joaquín Hernández. *Cojímar, pueblo de pescadores* (*Cojímar, Village of Fishermen*). Havana: Extramuros, 016.

Moore, Alex. *Fidel Castro: In His Own Words.* New York: Hollan, 2017.

Moorehead, Caroline. *Gellhorn: A Twentieth-Century Life*. New York: Henry Holt, 2003.

Mort, Terry. *The Hemingway Patrols: Ernest Hemingway and His Hunt for U-boats*. New York: Scribner, 2009.

Moruzzi, Peter. *Havana Before Castro: When Cuba Was a Tropical Playground*. Layton: Gibbs-Smith, 2008.

Munro, Dana Gardner. *The United States and the Caribbean Republics, 1921–1933*. Princeton: Princeton University Press, 1974.

Murphy, Charlene M. "A Shared Palette: Hemingway and Winslow Homer, Painters of the Gulf Stream." In *Hemingway, Cuba, and the Cuban Works*. Edited by Larry Grimes and Bickford Sylvester. Kent: Kent State University Press, 2014.

Nohlen, Dieter. *Elections in the Americas: A Data Handbook*. Vol. 1, *North America, Central*. Oxford: Oxford University Press, 2005.

Nuermberger, Gustave A., Victor J. Farrar, John G. Reid, and William R. Willoughby, eds. *Foreign Relations of the United States, 1932, The American Republics*, vol. V.

Washington, DC: US Government Printing Office, 1948.

Olson, Julius E., and Edward Gaylord Bourne, eds. *The Northmen, Columbus and Cabot, 985–1503, Original Narratives of Early American History*. New York: Charles Scribner's Sons, 1906.

Ortíz, Fernando. *Cuban Counterpoint: Tobacco and Sugar*. Durham: Duke University Press, 1995.

———. *Hampa Africana: Los negros esclavos*. Havana: Rivista bimester cubana, 1916.

Palmié, Stephan, and Francisco A. Scarano. *The Caribbean: A History of the Region and Its Peoples*. Chicago: University of Chicago Press, 2011.

Páporov, Yuri. *Hemingway en Cuba*. Mexico City: Siglo Veintiuno Editores, 1993.

Paterson, Thomas G. *Contesting Castro: The United States and the Triumph of the Cuban Revolution*. Oxford: Oxford University Press, 1994.

Perez, Louis A., Jr. *Cuba: Between Reform and Revolution*. New York: Oxford University Press, 1995.

———. *Cuba in the American Imagination: Metaphor and the Imperial Ethos*. Chapel Hill: University of North Carolina Press, 2011.

———. *Cuba Under the Platt Amendment, 1902–1934*. Pittsburgh: University of Pittsburgh Press, 1986.

———. "Image and Identity." In *Inside Cuba: The History, Culture, and Politics of an Outlaw Nation*. Edited by John Miller, Aaron Kenedi, and Andrei Codrescu. New York: Marlowe, 2003.

———. *On Becoming Cuban: Identity, Nationality & Culture*. Chapel Hill: Harper & Collins, 1999.

———. *To Die in Cuba*. Chapel Hill: University of North Carolina Press, 2005.

Perez-Lopez, Jorge. *The Economics of Cuban Sugar*. Pittsburgh: University of Pittsburgh Press, 1991.

Perkins, Maxwell. *Editor to Author: The Letters of Maxwell E. Perkins*. Edited by John Hall Wheelock. New York: Scribner's, 1950.

Pivano, Fernanda. *Hemingway*. Milan: Rusconi, 2001.

———. "Persona and Personalità di Hemingway." In *Hemingway e Venezia*. Edited by Sergio Perosa. Firenze: Olschki, 1988.

Poole, Sean. *Gattorno: A Cuban Painter for the World*. Miami: Arte al Dia International, 2004.

Putnam, Samuel. *Paris Was Our Mistress: Memoirs of a Lost and Found Generation*. Carbondale: Southern Illinois University Press, 1970.

Quirk, Robert E. *Fidel Castro*. New York: W. W. Norton, 1995. First published 1993.

Raeburn, John. *Fame Became Him*. Bloomington: Indiana University Press, 1984.

Ramonet, Ignacio. *In Conversation with Fidel*. Havana: Cuban Council of State Publications, 2008. First published in Spanish, 2006.

Reynolds, Michael. *An Annotated Chronology*. Detroit: Omnigraphics, 1991.

———. *Hemingway: The American Homecoming*. Hoboken: Blackwell, 1992.

———. *Hemingway: The 1930s*. New York: W. W. Norton, 1998.

———. *Hemingway: The Final Years*. New York: W. W. Norton, 1999.

———. *Hemingway's Reading 1910–1940: An Inventory*. Princeton: Princeton University Press, 1981.

———. *Hemingway: The 1930s Through the Final Years*. New York: W. W. Norton, 2012.

———. *Young Hemingway*. New York: W. W. Norton, 1996.

Reynolds, Nicholas. *Writer, Sailor, Soldier, Spy: Ernest Hemingway's Secret Adventures*. New York: William Morrow, 2017.

Rodenberg, Hans-Peter. *The Making of Ernest Hemingway: Celebrity, Photojournalism and the Emergence of the Modern Lifestyle Media*. Berlin: Lit Verlag, 2014.

Rodríguez, Osmar Mariño. *Hemingway: Un campeón en La Habana* [*Hemingway: A Champion of Havana*]. Havana: Editorial Desportes, 2006.

———. *La Habana de Hemingway y Campoamor* [*The Havana of Hemingway and Campoamor*]. Havana: Ediciones Extramuros, 2009.

Rollyson, Carl. *Beautiful Exile: The Life of Martha Gellhorn*. London: Aurum Press, 2001.

Ross, Lillian. *Portrait of Hemingway*. New York: Modern Library, 1999.

Russell, D.E.H. *Rebellion, Revolution, and Armed Force: A Comparative Study of Fifteen Countries with Special Emphasis on Cuba and Africa*. New York: Academic Press, 1974.

Russo, Peter D., and John H. Esperian. *Offshore Vegas: How the Mob Brought Revolution to Cuba*. New York: iUniverse, 2007.

Ryan, Frank L. *The Immediate Critical Reception of Ernest Hemingway*. Lanham: University Press of America, 1980.

Samuelson, Arnold. *With Hemingway: A Year in Key West and Cuba*. New York: Henry Holt & Co., 1988.

Sanford, Marceline Hemingway. *At the Hemingways: A Family Portrait.* Boston: Little, Brown, and Company, 1962. First published 1961.

Sarason, Bertram D. *Hemingway and the Sun Set.* Colombia: Bruccoli-Clark Layman, 1972.

Sayles, John, *Los Gusanos.* New York: Nation Books, 2004. First published by Harper Collins in 1991.

Schlesinger, Arthur M. *The Cycles of American History.* New York: Houghton Mifflin, 1999.

———. *A Thousand Days: John F. Kennedy in the White House.* New York: Houghton Mifflin, 2002.

Shakespeare, William. *Henry IV, Part I.*

Shoultz, Lars. *That Infernal Little Cuban Republic.* Chapel Hill: University of North Carolina Press, 2011.

Skwiot, Christine. *The Purposes of Paradise: U.S. Tourism and Empire in Cuba and Hawaii.* Philadelphia: University of Pennsylvania Press, 2010.

Smith, Earl T. *The Fourth Floor: An Account of the Castro Communist Revolution.* New York: Random House, 1962.

Smith, Tom. "Routes of Columbus's Second, Third, and Fourth Voyages, 1493–1504." In *Discovery of the Americas: 1492–1800.* Edited by John S. Bowman and Maurice Isserman. New York: Facts on File, 2005.

Sokoloff, Alice. *The First Mrs. Hemingway.* New York: Dodd Mead, 1973.

Spaulding, E. Wilder. *Ambassadors Ordinary and Extraordinary.* Washington, DC: Public Affairs Press, 1961.

Stein, Gertrude. *The Autobiography of Alice B. Toklas.* New York: Harcourt, 1933.

Szulc, Tad. *Fidel: A Critical Portrait.* New York: Avon, 1986.

Terry, Thomas Phillip, ed. *Terry's Guide to Cuba.* New York: Houghton-Mifflin, 1929.

Thomas, Hugh. *Cuba: A History.* London: Penguin, 2013.

———. *Cuba or the Pursuit of Freedom.* Cambridge: Da Capo, Press, 1998.

———. *The Cuban Revolution.* New York: Harper Collins College Division, 1977.

Todorov, Tzvetan. *The Conquest of America.* New York: Harper & Row, 1984.

Tomlin, Gregory. *Murrow's Cold War: Public Diplomacy for the Kennedy Administration.* Lincoln: University of Nebraska Press, 2016.

Villard, Henry Serrano, and James Nagel. *Hemingway in Love and War. The Lost Diary of Agnes von Kurowsky, Her Letters, and Correspondence of Ernest Hemingway.* Boston: Northeastern University Press, 1989.

Villarreal, René, and Raúl Villarreal. *Hemingway's Cuban Son: Reflections on the Writer by His Longtime Majordomo.* Kent: Kent State University Press, 2009.

Vivian, Thomas, and Ruel P. Smith. *Everything about Our New Possessions.* New York: R. F. Fenno and Co., 1899.

Wagner-Martin, Linda. *Ernest Hemingway: A Literary Life.* New York: Palgrave Macmillan, 2007.

———. *Ernest Hemingway: Six Decades of Criticism*. Ann Arbor: Michigan University Press, 1998.

———. ed. *A Historical Guide to Ernest Hemingway*. New York: Oxford University Press, 2000.

Watson, Emmett. *My Life in Print*. Seattle: Lesser Seattle Publishing, 1993.

Weyl, Nathaniel. *Red Star Over Cuba*. New York: Hillman, 1961.

Wilson, Edmund. *The Bit Between My Teeth*. New York: Farrar, Strauss and Giroux, 1965.

Wright, Philip. *The Cuban Situation and Our Treaty Relations*. Washington, DC: The Brookings Institution, 1931.

Wukovits, John F. *Eisenhower*. New York: Palgrave Macmillan, 2006.

Yaffe, Helen. *Che Guevara: The Economics of Revolution*. New York: Palgrave, 2009.

Yewell, John, Chris Dodge, and John DeSirey, eds. *Confronting Columbus: An Anthology*. Jefferson, NC: McFarland & Co., 1992.

Zanetti, Oscar, and Alejandro Garcia. *Sugar and Railroads: A Cuban History, 1837–1958*. Translated by Franklin Knight and Mary Todd. Chapel Hill: University of North Carolina Press, 1998.

Zinn, Howard. *A People's History of the United States: 1492–Present*. New York: Harper Collins, 2003.

LIBRARY COLLECTIONS

Anita Logs, Hemingway Personal Papers, John F. Kennedy Library.

Archibald MacLeish Personal Papers, Library of Congress.

Archives of Charles Scribner and Sons. Princeton University Library.

Bernice Kert Personal Papers, John F. Kennedy Library.

Carlos Baker Collection of Ernest Hemingway, Princeton University Library.

Confidential File, White House Central Files, Dwight D. Eisenhower Library.

Ernest Hemingway Collection, Princeton University Library.

Hemingway Miscellaneous Accessions Collection, John F. Kennedy Library.

Hemingway Personal Papers, John F. Kennedy Library.

Hemingway Reference Collection, John F. Kennedy Library.

James C. Hagerty Papers, Dwight D. Eisenhower Library.

Jane Mason Personal Papers, John F. Kennedy Library.

John Sherman Cooper Papers, Kentucky Digital Library.

Latin American Election Statistics, University of San Diego.

Mary Hemingway Personal Papers, John F. Kennedy Library.

Museum Ernest Hemingway Collection, John F. Kennedy Library.

Newspaper Clippings. Hemingway Collection. John F. Kennedy Library.

Patrick Hemingway Papers. Princeton University Library.

Pilar Logs, Hemingway Personal Papers, John F. Kennedy Library.

Raúl Chibás Collection, Hoover Institution Archives, Stanford University.

THESES AND DISSERTATIONS

Clinton, Richard Edgar, Jr. "The United States and the Caribbean Legion: Democracy, Dictatorship, and the Origins of the Cold War in Latin America, 1945–1950." Athens: Ohio University, dissertation, 2001.

Hargrove, Claude. *Fulgencio Batista: Politics of the Electoral Process in Cuba, 1933–1944.* Washington, DC: Howard University, dissertation, 1979.

Mickelson, Erik D. "Seattle By and By: The Life and Times of Emmett Watson." Missoula: University of Montana, thesis, 2002.

ACKNOWLEDGMENTS

• • • • •

I would like to thank the *directora* of the Finca Vigía, Ada Rosa Rosales, for encouraging me and supporting me when I inquired about studying in residence at the museum. By the same token, I must thank my assistant in Havana, Yavseny Roque Hernandez; and the staff of the museum, in particular Kenia Mascaró and Isbel Iseel Ferreiro Garit; the present *directora*, Grisell Fraga Leal; and the former *directora*, Gladys Rodrīguez Ferrero.

Thank you to the Durands, Clara Elena Serpa, Raúl Pérez, America Fuentes, and to the kind people of Cuba who showed me new perspectives, courage, and hospitality. I thank the minister of culture and staff, including Lisette Muruaga and Margarita Elorza. A special thanks to Cuban researcher Osmar Mariño Rodríguez for providing me access to Fernando G. Campoamor's Personal Papers.

Thank you, librarians of the John F. Kennedy Presidential Library—in particular, Susan Wrynn, Maryrose Grossman, and Arabella Matthews.

Thank you to my generous mentors, editors, and agents: Deborah Ritchken, Gay Claiborne, Susan Beegel, Mark Krotov, Ryan Harrington, and Melville House. Thank you to my mom, dad, and wife, Yelani.

INDEX

• • • • •